GLOBAL HUMANITIES READER

UNIVERSITY OF NORTH CAROLINA ASHEVILLE HUMANITIES PROGRAM

The Humanities Program at University of North Carolina Asheville explores what it means to be human. We examine the experiences of our shared humanity by looking at the oral, literary, and material expressions of our orientations and convictions, values and passions, and struggles and strategies for survival and thriving. In engaging with a wide and diverse set of perspectives, we consider both their original contexts and their ongoing influence on our times. These inquiries are strengthened through an interdisciplinary approach to Humanities that draws together faculty and subject matter across disciplines currently including: Africana studies, anthropology, arts, Asian studies, biology, chemistry, classics, economics, history, Indigenous studies, languages, literature, mathematics, philosophy, physics, political science, psychology, religious studies, sociology, and women, gender and sexuality studies. Humanities helps us to make educated and ethical decisions as we strive to understand multiple perspectives on human experience, engage in culturally appropriate and community-centered problem solving, and thrive as global and local citizens of our own communities.

The *Global Humanities Reader* is a three-volume work edited by a team of faculty from UNC Asheville. The three volumes are *Volume 1 - Engaging Ancient Worlds and Perspectives, Volume 2 - Engaging Pre-Modern Worlds and Perspectives*, and *Volume 3 - Engaging Modern Worlds and Perspectives.*

Katherine C. Zubko and Keya Maitra, General Editors

Brian S. Hook, Sophie Mills, and Katherine C. Zubko, *Engaging Ancient Worlds and Perspectives*, Editors

Renuka Gusain and Keya Maitra, *Engaging Pre-Modern Worlds and Perspectives*, Editors

Alvis Dunn and James Perkins, *Engaging Modern Worlds and Perspectives*, Editors

Cameron Barlow, Timeline and Source Preparation Editor

Global Humanities Reader

VOLUME I

Engaging Ancient Worlds and Perspectives

VOLUME EDITORS:

Brian S. Hook, Sophie Mills, Katherine C. Zubko, and Keya Maitra

University of North Carolina Asheville

ISBN 978–1-4696–6640–2 (paperback: alk. paper)
ISBN 978–1-4696–6641–9 (ebook)

Published by the University of North Carolina Asheville Humanities Program

Distributed by the University of North Carolina Press
www.uncpress.org

Cover photo credit: David Becker, licensed and used by permission of the photographer, https://beckerworks.de
Cover Design by Cameron Barlow

CONTENTS

CONTENTS BY INQUIRY

ACKNOWLEDGMENTS

As we sit down to compose these acknowledgments we are almost in disbelief that we have arrived at this point. We did not have a definitive roadmap when we started in 2017. Now a global pandemic later, we are at the finish line. Our student-centered approach served as our North Star. Working with many stakeholders we determined the steps of the process that brought us here. There were more than sixty people inside and outside of UNC Asheville who helped us with this project. Unfortunately we can't name every single one of them, but to them, using the South African expression, we say *ubuntu*! *"I am because you are; we are because you are."* This project is because you are!

This *Global Humanities Reader: Engaging Ancient Worlds and Perspectives,* would not be possible without the support of the following individuals and funding sources:

This project benefited from an amazing **Reader Support Team**. Jessica Park was the hub facilitating all connections and communications, keeping the project organized every step of the way. She often helped us reimagine what the project could be with her timely interventions and keen eye for detail. Jon Morris handled the copyright issues with such competence and precision that we never had to deal with the countless emails and loose ends with multiple publishers. Cameron Barlow, our student partner, actualized *all* the graphic timelines, and envisioned and created the comprehensive timelines from the ground up, in addition to his detail-oriented primary source preparation. It is no easy feat transferring pdfs of ancient sources into a Word format, undoing diacritical marks, weird spacing, and nineteenth- and twentieth-century publishing styles—ALL CAPS! The success of this project is due to their ability and willingness to routinely go beyond the call of duty exhibiting constant and tireless enthusiasm, unparalleled professionalism and a collaborative spirit that found solutions for every problem.

Our colleagues from the UNC Asheville Career Center, David Earnhardt and Chelsey Augustyniak, became a part of this project early on and read many of the primary sources in the process of their creative collaboration on the Beyond the Classroom feature. Tracey Rizzo agreed to compose the unique cross-cultural historical introductions for each volume, a task made even more difficult since we wanted her to tell a story that not only offered integrated contexts for our primary sources but also would inspire the reader to expand their engagement. Tracey not only delivered on our request but worked indefatigably on multiple drafts. One of our amazing art historians, Eva Hericks-Bares, curated the images for the introductions that Tracey wrote, and located usable high-resolution images with the appropriate licensing requirements. Her detailed captions bring these images into clear focus in relation to the overview of history. Amanda Bell provided tremendous research support by creating surveys and analyzing faculty and student data to support the shape of the primary guiding priorities and pedagogical features in the project. Our colleague, Lyndi Hewitt and her students offered support in designing the student survey instrument. We are grateful to Heather Hardy, a member of our Asheville community, for diligently fact checking all the timeline information. Finally, we are thankful to John McLeod from the UNC Press Office of Scholarly Publishing Services and his colleagues, including Lisa Stallings and her team at Longleaf Services, for helping us navigate this complex process.

We thank our various **funding sources**. The generous support from the Mellon grant allowed us to first conceive and then execute this audacious project. We thank our colleague Brian S. Hook for his crucial leadership in securing the grant and getting the project started as its first general editor. We also thank then-provost of UNC Asheville, Joseph R. Urgo, for his unwavering support for the project at its early stages. A Thomas W. Ross Fund Publishing Grant from UNC Press provided critical support that made the various design aspects possible. Finally, we thank Katherine C. Zubko who offered unfailing and constant support through her NEH Distinguished Professor in the Humanities funds whenever a supplementary need arose.

A number of other individuals offered unhesitating support for this project at various moments and we thank them for their steadfast encouragement: our colleagues Ameena Batada, Dee James and Melissa Himelein for providing important feedback on the General Editors' Welcome; Joevell Lee; Charlotte Smith; Steve Birkhofer; Wendy Mullis; Leah Dunn; Natalia Zubko; and peer reviewers for the cross-cultural introductions: UNCA History department colleagues, Saheed Aderinto (Western Carolina University), Steven Gerontakis (University of Florida), and Shawna Herzog (Washington State University).

Finally, we thank our **contributors**, who wrote source introductions and pedagogical features for all of the sources within this volume: Elena Adell, Mildred Barya, Agya Boakye-Boaten, Mustapha Braimah, Melissa Burchard, Joseph Cross, Barbara Duncan, Mark Gibney, Brian Graves, Grant Hardy, Eva Hericks-Bares, Marcus Harvey, Lora Holland-Goldthwaite, Brian S. Hook, Doria Killian, Dennis Lundblad, Keya Maitra, Sophie Mills, Sol Neely, Rodger Payne, Juan Sanchez-Martinez, Rob Tatum, Scott Williams, and Katherine C. Zubko.

In asking our contributors to craft the learning support items for each source, we asked them to do far more than simply writing a supporting introduction. Our contributors not only rose to the occasion but also revised their entries in response to the editorial feedback. Many of the contributors wrote multiple entries. Our colleague Grant Hardy modeled for us his devotion and excitement about student-centered pedagogy and thereby offered us crucial confidence to stay the course at various stages. And last, but not least, we thank our families who teased us for having too many tabs open on our computers, and were patient and only mildly irritated on our behalf at times as this project took over countless hours spilling over into many nights and weekends.

GENERAL EDITORS' WELCOME

Katherine C. Zubko and Keya Maitra

PART I: GETTING TO KNOW THE ELEPHANT

Welcome to the University of North Carolina Asheville's *Global Humanities Reader: Engaging Ancient Worlds and Perspectives*. Let us begin by sharing a story about the elephant and the blind men from South Asia:

> Several blind men are brought before a king and asked to describe an elephant. An elephant is brought to them and they proceed to feel it with their hands. One, who grasps the elephant's trunk, claims that an elephant is like a snake. Another, grasping a leg, claims it is like a tree. Yet another grasps the tail and says it is like a rope; and another, feeling the elephant's side, claims it is like a wall. The blind men then argue amongst themselves about the true nature of the elephant. Who is correct?[1]

You might be familiar with a different version of this narrative. What is instructive is that not only does the setting of the story shift based on who is engaging it, including Hindus, Buddhists, and Jains, but that the lesson of the narrative changes as well. Thus, while the Buddha takes it to reflect how the men "cling" to their individual "finding," the Jain view uses it as an example of their epistemological perspectivalism (*anekantavada*) or many-sidedness.

This version of the story is instructive also in what it does not emphasize; for example, it doesn't draw our attention to the ground where the elephant stands. Engaging with this narrative especially in the context of the United States, the land can no longer be ignored or taken for granted, but is central to one's becoming aware of our erased and fractured histories and our uncomfortable collective self-understanding. We want to acknowledge and honor that UNC Asheville is on *Anikituwag*i (Chero-

1. Anand Jayprakash Vaidya, "Making the Case for Jaina Contributions to Critical Thinking Education," *Journal of World Philosophies* 3 (2018): 61–62.

kee) ancestral land and that we continue to build mutual, respectful relationships with the Eastern Band of Cherokee (EBCI) who are ongoing stewards of this area, and from whom we continue to learn. Acknowledgment is not enough, however, and it is our hope that these Readers help us put our commitment to this relationship into action.

We want to use the elephant story to remind us of insights that emanate from our understanding of UNC Asheville's Humanities Program:

- Exploration of truth and meaning is a collaborative affair involving perspectives from various cultures and occupants of different viewpoints within a single culture.
- No one discipline might have the final exclusive claim on truth, especially when it comes to enduring questions.
- The inquiry model, where asking questions is centered, is the most effective approach for fostering informed, engaged and compassionate global citizens given its commitment to active, authentic, and open-minded learning.
- Finally, critical thinking has to be conceived in its global purview in order to open us to a wide spectrum of methodologies and epistemologies.

This welcome is primarily aimed at students so that the context for these Readers and the choices we have made may become more transparent.

Who We Are: The Humanities Program at UNC Asheville

On behalf of the editorial team—Brian S. Hook, Sophie Mills, Renuka Gusain, James Perkins, and Alvis Dunn—we are delighted to introduce three humanities primary source anthologies that have been created as the culmination of a multiyear faculty-led curricular revision process at the University of North Carolina Asheville. Our public liberal arts university's more than fifty-year-old Humanities Program consists of a four-course sequence taken by all of our students.[2] The Humanities Program serves as the hub of the wheel of our liberal arts mission. The different spokes of this mission are: critical thinking, interdisciplinarity, cross-cultural commitments to diverse perspectives: and inquiry-focused learning. They are held together by an integrative and open-minded sensibility embodied in its curriculum design, delivery and student learning outcomes.

Early on in the history of this program, faculty saw the need to create their own anthologies of diverse primary sources, as no other available anthology was suitable to meet their goals. These anthologies, published as the Asheville Readers, have periodically been revised over these past decades, as faculty continually engage in curricular

2. Margaret Downes, "The Humanities Program at University of North Carolina at Asheville," in *Alive at the Core: Exemplary Approaches to General Education in the Humanities*, edited by Michael Nelson et al. (San Francisco, CA: Jossey Banks, 2000), 203–24.

revision. The main audience for these Readers has always been our own university students who participate in our homegrown, interdisciplinary program.

Thanks to the generosity of a Mellon grant awarded in 2017, this new iteration of the Asheville Readers—renamed *Global Humanities Readers*—are able to evolve in ways that better support the needs of our students at UNC Asheville and beyond who find themselves in a complex, interconnected, and rapidly changing world. For the first time, the Readers will be available online free of cost not only to our students but also to high school, community college, and university students across North Carolina public educational online communities. These developments very much align with our own public liberal arts mission and that of the Humanities Program out of which these Readers have emerged.

Values That Guide Our Readers: Diverse Cross-Cultural Perspectives and Inquiry Focus

Informed by surveys and discussions with faculty and students, the editorial team identified two main principles that have guided the shaping of these new Readers. The first is a commitment to placing materials from multiple, diverse perspectives in conversation with one another. Second is a focus on providing ways to cultivate our ability to ask questions—to inquire—while deepening our cross-cultural and cross-disciplinary engagements with the materials. We believe both values help you to see your own points of view as emerging from particular contexts, assumptions, and experiences, and that your own is only one of many co-existing views.

Furthermore, we are interested in promoting an openness to *your* encounters with materials. At times we have intentionally encouraged new insights by offering competing perspectives or challenging traditional viewpoints. In some ways, we want to foment intellectual chaos, uncertainty, and struggle by challenging the obvious or the given. Our goal is to enable the potential for growth and help you develop skillful facility in holding multiple perspectives. This is not to encourage a form of relativism, but rather to foster a deeper understanding of context and position—whether disciplinary, cultural, and/or intersectional—that permeate your inquiry.

The Jain concept of *anekantavada* mentioned earlier speaks to these multiple co-existing perspectives, each limited to one's position and experience as exemplified in the parable of the elephant. But this story also speaks to the power of self-awareness of each perspective that in combination allows a different communal truth to emerge in contrast to a privileged pre-existent ideal Truth (Elephant).

In order to acknowledge that the nature of truth is both communal and multifaceted, students must engage in this study and effort as deeply as possible. Engaging deeply permits us to penetrate typical surface comparisons and unfounded generalizations. Better still, we are not trapped in judgments that perpetuate one dominant view of the world as the highest or only way to perceive it. To accomplish this requires the strengthening of a very important skill related to critical thinking, namely inquiry. It becomes crucial that we ask questions such as: How might the Jain concept help formulate new questions about the assumptions around an ideal pre-existent Truth and its consequences for human ways of knowing? How is knowledge characterized, who has access, and what might this reflect about human experience from these different worldviews? Each story, reflecting different ways of knowing, comes into sharper focus through the process of cross-cultural comparison. Take again for example another central concept in the study of humanities, namely, aesthetics. On the one hand, this term could be seen as having innately westernized constructs, but when we step back and ask, "How do humans create, define, and experience artistic expressions?," many possible approaches create multiple, contextualized case studies and interpretations that illuminate various underlying foundations.

The selections of primary sources included in each Reader reflect our unwavering commitment to the dual values of cross-cultural diverse perspectives and inquiry-focused engagements. We aim to course correct from some of the available humanities textbooks in which the defining narrative remains that of Western liberalism. For example, the ways that humanities textbooks have treated race and indigeneity have often furthered harm by excluding multiple perspectives on the difficult lived realities of what we now call racial injustices, as well as patronizing or whitewashing the experiences through stilted frameworks and terminology. In these volumes, there are, at times, gaps in source materials focused on experiences of race, slavery, and indigeneity that are curricular growth areas for the program. It is relevant to note here that in spite of coming from a large group of contributors, our selections are still reflective of the group's interests and areas of focus and we know that a different group might have come up with a different set of readings and perspectives. The choices made are a reflection of the times in which the editors and faculty contributors are living. Engaging in collaborative editing processes with faculty contributors provided us opportunities to have conversations about problematic framing, terms, and even the sources we decided to include. This process has made us aware that inclusivity need not be pitted against expertise or any of its cousins, such as rigor or standards, that are often used to police boundaries around knowledge. We don't always get it right, but we are working to bring more awareness, with honesty and humility, to correcting mistakes made in the past.

Our sincere attempt has been to anchor the framing narratives of each Reader in cross-cultural and interdisciplinary perspectives where no one single cultural ideology or disciplinary approach is privileged. However, it is important to acknowledge that each Reader is still temporally organized linearly, focused on written and primary source content, and clearly foregrounds a human-centered perspective that might be suspect from certain cultural viewpoints. These choices, especially the chronological framing of content, admittedly presuppose a linear understanding of time sometimes challenged by various cultures. Linear temporal systems value locating dates for events and people based on criteria that at times exclude cultural expressions of humanity in which orality is valued as much as or sometimes more than writing. The emphasis on time has had the impact of undervaluing sources that come to us through oral means because they could not be tied to a particular origin date. We have tried to address this exclusionary tendency by including more sources from oral traditions to honor cultures' own understandings of their ancient roots by not marking particular time periods in the titles of the volumes.

At the moment of compiling the Readers, for many institutional, program, and resource reasons, we moved forward with a chronological framing even though we are aware of ways of understanding time that diverge from this framing. Linda Tuhiwai Smith, for example, draws our attention to the fact that many Indigenous languages don't have a word for time. She takes this to reflect the fact that lineal or linear time does not operate as a foundational organizing principle in these cultures.[3] In order to disrupt a singular linear organizational model, we have included a second suggested grouping of sources by either theme, question, or some other category, and included sources in the Readers that are engaged across chronological timeframes.

We realize that each of our decisions, however intentional about inclusivity, has blind spots. Instead of treating this realization as a paralyzing hurdle, we want to approach it as an opportunity for self-reflection that makes explicit the reasoning behind and also the implications of our selections/choices. Indeed, this self-awareness commits us to an epistemic humility that is the hallmark of a pedagogy that foregrounds process and meaningful engagement. Thus, while we are confident that this revision project makes huge strides, there is always more work to be done. For example, because of a long-standing commitment to written sources, our introductory Humanities course has struggled to expand its understanding of "primary source" to include artefacts, material cultures and other aspects from the Global South. We do include these components, but they currently live on an online learning platform rather than in this Reader. It is our hope in the next revision that these materials will be incorporated more directly.

Finally, our ability to ask questions is often taken for granted, as a given without the need for cultivation. It is often assumed that we automatically learn how to ask questions without direct instruction on how we come to ask particular questions, in what contexts, based on what criteria, and for what purposes. The editorial team realized in talking with students that the skill of asking productive questions needed to be made more visible, with opportunities for practice, and thus decided to make it the central pedagogical focus of these Readers. The team began to test out several learning features that would support this noteworthy and transferable skill. In the following we discuss how inquiry-based learning is embedded in the support features of the Readers.

3. Linda Tuhiwai Smith, *Decolonizing Methodologies: Research and Indigenous People*, 2nd ed. (New York: Zed Books, 2012), 52.

PART II: HOW TO USE THIS READER: INTRODUCING THE LEARNING SUPPORT FEATURES

Over the past several years, faculty and staff collaborated across various disciplines, programs, and areas at UNC Asheville to globalize the content of courses that grew out of a westernized humanities model. In addition, to support effective and meaningful encounters with the ideas in these sources, faculty have embedded the insights of pedagogical research, namely creating learning environments that are culturally aware, active, inquiry-based and draw upon best practices in cultivating reflective spaces. The editorial team, in view of these aims, realized the need to create a thoroughly interactive text that actualizes our commitments to student success.

Like no other revision process in the past, the editorial team engaged in a research-based approach utilizing our faculty's and students' feedback through surveys, focus groups and pilot feedback cycles. The unique organization of these Readers emerged as a result of this process and we want to specifically mention how central students were to the final product design. Thus, in addition to the brief introductions to each primary source, which was a hallmark of previous Readers, these new Readers now incorporate several intentional learning support features students overwhelmingly identified as useful to their learning process. We hope the descriptions of each of these features serve to enhance your own particular nuanced engagement with the sources in these Readers.[4]

Cross-Cultural Historical Introduction to Each Volume

One of the most unique features that you will encounter in these Readers is a cross-cultural historical introduction at the beginning of each volume. Authored by our colleague Tracey Rizzo, from the History Department, these essays provide a perspective on a larger sweep of history during each time period, identifying key moments and concepts that shape a particular chronological era. These introductions are global in focus, weaving examples from various parts of the world together in order to exemplify how humans in different cultures and times experience, shape, and respond to their worlds. In acknowledging the historical orientation of these cross-cultural introductions, we understand that other disciplinary approaches might have used their own framing questions and criteria. What types of questions and criteria might scholars from other disciplines foreground when seeking to discuss human forms of experience, such as religious movements, war, or love?

These introductions are intended to be flexible in how they are used in classrooms. You may be asked to read the essay at the beginning of a semester to provide an historical disciplinary approach and contextualize the semester. You may also be

4. The description of learning support features has been edited from a document first drafted by Brian S. Hook and used to help guide faculty contributors who have written entries.

directed to segments as relevant to particular entries for each week, as they provide further context in addition to each entry's dedicated introduction.

Snapshot Boxes with Tags

We have included a small box at the beginning of each entry that provides some basic contextual information, based on scholarly consensus, for reading at a glance. Specific information may vary based on what is appropriate to the source but often includes the following: language of the original document; date; location or origin; genre; national/ethnic identity; and tags.

A unique feature developed for these entries is the set of "tags" listed in the snapshot box. Tags aim to highlight connections, for example, by offering a bird's-eye view of central concepts, within the course and possibly across courses. They are not places, names, and events; they also are not themes or keywords for that matter. Each course also contains a tag glossary that collects all the tags used in that course along with the readings in which they appear. We have come to think of the tags as hubs that offer an initial location for seeing, creating, and facilitating exciting new connections. We welcome you to enjoy exploring the trails that these tags help signpost and to create your own.

Introductions with Bolded Terms

Each course entry is accompanied by an introduction that invites you into the reading and offers a few navigational tools. These introductions are not SparkNotes summaries or comprehensive overviews like an encyclopedia or wikipedia article. Reading the introduction thus cannot replace reading the source itself, and much will be missed if this strategy is attempted. We also bolded a few terms to alert you to key concepts and frameworks.

We have modified the primary focus of these introductions to prioritize inquiry-based learning, and so you will note the inclusion of questions embedded directly in the introduction in order to prompt exploration of both the context and the source itself. Questions as opportunities of reflective pauses are often framed such that readers have an opportunity to make their own connections. Our aim is to provide much-needed contextual support while leaving room for you to engage a source without preemptively providing many of the interpretative possibilities. This moves away from "tell me what to think or what I should know" to "give me parameters that can guide my own productive engagement with the source."

In some cases, you will notice slightly different approaches to readings, especially if they are from typically underrepresented cultures in the curriculum. This might entail more notes to provide access to critical contextual sources, an expanded narrative timeline as part of the introduction, and/or different types of strategies for engaging the text. By allowing for differences in some of the entries, our intention is to provide more inclusive spaces for expert voices from the margins that our students have not usually heard or been able to find, and to build skills for working with multiple perspectives. It is a goal of the liberal arts and this project to put the values into practice that will foster, educate, and engage these skills as part of becoming global citizens.

Timelines

Most Reader entries include a timeline with three different types of chronological information: (1) black points relevant to the source directly; (2) orange points for comparison to other cultures during the same time period; and (3) larger historical time periods, eras, or movements relevant to the context of the source (as blue bands) or as cross-cultural comparisons (as orange bands). Timelines are a way to provide a type of context for each source, but with the important reminder of what else is going on in other parts of the world. Creating a timeline for ancient, oral storytelling traditions that are not matched to a particular date did not seem effective but rather revealed the assumptions of linear time frames. In a few other cases, we have added a timeline with more modern-day points to raise awareness about present-day contexts that have inherited these storytelling traditions. Sometimes we have also included a more substantial narrative timeline for underrepresented cultures.

At the beginning of each volume you will find a comprehensive timeline noting important points across all the sources in one place. To create a comprehensive timeline is by its very nature an impossible task, as no amount of space or organizational strategy could possibly capture so many concepts visually. However, we hope that the choices we made bring into perspective some of the most prominent chronological points.

Pre-PARs and Post-PARs

You will find a unique feature on either side of the primary source itself: Primed and Ready (PAR) activities placed just before you begin reading (pre-PARs) and again after your first read-through (post-PARs). After getting your contextual and chronological grounding with the introduction and timeline, the pre-PARs are a way for you to pause and spend a few minutes connecting to your prior knowledge of a concept or experience (e.g., "What do you think the role of a teacher is?") or on knowledge already learned in class through previous materials (e.g., "What kinds of models for imitation are the heroes of earlier myths?").

These are not intended to involve research, but rather invite you to gather your own thoughts before you start reading. There are no right or wrong answers. The goal is to encourage you to approach the readings with questions in mind, and to see in the works a resemblance or distance between your own responses and those you find in the work.

At the end of the source reading, you will often find post-PARs that might ask you to revisit the brief observations noted in the pre-PARs, but through the lens of the source directly. If a pre-PAR asks you to list five ideas that you associate with the "sacred," a post-PAR might ask you to identify how the work presents the "sacred." A second type of post-PAR may ask you to briefly practice a particular skill, such as becoming attentive to a particular feature, or to consider the reading with an analytical tool in mind, to help with comprehension and clarity. Strategies might include outlining a small portion of an argument, identifying evidence, looking for assumptions, listing dominant and missing perspectives, or locating initial comparative patterns.

PARs are not discussion or essay questions, deep-level critical thinking activities, or "busy work." The purpose is to move you from more passive to more active forms of processing the information with which you are engaging so that when you come to class, you have a starting point to enter into the discussion. Faculty may select a particular pre-PAR and/or post-PAR for you to complete prior to class, however they are all available for you to use to support your engagement with the materials.

Inquiry Corners

Another feature comes at the end of most entries: The Inquiry Corner.[5] As part of our commitment to supporting an inquiry-based focus, we developed this feature as a platform to bring awareness to what different types of questions do as pathways of inquiry. It is intended as a model for how to ask more productive questions in relation to inquiry processes and goals. The questions provided are not the only types of questions that can be asked, nor do they need to be asked in any particular order.

You may want to ask what certain questions can help you to do—clarify, compare, connect, or critically engage with a topic in which you can delineate the criteria and assumptions of what that question entails. While you may end up utilizing some of these questions in class discussion or in writing prompts—especially the comparative or critical forms—the idea is that with practice, you will gain facility in formulating your own versions of these questions and other types, including those from various disciplinary contexts.

The Inquiry Corner is not a set assignment meant to "be completed" before class, but your professor may guide you to engage this feature in various ways as a part of assignments or class preparation or to practice creating your own questions, or to

5. We are indebted to some inspirational models that supported the development of this inquiry-based learning feature, especially Keya Maitra's "Philosopher's Corner" as found at the end of each chapter in her *Philosophy of the Bhagavad Gita*. We are also grateful to Heather Laine Talley's question prompts that she used in her sociology classes and that served as a useful base for the development of this feature for our Humanities courses.

explore a source on your own. Here are some brief frameworks for the types of questions we chose to include:

- **Content Questions:** Models how to clarify an idea or term in the source, as part of close reading skills. (How is dharma being defined in the source?)
- **Comparative Questions:** Compares a topic between course materials for exploration. (How is nature viewed/depicted in the *Epic of Gilgamesh* and the *Daodejing*?)
- **Critical Questions:** Invites a source-grounded examination of a topic/subtopic with multiple possible perspectives/examples, within a source or across sources. This type of question builds analytical/interpretive/reasoning capacities utilizing evidence. (What forms of authority do leaders rely upon to support their positions of power?)
- **Connection Questions:** Bridges one's own knowledge/experience with ideas in the source; could also connect to student life experiences. (What rhetorical or aesthetic skills do you use when expressing your own authority? Your own doubts or vulnerabilities?)

Beyond the Classroom

In collaboration with colleagues from UNC Asheville's Career Center, in 20–25 percent of the entries, we have included questions that arise out of the content and approach of the reading but move into real-life, forward-looking engagement, thus allowing new contexts to explore, practice, and apply the active model of inquiry.

Maps

Maps are an important aspect of contextualizing our primary source materials. We decided that since there are rich and well-developed online map resources, it would be best to direct our students and faculty to their use, instead of trying to replicate them in not as detailed a form in these Readers. Some of the resources we recommend using are: Ancient World Mapping Center (http://awmc.unc.edu/wordpress/free-maps/), World History Encyclopedia (https://www.ancient.eu/mapselect/), and TimeMaps (https://www.timemaps.com/).

A Few Parting Notes

Finally, the time has come to turn it over to you, dear reader. Our hope is that you have as much fun as we had in compiling this, and we mean all of us—more than sixty people and more than twenty departments/programs/areas were involved in making this series possible. We engaged in a unique collaborative process at every stage, including in the editing of sources that centered dialogue between editors in real time, instead of an individualist approach. We have endeavored to not only bring the elephant into the classroom but to provide strategies to behold more than one aspect—the trunk, the ear, or the side—together and collectively while also becoming aware of the parts of the elephant we don't know how to see from our own cultural perspectives. May we all continue to find more perspectives to engage and respect. Enjoy!

Ancient Worlds

An Historical Cross-Cultural Introduction

Tracey Rizzo

Images curated by Eva Hericks-Bares

This brief introduction to the first volume of *Global Humanities Reader: Engaging Ancient Worlds and Perspectives* invites students to explore how people created diverse forms of community in various parts of the world from circa 8000 BCE to circa 300 CE. By providing basic historical context for the texts that follow, this introduction will help students locate abstract topics in the particular circumstances of their respective places and times. Historians identify the material conditions of the human experience and thereby organize our study of the past both geographically and chronologically: where and when something develops helps us understand what and why, all questions explored by scholars in many disciplines such as literary and art critics, anthropologists, and philosophers. In this brief overview, we can include only a handful of examples of such contexts that open windows into the distant past. In selecting examples, we have been particularly mindful of including perspectives that reflect diverse positionalities as well as highlighting some interdisciplinary opportunities that overlap with theories in neuroarchaeology and environmental studies. We hope this approach offers one of many contexts in which these insights help us understand our shared humanity.

To make sense of millennia of world history, scholars rely on categorizations that reflect our disciplinary standpoints. Categorizations are thus subjective, even when seemingly objective. Common dating such as BC or BCE still represents a calendar based on the birth of Jesus, for example. The determination of some dates is hard to approximate due to lack of corroborating or disputed evidence. Broader periodizations such as "ancient," "medieval," and "modern" are biased by Eurocentric epistemologies, and chronological understanding of time is not easily translated into other histories. Even place names and cardinal directions are labels that arise from culturally specific assumptions. The "Middle East," for example, is geographically nonsensical—middle to where? It was invented to describe cultures and countries midway between China and Europe. Geographically, these cultures and countries are located in Southwest Asia, but sometimes North African countries and cultures also count as the "Middle East." Following conventions in world history, we include this part of the world in "Afroeurasia," signaling its centrality as the crossroads of three continents.

Because this introduction supports student learning in the literatures and philosophies of distinct cultures, it provides an overview of political structures, including varieties of state formations from clans to empires. Institutions that organize human communities have different meanings in different contexts: the "family" is not always the family, an "empire" is not always an empire, at least not in the sense that first springs to mind. Political and institutional structures are the skeletons over which we drape the ideas and private experiences of peoples and cultures who dwell within them. Such terms are used here in as general and nonevaluative ways as possible. "Empire," for example, most basically describes large state formations that incorporate diverse populations. They develop in certain places and times because of a variety of factors, from climate to religion; it does not mean, however, that empires necessarily reflect better or more evolved states than other societal structures.

Because our emphasis is on what makes us human, we tell the story of the gradual integration of diverse cultures into something we recognize as the "world," a term that connotes cultures as opposed to "globe" or "planet." Here too a description of the process known as "integration" is used in the most neutral way possible. "Integration" may include assimilation—forced or voluntary—but is distinct from it. It describes broader forces that structure individual choice-making, while positing that such choice-making is itself constrained and fraught.

Our corpus of primary textual sources emerged in cultures both distinct and entwined. By "text" we mean primarily written sources, but these are not the only repositories of knowledge. We therefore include some images of archaeological fragments and works of art, and written versions of oral sources, marking their transmission histories. The perspectives of written, and in some cases oral sources often reflect those of the most powerful people during or after they were composed. Together, these sources constitute pieces of the story of humanity, a story that will constantly need to be rewritten as new ways of thinking about those sources, and new sources themselves, emerge.

Early Communities

The study of the humanities usually begins when complex and diverse cultures proliferated perhaps 15,000 years ago. While new discoveries by paleontologists continue to push back the origins of a distinct human species to at least 150,000 years ago, humanists study cultural expression from later periods with the aid of fragments

Long-neck turtles, pigment on natural rock surface at Ubirr, Kakadu National Park, Australia. Public Domain

While the tradition of carving and drawing on rock surfaces with pigment goes back more than 40,000 years in this northern region of Australia, this form of painting, known as x-ray art (for showing bones and internal organs) is probably only a few thousand years old. Yet it speaks to a long-established artistic practice of close observation and to the inspiration provided by the specific environment.

of pottery, cave paintings, and eventually texts and narratives transmitted orally and through written media that reveal the mental and material universes of diverse peoples. Rock art in caves, often depicting animals, has been discovered in Europe, Africa, Australia, and Indonesia and dates back to at least 40,000 BCE. Thousands of figurines, small sculptures of women with large breasts and genitals, also appeared around the same time in many locations. Although their exact function may never be known, all of these fragments attest to an enduring fascination with creation, the creation of the world and the creation of life. The stories people have told and continue to tell about creation reveal something fundamental about humanity: our need to generate diverse and culturally specific expressions of common human preoccupations.

Diversification is one of the major focuses of humanistic study. Diversification follows the spread of humans outward from East Africa into different climates. People crossed from Afroeurasia to the Americas by land bridge until glaciers melted them 11,000 years ago, isolating human groups, causing cultures to diversify. Further diversification came with a specialization of roles within and among groups, including, fundamentally, a nearly universal gender-based division of labor. Wielding tools and other weapons became the provenance of men who used them both for protection and to dominate other groups, while women provided greater diversity of sustenance through foraging. Other forms of in-group diversification include by age, ability, and status.

Diversification and its opposite, homogenization, characterize human development, the latter often facilitated by trade and political and military integration. Tensions between diversification and homogenization map closely to the expansion of centralized states, which sometimes forced homogenization, thus inadvertently becoming vulnerable to uprisings by both insider and outsider groups. These states used every tool at their disposal to legitimize their authority, maintain control, and define the realms over which they ruled—bodies of law, religious systems, ancestral lineages, kinship networks, and monumental architecture, for example—but they were seldom successful for more than a few hundred years. Studying the cycles of their expansion and contraction sheds light on the underlying structures shaping human experiences and how people recraft those structures in turn. By exploring the material conditions that influenced micro- and macro-level social, political, and economic structures, we can situate beliefs and other forms of cultural expression in their appropriate contexts.

Varieties of human communities dotted the world's landscapes 10,000 years ago when the end of the Ice Age created favorable conditions for agricultural settlements to form in river valleys across the globe. Farmers during this era were migratory, slashing and burning forests to clear land and then moving on when that land stopped yielding. While people living in resource-rich regions continued to provide for their subsistence needs by gathering and hunting, peoples in resource-poor regions (for example, the Central Asian steppes) continued to migrate with their herds in search of pasture land. Their coexistence suggests that human communities did not form in a linear or universal way but rather as a reaction to local environmental variables. Recent excavations at Göbekli Tepe (Turkey), the world's oldest known temple/astronomical observatory, dating back 12,000 years, have revealed that it was not constructed by sedentary people. The twenty-five-acre complex consists of geometrically arranged limestone pillars weighing up to fifty tons and decorated with images of animals, including scorpions and lions. Animal bones found at the site suggest that wild game was the food source for builders and worshipers. Remains of domesticated animals and wheat cultivation that date to centuries after the temple have been found twenty miles away. In this case, the subsistence needs of people engaged in meaning-making spurred innovation. While broad patterns and commonalities may tell the story of humanity on a universal scale, local examples often challenge historical generalizations and compel us to examine our assumptions more carefully.

Larger settlements could only be sustained by more intensive agriculture and animal domestication. Yet these developments also rendered such settlements vulnerable to overgrazing, soil exhaustion, and above all infectious diseases. Excavations at city-states such as Çatalhoyuk (Turkey), Jericho (Israel), Mohenjo Daro (Pakistan),

Excavated ruins of Mohenjo-daro, with the Great Bath in the foreground and the granary mound in the background, made of baked brick, Mohenjo-daro (now Larkhana, Sindh, Pakistan), c. 2500 BCE. Photograph by Saqib Qayyum/license CC-SA-3.0.

In the early twentieth century, excavations revealed a massive city as large as three square miles in what had first appeared to be a series of mounds. The baked brick used as the main building material ensured its survival and thus allows a glimpse into an organized, highly developed society, whose written records continue to remain inaccessible until its script is deciphered.

and Caral-Supe (Peru) reveal similarities in the types of households and architecture and the economic and religious practices of people primarily engaged in agriculture, which then led to specialization, permanent structures, and artistic expression. By 7000 BCE artisans learned to harden clay into useful storage vessels and decorated them—perhaps for commemoration, accounting, or enjoyment. A thousand years later, people began applying heat to copper, plentiful in many parts of the world, to produce molds for tools, decorative jewelry, and home ornamentation that conveyed degrees of social status, as burial sites attest. By 3500 BCE, a number of larger communities developed around river valleys on every continent. Archaeological sites confirm the exchange of products and illustrate how infrastructural networks integrated communities. Charting seasonal floodwaters, cultivators could grow enough varied food to support populations of tens of thousands. These societies reveal widespread iron tool use and the imagination to lay out settlements for commercial as well as ritual purposes—possibly including communication with deities and ancestors by means of religious specialists, as excavated burial sites attest.

Displacement occurred regularly when climate-related events destabilized these settlements. Additionally, herders, nomads, climate refugees, and invaders interacted with settlers, transforming or sometimes destroying settlements. Increasing competition among powerful clans and even larger entities resulted in persistent violence as weapons as well as fortifications and palace complexes became more sophisticated. When expanding towns or villages encroached on each other and competed for fertile land, militarism developed. Some gradually evolved into fortified cities, or city-states where victorious warriors might claim divine or supernatural powers or even assume the mantle of god-king. This concentration of political and economic power in one territorially bound entity that extended its reach through trade or conquest became the norm throughout most of the world in the coming centuries. Waves of invasion, transformation, or collapse gave way to other forms of community, including, much later, religions whose missionaries and monasteries achieved a cultural consolidation that fostered new forms of belonging as well as new tensions between homogenization and diversification.

South America

In the Americas, the transition to settled agriculture began around 8000 BCE. Maize may have been cultivated even earlier. In Peru, up to twenty settlements, some of them fully developed cities such as Caral, formed along the Fortaleza and Supe Rivers, constituting the Norte Chico territorial state (3700–1800 BCE). These cities had irrigation systems, apartment-style housing complexes, pyramids, and plazas. While archaeological evidence is limited, the region appears to have been ruled by a priestly caste. Sculptures and engravings suggest belief in a staff god, better documented in later Andean civilizations, who communicated through shamans. Craftsmen made musical instruments, such as flutes, from pelican, llama, and deer bones and decorated them with elaborate carvings. Some of these were found at burial sites, suggesting they were used in preparation for the afterlife. They also buried their dead with jewelry made of stones. Knotted strands of yarn known as quipus were an early form of recorded expression and accounting needed to support extensive trade. Located near the Pacific Ocean, Norte Chico cities benefited from coastal fishing as well as riverine crops such as beans, cotton, and squash. They traded these goods as far north as Ecuador and east into the Amazon rainforest. Indeed, trade may have underpinned relatively peaceful relationships in this region since the cities themselves were not fortified, no weapons have been found, and there is no evidence of warfare, such as charred structures or mutilated corpses.

By around 1000 BCE new communities flourished up the steep slopes and along the valley floor of the Andes mountains. Unlike their predecessors who do not appear to have practiced metallurgy, Chavin people forged precious metals into weapons and

Border fragment of a large textile, woven of cotton and camelid hair, Paracas peninsula (now Peru), c. 450–175 BCE. Public Domain

This rare surviving fragment highlights the ancient Paracas weavers' understanding of pattern, structure, and color. Though seemingly representing skeletal humans, the figures' actions have been debated to range from falling, to flying, dancing, or floating. While this may have been intentional on the artists' part, it may also speak to the lack of information modern interpreters have available to them to make such a determination.

decorative objects and traded obsidian and textiles along the Pacific coast. With a population of possibly 3,000 around 750 BCE, the site was stratified with elite dwellings consisting of stone and more common dwellings made of adobe arranged around a palace-temple complex replete with hidden passages and staircases and ventilation and drainage systems. They worshiped Lanzon as their chief deity and decorated his temple with images of jaguars, serpents, and hawks. Priests consumed hallucinogens derived from the San Juan cactus and appeared as jaguars in Chavin rituals that attracted pilgrims from the Amazon forest and the coast alike. More militarized than their Chico counterparts, the Chavin nonetheless continued to rely on trade to organize relationships up and down the Pacific coast and into the Andean highlands.

After the end of the Chavin civilization, the next major Andean civilization was Moche (100–700 CE). While its system of agriculture and trade and its rituals and town design clearly grew out of these earlier civilizations, it was further militarized, engaging in conquest and sacrificing prisoners to its gods. The causes of the instability that prompted a military response are unclear, but the region suffered from more frequent droughts, earthquakes, and El Niño monsoons. This more violent culture also produced more sophisticated art, craft, jewelry, and pottery that depicted gods and warrior-shamans not only in battle but also in erotic situations with gods and goddesses. The well-preserved and elaborate tomb of the Lord of Sipan, likely a ruler who died around 250 CE, included decorative objects made of gold, silver, and turquoise; pots full of food and drink; and the corpses of six other people—three young women, two young men, and one child; and a dog and llama to guide and support him in the afterlife. The corpse's name is unknown, nor is it clear that he was a king, although he did hold a scepter in the grave. While the civilization was likely patriarchal, one elite woman's tomb, the so-called Lady of Cao (d. c. 450 CE), contained similar objects, including staffs, war clubs, and spear throwers.

North America

The jaguar also appeared as a sacred animal in the rituals of the Olmecs to the north in Mexico around 1500 BCE. Decentralized settlements traded with each other but did not form a unified state. Instead, Olmec culture revolved around three cities whose sacred sites were guarded by sculptures of large human heads, jaguars, and were-jaguars—half human, half jaguar figurines found at burial sites. These figures appeared to be part of rain-making rituals that also included human sacrifice and a ball game. Their hierarchically organized society included rulers, craftsmen and merchants, a priestly class, and a large peasantry. Unlike other areas of extensive settlement, the decline of Olmec culture a thousand years later was not precipitated by invasion, rebellion, or a climate crisis. Instead, inhabitants gradually migrated, likely in search of more arable land to the south. Climate historians speculate that volcanic eruptions and over-siltation of rivers resulting from agricultural runoff decreased crop yield.

The mound-building cultures of North America's Midwest combined agricultural settlements near the Ohio and Mississippi Rivers with continued hunting and gathering. As elsewhere, plant cultivation, including pumpkins and other squashes, led to more durable settlements, which included mounds used for burial and other purposes, dating from around 3500 BCE to 1500 CE. Situated near river banks, the mounds used for burial grew in height as more deceased members were added, eventually achieving monumental status with a public function. Precious goods, usually decorative adornments, unearthed at these sites attest to the high status of the deceased, who were the most elite members of the community, including shamans. A widespread trading network linked settlements as far flung as the Great Lakes, the southern Appalachian Mountains, and the Gulf of Mexico as the variety of objects attest, including those made of copper, mica, volcanic glass, and conch. Along the Ohio River Valley, people laid out the mounds horizontally and formed them into precise geometric shapes. Some earthworks apparently had an astronomical function as well, typical of the layout of many ceremonial centers in the Americas and elsewhere. By 400 CE the small communities characteristic of this period began to disappear, possibly due to less reliable crop yield, decline in animals associated with the introduction of bow and arrow hunting, and attendant warfare. There is no one name to describe these ancestors of a score of different Indigenous cultures, but artifacts similar to those dating to this location and period suggest continuity to the Ojibwe and Chipewa, exonyms for the Anishinaabe peoples of the upper Midwest.

West Asia

Sumerian farmers used extensive artificial irrigation techniques to improve yield in the dry hot climate of Southern Mesopotamia, including networks of canals and reservoirs along the Tigris and Euphrates Rivers. By 3000 BCE, as many as 80,000

Serpent effigy, made from mica, Hopewell culture, Mound 4 (Little Miami Valley, Ohio), Peabody Museum, Harvard University, c. 200 BCE to 500 CE. Photograph by Daderot/license CC-SA-4.0.

Although the mounds from which this effigy hails were destroyed, the shape and symbolism of the serpent can be found in other sites throughout the area now known as the Ohio Valley. The meaning of snakes as a powerful symbol varies among tribes, and associations range from fertility, to death and re-birth.

people lived in Uruk, a walled city in modern-day Iraq. Sumerians also invented wheeled transportation and built watercraft that could navigate the Persian Gulf, down the coast of the Indian Ocean, making contact with merchants from East Africa and northern Indian subcontinent. Such over-land and over-sea exchanges knit together the societies of Afroeurasia. Expansion outside the walls to grow enough food to support such a population brought neighboring communities into conflict. Fortifications not only increased security but brought risks as well, including the transmission of diseases through close proximity with animals and waste, making walled cities environments ripe for epidemics.

Extensive agriculture, trade, and urbanization led to occupational specialization and the need for record-keeping. Carvings in hardened clay constitute the world's first-known writing system, called cuneiform. Mostly used for practical functions like accounting, early writing also compiled lists of rulers and gods. By 3200 BCE, symbols came to represent sounds. People could now convey change over time and use verbs in addition to objects and proper names. Engravings on tablets and stone or wooden pillars attest to the hierarchical structure of Sumerian and Mesopotamian society, as exemplified by the rule of Gilgamesh (2700 BCE), who claimed quasi-divinity. Written much later, *The Epic of Gilgamesh* narrates his legendary quest for immortality. As in many epic tales, lionized elite men wielded cruelty and charisma to secure their positions. Their prestige organized people, especially other elite men, within emerging social and political hierarchies. Private householders echoed these hierarchies in domestic life by subordinating women to men and children to elders,

The Law Code Stele of King Hammurabi, basalt, Babylonian Empire (now Louvre, Paris), c. 1792–1750 BCE. Photograph by Mbzt/license CC-BY-3.0.

In addition to the image of Hammurabi (standing) receiving his regal powers from the seated sun god Shamash, the stele contains more than three hundred laws written in Akkadian cuneiform. The details of many of the laws imply that they are based on legal precedent (i.e., not random decisions), and they take the form "if you take this action then this is the consequence." This is one of the first instances of recorded law and its connection to maintaining civil society.

while urban and rural labor arrangements also reflected patriarchy. Customs and laws followed.

This model spread throughout Southwest Asia as the Akkadian Empire, established by King Sargon (2334 BCE), absorbed much of the region. One of the first signed works of literature, a poem to the goddess Inana in Uruk, by then the world's largest cosmopolitan center, was written by Enheduanna (2286–2251 BCE), Sargon's daughter. In addition to poetry, engravings reveal an urban culture of leisure and entertainment, including music, beer drinking, and board games. Sargon commanded an army of up to 5,000 troops organized into phalanxes and augmented by charioteers and then cavalry. Weapons diversified across Afroeurasia as well. As a result of these conquests, the Akkadian Empire included as many as a million people out of a world population estimated at twenty-seven million. However, regular uprisings by conquered people who defended the autonomy of their city-states finally led to its demise around 2150 BCE.

By 2000 BCE, urbanization led to an ultimately unsustainable relationship with the land. Ever-intensifying demand created aqueducts, canals, and slash and burn forestry. Motivated by unpredictable shifts in climate, crop failures, and resulting famine, nomadic pastoralists regularly invaded settled communities. Collectively, invasions resulted in the destabilization and even disappearance of river valley cities around 2000 BCE. Afroeurasian nomads, such as the Hittites of Southern Anatolia, possessed the military advantage of the horse-drawn chariot and perfected their marksmanship and weaponry. While they sacked Babylon in 1595 BCE, they also engaged in diplomacy and agreed to the world's first-known written peace treaty with Egypt in 1258 BCE at Kadesh concerning the control of Syria.

Attempting to consolidate his power by means of law rather than solely by conquest, Hammurabi (r. 1792–1750 BCE) ruled over the Babylonian Empire, whose capital city may have had a population of 150,000. The empire lasted three hundred years and his code of law remained influential for centuries and was foundational to codes of law and religious teachings throughout Afroeurasia. While enshrining some equality before the law, this retaliatory code calibrated punishments to social rank. It also enshrined a gendered hierarchy with women considered as property and where adulterous wives could be killed by their husbands. Husbands, however, were free to engage in sex with concubines, prostitutes, and enslaved people. Veiling as a sign of modesty and ownership appeared in the Neo-Assyrian Empire; only prostitutes could appear without one. Indebted men could also sell their wives and children into slavery. While some enslaved laborers worked in agriculture, most were in domestic service.

Among the largest empires in world history, the Neo-Assyrian (911–609 BCE) and Achaemenid or Persian (550–330 BCE) empires encompassed populations of fifteen million and thirty-five million respectively. The former was established by violent subjugation while the latter included tribute collection and relative toleration of diversity. Neo-Assyrian kings launched holy wars in the name of their god Ashur and broke resistance by relocating up to four million people, some of them enslaved, conscripted, or merely dispersed, in a bid to break up tribal and kin loyalties. These disruptions also served to homogenize the empire as new and old communities intermingled. With millions of conscripted laborers building roads, mining metals, and engaging in siege warfare, the Neo-Assyrians eventually occupied most of Afroeurasia, including Egypt. Castrated men guarded harems of royal women and concubines, guaranteeing the legitimacy of the male line of succession and the seclusion of these women. Men in service to the king were divided by ethnicity into specific functions: Israelites were charioteers; Phoenicians were sailors; and conquered men provided servile labor in farming and construction. Partly due to geographic overreach, the vast military resources of the Neo-Assyrian Empire could not forestall civil war; indeed, revolts by generals combined with invasions by the Medes and Neo-Babylonians led to a period of chaos only ended by Cyrus the Great (r. 559–530 BCE), who established the Persian Empire.

Persians knit together their vast empire by means of infrastructural projects, toleration of the wide range of peoples and cultures living within their borders, efficient administration, and theocracy. They established trading networks, some of them actual roads, such as the Royal Road that extended to the Mediterranean. Branch roads eventually extended into Egypt and India. To demonstrate his commitment to pluralism and the rights of his subjects, Cyrus released the Jews from their captivity in Babylon in 538 BCE, an event detailed in the Hebrew Bible, possibly written down after their return to Jerusalem to build the second temple. Second Temple Judaism established an orthodoxy that included an embrace of monotheism; the independence of the community of believers from temporal authority; messianism; and the study of the Torah, which guided Jews in every aspect of their lives and separated them from the majority culture. Darius I (r. 522–486 BCE) required that all subjects pay tribute and profess loyalty to the king; otherwise he did not regulate their communities. Administrative innovations secured the vast holdings of the empire with the appointment of local governors personally appointed, and spied upon, by the king. Zoroastrianism, a religious system founded by Zoroaster, with both monotheistic and dualistic aspects, underpinned his rule. Continued warfare, the extended Graeco-Persian Wars from 499 to 449 BCE, drained Persia's treasury and discredited its rulers, leading to their defeat by Alexander the Great in 330 BCE.

Although his reign was short, Alexander (356–323 BCE) defeated the Persian Empire, overwhelmed the city-states of the Mediterranean, extended his reach briefly into the northern Indian subcontinent, and occupied Egypt. Using the Persian infrastructure to move his massive armies, he spread Hellenistic or Greek culture across Afroeurasia and encouraged intermarriage between his troops and local women. Raiding local coffers, his armies redistributed wealth from the treasuries of Cairo and Persepolis throughout the Mediterranean. His generals established hereditary dynasties: the Ptolemies of Egypt and the Seleucids of Southwest Asia, including Babylonia. They oppressed Jews who had enjoyed toleration under Persian emperors. The Maccabees revolted against the Seleucid king after he outlawed Jewish practices, including circumcision in 167 BCE. Their bid for independence was somewhat successful in that they gained control of Jerusalem, but some Jewish people had assimilated to Hellenism, provoking a division in one of the world's oldest faith communities. The spread of Greek culture was facilitated by the use of Greek language across Afroeurasia, the standardization of currency, and the spread of slavery. At the same time, mystery cults emphasized a more personal religious experience whether in Greece, Rome, Persia, or Egypt, perhaps as much a reaction to the suffering and fragmentation associated with war as to the syncretism produced by large-scale homogenization and cultural exchange.

Battles between the Ptolemies and Seleucids assured the fragmentation of the Near East until a semi-nomadic confederacy from Central Asia, the Parni, consolidated power in 247 BCE and forged the Parthian Empire that lasted five hundred years, centered in the Iranian plateau. As the Parthians battled many enemies, including Rome, to maintain their borders, their rule remained decentralized, herking back to their nomadic roots. They extended a system of satrapies, which allowed some measure of local autonomy. They dominated the Royal Road, an east-west route through all of Mesopotamia, including Baghdad in the west and Bactria in the east, bordering India and therefore eastern markets. Because of their rivalry with Rome, Parthians created a new blended architectural style signaled by the circular and floral motifs that would remain characteristic of Iranian architecture. With renewed assaults by Rome in 165 CE and 198 CE and Kush in 144 CE, the empire began to disintegrate, and a rival arose from within to topple the dynasty and establish a new one, the Sasanian Empire (224 CE–651 CE).

South Asia

Originating on the Iranian plateau, settlements spread along the Indus River valley by the third millennium BCE. The Indus River's regular flood patterns enabled sustainable agriculture for centuries, supporting the largest town, Harappa. The floodplain supported a swath of settlements at least double that of Mesopotamia, covering half a million square miles. Because its language has yet to be deciphered, and textual evidence is limited, its political organization cannot be known with certainty but the complex architecture of Harappa and Mohenjo Daro suggest a wealthy, stratified, and cultured string of cities in regular contact with other cities in Afroeurasia. Official seals depicting unicorns and animals have been found in Mesopotamia. Masons used large ovens to make bricks, which were then laid by tilers to build complex structures over underground drainage systems. Moving sewage away from the elite sections of towns, Harappan engineers planned communities that reflected the status of its many subgroups. Poorer neighborhoods were built of less durable sunbaked bricks; even in the earliest settlements survival correlated to socioeconomic status. Flooding wiped away traces of these communities. The absence of king lists and royal tombs could mean that their form of governance was less hierarchical, or even participatory. Instead of a palace-temple complex, the largest structure was a public bath, possibly indicating an emphasis on cleanliness and purity. Even before the Harappan collapse, Aryan nomads coming from between the Black and Caspian Seas were migrating into the region with cattle and horses, some making their way toward the Hindu Kush, and then into Indus Valley and beyond. As part of their cosmology, they sacrificed animals to their gods and chanted hymns known as the Vedas, hence the Vedic age beginning around 1500 BCE. Brahmanism, Hinduism's predecessor and one of the world's oldest living religions, evolved during this age. Brahmin priests recited Vedic hymns directed to specific gods when their patrons sought intercessions before battle or the birth of a child, for example. Their language, Sanskrit, is the oldest extant Indo-European language. With chariots and metallurgy they became expansionist and eventually occupied most of the Indian subcontinent.

Organized hierarchically, Vedic society came to include an increasingly rigid caste system. When professions became hereditary, intermarriage between different classes was prohibited, and few possibilities for socioeconomic mobility existed. Priests, members of the *brahmin* caste, held the highest positions; they helped kings maintain and carry out necessary rituals related to their relationships to the gods,

Seal with Pashupati figure, steatite/soapstone, Mohenjo-daro (now Larkhana, Sindh, Pakistan), 2600–1900 BCE. Public Domain

This type of stamp seal was widely used in the ancient world to indicate ownership (functioning like a signature pressed into clay), making such seals fairly common objects. The main image here is a seated figure surrounded by animals. Considering the posture, the name of Pashupati (lord of animals), and the multiple faces (three are visible), this has been interpreted as an early representation of later Hindu god).

often imparting legitimacy to a ruler who was a member of the warrior (*kshatriya*) caste. Their negotiation for religious and secular power is narrated in many stories within the Hindu epics of *Ramayana* and *Mahabharata*, the core stories depicting warrior values. As with other attempts at centralization and homogenization, various groups began to craft different and more inclusive spiritual traditions. By the fifth century BCE, a Himalayan prince, Siddhartha Gautama (c. 563–483 BCE), launched a doctrinal challenge to Brahmanical claims and founded the world's first universal religion, Buddhism. Abandoning the constraints of his social position, his family of origin, and his wife and child, he undertook study with other ascetics and teachers before his own solitary vow to experience enlightenment and alleviate suffering. He taught the Four Truths, of which the last was the Eightfold Path, offering hope to the poor and lower-caste people that they might escape suffering and achieve *nirvana* by renouncing attachments. His community of followers from all social castes became monks and nuns, taking a vow of poverty; wealthy merchants supported them, and monasteries proliferated and prospered in the following century. Buddhist missionaries spread their ideas and practices along the Silk Roads—the land routes that facilitated trade throughout Afroeurasia.

The Indus River valley communities and those that emerged later through the formerly nomadic Aryan settlers/Vedic age were decentralized and did not establish geopolitical empires. When the Macedonian armies led by Alexander the Great reached the Indus River valley, having crossed narrow Himalayan mountain passes, decentralized states proved unable to defend themselves. One of these states, the Magadha kingdom, organized a confederation to repulse Alexander, led by Chandragupta Maurya (r. 322–297 BCE). Rich in iron ore for mass-producing weapons, as well as in elephants for charging the enemy, the Gandhara region supported

Chandragupta's armies. He not only ousted Alexander's forces but established rule over surrounding states, creating the Mauryan Empire (322–185 BCE). Pressing against the Seleucids in the west, a truce was reached with the exchange of women for elephants and the mutual acceptance of ambassadors. This enabled Chandragupta's successor, his grandson Ashoka (r. 268–232 BCE), to concentrate his armies on southward expansion, forcing the submission of semi-independent states, such as Kalinga whose defeat resulted in the deaths of 100,000 soldiers and the forced relocation of 150,000 people. Ashoka then renounced violence and converted to Buddhism. In his Kalinga Edict he committed to toleration and respect for living things. He required obedience of his subjects and spread the teachings of the Buddha as a code for right living among all his subjects, Hindus and Greeks as well as Buddhists. He is known for sending Buddhist monks and nuns, including his daughter Sanghamitta and son Mahinda, to what is now Sri Lanka, beginning the spread of Buddhism outside of the Indian subcontinent, after being actively involved in determining orthodox aspects of Buddhism in the third council. He issued decrees in many languages, which were inscribed on pillars in public places; one of these banned the sacrifice of cattle as detrimental to agricultural progress. At its height, his empire stretched north to today's Pakistan and Iran, and south to the tip of the subcontinent, and included over fifty million people. After the Mauryan Empire disintegrated, tenets of a shared culture held the subcontinent together when armies and bureaucracies shrank.

Alexander's influence lasted longest in the many garrison towns he established connecting Iran to Pakistan. Soldiers settled there, marrying local women and raising bilingual families. Indo-Greek settlements and territorial states such as Bactria in the Gandhara region of the Indian subcontinent fused the Greek and Hindu pantheons of gods and goddesses. Cities were laid out similarly to those in Greece and included theaters, temples, and gymnasia. Coins attest to this fusion showing elephants on one side and Athena on the other. King Menander from Afghanistan (d. 130 BCE) not only styled himself a savior in the Zoroastrian tradition but also engaged in dialogue debating the teachings and nature of the Buddha. Gandhara art includes Greco-Roman influences, even in its depiction of the Buddha. Thus empires promoted both diversification and homogenization, sometimes resulting in a multicultural synthesis.

East Asia

In China, early communities formed along the Yellow and Yangtze Rivers and gradually developed agriculture. Variable microclimates meant that people settled into distinct zones with only occasional contact for trade. Excavations at one of these sites, the Banpo village, reveal a complex diet of pork and wild grains and fruits. Up to five hundred people lived in wooden houses built over storage pits that included kilns and pottery wheels as well as decorative pots and dishware. Dwellings were organized around a central plaza, a common feature of Neolithic villages. Some were multiple stories high and had covered front porches. Exterior to the dwellings was a moat to

Ritual Object (cong), jade (nephrite), Liangzhu culture (now China), c. 2400 BCE. Public Domain

Objects made from jade fulfilled many important roles in Neolithic China. Though their exact meaning is elusive, the congs' precious material, geometrically pleasing shapes, carved decorations, and arrangement in the tombs suggest that they not only marked wealth and social status but also had a ritual or religious function.

defend against snakes and other animals that may have also functioned as a drainage system. Burial grounds outside the village were divided by gender. Excavations reveal possible matrilineality with more numerous and diverse goods in women's tombs. Jade objects were found in elite burial tombs. Around 4000 BCE the Banpo village was abandoned suddenly, perhaps due to flooding as there is no evidence of attack. At other settlements, human remains attest to violence wrought upon settled peoples, including scalping and decapitation. By 2000 BCE regular incursions by Steppes people to the north influenced China's history for millennia. Steppes peoples domesticated horses and resumed nomadic pastoralism after briefly settling. Dunes filling in depressions in the Gobi Desert, prohibiting large-scale agriculture, may have been one of the root causes of the disappearance of settlements.

The roots of China's relatively unbroken system of governance date from around 1600 BCE where oracle bones and later annals of historiography describe the Mandate of Heaven, a doctrine legitimizing rule by one family, usually by conquest. Conquering rival clans, the Xia (2070–1600 BCE), Shang (1600–1046 BCE), and Zhou (1046–256 BCE) dynasties formed in part to organize the massive infrastructural projects required to mitigate the devastating floods of the Yellow River, first through levees, then canals. Increasing agricultural yield and prosperity enabled the early dynasties to enrich themselves, their wealth and power proving their possession of the mandate. The Zhou ruled for nearly eight hundred years, although a love triangle resulted in a split between the Eastern and Western Zhou in 771 BCE. War and instability marked its later years, referred to as the Warring States period (475–221 BCE); during this time meditations on the meaning of life proliferated. Chinese philosophy from 500–200 BCE included the emergence of Confucianism, whose doctrine is articulated in the *Analects*, a compilation of the teachings of the philosopher Confucius (551–479 BCE). Emphasizing duty, deference, family, benevolence, and social harmony, Confucius focused on this-worldly relationships rather than on notions of the afterlife. Deference was to be extended to one's forebears, accommodating earlier traditions of ancestor worship to form a highly adaptive and broad spiritual tradition that persists in China today. Furthermore, earlier shamanic traditions of reading lines on bones for oracles and other omens persisted. With its three obediences and four virtues, Confucianism underpinned patriarchy and the subordination of women, but mothers could have considerable influence over their adult sons and daughters-in-law, while royal wives and concubines, kept in seclusion and guarded by eunuchs, influenced politics at the highest levels.

While most people farmed, men in rural communities could be conscripted for military service and public works. Although urbanization was sporadic, a class of merchants emerged and a nascent bureaucracy promised opportunities for young men on the basis of merit. Traveling scholars spread Confucianism across Asia where it gradually merged with Mahayana Buddhism, a more devotional offshoot that deified the Buddha while also positing the existence of bodhisattvas, individuals on the path to becoming buddhas themselves. In contrast to Confucianism, Laozi and Zhuangzi criticized hierarchy and praised spontaneity in a nature-based and mystical belief system known as Daoism. Daoists described a cosmic unity that upended the rigid system of deference and hierarchy favored by the government.

Shi Huangdi (259–210 BCE), from the western state of Qin, conquered all the other Warring States to consolidate power over a unified China in 221 BCE and claim the Mandate of Heaven, establishing the Qin dynasty (221–206 BCE) with himself as First Emperor. His thirst for conquest resulted in Chinese armies extending control into today's Korea and Vietnam. Using war captives as slaves, particularly Vietnamese women trafficked into sexual slavery, the Qin extended Shang slavery whose original purpose was to stockpile victims for ritual sacrifice. To stabilize the population of nomads to the north, the Qin sent 30,000 colonists to settle in Mongolia. Though the dynasty only lasted fifteen years, it featured several significant innovations including the initial construction of the Great Wall of China, the molding of a life-size terracotta army for the First Emperor's tomb, and the standardization of currency and weights and measures. Most infamously, the Qin emperor burned books and executed Confucian scholars in 212 BCE in a bid to establish Legalism, which advocated a form of statecraft that justified extreme measures to advance the regime, as official doctrine. By 209 BCE, workers mutinied and joined forces with a wide range of enemies of the Qin: merchants, local governors, generals, and even Xiongnu tribesmen to the north who resented the colonists. The ensuing succession crisis, replete with fratricide, a coup, an uprising, and intrigue by eunuchs and concubines ended the dynasty in disgrace, at least according to the chroniclers of the succeeding Han dynasty.

Wresting the Mandate of Heaven away from the Qin, Liu Bang (r. 206–195 BCE), a policeman, founded the Han dynasty and installed himself as Emperor Gaozu. Han consolidation resulted in an even larger army, including 50,000 crossbowmen, some on foot, some on horseback—and an even larger persecution of dissenters. At the same time, the bureaucracy ballooned to 130,000, enabling stricter control of the populace and government jobs for ambitious men, some of whom were graduates of a new imperial university dedicated to this purpose, founded in 136 BCE by Emperor Wu (r. 141–87 BCE). Confucianism became the official governing doctrine and mastering it helped aspirants launch their careers. Scholars also made medical discoveries and invented paper and the magnetic compass. Government investments and monopolies stoked iron and silk production and the minting of copper coins. For the new urban elite, the seclusion of women became a marker of status; poorer women, some enslaved, served as domestics or silk spinners.

One of the most significant developments of the Han dynasty was the establishment of a series of trade routes known as the Silk Road, the term used to describe a network of royal roads to transport luxury goods produced in China to the West dating back to the Achaemenid Empire. Silk and coinage were among the most highly sought-after goods traversing the Silk Roads. When the West made contact with the land of silk, or China, around 200 BCE, the full extent of the integration of Afroeurasia was complete. Once Emperor Wu's forces divided the Xiongnu confederacy, Xiongnu horsemen functioned as middlemen in a network that moved goods along perhaps as many as 5,000 miles across Afroeurasia. Caravan cities on oases fed by irrigated water emerged to support long distance trade and attracted merchants from across Afroeurasia. They connected the Yellow Sea, and later South China Sea, and became cosmopolitan cities. Missionaries and ideas traversed the Silk Roads as well, which was crucial especially to the spread of Buddhism across Asia. Han prosperity held together the diverse districts of China for centuries but bids for local autonomy always threatened civil war, including in colonized Vietnam where two sisters led a protracted if ultimately unsuccessful rebellion in 40–43 CE. After a series of natural disasters ruined rural landlords and peasant families alike, Daoist mystics prophesied regime change and mobilized first the insurgents known as the Red Eyebrows and then the Yellow Turbans, named because of the dyes they used to distinguish themselves. They were joined by local lords and generals who resented growing wealth disparities, especially when flooding and famine reached beyond the peasantry and while court eunuchs enriched themselves and isolated the emperor. The Yellow Turbans numbered in the hundreds of thousands and their revolt lasted in pockets for twenty-one years, finally ending the Han dynasty in 220 CE.

Southern Europe

Micro-societies formed on the islands dotting the Aegean Sea as early as 2000 BCE, illustrating how environmental conditions resulted in a diversity of societies. Because the islands were rocky, hilly, and difficult to farm, they were connected via the sea and thus did not develop extensive agriculture or land-based territorial states. Trade with Southwest Asia and North Africa rendered the Mycenaean and Minoan cultures cosmopolitan and their accumulating wealth brought them into conflict with each other. The Mycenaeans, who had developed chariots most likely by the sixteenth century BCE, eventually prevailed over the seafaring Minoans by 1200 BCE, after which they began to dominate all of the Aegean islands. But they were in turn challenged by other sea-faring invaders, about whom little is known. The resulting three centuries (1200–900 BCE) of instability led to decentralization and the proliferation of the city-state—also known as the polis, an urban center where commercial and political interests intermingled. The city-state was a common form of community governance, known not only in Greece but in other cultures as well. Although the events of this period are hard to authenticate, Homer's detailed accounts of the warrior's life are the subjects of the *Iliad* and the *Odyssey*, epic poems composed in the eighth century BCE. Homer's identity is uncertain and the earlier versions of the poems were recited long before they were written down, as is true of all preliterate cultures. Nonetheless, the *Iliad* provides an embellished account of the last year of the Trojan War between Greece and Troy, fought in Turkey during the twelfth century BCE. After their successful siege of Troy, the *Odyssey* details the Greek warrior Odysseus's ten-year struggle to return home after the war.

Regularly assaulted by more powerful neighbors on either side of the Mediterranean, the Aegean islands formed defensive leagues that eventually fended off even the Persian Empire for nearly two hundred years. But these leagues never evolved into an empire since competitiveness and distinctiveness precluded homogenization. Competition between them was funneled into competitive sports, including the Olympic Games, established around 776 BCE. Eventually drought and the need for greater defense led to the concentration of power in the hands of oligarchic families in most poleis, and in some of them, even tyrants. An increasingly indebted and even enslaved population rose up to protest tyranny and wealth inequality. By 594 BCE the Athenian jurist Solon sought to avoid the brutal civil strife of other city-states by empowering male citizens to serve on elected councils, and by canceling debts and forbidding slavery. In Athens, free male citizens overthrew their oligarchic overlords in 507 BCE. Merchants and other free-born men selected their leaders. Athenians coined the word "democracy," although at the time it did not include women, foreigners, or any unfree persons such as slaves. Investments in public life, including the temples on the Acropolis, resulted in innovations in art, architecture, science, theater, and philosophy. Enslaved war captives mined the silver that funded this cultural

Vessel with Octopus decoration, ceramic, Minoan (Archaeological Museum Herakleion, Crete, Greece), c. 1500 BCE. Photograph by Wolfgang Sauber/license CC-SA-3.0.

Evidence of the close relationship the Minoan population had with the marine life encircling their island can be found in this object. Not only does it showcase a very lifelike octopus and other sea creatures (urchins, coral, shells), but it would have held freshwater and features handles so it could be tied to a boat during sea travel.

flourishing. In some city-states, up to 25 percent of the population was enslaved. The Peloponnesian War between the two most powerful city-states, Athens and Sparta, in 431–404 BCE, militarized both societies, exhausting resources, and occasioning philosophical speculation about the meaning of existence and right government. Although regularly challenged by usurpers, Athenian democracy endured in Greece until Alexander the Great of Macedon conquered it in 338 BCE.

On the Italian peninsula, Etruscan city-states formed in the Arno and Tiber river valleys by the eighth century BCE. They shared a language and a religion built on divination. The Etruscans were skilled artisans in iron and pottery and they gained prosperity through trade; and, from their surviving art it seems that women enjoyed more equality in their society than in Greek or Roman societies. In the eighth–sixth centuries they dominated their neighboring city-states, including Rome. But in the late sixth century BCE, Rome asserted its right to self-governance by ousting the Etruscan kings and establishing a Roman identity, which borrowed heavily from Etruscan influences. Roman domination of Etruria continued for the next six centuries until Etruscan culture was largely erased and their language lost by the first century CE.

The Roman government that followed the expulsion of kings was one of checks and balances. Annually elected magistrates carried out the daily exercise of government; following their year in office they served on a ruling council, the senate, where they deliberated policy on trade, treaties, and wars and proposed legislation; popular assemblies voted on the legislation and the annual magistrates. The Romans referred to this system as a *republic*, or "people's government," though it was in most ways an aristocracy of wealth and status. It lasted for five hundred years, through social unrest and external challenges from Greece, Gallic peoples migrating from across the Alps, and especially from Carthage in North Africa. Remarkably, the republic, suitable to the small-scale city-states of the Mediterranean, endured even as Rome pursued military expansion. Three Punic (Carthaginian) Wars, occurring intermittently for over a century, resulted in the final defeat of Carthage (264–146 BCE). After Carthage's second defeat in 202 BCE, Rome defeated the Hellenistic kingdoms in Greece and sold into slavery enormous numbers of Greeks; we read of the enslavement of 150,000 following the defeat of Epirus in 167 BCE. Consolidation in the north on the Italian and Gallic sides of the Alps under Julius Caesar from 59–51 BCE resulted in more wars, more wealth, and more slaves.

Roman militarism did not preclude genuine participatory government or cultural flourishing. Rome freely borrowed from conquered peoples, including the Etruscans and Greeks, which underpinned developments in the arts, engineering, and bureaucratic governance. Its system of representative government was the first large-scale alternative to kingship. Adult male citizens could enjoy constitutional rights to representation and fair trial. As the republic expanded its influence, senators accrued more wealth and power beginning especially in the second century BCE. Their wealth usually took the form of land, which led to the growth of slavery in Italy. From 133–121 BCE, brothers Tiberius and Gaius Gracchus, two magistrates, or tribunes, proposed legislation to redistribute land and cap wealth. Gaius Gracchus also proposed a path to Roman citizenship for Italians. This move divided his base of support; poor Romans were defensive of their citizenship, the only privilege they had. The increasingly reactionary senate took advantage of this divide and promoted the assassination of both men and three thousand of their followers.

Roman citizenship excluded slaves, and the late Republic and early Empire depended upon slavery, both to devastate defeated populations and to use their labor, even for entertainment. Gladiatorial contests demonstrated the brutality men might exact against other men; in one of Caesar's triumphal games, 2,000 men fought to the death. Owned by patrons who trained them to win in the arena, gladiators were chattel slaves boarded in training schools. Two significant slave rebellions took place in Sicily in 135–132 and 104–101 BCE. A third rebellion in southern Italy was led by Spartacus (111–71 BCE), which began with seventy enslaved trainees at the school and grew to 70,000 rebels. It lasted over a year. At the same time, Roman legions were dispersed to frontiers in Spain to suppress anticolonial uprisings and in Turkey to fight wars with the Seleucid Empire. When Roman legions finally captured Spartacus's rebels, they crucified 6,000 survivors along the Appian Way.

Although military conquests and slavery fostered a culture of violence, the Ro-

Altar of Augustan Peace (Ara Pacis Augustae), marble, Rome, Italy, 9 BCE.

Photograph by Amphipolis/license CC-SA- 2.0.

Commissioned in 9 BCE for Augustus's return from three years of war, the *Ara Pacis* was ostensibly a monument to the period of peace Augustus had given the Roman Empire (rather than a commemoration of a victorious battle or war). This altar is decorated with scenes of a procession that features representatives of different groups associated with the imperial household. The figures are carved in marble, which makes this ritual procession one they will carry out in perpetuity.

man Empire was fundamentally urban and settled. The arts, architecture, trade, and a high standard of living thrived during the late republic and empire. Caesar's successor, Octavian (63 BCE–14 CE), who received the title Augustus in 27 BCE, became the first Roman emperor and initiated a peace—the Pax Romana—that lasted for more than two hundred years. Sixty–seventy million people inhabited the Roman Empire in the early second century CE, from Scotland to the Caucasus to Sudan and North Africa, while Roman military garrisons protected its borders from invasion. Efficient administration, censorship, and the quashing of dissent largely prevented internal uprisings, especially as long as prosperity and good harvests satisfied most people's needs. Rome itself was the largest city in the world until the eighteenth century, with one million people, necessitating sophisticated transportation, sanitation, and revenue infrastructure. A complex body of law delineated the status-based rights and duties of citizens; its basic structure influenced western law for centuries. Romans worshipped a pantheon of gods and goddesses, similar to the Greeks who inspired them. Poorer Romans were generally attracted to popular mystery cults that emphasized personal salvation from this-worldly suffering in the afterlife.

Christianity took root in this context. The trial of the Jewish prophet Jesus of Nazareth for sedition resulted in his crucifixion around 30 CE. Within a decade, the preacher Paul of Tarsus (Syria) traveled widely telling stories of the messiah, the Christ, and the miracles of Jesus's life and death, gathering converts. The spread of Christianity threatened Roman rulers in Italy and across the empire, resulting in increasing persecutions by the third century CE. The outbreak of disease exacerbated the centrifugal forces threatening the empire: the Antonine Plague, or Plague of Galen, probably smallpox, from 165–180 CE, was a turning point. Increased suffering and poverty may have led more people to embrace mystery cults; unsustainable mining and agricultural practices depleted natural resources; and decadent and ineffective leadership delegitimized the regime. Above all, Huns and Persians pressed Rome's borders, tempted by its wealth, seeking to enlarge their own territories or fleeing from climate instabilities.

Sub-Saharan Africa

Some of the world's largest and earliest migrations occurred in sub-Saharan Africa as Bantu-speaking peoples spread south and east from the confluence of the Niger and Congo Rivers at least over a millennium. Migrants traded with Nubians and Sudanic people to the north who then traded in Egypt and then the Mediterranean, thus illustrating the crucial role played by migrants in connecting diverse peoples through transregional trade. Originating near major bodies of water in Nigeria/Cameroon and in Congo, some five hundred Niger Congo languages date back to 4000 BCE and are spoken by nearly 100 million people today. The immense diffusion of their languages, skills, and beliefs can be traced from the linguistic, archaeological, and genetic records. Bantu speakers settled near rivers that they navigated by canoe. They cultivated yams, okra, millet, and palm oil, which they traded with forest dwellers for meat and honey. Conflict and disease, brought by the migrants, took their toll on forest dwellers; some populations were decimated by domesticated animal-born diseases to which they had no immunity. The settlements gradually subsumed surviving hunter-gatherers into their communities—clan-defined villages headed by chiefs who governed by age-structured councils.

By 1000 BCE, Bantu-speaking migrants followed iron deposits as their interests in metallurgy grew. Some metal workers, usually male, called upon female spirits to give them power, suggesting a high degree of respect for women's reproductive and creative powers. Bantu peoples worshipped territorial and ancestral gods and women could be spirit mediums and ritual specialists alongside men. They officiated over ancestor rituals, including the sacrifice of cattle in some areas, and accessed visions and trances to offer counsel, healing, and remedies for evil. Because of the extent

Pyramids of Meroe, granite and sandstone, Kingdom of Kush (now Sudan), 300 BCE–300 CE. Photograph by Laurent de Walick/license CC-SA-2.0.

Though not initially as impressive as the Old Kingdom Pyramids at Giza, the adoption of this Egyptian burial practice—complete with pylon gates flanking the processional causeway—by the Kushite rulers two millennia later shows the staying power of the Egyptian worldview. Even after losing control over the larger empire, the rulers of Meroe still followed many of the habits their pharaonic ancestors had adopted as rulers of the Twenty-fifth dynasty (712–653 BCE).

and duration of the migration, there was a high degree of intermingling from Sudan to South Africa. The resulting diffusion of a common set of beliefs and practices informed the distinctive societies that followed.

Societies formed to the west as well. By the sixth century BCE the Nok culture of Nigeria spread over an area of 30,000 square miles, as indicated by the discovery of distinctive iron and terracotta objects. Iron weapons and decorative objects suggest both commercial and military purposes. Smelters, whose practices may have derived from the Nubians, skipped the bronze age and went straight from stone to iron, likely because of the availability of material. Dwellings were built on rings of stone, which have survived, and there is evidence of pumpkin and sorghum cultivation, indicating the organization of village life around agriculture, ritual, and defense. Terracotta figurines representing animals and people illustrate artistic accomplishment and provide clues to the social and spiritual systems of the Nok. Sculptors produced life-

Seated figure, terracotta (ceramic), Nok civilization, West Africa (Louvre Museum, Paris, France), c. sixth century BCE–sixth century CE. Public Domain

With its emphasis on the portrayal of the head, this seated figure highlights the symbolic significance of stylized and idealized features. Attributes such as jewelry and braided hair speak to the importance of these kinds of markers (of wealth, social and/or political standing), while the position itself, where the chin rests on one knee while the other leg is tucked under, shows the power of body language.

sized heads with realistic and detailed features. They sculpted jewelry, facial hair, and clothing onto the smaller figurines, some of whom held weapons or other symbols of leadership. Some figures are part animal and part human. The culture seems to have been in decline by 200 CE as indicated by the age and declining number of pottery fragments for reasons that are unclear, although its influences on later cultures in the region are clear.

North Africa

As early as 10,000 BCE migrants collected wild grains, and cultivation eventually followed in the Nile River valley. Gourds and watermelons appeared around 5000 BCE and trade with Mesopotamia spread wheat and barley. To support the growing Egyptian population, irrigation innovations such as catchment basins and dikes helped control water flow and increased access to arable land. The two distinct areas of Egypt, the Nile Delta (known as Lower Egypt) and the extensive Nile Valley (known as Upper Egypt), were first united by a legendary ruler in around 3100

Pyramid of Khufu, limestone, Giza Plateau, Egypt, 2551–2528 BCE. Photograph by Francisco Anzola/license CC-SA-2.0.

One of the wonders of the world since the third millennium BCE, the first and largest of the three pharaonic pyramids at Giza accomplished a kind of immortality for its owner, despite the fact that the mummy itself did not rest there for the intended eternity. A marvel in many fields, from the sciences (including mathematics, astronomy, and physics), to engineering, management, and logistics, it remains one of the most impressive representations of the power associated with being pharaoh and shows why the role was so desirable even to foreign rulers.

BCE—possibly an individual named Narmer, who is commemorated in a number of votive objects for exactly this feat. The *Palette of Narmer* is one of the first instances that identifies the pharaoh's hieroglyphic name in a cartouche and begins the tradition of documenting a ruler's accomplishments in both verbal and visual form. As early as the Third dynasty, rulers began to be buried in pyramid complexes, first as stepped pyramids (Djoser, r. 2630–2611 BCE), and then in the Fourth dynasty in the massive pyramids at Giza. The largest pyramid at Giza was built for the Pharaoh Khufu (2551–2528 BCE) by paid laborers and encompasses 2.3 million limestone blocks weighing 2.5 tons each, which were quarried on site. Pharaohs were now understood to be living gods and the close relationship between the ruler and the sun god is visible in the shape of the pyramid as a solar symbol, and in its alignment on an east-west axis mimicking the path of the sun.

Over the course of four millennia, pharaonic Egypt experienced several periods of decentralized power—known as "intermediate periods"—and subsequent periods of reunification. Such breakdowns in central government often followed exceptionally long reigns of an individual; economic struggles; or external threats that were not met, thus allowing smaller, regional powers or outside forces to gain importance and influence. While the intermediary periods following the Sixth dynasty (ending the Old Kingdom), the Thirteenth dynasty (ending the Middle Kingdom), and the Twentieth dynasty (ending the New Kingdom), turned Egypt upside down, they also resulted in advances and innovations that the conservative sociopolitical system of Ancient Egypt would not have permitted otherwise. For example, the Hyksos warriors introduced horses and chariots to Egypt, which changed both warfare and royal representation in the subsequent New Kingdom.

Among the many pharaohs of ancient Egypt's thirty dynasties, three New Kingdom pharaohs stand out: Hatshepsut (1479–1458 BCE), Amenhotep IV (aka Akhenaten) (1353–1336 BCE), and Ramesses II (1279–1213 BCE). As one of the few women to rule as pharaoh (a male-gendered position), Hatshepsut sought to affirm her legitimacy by claiming divine birth; erecting monuments touting her accomplishments, which included an expedition to the wealthy land of Punt; and building temples to ensure her immortality. She was generally portrayed in the traditional pharaonic garb, which includes a headdress, royal insignia, and a false beard, which usually downplayed any female attributes. Still, the presumption did not sit well with the establishment, and under her successor and stepson, Thutmose III, most visual and verbal references to her were destroyed.

The Eighteenth dynasty pharaoh Amenhotep IV changed his name to Akhenaten to signal his connection to the worship of the sun disk Aten, which he proclaimed as the new and only cult (against the long tradition of a broad Egyptian pantheon with many local cult centers). To enforce this change, he also relocated the capital city, which was to be built from scratch on an uninhabited site now known as Amarna. This experiment ended after his death, when his young son Tutankhaten (better known by his new name Tutankhamun) overturned all changes and signaled to the nation yet another instance of return to order and tradition. In the Nineteenth dynasty, the almost seven-decade-long rule of Ramesses II allowed him to embark on ambitious building and military campaigns, commissioning the most structures and monuments of any reign and stabilizing the power for his dynasty for another century. The remaining millennium of Pharaonic Egypt shows the allure of the country to other powers: it was ruled in succession by Libyans (Twenty-second dynasty), Nubians (Twenty-fifth dynasty), Saite (Twenty-sixth dynasty), Persians (Twenty-seventh dynasty), and Greeks (who founded the Ptolemaic period after the Thirtieth dynasty), until it was eventually absorbed into the Roman Empire in 31 BCE.

Egyptian pharaohs also engaged in sometimes bloody conflicts with Nubians to the south. Nubians possessed trading monopolies on ivory, gold, ebony, and access to animals and goods from tropical Africa, including panthers and monkeys. A Nubian king, Piye, defeated Egypt and became the first pharaoh of the Twenty-fifth dynasty (712–664 BCE). Eventually defeated, Nubians retreated farther south and established a new capital at Meroë where a syncretic culture survived until 400 CE. Adopting burial practices from Egypt, Nubians built pyramids and buried thirty kings and eight queens. Although defeated by Rome in a five-year war at Aswan in 22 BCE, Meroë continued on in peace until it gradually declined due to desertification and loss of trade routes. New cultures emerged from the spread of Christianity in the Sudan, including the kingdom of Makuria marked by monasteries, cathedrals, and the adoption of the Coptic language alongside "Old Nubian."

Conclusion

The diversity of cultures maps closely to the diversity of environments in which they took root. Where resources were abundant, as they were on most of the planet in the period to 300 CE, foragers and herders predominated. Where agriculture could be supported, farmers and city-dwellers predominated. In the harshest climates, nomads predominated. Through trade, people interacted in an increasing number of contact zones. Climate change disrupted every culture, but urban and imperial societies were the most vulnerable to ensuing famine or disease because their populations were not self-supporting and their wealth attracted outsiders. In moments of instability, people sought new understanding of human fragility and new forms of community. In all regions of the world, practices and beliefs formed in this period provided a foundation for successive generations. The increasing interconnectedness of the three continents constituting Afroeurasia is one of the major developments in world history, where "the world" as a cultural phenomenon (as opposed to "earth" or "planet") came into being. Interconnectedness may have been both cause and consequence of increasingly large state formations, yet even where cultures existed geographically apart from Afroeurasia, methods of living on the land, of making meaning, of forming community, share similarities.

Comprehensive Timeline

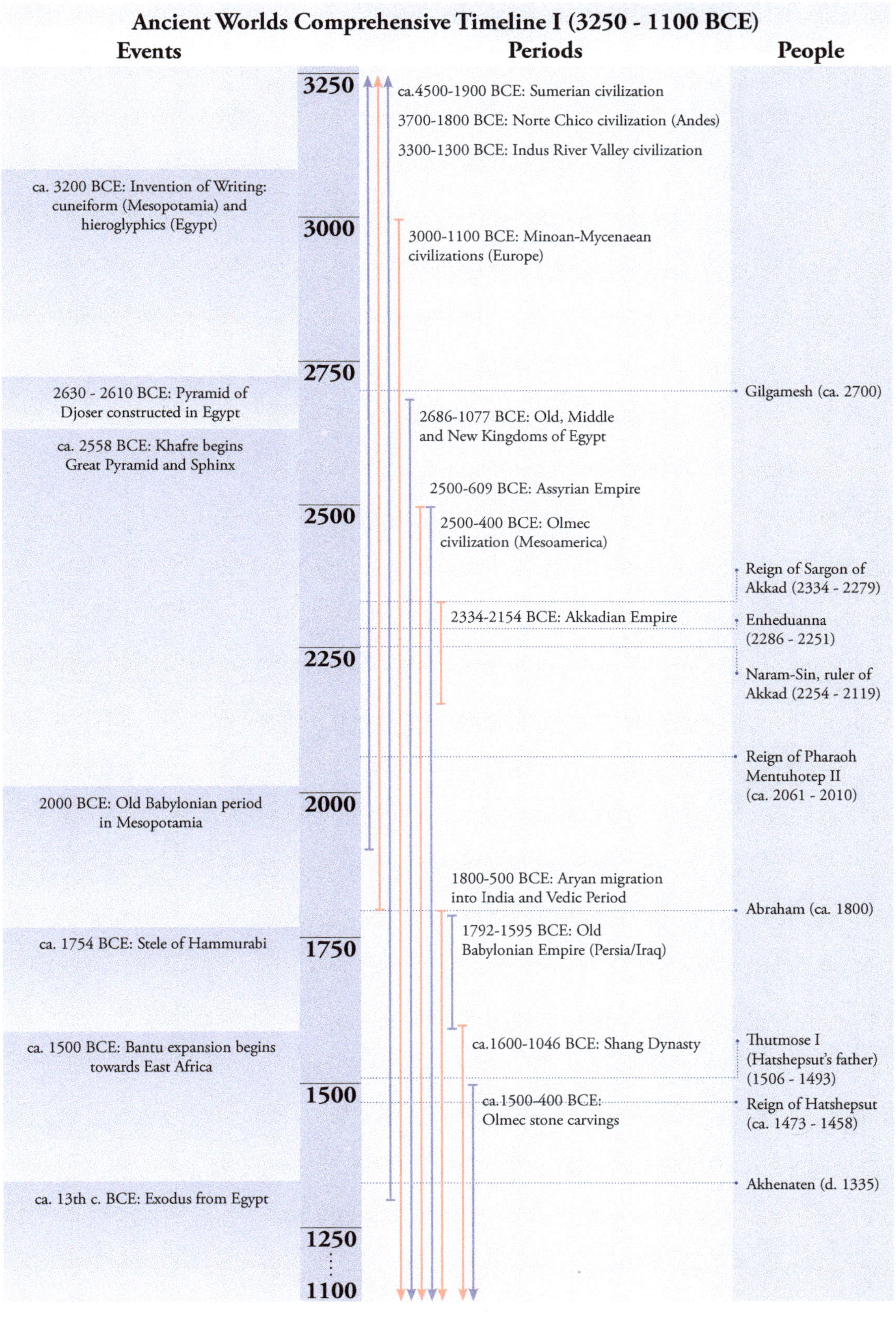

Ancient Worlds Comprehensive Timeline II (1100 - 500 BCE)

Events

- ca. 1100 BCE: *Instruction of Amenemope*
- 1070 BCE: Nubia regains independence from Egypt
- 814 BCE: Traditional founding of Carthage in North Africa by Phoenicia
- 800 - 600 BCE: Early Shramana Movements
- 722 BCE: Assyria defeats northern kingdom of Israel
- 7th c. BCE: Library of Ashurbanipal (in Nineveh)
- 7th c. BCE: Earliest compositions of Hebrew Book of Proverbs
- 586 BCE: First Temple in Jerusalem destroyed, Babylonian exile
- 539 BCE: Cyrus' conquest of Babylon
- ca. 532 BCE: First tragic dramas in Athens
- 516 BCE: Second Temple completed in Jerusalem
- 508 - 507 BCE: Establishment of democracy in Athens

1100 · **1025** · **950** · **875** · **800** · **725** · **650** · **575** · **500**

Periods

- 1050-930 BCE: United monarchy in Israel
- 1046-256 BCE: Zhou Dynasty (China)
- 1000-800 BCE Bantu migrations across sub-Saharan Africa
- 911-609 BCE: Neo-Assyrian Empire
- 900-200 BCE: Chavin Culture (Andes)
- ca. 900-300 BCE: *Upanishads*
- ca. 800-480 BCE: Archaic Greece
- 771-476 BCE: Spring and Autumn Period in China
- 626-539 BCE: Neo-Babylonian Empire
- ca. 6th-3rd c. BCE: *Daodejing*
- 550-330 BCE: Achaemenid Period (Persia)

People

- Homer (8th c.)
- Rule of Kings at Rome (753 - 509)
- Sappho (ca. 630 - 570)
- Cyrus the Great (ca. 600 - 530)
- Pythagoras (ca. 570 - 495)
- Confucius (551 - 479)
- Mahavira (ca. 6th - 5th c.)
- Laozi (ca. 6th - 4th c.)

Ancient Worlds Comprehensive Timeline III (500 - 100 BCE)

Events

- 500 BCE: Ile Ife - Ancient Yoruba city founded
- 490-479 BCE: Persian Wars
- 450 BCE: Hebrew Bible (Tanakh) compilation completed
- ca. 440 BCE: Beginning of Mohism in China
- 415 BCE: Destruction of Melos
- 387 BCE: Plato founds the Academy
- ca. 300 BCE: Mahayana splits from Theravada
- 3rd. c. BCE: Great Wall of China begins construction
- 256 BCE: Ashoka's earliest rock edicts
- 213 BCE: Burning of the *Book of Songs*
- 167 BCE: Antiochus IV outlaws Judaism, Maccabean revolt begins
- 100 BCE - 200 CE: Buddhist dialogues: "Questions of Milinda"

Periods

500

- ca.500 BCE-200 CE: Ancient Nok Culture (Africa)
- 500-200 BCE: Hieroglyphs at Zapotec (Mexico)
- 5th-1st c. BCE: Oral Pali Canon
- 475-221 BCE: Warring States Period (China)

450

- 431-404 BCE: Peloponnesian War

400

- 400 BCE - 400 CE: *Ramayana* and *Mahabharata*
- 400 BCE - 250 CE: Late Pre-Classic Maya Period (Mesoamerica)

350

- 332-160 BCE: Judea under Greek rule
- 322-185 BCE: Mauryan Empire (India)

300

250

- 247 BCE - 224 CE: Parthian Empire (Present-day Iran)
- 221-206 BCE: Qin Dynasty (China)
- 202 BCE - 220 CE: Han Dynasty (China)

200

- 200 BCE - 200 CE: *Natyasastra* compiled

150

- 150 BCE - 200 CE: Construction and rise of Teotihuacan (Mexico)
- 140-37 BCE: Hasmonean Dynasty

100

People

- Siddhartha Gautama (5th c.)
- Socrates (ca. 470 - 399)
- Thucydides (ca. 460 - 400)
- Plato (ca. 427 - 348)
- Euripides (d. 406)
- Zhuangzi (ca. 4th c.)
- Aristotle (384 - 322)
- Alexander the Great (356 - 323)
- Ashoka (304 -232)
- Han Feizi (ca. 280 - 233)
- Qin Shi Huang (259 - 210)
- Judas Maccabeus (d. 160)

Ancient Worlds Comprehensive Timeline IV (100 BCE - 300 CE)

Scale	Events	Periods	People
100		100 BCE-500 CE: Hopewell cultures in North America	
		57 BCE-668 CE: Three Kingdoms of Korea	
50			Reign of Herod the Great (37 - 4)
		27 BCE-476 CE: Roman Empire	Reign of Augustus (27 BCE - 14 CE)
	19 BCE: Virgil's *Aeneid*		
	1st c. CE: Asvaghosha's *Buddhacharita*		
1 CE	ca. 1st c. Buddhism introduced to China (Mahayana)		Jesus (ca. 4 BCE - 30 CE)
			Ban Zhao (ca. 45 - 116 CE)
50	50-57 CE: Apostle Paul's letters to churches		Epictetus (50 - 135)
	70 CE: Second Temple destroyed by Rome	70-110 CE: Gospels composed	
		100-700 CE: Moche civilization (Present-day Peru)	
100		100-700 CE: Kingdom of Aksum (Ethiopia)	Reign of Trajan (98 - 117)
		100-1600 CE: Ancestral Puebloans flourish in present-day Four Corners Region	Reign of Kanishka, Kushan Emperor (127 - 150)
			Emperor Keiko (d. 130)
150			
	ca. 200 CE Mishnah compiled		
200	203 CE: Martyrdom of Perpetua and Felicity	ca. 3rd-6th c. CE: sacred text *Avesta* collated (Zorastrian)	Bhasa (3rd c.)
250		250-900 CE: Classic Maya Period (Mesoamerica)	
300		ca. 300-1100 CE: West African Wagadou (Ghana) Empire	Kalidasa (4th - 5th c.)
	313 CE: Edict of Milan		

Cosmogonic Myths

Introduction

What does it mean to label a story a **myth**? For many, the word denotes some type of false narrative, a tale left over from a prescientific age, when people invented stories to explain what they could not understand. In more contemporary times, we use the term to indicate ideas that wield great social and political influence by those in power, but that are nonetheless often distorting or problematic. Take, for example, the "myth of the American frontier" that was used to justify settler colonialist expansion and genocide. Or, in another example, the "myth of the melting pot" romanticizes conformity or assimilation to hegemonic ideas about race, religion, and ethnic identity by undermining the value of diversity. Other contemporary forms of myth might include the Star Wars, Harry Potter, and the Marvel heroes of comics, graphic novels, and films. Myth, especially as interpreted, applied, and adapted from dominant cultures, can have a powerful influence in the ways that people think and act, conceive and dream, even live and die.

Ancient peoples certainly engaged in mythmaking, and there can be little doubt that their myths were often attempts to explain the world in which they lived. The modern connotation of "myth" as "not true" does not capture the impact of these stories in peoples' lives, and yet it would be a misreading and misunderstanding if we read them literally. Myths are not mathematical proofs or scientific formulae; they are better viewed as works of art, as creative products of the human imagination to try to order the otherwise chaotic experience of human beings in the natural world. They are evocative rather than demonstrable, symbolic rather than factual; myths are **metaphors** in narrative form. They are also sparse, even skeletal, and can be developed according to the circumstances of the teller and the audience. Consider, for example, the strange Greek myth of the Titan Kronos, who devours his own children. It is the gruesome tale of a deranged and very dysfunctional father, but tragic writers use this myth as a metaphor for conflict between generations. Philosophers use it as a metaphor for the relationship between tyrannical rulers and their people. And other Greek and Roman writers noted that Kronos was similar to *chronos* (time), and thus, through wordplay, the myth expresses a truth with which modern physics still grapples: Why does time move only in one direction, and why are we all subject to its toll? Truly, time does eventually consume us all.

Scholars who have studied myths have identified at least three main types. **Archetypal myths** present patterns for some forms of human behavior, especially ritualized behaviors. In the Jewish Passover Seder, the youngest child asks a series of questions such as: Why is this night different from other nights? And why do we engage in certain activities only on this night? To answer, the one leading the ritual tells the story of the first Passover, found in the biblical Book of Exodus, and explains that their actions are reenactments of this original event. The hero myth, which often includes the hero's birth, challenges, and victories, is a nearly universal form of the archetypal myth. **Etiological myths** tell of the cause or origin of some particular thing, usually, but not always, a natural phenomenon. "How the Tiger Got His Stripes" (Asian) or "How the Raven Became Black" (Native American) would be examples of this type of myth; these stories also usually contain an appropriate moral reminding people how to behave.

Creation stories or **cosmogonic myths** concern how the world in which we humans live came to be, or at least how it came to be a meaningful place for human habitation. The term "cosmogonic" is a combination of two Greek words—*cosmos* (the ***ordered*** universe) and the suffix *-gony* (birth or beginning). Cosmogonic myths focus on the ways in which the world we live in was ordered and structured for human beings, rather than explaining the ultimate origin of everything. A cosmogonic myth may begin, therefore, in the habitation of the gods, or with a primeval ocean filled with animals, in a cave deep beneath the earth, or with a supernatural figure or figures who may think or speak the world that we know into existence or generate it through sexual activity. To probe behind these beginnings, to ask about the origins of the gods or the first animals, or what existed before the primeval waters is to ask an unanswerable and even a meaningless question, not unlike the claim by modern physicists like the late Stephen Hawking that to inquire of what came before the Big Bang—that is, what came before time and space existed—is to ask that which we cannot answer.

The history of the study of myths sometimes reveals more about the cultural position and perspective of the scholar rather than the engagement with how people within the culture understand them. For example, the Scottish mythologist Sir James Frazer (1854–1941) collected myths from all over the world to write his famous study *The Golden Bough* (orig. pub. 1890) and noticed that despite the wide variety of myths he was able to obtain, they displayed only a small number of varied themes based on categories most prominent in Christian sources, such as floods and the presence of a singular all-powerful creator deity. Through the narrowing of these viable themes, proof of a possible common pattern emerged that scholars took to undergird all human experience. For Sigmund Freud (1856–1939) and Carl Jung (1875–1961), the founders of psychoanalysis, these recurrent figures and themes provided insight into the "universal" human subconscious—they were the shared symbols that connoted the ability of a maturing humanity to think in abstract terms and thus to locate themselves in time and in space. How does this approach to the study of myths reflect the Western values of these scholars? How might an approach embodying different cultural values impact our engagement with these narratives? How might employing multiple perspectives enable your reading of the following selection of myths from different cultures?

Rodger Payne
Department of Religious Studies

PRE-READING PARS

1. What informs your ideas about the origin of the cosmos? Science? Religion? Philosophy?
2. Identify three to five details of the Star Wars or Harry Potter series (or similar stories) that could be described as elements of archetypal hero myths. What patterns for human behavior do they suggest?
3. Identify two or three ways that you respond differently to an oral rather than written narration.
4. How do you use common narratives like origin stories to understand yourself or the world around you?

Cosmogonic Myths

How the World Was Made, as told by Kathi Smith Littlejohn, Cherokee storyteller

Remember that all myths were originally oral traditions and were intended to be heard rather than read. Storytelling is a performance art that draws the audience into the narrative, and the storyline may be further embellished and amended by the storyteller. Kathi Smith Littlejohn of Cherokee, North Carolina, is among the best known of contemporary storytellers, and this version of the Cherokee cosmogonic myth was initially delivered orally to children. The myth itself exemplifies a theme known as the "earth-diver," in which an animal is responsible for creating the land upon we as humans live. What experiences might have informed such an idea? What does this myth suggest about the relationship between human beings and the natural world?

This is another legend about mud.
We like legends about mud.
A long time ago,
  there were only two people and the animals.
And they all lived together
    on a tiny little rock in the middle of the water.
One was a grandfather,
    and one was his grandson, a little baby.
And as babies do,
    he started to grow.
Can you still wear the shoes that you wore when you were in
    Kindergarten?
No.
Why?

What happened?
You grew, that's right.
What about, does anybody wear diapers in here?
No.
Because why?
That's just for babies and you got too big, didn't you?
Well, that's what started happening with this baby. He started growing,
    and he started learning to crawl,
    and then he started learning to walk,
    and then he began to play.
And when he was about your age,
    there was no more room on the rock.
He said,
    "Grandfather, I really wish I had some more room to play.
    I can't do anything, I bump into you, I bump into the animals,
    they bump into me,
    and I'm still growing."
The grandfather thought,
    "You know that is—that's going to be a real problem
    because, what's going to happen when he's sixteen?"
So all the animals started talking about,
    "This is a real problem. What are we going to do?"
So the animals decided that they would dive down into the water
    and try to find some more land.
One tried,
    and went all the way down as far as he could
    and came back and said,
    "I ran out of air. I just can't go any further."
Nobody else wanted to try.
Finally Mr. Turtle said,
    "I can.
    I can stay on the bottom of water for a long time without air.
    Maybe I can find some more land."
So he went down into the water,
    and they all watched him go out of sight,
    and he was gone for seven days.
Finally, on the seventh day,
    they saw some bubbles coming up out of the water,
    and they all ran to look and see if he was coming back.
And slowly they began to see him come into sight,
    and they were very sad
    because he was dead.

The water had killed him.
He'd run out of air and he died.
But then they saw
    that on the bottom of all four of his feet
    there was some mud.
And they carefully got all the mud off,
    and they laid it out on the rock to dry,
    and they watched it carefully.
And when it was dry enough,
    Grandfather threw it out into the water,
    and it became land,
    just as we have land today,
    except it was very soft and very muddy.
And the buzzard flew off of the rock with his great wings,
    and said,
    "With the air from my wings,
    I'll make a fan and dry it
    so we can walk on this new land."
But
    each time when his wings went down,
    it would make a big valley,
    and each time the wings would go up,
    it would make a big mountain.
And pretty soon the animals said,
    "If we don't stop him
    there's not gonna be any land flat enough to walk on."
So they called him back,
    and today,
    when you look all around us,
    what do we have here?
Mountains
    where his wings went up and made the mountains,
    and valleys
    when they went down.
But if they hadn't stopped him,
    the whole world would look just like Cherokee.
And that's how the world was made.

Genesis 1–2: Creation

There are two accounts of creation in the biblical Book of Genesis, which forms a part of the **canon** of scripture (authoritative writings) for both Jews and Christians.

Both versions can be ascribed as stories of ***creation ex nihilo***, a Latin term meaning "creation from out of nothing," since God alone exists before anything else. The first account (chapters 1:1–2:3) is highly structured, even poetic in its description; the second—and probably older—account (chapter 2:4–25) reverses the order of the preceding by placing human beings as the first among God's creations, who are made using the "dust of the ground." What other differences can you find? What do you think are the various meanings suggested in each account? How are human beings related to nature here?

Chapter 1

1 When God began to create heaven and earth— 2 the earth being unformed and
void, with darkness over the surface of the deep and a wind from God sweeping over
the water— 3 God said, "Let there be light"; and there was light. 4 God saw that
the light was good, and God separated the light from the darkness. 5 God called the
light Day, and the darkness He called Night. And there was evening and there was
morning, a first day.

6 God said, "Let there be an expanse in the midst of the water, that it may separate
water from water." 7 God made the expanse, and it separated the water which was
below the expanse from the water which was above the expanse. And it was so. 8 God
called the expanse Sky. And there was evening and there was morning, a second day.

9 God said, "Let the water below the sky be gathered into one area, that the dry
land may appear." And it was so. 10 God called the dry land Earth, and the gathering
of waters He called Seas. And God saw that this was good. 11 And God said, "Let
the earth sprout vegetation: seed-bearing plants, fruit trees of every kind on earth
that bear fruit with the seed in it." And it was so. 12 The earth brought forth vegetation: seed-bearing plants of every kind, and trees of every kind bearing fruit with the
seed in it. And God saw that this was good. 13 And there was evening and there was
morning, a third day.

14 God said, "Let there be lights in the expanse of the sky to separate day from
night; they shall serve as signs for the set times—the days and the years; 15 and they
serve as lights in the expanse of the sky to shine upon the earth." And it was so. 16
God made the two great lights, the greater light to dominate the day and the lesser
light to dominate the night, and the stars. 17 And God set them in the expanse of the
sky to shine upon the earth, 18 to dominate the day and the night, and to separate
light from darkness. And God saw that this was good. 19 And there was evening and
there was morning, a fourth day.

20 God said, "Let the waters bring forth swarms of living creatures, and birds that
fly above the earth across the expanse of the sky." 21 God created the great sea monsters, and all the living creatures of every kind that creep, which the waters brought
forth in swarms, and all the winged birds of every kind. And God saw that this was
good. 22 God blessed them, saying, "Be fertile and increase, fill the waters in the

seas, and let the birds increase on the earth." 23 And there was evening and there was morning, a fifth day.

24 God said, "Let the earth bring forth every kind of living creature: cattle, creeping things, and wild beasts of every kind." And it was so. 25 God made wild beasts of every kind and cattle of every kind, and all kinds of creeping things of the earth. And God saw that this was good. 26 And God said, "Let us make man in our image, after our likeness. They shall rule the fish of the sea, the birds of the sky, the cattle, the whole earth, and all the creeping things that creep on earth." 27 And God created man in His image, in the image of God He created him; male and female He created them. 28 God blessed them and God said to them, "Be fertile and increase, fill the earth and master it; and rule the fish of the sea, the birds of the sky, and all the living things that creep on earth." 29 God said, "See, I give you every seed-bearing plant that is upon all the earth, and every tree that has seed-bearing fruit; they shall be yours for food. 30 And to all the animals on land, to all the birds of the sky, and to everything that creeps on earth, in which there is the breath of life, [I give] all the green plants for food." And it was so. 31 And God saw all that He had made, and found it very good. And there was evening and there was morning, the sixth day.

Chapter 2

1 The heaven and the earth were finished, and all their array. 2 On the seventh day God finished the work that He had been doing, and He ceased on the seventh day from all the work that He had done. 3 And God blessed the seventh day and declared it holy, because on it God ceased from all the work of creation that He had done.

4 Such is the story of heaven and earth when they were created. When the Lord God made earth and heaven—

5 when no shrub of the field was yet on earth and no grasses of the field had yet sprouted, because the Lord God had not sent rain upon the earth and there was no man to till the soil, 6 but a flow would well up from the ground and water the whole surface of the earth— 7 the Lord God formed man from the dust of the earth. He blew into his nostrils the breath of life, and man became a living being. 8 The Lord God planted a garden in Eden, in the east, and placed there the man whom He had formed. 9 And from the ground the Lord God caused to grow every tree that was pleasing to the sight and good for food, with the tree of life in the middle of the garden, and the tree of knowledge of good and bad. 10 A river issues from Eden to water the garden, and it then divides and becomes four branches. 11 The name of the first is Pishon, the one that winds through the whole land of Havilah, where the gold is. 12 (The gold of that land is good; bdellium is there, and lapis lazuli.) 13 The name of the second river is Gihon, the one that winds through the whole land of Cush. 14 The name of the third river is Tigris, the one that flows east of Asshur. And the fourth river is the Euphrates. 15 The Lord God took the man and placed him in the garden of Eden, to till it and tend it. 16 And the Lord God commanded the man, saying, "Of

every tree of the garden you are free to eat; 17 but as for the tree of knowledge of good and bad, you must not eat of it; for as soon as you eat of it, you shall die."

18 The Lord God said, "It is not good for man to be alone; I will make a fitting helper for him." 19 And the Lord God formed out of the earth all the wild beasts and all the birds of the sky, and brought them to the man to see what he would call them; and whatever the man called each living creature, that would be its name. 20 And the man gave names to all the cattle and to the birds of the sky and to all the wild beasts; but for Adam no fitting helper was found. 21 So the Lord God cast a deep sleep upon the man; and, while he slept, He took one of his ribs and closed up the flesh at that spot. 22 And the Lord God fashioned the rib that He had taken from the man into a woman; and He brought her to the man. 23 Then the man said, "This one at last is bone of my bones, and flesh of my flesh. This one shall be called Woman, for from man was she taken." 24 Hence a man leaves his father and mother and clings to his wife, so that they become one flesh. 25 The two of them were naked, the man and his wife, yet they felt no shame.

Rig Veda: Purusa-sukta/Cosmic Man

"Hinduism" is a colonial term meant to combine the multitude of ideas and practices that originated on the Indian subcontinent into a single religion. Thus, unlike Judaism and Christianity there is no single myth that can be called *the* Hindu cosmogonic myth; indeed, sacred writings such as the Vedas contain many variants of cosmogonic narratives. This Vedic account narrates a primordial sacrifice from which both the cosmos and human beings arise. Cosmogonic myths from many other cultures—such as Mesopotamian, Norse, and some African cultures—similarly narrate the necessity of a primordial sacrifice. What might make this such a widespread claim in such different times and places?

1 Purusa[6] has a thousand heads, a thousand eyes, a thousand feet. He pervaded the earth on all sides and extended beyond it as far as ten fingers.

2 It is Purusa who is all this, whatever has been and whatever is to be. He is the ruler of immortality, when he grows beyond everything through food.[7]

3 Such is his greatness, and Purusa is yet more than this. All creatures are a quarter of him; three quarters are what is immortal in heaven.

4 With three quarters Purusa rose upwards, and one quarter of him still remains

6. Purusa is a giant, cosmic man whose different parts shape the world. While some scholars have referred to this as a "dismemberment myth" in comparison to Osiris, Ymir, and others, it is important to see these gods and figures as being both the whole and their parts simultaneously.

7. This rather obscure phrase seems to imply that through food (perhaps the sacrificial offering) Purusa grows beyond the world of the immortals, even as he grows beyond the earth (v. 1 and v. 5). He himself also transcends both what grows by food and what does not (v, 4), i.e., the world of animate and inanimate creatures, or Agni (eater) and Soma (eaten).

here. From this[8] he spread out in all directions, into that which eats and that which does not eat.

5 From him Viraj[9] was born, and from Viraj came Purusa. When he was born, he ranged beyond the earth behind and before.

6 When the gods spread the sacrifice[10] with Purusa as the offering, spring was the clarified butter, summer the fuel, autumn the oblation.

7 They anointed[11] Purusa, the sacrifice[12] born at the beginning, upon the sacred grass. With him the gods, Sadhyas,[13] and sages sacrificed.

8 From that sacrifice in which everything was offered, the melted fat was collected, and he made it into those beasts who live in the air, in the forest, and in villages.

9 From that sacrifice in which everything was offered, the verses and chants were born, the metres were born from it, and from it the formulas were born.

10 Horses were born from it, and those other animals that have two rows of teeth; cows were born from it, and from it goats and sheep were born.

11 When they divided the Man, into how many parts did they apportion him? What do they call his mouth, his two arms and thighs and feet?

12 His mouth became the Brahmin; his arms were made into the Warrior, his thighs the People, and from his feet the Servants were born.[14]

13 The moon was born from his mind; from his eye the sun was born. Indra and Agni came from his mouth, and from his vital breath the Wind was born.

14 From his navel the middle realm of space arose; from his head the sky evolved. From his two feet came the earth, and the quarters of the sky from his ear. Thus the gods set the worlds in order.

8. That is, from the quarter still remaining on earth, or perhaps from the condition in which he had already spread out from earth with three quarters of his form.

9. The active female creative principle, Viraj is later replaced by Prakrti or material nature, the mate of Purusa in the Sankhya school of philosophy.

10. This is the word used to indicate the performance of a Vedic fire sacrifice, spread or stretched out (like the earth spread upon the cosmic waters) or woven (like a fabric upon a loom). What follows describes Purusa as an offering made to the fire sacrifice. Early Vedic rituals sometimes included animal offerings in addition to flowers, rice, butter, soma (juice of a type of possibly hallucinogenic plant), and other items given to the fire. In response to Buddhist (and likely Jain) critiques, Vedic sacrifices eventually ceased using animals.

11. The word actually means "to sprinkle" with consecrated water, but indicates the consecration of an initiate or a king.

12. Here "the sacrifice" indicates the sacrificial victim; they are explicitly identified with one another (and with the divinity to whom the sacrifice is dedicated) in verse 16.

13. A class of demi-gods or saints, whose name literally means "those who are yet to be fulfilled."

14. The four classes of *varnas*, or castes, of classical Indian society. This is the earliest extant mention of this social system.

15 There were seven enclosing-sticks[15] for him, and thrice seven fuel-sticks, when the gods, spreading the sacrifice, bound Purusa as the sacrificial beast.

16 With the sacrifice the gods sacrificed to the sacrifice.[16] These were the first ritual laws. These very powers reached the dome of the sky where dwell the Sadhyas, the ancient gods.

Chāndogya Upanishad: The Cosmic Egg

The *Upanishads*, as part of the *Vedas*, reflect the last layer of development that provides further interpretations on earlier Vedic ideas. As with the theme of the earth-diver or the primordial sacrifice, the use of the egg as a metaphor for creation is one common to many cultures. What might be the experience or reasoning behind this? Could you compare the idea of the cosmic egg to any contemporary concepts of the beginning of the universe?

1. The Sun is Brahman—this is the teaching. An explanation thereof (is this). In the beginning this (world) was non-existent. It became existent. It grew. It turned into an egg. It lay for the period of a year. It burst open. Then came out of the egg-shell, two parts, one of silver, the other of gold.

2. That which was of silver is this earth, that which was of gold is the sky. What was the outer membrane is the mountains; that which was the inner membrane is the mist with the clouds. What were the veins were the rivers; what was the fluid within is the ocean.

3. And what was born from it is the yonder sun. When he was born, shouts and hurrays as also all being and all desires arose. Therefore at his rise and his every return, shouts and hurrays as also all being and all desires arise.

4. He, who knowing thus, meditates on the sun as Brahman, pleasant shouts will come unto him and delight him, yea, delight him.

Why the Sun and Moon Live in the Sky (Ibibio/Nigerian)

As narratives that indicate the human relationship to the cosmos, myths are filled with elements and symbols drawn from the natural world. Our ancient ancestors knew that both the sun and water were essential for life, and so many myths are concerned with understanding this significance. This myth, from the Ibibio people of present-day Nigeria, offers an explanation of the separation of these important forces. What type of myth is this? What truths about the natural world are expressed here? Do you think that the myth is meant to be intentionally humorous?

15. The enclosing-sticks are green twigs that keep the fire from spreading; the fuel-sticks are seasoned wood used for kindling.

16. The meaning is that Purusa was both the victim that the gods sacrificed and the divinity to whom the sacrifice was dedicated; that is, he was both the subject and the object of the sacrifice. Through a typical Vedic paradox, the sacrifice itself creates the sacrifice.

Many years ago the sun and the water were great friends, and both lived on the earth together. The sun very often used to visit the water, but the water never returned his visits. At last the sun asked the water why it was that he never came to see him in his house. The water replied that the sun's house was not big enough, and that if he came with his people he would drive the sun out.

The water then said, "If you wish me to visit you, you must build a very large compound; but I warn you that it will have to be a tremendous place, as my people are very numerous and take up a lot of room."

The sun promised to build a very big compound, and soon afterward he returned home to his wife, the moon, who greeted him with a broad smile when he opened the door. The sun told the moon what he had promised the water, and the next day he commenced building a huge compound in which to entertain his friend.

When it was completed, he asked the water to come and visit him the next day.

When the water arrived, he called out to the sun and asked him whether it would be safe for him to enter, and the sun answered, "Yes, come in, my friend."

The water then began to flow in, accompanied by the fish and all the water animals.

Very soon the water was knee-deep, so he asked the sun if it was still safe, and the sun again said, "Yes," so more water came in.

When the water was level with the top of a man's head, the water said to the sun, "Do you want more of my people to come?"

The sun and the moon both answered, "Yes," not knowing any better, so the water flowed in, until the sun and moon had to perch themselves on the top of the roof.

Again the water addressed the sun, but, receiving the same answer, and more of his people rushing in, the water very soon overflowed the top of the roof, and the sun and the moon were forced to go up into the sky, where they have remained ever since.

Duncan, Barbara. "How the World Was Made," as told by Kathi Smith Littlejohn. In *Living Stories of the Cherokee*, 40–43. Chapel Hill: University of North Carolina Press, 1998.

"Genesis 1–2." In Tanakh: A New Translation of the Holy Scriptures According to the Traditional Hebrew Text, 3–5. Philadelphia, PA: The Jewish Publication Society, 1985.

"Purusa-Sukta." In *The Rig Veda: An Anthology*, selected, translated, and edited by Wendy Doniger O'Flaherty, 29–32. New York: Penguin Books, 2005.

Radhakrishnan, Sarvepalli. "Section 19: The Cosmic Egg." In *The Principal Upanisads*, 399–400. Atlantic Highlands, NJ: Humanities Press, 1992.

Dayrell, Elphinstone. "Why the Sun and Moon Live in the Sky." In *Folk Stories from Southern Nigeria West Africa*, 64–65. London: Longmans Green, 1910.

POST-READING PARS

1. How does divine agency work in these myths? Is creation always an act of a divinity? Do these myths seem to encourage human creativity?
2. What features of archetypal hero myths do you see in these narratives?
3. What etiologies, or causes of things, did you find in these myths?
4. How does your reading of these stories affect the way you view being human, or your connection to the natural world?

African Family Songs: "Mother's Song" (Loma), "Blessings Upon an Infant" (Ga), and "A Mother to Her First-Born" (Lango)

Introduction

The original authors of these three poems, "Blessings Upon an Infant," "Mothers' Song," and "A Mother to Her First-Born," remain unknown because of the nature of oral literature, which is the traditional source of the poems. As such, they were passed on from generation to generation through **memorization** and performed as **songs** or **chants.** Unlike today's literary production, which emphasizes individual copyrights, in traditional African societies, poetry and songs belonged to everyone. Although there were official storytellers, like the griot in West Africa, any member of the community could become a great storyteller based on how well they could recite, embellish/improvise, and transmit through voice a well-known song or poem. This art and craft of storytelling—**orature**—is a combination of orality and literature and embodies the creative power and skill of the narrator who often would be expressing communal narratives that highlight the values, beliefs, rituals, and fears of the community. What other examples of orature come to your mind?

Since these poems go back several generations when African languages and cultures were not yet impacted by European influences, they reflect **African aesthetics** (sensibilities involving the nature of beauty and the manner of its appreciation and value of artistic expressions from African perspectives) in subject matter, imagery, voice, and perspective. All three are from **sub-Saharan Africa**, the parts of the African

SNAPSHOT BOX

LANGUAGE: Loma, Ga, and Lango

DATE: Oral sources

LOCATION: Present-day Ghana, Liberia, Uganda, and Southern Sudan

GENRE: Poems, songs

Ethnic identities: Ga, Loma, and Langi (singular: Lango) peoples

CONTEXTUAL INFORMATION: Transcribed from African languages and published in the 19th–20th centuries

TAGS: Desire and Happiness; Family; Music; Oral Histories and Storytelling; Women and Gender

Timeline

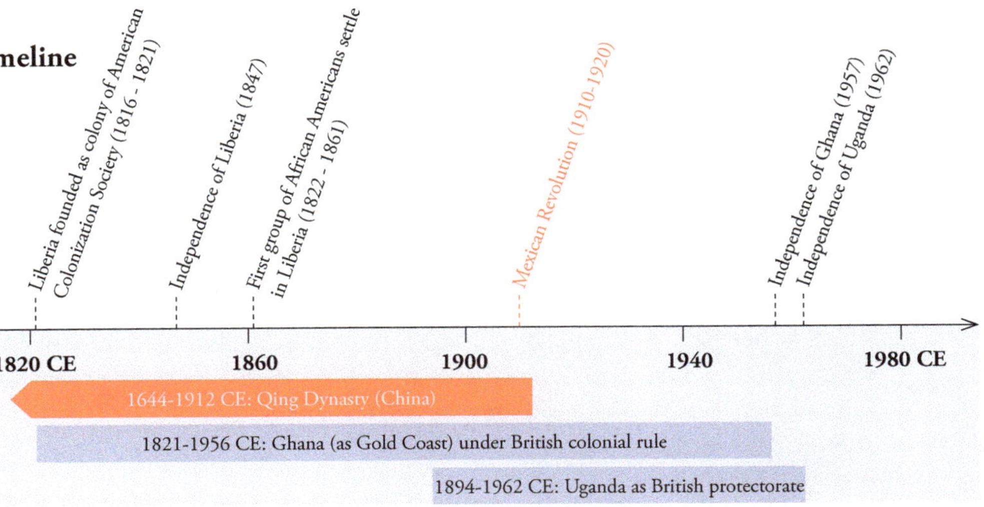

continent that lie south of the Sahara Desert. These Anglophone areas were colonized by the British who introduced English as a language of business and government, which explains how or why the transcribers of the poems you will read were living in these regions.

The first poem, "Blessings Upon an Infant," was transcribed by the social anthropologist Margaret Joyce Field (born in Gloucester; 1899–1971) when she was stationed in Ghana (then called the Gold Coast while under British colonial rule from 1821–1956) as a British government correspondent. In March 1957, the Gold Coast became independent and renamed itself Ghana after the ancient West African Empire it had formerly been a part of. Field first published this poem in her book ***Religion and Medicine of the Ga People*** published by Oxford University Press, first in 1937, and later in 1961. In most traditional African cultures, the birth of a child was a special occasion for celebration, and this poem celebrates that event. It is a prayer that is chanted on the eighth day after a child is born among the Ga. For the first seven days, the baby is believed to wander between the spiritual and physical world and can decide to return to the former. On the eighth day, the infant is likely to survive and consequently brought outside to be publicly acknowledged in what is called the outdooring ceremony, when the baby is given a day name, which corresponds to the day of the week it was born. Relatives and friends gather at dawn when the baby is brought outside for the first time. The speaker in the poem is often an elder who holds the baby and chants the prayer.

The second poem, "Mother's Song," was recorded by American artist and Iowa-born writer Esther Warner (1910–2002) while living among the Loma people in Liberia with her husband, who worked with the Firestone Rubber Plantation founded in the 1920s during World War II in 1941–1944. Liberia was founded in 1816 as a colony of the American Colonization Society for the intention of resettling former US enslaved persons. The first group of African Americans arrived and settled in Liberia in 1822. Liberia declared its independence from the American Colonization Society in 1847 but was not recognized as a nation by the United States until 1862. This poem first appeared in ***Seven Days to Lomaland***, in 1954. In this poem, some of the beliefs, values, and fears of the Loma people are captured. The last line, "In the town of the Dead," is a reference to the realm of ancestral spirits.

Jack H. Driberg (1886–1946) was an Assam-born British colonial administrator in Uganda from 1912 to 1921; he then transferred to Sudan until his retirement from colonial service in 1925. Between 1884 and 1885, during the scramble for Africa when the continent was partitioned at the Berlin Conference, Uganda was assigned to the British. In 1894, Uganda became a British protectorate until it fought for independence, which was recognized in October 1962. Driberg spent six years among the Langi people in Northern Uganda and the neighboring areas of Southern Sudan from whom the third poem, "A Mother to Her First-Born," originates. It was first published in ***Initiation: Translations from Poems of the Didinga and Lango Tribes*** in 1932. This poem celebrates the birth of a son from a mother's point of view. It is written in the traditional style and aesthetics of the East African song genre—strong lyricism and dramatic, narrative verse. In the poem, the mother sings to the child with love and pride, while perhaps working in the field or preparing a meal while the baby is strapped on her back.

As you read these poems/songs, consider what might have gotten lost in the process of transcription into English.

Mildred Barya
Department of English

PRE-READING PARS

1. Do you remember any songs that your mother or guardian sang to you? If so, what were they about?
2. What are two hopes you would have for children who are being born now?
3. Tell the story about how your parents decided to give you your name.

African Family Songs

Mother's Song [A Loma poem from Liberia]

When a son leaves our womb,
We are joyously glad;
The gladness heals us.
When he leaves our larger womb,
The village, we lie torn, bleeding:
There is no healing, no healing
Until a son returns to us,
There is no healing;
Only when he returns
Can there be healing.
Oh, oh, our sons,
Stay with us now
Until we come together
In the town of the Dead.

Blessings Upon an Infant [A Ga poem from Ghana]

Rites During the Childhood of Ordinary Children

After the child is born it is 'kept like an egg' indoors for seven days. It is then held to have survived seven dangers, and is worthy to be called a person.

On the eighth day very early in the morning, about four o'clock, two women of the father's family are sent to bring the child from the mother's home, where it was born and where it will be suckled, to its father's house. The friends and relatives assemble in the yard outside the house for the *kpodʒiemɔ* or 'going-out' ceremony.

An elder, chosen for their admirable character, asks a blessing with rum and then takes the child in their arms and lifts it upwards three times. Then they make a speech of which several variations have been given to me. The assembled company chime in between each phrase with '*Yao!*,' or some other exclamation of assent.

[...]

Hail, hail, hail! May happiness come. Yao!

Are our voices one? Yao!
Hail, let happiness come. Yao!
The stranger who has come, their back is towards the darkness. Yao!
Their face is towards the light. Yao!
May they work for their father. Yao!
May they work for their mother. Yao!
May they not steal. Yao!
May they not be wicked. Yao!
The children of this family forgive everything that can be forgiven. Yao!
May they eat by the work of their five fingers. Yao!
May they come to respect the world. Yao!
Upon their mother's head, Life. Yao!
Upon their father's head, Life. Yao!
If we should join up to make a circle, may our chain be complete. Yao!
If we dig a well may we come upon water. Yao!
If we draw water to bathe our joints may they be refreshed. Yao!
Circumspect Gã, like the blowing wind, be better than your word. Yao!
You see, but you have not seen.[17] Yao!
You hear but you have not heard. Yao!
A circumspect Gã does not lie. Yao!
If you lie down, think about your work. Yao!
Today if any person who wishes harm is passing by and asks what we are doing and they tell them and they say any evil word or wishes that the child lying here shall die, shall this blessing be to bless him? Oho!
Let us shout upon their head. Ho-o-o.
Hail! Let happiness come. Yao!
Are our voices one? Yao!
Hail! Let happiness come. Yao!

Then the child is laid naked on the ground under the eaves. Eminent families have a slab of stone on which it is laid and under this stone 'something was buried long ago,' but no one remembers what. Then the elder takes water in a calabash and flings it three times on the roof, so that it trickles down on the child like rain. This is to introduce the child to the rain and to the earth. Then the child as it lies on the ground is blessed.

[...]
I bless you. Yao!
I bless you. Yao!
I bless you. Yao!
May you be blessed and may you receive blessing always. Yao!

17. Be discreet. Do not babble about everything you see.

Then they brush the child gently with their left foot, saying, '*Mi t ʃwao nane*' (I am striking you with my foot, an idiom meaning, I am impressing you with my character). Then the elder does it again with the right foot and then says, '*Kɔ mi nane*' (Take hold of my foot—become like me).

Then the elder takes the child up again and, if they like, makes a long extempore speech detailing the good points in their own character and telling the child to copy them, then modestly discovering a few bad points and cautioning the child to avoid them.

Then a second representative of the father's family and one of the mother's come forward, and the leader recites the *Dʒɔmɔ* or Blessing, the community chiming in with responses of '*Yao*.'

Then everybody drinks corn wine and rum, after, of course, giving some to the ancestors. The *kpodʒiemɔ* ceremony, carried out at the father's house, is the seal of respectable paternity.

The child is now a member of the family and has assumed its own name. If it dies before the eighth day it is considered as having never been born and has no name, but it can die on the ninth day and its father and mother for the rest of their lives be called by its name—'*Dede* mother,' '*Tete* father.'

A Mother to Her First-Born [A Lango poem from Northern Uganda and/or Southern Sudan]

Speak to me, child of my heart.
Speak to me with your eyes, your round laughing eyes,
Wet and shining as Lypeyo's bull-calf.

Speak to me, little one,
Clutching my breast with your hand,
So strong and firm for all its littleness.
It will be the hand of a warrior, my son,
A hand that will gladden your father.
See how eagerly it fastens on me:
It thinks already of a spear:
It quivers as at the throwing of a spear.
O son, you will have a warrior's name and be a leader of men.
And your sons, and your sons' sons, will remember you long after you have slipped into darkness.
But I, I shall always remember your hand clutching me so.
I shall recall how you lay in my arms,
And looked at me so, and so,
And how your tiny hands played with my bosom.
And when they name you great warrior, then will my eyes be wet with remembering.

And how shall we name you, little warrior?
See, let us play at naming.
It will not be a name of despisal, for you are my first-born.
Not as Nawal's son is named will you be named.
Our gods will be kinder to you than theirs.
Must we call you "Insolence" or "Worthless One"?
Shall you be named, like a child of fortune, after the dung of cattle?
Our gods need no cheating, my child:
They wish you no ill.
They have washed your body and clothed it with beauty.
They have set a fire in your eyes.
And the little, puckering ridges of your brow—
Are they not the seal of their fingerprints when they fashioned you?
They have given you beauty and strength, child of my heart,
And wisdom is already shining in your eyes,
And laughter.

So how shall we name you, little one?
Are you your father's father, or his brother, or yet another?
Whose spirit is it that is in you, little warrior?
Whose spear-hand tightens round my breast?
Who lives in you and quickens to life, like last year's melon seed?

Are you silent, then?
But your eyes are thinking, thinking, and glowing like the eyes of a leopard in a thicket.
Well, let be.
At the day of naming you will tell us.

O my child, now indeed I am happy.
Now indeed I am a wife—
No more a bride, but a Mother-of-one.
Be splendid and magnificent, child of desire.
Be proud, as I am proud.
Be happy, as I am happy.
Be loved, as now I am loved.
Child, child, child, love I have had from my man.
But not, only now, have I the fullness of love.
Now, only now, am I his wife and the mother of his first-born.
His soul is safe in your keeping, my child, and it was I, I, I, who made you.

Therefore am I loved.
Therefore am I happy.
Therefore am I a wife.
Therefore have I great honour.

You will tend his shrine when he is gone.
With sacrifice and oblation you will recall his name year by year.
He will live in your prayers, my child,
And there will be no more death from him, but everlasting life springing from your loins.
You are his shield and his spear, his hope and redemption from the dead.
Through you he will be reborn, as the sapling in Spring.
And I, I am the mother of his first-born.
Sleep, child of beauty and courage and fulfilment, sleep.
I am content.

"Mother's Song." In *Seven Days to Lomaland*, translated by Esther Warner, 180. Boston: Houghton Mifflin, 1954.

Field, M. J. "Blessings Upon an Infant." In *Religion and Medicine of the Gã People*, 171–73. Oxford: Oxford University Press, 1961.

"A Mother to Her First-Born." In *Initiation: Translations from Poems of the Didinga and Lango Tribes*, translated by J. H. Driberg, 16–17. London: Golden Cockerel Press, 1932. Reprinted by permission of Associated University Presses.

POST-READING PARS

1. What are two or three hopes for children that are expressed in the poems?
2. Identify what the primary emotions are in each poem.
3. List two or three cultural values that are highlighted in each poem.
4. Give two examples of how the collective voice is amplified in each poem.
5. Compare how you were named with the way naming is conducted in the poem "A Mother to Her First-Born."

Inquiry Corner

Content Question(s):	**Critical Question(s):**
How is figurative language and repetition used in these poems? In the song "A Mother to Her First-Born," what reasons are highlighted or justified for giving a child a bad name like "Insolence" or "Worthless One"?	How does the perspective of the narrator/first-person perspective in each poem shape our perception of the child? Given the time period in which Esther Warner lived in Liberia, comment on the significance of the last four lines of the poem "Mother's Song."
Comparative Question(s):	**Connection Question(s):**
Compare and contrast the aspirations parents have for children in these poems with those found in other sources, such as *Life of the Buddha*, *The Recognition of Shakuntala*, *Lessons for Women*, *Epic of Gilgamesh*, and so on.	Write a fourteen-line poem that highlights a "coming-of-age" or turning point in your life that deserves ceremony or recognition. Imagine the kinds of future that children being born now can aspire to and what obligations we as adults have to make those aspirations come true.

African Work Songs for Pounding Grain: "Lazybones" and "A Shared Husband I Do Not Want" (Chichewa)

SNAPSHOT BOX

LANGUAGE: Chichewa

DATE: Oral tradition

GENRE: Song

ETHNIC IDENTITY: Chichewa (in present-day Malawi, Zambia, Mozambique, Zimbabwe, Eswatini, and Botswana)

TAGS: Body; Community/Communal Identity; Education; Family; Music; Ways of Knowing

Introduction

In most African cultures, singing and drumming is not art for art's sake; it is functional, it is interwoven in the social fabric, it reveals hidden cultural construction, and it displays often unacknowledged forms of creativity. As an artist, educator, and accomplished researcher of many sub-Saharan Africa dance forms, and Ghanaian born and bred, I concur with this idea. To us, singing while working is not ordinary but a verbal art form. Songs, chants, and ululations (a type of trilling sound connected to both grief and celebration) can be creative participatory expressions that are prevalent during chores and farming as a means of entertainment to essentially ease hard work. Those who are working choose songs selectively as the songs reflect an assessment of the particular experiences of the moment, which may speak directly to one's current relationships, observations, grievances, and other life matters.

Songs related to work are without a single composer. Instead the songs, chants, and gestures are viewed as communal property and are sometimes associated with a particular clan. While many musicians also acknowledge divine inspiration, there is strong evidence to suggest that song creation, dance patterns, and drumming are communally invented, assessed, and passed along. The two songs you will read below are from the Chichewa people, who occupy sub-Saharan African countries such as Malawi, Zambia, Mozambique, Zimbabwe, Eswatini, and Botswana.

The two Chichewa songs are connected to the particularly demanding household chore of pounding grains through a large mortar (bowl) and pestle (a long heavy pole) made of wood. Placed in the middle of the thatch-compound house,[18] the mortar and pestle are used to break down the grains into a powder form through repeatedly raising the pestle up high and letting it drop onto the grains. This resulting powder can be used like a flour to make various foods. Pounding is done in groups with partners working each mortar and pestle, making coordination between people working the same pestle necessary for efficient pounding. Singing helps create a shared underlying rhythmic metronome to guide the work but also makes it more refreshing and omits procrastination and pessimism. What strategies do you use to make repetitive forms of work go by faster or to coordinate work with other people?

18. This refers to a cluster of buildings in an enclosure, having a shared or associated purpose, such as the houses of an extended family. Grant Macloly Moloko Nthala, *The Chewa Arts of Drumming and Its Influence on Modern Malawian Music*. PhD diss., University of the Free State, Bloemfontein, South Africa, 2009.

The first of the two songs, "Lazybones," serves as a guide to the pounder to keep going until the job is fully accomplished. A pounder cannot afford to be lazy. Singing this song brings the group together, working as a team, to motivate themselves. They do all these to tap into each other's energy as a lazy person is frowned upon in the community. This song is sung as a group (of pounders and nonpounders) using a call-and-response approach. There are people in the community who come to these pounding spots to show their appreciation by singing, clapping, and ululating. Call and response is a succession of two distinct phrases usually written in different parts of the music, where the second phrase is heard as a direct commentary on or in response to the first. In the case of this song, the caller pounds while "calling," then the rest of the group "responds" as a chorus.

This song appears straightforward in supporting the rhythms of work but has a lot of other layers of meaning that publicly nurture community cooperation and call out nuisances in the community. For example, this song is also used to ask for help if you need it and cultivates the instinct to offer a helping hand to the pounder(s). This is a clarion call to keep lazy and uncooperative people in the community on their toes. In addition, the lazybones (whom the song is intended for) complains of having a headache and legs and hands that are malfunctioning. The aforementioned body parts are the most important during the process of pounding. But when lazybones is called to partake in the fruits of the community labor produced by pounding, their personality and intentions are revealed. The singer manipulates and rearranges units of a given vocabulary within the song to suit the occasion and the people who are present, including anyone who might not have been doing their share of the work recently. When someone is not contributing, what socially viable ways do you have to address their lack of teamwork?

This song reminds me of a story that was told around the fire pit in the chilly evenings after dinner, which was the best part of my day when growing up in the southern part of Ghana, West Africa. Our elders modeled an atmosphere where differences are embraced and celebrated no matter its form, a type of wisdom from their forebears passed along through community storytelling and songs, such as this story of Hawk and Hen:

> Once upon a time, there lived a Hawk and Hen who lived together in a little house. They were best friends and did everything together. These two friends loved to play drums, so they decided they're going to make their own, but Hen was lazy. One day Hawk asked Hen, let's go into the forest to cut wood and make some drums. Hen replied, sorry I am very sick, I can't come with you. Then Hawk said, lend me your axe and machete so I can chop and carve the wood for the drum. Again, Hen said I am sorry my axe and machete are sick so they can't work. Hawk became furious and stormed away to borrow tools elsewhere. Without Hen's help, Hawk persisted and hauled the wood home from the forest to successfully make the drum. One afternoon, Hawk was away from home and heard

> the unique sound of the drum afar and flew quickly to the house only to find Hen playing the drum. Hen, upon seeing Hawk, fled the house, never to be spotted by Hawk again. Until today, Hen lives in fear as Hawk continues to haunt her.

How might this story give new insights or perspectives to the song, "Lazybones"?

The second song, "A Shared Husband I Do Not Want," is sung by a Chichewa married woman who hasn't yet had children. The pounding song is one of the most powerful modes of verbal expression for her relationship concerns. The pounding is a verbal strategy that the woman employs to negotiate with and influence others to effect change within her environment and the community at large. This song directs its listeners to develop an integral voice in the strategic efforts toward building more diverse, inclusive, supportive, and equitable spaces in all spheres of life.

In the song's introduction, she establishes her revulsion about the current situations in the house. She is directly referring to her husband and/or in-laws while pounding grains for dinner. The woman is lamenting, through the song, a plethora of caveats to her husband and in-laws about their decision to bring a second wife into the household. At the same time, she is addressing concerns she has about her husband, and how she is being treated as a wife even with all the hard work she puts into the family. She is yearning for appreciation, care, and love that the song suggests she is getting less of or none. Seeing the Chichewa women (physically) pounding the grains in their community—the speed of the melody, the intensity of the pestle, the movement of the arm in connection with the scapular, and how it affects the torso—provides embodied clues to capture the intent and meaning of the song for the person who is pounding in that moment. A song about bringing a second wife home may be a metaphor for other obstacles, such as work, that take away one's attention and thus are getting in the way of a thriving household.

While noting her grievances, at the same time she expresses her love for her husband and her desire to create the optimal social, emotional, and physical conditions within the household for expanding and nurturing her family. Besides her husband and in-laws, she may also be petitioning the ancestors, using the grain as a sacrificial offering as part of her song. Can you think of songs that speak to the difficulties of a situation and also constructively name the positive aspects that can help navigate the difficulties?

Mustapha Braimah
Center for Dance, Music and Theatre, Goucher College

PRE-READING PARS

1. List three things that re-energize you to overcome procrastinating.
2. When friends or family are not providing support or pitching in when you need them to, what strategies do you use to try to get them to help? What role do communal expectations play in those appeals?
3. What have you or will you do today to promote diversity, equity, and inclusion?
4. Do songs you sing thematically sync with an issue you're grappling with? How do songs affect your daily activities? How do we use songs as a medium of expression?
5. Write down four ways of communicating an idea/opinion indirectly to someone.

African Work Songs for Pounding Grain

Lazybones

Lazy bones, let's go to the farm
Sorry, I've got a headache
Lazy bones, let's go pounding grains
Sorry, my leg isn't right
Lazy bones, let's go fetch firewood
Sorry, my hands are hurting
Lazy bones, come and have some food
Hold on, let me wash my hands!

A shared husband I don't want!

A shared husband I don't want!
I want my own
Who looks on proudly as I pound,
Not somebody else's
Who when I pound
Turns his back on me!
I want a beautiful child
Who sleeps on a mattress
In a house with a wooden door!

"Pounding Songs." In *Oral Poetry from Africa: An Anthology*, compiled by Jack Mapanje and Landeg White; adviser, Isidore Okpewho, 55, 93. New York: Longman, 1983.

Ananseɛm (Stories for Ananse)

SNAPSHOT BOX

LANGUAGE: Akan (Twi/Fante)

DATE: Oral traditions

LOCATION: Present-day Ghana and Cote d'Ivoire

GENRE: Storytelling

ETHNIC IDENTITY: Akan (thirty or more different groups)

TAGS: Body; Conflict and War; Death; Deities and Spirits; Education; Ethics and Morality; Family; Identity; Journey; Nature; Oral Histories and Storytelling; Ways of Knowing

Introduction

Ananse, also known as Kwaku, an Akan name given to a male born on Wednesday, is considered a legend and a trickster, who is full of deception. *Ananseɛm*—folklore of Ananse—are used in teaching life lessons and are an important tool for the transmission of social values, mores, and the ontology (constituents of reality) of Akanfuo (Akan people). As a child, I grew up listening to many *Ananseɛm* as told by my father, who was a chief and an amazing storyteller. As in many traditional African societies, stories are used as an important enculturation tool. The lessons from these *Ananseɛm* still undergird many of my decisions and my choices in life, the exact impact these stories are supposed to have. Are there stories from your childhood that play a role in your everyday decisions?

Ananseɛm are mostly told by elders to children across many different Akan groups, typically with an opening in a form of call and response. For example, before an Mfantsenyi (a Fantse person from the Akan linguistic group) storyteller starts with the *Ananseɛm*, they announce to the audience "*kodzi wonngye ndzi* (fables are not to be believed)," to which the audience responds, "*wogye sie* (we keep them)." The Asantefuo (Asante group of Akan) have a similar call and response for the beginning of *Ananseɛm*. The storyteller begins with "*Ananseɛm nseseɛ* ooo (Ananse's story is about to begin)," and the audience responds, "*yɛsesa soa woara* (we're ready to carry it)." These calls and responses also serve as a reminder to the listeners to be attentive and not disrupt. This teaches children to be focused and good listeners. After each story, the children are encouraged to ask

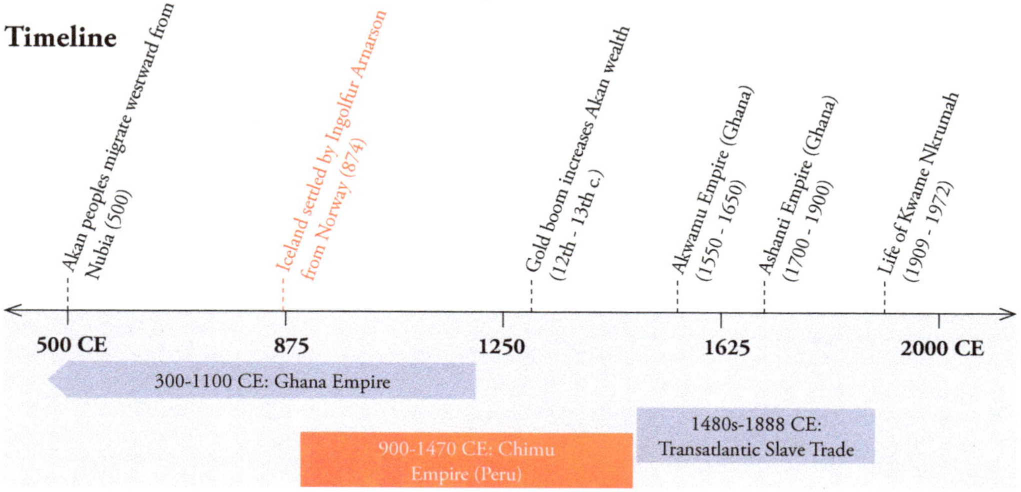

questions, give answers, and consider possible moral lessons. Why might the call-and-response strategy be effective in getting the listeners to focus their attention?

Anansesɛm highlight the importance of cleverness and not necessarily intelligence. Ananse, which is the Akan name for spider, is a complex imaginary in Akan mythology. Ananse is credited with teaching Asantefuo the art of weaving the famous and internationally acclaimed Asante patterned textile cloth, ***ntoma***. Legend has it that two farmers keenly observed the spider weaving its web in the forest. After several days of observation, they learned the intricate weaving techniques of the spider. The spider's method of weaving birthed the first weaving technique of the Asante ***ntoma***, now known as the Kente cloth. This is where Kwaku Ananse gets his legendary status, inspiring the weaving of cloth as well as the weaving of stories that ultimately help shape Akan minds and social behaviors.

Anansesɛm are much more complicated than just stories about a spider who is clever and full of tricks. ***Anansesɛm*** have both etiological (causal explanation) and etymological (how things got their names) aspects. Etiological ***Anansesɛm*** are used to explain our natural world, how things came to be as they are. For example, why is the spider always seen in a web in the ceiling? According to one story, Kwaku Ananse, after he had been outed for many of his clever tricks, became so ashamed that he found a hiding place in the ceiling. That is why the spider is always building its web in the ceiling. In another Anansesɛm, humans were originally created as half beings. However, they were always fighting. During one of those fights, Kwaku Ananse hit the heads of the two half beings with a whisk, resulting in the two becoming one, ***nipa baako*** (one human). This story highlights the etymological function of Anansesɛm.

Anthropomorphized Kwaku Ananse navigates a world in which he thinks of himself as a very clever person. In one such story, Kwaku Ananse was granted all the knowledge in the world after completing some improbable tasks for ***Nyankopong*** (the Sky-god). This knowledge was contained in a gourd. In his selfish quest to secure the knowledge of the world only for himself, he decided to hide the gourd in a tree. In the process of climbing the tree, the gourd fell, making knowledge available to everyone around the world. It is only the ***kwasia*** (the fool), who either delays or refuses to go get some of the available knowledge. This is how the world gained access to knowledge, according to the ***Anansesɛm***. What other stories that you know explain how humans gain access to knowledge? Do these stories convey positive or negative messages about gaining access to knowledge?

At the end of ***Anansesɛm***, the storyteller finishes with, "***Anansesɛm a metoeɛ yi, sɛ ɛyɛ dɛ oo sɛ ɛnyɛ dɛ oo, ebi nkɔ na ebi mmra*** (The Ananse story I share, whether is sweet to you or not, take it somewhere, and bring some back)." ***Anansesɛm*** are collective stories of our shared experiences of humanity told through the worldview of most Akanfuo (Akan people).

Agya Boakye-Boaten
Africana Studies and Department of Interdisciplinary Studies

Ananseseɛm: Stories of Ananse

Ananse and Ntikuma

Ntikuma became totally astonished when he saw Ananse's large farm. Ananse, who used to idle about, had at this time grown vegetables and other crops. Being startled by the blooming crops, Ntikuma approached Ananse respectfully for some advice on good farming. By nature, Ananse was very inconsiderate; so instead of helping Ntikuma to improve his farm, Ananse rather decided to mislead him. That way, he would be able to eliminate any farmer who would like to compete with him. Ananse told Ntikuma that he fried his corn and salted his vegetables before he planted them.

The following planting season, Ntikuma followed Ananse's advice when he sowed his fried corn. Two months passed but none of the corn germinated. The large quantity of corn and vegetables he was expecting to bloom became rotten in the ground. Ntikuma vowed to get Ananse for the big swindle. Three days after this incident, Ntikuma covered his entire body with pieces of roasted pork. He looked exactly like a burned person after this act. Ntikuma then sent messengers to Ananse's village and informed him that he had had a fire accident and burnt his body. On hearing the sad news, Ananse immediately visited Ntikuma, his son. At dinner time Ntikuma asked his family to use some of the meat on his back for making soup. Ananse was served with some of the soup which he enjoyed very much. Due to the delicious meals he was enjoying, Ananse extended his visit to a whole week. Before he left, Ananse asked Ntikuma to tell him the secret for turning his body into such tasty meat and still live. Ntikuma said he instructed his family to throw him into a burning fire. They then turned him round and round until he became well roasted.

Anxious to change his body into roasted meat, Ananse followed Ntikuma's instructions as soon as he returned to his village. His family set a fire ablaze and threw Ananse into it as he told them to do. But Ananse could not bear the intense heat from the fire. By the burning pains, Ananse knew that he had blundered. He therefore yelled to his family to pull him out of the fire. They paid no heed to him because Ananse forced them to become intoxicated before putting him in the fire. By the time Ananse struggled out of the fire by himself, he had suffered severe burns all over his body. News about Ananse's fire accident reached Ntikuma. On arrival, Ntikuma saw that his father Ananse had actually burned himself senselessly. Although he pitied Ananse for his pains, he rejoiced in his heart for having his revenge against his wicked father.

Trying to show off, Ananse instructed his children to cut part of his burnt body for roasted meat for making soup for his guest. But, he kept withdrawing his instructions each time they started to cut his body. The open sores on Ansnse's body became infected and a few days later Ananse went to his village and passed away.

Ananse and the Fisherman

Ananse loved fishing before he became blind at an advanced age. His fellow fishermen advised him to stop fishing since he could not see. But Ananse would not listen. Because of Ananse's determination and insistence, three of his friends decided to help him to fish. Ananse was walked to the sea, helped into the boat and helped to cast his net. The fellow fishermen thought that Ananse would appreciate their kind help. But, instead Ananse became rude and disrespectful to them each day. Whenever they told Ananse to step into the boat in the morning, he replied, "I already know where the boat is." The fishermen became displeased with Ananse's insulting behavior.

One day when Ananse was being helped to cast his net at a very good spot he asked his helpers rudely, "Don't you think I have enough sense to tell where the fish are?" They continued fishing until they made enough catch for the day. Instead of rowing back to the shore, the angry fishermen rowed the boat into the deep waters. They stopped the boat as usual and told Ananse that they had reached the shore so he could step out of the boat. Ananse quickly retorted, "Do you think I am dumb? Why do you keep telling me when to get off the boat? Don't you know I already know that we are at the shore so I have to get off the boat? Aren't you being foolish to tell me what to do every day?" Being as proud as a peacock, Ananse confidently jumped out of the boat, hoping to land on the beach. But, he rather found himself drowning. He began to shout "You fools, what have you done to me? Get me out quickly!" Even at the point of drowning, Ananse was too proud to say "Please help me." His friends quickly turned the boat round and rowed away. Ananse tried to swim to the shore. But, instead of swimming towards the beach, he rather swam farther into the sea because of his blindness. Nothing was heard of Ananse again. It therefore became a saying that 'Pride does not pay, it only gives its owner away.'

Ananse and the Greedy Lion

Being king of the beasts, the lion sometimes became a bully to some of the small animals. One day, the lion said to Ananse, "I have heard that you are very clever, I will therefore want you to hunt for me." Out of fear, Ananse replied, "Yes master, I have been looking forward to hunting for you." A few hours later, the lion went to hunt with Ananse. "We should dig a long trench for trapping the animals," suggested Ananse. The lion said, "Since the trench is your idea, go ahead and dig it." Ananse had no choice but to dig the trench by himself while the lion took a nap under some shady trees. Ananse dug a deep trench in which he planted sharp stakes and poisonous thorns. He then covered the trench with light palm branches, a thin layer of soil and dry leaves.

Ananse told the lion to go to the other end of the forest to roar to scare the animals to run southward towards the trap. Following the lion's roar, many animals got trapped and killed in the trench. Now Ananse and the lion had more meat than they could handle. By order, Ananse carried most of the meat to the lion's house. After a long day's work, the lion did not allow Ananse to eat at all. This infuriated Ananse. He felt like hitting his head against the wall, but being afraid of the lion, Ananse kept quiet without any lunch. Later in the afternoon, the lion ordered Ananse to cook dinner for him. Although Ananse was hungry, angry and tired, he was compelled to do his master's wish. This time Ananse used his head in order to regain freedom from the wicked lion.

From the trench, Ananse found a dead, fat deer which he brought home and cooked for his master, the lion. Ananse smeared the meat with poison which he squeezed from some deadly plants. After a long nap, the lion called for his dinner. Ananse hurriedly served the poisonous food to the lion who had bullied and starved him for two consecutive days. After devouring the poisoned meal, the lion remarked to Ananse, "That was the most delicious meal I have eaten for a long time..." But a few minutes later the lion complained of a stomach ache. Before the medicine man could arrive, the lion died of meat poison. Ananse once more became free. He and his family went to the trench daily to collect game for meat. Since that time, lions have feared spiders for sure; and a lion will not live in a cave in which cobwebs could be found.

Ananse the Daring Messenger

Long time ago, God, Nana Nyankopon, sent Ananse out on a risky mission, because he thought that Ananse was then the only person who had guts and was smart enough to undertake a herculean task. To get to Nyankopon in the sky, Ananse used his head by plumbing his body so that he could fly there. On arrival, Nyankopon sent Ananse back to bring him Death's golden sandals, golden snuff box and golden switch with which he whips his victims from the underworld.

Packing for this dangerous trip, Ananse took with him seasoned mashed potatoes. On his way he came to a dead end where there was no one except the road. To Ananse's surprise, the Road asked him for some food. Being selfish, Ananse was at first reluctant in sharing his food. But after the Road had promised to help him on his returning trip, Ananse gave the Road some of his food. Later on during the trip, Ananse was again compelled to share his delicious mashed potatoes with the River, Black Ants, Antelope and a Fence, all of whom promised to help him when returning home from scary Death's village.

When Ananse got to Death's village, his host Death asked, "What brings you here Ananse? No one has been here before. If you have come with a clear conscience then enjoy your stay indeed. Otherwise I cannot promise you a safe return home." From that moment, Ananse realized the danger ahead and began to put on his thinking cap. After they had gone to bed, Death sneaked into Ananse's room to see if he was fast asleep so that he would chop off his head. But there sat Ananse talking to himself and scratching his body. When Death asked him why he was still not asleep, Ananse said he forgot to bring his golden sandals which he always wore if he wanted a sound sleep. Death quickly gave his golden sandals to Ananse to wear. He was hoping that his guest would then fall into a deep sound sleep for him to take care of him in his sleep. But Ananse hid the sandals in his bag and still stayed awake till morning. The following night, Death made his second attempt to kill Ananse. But wise Ananse pretended to be shivering with fever when Death entered the guest room. Death therefore gave his golden snuff box to Ananse to use some of the powerful snuff. Again, Ananse slipped it into his pocket and paced the room until day break. On the third day, Ananse let loose some tse-tse flies. Ananse said, "If I could get a fly-switch, I would quickly take care of all these harmful flies." Death quickly gave his golden switch to Ananse to use. But Ananse chased the tsetse flies from the house to the backyard and finally escaped. When Death realized that Ananse had tricked him and run away, he gathered his men and began to chase after Ananse.

The first obstacle on the way, which was no problem for Ananse, was the Fence (pampin). But it took Death and his men some time to tear the Fence down. This gave Ananse time to widen the gap between them. Since all the obstacles had promised to help Ananse, his problems became extensively minimized. After Ananse had run past a hill, an army of Black Ants (nkrane) quickly covered the road behind him to slow down Death and his men. When Ananse was getting tired of running and his assailants were closing in on him, one of his accomplices, the Antelope made a scratching sound on the wrong track. And Death and his men deviated from the right road on which Ananse was running. When Death later found the right track, he could see Ananse running slowly ahead of them. But when they got to a river that was on Ananse's side and had helped him, Death could not cross because it suddenly over flooded its banks in protection of Ananse. Death and his gang had to cut tree-trunks to make bridges before they could cross it. This cost them a lot of time in their effort to catch up with Ananse. Finally the road that Ananse helped multiplied itself after Ananse had passed. Death did not therefore know which road to follow when they reached that intersection. Each road that they followed led them to a dead end until they became completely exhausted and gave up the chase.

By this time, Ananse had reached home. The next day, at a great gathering on earth, Ananse presented Death's golden sandals, golden snuff box and golden switch to God, Nana Nyankopon. As his prize for accomplishing the dangerous mission successfully, Nyankopon gave Ananse a title of popularity. That was how Ananse became popular throughout the land and his name is mentioned in many folk tales.

Asihene, Emmanuel V. Selections from *Traditional Folk-Tales of Ghana*, 17–18, 33–36, 55–57. Lewiston, NY: Edwin Mellen Press, 1997.

Ifá Divination Poetry (Yorùbá)

SNAPSHOT

LANGUAGE: Yorùbá

LOCATION: Yorùbáland (modern-day Southern Nigeria)

TAGS: Aesthetics; Conflict and War; Death; Deities and Spirits; Divination; Family; Identity; Journey; Oral Histories and Storytelling; Religion; Sacrifice

Introduction

Ifá divination poetry forms a significant part of a vast sacred oral literary corpus known in the Yorùbá tradition of southwestern Nigeria as **Odù Ifá**. Likely predating the era of Islam and Christianity in West Africa and numerous West African kingdoms of antiquity, these poems (**ẹsẹ Ifá**) are believed to have a mythical origin in the sacred Yorùbá city of Ilé-Ifẹ̀.[19] The poems serve as the dynamic basis for communication between humans and their divinities as part of divination rituals. What might be some of the reasons why people may want to communicate with their divinities?

Divination—typically understood as the practice of learning about the future or the unknown by some supernatural means—is common to many ancient cultures. Each culture employs different forms. For example, in ancient China, bones or shells were inscribed and then heated, and the cracks were then interpreted. In Hebrew culture, lots were drawn (see Proverbs 16:33; Jonah 1:7). The Greeks consulted oracles, like that at Delphi. The Romans, borrowing from the Etruscans, consulted the livers and entrails of sacrificed animals. Astrology was essential for the Persians, South Asians, Maya, and others already mentioned. And texts, once they were written down, became important sources of guidance—though they often

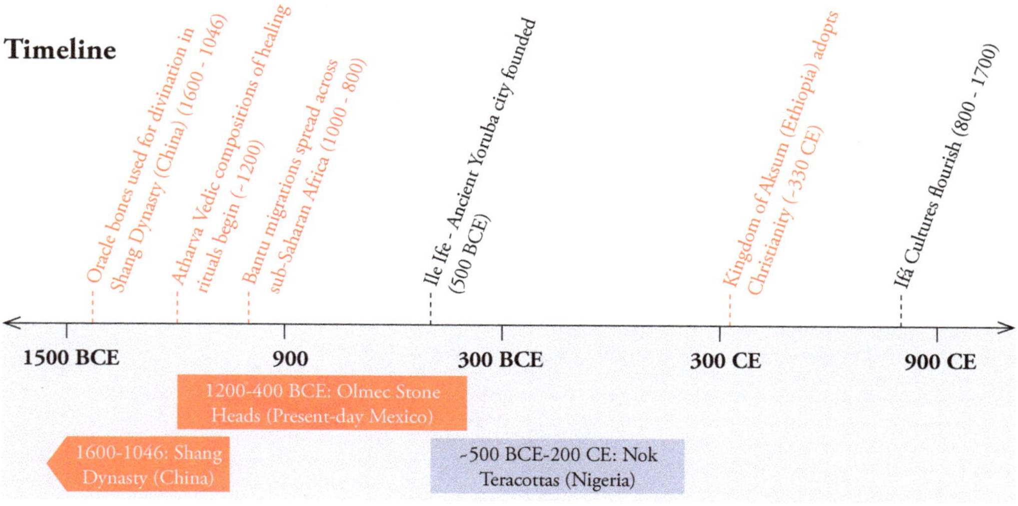

19. Jacob Olúpọ̀nà, *City of 201 Gods: Ilé-Ifẹ̀ in Time, Space, and the Imagination* (Berkeley: University of California Press, 2011), 2, 14, 68.

required interpretation. Into this category of poetry and interpretation we can put the Ifá tradition. And yet, Ifá divination is not always about the future but rather a negotiation of atemporal knowledge from the spiritual realm that informs present circumstances and ongoing relationships between the spiritual and physical worlds.

The terms ẹsẹ Ifá and Odù Ifá mark the two primary divisions of this Ifá poetic corpus: the Odù, which refers to 256 "books" or "volumes," and ẹsẹ, subdivisions, "chapters," or poetic verses of the Odù whose total number is unknown due to regular augmentation. Of the 256 Odù, sixteen are considered "principal," and thus of greater importance, and the remaining 240 are considered "minor." Yorùbá diviners (***Babaláwo*** **— male diviner; Ìyálòrìṣà — female diviner**) are expected to commit to memory and be able to chant and interpret as many verses of ẹsẹ Ifá as they can in order to assist clients seeking spiritual counsel from Yorùbá divinities (Òrìṣà).[20] Professor Wándé Abímbọ́lá, a world-renowned Babaláwo and scholar of **Yorùbá** language and literature, translated the poems that follow from Yorùbá to English in the 1970s.

Babaláwo and *Ìyálòrìṣà* both rely heavily on their extensive knowledge of ẹsẹ Ifá in the technical performance of **Ifá dídá (Ifá divination)**,[21] a complex divinatory system believed to have been bequeathed to the Yorùbá people by **Ifá**, the Yorùbá divinity of wisdom. An occurrence of divination begins when a client brings a question or concern to a priest or priestess that involves wanting to remedy ill health, changing jobs, resolving family troubles, or seeking advice on navigating important decisions in life. The Ifá divination process involves intricate, collaborative techniques used to determine the insight to proceed. They entail the casting of lots, or devices, that indicate a course of action through one of two different methods. The first method involves the transfer of sixteen palm nuts from hand to hand eight times, or alternatively an opele chain with eight individual palm nuts is thrown. Either way, there are 256 possible outcomes that point to a particular Odù Ifá that the *Babaláwo Ìyálòrìṣà* begins to sing.

The client who is seeking knowledge from the Òrìṣa about their situation listens to the sung poems until one resonates with them in relation to their present-day question. The religious specialist and the client work together to interpret the poem, originally provided by the Òrìṣà to resolve problems in the physical world. What does the use of Odù Ifá by Yorùbá diviners within the context of Ifá dídá tell us about how Yorùbá communities understand the relationship between the spiritual and physical worlds as a form of collaborative endeavor? A sacrifice, consisting of various offerings, such as tobacco, foodstuffs, money, a fowl, or a bottle of Schnapps, concludes

20. Wándé Abímbọ́lá, *Ifá: An Exposition of Ifá Literary Corpus* (Ibadan: Oxford University Press Nigeria, 1976), 15, 26–27.

21. Kọ́lá Abímbọ́lá, *Yorùbá Culture: A Philosophical Account* (Birmingham, UK: Iroko Academic Publishers, 2006), 47.

the divination process as a way to acknowledge the Òrìṣà, as well as the *Babaláwo/Ìyálòrìṣà*, for their assistance.

Because Yorùbá cosmology envisions the world as one of conflict and mystery (no one being knows all that there is to know), the intentional cultivation of relationships helps one to access and participate in collaborative knowledge, thereby mitigating conflicts that will naturally arise. The divination system enacts a technology for sustaining relationships between *Òrìṣa* and humans through effective communication, mutual knowledge creation, and acknowledgment of assistance through offerings of sacrifice and remembrance of ancestral rites. What is the Yorùbá understanding of sacrifice and ancestral rites in their contributions to collaborative knowledge production and conflict resolution? The Yorùbá religious tradition has been described as "elastic,"[22] suggesting its adaptability and relevance to contemporary challenges facing human communities. How does American society today manage conflict, existential danger, and the unknown? How might this compare to the management of these realities in Ifá dídá?

Marcus L. Harvey
Department of Religious Studies

22. During a lecture given at Emory University in 2007, Wándé Abímbọ́lá used this word in explaining both the adaptability of Yorùbá religion and its openness to interreligious engagement.

PRE-READING PARS

1. Write down three to five ways sacrifice is present in one form or another in your daily life.
2. Outline three to five ways you understand the past as related to the present.

Ifá Divination Poetry

IV Odu Meji

(a) Gateman, Open the Gate Intelligently

We build a tiny house,
And ask a divinity to accept it as his dwelling place,
If the divinity refuses to accept it,
Let him go into the forest to cut building poles,
Let him go into the grassland to fetch building ropes,
And see for himself the difficulties involved.
Ifá divination was performed for he who cuts palm fronds,
Ifá divination was also performed for he who ties palm fronds together,
On the day both of them were coming from heaven to earth.
The cutter of palm fronds was told to perform sacrifices,
The one who ties palm fronds together was also told to perform sacrifice.
Both of them performed sacrifice.
After they had performed sacrifice, all evil things
Could no longer go to them.
They said, "We build a tiny house,
And ask a divinity to accept it as his dwelling place.
If the divinity refuses to accept it,
Let him go into the forest to cut building poles,
Let him go into the grassland to fetch building ropes,
And see for himself the difficulties involved.
Ifá divination was performed for he who cuts palm fronds,
Ifá divination was also performed for he who ties palm fronds together,
On the day both of them were coming from heaven to earth.
You, who tie palm fronds together, tie them securely.
Tie them securely against death,
Tie them securely against disease.
You, who tie palm fronds, tie them well.
Gateman, open the gate intelligently.
Gateman, open the gate intelligently.
Open the gate for money,
Open the gate for wife.
Gateman, open the gate intelligently.

(b) The Important Stranger in the City of Benin

I arrive well,
I travel well.
I am he who usually travels and comes across fortune.
Just as they were laying down riches,
I entered unannounced like the owner's son.
I am not the owner's son;
I only know how to travel and come across fortune.
Ifá divination was performed for the important stranger
Who would enter the city unannounced
On the day they were sharing the wealth of the king of Benin.
The important stranger was going to the city of Benin on divination practice.
He added two cowries to three,
And went to consult another Ifá priest.
He was told that the journey would be good for him.
But he was told to perform sacrifice.
After he had performed the prescribed sacrifice,
He went on the road to Benin.
The time he entered the city,
Happened to be the time their king died.
He wondered if he, an experienced Ifá priest,
Should not go and sympathize with them.
The important stranger entered just as they were dividing the properties of the dead king.
And after they finished dividing the property,
A portion of it usually went to a stranger,
The citizens of Benin
Therefore gave a portion of the riches to the important stranger.
As soon as the important stranger gathered all the riches,
He went back to his own town.
He started to praise his Ifá priests,
And his Ifá priests praised Ifá.
They applied drumstick to *aran*,
And it brought forth its pleasant melodies.
As he stretched out his legs,
Dance caught them.
As he opened his mouth,
The song of Ifá came out therefrom.
He said it happened exactly as his diviners predicted.
"I arrive well,
I travel well.

I am he who usually travels and comes across fortune.
Just as they were laying down riches,
I entered unannounced like the owner's son.
I am not the owner's son,
I only know how to travel in order to come across fortune.
Ifá divination was performed for the important stranger
Who would enter the city unannounced
On the day they were sharing the wealth of the king of Benin.
Who then will help us improve this city?
It is the important stranger
Who will help us improve this city."

(c) When Two People Laugh at Each Other, It Results in a Quarrel

We laugh at those people who laugh at us;
As for those who do not laugh at us,
We never laugh at them;
When two people laugh at each other, it results in a quarrel.
Ifá divination was performed for *Erintunde*,
Offspring of *Elerin* in the city of *Sajeje*.
He was told to perform sacrifice
Because of people who know one and yet harm one
And he performed the sacrifice.
After he had performed sacrifice,
He started to triumph over his enemies.
When he became happy,
He said that was exactly what his Ifá priests predicted.
"We laugh at those people who laugh at us;
As for those who do not laugh at us,
We never laugh at them;
When two people laugh at each other, it results in quarrel,
Ifá divination was performed for *Erintunde*,
Offspring of *Elerin* in the city of *Sajeje*.
He was told to perform sacrifice because of people who know one and yet harm one.
Travellers to the city of *Ipo*,
Travellers to the city of *Ofa*,
There is nothing in my own life to be laughed at."

(d) Oya Is More Dangerous Than Sango; The Wife Is More Dangerous Than the Husband

When we see one *Okanran* this way,
And we see another *Okanran* that way,
The signature is that of *Okanran Meji* which means good luck.
Ifá divination was performed for *Sango*, nick-named *Oluorojo.*
'Bambi, offspring of those who use two hundred thunder stones to defeat their enemies.
When he was going to marry *Oya* as a wife.
Sango was told to be very careful
Because the wife he was going to marry
Would be more successful than he.
But *Sango* refused to perform sacrifice.
He wondered how his own wife
Could be more successful than himself.
If *Sango* threw thunder stones into any place,
Everybody would start shouting his name.
But if *Oya*, his wife,
Killed two people the same day,
Nobody would hear of the incident.
If she liked,
She would blow a strong wind against a wall,
And the wall would fall on people and kill them.
If she liked,
She would fell trees on many people, and kill them.
But if *Sango* kills only one person,
All the world would hear of the incident.
He said that was exactly how his Ifá priests
Employed their good voices in praise of Ifá.
"When we see one *Okanran* this way,
And we see another *Okanran* that way,
The signature is that of *Okanran Meji* which means good luck.
Ifá divination was performed for *Sango*, nick-named *Oluorojo*,
'Bambi, offspring of those who use two hundred stones to defeat their enemies.
When he was going to marry *Oya* as a wife.
The wife is more dangerous than the husband.
The wife is more dangerous than the hundred.
Oya is more dangerous than *Sango.*
The wife is more dangerous than the husband."

XI Ogunda Meji

(a) Ojontarigi, *The Wife of Death*

He who dashed suddenly across the road,
Performed Ifá divination for *Orunmila*
Who was going to snatch away *Ojontarigi*,
The wife of Death.
Ojontarigi was the only wife of Death.
Yet *Orunmila* wanted to snatch her away.
Orunmila was told to perform sacrifice,
And he performed it.
After he had performed sacrifice,
He snatched *Ojontarigi* away from Death.
Death then took his club,
And went towards Orunmila's house.
He met *Esu* in front of the house.
Esu said, "How are you,
Death, nick-named *Ojepe*, whose garment is dyed in *osun*."
After they had exchanged greetings,
Esu asked from him, "Where are you going?"
Death answered that he was going to Orunmila's house,
Esu asked, "What is the matter?"
Death said that *Orunmila* took his wife,
And he must kill Orunmila that very day.
Esu then implored Death to sit down.
After he had sat down,
Esu gave him food and drinks.
After Death ate to his satisfaction,
He stood up,
Got hold of his club,
And started to go.
Then *Esu* asked again, "Where are you going?"
Death answered that he was going to Orunmila's house.
Then *Esu* said, "How can you eat a man's food and turn round to kill him?
Don't you know that the food you have just eaten belongs to *Orunmila*?"
When Death did not know what else to do,
He said, "Tell *Orunmila* that he can keep the woman."
Orunmila started to dance,
He started to rejoice.
He said, "He who dashed suddenly across the road,
Performed Ifá divination for *Orunmila*
When he was going to marry *Ojontarigi*,

The wife of Death.
The matter over which you made a lot of noise,
It was last night that I put it in wine,
And drank it away.
Just like that.
We smoked this matter away with tobacco.
We smoked this matter away with tobacco,
We will not die again.
Just like that.
We smoked this matter away with tobacco."

(c) Oyeepolu, *Offspring of Those Who Perform the Ancient Rites of the City of Ife*

Pepe, Ifá priest of the inside of the house;
Otita, Ifá priest of Outside;
It is the sparrow which builds its own nest
And puts its entrance face-down in a curve;
The nest neither touches water nor rests on dry land;
But its entrance points down in a curve.
Ifá divination was performed for *Oyeepolu*,
Offspring of those who perform the ancient rites of *Ife*;
Whose mother left all alone
When he was very young.
When *Oyeepolu* grew up,
He did not know all the rites of his family.
His life became unsettled.
He sought a wife to marry but found none.
And he did not have peace in his own home.
He therefore added two cowries to three
And went to an Ifá priest to perform divination.
He was told that it was because of the ancient rites of his family
Which he had forgotten
That he was in such confusion.
He was told to go
To the graves of his fathers,
And ask his ancestors for power and authority.
After he had done so,
He started to enjoy his own life.
He had money,
He married a wife,
And he produced children as well.

He said that was exactly what his Ifá priests predicted.
"*Pepe*, Ifá priest of the inside of the house;
Otita!, Ifá priest of Outside.
It is the sparrow which builds its own nest
And puts its entrance face-down in a curve;
The nest neither touches water nor rests on dry land;
But its entrance points down in a curve.
Ifá divination was performed for *Oyeepolu*,
Offspring of those who perform the ancient rites of *Ife*;
Oyeepolu did not know anything.
If oil is the first thing to be poured on the ground,
I do not know.
If kolanut is the first thing to be put on the ground,
I do not know.
If wine is the first thing to be poured on the ground,
I do not know.
Oyeepolu did not know anything.
All the divinities and ancestors of heaven,
Hasten here,
And help us perform this ritual."

(d) Ori, *The Divinity Responsible for Predestination*

No wise man can tie water into a knot on the edges of his garment.
No sage knows the number of the grains of sand on the earth.
Ifá divination was performed for *Ori*,
Ifá divination was also performed for Character.
Ori asked from his diviners whether he could have all the good things of life.
He was asked to perform sacrifice,
And he performed it.
After he had performed sacrifice,
He had all the good things that he wanted.
He said that was exactly how his Ifá priests
Employed their good voices in praise of Ifa.
"No wise man can tie water into a knot on the edges of his garment.
No sage knows the number of the grains of sand on the earth.
Ifá divination was performed for *Ori*.
Ifá divination was also performed for Character.
Ori, we hail you;
You are the one who allows children to be born alive.
A person whose sacrifice is accepted by *Ori*
Should rejoice exceedingly."

XVI Ofun Meji

(a)He Who Cannot Be Subdued

The sole of the feet is always flat.
Ifá divination was performed for he who cannot be subdued.
He who cannot be subdued is another name for the hill.
Twenty years from today,
The hill remains alive and as strong as ever.
The hill is always found to be as strong as ever.
The hill, the hill, who is strong and firm.
Thirty years from today,
The hill remains as strong as ever.
The hill is always found to be as strong as ever.
The hill, the hill who is strong and firm.

(b) Ifa's Life Was Cooler Than Water

Adeyeri, Ifá priest of *Alaraan*,
Adetutu, Ifá priest of *Ajiforogbogbola*,
Performed Ifá divination for *Orunmila*
Who woke up early in the morning,
And was going to marry she who bathes only with cold water.
Ifá's life was cooler than water.
Ifá's life was certainly cooler than water.
Ifá's life was cooler than water.
The speaker of all languages was the one who married she who bathes only with cold water.
Ifá's life was cooler than water.

(c)The Tall Plantain Living among Enemies

When the wasp wants to sting, it dips its anus into its hive;
When the sword wants to strike, its handle points in the direction of the scabbard;
Ifá divination was performed for the tall Plantain Plant
When he was living among enemies.
The Plantain was told to perform sacrifice,
And he performed sacrifice.
As a result, he conquered his enemies.
He praised his Ifá priests
And his Ifá priests praised Ifá.
He said, "When the wasp wants to sting, it dips its anus into its hive;
When the sword wants to strike, its handle points in the direction of the scabbard;

Ifá divination was performed for the tall Plantain Plant
When he was living among enemies.
Orunmila said that he would repeatedly dip into water,
The head of the enemy."

(d) Orangun Meji, *The Sign of Fortune*

The palm trees which are so conspicuously bent
That some dip their heads in water,
And others dip their heads inside farmland.
Ifá divination was performed for *Orangun* who lived in the city;
Ifá divination was also performed for *Orangun* who lived in the village.
Both of them were told to perform sacrifice,
And they performed it.
After they had performed sacrifice,
They started to have different kinds of good things.
They said, "The palm-trees which are so conspicuously bent
That some dip their heads in water,
And others dip their heads inside farmland.
Ifá divination was performed for *Orangun* who lived in the city.
Ifá divination was also performed for *Orangun* who lived in the village.
Travellers to the city of *Ipo*,
Travellers to the city of *Ofa*,
When we see *Orangun Meji*,
We begin to have fortune."

Abimbola, Wande. *Ifá Divination Poetry*, 61, 63, 65, 79, 99, 101, 103, 121, 123, 125, 151, 153. New York: NOK Publishers, 1977.

POST-READING PARS

1. Identify two or three examples of how these poems incorporate sacrifice.
2. Identify two or three ways these poems might address the concerns of people in different eras, situations, and so forth.

Inquiry Corner

Content Question(s):	**Critical Question(s):**
What are the sources of conflict that show up in the poems and how are conflicts resolved? What is the role of the unknown in these poems?	What distinction between prosperity and well-being is being made in these poems? How is remembrance related to well-being here?
Comparative Question(s):	**Connection Question(s):**
How does the role of sacrifice in the poems compare to the role of sacrifice in other texts in this Reader (e.g., Genesis 22, *Epic of Gilgamesh*, *Life of the Buddha*)?	In what ways do relationships help you navigate conflict and/or the unknown?

Instruction of Amenemope

Introduction

The sole complete copy of the *Teaching of Amenemope*[23] is on a **papyrus scroll** inscribed in the seventh century BCE, when Egypt was reunited under a single pharaoh after a period of disunity and anarchy. It was likely composed several centuries earlier in the New Kingdom, at the height of Egypt's political power and cultural influence. *Amenemope* is a collection of proverbial sayings or **maxims** for virtuous living that were clear in intent yet profound in meaning, deserving of rereading, memorization, and continual reflection. Egyptologists call works like this "instructional" or "wisdom literature." Are there any cultural sources for virtuous living or wisdom that you use in your daily life?

We do not know *Amenemope*'s author, but the scroll we have was inscribed by Senu, son of Pemu. His name can be found in the **colophon**, a short label found at the ends of scrolls that confirm it was copied completely and identify the person who did it. Senu may have copied it for private use or for a local library. *Amenemope* could have been authored by the individual named Amenemope who speaks for the entirety of the text, but

SNAPSHOT BOX

LANGUAGE: Ancient Egyptian

DATE: c. 7th century BCE

LOCATION: Egypt

GENRE: Wisdom literature

TAGS: Class and Wealth; Desire and Happiness; Education; Ethics and Morality; Family; Wisdom

Timeline

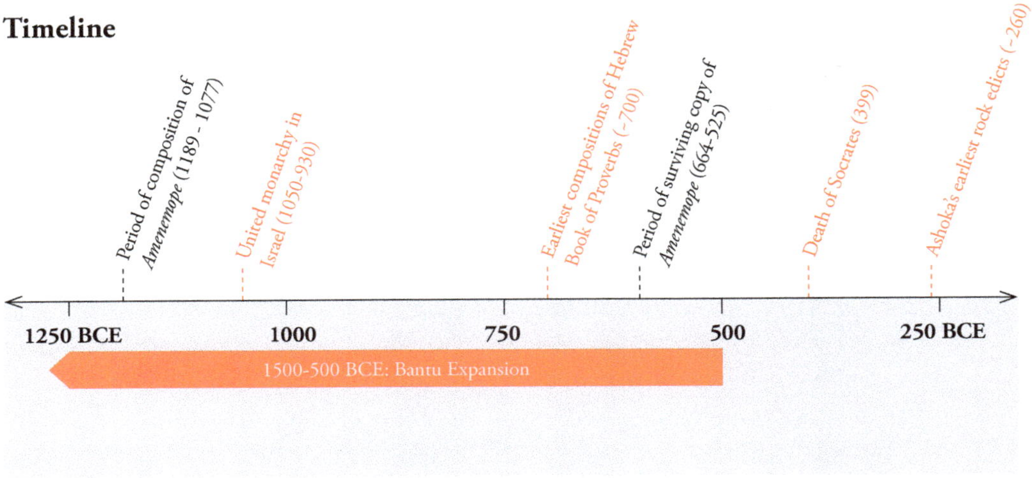

23. Because the Egyptian hieroglyphic writing system recorded only consonants, not vowels, we are not always sure of the exact way any Egyptian word would have sounded. The popular Egyptian name "Amenemope" survives later in Greek texts, which allows us to be certain of its pronunciation: "Ah-men-em-OH-puh."

he also may be purely literary. In the prologue, Amenemope identifies himself as a state official and says that the instructions that follow are for his son.

Amenemope's readership was quite small: approximately 1 percent of the population was literate. These individuals, called **scribes**, were trained from a young age to do the difficult task of learning the complex **hieroglyphic** writing system in which pictures stood for sounds, words, and concepts. Formal schools for scribes probably existed, but many were trained by their fathers or caregivers. Instructional literature like *Amenemope* was a cornerstone of advanced education: students would copy out passages by dictation or memory. In order to become a professional scribe, the student must not only be able to read and write hundreds of hieroglyphic signs but also create elegant and readable documents. This skill came not only through rote memorization but from a great deal of practice, hence the number of practice copies that have survived of texts like *Amenemope*. For this reason, it can rightly be called a **school text** as well as a work of literature. The result of knowing a work like *Amenemope* backward and forward is that the student becomes inculcated with attitudes considered important for participating in elite Egyptian society. *Amenmeope* was likely popular as a school text because of the way it presents the ideal citizen as deferent to authority and careful in speech. Education was therefore not only a process of professionalization but also of inculturation. Do you think that your education has trained you to hold certain cultural values, or to question those values? Or do you think that education promotes values at all?

A central theme of the work is the "heated" versus the "silent" person. In characterizing these types, the author is especially concerned with speaking, in both conversational and formal settings (for example, in court). A heated person will talk without deliberation and argue, causing anger and strife. The metaphor of "heat" to describe a person who cannot control himself and who harms others is carefully chosen. What colors, similes, and contexts do you associate with "heat"? Perhaps similar to some of our own ideas, Egyptians identified heat with the color red as well as with cheeks flushed in anger. Finally, they also associated heat with the poison of snakes and scorpions. The silent person, on the contrary, heeds the warning to "not separate your heart from your tongue" (ch. 10). For the Egyptians, controlling one's tongue means allowing your heart, which they believed to be the seat of intellect and emotion, to guide your actions. Moreover, the heart is considered a place of divine intervention in human affairs: "The tongue of a person is the steering oar of a boat, / But the Lord of All is its pilot." The silent person is therefore a channel for divine influence. In one of *Amenemope*'s most forceful statements, we are told, "The heart of a man is the nose of god, / Beware of neglecting it" (ch. 24).[24] The odd equa-

24. The Egyptians, keen practitioners of medicine, also believed that the heart was the seat of a network of vessels that led throughout the body, pumping blood (and, they thought, water and air) through them in order to regulate and cool the body. In other words, they theorized something like the circulatory system, centuries before the Greek physician and

tion of the human heart with the god's nose is based on the belief that the nose, as the conduit of breath, ... life to humanity.[25]

Amenemope expre... into the everyday life of a scri... archy in society is affirmed, a... irness in dealing with courts ... constant concern for the poor ... corrective to ableism: In chapte... nature of human life, which is ... superior to disabled persons. A... deteriora- tion: "God is ever i... 18). What does this suggest a...

...oseph Cross
...ies Program

---

philosopher Galen did. The Egyptians believed that a circulatory system overloaded by heat would lead to general malaise.

25. An alternate ancient copy of *Amenemope* replaces "nose" with the similar-sounding "gift," perhaps to make the point more forceful, or to avoid the stark image!

hum readings
- apology to socrates → moodle
- GHYC - nicomachaen pg 409-422

PRE-READING PARS

1. Write down two examples of advice you were given before starting college.
2. Identify two ways you are most likely to respond to the world. What kind of impact does your approach have on yourself and others?

Instructions of Amenemope

Introduction

The beginning of the instruction about life,
The guide for well-being,
All the principles of official procedure,
The duties of the courtiers;
To know how to refute the accusation of one who made it,
And to send back a reply to the one who wrote;
To set one straight on the paths of life,
And make one prosper on earth;
To let their heart settle down in its shrine,
As one who steers him clear of evil;
To save them from the talk of others,
As one who is respected in the speech of humankind.
Written by the superintendent of the land, experienced in his office,
The offspring of a scribe of the Beloved Land,
The superintendent of produce, who fixes the grain measure,
Who sets the grain tax amount for his lord,
Who registers the islands which appear as new land over the cartouche of His Majesty,[26]
And sets up the landmark at the boundary of the arable land,
Who protects the king by his tax rolls,
And makes the Register of the Black Land.[27]
The scribe who places the divine offerings for all the gods,
The donor of land grants to the people,
The superintendent of grain who administers the food offerings,
Who supplies the storerooms with grain.
A truly silent man in Tjeni in the Ta-wer nome,[28]

26. When the annual inundation of the lands subsided, the newly formed islands in the Nile were immediately designated as royal property.

27. The usual name for Egypt.

28. Tjeni in the Ta-wer nome (Abydos) was the great temple and cult site of the god Osiris, where many royal and private memorial buildings were dedicated. Ipu and Senut are in the Panopolite nome to the north of Abydos, the area of modern Akhmim, of which the patron god was Min-Kamutef.

One whose verdict is "acquitted"[29] in Ipu,
The owner of a pyramid tomb on the west of Senut,
As well as the owner of a memorial chapel in Abydos,
Amenemope, the son of Kanakht,
Whose verdict is "acquitted" in the Ta-wer nome.
For his son, the youngest of his children,[30]
The smallest of his family.
[...]
Horemmaakheru is his true name,
A child of an official of Ipu,
The son of the sistrum player of Shu and Tefnut,
The chief singer of Horus, the lady Tawosret.

He Says: Chapter 1

Give your ears and hear what is said,
Give your heart over to their interpretation:
It is profitable to put them in your heart,
But woe to one who neglects them!
Let them rest in the shrine of your belly
That they may act as a lock in your heart;
Now when there comes a storm of words,
They will be a mooring post on your tongue.
If you spend a lifetime with these things in your heart,
You will find it good fortune;
You will discover my words to be a treasure house of life,
And your body will flourish upon earth.

Chapter 2

Beware of stealing from one who is miserable
And of raging against the weak.
Do not stretch out your hand to strike the aged,
Nor snip at the words of an elder.
Don't let yourself be sent on a fraudulent business,
Nor desire the carrying out of it;

29. The Egyptians believed that a deceased person would receive the verdict of "acquitted," literally "true of voice," in a court hearing before the god Osiris, so long as the person was pure of heart and gave truthful witness to having led a worthy life. The verdict allowed them to enjoy eternal life in the realm of the dead.

30. The addressee is the man's son, in this case Hor-em-maakheru, whose name means "Horus is vindicated," the son of Amenemope and Tawosret.

Do not get tired because of being interfered with,[31]
Nor return an answer on your own.
The one who does evil, throw them <in> the canal,
And 'they will bring back its slime.'
The north wind comes down and ends its appointed hour,
It is joined to the tempest;
The clouds are high, the crocodiles are nasty,
O heated one, what are you like?
They cry out, and their voice (reaches) heaven.
O Moon, make their crime manifest![32]
Row that we may ferry evil away,
For we will not act like one of his kind;
Lift them up, give them your hand,
And leave them <in> the hands of god;
Fill their belly with your own food
That they may be sated and weep.
Something else of value in the heart of god
Is to stop and think before speaking.

Chapter 3

Do not get into a quarrel with the hot-mouthed
Nor incite them with words;
Proceed cautiously before an opponent,
And give way to an adversary;
Sleep on it before speaking,
For a storm come forth like fire in hay is
The heated one in their appointed time.
May you be restrained before them;
Leave them to themselves,
And god will know how to answer them.
If you spend your life with these things in your heart,
Your children shall observe them.

31. Or, "do not revile someone you have hurt," or "do not act the part of a tired one (be downcast) toward the one you deceive."

32. The moon here stands for Thoth, who was the god of writing, accounting, and mathematics. The Egyptians believed that Thoth would deliver the verdict in the afterlife for whether one's soul was worthy to live forever in eternity.

Chapter 4

The heated one in the temple
Is like a tree grown in an enclosed space;
In a moment is its loss of foliage.
It reaches its end in the carpentry shop;
It is floated away far from its place,
Or fire is its funeral pyre.
The one who is truly temperate sets themselves apart,
They are like a tree grown in a sunlit field,
But it becomes verdant, it doubles its yield,
It stands before its owner;
Its fruit is something sweet, its shade is pleasant,
And it reaches its end in a grove.

Chapter 5

Do not take by violence the shares of the temple,
Do not be grasping, and you will find abundance;
Do not take away a temple servant
In order to do something profitable for another man.
Do not say today is the same as tomorrow,
Or how will matters come to pass?
When tomorrow comes, today is past;
The deep waters become a sandbank.[33]
Crocodiles are uncovered, the hippopotamuses are on dry land,
And the fishes gasping for air;
The wolves are fat, the wild fowl in festival,
And the nets are 'drained.'
Every temperate man in the temple says,
"Great is the benevolence of Re."[34]
Adhere to the silent one, you will find life,
And your body shall flourish upon earth.

Chapter 6

Do not displace the surveyor's marker on the boundaries of the arable land,
Nor alter the position of the measuring line;
Do not be covetous for a single cubit of land,
Nor encroach upon the boundaries of a widow.

33. Possibly meaning that the time for action is now past.
34. Re is the standard name for the sun god.

One who transgresses the furrow shortens a lifetime,
One who seizes it for fields
And acquires by deceptive attestations,
Will be lassoed by the might of the Moon.
To one who has done this on earth, pay attention,
For they are an oppressor of the weak;
They are an enemy worthy of your overthrowing;
The taking of Life is in their eye;
Their household is hostile to the community,
Their storerooms are broken into,
Their property is taken away from their children,
And their possessions are given to someone else.
Take care not to topple over the boundary marks of the fields,
Not fearing that you will be brought to court;
One pleases god with the might of the lord
When they set straight the boundaries of the arable land.
Desire, then, to make yourself prosper,
And take care for the lord of all;
Do not trample on the furrow of someone else,
Their good order will be profitable for you.
So plough the fields, and you will find whatever you need,
And receive the bread from your own threshing floor:
Better is a bushel which god gives you
Than five thousand deceitfully gotten;
They do not spend a day in the storehouse or warehouse,
They are 'no use for dough for beer';
Their stay in the granary is short-lived,
When morning comes they will have vanished.
Better, then, is poverty in the hand of god
Than riches in the storehouse;
Better is bread when the heart is at ease
Than riches with anxiety.

Chapter 7

Do not set your heart upon seeking riches,
For there is no one who can ignore Destiny and Fortune;
Do not set your thoughts on superficial matters:
For every man[35] there is his appointed time.

35. In this translation, "man" is used only when the specific gendered term is used in the original text. More often than not, *Amenmope* uses a generic word like our "person" or "human." With most epithets, such as the "hot-mouthed," a word like "man" or "person" is not specified.

Do not exert yourself to seek out excess
And your allotment will prosper for you;
If riches come to you by thievery
They will not spend the night with you;
As soon as day breaks they will not be in your household;
Although their places can be seen, they are not there.
When the earth opens up its mouth, it levels him and swallows him up,
They will plunge in the deep;
They will make for themselves a great hole which suits them.
And they will sink themselves in the underworld;
Or they will make themselves wings like geese,
And fly up to the sky.
Do not be pleased with yourself (because of) riches acquired through robbery,
Neither be sorry about poverty.
As for an officer who commands one who goes in front of him,
His company leaves him;
The boat of the covetous is abandoned <in> the mud,
While the skiff of the truly temperate one 'sails on.'
When he rises you shall offer to the Aten,[36]
Saying, "Grant me prosperity and health."
And he will give you your necessities for life,
And you will be safe from fear.

Chapter 8

Set your deeds throughout the world
That everyone may greet you;
They make rejoicing for the Uraeus,[37]
And spit against the Apophis.[38]
Keep your tongue safe from words of detraction,
And you will be the loved one of the people,
Then you will find your (proper) place within the temple
And you will share in the offerings of the lord;
You will be revered, when you are concealed <in> your grave,
And be safe from the might of god.
Do not accuse a person of a crime,
When the circumstance of (their) flight is unknown.
Whether you hear something good or bad,

36. The disk of the sun, Aten is a distinct aspect of the solar god Re.

37. The Uraeus is the protective cobra snake depicted on one of the pharaoh's crowns.

38. Apophis is a snake demon associated with Seth (god of the desert) and represents darkness. Apophis threatens the barge of the sun-god as it navigates through the night.

Put it outside, until they have been heard;
Set a good report on your tongue,
While the bad thing is concealed inside you.

Chapter 9

Do not fraternize with the heated one,
Nor approach them to converse.
Safeguard your tongue from talking back to your superior,
And take care not to offend them.
Do not allow them to cast words only to entrap you,
And be not too free in your replies;
With a man of your own station discuss the reply;
And take care of 'speaking thoughtlessly';
When one's heart is upset, words travel faster
Than wind over water.
One is ruined and created by their tongue,[39]
When they speak slander;
One makes an answer deserving of a beating,
For their freight is damaged.
They sail among all the world,
But their cargo is false words;
They act the ferryman in twisting words:
They go forth and come back arguing.
But whether they eat or whether they drink inside,
Their accusation (waits for them) outside.
The day when their evil deed is brought to court
Is a disaster for their children.
Even Khnum will straightway come against them,[40]
The potter of the hot-mouthed,
It is to knead and bake the hearts that he molds.
They (the hot-mouthed) are like a wolf cub in the farmyard,
And they turn one eye to the other (squinting),
For they set families to argue.
They go before all the winds like clouds,
They change their hue in the sun;
They crock their tail like a baby crocodile,
They curl themselves up to inflict harm,

39. He makes and breaks reputations.

40. The ram-headed god Khnum was (according to one popular myth) the creator of gods, humans, and animals, and is depicted molding creatures using a potter's wheel.

Their lips are sweet, but their tongue is bitter,
And fire burns inside them.
Do not fly up to join that one
Not fearing you will be brought to account.

Chapter 10

Do not force yourself to greet the heated one
Nor destroy your own heart;
Do not say to them, "May you be praised," not meaning it
When there is fear within you.
Do not converse falsely with a person,
For it is the abomination of god.
Do not separate your heart from your tongue,
All your plans will succeed.
You will be important before others,
While you will be secure in the hand of god.
God hates one who falsifies words,
His great abomination is duplicity.

Chapter 11

Do not covet the property of the poor
Nor hunger for their bread;
The property of the poor is an obstruction to the throat,
It makes the gullet throw it back.[41]
It is by false oaths that one has brought themselves up,
While their heart slips back inside them.
Do not let disaffection wear away success,
Or else evil will topple good.
If you are 'at a loss' before your superior,
And are confused in your speeches,
Your flatterings are turned back with curses,
And your prostrations by beatings.
Whoever fills the mouth with too much bread swallows it and spits up,
So you are emptied of your good.
To the overseer of the poor pay attention
While the sticks touch them,
And while all their people are bound in chains:

41. Perhaps meaning that the limited property of a poor man is barely enough to keep him alive, like moisture in his throat.

And they are led to the executioner.
When you are too free before your superior,
Then you are in bad favor with your subordinates.
So steer away from the poor on the road,
That you may see them but keep clear of their property.

Chapter 12

Do not covet the property of an official,
And do not fill (your) mouth with too much food arrogantly;
If he sets you to manage his property,
Respect his, and yours will prosper.
Do not deal with the heated one,
Nor associate yourself to a disloyal party.
If you are sent to transport straw,
Abstain from profiting thereby,
If a man is detected in a dishonest transaction,
Never again will he be employed.

Chapter 13

Do not lead a person astray (with) reed pen on papyrus:
It is the abomination of god.
Do not witness a false statement,
Nor remove another (from the list) by your order;
Do not reckon with someone who has nothing,
Nor make your pen be false.
If you find a large debt against a poor person,
Make it into three parts;
Release two of them and let one remain:
You will find it a path of life;
You will pass the night in sound sleep; in the morning
You will find it like good news.
Better it is to be praised as one loved by people
Than wealth in the storehouse;
Better is bread when the heart is at ease
Than riches with troubles.

Chapter 14

Do not ingratiate yourself with a person,
Nor exert yourself to seek out their hand,

If they say to you, "take a bribe,"
There is no need to respect them.
Do not be afraid of them, nor bend down your head,
Nor turn aside your gaze.
Address them with your words and say to them greetings;
When they stop, your chance will come;
Do not repel them at his first approach,
Another time they will be apprehended.

Chapter 15

Do well, and you will attain influence.
Do not dip your pen against a transgressor.
The beak of the Ibis is the finger of the scribe;[42]
Take care not to disturb it;
Thoth dwells (in) the temple of Khmun,
While his eye travels around the Two Lands[43];
If he sees one who cheats with his finger (that is, a false scribe),
He takes away his provisions by the flood.
As for a scribe who cheats with his finger,
Their son shall not be enrolled.
If you spend your life with these (words) in your heart,
Your children shall observe them.

Chapter 16

Do not tilt the scale nor falsify the weights,[44]
Nor diminish the fractions of the grain measures;
Do not wish for the grain measures of the fields
To cast aside those of the treasury.[45]
The Ape[46] sits by the balance,
While his heart is the plummet.
Who is a god as great as Thoth,
The one who discovered these things, in order to create them?

42. The Ibis here is Thoth, patron god of the scribe. An Ibis is a marsh bird common in Lower Egypt. Thoth invented writing and is the scribe of the gods. Thoth is also depicted as an ape.

43. A name for Egypt, whose two parts were the Nile Delta in the north (Lower Egypt) and the Nile Valley in the south (Upper Egypt).

44. Absent coinage, which was invented in the seventh century BCE in Lydia (modern-day Turkey), an accurate scale was the only way to record and assess the economic value of goods.

45. Do not use different measures to your own benefit.

46. The ape was one of the forms of the god Thoth, along with the ibis bird.

Do not get for yourself short weights;
They are plentiful, yea, an army by the might of god.
If you see someone cheating,
At a distance you must pass him by.
Do not be avaricious for copper,
And desire fine clothes;
What good is one cloaked in fine linen,
When he cheats before god.
When faience are heaped upon gold,[47]
At daybreak they turn to lead.

Chapter 17

Beware of tampering with the grain measure
To falsify its fractions;
Do not act wrongfully through force,
Cause it not to be empty inside,
May you have it measured exactly as it arrived,
Your hand stretching out with precision.
Make not for yourself a measure of two capacities,[48]
For then it is toward the depths that you will go.
The measure is the eye of Re,[49]
Its abomination is the thief.
As for a grain measurer who multiplies and subtracts,
Their eye will seal up against him.
Do not receive the harvest tax of a cultivator,
Nor set a papyrus against them to harm them.
Do not enter into collusion with the grain measurer,
Nor defraud the share of the Residence,[50]
More important is the threshing floor for barley
Than swearing by the Great Throne.

Chapter 18

Do not go to bed fearing tomorrow,
For when day breaks how will tomorrow be?
Man knows not what tomorrow will be!

47. Faience is glazed earthenware. Egypt is known for vivid blue faience.
48. A measure that can be read two ways.
49. The most common name for the sun god.
50. A name for the palace where the pharaoh resided.

God is ever in his perfection,
While man is ever in his failure.
The words which people say pass on one side,
The things which God does pass on another side.
Do not say, "'I am' without fault,"
Nor try to seek out trouble.
Fault is the business of god,
It is sealed with his finger.
There is no success in the hand of god,
Nor is there failure before them;
If one turns oneself about to seek out success,
In a moment he (the god) destroys them.
Be strong in your heart, make your inmost firm,
Do not steer with your tongue;
The tongue of a person is the steering oar of a boat,
But the lord of all is its pilot.

Chapter 19

Do not enter the council chamber in the presence of a magistrate
And then falsify your speech.
Do not go up and down with your accusation
When your witnesses stand readied.
Do not 'overstate' <through> oaths in the name of your lord,
(Through) pleas (in) the place of interrogation.
Tell the truth before the magistrate,
Lest he gain power over your body;
If you petition before him the next day,
He will concur with all you say;
He will present your case <in> court before the Council of the Thirty,[51]
And it will be 'decided' another time as well.

Chapter 20

Do not defraud a person in the law court
Nor put aside the one who is just.
Do not pay attention to garments of white.
Nor scorn one in rags.
Take not the bribe of the strong,
Nor repress the weak for them.

51. The name of a standard judicial body made up of thirty men.

As for the just who bears the greatness of god,
They will render himself as he wishes.
The strength of one like them
Saves a poor wretch from their beatings.
Do not make for yourself false 'enrollment' lists,
For they are punishable offenses (deserving) death;
They are serious oaths which promote respect;
And they are to be investigated by a reporter.
Do not falsify the oracles on a papyrus
And (thereby) alter the designs of god.
Do not arrogate to yourself the might of god
As if Destiny and Fortune did not exist.
Hand property over to its (rightful) owners,
And seek out life for yourself;
Let not your heart build in their house,
For then your neck will be on the execution block.

Chapter 21

Do not say, find for me a strong patron,
For a man in your town has afflicted me.
Do not say, find for me an active intercessor,
For one who hates (me) has afflicted me.
Indeed, you cannot know the plans of god;
You cannot perceive tomorrow.
Sit yourself at the hands of god:
Your tranquility will overthrow them (the adversaries).
As for a crocodile deprived of 'his tongue,'
His significance is negligible.
Empty not your soul to everybody
And do not diminish thereby your importance;
Do not pour out your words to others,
Nor fraternize with one who is too rash.
Better is a man whose report is inside him
Than one who tells it to disadvantage.
One cannot run to attain perfection;
One cannot create (only) to destroy it.

Chapter 22

Do not provoke your adversary,
And do not <let> them say their innermost thoughts;
Do not fly up to greet them
When you cannot see 'how they act.'
May you first comprehend their accusation;
Be calm and your chance will come.
Leave it to them and they will empty their soul;
'Sleep knows how to find them out';
Touch their feet, do not disrespect them;
Fear them, do not underestimate them.
Indeed, you cannot know the plans of god,
You cannot perceive tomorrow.
Sit yourself at the hands of god;
Your tranquility will overthrow them.

Chapter 23

Do not eat a meal in the presence of a magistrate,
Nor set to speaking first.
If you are sated, pretend to chew,
Enjoy yourself with your saliva.
Look at the cup in front of you,
And let it suffice your need.
Even as a noble is important in his office,
So they are like the abundance of a flooded well.

Chapter 24

Do not listen to the proposition of an official indoors,
And then repeat it to another outside.
Do not allow your discussions to be brought outside
Lest your heart be grieved.
The heart of a person is the nose of god,
So take care not to slight it;
A person who stands <at> the side of an official
Should not have their name known (in the street).

Chapter 25

Do not laugh at the blind nor taunt a little person,
Neither interfere with the condition of the disabled;
Do not taunt a man who is in the hand of god,[52]
Nor scowl at him if he errs.
A person is clay and straw,
And god is their potter;
They (the god) overthrow and build daily,
Impoverish a thousand if they wish,
But make a thousand people into officials
When they are in their hour of life.
How fortunate is the one who reaches the West,[53]
When they are safe in the hand of god.

Chapter 26

Do not sit in the beer hall
Nor join someone greater than you,
Whether they be low or high in their station,
An old or a young person;
But take as a friend for yourself someone compatible:
Re is helpful though he is far away.
When you see someone greater than you outside,
Follow them, respect (them).
And give a hand to an old person filled with beer:
Respect them as their children would.
The strong arm is not ‘weakened’ when it is uncovered,
The back is not broken when one bends it;
A man is not denigrated when he speaks sweet words,
More so than a rich man whose words are straw.
A pilot who sees into the distance
Will not let their ship capsize.

Chapter 27

Do not reproach someone greater than you,
For they have seen the Sun before you;

52. This may refer to what we would today diagnose medically as epilepsy, or to a religious experience like ecstasy.

53. The common euphemism for the realm of the afterlife, associated with the place of the setting sun as well as with the uninhabitable desert which lay west of the Nile.

Do not let yourself be reported to the Aten when it rises,
With the words, "Again a young man has reproached an elder."
Very painful in the sight of Re
Is a young person who reproaches an elder.
Let them beat you with your hands folded,
Let them reproach you while you keep quiet.
Then when you come before them in the morning
They will give you bread freely.
As for bread, the dog of his master
Barks to the one who gives it.

Chapter 28

Do not identify a widow if you have caught her in the fields,
Nor fail to give way if she is accused.
Do not turn a stranger away from your oil jar
Double it (more than) for your (own) family.
God loves the one who cares for the poor,
More than the one who respects the wealthy.

Chapter 29

Do not turn people away from crossing the river
When you have room in (your) ferryboat;
If an oar is given you in the midst of the deep waters,
So bend back your hands <to> take it up.
It is not an abomination in the hand of god
If the crew does not agree.
Do not acquire a ferryboat on the river,
And then attempt to seek out its fares;
Take the fare from the person of means,
But (also) accept the destitute (without charge).

Chapter 30

Mark for yourself these thirty chapters:
They please, they instruct,
They are the foremost of all books;
They teach the ignorant.
If they are read before the ignorant,
They will be purified (of their ignorance) through them.
Fill yourself with them; put them in your heart

And get people to interpret them.
As for a scribe who is experienced in his position,
They will find themselves worthy of being a courtier.
It is finished.
By the writing of Senu, son of the god's father Pamiu.

Simpson, W. K., and R. K. Ritner. *The Literature of Ancient Egypt: An Anthology of Stories, Instructions, Stelae, Autobiographies, and Poetry*, 223–43. New Haven, CT: Yale University Press, 2003.

POST-READING PARS

1. Did you find any advice in *Amenemope* that rings true in your experience or could be useful today? Is any of the advice similar to what you received?
2. Identify two conceptions about the human body or human nature that are reflected in the reading. How are they different from what you think?

Inquiry Corner

Content Question(s):

What metaphors and imagery are used to describe the heated versus the silent person?

What role does the divine play in ethical life?

Critical Question(s):

What effect does the framing of *Amenemope*'s teaching as from a father to a son have?

What could be the purposes of *Amenemope* given its critical perspective on success and wealth?

Comparative Question(s):

Would the ideal person envisioned by *Amenemope* follow the ideals of *ren* ("human-heartedness" or kindness) and of being a gentleman (*junzi*) in the *Analects*?

Connection Question(s):

Do you think that you can have a successful career and also be a good person? What are the challenges involved?

What role does codified advice play in the contemporary world? (e.g., identifying which academic majors lead to financial security). Can such advice restrict freedom?

BEYOND THE CLASSROOM

- What are some specific ways you would deal with a colleague or boss whose communication style was consistently caustic, abrasive, or disrespectful?
- Much of the morality described here could be seen as self-serving, from the perspective of power. It was written by "the divine" and demands subservience to those with wealth and position. Do you agree with the moral tenets prescribed here, even though there is a power dynamic at play?

Egyptian Love Poetry

SNAPSHOT BOX

LANGUAGE: Ancient Egyptian

DATE: c. 11th century BCE

LOCATION: Egypt

TAGS: Aesthetics; Emotion; Family; Love

Introduction

Several anonymous collections of love poetry have survived from Ancient Egypt, totalling about fifty poems, all dating from the late New Kingdom. The poem given here is found on the back of a **papyrus scroll** currently held in the British Museum, called Papyrus Chester Beatty I, named for the individual who purchased it on the antiquities market in Egypt. The scroll is a compilation of several works of literature and even includes a copy of a receipt for the purchase of an ox! While some love poetry personifies and expounds upon the idea of love itself, Egyptian love poems portray the thoughts and emotions of people who are in love from the first-person perspective. The present selection is a single poem made up of seven stanzas, each with a single speaker, alternating between a female and a male voice.

The professional book maker who copied the poems onto the scroll gave them a title at the beginning: "The Sayings of the Great Happiness." Explicit titles are rare for ancient works of literature. The Egyptian word for happiness also means "entertainment." One scholar has suggested that it should be read as "The Great Entertainer," referring to the poem's author.[54] Furthermore, since the gender of the noun "entertainer" in Egyptian is written here as feminine (the noun usually being masculine), this poem may be a rare ancient example of a work of literature authored by a woman. Prominent Egyptian women were priestesses as well as professional singers and harp players in temples, and thus would have been literate,

Timeline

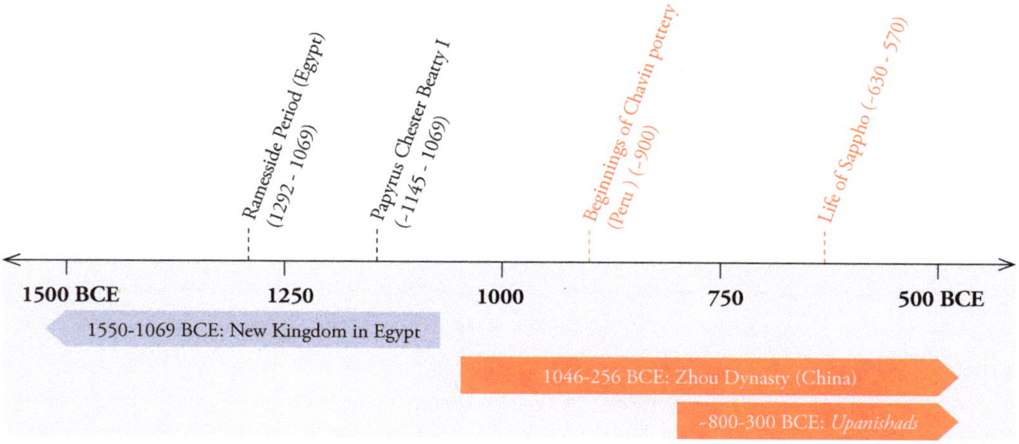

54. Michael V. Fox, *The Song of Songs and Ancient Egyptian Love Poetry* (Madison: University of Wisconsin Press, 1985), 55–56.

inviting a comparison with the Mesopotamian high priestess Enheduanna. Naming the author of these poems would be striking, since, as a rule, ancient Egyptian literature was anonymously written. Regardless of whether the author is named, can you find any clues to support an argument for female authorship based on the text of the poem alone?

The word "entertainment" literally means "make the heart forgetful" in Egyptian. For the reader or hearer, this poem provided a break from the difficulties of life. Forgetfulness of the heart is also relevant to the portrayal of the lovers in the poem. They take turns speaking at length (about twenty lines at a time) about their beloved, but instead of speaking directly to them, they address others who are listening, or their own hearts in soliloquy. They appear to be young and in the beginning stages of falling in love with each other. They call each other "brother" and "sister" out of affection, much like we use the same terms today, though in our case with friendly, not romantic, connotations. The young lovers reproach their own heart for its foolishness, describing it as fluttering, leaping, and exulting at the presence or even mere thought of their beloved. At times, the heart is treated like an independent entity with thoughts and feelings of its own. How does the author's description of the experience of love compare to your own? Love also leads to an exuberance of language, making the creative medium of poetry particularly apt. A striking example of the typical descriptive language of Egyptian love poetry is the first stanza, where the young man describes his beloved from head to toe with a concoction of adjectives, metaphors, and similes drawn from a wide range of human experience.[55]

This love poetry would have been read and copied by students learning how to write hieroglyphs as they become trained to be **scribes**, similar to *Amenemope* (see page 77). Copies of Egyptian love poems have been found on chips of stone or shards of pots useful as scratch paper for students. For us, the idea of entertainment is often considered to be at odds with education. However, as you read the verses, how might this poetry be interpreted as conveying lessons about love? It also served as an engaging medium for practicing vocabulary as seen in its use of difficult language and rare words (which do not come across in the translation). An intriguing feature of this poem is how each stanza begins and ends with a pun or wordplay on its number. For example, in stanza 2, the word "brother" resembles the Egyptian word for the number "2."

It is also possible that the scribe who created the surviving copy of this poem adapted it from another source, such as folksong. As you read, you should ask yourself if this poetry shows any indications of an original oral context of performance. Look for signs not only in the words but also in the way you imagine the poem could

55. A similar type of poetic description of a beloved can be found in the biblical Song of Songs (also known as the Song of Solomon, after its legendary author), chapters 4–6. This work of ancient Hebrew love poetry is akin to the Egyptian, though written centuries later.

have been performed. Re-create this by reading the poem out loud, taking note of how long it takes you from start to finish, as well as how long each speech takes to read. Would this be appropriate as a staged dialogue performed in front of an audience? Or could the individual speeches by the lovers be performed as actual serenades?

Joseph Cross
Humanities Program

From Papyrus Chester Beatty I: A Cycle of Seven Stanzas

Beginning of the sayings of the great happiness (First Stanza)

The One, the sister without peer,
The handsomest of all!
She looks like the rising morning star
At the start of a happy year.
Shining bright, fair of skin,
Lovely the look of her eyes,
Sweet the speech of her lips,
She has not a word too much.
Upright neck, shining breast,
Hair true lapis lazuli;
Arms surpassing gold,
Fingers like lotus buds.
Heavy thighs, narrow waist,
Her legs parade her beauty;
With graceful step she treads the ground,
Captures my heart by her movements.
She causes all men's necks
To turn about to see her;
Joy has he whom she embraces,
He is like the first of men!
When she steps outside she seems
Like that other One!

Second Stanza

My brother torments my heart with his voice,
He makes sickness take hold of me;
He is neighbor to my mother's house,
And I cannot go to him!
Mother is right in charging him thus:
"Give up seeing her!"
It pains my heart to think of him,
I am possessed by love of him.
Truly, he is a foolish one,
But I resemble him;
He knows not my wish to embrace him,
Or he would write to my mother.
Brother, I am promised to you
By the Gold of women!
Come to me that I see your beauty,

Father, Mother will rejoice!
My people will hail you all together,
They will hail you, O my brother!

Third Stanza

My heart devised to see her beauty
While sitting down in her house;
On the way I met Mehy[56] on his chariot,
With him were his young men.
I knew not how to avoid him:
Should I stride on to pass him?
But the river was the road,
I knew no place for my feet.
My heart, you are very foolish,
Why accost Mehy?
If I pass before him,
I tell him my movements;
Here, I'm yours, I say to him,
Then he will shout my name,
And assign me to the first ...
Among his followers.

Fourth Stanza

My heart flutters hastily,
When I think of my love of you;
It lets me not act sensibly,
It leaps (from) its place.
It lets me not put on a dress,
Nor wrap my scarf around me;
I put no paint upon my eyes,
I'm even not anointed.
"Don't wait, go there," says it to me,
As often as I think of him;
My heart, don't act so stupidly,
Why do you play the fool?
Sit still, the brother comes to you,
And many eyes as well!
Let not the people say of me:

56. By some accounts Mehy was a fictional character, by others a historical figure. Recent studies have identified a historical personage with this name, a military commander under the New Kingdom, King Seti I (c. 1295–1280 BCE). In literature, Mehy may have become a romantic hero.

"A woman fallen through love!"
Be steady when you think of him,
My heart, do not flutter!

Fifth Stanza

I praise the Golden, I worship her majesty,
I extol the Lady of Heaven;
I give adoration to Hathor,[57]
Laudations to my Mistress!
I called to her, she heard my plea,
She sent my mistress to me;
She came by herself to see me,
O great wonder that happened to me!
I was joyful, exulting, elated,
When they said: "See, she is here!"
As she came, the young men bowed,
Out of great love for her.
I make devotions to my goddess,
That she grant me my sister as gift;
Three days now that I pray to her name,
Five days since she went from me!

Sixth Stanza

I passed before his house,
I found his door ajar;
My brother stood by his mother,
And all his brothers with him.
Love of him captures the heart
Of all who tread the path;
Splendid youth who has no peer,
Brother outstanding in virtues!
He looked at me as I passed by,
And I, by myself, rejoiced;
How my heart exulted in gladness,
My brother, at your sight!
If only the mother knew my heart,
She would have understood by now;
O Golden, put it in her heart,

57. Though Hathor is best known as the goddess of the sky, she was also the goddess of music, beauty, and love.

Then will I hurry to my brother!
I will kiss him before his companions,
I would not weep before them;
I would rejoice at their understanding
That you acknowledge me!
I will make a feast for my goddess,
My heart leaps to go;
To let me see my brother tonight,
O happiness in passing!

Seventh Stanza

Seven days since I saw my sister,
And sickness invaded me;
I am heavy in all my limbs,
My body has forsaken me.
When the physicians come to me,
My heart rejects their remedies;
The magicians are quite helpless,
My sickness is not discerned.[58]
To tell me "She is here" would revive me!
Her name would make me rise;
Her messenger's coming and going,
That would revive my heart!
My sister is better than all prescriptions,[59]
She does more for me than all medicines;
Her coming to me is my amulet,
The sight of her makes me well!
When she opens her eyes my body is young,
Her speaking makes me strong;
Embracing her expels my malady—
Seven days since she went from me!

"Egyptian Love Poems (From Papyrus Chester Beatty I, Poem 1)." In *Ancient Egyptian Literature. A Book of Readings: The New Kingdom*, edited by Miriam Lichtheim, 182–85. Berkeley: University of California Press, 2006.

58. In Ancient Egypt, both physicians and religious healers or magicians worked together in medical practice.

59. Medical manuals from Egypt describe numerous prescriptions like the one referenced here. These would include a pharmaceutical concoction, with instructions for preparation and application, often accompanied by a prayer, or even short mythological story, to be recited when the medicant was applied.

"Song for Dance of Young Girls" (Didinga)

Introduction

The recent burgeoning demand for African music and dance in mostly Western institutions highlights the need to clarify its purpose, invaluable contribution, and significance to its practitioners within its particular African context. As Albert Mawere Opoku, an African scholar-dancer describes,

> To us, life, with its rhythms and cycles, is Dance. [. . .] Dance is a language, a mode of expression, which addresses itself to the mind, through the heart, using related, relevant and significant movements which have their basic counterparts in our everyday activities. [. . .] For a deeper insight into our way of life—our labors, material cultures, aspirations, history, social and economic conditions, religious beliefs and disbeliefs, moments of festivity and sadness—in short, our life and soul, and the realities, perceived, conceived or felt, that make us the people that we have been and are at present, are revealed to the serious seeker, in our dance.[60]

SNAPSHOT BOX

LANGUAGE: Didinga

LOCATION: Present-day South Sudan, Uganda, and Kenya

GENRE: Song

ETHNIC IDENTITY: Didinga

TAGS: Aesthetics; Body; Emotion; Family; Friendship; Identity; Oral Histories and Storytelling; Women and Gender

Timeline

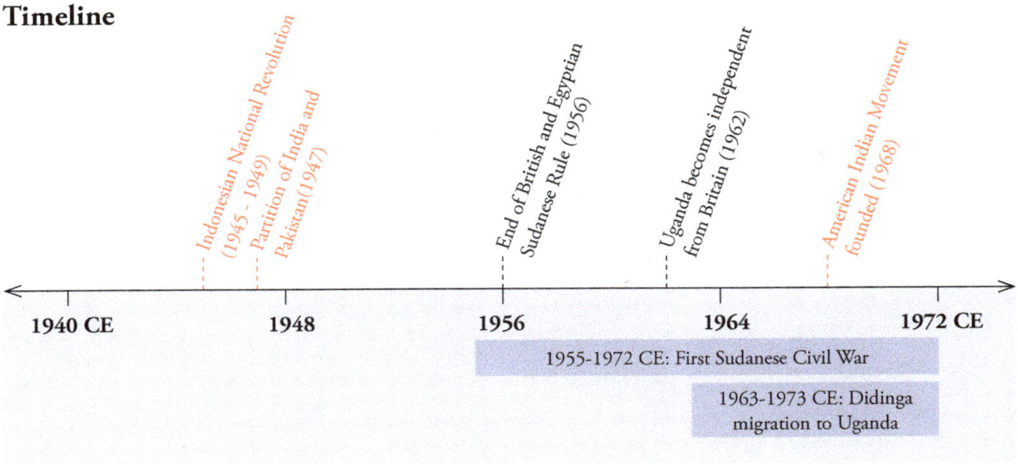

60. Albert Mawere Opoku, "The African Choreographer's Problems." *Institute of African Studies Research Review* (1969): 5–12. Opoku was a dance professor at the University of Ghana and Founding Artistic Director of the Ghana Dance Ensemble. See also Veronica Tadjo, *Talking Drums: A Selection of Poems from Africa South of the Sahara* (New York: Bloomsbury USA Childrens, 2004).

This is a depiction of the role of dance and music, and how it is woven into the fabrics of African societies. For the African, music and dance coupled with its related ceremonies are important rites of passage, marking important times of transition in one's personhood in relationship to their self and community, such as becoming an adult, marriage, and so on.

The song, "Song for Dance of Young Girls," is a work song focused on the art of pottery making being passed down from a mother to her children, including young members of the extended family. This song highlights the working songs of the Didinga people of East Africa. They are mostly subsistence farmers who occupy the geographical location of where the borders of Kenya, South Sudan, and Uganda meet. Apart from farming, the Didinga people are vested in raising and trading livestock (cattle and sheep) as well as the making of pottery, which they inherited from their ancestors.

"Song for Dance of Young Girls" is a song from a young girl to her mother with an immense appreciation for the gift of pot moulding, the shaping of pots by hand, as a livelihood. Pots are of utmost importance in the homes of Didinga people. They are skilled in pot moulding as it is embedded in their cultural norms. It has multipurpose uses: storing and preserving perishable agricultural products; storing and keeping water cooler than room temperature; cooking; fetching water; preparing and preserving Indigenous medicine; storing beverages, and the like. The song is sung by an individual or group of potters while moulding to stimulate their energy and concentration through a call-and-response form of music. This music is meant to guide, support, and accelerate the skill set that has specifically been passed on by a mother. This song fosters social cohesion and inspires communal identities. This song, among many others, is meant to inspire, motivate, as well as send a message (market themselves) about how they have learned to be potters from their (teacher) mother. When performed in nontypical staged settings, observers in the audience become participants through the call and response within this fundamentally participatory artistic form.

The song has four verses, with each one addressing a unique set of ideas yet deepening the reciprocity with the other. The first verse evokes nostalgia, especially involving memories of spending time with one's mother while learning to mould. The following verse reveals that their mother taught them not only the acquisition of potter skills but about life in general, including their cultural norms. Using pot moulding as an example, each mother taught their children about life and everything it brings. The words in the song may serve as a manual for the process of making a desirable pot. It is up to the singer(s) to decide the enactment of emotions, but the memory is always there to guide them through the song. In the third verse, people reminisce about their mothers and show appreciation in a variety of ways based upon whether their mother is physically present, dead, or alive. Thus, for example, through their singing, they evoke the spirit of their mother from the ancestral world if she had passed on. The fourth and final verse of the song is in the form of a prayer — libation and appreciation for the gods that protect and provide the land with rain and abundance of rich clay. Pot making is a combination of all-natural elements such as clay, water, wood, fire, and the sun, all elements seen as possessing life. The conclusion of the song "Oh, clay of the river, bend to our hands" changes the mood; it becomes solemn to show indebtedness for strength and skills.

In most African societies, mothers (women) wield social power and influence in the lives of their children and the community at large.[61] For example, the Yoruba saying, "Iya ni wura, baba ni jigi" (mother is gold, a father is a piece of mirror) is a testament to the importance of motherhood in African societies. Mother is gold: strong, valuable, true, central to their children's existence. Thus their mother uses her powers, privileges, and entitlements to nurture them into adulthood. In "Song for Dance of Young Girls" this process involves the concept and creative process of the pot.[62] For example, one of the lines, "its belly swells like the mother of twins" is repeated and exaggerated, because the more the pot's belly is swollen, the easier it becomes balanced with little to no chance of falling. The inheritor will pass on knowledge and wisdom about life, embodied in this simile and pot-making practice, to the next generation.

The Didinga people are acutely aware of their surroundings. The entire song clearly establishes the use of a simile, especially with the suggestion that the pot "swells like the paunch of a hyena." The mention of a hyena in this verse is a testament to their environment and connection to wildlife. Hyenas inhabit savannahs, grasslands, woodlands, and forest edges across sub-Saharan Africa. These predators use their nocturnal prowess to hunt the Didinga livestock. Over the years, the people have developed innovative mechanisms to prevent their livestock from being killed by hyenas. One of these preventive measures is lighting a fire in a pot to burn through the night.

Finally, it is noteworthy that the microcosm of music, work, and dance is a direct response to the social macrocosm in many African societies. Although this is a song for dance of young girls, its execution affects the entire community. However, the focus is all about celebrating women — for example, our mothers for their resilience. Apart from pottery, many life events could inspire similar songs among the Didinga people: when a girl reaches adolescence, celebrates an achievement, or gets married; it also could celebrate women in leadership positions, and farming, among oth-

61. Akujobi Remi, "Motherhood in African Literature and Culture," *Comparative Literature* 13, 1 (2011): 2–7.

62. Peter Karubi Nwanesi, "Development, Micro-credit and Women's Empowerment: A Case Study of Market and Rural Women in Southern Nigeria," *Researchgate* (2006): 20–57.

ers. This performance often serves as a platform where societal issues are addressed by the queen-mother or chief and elders of the community.

Mustapha Braimah
Dance Program and Department of Drama

PRE-READING PARS

1. What skill sets have you learned from your mother or any member of your family?
2. What types of events happen that mark the transition to being an adult (e.g., getting your driver's license, etc.)? What skills or knowledge do you think are valuable to pass on to the next generation?
3. List two to three special occasions that highlight a milestone in your life.
4. If we agree that songs are the manual for our daily activities, what songs from your playlist would support that statement?

Song for Dance of Young Girls

A hot sun was beating down on the river's bank where the girls were playing. They could just see their village standing out over the treetops, the newly thatched roofs shining a golden-yellow in the sunlight. They had already scoured their gourds in the river and they had bathed and were becoming grimy once more with sweat and the dust which their feet trampled up. Round and round the girls danced in a circle, their arms linked together, their legs criss-crossing in an ever-shifting kaleidoscope of movement, broken by a heavy stamp and a pause to mark the rhythm at the end of each line of the song ... [And then], down they sat cross-legged in a circle, holding hands, and one sang very slowly:

[Verse 1] *We mould a pot as our mothers did.*
The pot, where is the pot?
And they all answered, thrusting their clasped hands to the centre:
The pot, it is here.
We mould the pot as our mothers did.
First, the base of the pot.

They leaned forward again, all their hands touching in the centre.

[Verse 2] *Strip by strip, and layer by layer.*
Supple fingers kneading the clay,
Long fingers moulding the clay,
Stiff thumbs shaping the clay,
Layer by layer and strip by strip,
We build up the pot of our mother.

As she sang, all hands, still clasped, were withdrawn, and the whole circle swung first to the left and back to the right, then left and right again with a slow rhythmic motion, while all the children chorused:

[Verse 3] *We build up the pot of our mother,*
Strip by strip and layer by layer.
Its belly swells like the paunch of a hyaena,
Of a hyaena which has eaten a whole sheep.
Its belly swells like a mother of twins.
It is a beautiful pot, the pot of our mother.
It swells like a mother of twins.

They all sang, as they leaned far back from their hips and raised their arms outwards.

[Verse 4] *Oh clay of the river, bend to our hands,*
Curve delicately.
See the strong shoulder and narrow neck.
(In, children, in)
Strip by strip and layer by layer,
Supple fingers kneading,
Long fingers moulding,
Stiff thumbs shaping,
The beautiful pot, the pot of our mother.

Leaning forward again, the children swayed in time to their leader's song, swayed left and right, their glistening backs curving and their arms straining more and more forward to shape the pot down to its mouth.

Suddenly their hands met and they leaped up all together with a shout
The pot, the pot of our mother.

Driberg, J. H. "Song for Dance of Young Girls." In *People of the Small Arrow*, translated by A. Sakyiama, 320–24. New York: Payson and Clarke, 1930.

"Song of Gimmile" (Mandinka/Mande)

Introduction

SNAPSHOT BOX

LANGUAGE: Mandinka

DATE: Oral tradition

LOCATION: Mali

GENRE: Storytelling, song

ETHNIC IDENTITY: Mandinka/Mande

TAGS: Authority and Leadership; Music; Oral Histories and Storytelling

The "Song of Gimmile" is an oral source that originates from the inhabitants of the great Mali Empire (c. 1230s–1610), also known as Mandinka or Mandingo Kingdom.[63] It spanned across parts of the modern-day countries of Guinea, Niger, Guinea-Bissau, Mauritania, Burkina Faso, Nigeria, Ivory Coast (Côte d'Ivoire), Senegal, Gambia, Sierra Leone, and Ghana, thus making it the largest **Sudanic** empire in West Africa. It gets its name from the Arabic term, ***bilad al-sudan***, meaning "the land of the blacks." This was a term that Arab travelers going from the north of Africa to the west of the continent for trade used to refer to the stretch of land south of the Sahara Desert. For almost 1,000 years, the Sudanic empires of Ghana, Mali, and Songhai (also Songhay) dominated western Africa. They thrived in commerce, scholarship, and military prowess; the ***Epic of Sundiata***, for example, extols the military ingenuity and valor of King Sundiata, the founder of the Mali Empire. Sudanic empires' success was largely due to their ability to control the trans-Saharan trade routes; to establish universities and learning centers in cities like Timbuktu, Djenne, and Gao; and to command allegiance from numerous tributary states. What other factors or features might contribute to an empire's success?

Timeline

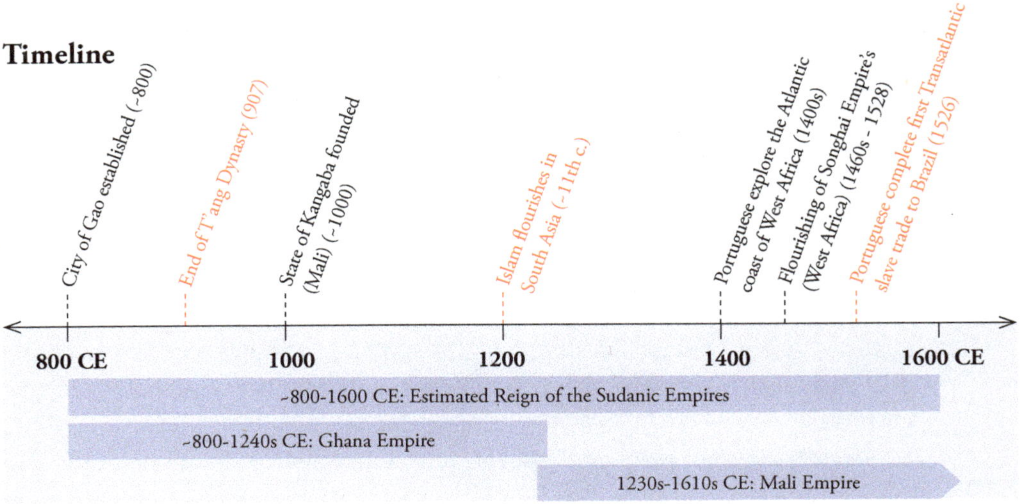

63. The story itself mentions the "Gindo people" but Mandinka is the common term used consistently. It may be that it could have been originally "Ndingo" derived from "Mandingo" and the transcriber may have written Gindo.

The oral tradition that generated the "Song of Gimmile"[64] was located in the Mali Empire, which followed the Ghana Empire. The Ghana Empire was founded by the Soninke people and thrived from the 800s to 1070 CE. When it ended in 1240 CE, it was succeeded by the Mandingo state of Kangaba, which became known as Mali, and absorbed ancient Ghana, including new territories stretching north into the Sahara, then eastward beyond the bend of the Niger, and westward to the Atlantic coast. The Mali Empire flourished between circa 1235–1430s CE. Subsequently, it was subsumed by the Songhai Empire, which had begun as the bustling city of Gao as early as 800 CE. The Songhai Empire peaked between 1460–1528 CE and took over a large part of what had been the Mali Empire and other territories farther west.

The narrative represents a fragment of an ancient tradition of storytelling that incorporates themes, ideas, and cultural values from the viewpoint of the Mandinka people who lived in ancient Mali. By highlighting their day-to-day lives and perspective—what's fair or unjust, good or wicked, absurd or reasonable, admired or contemptible, hospitable or mean—the narrative invites readers to think about their own standards of behavior or truths, strength, and weaknesses, and how they might be shared widely by a larger group or community. What other stories or songs come to mind that artfully evoke a wide range of community values?

Oral tradition narratives in ancient African cultures often contain rhetorical strategies that enable the audience to remember the story and pass it on. In this case, a song is embedded in the narrative for easy memorization, and it becomes the vehicle that transports the story far beyond the territory from which it originates. The song gains a broader function outside the tale when it's sung and popularized not only by the bard, who in this case would be the **griot** (the official storyteller, historian, and traveling musician), but also any ordinary person who enacts it like a work song, similar to the pounding songs also found in this Reader (See page 54). Herein lies the art of **orature** and storytelling—what's orally passed on comes to life through enactment in a living community and social setting. How might music or any other art impact social change when it is heard and performed by others in a larger community?

In addition to the literary stylistic conventions, it would be helpful to consider both the moral and entertainment qualities of the narrative, which involve the law of cause and effect. An inquiring reader might ask: How is the tale informing us about our own condition, if not literally, then metaphorically? Have we faced the escalation of an issue that with a little foresight could have been avoided by a simple gesture?

Readers can also reflect on the beliefs or assumptions that have caused them to

64. The "Song of Gimmile" was first recorded in German by an ethnologist and archaeologist, Leo Frobenius (1873–1938), and published in "Atlantis; Volksmärchen und Volksdichtungen Afrikas," in 1921–28. The English version appeared in the anthology, *The King's Drum and Other African Stories*, edited and translated by Harold Courlander.

complain about or ridicule an injustice, or they can question why they exercised a particular judgment or took a particular course of action. What are some of the actions taken or words spoken that you wished you could take back when you realized their consequences? What narratives about power are held in American culture that match some of the views expressed in this story?

Mildred Barya
Department of English

PRE-READING PARS

1. What do you think the role of an artist (musician, writer, or storyteller) is? Brainstorm three to five ideas.
2. Make a list of three to five characteristics that you think a person who is in a position of authority or leadership over you must have. Why are those qualities important to you and others?
3. Identify two or three avenues you use to find news of what's happening around you or critical events shaping your world.

Song of Gimmile

The Song of Gimmile

[A Gindo song from Mali]

Once there was Konondjong, a great king of the Gindo people. One day a singer from Korro came to Bankassi, where Konondjong lived. He went to the king's house and sang for him. He played on his lute and sang about famous warriors and their deeds, about things that had happened in the world, and about the accomplishments of the chiefs of former times. King Konondjong was entertained by what he heard. When the singing finished, Konondjong asked the singer what he wanted in Bankassi. The bard replied, "Oh, sir, all I want is a small gift from you."

The king said in surprise, "You ask the king of the Gindo people for a gift?"

"Only a small gift, a token in exchange for my singing," the bard answered.

"Ah!" Konondjong said with exasperation. "Here is a homeless bard who presumes to ask the king of the Gindo for a present! Many famous bards come and sing for the honor of being heard, but this man asks for something in return! Whoever gave me such disrespect before? Take him away and give him fifty lashes."

So King Konondjong's servants took the bard and beat him with a knotted rope for punishment. The singer then made his way home to Korro.

In Korro there lived a man by the name of Gimmile. Gimmile heard the story of what happened to the bard who sang for King Konondjong. So he composed a song of contempt about the king. It went:

"Konondjong, king of the Gindo,
He is fat, his neck is flabby.
Konondjong, king of the Gindo,
His teeth are few, his legs are swelled.
Konondjong, king of the Gindo,
His knees are bony, his head is bald.
Konondjong, king of the Gindo."

This was the song made by Gimmile. He went out where the people were, taking his harp with him, and he sang his song. Gimmile's voice was good. The music of his song was catching. Soon other people of Korro were singing this song. It became popular among the people and the bards. Travellers who came to Korro took the song away and sang it elsewhere. It was heard at dances and festivals. Among the Gindo people it was known everywhere.

"Konondjong, king of the Gindo,
He is fat, his neck is flabby.
Konondjong, king of the Gindo,
His teeth are few, his legs are swelled.
Konondjong, king of the Gindo,
His knees are bony, his head is bald.
Konondjong, king of the Gindo."

Women sang it while grinding corn. Girls sang it while carrying water. Men sang it while working in the fields.

King Konondjong heard the people singing it. He was angered. He asked, "Who has made this song?"

And the people replied, "It was made by a singer in Korro."

Konondjong sent messengers to Korro to the bard whom he had mistreated. The bard came to Bankassi, and the king asked him, "Who is the maker of this song?"

The bard replied, "It was made by Gimmile of Korro."

The king gave the bard a present of one hundred thousand cowry shells, a horse, a cow, and an ox. He said, "See to it that Gimmile's song is sung no more."

The bard said: "Oh, sir, I was whipped with a knotted rope when I sang for you. Even though you are a king, you cannot retract it. A thing that is done cannot be undone. A song that is not composed does not exist; but once it is made, it is a real thing. Who can stop a song that travels from country to country? All of the Gindo people sing it. I am not the king. If the great king of the Gindo cannot prevent the song of Gimmile from being sung, my power over the people is certainly less."

The song of Gimmile was sung among the people, and it is preserved to this day, for King Konondjong could not bring it to an end.

The king was not compelled to beat the bard, but he did, and then it could not be undone.

Gimmile did not have to make a song about the king, but he did, and it could not be stopped.

Courlander, Harold. "Song of Gimmile." In *The King's Drum and Other African Stories*, 9, 11–12. San Diego, CA: Harcourt Brace Jovanovich, 1962.

POST-READING PARS

1. Compare and contrast your understanding of the role of artists with the role played by Gimmile and the bard from Korro.
2. Reflect on your qualities of a leader and compare and contrast them with those demonstrated by Konondjong.

Inquiry Corner

Content Question(s):

What assumptions does the king make about the bard from Korro? Why is he unable to suppress the song?

Was Gimmile justified in making a mocking song about a stingy king who refused to show generosity to the bard?

Critical Question(s):

What's the difference between narrative truth and narrative persuasion? When is it important to do one and not the other?

Comparative Question(s):

In what ways do other sources we have read incorporate a critique of those in power?

Connection Question(s):

Why does banned music or literature become more popular?

Think of a current hot debate/topic in the media or political environment that you care about and provide different perspectives about it.

BEYOND THE CLASSROOM

» The idiom "a thing that is done cannot be undone" has many analogs: "Once the die is cast" or "it is what it is" reflect a similar attitude. When making decisions, for example as an employee with leadership responsibilities, what is the value of deliberation and planning? What is the value of staying the course even when it appears things are not going according to initial plans?

"Speech of the Queen" by Hatshepsut

Introduction

The Eighteenth dynasty Egyptian pharaoh Hatshepsut, or as some writers have referred to her, the "King herself," is one of the best-known female ancient rulers. The dynasty established by Hatshepsut's family is credited with restoring order after a century of foreign rulers in Egypt. Through construction of monuments, temples, obelisks, and **pylons** (monumental gateways decorated with scenes of the pharaoh in action), the Eighteenth dynasty rulers showcased this return of order. They also created the perception of a new golden age, building on the stable, powerful Egypt of the past through architecture, particularly the pyramids built during the Fourth dynasty and funerary temples of the Twelfth dynasty. In what ways do you think public monuments create a sense of national identity or order?

In ancient Egypt, order is often expressed through **binaries**, pairs that are opposed or complementary. Binaries could be found in the land itself, which was divided into lower (North) and upper (South) Egypt, and in the fertile Nile region and infertile desert areas. Dominant among the pairings were natural binaries (day/night, life/death), seasonal ones (flooding/nonflooding), as well as social binaries such as that between the royal family and ordinary Egyptians. How might preserving these dualities ensure Egypt's continuity? Not all binaries were seen as absolute or rigid; some, like life and death, were permeable and fluid. In fact, the entire royal family

SNAPSHOT BOX

LANGUAGE: Egyptian hieroglyphs

DATE: c. 1479–1458 BCE

LOCATION: Temple of Amun in Karnak, Egypt

CONTEXTUAL INFORMATION: Dedication, inscription

TAGS: Authority and Leadership; Monument and Artifact; Rhetoric and Propaganda; Women and Gender

Timeline

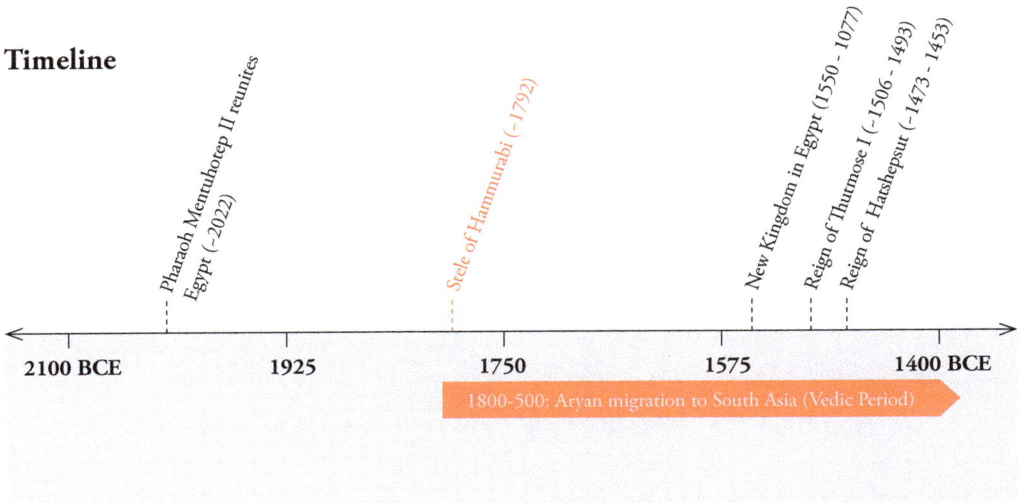

operated in a space between human and divine through the pharaoh. For example, he inhabited a human body but was considered the offspring of the gods and was expected to join the gods in the afterlife and thus continue to serve Egypt.

Gender and authority were similarly not dualistic but often rather deftly negotiated within the royal family. For example, the founder of the Eighteenth dynasty, Ahmose, first bestowed on his wife/sister Ahmose Nefertari the title of ***god's wife of Amun***. In this role she served as priest of one of the main gods, Amun, and she was deified and worshipped after her death.[65] Unlike the usual queenly titles such as ***king's wife***, ***king's principal wife***, or ***king's mother***, the title of ***god's wife*** allowed the individual to be acknowledged on her own divine terms, rather than through her relationship with the pharaoh. It is probably no surprise that Hatshepsut preferred to use "god's wife" as her original title, before claiming the full royal and divine title of pharaoh. Since divine kingship was built into the very fabric of the ancient Egyptian worldview—requiring the close connection between the royal family and the Egyptian pantheon—Hatshepsut's position as female king was possible.

Hatshepsut also established her authority over Egypt through claiming Amun-Re, a sun god, as her father. While the number of Egyptian gods grew as each new dynasty added their favored local deity, the pantheon had always included a solar deity and gods with attributes of the sun. Amun-Re was worshipped at Thebes, combining the local deity Amun with the solar deity Re, as the primary god of the Eighteenth dynasty. Already in the Old Kingdom Fourth dynasty, pharaohs had begun to be called "Sons of Re." In Hatshepsut's mortuary temple at Deir el-Bahri, which is a three-tiered structure, surrounded on each level by a **colonnade** (a row of columns that creates a porch space), the innermost shrine is dedicated to Amun-Re, while a relief in the mid-level colonnade depicted Hatshepsut as the daughter of Amun-Re, thus laying definitive claim to the divine lineage of Egypt's kings. What type of worldview allows for the addition of new gods?

Hatshepsut's role was unprecedented in Egypt and utilized aspects from female and male binaries to create authority. Traditional authority in Egypt and its iconography was male and so Hatshepsut is sometimes portrayed in male guise and appropriated male prerogatives, such as the creation of obelisks, including the one at the Temple of Amun at Karnak on which this queen's speech is inscribed. However, some sculptures showing her in female garments and royal attributes do survive, and in some instances the written record also employed feminine pronouns and forms of words, making it clear that it was not anathema to represent her as a woman. What could these representations mean about the gendered nature of power in Egypt and about Hatshepsut's identity?

Eva Hericks-Bares
Department of Art and Art History

65. See Gay Robbins, *Women in Ancient Egypt* (Cambridge, MA: Harvard University Press, 1993), 43–44.

PRE-READING PARS

1. Consider a structuring mechanism in your own life (daily schedule, rituals, or guiding principles). How does this structure help you navigate your daily life?
2. Think of a public monument you have visited. What do you remember being written on it?

"Speech of the Queen"

I have done this with a loving heart for my father Amun;
Initiated in his secret of the beginning,
Acquainted with his beneficent might,
I did not forget whatever he had ordained.
My majesty knows his divinity,
I acted under his command;
It was he who led me,
I did not plan a work without his doing.
It was he who gave directions,
I did not sleep because of his temple,
I did not stray from what he commanded.
My heart was Sia[66] before my father,
I entered into the plans of his heart.
I did not turn my back to the city of the All-Lord,
Rather did I turn my face to it.
I know that Ipet-sut is the lightland on earth,
The august hill of the beginning,
The Sacred Eye of the All-Lord,
His favoured place that bears his beauty,
That gathers in his followers.
It is the King himself who says:
I declare before the folk who shall be in the future,
Who shall deserve the monument I made for my father,
Who shall speak in discussion,
Who shall look to posterity—
It was when I sat in the palace,
And thought of my maker,
That my heart led me to make for him
Two obelisks of electrum,

66. The personification of the concept of understanding.

Whose summits would reach the heavens,
In the august hall of columns,
Between the two great portals of the King,
The Strong Bull, King Aakheperkare, the Horus triumphant.[67]
Now my heart turns to and fro,
In thinking what will the people say,
They who shall see my monument in after years,
And shall speak of what I have done.
Beware of saying, "I know not, I know not:
Why has this been done?
To fashion a mountain of gold throughout,
Like something that just happened."
I swear, as I am loved of Re,
As Amun, my father, favours me,
As my nostrils are refreshed with life and dominion,
As I wear the white crown,
As I appear with the red crown,
As the Two Lords have joined their portions for me,
As I rule this land like the son of Isis,
As I am mighty like the son of Nut,
As Re rests in the evening bark,
As he prevails in the morning bark,
As he joins his two mothers in the god's ship,
As sky endures, as his creation lasts,
As I shall be eternal like an undying star,
As I shall rest in life like Autumn—
So as regards these two great obelisks,
Wrought with electrum by my majesty for my father Amun,
In order that my name may endure in this temple,
For eternity and everlastingness,
They are each of one block of hard granite,
Without seam, with joining together!

My majesty began work on them in year 15, second month of winter, day 1, ending in year 16, fourth month of summer, last day totalling seven months of quarry work. I did it for him out of affection, as a king for a god. It was my wish to make them for him gilded with electrum. "Their foil lies on their body," is what I expect people to say. My mouth is effective in its speech; I do not go back on my word. Hear ye! I gave for them of the finest electrum. I measured it by the gallon like sacks of grain.

67. Thutmose I had built the two pylons now numbered IV and V, and a hypostyle hall between them. Hatshepsut removed its wooden ceiling, thus turning the hall into a colonnaded court, and erected her two obelisks in it.

My majesty summoned a quantity beyond what the Two Lands had yet seen. The ignorant and the wise know it.

Nor shall he who hears it say,
"It is a boast," what I have said;
Rather say, "How like her it is,
She is devoted to her father!"
Lo, the god knows me well,
Amun Lord of Thrones-of-the-Two-Lands;
He made me rule Black Land and Red Land as reward,
No one rebels against me in all lands.
All foreign lands are my subjects,
He placed my border at the limits of heaven,
What Aten encircles labours for me.
He gave it to him who came from him,
Knowing I would rule it for him.
I am his daughter in very truth,
Who serves him, who knows what he ordains.
My reward from my father is life-stability-rule,
On the Horus throne of all the living, eternally like Re.

Hatshepsut. "Speech of the Queen." In *Ancient Egyptian Literature*, edited by Miriam Lichtheim, 337–39. Oakland: University of California Press, 1973–1980.

POST-READING PARS

1. In what ways do you see aspects of "order" and continuity showing up in the format or content of the speech?
2. What did you notice about the use of pronouns and "I" statements in terms of gender and authority?

Inquiry Corner

Content Question(s):	**Critical Question(s):**
How does the inscription lay out the divinely ordained role of the pharaoh? Who is the implied audience—and why does that matter?	Critically evaluate the strategies Hatshepsut uses to create authority through gender fluidity.
Comparative Question(s):	**Connection Question(s):**
How does the "Speech of Hatshepsut" relate to writings or carved inscriptions we have from other rulers, like the Code of Hammurabi? Consider the use of celestial bodies and description of natural phenomena in this passage in comparison with creation myths from other cultures.	Commemoration is an important aspect of Egyptian life (as is evident in their elaborate funerary practices). What kind of measures do we take to ensure our own "immortality"?

BEYOND THE CLASSROOM

» In describing the obelisks, Hatshepsut tells how long they took to build, how seamlessly the stones were connected, how ornately they were decorated, and so on. How would someone involved in part of this project describe their accomplishment so that the reader knows what they did, how they did it, and what results they got?

Eastern Band of Cherokee Origin Stories

Introduction

The two stories you will read, "The Origin of Legends" and "The Origin of Strawberries," are told by three Cherokee storytellers, Kathi Smith Littlejohn, Davy Arch, and Freeman Owle. All three are members of the **Eastern Band of Cherokee Indians**, a federally recognized tribe whose homeland encompasses southern Appalachia, and grew up on the **Qualla Boundary**, home of the Eastern Band, surrounding the town of Cherokee, North Carolina. They learned to tell stories from the elders of the tribe, which included their parents and grandparents, though their own personal storytelling styles differ. These storytellers draw on **oral tradition** (the knowledge of a group of people passed on by word of mouth) but their sources may include written material, like American anthropologist James Mooney's *Myths and Legends of the Cherokees*,[68] stories collected on the Qualla Boundary in the 1880s, including a version of the story you will read below by Dagwadihi, Catawba Killer (Dah-gwah-DEE-hee). In addition to their tribal education, Kathi Littlejohn and Freeman Owle have degrees in education, and Davy Arch is a master artist who practices Cherokee crafts, such as masks, carving, pottery, and textiles.

"The Origin of Strawberries" is a popular narrative **folktale** told here by three different storytellers and imparts an important cultural value. A folktale is a story passed through generations by oral transmission, and there is no single authoritative version of the story. Cherokee people often refer to their myths, legends, folktales, and oral histories as **legends**. What differences and similarities do you see among the storytellers' versions?

All of the stories have been transcribed in the exact words of the storytellers, and most were recorded at storytelling events with a live audience. When they tell stories, these storytellers' speech becomes rhythmic in subtle ways and begins to sound like poetry. To represent this on the page, stories are written in lines like poetry. This transcription technique is called **ethnopoetics** and was developed to more accurately represent the words and creativity of American Indigenous storytellers. Whenever the storyteller pauses, a new line is begun. If you read their stories aloud, pausing slightly at the end of each line, you will hear a little of the rhythm they use to tell the stories.

68. James Mooney, *Myths, Legends, and Sacred Formulas of the Cherokees* (Washington, DC: Government Printing Office, 1900). Reprinted in many versions.

SNAPSHOT BOX

LANGUAGE: Cherokee, told in English

DATE: Oral tradition

LOCATION: Southern Appalachia, Cherokee homeland

CONTEXTUAL INFORMATION: Cherokees have lived in southern Appalachia since 12,000 BCE. During that time, they developed agriculture, textiles, and pottery; built mounds in towns along the rivers; and participated in trade networks spanning thousands of miles. The United States removed most of them in 1838 on the Trail of Tears, but a small group, the Eastern Band of Cherokee Indians, remained and live here today.

TAGS: Community/Communal Identity; Conflict and War; Deities and Spirits; Education; Ethics and Morality; Family; Indigeneity; Journey; Love; Nature; Oral Histories and Storytelling; Origin Stories; Wisdom

Timeline[69]

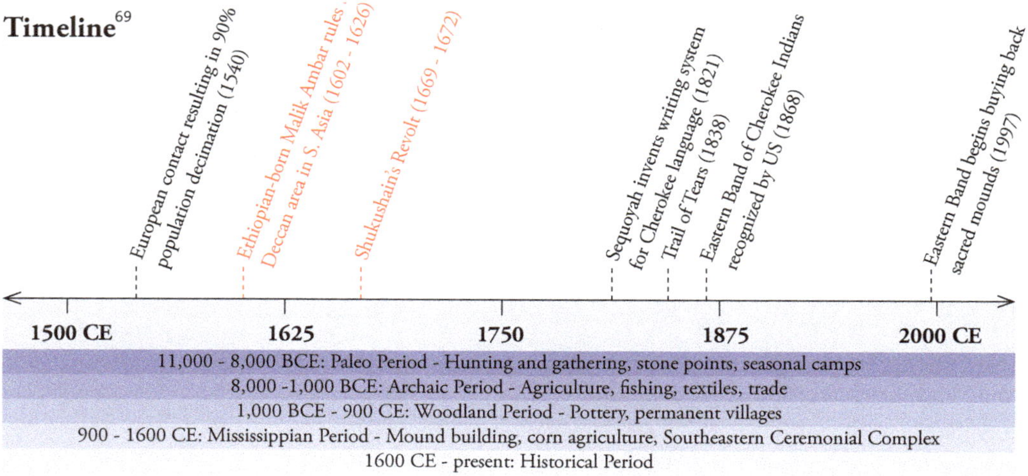

Storytellers in the oral tradition use repetition—especially **motifs** and **formulaic numbers**—to help them remember long stories and to engage their audience. Motifs are details that repeatedly appear in the oral tradition of a particular culture. What devices help you remember stories or songs? In American Indigenous folktales, different motifs appear, such as an animal who helps the people by providing information. Similarly, a motif in a European folktale might be a magic animal that supplies treasure, like the goose who laid the golden egg. Different cultures also have formulaic numbers that embody their worldviews. In permeating the oral traditions, they also shape the most foundational aspects of cultural knowledge. For example, in American Indigenous cultures the numbers 4 and 7 are most important for many communities and reflect the four cardinal directions as part of the overall orienting framework of seven directions: east, north, west, south, above, below, and in the center. In these Cherokee folktales, you will see that the storytellers may repeat phrases in fours, or give four details. In comparison, in many European folktales, the number three is important: three brothers go on a quest; three wishes are granted, and so on.

In the "Origin of Strawberries," the main figures are often considered to be the first man and woman from within the Cherokee worldview; some storytellers, such as the version by Dagwadihi, Catawba Killer in Mooney's collection of stories from 1880s, name them Kanati and Selu, and note that this first couple lived at Shining Rock (above off the Blue Ridge Parkway in present-day Haywood County). This first

69. The bottom timeline provides the generally accepted phases for material culture and social organization for Indigenous communities in North America, although not all groups followed this trajectory, including some groups within the Piedmont and coastal areas of present-day North Carolina who did not participate in the activities connected to the Mississippian Period within the southeast region.

couple are part of a mythic cycle that explains the origin of corn and game, in addition to strawberries (and other fruits such as huckleberries, blackberries, and service berries in Dagwadihi's version) and chronicles the quests of their two sons. How might the fact that this story has different versions reflect the core story's importance in capturing a primary Cherokee cultural value?

Barbara R. Duncan
Department of Languages and Literatures

PRE-READING PARS

1. What is the role of oral tradition in your culture? Think about not just myths, folktales, and legends, but stories and other knowledge that you have learned mainly from other people telling you or showing you.
2. What is the place of anger in your culture or religion? Is it acceptable or not?

Eastern Band of Cherokee Origin Stories

"The Origin of Legends" as told by Kathi Smith Littlejohn

Today, I'm going to tell you some Cherokee legends.
We were just talking a little bit about what people did a long time ago.
They didn't have books did they? They didn't go to school,
so they needed legends to teach people
about different animals
with stories
and how things came to be
and about the rules that everybody was supposed to go by
so they would treat each other with a lot of respect
and take care of one another.
That's why we have legends.
>>
Why do you think I'm here today?
To tell us legends.
What are legends?
Very good, a tale that was long ago that was true.
But does anybody know how the legends came to be?
How did we get legends?
From your grandfather, very good.
And I'm gonna tell you the first legend
about how we got legends,
because at one time there were no grandfathers.
In fact, it was such a long time ago,
they were young themselves.
A long long long time ago,
there was a group of people
that lived by themselves in the world
with all of the animals.
And they could all talk to one another,
they could talk to the animals,

and they had the same language,
and everybody got along.
And then one day,
as people will do,
they started to fight.
One thing led to another,
and this person wasn't talking to this person.
Another thing happened,
and this person pushed this person.
Somebody wasn't very nice to somebody,
and somebody stole something from somebody,
and they were really really angry at one another.
So angry that they hit each other,
and they were going to kill one other.
The Creator didn't like this at all.
And so
he sent them
—divided them up into groups of four—
and sent
one group to the north,
one to the south,
one to the east
and one to the west.
All around to the corners of the world.
And once they got there,
they were very confused,
because they didn't know how to live
in this part of the world.
They weren't familiar with these things.
They didn't know where the water was.
They didn't know what kind of plants these were.
They didn't know how to get ready for the winter
because they didn't know what the winter was gonna be like.
So the Creator felt very sorry for them,
and he wanted to help them,
but he wanted them to learn their lesson.
So he sent them a gift.
He sent them dreams
that told them about each of the animals,
what to eat,
what to do,
what kind of plants they could use for medicine,

and what kind of plants, if they ate them, would make them sick,
how to catch that kind of fish,
how to look at these different kind of animals and use them.
So they began to learn,
and they began to grow,
and they began to live in their new home,
and they got along with each other this time.
Then he sent them another gift
so they would never forget these things.
He sent them legends,
about all of these animals
and all of these plants.
So that each time they told the legend,
they would remember these animals
and take better care of them
and take better care of each other.
And that's how the legends came into the world.
Okay? Now you know? Okay, let's tell another legend.

First Man and First Woman (Origin of Strawberries), as told by Kathi Smith Littlejohn.

Now,
how many of you have ever had a fight
with your brother or sister,
your best friend or teacher?
Oh no, no, now you better not tell me you had a fight with your teacher.
Oh my goodness.
Did—
before you know it—
you were yelling ugly mean things
that you really didn't mean to say,
mainly about what they looked like and smelled like,
they were kind of stupid,
and you hated them,
and you really didn't,
but when we get angry
we say these things without thinking first, don't we.
Well, a long time ago,
that's exactly what happened between first man and first woman.
And they were so much in love,

and they loved one another,
and they loved their animal friends.

What happened that day
nobody can even remember,
but all of a sudden first woman said,
"You are the slowest man on the face of the earth.
I asked you two days ago to help me with this,
and now look what happened."
"Well, you call me slow, you're as slow as an old turtle."
"I asked you if you'd do this."
"And not only that, but you're fat."
"Fat, well you're ugly."
Oh, the ugly things they said about one another,
and oh, he got so mad,
and they were yelling and screaming.

First woman burst into tears,
and she ran out the door.

He ran after her,
and he hollered,
"You go on and don't you ever come back."
Oh, and he was still so angry,
and he stomped around,
and he thought,
"She called me fat! Fat? How dare she?
She ought to look at herself before she—
Oh, don't you ever come back and tell me that."

Then it got later and later,
and he got a little more worried about her.

So he went to the edge of the clearing and kinda called her name,
and no answer.

And he thought,
"That's all right.
You stay out there all night.
See if I care."

And he walked back in and slammed the door,
and it got real late, and real dark.

There were no lights then,
and he was really worried, and he thought,

"Gosh, what if something really has happened to her?
Oh no, oh I can't wait to see her and tell her I'm sorry.
I told her she was ugly. She's not ugly.
Oh, I'm so sorry."

And at first light, the next day,
he started out to try to find where she was,
and he began to see little signs,
and he found a broken leaf or a broken branch,
and he could see the bent grass where she ran.

So pretty soon,
he started noticing that there was a little flower,
just about the space of a woman's foot if she was running,
and it was in a straight line.

He'd never seen these flowers before,
and he followed the little white flowers
that led him straight to where she was.

She had lain down and gone to sleep.

She stayed right there so he could find her.

He woke her up and said,
"Oh, my baby, I'm so sorry."

And she went,
"Oh, smooch smooch honey darlin.'"

Oh, mushy mushy.

And they promised they wouldn't fight any more,
they put their arms around each other,
and started walking back home, lovey-dovey.

And as they stepped over each of the white flowers,
they bloomed out into a strawberry.

And the strawberries are supposed to remind us now
not to ever fight with the people that we care about.

They're just a reminder
about the first man and first woman's fight,
and how we got strawberries in the world.
That's how the Cherokee people got the first strawberries.
And the legend goes on to tell us
that we should keep them in our home at all times:

maybe a picture,
maybe jelly,
it may be strawberry jam.
To remind us not to argue
as first man and first woman did.

The Origins of Strawberries, as told by Freeman Owle

One of the ones that I like to tell to people here—
and through my storytelling
I've tried to sort of analyze what the stories really meant
when they were presented to the children back in the old times.
And I found specifically that stories
like the story of the creation of strawberries
have special meanings, and I'll try to convey that.
They say once there was a man who,
in this matrilineal society,
his wife had told him to go out and kill a deer that day.
And he went out with good intentions of bringing back a deer,
because her family was coming that evening to have dinner with them,
and the grandmother, her mother, was a very important person in that society.
So he went out that day and he was looking for a deer,
preferably the best one he could find.
And he happened to come across a fellow who had fallen into a ravine,
and his leg was broken,
and so he went down in the ravine and helped him out
and carried him back to his village,
and by the time he made it back to the village,
it was very late in the day.
So he went back to the forest real quickly and started to hunt.
And by that time all of the deer had gone in and he couldn't find one.
So he came back to his village where his wife was living.
And she saw him coming on the hillside.
And he didn't have a deer.
So she got very angry,
and she began to throw things,
and she ran away out of the village and left
and went back toward her own village, her mother's village.

And he came back
and was praying to the Great Spirit
and was telling him that he would like for the Great Spirit to slow her down,
so he could tell her what happened that day
and the reason for him not bringing the deer back.
She was moving very quickly, and the Great Spirit said that he would.
So he began to put beautiful flowers in her path.
And this didn't slow her down at all,
she just kept right on running
as fast as she could go.
And so he began to put fruit trees in her path,
and she would go around them
and was not even interested in the fruit.
So the Great Spirit said that he would have to put something in the path
that smelled delicious,
that looked beautiful to the eye,
and tasted very, very good.
So he put this little plant right down near her feet,
because she was angry and looking down.
And she saw these beautiful little white flowers,
and then began to see a red fruit on the ground.
Then eventually she smelled it, and it was wonderful.
And then she began to pick some of them and taste them,
and they were so good that she sat down in the middle of the patch.
And the young man caught up with her
while she was eating the strawberries,
and he apologized to her
and told her what had happened.
So she realized that she had left in anger
and went on back to the village.
I think this is a teaching to the children
that we shouldn't in the heat of anger
jump up and run away
and make real drastic decisions or actions at that point.
And so each and every story had a real reason for it.
The Cherokees did not have schools,
so they had to tell stories to teach their children.

The Origin of Strawberries, as told by Davey Arch.

One of my favorite stories,
    that Mary Chiltoskey used to tell,
    is the story of the origin of the strawberries.
And she said that first man and woman were living together,
    and they got mad at one another, and the man left.
No, the woman left, that's the way it was.
And went to live somewhere else.
The man began to miss her, so he prayed.
And God told him about the strawberries,
    and told him he would line the trail along to where the woman
        was staying,
    and she would begin to eat the strawberries,
    follow the trail of strawberries back to where he was at.
And they were reunited.
They say that's why. the strawberries bloom so early in the spring,
    they're the first berry,
    they come out,
    they were the first berry that man presented to woman,
    to gain her affection, or regain her affection.
And all the old people
    keep some strawberry preserves around
    to remind them
    and to keep peace in the house.

Duncan, Barbara. *Living Stories of the Cherokee*, 32–34, 55–58, 100–101, 226–28. Chapel Hill: University of North Carolina Press, 1998.

POST-READING PARS

1. Compare the role of oral tradition in your culture with Cherokee culture.
2. Compare the place of anger in your culture with Cherokee traditional teachings as revealed in these folktales.

Inquiry Corner

Content Question(s):	**Critical Question(s):**
What is the purpose of legends in Cherokee culture? What was the origin of strawberries? How do the storytellers use formulaic numbers?	Compare and contrast the three versions of "The Origin of Strawberries." Why do you think the storytellers told it differently? What details did they include or omit? Is it still the same story?
Comparative Question(s):	**Connection Question(s):**
Compare and contrast the role of nature in these Cherokee stories with other sources that include nature prominently (e.g., Shakuntala, Bacchae, *Pop Wuj*, *Epic of Gilgamesh*, Genesis, Purusa, etc.).	What insights about conflict resolution displayed in the Cherokee version of "Origin of Legends" and "The Origin of Strawberries" are relevant to our contemporary contexts?

BEYOND THE CLASSROOM

» Remember the story of the man on a hunt for a deer. What is an example of a time you were given a task but outside forces prevented its completion. What happened? Who was affected? What were the results of not completing the task? How did you recover?

Eastern Band of Cherokee Nature Stories, as told by Freeman Owle

Introduction

The Cherokee traditional stories involving nature you are about to read are told by Freeman Owle, a member of the **Eastern Band of Cherokee Indians**, a federally recognized tribe whose homeland encompasses the cultural region of southern Appalachia. Owle grew up in the Birdtown community on the **Qualla Boundary**, located around the town of Cherokee, North Carolina. Owle has a master's degree in education and is a master artist in stone carving. The sources of his stories include his parents, grandparents, Cherokee oral traditions, and written sources. Anthropologists and folklorists note that oral traditions reflect the culture of a people: their values, their expectations for how people are supposed to behave, and encoded scientific information. This information is also described as **traditional ecological knowledge** or TEK, and includes information about the place where they live, including geography, plants, animals, astronomy, symbolic and poetic explanations for the mysteries of life, death, and creation. Owle is primarily an educator of Cherokee history and culture, who uses stories to educate both Cherokee people and the public about language, beliefs, and traditions that are shared by the Eastern Band of Cherokee people. His stories highlight values such as spirituality, group harmony, strong individual character, sense of place, honoring the past, educating the children, and humor—values cherished by Cherokee peoples.

These six stories, originally told by Owle to an audience of adults, show aspects of the relationship between Cherokee people and the natural world and also convey Cherokee values and lessons. Before contact with Europeans, Cherokees lived on more than 140,000 square miles encompassing southern Appalachia. Among the various ways that Cherokee peoples related to nature included hunting mastodons with stone points; developing agriculture, using plant fibers to create sophisticated textiles; managing woodlands with prescribed burns; semi-domesticating white-tailed deer and turkey; building mounds along rivers; watching the stars; and practicing intensive gardening and crop rotation. In contrast, when Europeans arrived in the Southeast in 1540, they described a wilderness in need of being subdued or tamed. This "wilderness," however, had been carefully managed for generations through an inter-relational interdependency between the Cherokee peoples and nature. This symbiotic balance was broken only by the arrival of

SNAPSHOT BOX

LANGUAGE: Cherokee, told in English

DATE: Oral tradition

LOCATION: Southern Appalachia, Cherokee homeland

CONTEXTUAL INFORMATION: Cherokees have lived in southern Appalachia since 12,000 BCE. During this time, they developed agriculture, textiles, and pottery, built mounds in towns along the rivers and participated in trade networks spanning thousands of miles. The United States removed most of them in 1838 on the Trail of Tears, but a small group, the Eastern Band of Cherokee Indians, remained and live here today.

TAGS: Aesthetics; Cosmology; Death; Deities and Spirits; Education; Emotion; Ethics and Morality; Family; Freedom and Harmony; Indigeneity; Journey; Music; Nature; Oral Histories and Storytelling Philosophy; Religion; Ways of Knowing; Women and Gender

Timeline[70]

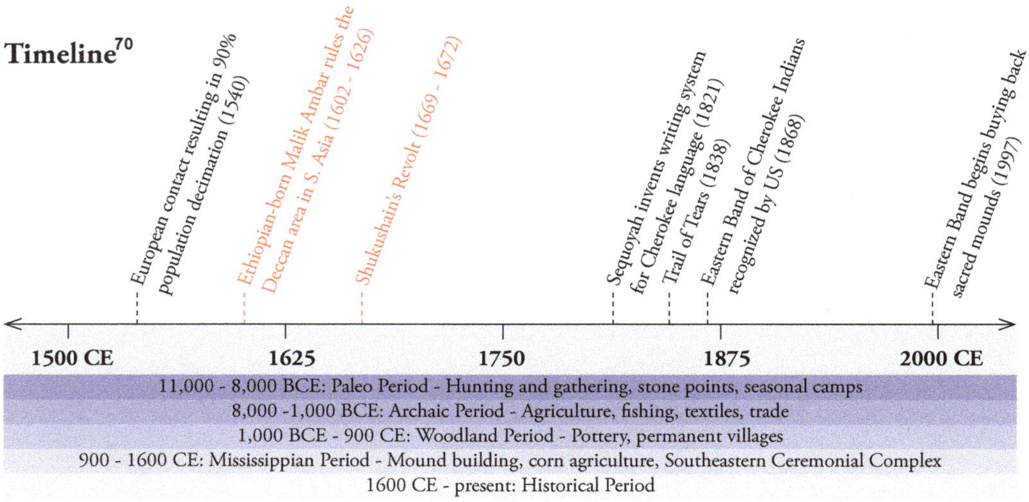

European diseases, which killed at least 90 percent of American Indigenous people between 1500–1650, as well as invasive species that destroyed parts of the ecosystem. Europeans missed the evidence of careful land stewardship because, unlike their model of dominance over nature, the Cherokees and other Indigenous communities do not dominate or control nature. Cherokee peoples understand human beings to be part of nature, but with a special responsibility to take care of the plants and animals and each other.

Traditional environmental knowledge is encoded in traditional beliefs and stories. For example, the story of "Going to Water" features the Long Man, Yvwi Gunahita (Yunh-WEE Goo-nah-HEE-tah). The river is his body, with his head in the mountains and his feet in the sea. The Long Man has the power to cleanse people both physically and spiritually and because of this, his body is sacred. People are forbidden from throwing waste, including bodily waste, in the river. Early European explorers and missionaries labeled these beliefs as superstitions while putting their waste into their drinking water, causing many deaths from typhoid and dysentery. As you read the other stories, what kinds and dimensions of relationalities between humans and nature do you see described?

After a long history of struggle to reclaim their land-based ways of life after forced displacement, special laws, as only a partial form of reparations, have been enacted to protect the rights of American Indigenous peoples to practice their tra-

70. The bottom timeline provides the generally accepted phases for material culture and social organization for Indigenous communities in North America, although not all groups followed this trajectory, including some groups within the Piedmont and coastal areas of present-day North Carolina who did not participate in the activities connected to the Mississippian period within the southeast region.

ditional forms of religion. The Native American Indian Religious Freedom Act (1979) and the UN Declaration of the Rights of Indigenous Peoples (2007) both affirm the need for Indigenous peoples to have access to their sacred sites for ceremonies and to be allowed to possess certain items that might otherwise be protected, such as eagle feathers. How might these stories provide insight into these ongoing struggles for access to land and practices related to nature?

Barbara R. Duncan
Department of Languages and Literatures

PRE-READING PARS

1. What attitudes toward nature did you learn from your culture, religion, or stories in your family?
2. In the last twenty-four hours, what are some concrete ways you interacted with nature?

Eastern Band of Cherokee Nature Stories

"The Daughter of the Sun"

The daughter of the Sun was another legend the Cherokees told.
And this one is not told as much,
    but it has a lot of very interesting meanings and values to teach,
    and it's unusual that the Sun would be a woman.
The Sun and her daughter the Moon are crossing the sky.
And one day the Sun looked down and noticed
    that all the people were looking at her rather squinch-eyed
    and with ugly faces every time they looked at her
    because of her great brightness.
So the Sun got very angry
    and said that she didn't like for people to look at her like that.
    And the Cherokees were making fun of her
    by making faces at her.
And she got very angry,
    and she began to increase her heat
    coming down upon the earth.
And the people were so hot their crops began to dry up,
    and they began to pray to the Great Spirit
    to get the Sun to stop making it so hot.
And it continued on.
So they began to turn to their medicine people,
    and they went to this old medicine man, and he said,
    "Well, we can talk to the Sun,
    and we can sing to her,
    and see if we can get her to calm down
    and lessen her heat."
So they began to sing to the Sun.
But of course when they looked at her
    their faces were still all squinched and drawn.

And she was not very happy,
        and she didn't like the music,
        so she made it even hotter.

And the streams began to dry up,
        and the trees began to die,
        and the crops they planted wouldn't even come up,
        so the Cherokees had real problems.
And they decided, through their medicine people,
        that they would kill the Sun.
And so the medicine man changed a person into a rattlesnake,
        and he was supposed to go up into the heavens
        and find his way to where the Sun crossed the sky,
        and when she went in to visit her daughter the Moon,
        the next morning when the Sun came out,
        the rattlesnake was to bite her and kill her.

So sure enough,
        he made his way into the heavens
        and found the house of the Moon,
        and he sat out by the doorway
        and waited for the Sun to come out.
And she came out that morning,
        and she came out so quickly
        that he struck—
        and she was so bright,
        and he missed.
So he came back to the earth
        and told the medicine people what had happened.
So they were very upset with him
        and told him that the next day they would send a copperhead.
So the copperhead went up and he hid by the doorway,
        and the Sun came out,
        and he struck—
        and he was to try to get her before she came out—
        and he struck too soon
        and missed,
        and the Sun went on its way.

So the next day they sent both of them up
        and told them that they would have to kill the Sun,
        that they would both strike
        just before she came out,

as soon as the door was open, they would strike.
And sure enough, the door opened that morning,
and they struck,
and all of a sudden they hit something and looked,
and it fell to the ground,
and it was the daughter of the Sun.
The Moon had come up that day.
And so they were very upset.
And when the Sun saw this,
she was very, very angry,
and she began to burn
and even set fires on the earth with her great heat.
The people were digging into the earth trying to save themselves.
And the rattlesnake came back, and the copperhead,
and they changed themselves back into people,
and they told the people what had happened.
So the medicine man said the only way they could make things
right
would be to go to the land of the dead.
Take seven sourwood sticks
and find the daughter of the Sun
dancing in the great circle of the dead,
and when she came around
they would touch her
seven times
with those sticks,
and she would fall down asleep,
and they would put her into a great basket
and carry her back to the land of the Cherokee.
But the medicine man said,
"Under no conditions should you open the basket
even just a little bit."

So they had gone to the land of the dead;
after many, many days' journey
and great problems finding their way there,
they finally made it.
And sure enough,
there was that great circle of death
where the people were dancing,
and they saw the daughter of the Sun.
She danced around to where they were,

and they touched her the first time,
and seven times they touched her
with those sourwood sticks,
and she didn't even know it.
On the seventh time she fell to the ground.
They picked her up and put her in the basket
and started their long journey back to the land of the Cherokee.
On the way back, the daughter of the Sun began to talk
in the basket.
Said she was getting very warm inside,
and would they please open it just a little bit.
But they wouldn't do that;
they remembered their instructions.
After a while she began to say she was getting thirsty,
and then they ignored that.
Then she said she was hungry,
and they sort of thought,
"Well, if we let her starve to death, we'll really be in trouble,"
and they were tempted to open the basket,
but they didn't.
After a while she began to say
in a very weak voice,
"I'm hungry
and I'm smothering to death.
I need air."
So one of the people in the group decided they could open it
just a little bit
to give her some air.
When they opened it
there was a red light,
a flittering coming out of the basket,
and it went off into the forest.
And they closed it back real quickly
and said,
"Well, we can't do that.
We better follow instructions."
They carried the big basket
all the way back to the village,
and when they got there,
immediately the medicine man knew they'd opened the basket.
So when he looked inside he was very angry
because there was nothing inside at all.

They began to wail in their great sadness.
They looked outside, and the Sun was scorching the earth.
All of a sudden they noticed that it began to cool off a little bit.
They looked out, and the lady Sun was smiling.
And they listened,
    and they heard this sound
    of a beautiful song
    coming from a bird in the bush.
They looked over to the bush,
    and there was
    a beautiful redbird.
And as it sang,
    the Sun smiled,
    and the heat decreased.
They then knew that the redbird
    was the daughter of the Sun.
From that day forward,
    the Sun has been good to the Cherokee people.

"Corn Spirit Woman"

Another story that gives some respect to the women in the tribe—
    and I mentioned that it is a matrilineal society.
There's a story of the Corn Woman.
And she is a spirit that is sent down from heaven every year
    to come and walk in the fields of the Cherokee.
And when she walked in the fields
    the corn began to grow,
    and it grew tall and beautiful.
And the Cherokee corn is a corn that is very, very special,
    because it is a corn that has ten rows of kernels on it.
And most other ears have thirteen,
    that we are familiar with today.
So the Cherokee corn will grow ten, almost ten feet tall,
    and on those stalks it will have three or four ears of corn,
    where most [other kinds of] stalks have one or two,
    and it's beautiful in color.
It's all the colors of the rainbow.
And many people ask, "How did you paint that?"
And the Cherokees ate it.
It's a very good corn.
Anyway, this Corn Woman would walk in the fields,

and the corn would grow beautifully.
One year they planted their corn
and had gone out to watch it come up,
and it didn't come up.
And they waited a week,
and then two weeks,
and it still hadn't come up.
So they prayed to the Great Spirit
and asked where the Corn Woman Spirit was.
And he said that he had sent her down two weeks before,
and she was missing, evidently.
And so the people began to look.
And they looked all over the earth known to them at that time,
and they couldn't find her.
So they began to ask the animal kingdom
if they would help search for her.
So all the animals were searching for this beautiful Corn Woman Spirit
when all of a sudden the raven dived down into a dark cave
and was looking for her.
And he found her in the bottom of the cave, all tied up.
She was captured and prisoner
of the evil spirit Hunger.
And he was dancing around her and laughing,
knowing very well that if she didn't get out,
that the Cherokee people would starve the coming winter.
So the raven went back and reported to the people
that he had found the Corn Woman Spirit.
And they told the raven
that only he and his family could get her free.
So they told him to go down into the cave
and perch on the ledges
and hide from the evil spirit,
and he did.
He took all of his brothers and sisters into the cave,
And they were so black they couldn't be seen by the evil spirit,
and they perched on the ledges and the rocks.
When the signal was given they all leaped down
and pecked the evil spirit
and made such terrible noises
that they frightened him out into the sunlight.
And like most evil,

when he hit the sunlight he just melted away
and disappeared.
They freed the Corn Woman Spirit with their big strong beaks,
and when she walked out into the sunlight
the corn of the Cherokees began to grow.
From that day forward, the Great Spirit in the heavens
would not let her come down in person.
And so it is today.
So when you look out at the cornfields
and see the stalks of corn
and their leaves waving in the wind,
you'll know that the Corn Woman Spirit
is walking though the fields of today.
Cherokees are unlike the Appalachian people,
they don't take the raven
and hang him up on a stick and expect the other ravens to deduce,
"Well I can't go to that field, that raven ate corn and he was killed."
That wouldn't stop them.
But the Cherokees give the raven a very special place:
that he was the one that saved the fields of the Cherokee.
So therefore they feel that if he takes a few kernels of corn, that's ok.
But if the raven is in the field, and an animal comes into the field,
the crows and the ravens will pitch such a fit
that the people will know
that someone is stealing their corn,
so they can go down and chase them away.
So I imagine it's all in the way you look at animals and the circle of life
as to whether they're necessary or need to be destroyed.
The Cherokee saw the importance of all animals and all people
and so therefore they had a very special place.
And that story, I feel, is told to teach those lessons.

"The Earth"

So the Cherokee people still believe that the earth has a lot to give.
They still believe that it's important to take care of the waters,
to preserve the air,
to preserve the forest,
to preserve the life of people themselves.

When I was a child growing up on the reservation,
it was not beyond the times of beauty.
It was a time early in the morning,
when my father would awaken me
and tell me that it was time to go to the forest.
We would get up before daylight and head to the mountaintop.
As we walked, I wondered why.
As I walked, I would sometimes place my foot upon a twig,
and it would break and snap,
and he would turn very quietly and say, "Shh."
I would place my feet more carefully,
and after a while
I noticed that I was able to place them by feeling where they were going,
without making a sound.
We walked in the darkness for a long time and finally came to a clearing,
and I noticed the beautiful stars in the sky early that morning.
And he said,
"Sit down."
I sat down upon the ground,
and I began to look at the beautiful heavens,
and after a while I began to hear noises, all around.
And he said,
"Be quiet."
There was a noise off to the left,
then a noise in the front,
and then the leaves were rattling in the trees up to the right,
but I remained still.
After a while,
the rays of sunlight began to take over the skies,
and the stars disappear.
The rays of sun revealed to me
that off on the right were squirrels jumping in the hickory nut trees,
revealed to me
that in front of me in the forest there was a deer, with its baby,
and off to the left the grouse was shuffling in the leaves with baby chicks.
And no sooner had the sun come,
than my father said,
"We're ready to go."

We got up from the clearing,
    and we walked out of the forest,
    and in my mind was a question of
    why that we had done this.
But after I returned home,
    he told me,
    "What have you learned?"
I said,
    "I've learned, Father, that if you're quiet enough,
    still enough, long enough,
    that you become part of nature."
And he said,
    "You've learned well, son."
He loved the forest.
He loved to tell the stories of the Cherokees.
And one of the ones he told me many times was the story of the
        magic lake.

"The Magic Lake"

He said
    there was a young lad walking in the forest one day.
I remember these stories because a lot of times at night,
    we were sitting in front of an old wood heater—
    all nine of my brothers and sisters and I—
    having corn.
And I don't know if you've ever done this or not,
    but you'd take a little bit of oil and put it into a frying pan,
    and you'd put it on that very hot stove and put kernels of corn
        in it.
They didn't pop but they parched.
Then after a while
    when they got done you could crunch those,
    and listen to the stories.
And this young Cherokee boy was walking in the woods,
    and he saw droplets of blood upon the leaves,
    and he began to follow those
    because he was concerned with something being hurt,
    because all the animals were important.
He followed them up the hillside
    and eventually came upon a small bear cub
    who had been wounded, and his leg was bleeding.

And up the hill he went, following it,
        and it would stumble and fall,
        and make its way to its feet again,
        and it was struggling, going in one direction,
        to the great mountain that the Cherokees call Shakonige,
        which is the Blue Mountain
        or, today, Clingman's Dome.
And it was a sacred mountain to the Cherokee
        and a very special place.
Eventually nightfall came and the bear lay down.
The young man stayed close by that night,
        and early in the next morning
        the little cub again got up
        to go up to the top of the mountain,
        and this time made it to the top.
And the fog was covering everything
        except for the very peaks of the mountains.
The little cub goes over, and it jumps into the fog.
And the young man says,
        "Surely he's gone now."
But all of a sudden
        the fog turns to water,
        and the little bear begins to swim.
He swims out a ways,
        and then he comes back,
        and when he gets out of the water,
        his leg is completely healed.
And the young man is very confused.
He looks,
        and a duck swims in the water with a broken wing,
        and his wing is made well.
And animals are coming from all directions
        and coming to the water,
        and they're swimming and being healed.
He looks up at the Great Spirit,
        and he says,
        "I don't understand."
The Great Spirit says,
        "Go back and tell your brothers and sisters the Cherokee,
        if they love me,
        if they love all their brothers and sisters,
        and if they love the animals of the earth,

when they grow old and sick,
they too can come to a magic lake and be made well again."
This was a belief that was "savage."

"Going to Water"

The same "savage" would go down to the waters of the Tennessee,
right down here,
early in the morning every morning,
wade out waist deep,
take the waters of the river and throw it up over his head.
And say,
"Wash away any thoughts or feelings
that may hinder me from being closer to my God.
Take away any thoughts or feelings
that may hinder me from being closer to all my brothers and sisters on the earth,
and the animals of the earth."
And they would wash themselves
and cleanse themselves
every morning,
and then they would walk out of the water.
And you see many people using crystals today,
but the only use I know—
the Cherokee had pure crystal.
They would hold it in front of the individual,
and if he saw himself upside down in it,
he had to go back into the water and do the same thing over again.
But if he was upright, he was cleansed, and free to go about his daily work.
Those people loved the earth.

Duncan, Barbara. Stories as told by Freeman Owle and Kathi Smith Littlejohn. In *Living Stories of the Cherokee*, 40–43, 201–12, 228–31. Chapel Hill: University of North Carolina Press, 1998.

POST-READING PARS

1. What attitudes toward nature did you learn in these stories?
2. Which local western North Carolina landmarks are referenced in these stories?

Inquiry Corner

Content Question(s):	Critical Question(s):
Identify two or three themes that these stories share. How would you describe the ecological world of the southern Appalachians?	What are some inherent biases of science? Can science adequately describe nature? Are there ways that traditional ecological knowledge (TEK) reveals aspects of nature that science doesn't?
Comparative Question(s):	**Connection Question(s):**
Compare and contrast the approach to nature in these stories with other sources we've read in this Reader (e.g., *Daodejing*, *Ananseseɛm*, Potlatch, and *Book of Songs*).	If you had to communicate a scientific belief in the form of an oral story that would be remembered for generations, how would you tell it?

"Laughing Warrior Girl" (Ohkay Owingeh/Tewa)

> **SNAPSHOT BOX**
>
> LANGUAGE: Tewa/Tano
>
> DATE: Oral tradition
>
> LOCATION: Tewa Basin on northern Rio Grande river/Southwest United States
>
> GENRE: Storytelling
>
> ETHNIC IDENTITY: Pueblo/Ohkay Owingeh
>
> TAGS: Authority and Leadership; Conflict and War; Deities and Spirits; Indigeneity; Oral Histories and Storytelling; Religion; Women and Gender

Introduction

The story, "Laughing Warrior Girl," is part of Ohkay Owingey/Tewa culture. Tewa are one of many Indigenous groups whose ancestral and current home is located on the lands of present-day Southwest United States. The term is used also to refer to the Tewa language and culture to distinguish from many other unique Pueblo groups such as Laguna, Zia, and Zuni. *Pueblo*, "village" in Spanish, is the term applied to all Indigenous peoples living in Arizona, New Mexico, Utah, and Colorado whom the colonizing forces came into contact in the 1600s. What might be the reasons for this region to be also called the Four Corners?

Ancestral Puebloans were in this area as early as 100 CE, with the Tewa peoples likely migrating from the Mesa Verde region to the Tewa Basin along the Northern Rio Grande (present-day northeast New Mexico) in 1280 CE. The history of Pueblo migration becomes integrally linked to the colonization process after contact with Europeans. One smaller group of Tewa migrated to First Mesa (present-day northeast Arizona) in 1696 CE to aid the Hopi peoples in their fight for survival against the Spanish colonizers. The Spanish had returned to decimate the groups that had been successful in the earlier Pueblo Revolt of 1680. Some Tewa peoples continue to live in the communities on First Mesa, as well as in five Tewa villages in Tewa Basin, each designated with their own separate tribal names, including the Ohkay Owingey, formerly known as Tewa San Juan Pueblo, a name given by the Spanish.

Oral history is the contemporary term used in Indigenous Studies for storytelling.

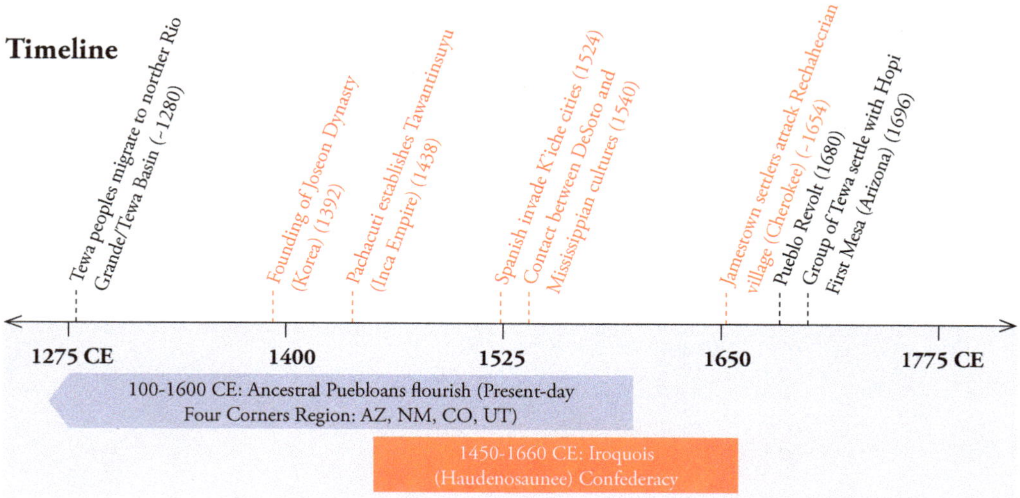

Oral histories are often miscategorized by state government officials, anthropologists, and missionaries as myths or tales (as in "tall tales" = not true). However, for Indigenous cultures, these oral histories are a rich living storytelling tradition that transmits sacred knowledge about community values, origins, and relationships to ancestors, spirit beings, plants, and animals. Oral histories dynamically change based on the teller, audience, and context, and so when they are written down, these stories appear to be more fixed than they are meant to be. This is true of oral histories across times and cultures.

The written versions of oral histories often reveal more about the perspectives and frameworks of the collectors who then analyze patterns in the stories according to criteria of dominant cultures' written sources. For example, folklorist Elsie Clews Parsons noted an "original" and "variants," when recording stories with the help of her Tewa translators in the largest published text, ***Tewa Tales***, in 1929. The written version of this oral history of "Laughing Warrior Girl" is from Parsons's volume, which continues to be used by both Indigenous and non-Indigenous scholars, not without critique. What criteria do you think might determine what was an "original" and what made a story a "variant"? What does this categorization indicate about who is making these distinctions and why? What other criteria could shape an approach in translating oral histories?

The following oral history, "Laughing Warrior Girl," reflects a Tewa cultural perspective on gender. In the narrative, the main character, Pohaha, is labeled as not a "good girl" by family elders. And yet because of her behaviors, those family elders approach her while she is grinding corn, a traditionally female activity in Tewa culture. They ask her to provide leadership in a battle because she is both "a girl and a man." Pohaha goes into battle, like her grandmother did, with only one side of her hair butterfly whorled in a side knot. (Women usually styled their hair with side knots on both sides.) Pohaha's face also turns into a mask when in battle, a mask that Pohaha removes and hangs on the wall when at home and is given to her community after her death. Pohaha is declared a "good girl" for her behaviors and also is designated as an ***okuwa/oxua*** (Oak-u-wah). ***Okuwa/oxua*** is a word translated as "cloud being," by Ohkay Owingeh anthropologist Alfonso Ortiz. ***Okuwa/oxua*** is similar to the ***kachinas***, or spirits, of nearby Diné (Navajo), Hopi, and Zuni Indigenous communities. Cloud-beings and kachinas are spirits embodied by masked dancers as part of ceremonies, especially related to the bringing of rain that is needed to grow corn in the high mountain altitudes of pueblo communities.

As you read, pay careful attention to the aspects being used to construct an understanding of gender. Gender binaries are embedded in dominant, Western ideologies—how might Elsie Clews Parsons's translation of this oral history be influenced by the binary frameworks she brings to her work as a twentieth-century American folklorist? How might this oral history provide insight into a Tewa understanding of gender?

Katherine C. Zubko
Department of Religious Studies

Laughing Warrior Girl

Where they were living lived Laughing Warrior Girl,[71] a girl who would not mind her mother or father or uncle. They were telling her to be a good girl, but she got angry quickly. Then they got tired telling her to be good so they just let her go. One time she was grinding corn, and many enemies were coming, very close to the village. Her uncle came to her house and asked her mother where she was. Her mother said she was grinding corn. He went to where she was grinding and caught her arm and said, "Take your bow and arrows and go and fight with the enemies who are coming. You would not mind us and behaved like a boy. Now is the time for you to go and fight and be brave," said the uncle to the girl. She laughed ha! ha! "I am very glad to go," she said. "I am very anxious to go and fight the enemies. I am not afraid. I will do all I can."—"That is why I tell you. Come out!" said the uncle. "I will," she said. She stood up and her uncle gave her bow and arrows and hung the bandolier[72] around her. Then she looked around and there was a rattle hanging on the wall. She stepped up and got it. Then she started to sing. As soon as she stopped singing, she laughed ha! ha! She sang four times in the room. Then she went out and sang outdoors four times. Whenever she paused in singing she laughed ha! ha! because she was not afraid to fight. Then she started, and the men followed her. People were saying, "The Cottonwood People (clan) girl (*te'towa*) is going to fight." Some of them laughed at her. But she just went on, singing and laughing ha! ha! happy she was going to fight. Before she met the enemies, she pulled her dress up, four times, to show the enemies that she was a girl.

Then she fought. She killed all the enemies that same day. After that the fighting was over and she turned back. The men fighting with her saw she had turned *okuwa*: she was wearing a mask, one side was blue, and one side was yellow, and she had long teeth. They were afraid of her, she looked strange, she no longer looked like a girl. But she kept on singing her song, ending with ha! ha! She kept on going home, and the men followed her. When they got to the village, all the people came out and watched the girl, how she had become some sort of a [new] person. When she went to war, she did not look like that. She went to her house and went in, and then she took off her mask and hung it on the wall, and she hung her rattle in the same place and the bow and arrow close, too. That is the way that girl became Laughing Warrior Girl. Her uncles came to the house at night. They had been talking about her. All day they had been thinking that she must be a man. So they went in there, all gathered

71. Chakwena mui su'amo (their grandmother) was similarly a girl, sent to war by her uncles, and also, while she was fighting, her face turned into a mask. Her mother was combing her hair and had only one side whorled, and the stick she used was still in the whorl. Then her uncle came in. (The scene between Pohaha and her uncle is repeated.) In this case the uncle also gives a quiver of mountain lion skin and the mask is different, too, black, with yellow eyes and tongue hanging out.

72. A belt with pockets hung over the shoulder to hold ammunition, in this case, arrows.

together, the oldest uncle[73] said they would put her in as Pota'i (war chief). Even if she was a girl, she was a man, too. So they said that whenever enemies came she was to be the leader in war. "You have to watch for the people," they told her. "If any sickness comes, you have to drive the sickness away from the people. And consider that the people are all your children. Treat them right," they told her. After that she became a good girl, she no longer acted as she used to. When war came, she went first and dressed as she did before in war. After she died, she left her mask and said that it would represent her. She would always be with the people, even if dead. "I will be with you all the time," she said, "the mask is me," she said. That is why those Cottonwood People keep that mask.

Selection from *Tewa Tales*, edited by Elsie Clews Parsons, 191–92. New York: American Folk-Lore Society and G. E. Stechert and Co., 1926.

73. The characteristic Hopi-Tewa maternal family is being referred to, the English term "uncle" always meaning mother's brother or mother's mother's brother. The influence of the "uncle" comes out clearly in this tale, as well as the relation between maternal family and clan.

from *Pop Wuj* (K'iche' Maya)

SNAPSHOT BOX

LANGUAGE: K'iche' Maya

DATE: Oral/Ts'íib tradition; written version c. 1550 CE

LOCATION: Pre-Columbian Mesoamerica, Iximulew/ Guatemala

GENRE: Ts'íib (multimodal text)

ETHNIC IDENTITY: K'iche' Maya/Pan-Maya

TAGS: Conflict and War; Cosmology; Death; Deities and Spirits; Empire and Colonialism; Family; Identity; Indigeneity; Journey; Oral Histories and Storytelling; Origin Stories; Sacrifice

Introduction

You may find that sometimes Indigenous peoples and their expressions are pictured and analyzed as if they were from vanished peoples and practices. Indigenous scholars call those narratives "colonial." On the contrary, it is important to remember that today at least six million people identify as Maya in Mexico, Guatemala, Belize, Honduras, El Salvador, and the United States; and they speak more than thirty languages older than English and Spanish. Both big cities such as Guatemala City and small communities such as Momostenango are located on ancestral Maya territory, whose biodiversity and human geography are encoded in the *Pop Wuj*.

The *Popol Wuj* or *Pop Wuj*[74] you are reading is not about the past nor about the Maya, but the creation of everything and everybody on **Iximulew**, the land of maize, associated with present-day Guatemala. Poet Humberto Ak'abal describes the *Pop Wuj* as a foundational text that describes the creation process of the earth, animals, and human beings (a cosmogony), the formation of the first communities and villages, and the origins of the earliest families who inhabited the land of the K'iche' Maya. Ak'abal also pronounces the narrative as **mystic**: it reveals the importance of ritual and acknowledges that some things remain a mystery and are difficult to elucidate from our contemporary sensibilities.[75] Andres Xiloj, an **Aj q'ij** (Maya daykeeper[76]), also notes that the *Pop Wuj* is actually an **ilbal**, a kind of crystal/stone that can reveal "everything under the sky and on the earth, all the way out to the four corners."[77] During the creation process, several times the creators have to ask guidance from the grandparents Ixmucane and Ixbalanque, the masters of the tz'ite seeds, "bright-red beanlike seed of the coral tree."[78] From the beginning, divination ceremonies are at the core of the *Pop Wuj*, and they

74. For a guide to pronounce the K'iche' Maya language, see http://www.famsi.org/mayawriting/dictionary/christenson/quidic_complete.pdf.

75. Humberto Ak'abal, *Paráfrasis del Popol Wuj* (Maya' Wuj, 2016), 12.

76. Aj q'ij literally means "the one who knows about the days." The Aj q'ij follows carefully the Maya ritual calendar, and based on this knowledge, offers fire ceremonies and provides advice to the community.

77. Dennis Tedlock, *Popol Vuh: The Definitive Edition of the Mayan Book of the Dawn of Life and the Glories of the Gods and Kings* (New York: Touchstone, 1996), 18.

78. Allen Christenson, *Popol Vuh: Sacred Book of the Quiché Maya People* (Norman: University of Oklahoma Press, 2007), 68. Electronic version of *Popol Vuh: The Sacred Book of the Maya* can be accessed at www.mesoweb.com/publications/ Christenson/PopolVuh.pdf.

Timeline

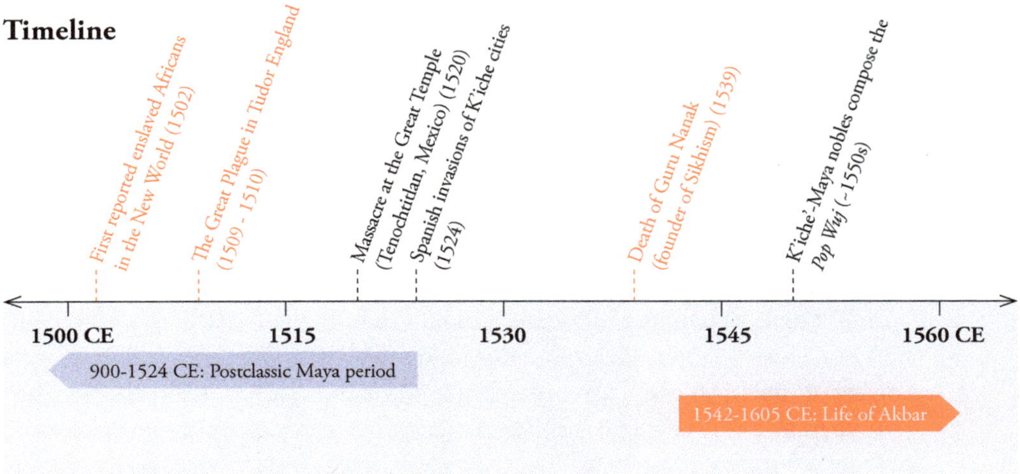

are still practiced by the Aj q'ij, who use the tz'ite, sometimes surrounded by stones and crystals. What types of guidance might you ask for from your grandparents?

You are here reading an episode that takes place after the first failed attempts to create humanity from the animals, then from mud, and finally from carved wood. Humanity will finally be created from white and yellow maize. That final successful attempt is narrated, in the written version of the *Pop Wuj*, right after the episode in Xibalba—the one you are reading here. Xibalba, translated as the "place of fear" or "place of awe," has captivated Western imagination for centuries. Most translators have chosen "underworld/inframundo" as a way of placing this complex realm. On the one hand, Xibalba is home of the Lords of Death; on the other hand, Xibalba is also home of Ixquic (Lady Blood in Christenson's translation), who is the Mother of the twins, Sun and Moon, and the one responsible for the "miracle of the maize." Xibalba is both a place of blood and pain and a place of gardens, flowers, and laughter.

Before the descent to Xibalba, the text introduces us to key episodes with Seven Macaw and his sons Zipacna and Cabracan. They are defeated by the Hero Twins, Hunahpu and Xbalanque, the same way these twins defeat the lords of Xibalba. Note that all these events, including the episode in Xibalba, are happening in the dark, at night, "While the face of the earth was only a little brightened, before there was a sun."[79] Note, as well, the importance in this episode of the ball game. The ball game was played widely throughout pre-Columbian Mesoamerica, and it is here being represented as a space with ceremonial and religious significance. Throughout Classic Maya–era cities, such as Tikal and Copan, and post-Classic Maya cities such as Iximche' and Q'umarkaj, today we still find I-shaped stone courts dedicated to this game, which demonstrate how central it was for the Maya governance and social organization for millennia. It used to be played between two teams, dressed

79. Christenson, *Popol Vuh*, 76.

in ceremonial regalia. Players hit a solid rubber ball with their bare hips only while re-enacting the cosmic battle between death and life, trying to push the other team out of the court. There are multiple layers of meaning in the ball game, including balancing creation and destruction, which are in constant flux in the Maya worldview. For instance, as the heart beats and irrigates blood through the full body during the gymnastic movement of the ball game, players both in Xibalba and the ball court, ancestors and descendants come together to re-enact the sacrifice and resurrection of the maize god.[80]

In Pre-Columbian times, multiple episodes from the *Pop Wuj* such as the twins battling Seven Macaw were represented in stelae, altars, murals, ceramics, and codices throughout what has been called "Mesoamerica." As **Abiayala** has been reclaimed as a Native name for the Americas, Indigenous peoples have proposed specific words from Native languages to name Indigenous literatures. Gaspar Pedro González, Maya poet and novelist, stated that **kotz'ib'** ("our literature") encompasses different ways of expressing Maya thought through signs, symbols, colors, fabrics, and lines. For example, an ideal way to begin to recognize the complexity and multidimensional nature of these narratives is lifting our gaze to the skies, acknowledging the deep connections that first Mesoamericans had with the stars, planets, and the moon that allowed them to be aligned with the cosmic cycles. Patterns of the stars of the northern sky hold a key for those seeking to begin to understand the origins and the inspiration of some of the events and beings mirrored in the *Pop Wuj*.[81] What types of narratives do you know that are connected to the stars?

The *Pop Wuj* manuscript that we have originated around 1550 CE, written by K'iche' who were then under Spanish colonial occupation. The anonymous manuscript was written in the K'iche' language with our Latin alphabet and was transcribed and translated into Spanish by the priest Francisco Ximénez at the beginning of the 1700s. Therefore, the text that we have is a K'iche' version of an ancient Mesoamerican saga, written under the Christian siege of Spanish colonization.

More recently, researchers have defined **ts'íib** as a multimodal "recorded knowledge."[82] This Maya literary alphabetic/nonalphabetic understanding of expression has opened multiple approaches for readers of Maya ts'íib. In this context, the *Pop Wuj* is not just a book nor just a colonial text, but a foundational story expressed throughout centuries in many codes, languages, and materials. These multimodal textualities, ts'íib, including orality and the colonial book itself, constitute the *Pop*

80. David Freidel, Linda Schele, and Joy Parker, *Maya Cosmos: Three Thousand Years on the Shaman's Path* (New York: William Morrow Company, 1995), 341.

81. Freidel, Schele, and Parker, *Maya Cosmos*, 9.

82. See Paul Worley and Rita Palacios, *Unwriting Maya Literature: Ts'íib as Recorded Knowledge* (Tucson: University of Arizona Press, 2019).

Wuj, whose ***tzij***, "truths, stories, narratives, wisdom, and traditions,"[83] are still in practice today among some Maya both in Guatemala and abroad. Contemporary Maya traditionalists remember its stories and philosophy via orality and ceremony even without having read the surviving *Pop Wuj* manuscript.

Contemporary Indigenous thinkers have suggested that one way for non-Indigenous readers to enter this ts'íib/literature is to hold space for Indigenous perspectives. Instead of absolute oppositions such as good/bad, light/darkness, life/death, a view of relational mutuality has been emphasized. For example, Gloria Chacón proposes that the ancient Maya methodology of double gaze, or **kab'awil**, is one such relational view being founded on the connections among cosmos, land, and body.[84] From a kab'awil reading, the creation story of the maize-people is also the story of their land and their way of being. Both certainty and intuition, as well as humility, guide Hunahpu and Xbalanque throughout the cycle of death and rebirth while crossing Xibalba. In what contexts would it be beneficial to hold certainty, intuition, and humility together?[85]

Juan Sánchez-Martínez and Elena Adell
Department of Languages and Literatures

83. Carlos M. López, "The Popol Vuj: The Repositioning and Survival of Mayan Culture," in *A Companion to Latin American Literature and Culture*, edited by Sara Castro-Klaren (Hoboken, NJ: Blackwell Publishing, 2008), 68.

84. Gloria Elizabeth Chacón, *Indigenous Cosmolectics: Kab'awil and the Making of Maya and Zapotec Literatures* (Chapel Hill: University of North Carolina Press, 2018).

85. For a complete experience of the *Pop Wuj*, we recommend K'iche' dictionaries and translations by K'iche' writers such as Adrián Inés Chávez and Sam Colop (see Nathan C. Henne, *Reading Popol Wuj: A Decolonial Guide* [Tucson: University of Arizona Press, 2020]), as well as the original manuscript in K'iche' available online. Allen Christenson's English translation from K'iche', including its footnotes, is recommended. Also, if you want to research further pre-Columbian Maya Ts'íib'/multimodal textualities, see Dennis Tedlock, *2000 Years of Mayan Literature* (Berkeley: University of California Press, 2010). See also Ann González, "The Popol Vuh for Children: Explicit and Implicit Ideological Agendas," *Children's Literature Association Quarterly* 39, 2 (Summer 2014): 216–33, and Víctor Montejo, "Heart of Heaven, Heart of Earth: The Maya Worldview." In *Native Universe: Voices of Indian America* (Washington, DC: National Museum of the American Indian, 2004).

The points and bands on the graphic timeline on page 155 are unable to capture the full story, so we are including an extended narrative timeline. For example, while the Classic Maya period includes Long Count calendar inscriptions on stelae, murals and ceramics found in Maya cities such as Tikal, Palenque, and Copan, the post-Classic Maya period includes syllabic and calendric writing on codices made of amate bark paper, in which Maya astronomy related with Venus, Mars, and eclipses is registered. From that point on the story unfolds as follows:

1520: Pedro de Alvarado is responsible for the Massacre of the Great Temple (Tenochtitlan, Mexico), in which the Aztec elite was assassinated by the Spanish army during the Tezcatlipoca ceremony.

1524: Spanish invasion of K'iche' cities. Between February and March, Pedro de Alvarado and around four hundred Spanish soldiers invaded the K'iche' cities of Xelaju Noj (Quetzaltenango) and Q'umarkaj (Cumarcah).

1550s: Anonymous K'iche'-Maya nobles composed *Pop Wuj* manuscript in Santa Cruz del Quiche.

Early 1700s: In Santo Tomás de Chuila, Dominican friar Francisco Ximénez copied the manuscript and translated it in two columns; one in K'iche,' and one with the text translated into Spanish.

1821: The Captaincy General of Guatemala, formed by Chiapas, Guatemala, El Salvador, Nicaragua, Costa Rica, and Honduras, officially proclaimed its independence from Spain.

1800s: In 1829–1830, Ximénez's manuscript is placed in the library of the University of San Carlos, in Guatemala City. In 1856–1857 and in 1861 a Spanish and a French translation of the text are published in Europe. Carl Scherzer and Charles Etienne Brasseur de Bourbourg are responsible for those, respectively. There are different versions of what happened with the manuscript from San Carlos, and questions about whether Brasseur's manuscript is the same as the one Scherzer had. Regardless, there is a K'iche' manuscript in the Newberry Library of Chicago that Guatemalan historian Adrián Recinos discovered there in 1941 (A. González, 217–18).

The story of the text—its *colonial archaeology*—does not stop there. Ann González explains how, during a good part of the twentieth century, the text (as a cultural artifact) was silenced, appropriated, and adapted by Guatemalan authorities depending on circumstances. The reason for these was to force the *ladino*, a non-Indigenous mestizo identity, as the marker of a modern Guatemalan nationhood. It is only after the Peace Accords of the 1990s that the Indigenous communities re-appropriated the written colonial version of the *Pop Wuj* for the benefit of their social organizations and communities. Nevertheless, what cannot be ignored is the way the *Pop Wuj* has survived regardless of the geopolitical conditions.

1944–1954: Guatemala revolution. Presidents Juan José Arévalo Bermejo and Jacobo Árbenz Guzmán opened the possibility (for the first time in Guatemala) of a strategic alliance among Indigenous youth, Afro-descendants, peasants, and ladinos (mixed-race).

1954: Coup d'état supported by US president Dwight D. Eisenhower. A right-wing dictatorship is installed; the civil war begins.

1980–1982: Guatemala general Efraín Ríos Montt, supported by US president Ronald Reagan, is responsible for the most violent years of the Maya genocide. Around 200,000 Maya people were killed and thousands were "forced disappeared."

1985: Kaqchikel writer Luis de Lion published *El tiempo principia en Xibalba*. In 2012 it was translated into English by Nathan C. Henne and published as *Time Commences in Xibalba*.

1992: Rigoberta Menchú, K'iche' activist, poet, and spokesperson, receives the Nobel Peace Prize.

1995: Agreements on Guatemalan Indigenous Peoples and Identities. Twenty-one Maya nations, as well as the Garífuna and the Xinca, were recognized for the first time by the nation-state as part of its multiethnic and multilingual history to the present.

1996: Guatemalan Peace Accords. During Alvaro Arzú's presidency, representatives from the nation-state and the Guatemalan National Revolutionary Unity (UNGR) signed them. Acknowledgment of Indigenous identities was decisive in seeking peace and unity.

2012: Efraín Ríos Montt is brought to court as responsible for the Maya genocide in the 1980s.

PRE-READING PARS

1. Identify two aspects that you typically notice when you read your favorite poetry (e.g., in relation to language, tone, structure, imagery, etc.). Notice how remaining open to the language and imaginary enhances your reading. On the one hand, be aware of how symbols and their interpretation often vary among different worldviews. On the other, reflect on the images and events, and on your reactions to them, just that. It is all right to step away from analytical interpretations.
2. What does "underworld" mean to you? Name a story you read or watched that describes an underworld.
3. How do you represent time? Try to not write but instead create a graphic or design.

From Pop Wuj, Descent to Xibalba

The Summons of Hunahpu and Xbalanque to Xibalba

And so they went rejoicing as ballplayers to the ballcourt. For a long time they played ball there alone, sweeping clear the ballcourt of their father.

Then the lords of Xibalba heard it:

"Someone has begun to play again over our heads. Have they no shame, stomping about up there? Did not One Hunahpu and Seven Hunahpu die when they desired to puff themselves up before us? Go then to summon them here once again," said One Death and Seven Death, along with all the lords.

"Summon them here," they said to their messengers. "Tell them, 'They must come, say the lords. Here we shall play ball with them. In seven days, we will play, say the lords.' Tell them this when you arrive there," the messengers were told.

Thus they came along the great cleared pathway, the road that led to the home of the boys. The messengers pursued them into the home of the Grandmother, but the boys were still playing ball when the messengers of Xibalba arrived.

"The lords say, 'They must surely come,'" said the messengers of Xibalba.

Then the messengers of Xibalba set the date:

"In seven days, they will be expected." Such was the word left with Xmucane.

"Very well then," replied the Grandmother. "They shall go as summoned, you messengers."

Thus the messengers returned again, leaving the Grandmother heartbroken:

"How shall I tell my grandsons of their summons? Were these not truly from Xibalba? They are just like the messengers who arrived in the past when their fathers went away to die," said the Grandmother.

Thus she wept bitterly in the house alone.

Then a louse fell down on her. It itched, so she picked it up and put it in her hand. The louse scuttled as it went along.

"My grandchild," she asked the louse, "would you like me to send you to summon my grandsons at the ballcourt?"

Thus he left as a summoner with this message:

"Messengers have arrived with your grandmother saying that you are to come. The messengers of Xibalba declare, 'In seven days you are to come,' says your grandmother."

Such was the message given to the louse. And so he went, scuttling along the way. Now sitting in the road was a youthful toad by the name of Tamazul.[86]

"Where are you going?" asked the toad of the louse.

"I am going to give the boys a message that is in my belly," said the louse to Tamazul.

"Very well then, but I see that you are not going very fast," the toad said to the louse. "Wouldn't you like me to swallow you? Then you would see how fast I could go. We would get there quickly."

"Very well," said the louse to the toad.

Thus he was licked up by the toad, who went hopping along his way. But he did not go fast. Presently, he was met by a great snake whose name was White Life.

"Where are you going, boy Tamazul?" asked White Life.

"I am a messenger with a message in my belly," said the toad to the snake.

"But I see that you aren't going very fast. Perhaps I would arrive there more quickly," said the snake to the toad.

"Go right ahead," he was told.

Thus the toad was swallowed up by White Life. The snake, then, received his food and they still swallow toads today.

Now this snake went quickly along his way. Then again the snake was met by the falcon, a great bird.[87] And the snake was swallowed by the falcon.[88] Then he arrived atop the ballcourt. Thus the hawk received his food, so that he still eats snakes in the mountains.

When the falcon arrived, he alighted atop the edge of the ballcourt while Hunahpu and Xbalanque were rejoicing and playing ball.

86. The name Tamazul is derived from the Nahuatl tamasolli (toad), perhaps indicating a central Mexican origin for portions of this tale.

87. Wak. The name of this bird is closely related to the Nahuatl word for falcon, *oactli*. It is likely the bird known as the Laughing Falcon. Karen Bassie-Sweet points out that the call of the laughing falcon is an indication of the coming of the rains in Mesoamerica (personal communication). She suggests that the twins' clearing of the maize field implies the dry season when the fields are cleared for burning. The subsequent descent into Xibalba would coincide with this period of death and sterility.

88. This humorous story may have prophetic significance as well. The louse represents corruption and decay. The toad is associated with the watery underworld and the fertility of the Earth's interior as a source of renewal. The serpent is a common symbol of regeneration because of its tendency to periodically shed its old skin to uncover a new one. Finally, the falcon is a common symbol of the reborn sun at dawn. Thus the sequence of animals may presage the events to happen in the underworld.

Then the falcon cried out:
"Wak-ko! Wak-ko!" was the cry of the falcon.
"What is that which is crying out? To our blowguns!" they said.

Hunahpu and Xbalanque Receive the Summons to Xibalba

So then they shot the falcon. The pellet from the blowgun buried itself straight into his eye,[89] knocking him down. Thus he fell, and they went out to grab him and question him:

"Why have you come?" they asked the falcon.

"I have a message in my belly. But surely you must first cure my eye, and then I will tell it," said the falcon.

"Very well then," they replied.

So they took off a little of the surface of their rubber ball and put it in the face of the falcon.[90] This they called Sliced Rubber. Immediately he was cured by them, making good again the sight of the falcon.

"Tell it then," they said to the falcon.

Thus he vomited the great snake.

"Speak!" they said again to the snake.

"All right," he replied. And so he vomited the toad.

"What is your errand? Speak!" the toad was told.

"My message is here in my belly," said again the toad.

Then he tried to throw up, but he did not vomit. His mouth just drooled. He tried, but nothing did he vomit. Thus the boys wished to beat him.

"You are a deceiver," he was told.

Then they squashed his rear end with their feet, crushing the bones of his backside with their feet.

Again he tried, but he just salivated at the mouth. So they pried open the mouth of the toad. It was pried open wide by the boys. They searched in his mouth and found that the louse was merely stuck in front of the toad's teeth. He was just in his mouth. He hadn't really been swallowed. It was merely as if he had been swallowed.

Thus the toad was defeated. As a result, it is not obvious what food was given to him. He could not go fast; thus he merely became spoil for the snake.

"Speak!" the louse was told.

Thus he spoke his word:

"The Grandmother says to you boys, 'Go and summon them. Messengers have arrived from Xibalba, the messengers of One Death and Seven Death. 'In seven days[91]

89. This is a play on words in the original Quiché, since "eye" is u b'aq' u wach (its pellet or seed on his face).

90. The laughing falcon has a black patch around the eyes.

91. The number 7 has ritual significance in the Mayan worldview. In this case, it may refer to the seven levels of the Earth that were believed to exist above the underworld. Thus the twins

they will come here to play ball with us. They must bring their gaming things—the rubber ball, yokes, arm protectors, and leathers. They will liven up this place, say the lords.' 'This is their word that has come,' says your grandmother. 'Thus you must come,' the Grandmother truly says. Your grandmother weeps. She calls out that you must come."

"Is it not true?" they asked in their hearts when they heard this. And immediately they returned to advise their grandmother.

The Descent of Hunahpu and Xbalanque into Xibalba

"Surely we must go, our grandmother. But first we will advise you. This is the sign of our word that we will leave behind. Each of us shall first plant an ear of unripe maize[92] in the center of the house.[93] If they dry up, this is a sign of our death. 'They have died,' you will say when they dry up. If then they sprout again, 'They are alive,' you will say, our grandmother and our mother. This is the sign of our word that is left with you," they said.

Thus Hunahpu planted one, and Xbalanque planted another in the house.

They did not plant them in the mountains or in fertile ground. It was merely in dry ground, in the middle of the interior of their home, that they planted them.

Then they left, each with his blowgun, and descended to Xibalba. They quickly went down the steps, passing through various river canyons. They passed through the midst of many birds. "Flocks" was the name of the birds.

And again they passed over Pus River and Blood River. In their hearts, the Xibalbans had intended these as traps. But they were not troubled. They just passed over them, floating on their blowguns.

When they came to the four crossroads, they already knew the roads of Xibalba—the Black Road, the White Road, the Red Road, and the Blue/Green Road.

Then they sent an insect named Mosquito. They sent him on ahead to obtain for them what he could hear:

---

were allowed a day to pass through each of these layers on their journey downward into Xibalba. It may also refer to the seven sacred directions of the Maya universe—the four cardinal directions plus the sky, center, and underworld.

92. Aj. This is an ear of unripe maize, or maize that is still soft on the cob. Alternatively, it may also refer to the stalk of the maize plant.

93. Although this incident seems odd, it is consistent with the ancient Maya conception of the universe in which all creation is seen as a house. The four corners represent the cardinal directions while its walls and ceiling form the vault of the sky. The foundation posts thus form the boundaries of the underworld. The maize plant is often depicted as a divine axis mundi standing at the center point of the universe with its roots extending downward into the underworld while its stalk reaches into the sky. The ancient Maya often erected colossal stone monuments of their revered kings decorated with tree and maize elements to emphasize the rulers' identity with this sacred living center. Thus the Quichés would see nothing odd in the twins identifying themselves with a maize stalk planted at the center of a divine household.

"You shall bite each one of them in turn. Bite the first one seated there and then keep on biting them until you have finished biting all of them. It will be truly yours then to suck the blood of people on the road," the mosquito was told.

"Very well then," said the mosquito.

So then he went along the Black Road until he alighted behind the effigies of carved wood. The first ones were all dressed up. He bit the first one, but there was no response. Then he bit the second one seated there, but he did not speak either.

Next he bit the third one seated there, who was One Death—"Ouch!" said each one when he was bitten. "What?" was their reply:

"Ow!" said One Death.

"What, One Death? What is it?"

"I am being bitten!"

"It's just . . . Ow! What was that? Now I am being bitten!" said the fourth one seated there.

"What, Seven Death? What is it?"

"I am being bitten!"

Next, the one seated fifth said, "Ow! Ow!"

"Flying Scab," asked Seven Death, "what is it?"

"I am being bitten!" he said.

Then the sixth one seated there was bitten.

"Ow!" "What, Gathered Blood? What is it?" asked Flying Scab.

"I am being bitten!" he said.

Next, the seventh one seated there was bitten. "Ow!" he said.

"What, Pus Demon? What is it?" asked Gathered Blood.

"I am being bitten!" he said.

Then the eighth one seated there was bitten. "Ow!" he said.

"What, Jaundice Demon? What is it?" asked Pus Demon.

"I am being bitten!" he said.

Then the ninth one seated there was bitten. "Ow!" he said.

"What, Bone Staff? What is it?" asked Jaundice Demon.

"I am being bitten!" he said.

Then the tenth one seated there was bitten. "Ow!"

"What, Skull Staff? What is it?" asked Bone Staff.

"I am being bitten!" he said.

Then the eleventh one seated there was bitten. "Ow!" he said next.

"What, Wing? What is it?" asked Skull Staff.

"I am being bitten!" he said.

Next, the twelfth one seated there was bitten. "Ow!" he said.

"What, Packstrap? What is it?" asked Wing.

"I am being bitten!"

Next was bitten the thirteenth one seated there. "Ow!"

"What, Bloody Teeth? What is it?" asked Packstrap.

"I am being bitten!" he said.

Then the fourteenth seated one was bitten. "Ow!"

"What, Bloody Claws? What is it?" asked Bloody Teeth.

"I am being bitten!" he said.

Thus their names were named. Each of them revealed the name of the other. Each of the individuals in order of their rank had his name revealed by the one who sat next to him.[94] Not one of their names was missed until all of the names were named when they were bitten by a hair that Hunahpu had plucked from the front of his knee. It wasn't really a mosquito that had bitten them. And so Hunahpu and Xbalanque heard the names of all of them.

Thus they came to where the Xibalbans were.

"Hail these lords who are seated there," said a tempter.

"These are not lords. These are merely effigies carved of wood," they said. Then they hailed each one of them:

"Morning, One Death. Morning, Seven Death.[95]
Morning, Flying Scab. Morning, Gathered Blood.
Morning, Pus Demon. Morning, Jaundice Demon.
Morning, Bone Staff. Morning, Skull Staff.
Morning, Wing. Morning, Packstrap.
Morning, Bloody Teeth. Morning, Bloody Claws," they said when they arrived there.

All of them had their faces revealed, for all of their names were named. Not one of their names was missed. When they were called upon, they gave the names of each one without leaving any of them out.

"Sit down here," they were told, for it was desired that they sit on top of the bench. But they didn't want to:

"This isn't a bench for us. It is merely a heated stone," said Hunahpu and Xbalanque. Thus they were not defeated.

"Very well then, just go into that house," they were told.

So then they entered into the House of Darkness. But they were not defeated there either. In their hearts, the Xibalbans ordained that they would be defeated there in this, the first of the trials of Xibalba.

Thus they entered first into the House of Darkness. There the messenger of One Death gave to them a torch, already burning, and a cigar for each of them. And the messenger said when he arrived:

94. There is a definite hierarchy among the lords of Xibalba, exemplified by the order in which they are seated on the palace bench. During Mayan ceremonial occasions, elders sit in the order of their rank of authority.

95. The greeting in each case is q'ala ta. Q'ala is a shortened version of "it is clear," related to the common modern Quiché greeting in the morning, saqirik (it has dawned). Ta may simply mean "then," a frequently used word in the text. It may also be a shortened form of tat (father), a term commonly used when addressing highly ranked or older persons.

"Thus says the lord: 'Here is their torch. It must be given back at dawn along with the cigars. They must return them.'"

"Very well," they replied.

But they didn't light the torch. They just placed the red tail feather of a macaw on it as a substitute for flame. Thus the night watchmen saw it as if it were burning.

As for the cigars, they just put fireflies on their tips. All night they would glow brilliantly because of them.

"We have defeated them," said the night watchmen. But the torch was not used up, for it was only an illusion. Neither did the cigars have anything burning on them. It was merely an illusion as well. Thus they returned them whole to the lords:

"What becomes of them? Where did they come from? Who begat them? Who gave them birth? Truly our hearts are troubled, for it is not good what they are doing to us. Their appearance as well as their nature are unique," they said one to another.

Then they summoned all of the lords:

"Let us play ball, boys," they were told.

But first they were questioned by One Death and Seven Death:

"Where did you really come from? Would you tell us, boys?" they were asked by the Xibalbans.

"We must have come from somewhere, but we don't know." Only this they said. They told them nothing.

"Very well then. We will just go and play ball,[96] boys," the Xibalbans said to them.

"Fine," they replied.

"Here is our rubber ball that we will use," said the Xibalbans.

"No, we will use ours," said the boys.

"Not so. We will use this one that is ours," said again the Xibalbans.

"Very well," said the boys.

"It appears to be a skull, but it is merely drawn on the ball,"[97] said the Xibalbans.

"It is not. It is a skull we tell you," said the boys.

"Not so," replied the Xibalbans.

"Very well then," said Hunahpu.

Thus the Xibalbans threw down their rubber ball, which landed before the yoke of Hunahpu. And when the Xibalbans saw this, the White Dagger came out of their rubber ball. It clashed about over the ground of the entire ballcourt, threatening the boys.

"What is that?" asked Hunahpu and Xbalanque. "You just want death for us. Did

96. The ball game was played throughout Mesoamerica beginning at least by the time of the Olmecs circa 1500 BCE. Although the rules varied over time and from region to region, it generally involved opposing teams of two or more players attempting to bounce a solid rubber ball without the use of hands through a ring placed vertically along the ball court's walls.

97. The verb root, juch' means "to draw lines or to adorn with figures." Thus the Xibalbans try to convince the twins that their ball looks like a skull only because it has had skull-like features drawn on it.

we not answer your summons when your messenger came? Have pity on us. We will just go, then," said the boys to them.

It was their desire that the boys would straightaway die there because of the blade. They were to have been defeated. But it was not so. It was the Xibalbans who were now defeated by the boys.

"Don't go, boys. We will just play with your ball," the boys were told.

"Very well then," they replied.

Thus they took out their rubber ball, and it was thrown down. Then their prizes were chosen:

"What will we win?" the Xibalbans asked.

"Surely it is your choice," the boys said.

"Our prize[98] shall be merely four bowls of flowers," said the Xibalbans.

"Very well. What kinds of flowers?" the boys asked the Xibalbans.

"One bowl of red petals,[99] one bowl of white petals, one bowl of yellow petals, and one bowl of the large ones," said the Xibalbans.

"Very well," replied the boys.

So then the ball was dropped into play. They were equal in strength, but the boys made many plays with the ball for they played with all their hearts. At last, the boys gave themselves up to be defeated, and the Xibalbans thus rejoiced at their defeat:

"We have done well. We have already defeated them at the first attempt," said the Xibalbans. "Where shall they go to get the flowers?" they asked in their hearts.

"You will give to us the flowers as our prize early in the morning," the boys Hunahpu and Xbalanque were told by the Xibalbans.

"Very well. We will play ball again early in the morning," they said. Then they made their plans together.

Thus the boys entered into Blade House, the second trial of Xibalba. Here it was desired that they would be sliced apart by the blades. They were to have died quickly in their hearts. But they did not die. They spoke to the blades, instructing them in this way:

"Yours shall be the flesh of animals," they said to the blades.

Thus they stopped moving. As one they all lowered the points of their blades.

And while they were passing the night in Blade House, they called out to all the ants:

"Cutting ants,[100] conquering ants, come! Go and get flower blossoms as prizes for the lords."

"Very well," they said.

98. This is likely a play on words between ch'ako'n (prize, spoils) and related words such as ch'akom (cuttings of flowers or plants), and chakaj (bouquet, bunch of flowers according to Varea).

99. This reading for much'ij is based on much' (to break apart, crumble, break into pieces). Flower petals are commonly given as offerings in modern highland Maya ceremonies, often broken off the flower as part of the ceremony as prayers are made.

100. These are large, leaf-cutting ants, known in Guatemala as zompopos.

Then the ants went to get flowers from the garden of One Death and Seven Death. Now the Xibalbans had previously instructed the guardians of their flowers:

"Look after our flowers with all vigilance. Do not allow them to be stolen. For by these we have defeated the boys. What if they were able to obtain these as our prize? Thus do not sleep all night."

"Very well," they said then.

But the guardians of the garden did not notice anything. They would just cry out aimlessly in the branches of the trees. They just toddled along through the garden repeating their song:

"Shpurpuwek, shpurpuwek," said the one when he called.

"Puhuyu, puhuyu," said the other, the whippoorwill by name, when he called.

These two were the guardians of the garden of One Death and Seven Death. They didn't notice the ants stealing that which they were guarding. They swarmed[101] and thronged, carrying away the flowers. They went to cut down flowers from the tops of trees, gathering them together with those from below the trees. All this they did while the guardians were crying out, not noticing that their tails and wings were being gnawed on as well.

The flowers were thus loosened until they fell down to be gathered up. The four bowls were thus quickly filled with their flowers. By dawn they had all been collected.

Then the messengers arrived to summon them:

"'Come!' says the lord. 'May they straightaway bring hither our prize,'" the boys were told.

"Very well," they answered.

For they had collected the flowers into the four bowls. Thus they went, arriving before the lords. Now the lords received the flowers with woeful faces. Thus the Xibalbans were defeated. The boys had just sent ants, and in one night they had collected the flowers in the bowls. Thus the Xibalbans all turned pale. Their faces were pallid because of the flowers.

And so they summoned the flower guardians:

"For what reason have you allowed our flowers to be stolen? These flowers that you see are ours," the guardians were told.

"We noticed nothing, O lords. But our tails have surely suffered[102] for it," they replied.

Then their mouths were split open[103] as punishment for allowing that which they were guarding to be stolen. Thus One Death and Seven Death were defeated by Hu-

101. B'olowik is literally "to boil." It is also used to describe the swarming of insects.

102. Kuyu is "to suffer, or endure." It is also used to describe something "bent, crooked, or crippled." Either reading would be applicable here. Whippoorwills have very short wing and tail feathers.

103. This is apparently meant as a play on words. The whippoorwills are said to have "cried out" in song when they should have been guarding the gardens of Xibalba. The Quiché phrase is "they broke open their mouths." Now the Xibalba lords "split open their mouths" as the punishment chosen to match the birds' crime.

nahpu and Xbalanque. And this is the reason why the mouths of whippoorwills gape wide open to this day.

Then the ball was dropped into play again, but the game was even. And when they had finished playing ball, they planned together once more:

"At dawn again," said the Xibalbans.

"Very well," said the boys when they had finished.

Hunahpu and Xbalanque in the House of Cold

And so they now entered the House of Cold. The cold here was immeasurable. The interior of the House of Cold was thick with hail.

But straightaway the boys caused the cold to dissipate.[104] They did it in. They ruined and destroyed the cold. Thus they did not die, but rather were alive when it dawned again. The Xibalbans had wanted them to die there, but this was not to be. Instead they were just fine when the dawn came.

So then their guardians came again to summon them.

"What is this? Haven't they died?" asked the lords of Xibalba.

And again they marveled at the deeds of the boys, Hunahpu and Xbalanque.

Hunahpu and Xbalanque in the House of Jaguars

Next they entered into Jaguar House, which was crowded inside with jaguars:

"Do not eat us. We will give you what is yours," the jaguars were told.

Then they scattered bones before the beasts, who voraciously crunched them.[105]

The hearts of the night watchmen found this sweet, saying, "They are finished. They have given themselves up. They have eaten their hearts, and now these are their skeletons that are being gnawed upon."

But they didn't die. They were just fine when they came out again from Jaguar House.

"What kind of people are these? Where have they come from?" asked all the Xibalbans.

Hunahpu and Xbalanque in the House of Fire

Next they went into the fire, for there was a House of Fire. There was nothing but fire inside. But they were not burned. They were to have been roasted and set aflame. Instead they were just fine when dawn came. It had been desired that they would straightaway die when they passed through there, but it was not so. Thus all the Xibalbans lost heart as a result.

104. Tzaj is to "evaporate, dry up, dissipate, exhaust."

105. Paq'aq'ik refers to the sound of crunching, gnawing, or eating rapidly. It is also used to describe the sound of walking over dry leaves.

Hunahpu and Xbalanque in the House of Bats

Next they were put inside Bat House, which had only bats inside. It was a house of death bats. These were great beasts with snouts like blades that they used as murderous weapons.

When they arrived there, they were to be finished off. They had to crawl inside their blowguns to sleep so that they would not be eaten there in this house.

Nevertheless, it was because of a single death bat that they gave themselves up in defeat. It came swooping down. But this was merely a way to manifest themselves when it occurred.

Thus they pleaded for wisdom all that night as the bats made a din with their flapping wings.

"Keeleetz! Keeleetz!" they said all night long.

At length things quieted a little, and the bats became motionless.

Thus one of the boys crawled to the end of his blowgun. Xbalanque said, "Hunahpu, do you see the dawn yet?"

"I will go and see for certain if it has happened," he replied.

Hunahpu truly wanted to look out of the mouth of his blowgun to see the dawn. But when he did so, his head was cut off by the death bat,[106] leaving the greater part of his body behind.

"What? Hasn't it dawned yet?" asked Xbalanque. But Hunahpu did not move.

"What is going on? Hunahpu wouldn't have left. What then has he done?"

But nothing moved; only the rustling of wings was heard. Thus Xbalanque was ashamed:

"Alas, we have given in already," he said.

At the word of One Death and Seven Death, the head was placed atop the ballcourt. Thus all the Xibalbans rejoiced because of the head of Hunahpu. Then Xbalanque summoned all of the animals—the coati and the peccary, and all the animals both small and great—while it was still dark, early in the morning. He then entreated them for their food:

"I send each of you to bring the food that belongs to you," said Xbalanque to them.

"Very well," they said.

Then they all went to obtain what was theirs. When they returned they were many. One brought back rotten things, another brought leaves, another brought stones, and yet another brought dirt. Thus the animals, both small and great, each brought their various foods.

Now after many had come, the coati arrived last of all bringing a chilacayote

106. The ability of bats to cut down fruit from trees while in flight associated them in the mind of the ancient Maya with decapitation sacrifice. Bats are often seen painted on ancient Maya vessels as underworld denizens of death, decorated with crossed bones and extruded eyeballs that have their optic nerves still dangling from them.

squash. She[107] came rolling it along with her nose. This was to be transformed into the head of Hunahpu. Immediately its eyes were carved upon it. Numerous sages came down from the sky. For Heart of Sky, he who is Huracan, appeared here. He arrived here in Bat House.

But the face wasn't completed successfully in time. Only its beautiful covering had appeared. It only had the ability to speak by the time the horizon of the sky began to redden, for it was about to dawn.

"Blacken it again with soot, old man,"[108] the possum[109] was told.

"Fine," replied the Grandfather.

And he blackened the sky with soot until it was dark again. Four times the Grandfather blackened it with soot. Thus today people say, "The possum blackens it with soot."

Finally the sky succeeded in turning red, and then blue when it began its existence.

"Is it not good?" Hunahpu was asked.

"Yes, it is good," he replied.

For his head was well supported. It became just like a true head. Then they planned a deception;[110] they took counsel together:

"Don't play ball. Just look threatening. I will surely be the one to accomplish it," said Xbalanque to him.

Then he instructed a rabbit: "Be there at the head of the ballcourt in the tomato patch," the rabbit was told by Xbalanque. "And when the rubber ball comes your way, hop away until I accomplish my task," the rabbit was told. Thus he was given his instructions there in the night.

And when it dawned, the both of them were well.[111]

107. The coati is consistently associated with females in the text, just as the peccary is associated with males. They are particularly identified as the grandmother and grandfather deities respectively.

108. Ama' is a general term for "male," whether human or animal. In this case, it is used as a nickname for the aged possum deity. Because of the possum's gray coat, awkward gait, and snaggly teeth, the Maya associated this animal with old age.

109. Vuch (possum) is the darkness of night just prior to the dawn. This is perhaps a manifestation of the creator deity Xpiyacoc, one of whose principal titles is Hunahpu Possum. In the Tzotzil area, a grandfather possum, called "Old Man Possum," is associated with the dawn at the beginning of the planting season, and that the red light of the east is said to be one of his manifestations: "'Uch [Possum] is greatly respected, because it has fire, because at dawn it lights up the hills. It is not the sunlight, for the sun rises later [. . .]" (Guiteras-Holmes 1961, 195–97; cf. 33, 206, 292).

110. Xkib'an ki tzij (they made their words). To "make" words is to deceive or to lie.

111. Literally "good their faces both of them," the standard way of saying that they were "fine," but also in this context a clever play on words considering the newly made "face" of Hunahpu.

The Head of Hunahpu is Restored

So the ball was again dropped into play. The head of Hunahpu was first placed atop the ballcourt.

"We have already triumphed. You are finished. You gave in, so give it up," they were told.

But Hunahpu just called out: "Strike the head as if it were a rubber ball," they were told. "No harm will come to us now, for we are holding our own."

Thus the lords of Xibalba threw down the ball where it was met by Xbalanque. The ball landed before his yoke and bounced away. It sailed clear over the ballcourt. It just bounced once, then twice, landing in the tomatoes. Then the rabbit came out, hopping along.[112] All the Xibalbans thus went after him. The Xibalbans all went after the rabbit, shouting and rushing about.

Thus the twins were able to retrieve the head of Hunahpu, replacing it where the chilacayote squash had been. They then placed the chilacayote squash on the ballcourt, while the true head of Hunahpu was his once more. Therefore they both rejoiced again. While the Xibalbans were out searching for their rubber ball, the twins retrieved it from the tomato patch. And when they had done so, they called out:

"Come on! We found our rubber ball!" they said. Thus they were carrying the round ball when the Xibalbans returned.

"What was it that we saw?" they asked.

And so they began again to play ball, both teams making equal plays until at last Xbalanque struck the chilacayote squash, strewing it all over the ballcourt. Thus its seeds were scattered before them.[113]

"What is this that has been brought here? Where is he that brought it?" asked the Xibalbans.

Thus the lords of Xibalba were defeated by Hunahpu and Xbalanque. They had passed through great affliction, but despite everything that had been done to them, they did not die.

The Deaths of Hunahpu and Xbalanque

This, then, is the memorial to the deaths of Hunahpu and Xbalanque. We shall now tell it in memory of their death.

What they had planned to do, they had done despite all their afflictions and misfortunes. Thus they did not die in the trials of Xibalba. Neither were they defeated by all the ravenous beasts that lived there.

112. The hopping of the rabbit thus confuses the lords of Xibalba into thinking it is the bouncing ball.

113. A play on words is made here between saqiram (scattered) and saqilal (squash seeds). If one did not recognize the pun in the original Quiché, the choice of words would be confusing.

And then they summoned two seers. Visionary persons they were. The names of these sages were Descended[114] and Ascended:

"The lords of Xibalba may inquire of you concerning our death. They are even now putting together their thoughts on the matter, because we have not yet died. We have not been defeated. We confounded their trials. Nor have the animals seized us. This, therefore, is the sign that is in our hearts. Heated stones will be the means by which our murder will be accomplished. Thus when all Xibalba has gathered together to determine how to ensure our death, this shall be the idea that you will propose. If you are asked about our death when we are burned, this is what you shall tell them, you, Descended and you, Ascended, if they should speak to you about it:

"'Wouldn't it perhaps be good if we scatter their bones in the canyon?'

"Then you are to say, 'This would not be good, for they would merely arise again to new life.'

"Then they will say to you, 'Perhaps it would be good to merely hang them in the top of a tree?'

"You will then reply, 'Certainly that would not be good, for you would see their faces before you.'

"Then the third time they will say, 'Would it be a good thing if we merely scatter their bones in the course of the river?'

"If then you are asked this, you will reply, 'It is good that they should die. And it would be good if their bones were ground upon the face of a stone like finely ground maize flour. Each one of them should be ground separately. Then these should be scattered there in the course of the river. They should be sprinkled on the river that winds among the small and great mountains.'

"This, then, is what you will say. Thus will be made manifest what we have said to you in counsel," said Hunahpu and Xbalanque.

For when they had thus counseled them, they already knew of their death. The Xibalbans were even then putting together the great heated stones in the form of a pit oven,[115] placing large hot coals within it.

Then came the messengers of One Death and Seven Death to accompany them:

"The lords say to us: 'May they come! Bring them so that they may see what we have cooked up for them.'[116] This is the word of the lords unto you, boys," they were told.

"Very well," they replied.

114. The Colonial period Varea dictionary lists Xulu (Descended) as "[spirit] familiars appearing alongside rivers." Basseta lists ah xulu as "a diviner," consistent with the statement in the *Popol Vuh* that he is a visionary seer.

115. Chojib'al (pit oven) is dug into the ground and filled with hot stones or coals to roast meat.

116. This is a play on words. Chojij means "to cook, broil, or set fire to something"; but it also means "to straighten out, take a direct route, or rectify something." Thus the Xibalbans were trying to trick the twins by saying that they were going to settle things, while at the same time hinting at the means by which they intended to kill them.

Thus they went quickly to the mouth of the pit oven. There the Xibalbans wanted to force them into playing with them:

"Let us jump over this our sweet drink. Four times each of us will go across it, boys," they were told by One Death.[117]

"You cannot trick us with this. Do we not already know the means of our death, O lords? You shall surely see it," they said.

Then they turned to face one another, spread out their arms and together they went into the pit oven. Thus both of them died there. Then all the Xibalbans rejoiced at this. They contentedly shouted and whistled:

"We have defeated them. None too soon have they given themselves up," they said.

Then they summoned Descended and Ascended, with whom word had been left by the boys. And the Xibalbans divined of them what was to be done with their bones. Thus according to their word, the bones were ground up and strewn along the course of the river. But they did not go far away; they just straightaway sank there beneath the water. And when they appeared again, it was as chosen boys, for thus they had become.

The Resurrection of Hunahpu and Xbalanque

On the fifth day they appeared again. People saw them in the river, for the two of them appeared like people-fish. Now when their faces were seen by the Xibalbans, they made a search for them in the rivers.

And on the very next day, they appeared again as two poor orphans. They wore rags in front and rags on their backs. Rags were thus all they had to cover themselves. But they did not act according to their appearance when they were seen by the Xibalbans. For they did the Dance of the Whippoorwill and the Dance of the Weasel. They danced the Armadillo and the Centipede.[118] They danced the Injury, for many marvels they did then. They set fire to a house as if it were truly burning, then immediately recreated it again as the Xibalbans watched with admiration.

Then again they sacrificed themselves. One of them would die, surely throwing himself down in death. Then having been killed, he would immediately be revived. And the Xibalbans simply watched them while they did it. Now all of this was merely the groundwork for the defeat of the Xibalbans at their hands.

117. The Xibalbans are lying about the purpose of the pit. They are suggesting that it is an underground vat for making some intoxicating drink, whereas in reality it is a pit oven into which they hope to trick the twins into falling.

118. Xtz'ul is a centipede. The Varea dictionary lists xts'ul as "a dance with small masks and macaw tail feathers." During this dance, participants put sticks down their throats (like sword swallowers), bones in their noses, and give themselves hard blows on their chests with a large stone.

The Summons of Hunahpu and Xbalanque Before the Lords

At length the news of their dances came to the ears of the lords One Death and Seven Death. And when they had heard of it, they said:

"Who are these two poor orphans? Is it truly delightful? Is it true that their dancing and all that they do is beautiful?"

For the lords were delighted with the account when they heard it. Thus they entreated their messengers to summon them to come:

"Say this to them: 'May they come so that we may watch them, for we marvel at them,' say the lords."

Thus the messengers went to the dancers and repeated the words of the lords to them.

"We don't want to, for in truth we are timid. We would be ashamed to enter into such a lordly house! Our faces are truly ugly,[119] and our eyes are just wide in poverty. Don't they see that we are merely dancers? What then would we say to our fellow orphans? We have responsibilities. They also desire our dances, for they revive their faces with us. It is not right that we should do the same with the lords. Therefore we do not want to do this, O messengers," said Hunahpu and Xbalanque.

But they were pestered, threatened with misfortune and pain. And so they went with apprehension, for they didn't want to be going too soon. Many times they had to be prodded because they just walked along slowly, making little progress, while the messengers who brought them led the way to the lords.

Hunahpu and Xbalanque Dance Before the Lords of Xibalba

At length they arrived before the lords. They pretended to be humble,[120] prostrating themselves when they came. They humbled themselves, stooping over and bowing. They hid themselves with rags, giving the appearance that they were truly just poor orphans when they arrived. Then they were asked where their home mountain was[121] and who their people were. They were also asked about their mother and their father:

"Where do you come from?" they were asked.

"We do not know, O lord. Neither do we know the faces of our mother or our father. We were still small when they died," they just said. They didn't tell them anything.

"Very well then. On with the spectacle. What do you want us to give you as payment?" they were asked.

119. Literally "evil/bad/filthy our faces," a common expression for "ugly" among modern Quichés as well.

120. Moch'och'ik is "to humble one's self hypocritically."

121. The Quichés still give directions by indicating which mountain is located nearby the destination. It is not uncommon to ask the location of a town or a person's house and be told, "go two mountains to the west and one to the north."

"We don't want anything. Truly we are frightened," they said again to the lord.

"Do not be afraid or timid. Dance! First you will do that dance in which you sacrifice yourselves. Then burn down my home. Do everything that you know. We would watch this, for it was the desire of our hearts that you be summoned. Because you are poor orphans, we will pay whatever you ask as your price," they were told.

Thus they began their songs and their dances, and all the Xibalbans came until the place was overflowing with spectators. They danced everything. They danced the Weasel. They danced the Whippoorwill. They danced the Armadillo.

Then the lord spoke to them:

"Sacrifice my dog, then revive him again," they were told.

"All right," they replied. So they sacrificed his dog and then revived him once more. The dog was truly happy when they revived him. He vigorously wagged his tail when they brought him back to life.

Then the lord spoke again to them: "Now you must surely burn my home," they were told.

So then they burned the home of the lord. The house was overflowing with all the lords, yet none were burned. Immediately it was restored again. Thus the home of One Death was not lost after all.

All the lords marveled, therefore, and greatly rejoiced at their dances. The lord thus spoke again to them:

"Now kill a person. Sacrifice him, but not so that he really dies," they were told.

"Very well," they said.

So they grabbed a person and sacrificed him. They extracted the heart of one of them and placed it before the lords. Now One Death and Seven Death marveled at this, for immediately that person was revived again by them. When he had been revived, his heart greatly rejoiced. And again the lords marveled at it:

"Now sacrifice yourselves. We would see this. Truly it is the desire of our hearts that you dance," said again the lords.

"Very well then, O lord," they replied.

So then they sacrificed themselves. Hunahpu was sacrificed by Xbalanque. Each of his legs and arms was severed. His head was cut off and placed far away. His heart was dug out and placed on a leaf.[122] Now all these lords of Xibalba were drunk at the sight, as Xbalanque went on dancing.

"Arise!" he said, and immediately he was brought back to life again. Now the lords rejoiced greatly. One Death and Seven Death rejoiced as if they were the ones doing it. They were so involved that it was as if they themselves were dancing.

122. Tz'alik is a leaf used for wrapping maize tamales. The implication is that the heart was placed on a leaf prior to wrapping it as an offering. An alternative reading would have this word derived from tz'alam, a flat stone or altar.

The Defeat of the Lords of Xibalba

For it was the desire of the lords to abandon their hearts to the dances of Hunahpu and Xbalanque. Then came the words of One Death and Seven Death:

"Do it to us! Sacrifice us!" they said.

"Sacrifice us in the same way," said One Death and Seven Death to Hunahpu and Xbalanque. "Very well then. Surely you will be revived. Are you not death? For we are here to gladden you, O lords, along with your vassals and your servants," they said therefore to the lords.

The first to be sacrificed was the very head of all the lords, One Death by name, the lord of Xibalba. He was dead then, this One Death. Next they grabbed Seven Death. But they didn't revive them. Thus the Xibalbans took to their heels when they saw that the lords had died. Their hearts were now taken from their chests. Both of them had been torn open as punishment for what they had done. Straightaway the one lord was executed and not revived. The other lord had then begged humbly, weeping before the dancers. He would not accept it, for he had become disoriented:

"Take pity on me," he said in his regret.

Then all of their vassals and servants fled into the great canyon. They packed themselves into the great ravine until they were piled up one on top of the other. Then innumerable ants swarmed into the canyon, as if they had been driven there. And when the ants came, the Xibalbans all bowed themselves down, giving themselves up. They approached begging humbly and weeping. For the lords of Xibalba were defeated. It was just a miracle, for the boys had transformed themselves before them.

And then they declared their names. They revealed their names before all Xibalba.

The Miraculous Maize of Hunahpu and Xbalanque

"Hear our names![123] We shall now declare them. We shall also declare the names of our fathers to you. We are they whose names are Hunahpu and Xbalanque. Our fathers are they who you killed, One Hunahpu and Seven Hunahpu by name. We are the avengers of the misfortune and affliction of our fathers. For this reason, we have endured all the tribulations that you have caused us. Thus we shall now destroy you all. We will kill you, for none among you shall now be saved," they were told.

Then all Xibalba begged humbly, weeping.

"Take pity on us, you, Hunahpu and Xbalanque. Truly we have wronged your fathers that you have named—they who are buried at Crushing Ballcourt," they said.

"Very well. Here then is our word that we declare to you. Hearken all you of Xibalba; for never again will you or your posterity be great. Your offerings also will

123. It was traditional in Mesoamerican societies to declare one's name when a victory has been won in battle or when superiority has been established.

never again be great. They will henceforth be reduced to croton sap.[124] No longer will clean blood be yours.[125] Unto you will be given only worn-out griddles and pots,[126] only flimsy[127] and brittle things.

"You shall surely eat only the creatures of the grass and the creatures of the wastelands. No longer will you be given the children of the light, those begotten in the light. Only things of no importance will fall before you.

"Only the sinner and the malevolent, the wretch and the molester who clearly have sinned, will be given to you. No longer will you be able to seize suddenly just any person.[128] You will be called upon only over the sap of the croton," they were told, all they of Xibalba.

Thus began their devastation, the ruin of their being called upon in worship. Their glory was not great in the past, for they wanted only conflict with the people of ancient times. Surely they were not true gods. Their names merely inspired fear, for their faces were evil. They were strife makers, traitors, and tempters to sin and violence.[129] They were also masters of deception,[130] of the black view and the white view. They were called masters of harm[131] and vexation. Fundamentally their faces were hidden. Thus their greatness and glory were destroyed. Never again would their dominion become great. This was the accomplishment of Hunahpu and Xbalanque.

Now at the same time, the Grandmother was weeping, crying out[132] before the ears of unripe maize that had been left planted. They had sprouted, but then they dried up when they were burned in the pit oven. Then the ears of maize had sprouted once

124. This fulfills the prophecy of Lady Blood, in which she declared that the lords of Xibalba would no longer be allowed to receive human hearts in sacrifice but rather would have to accept the red sap of the croton tree.

125. The ancient Maya offered their own blood to the gods to give them a portion of their life force. This would be fresh, clean blood. Andrés Xiloj commented that the Xibalbans are allowed to collect only blood that has been spilled on the ground (through injury, illness, or violence), thus making it dirty.

126. At the end of each ritual year, broken bits of pottery are left at shrines to symbolize the passing of one age to another. New pots and utensils represent a new beginning and an opportunity for a fresh start in life.

127. The adjective ch'uch' describes something that is soft and flimsy and thus unable to hold its shape.

128. The Quichés believe that the lords of Xibalba have power only over those who have truly committed punishable offenses and have thus submitted themselves to the powers of the underworld.

129. Lab'al is "war, violence, offense." In modern Quiché society it refers to a violent person.

130. Literally "masters of the buried heart."

131. Mox wach is "left face" or "crazy face." In modern usage it may refer to insanity as well as "violence, harm, or mischief."

132. As a goddess of fertility and the seasons, the weeping of Xmucane may have been associated by the Quichés with life-giving rains that helped the dry maize stalks to sprout again.

again, and the Grandmother had burned copal incense[133] before them as a memorial. The heart of their grandmother rejoiced when the maize sprouted a second time.

Thus they were deified by their grandmother. She named it Center House, Center Ancestral Plot, Revitalized Maize, and Leveled Earth.

She named it Center House and Center Harvest for it was in the very center of the interior of their home where they had planted the ears of maize.

She named it Leveled Earth and Revitalized Maize for it was upon level ground that the ears of maize had been planted. She named it Revitalized Maize because the maize had sprouted again. These names were given by Xmucane to what Hunahpu and Xbalanque had left planted. This was a memorial to them by their grandmother.

Now their fathers, One Hunahpu and Seven Hunahpu, had died long ago. They now went, therefore, to see the face of their father there at Xibalba. Their father spoke to them when Xibalba was defeated.

The Apotheosis of the Sun, Moon, and Stars

Here now is the adornment of their father by them, along with the adornment of Seven Hunahpu. For they went to adorn them at Crushing Ballcourt.

They merely wanted his face to be restored. Thus they asked him to name everything—his mouth, his nose, and his eyes. He was able to recover the first name, but then little more was said. He did not say the corresponding names for that which is above the mouth. Still, this had been said, and thus they honored him.

Thus the heart of their father was left behind at Crushing Ballcourt. His sons then said to him:

"Here you will be called upon. It shall be so."

Thus his heart was comforted.

"The child who is born in the light, and the son who is begotten in the light shall go out to you first. They shall worship you first. Your name shall not be forgotten.[134] Thus be it so," they said to their father when they comforted his heart.

"We are merely the avengers of your death and your loss, for the affliction and misfortune that were done to you." Thus was their counsel when they had defeated all Xibalba.

Then they arose as the central lights. They arose straight into the sky. One of them arose as the sun, and the other as the moon. Thus the womb of the sky was illuminated over the face of the earth, for they came to dwell in the sky.

133. Pom (copal incense) is made from the resin of the palo jiote tree. Copal is still burned by the Quichés as an offering to both Christian and traditional Maya deities.

134. Hunahpu is one of the twenty named days of the Quiché calendar. It is dedicated especially to the memory of ancestors. Hunahpu days are the chosen times to visit the graves of relatives and leave offerings of food, drink, flower petals, or incense. The twins are instituting this practice, beginning with the burial place of One Hunahpu himself.

The four hundred boys who had died at the hands of Zipacna also rose up to become their companions. They became a constellation of the sky.

Popol Vuh: The Sacred Book of the Maya. Translated by Allen J. Christenson, 141–77. Norman: University of Oklahoma Press, 2007.

POST-READING PARS

1. Identify two or three poetic elements you noticed in the reading of the *Pop Wuj*.
2. How is the Mayan underworld different from the ones you have encountered in your reading or viewing?
3. What "happens" in Xibalba that is of crucial importance to understand aspects of the Mayan worldview? Where and how do you see the balance between creation and destruction in this episode? Where and how do you see the cycle of birth–death–rebirth represented?

Inquiry Corner

Content Question(s):

Based on the story of Hunahpu and Xbalanque, how does maize represent humanity?

How would you describe Xibalba (the Houses, the dwellers, the environment, the rules)?

Critical Question(s):

How do the twins relate to the first sunrise? What conclusions can you make based on this relational way of being?

Why are the reenactments of the ball game considered to be cathartic and renewal rituals and important empowering ceremonies?

Comparative Question(s):

What other cultural perspectives resemble the Mayan understanding of the connections among the cosmos, land, and body?

Compare and contrast the relationship between the twins and the animals and insects with another source that features humans interacting with the animal world.

Connection Question(s):

Why, in the context of the university, do we give so much weight to writing and books, and less space for nonalphabetic ways of expression? Do you find a relationship between colonization and literacy?

How does your own understanding of death, time, and humanity resonate with the Mayan worldview?

Potlatch (Tlingit)

Introduction

Potlatch,[135] or ***ku.éex'*** (coo-TEE-yuh) in the language of the Tlingit peoples of the Pacific Northwest coast (*Lingít Yoo X̱'atángi*),[136] is a traditional practice/protocol of "giving" or a redistribution of resources. Particular relational and situational contexts important to the community, such as dedications, marriages, restoring or raising social status, and memorials serve as typical moments to convene a potlatch event. It is practiced with variations across several Indigenous communities in the Pacific Northwest and was banned by Canada from 1884–1951 and forbidden in many Northwest communities of the United States and Alaska during this time. The following reading offers a richly embellished account of a *ḵu.éex'* based on the research that Mary Giraudo Beck conducted on a mid-nineteenth-century *ḵu.éex'* hosted by Kaawishté (Kowishte), an important Tlingit historical figure. This was a culminating event of a year-long cycle of mortuary rituals connected to a funeral. Beck's literary re-creation intends to bring to life an example of a much older set of traditions prevalent within the Tlingit culture prior to Christianization and the United States's acquisition of Alaska from the Russian Empire in 1867. What sources might have contributed to this narrativized oral history account? What kinds of issues related to language and perspectives do such historicized re-creations often perpetuate? How might re-creations contribute to or detract from an understanding of Tlingit perspective and culture?

SNAPSHOT BOX

LANGUAGE: English, words from Tlingit language

DATE: Oral history of 19th century

LOCATION: Lingít Aaní (Tlingit Territory), near Wrangell, Alaska (Stikine River)

GENRE: Storytelling

ETHNIC IDENTITY: Tlingit, Pacific Northwest coast

CONTEXTUAL INFORMATION: Composed in 1993 by Mary Giraudo Beck as a historical literary re-creation

TAGS: Authority and Leadership; Class and Wealth; Community/Communal Identity; Death; Empire and Colonialism; Family; Indigeneity; Nature; Oral Histories and Storytelling

The Tlingit people have lived in what is today referred to as Southeast Alaska since time immemorial. Prior to colonial contact, they were the original occupants and guardians of the land, and they cultivated and harvested the rich natural resources of the land with respect, balance, and good stewardship. In fact, it is more common to talk of "relations" than "resources" when describing this rich cultural stewardship of the land. At the same time, the Tlingit traded and interacted with Indigenous cultures spanning a large area from what is today southcentral Alaska to Northern California. In every instance, claims of jurisdiction and **sovereignty** were enacted through robust ceremony and protocol—which is evident in aspects of the story told here. Today, in different forms, such protocol (as an expression of sover-

135. The word "potlatch" is thought to be derived from a word in Chinook Jargon, an important trade language of the Pacific Northwest coast, meaning "to give."

136. For resources on pronunciation, see: http://ankn.uaf.edu/curriculum/tlingit/salmon/dauenhauerarticle.pdf; https://tlingitlanguage.com/resources/beginning-materials/

eignty) and ceremony (as an expression of jurisdiction) continue. What are some of the ceremonies you celebrate in your life?

Like many Indigenous cultures of the Pacific Northwest coast, the imperatives of balance and reciprocity with the land are reflected in the cultural organization of Tlingit culture into two distinct but reciprocal **moieties** (or **"phratries"**): Raven (*Yéil*) and Eagle (Ch'aak'). This social division played a significant role not only in social and ceremonial life but also in everyday life since, in traditional custom, marriage was only allowed between individuals of different moieties. Each moiety was further divided between clans and clan houses. In this selection, prominent clans responsible for staging the ***k̲u.éex'*** include the Frog Clan (***kiks.ádi***) and Dog Salmon Clan (***l'eeneidí***), and their respective houses include "tina hit" (or ***Tináa Hít***, "copper shield house"); "gagan hit" (or ***G̲agaan Hít***, "sun house"); and "til hit" (or ***Téel Hít***, "dog salmon house"). Insofar as the Tlingit people are united in language and customs, clans participate in a complex legal system that includes well-defined property laws so that clans, and not individuals, can maintain collective ownership.

In this selection, we witness a description of a ***k̲u.éex'*** hosted by Kaawishté (Kowishte), a leader of the Chief Shakes Tribal House, located on Shakes Island in the middle of Reliance Harbor near Wrangell, Alaska, also known as the gateway to the Stikine River (***Shtax'héen*** in Tlingit, meaning "bitter river"). This great regional river is mentioned in the opening Raven story in which Raven "sends fish to the streams." Kaawishté ("Chief Kowishte") carried the title of "Shakes" (Tlingit leader) from 1840–1878, longer than any other—and his cultural rank, enacted through cultural protocol discussed below, is well accounted for in this story.

The story of this memorial potlatch ends with Kaawishté (Kowishte) conferring names upon his nephews, each of which is bestowed and accepted with reverence and a sense of responsibility that outlives the individual. In the same way that Kaawishté (Kowishte) carries the title of Chief Shakes V, Tlingit names survive across generations and ancestors. In Tlingit culture, it is not uncommon to hear someone say, "I do not carry my name. My name carries me." Similarly, the ethnographer Georges Emmons observed in 1916, "a name once given (to a clan house) survive(s) the mere structure." What names have you been given and how might they "carry you" beyond or outside of just your own individual life?

A central feature of the ***k̲u.éex'*** told in this story is the display and reverence for sacred ceremonial objects, called ***at.oow*** in Tlingit. ***At.oow*** are the most sacred possessions of a clan, and they can range in kind from the material to the immaterial—including sacred sites and land, songs, crests, regalia, names, and even celestial bodies. In Tlingit culture, everything has a spirit, including ***at.oow***. As we see in this story, the history and ownership of a clan's ***at.oow*** are recounted and validated through protocol and ceremony. After colonial contact, many explorers and early salvage anthropologists would scramble to acquire Tlingit sacred artifacts.

It is important for the reader of this story to bear witness to the numerous enactments of Tlingit protocol and ceremony dramatized here. Protocol is an expression of sovereignty just as ceremony is an expression of jurisdiction. While much of this cultural integrity was attacked through the forces of settler colonialism, Tlingit cultural practices rooted in these political and cultural genealogies have been reinstated and are protected now.

Sol Neely
Heritage University, Yakama Nation Reservation

PRE-READING PARS

1. How can non-Indigenous readers and audiences prepare themselves "to hear" the wisdom of Indigenous oral histories and literatures?
2. What are two most likely mistakes a researcher employing a Western perspective would make while trying to understand Indigenous cultures? In your own education, how have you been taught to understand the histories and futures of Indigenous sovereignty?
3. Identify two protocols, or types of expected behaviors, that would help to facilitate a balanced or reciprocal exchange or interaction between two people.

Potlatch

Raven Sends Fish to the Streams

One day Raven came to a place where he could see a house floating far out at sea, where Nascakiyel had put it for safekeeping. Raven knew this house was full of all kinds of fishes, but he did not know how to get at them. While puzzling over his dilemma, he saw a monster with a spear like the arm of a devilfish. Raven was fascinated by this weapon and agreed to marry the monster's daughter in order to obtain it.

Taking his new weapon with him, Raven paddled his canoe out to the house and sent his spear through it. He could hear all kinds of songs sung by different voices coming from the house, songs people now sing during the fishing season. When Raven threw his spear, it became very long and wrapped itself around the house so firmly that he could pull it toward his canoe. But he had to keep singing, "I think so! I think so!" a song known to all Raven people. Whenever he let up, the house would move back to the original place.

Three times it went back, but the fourth time Raven was able to pull it in far enough to beach his canoe. The door of the house opened and out came various kinds of fishes. Raven sang out to them, "Some of you go to Stikine River. Some of you go to Chilkat River," and the fishes did as he commanded. Then he sang, "Some go to the small creeks to feed the poor people." That is how fish came to the rivers and streams.

The Potlatch

After the four days of feasting and entertainment, the time came for the serious memorial potlatch celebration at the house built for this ceremony, when host groups mourned the deceased chief and all their dead.

The nakani ushered guests and hosts to their assigned seats, making every effort to avoid conflict among guests, treating all with equal solemnity. The nakani sat both chiefs side by side. First came the Frog clan chief Qoxkan of Tina Hit with regal stride and solemn bearing, his head high and eyes straight ahead. With equal courtesy and decorum the nakani escorted Dog Salmon chief, Tanaxh of Til Hit, to his place next to the Frog clan chief. Then members of these houses were led to the seats that their rank required.

The next-ranking Frog clan chief, Qalaktc of the local Gagan Hit, was then seated on the other side of Chief Qoxkan, and his house members after him. The remaining guest chiefs and their houses were seated with the same careful attention to rank and lineage. Finally the remaining house groups of the local village, led by their chiefs, were seated with their Raven or Eagle phratries.

Kowishte, the host chief, stood at the door, flanked on each side by nakani. Kitlen stood directly behind him, ready to prompt him with a suitable reply to a guest chief so that no insult would be inferred from the chief's answer. Kitlen had exceptional understanding of protocol and the quick-thinking; diplomatic ease necessary for this sensitive position. The rest of the Grizzly Bear men stood behind these dignitaries at the front of the house. As before, the nakani remained watchful; even in the midst of celebration, the intense competition among houses and clans could lead to hostile behavior that, becoming violent, could result in war.

The hosts, whose heritage was being celebrated in the telling of their stories, wore their most elaborate costumes. The Eagle, Grizzly Bear, and Killer Whale crests appeared in various forms on blankets and hats of the house chiefs. On display along the wall behind the guests were the many possessions of the clan: a Chilkat blanket; several button blankets depicting the crest Eagle, Grizzly Bear, Dogfish, Shark, and Killer Whale; and a large carving of the serpent-like sea monster Gonakadet. The house posts depicted the shark. Displayed in the center of the room was the preserved bearskin and head, a replica of the clan crest Bear. An antlered headdress representing the Deer of the Peace Dance ceremonies stood next to the famed Killer Whale drum acquired along with the crest, story, staff, Kit (Killer Whale) Canoe, and other related properties acquired in settlement of a war with the Tsimshian Blackfish clan.

Against the wall stood the Killer Whale staff, symbol of the authority of the head Grizzly Bear chief. Woven hats and baskets and carved hats and food dishes lay among carved animal masks and killer whale figures. Large bentwood boxes, coppers, and carved paddles lined the walls. Galge, the chief's nephew, sat in ritual garb in the honored position among all these luxury items that attested to his family and clan wealth.

The display of wealth and the songs and dances accompanying it offered the people opportunity to affirm rights that went with these things—the rights acquired by dead ancestors by purchase or gift to stories, songs, dances, and crests as well as streams, hunting grounds, and berry patches, and sometimes even rights to the house itself. The chief would reaffirm these rights in his speeches after each of the ritual songs.

The guests wore ordinary clothes, the men in long buckskin shirts and trousers and the women in buckskin shirts, long skirts, and cloaks of woven soft cedar bark or animal fur. The children wore long buckskin shirts, some with cedar-bark cloaks over them. Some of the adults and children wore cedar-bark hats, and everyone wore moccasins. The guests would not put on their ceremonial garments until their turn came to entertain the hosts at the feasts after the distribution of gifts. Then they would appear in splendid fur-trimmed headgear, beaded moccasins, and blankets emblazoned with beaded and button-worked clan crests. A few would carry beaded octopus bags—skin purses with long beaded tendrils hanging from the bottom.

When all were seated, a shrill cry of an eagle went up to announce the arrival of the Grizzly Bear head chief. The crowd fell silent as Chief Kowishte appeared before them in his ermine headdress with the carved Eagle frontlet and his Chilkat blanket woven with the Killer Whale crest. He now carried the sacred Killer Whale staff, symbol of his authority and might.

"To the warmest place under my wings I welcome you." Stretching out his arms, Kowishte repeated to the assembled company the welcome he had given earlier to the Frog people.

"To the warmest place under my feathers I welcome you." This time, the occasion was more solemn. He spoke of his sorrow and recounted the reasons for the potlatch.

"Last year my uncle, head chief of the Grizzly Bear clan, died. After his death we mourned him for many days. Then we burned his body. Many of you were here for the funeral ceremony performed by the Frog people. Then the Dog Salmon people were called upon to carve my uncle's mortuary pole and to build this house for the anniversary potlatch. The bones of the deceased chief, gathered after the cremation and stored in the grave house, have just been placed in the newly raised mortuary pole by the Dog Salmon nakani. We are gathered today to honor the anniversary of this great chief's death."

Chief Kowishte stood awhile as if in meditation. Then he intoned the first of the eight ritual mourning songs, relating ancestral history and the arrival of the clan at the present location.

...

Hīn yîx "gwasā'x îkAnē'k Axkā'k

The noise of your death, my uncle, will come down through the river.

NādadA'x gAdjîxā'n nādāgawu.'

From the nation has fallen down the nation's drum.

...

Phrases of these verses were repeated over and over as the dancers swayed to the rhythm of the song. At a signal from the song-leader, the entire host group joined in the singing. All present united in remembering the dead and weeping for them.

The deep tones of a large box-shaped drum, its sides formed by a single bent plank of cedar sewn together at the side with sinew and painted with a killer whale in red and black, marked a mournful rhythm to the songs. On its top was carved a large dorsal fin inlaid with opercula and eight tufts of hair. On each side of the fin was carved a human figure seated on a human head, memorializing Natasee, the hero who had aided a killer whale stuck on a rock and who later, similarly marooned, was then rescued by a killer whale. The drummer had his hand thrust through an opening in the back of the drum, which he beat from the inside to produce its deep, vibrating tones.

When the song ended, Chief Kowishte came forward to address the crowd. He began with the ritual recounting of the history of the Grizzly Bear clan, which the people had heard many times before and knew by heart.

"We came originally from the south, but more recently from the Taku. A family dispute caused us to move from the Taku, and we stopped first on an island at the mouth of the Stikine. But storms forced us to move to the mainland near the river. There the Grizzly Bear people thrived under the two brothers, Koxcu and Shaddesty, until Koxcu's son insulted his uncle Shaddesty by cutting his face in an argument. In reparation to his brother, Koxcu offered twenty slaves, but Shaddesty demanded instead the Grizzly Bear dancing hat. Koxcu refused to give it up, but to keep peace, he went with his family, slaves, and all his possessions in search of a new home. After considering various sites, Koxcu spied a cluster of trees that reminded him of their old home, and the clan settled at that place, our present home. They called it Kotslitan, our name for the poplar trees that were cut down to build the houses.

"When Koxcu died, his sister's son became Grizzly Bear chief. During this time we won the right to the Killer Whale crest from the Blackfish people." The chief held forward his staff surmounted with a carved killer whale.

"The former owners of the Killer Whale crest and all the property that went with it, people with whom we had traded oil for animal skins, started the war by taking the head of Koxcu, preserved in honor in a magnificent carved box, to demand ransom for it."

Chief Kowishte, who had controlled himself thus far, began to weep at the memory of this humiliation and grief. Then he intoned another mourning song:

...

Help me with your believing, Grizzly Bear children. It is as if my grandfathers' house were turning over with me. Where is the person who will save me?

...

When the song was finished, Kowishte went on with the story of the conflict.

"Unable to tolerate this abominable insult, the Grizzly Bear people set upon the Blackfish men when they returned the next spring to trade and took several of them captive. Then our great shaman told us to prepare for war. So the following spring when the Blackfish came to rescue their people we were prepared and defeated them easily, capturing their prized Kit Canoe. To make peace the following year, our conquered enemy gave us the right to the canoe as well as the Killer Whale crest and story."

The chief then began the story of the master carver and hunter Natsilane and the Killer Whale.

...

Natsilane was supreme in his craft of spear-making. He fit each spear for length and weight to the man who ordered it. He used the same care in everything he did. But Natsilane, by his skill and zeal to please his wife's family, instead only antagonized his wife's brothers. On sea lion hunts, Natsilane always leaped first onto the rocks, so that when his brothers-in-law arrived, all the animals he had failed to kill had escaped into the water. Soon Natsilane's reputation as a hunter began to overshadow theirs. Envious, they plotted to get rid of him.

On their next seal-hunting trip Natsilane was again the first to leap ashore. But the brothers-in-law paddled away, leaving him there to die. Only the youngest boy cried out for them to go back.

When Natsilane realized he had been left without food and clothing, he tried to spear a sea lion, but his spearhead broke off inside it. Tired and hungry, Natsilane fell asleep. He was awakened by a man, who led him to a den of sea lions beneath the rock. There he was able to save the son of the sea lion chief from death by removing his own spearhead from the animal's side. As a reward, the sea lion chief sent Natsilane home in an inflated sealskin bladder.

"Keep your thought on your home," the chief told him, and Natsilane did so, eventually arriving at a beach a few miles from his village. In secret he gathered his carving tools and returned to the beach, where he set about carving a blackfish or killer whale. His first attempt was in spruce, but when he tested it in the chain of four ponds he had made, the blackfish floated long enough to jump from the first pond to the second but then sank. A second blackfish of hemlock made it to the third pool, and a third, of red cedar, got to the fourth pond. Only the yellow-cedar blackfish jumped from pond to pond and then into the sea.

Natsilane called the blackfish to him and instructed it to find his brothers-in-law and drown them by destroying their canoe, but to save the youngest boy whom he had heard begging them to return to the rock. When this was done, Natsilane commanded the blackfish to do only good to humans in the future, making it an omen of good luck.

...

"That is why the Killer Whale is carved on the Grizzly Bear staff, the symbol of Grizzly Bear authority," Chief Kowishte concluded. "And that is why we have the Kit or Killer Whale canoe and use this crest for our hats and blankets and ceremonial garments."

"But older than the Killer Whale crest is the Grizzly Bear, our main crest, acquired at the time of the Flood." Then he began to relate the sacred Grizzly Bear story.

...

At the time of the flood the people saw the waters rising higher and higher until it covered the whole beach. They left their possessions and ran deeper into the woods to reach higher ground and escape the water rushing toward them. Soon they reached the base of a mountain.

"We will have to climb the mountain. The water keeps rising and will soon cover this ground," the chief said. He looked for a cleared place to go through the woods. As they went through the undergrowth, they came upon a bear.

Their first reaction was to pull away and start back toward the beach. Then they realized that the bear was also headed up the mountain. It seemed that he motioned to them to follow and called to them.

"Do not be afraid," they heard him say. "I have come to save you."

So they formed a line behind him. The bear knew the swiftest, most direct way to spiral up the mountain. As he plunged ahead of the people, his weight matted down the brush and made the walking faster and easier for them.

The grizzly bear stayed with the people for some time, and they were very grateful to him for saving them. But soon they were in need of food, for there was almost nothing edible on the mountain peak. So they were forced to sacrifice the bear to save themselves from starving. They used the meat sparingly so that it would last until the waters subsided. They had taken great care in skinning the bear and were able to preserve the hide with the claws and teeth and skull intact for many years after the flood. When the original hide wore out, they replaced it with the hide of another bear and continued to do so until the present.

...

"Because it had led them to safety and then sacrificed its life to feed them, the grizzly bear is highly respected by the Grizzly Bear people and became our main crest animal," Kowishte concluded. The chief finished by chanting the song of the legendary Grizzly Bear, which began: "Come here, you Bear, highest of all bears."

When Kowishte had finished his eight mourning songs interspersed with stories of lineage and status, he called on his nephew Galge to sing a song honoring one of his ancestors. These memorial songs were very solemn, often commemorating the mishaps and deaths that ensued as their ancestors carved out the clan history.

The Grizzly Bear chief's nephew seemed to grow in dignity and stature as he came forward in his Chilkat blanket with its all-over pattern of killer whales and his ermine headband with eagle frontlet. He began to sing a mourning song for a Frog clan bride:

...

This Eagle has taken his Raven bride to a good sandy beach. It is enough to make one cry. A Raven, however, always comes to amuse her.

...

As Galge repeated these verses over and over he took several small steps first to the right and then to the left, turning each way slightly. Grizzly Bear women swayed, moving their feet in place to the rhythm.

After Galge's song, Chief Kowishte then invited each member of the Grizzly Bear clan to sing and give a speech, introducing each by his potlatch name, his name of honor. These songs and accompanying dances were done to exhibit a crest or heirloom acquired in a particular way.

Once the singer had started the song, the rest of the clan joined in. Some were mourning songs composed for the dying or the dead in the legendary past or at least a generation ago. The words were sorrowful, and the tunes solemn with heavy, slow rhythms. Each told the story of what had happened to the singer's lost relatives and mentioned each of their names.

"It is not Raven's town I am crying about," one of the singers mourned. "It is my own grandfather's town I am crying about. Poor Dorsal-Fin-of-the-Killer-Whale-Seen will die before he reaches it."

"This is the song the Grizzly Bear Gucdutin sang when he was caught in a storm going to visit his Raven in-laws," the singer explained. "Gucdutin thought he was drowning and would not see his wife's relatives."

Singing a mourning song also required that much wealth be given away. One Grizzly Bear house chief, who had donated many large baskets and boxes to the potlatch gifts, sang a mourning song for his brother who had died in a hunting accident. All members of the host clan stood and swayed back and forth as they sang in harmony. "My little brother, where are you? Come back to me!" they sang over and over, varying the order of words a little and stressing various syllables.

As well as mourning, some songs related incidents from clan legends, often those concerned with the acquisition of a crest. Their words were not necessarily mournful, but the tunes and rhythms were somber. Most were accompanied by tambourine-type drums with deerskin heads. Some had crests painted inside the drumhead, where they would not be worn off from being beaten.

While the Grizzly Bears sang their clan songs, the host women danced. They wore doth headbands with feathers inserted and long beaded earrings, and their faces were painted with designs of the clan crest. One woman had a stripe of red the width of her eye painted from the hairline down to the mouth and then across the lips and chin, depicting the upright bar of the killer whale's dorsal fin. Another had a narrower red stripe from hairline to chin passing over each eye, illustrating the vapor jet of the blowing killer whale.

Over their long skirts most of the women wore blankets of blue serge with red borders, and button designs of a killer whale or grizzly displayed on the backs. A few women of higher caste wore Chilkat blankets. When the floor was crowded, they danced only with their arms and body, not moving their feet.

Nobody left the potlatch while the songs were being sung. After the singing had gone on for many hours, the Frog clan chief Qoxkan addressed Kowishte.

"Would the Eagle chief step out of the way?" This was an acceptable way of asking for a recess.

The host chief Kowishte did not move, continuing instead to watch the activity. Recognizing this behavior as part of the protocol, Chief Qoxkan remained unruffled and did not repeat the request. A little later the host chief looked in the Frog chief's direction.

"I'll move out of your way," Kowishte said. Then everybody rose and went outside for half an hour.

On their return, the singing of memorial songs continued until all who wanted to commemorate their dead had sung. Kowishte then came forward to announce the names of honor he was bestowing on his grandchildren and nephews. But first Kitlen, the ranking member of the council of his brothers and sisters, came forward to address the Grizzly Bear host chief.

"You, my nephew, are now officially named head chief of the Grizzly Bear clan," Kitlen said. "After our honored chief's funeral ceremony, the council met to choose the nephew most worthy to succeed him. For your knowledge of clan traditions and devotion to clan customs, for your steadfast character and sense of what is right, and for your strength of body and will, you were chosen. Now that the anniversary potlatch has been given, you inherit the name acquired from the Blackfish people in battle and passed on through many Grizzly Bear chiefs."

At a signal from the song leader, the Grizzly Bear people broke out in song.

When the singing finished, Chief Kowishte spoke. "For this honor I thank all of you," he said. "I know what great responsibility this honor brings. To prepare for receiving it, I fasted many days before this potlatch. With the help of the Eagle, Grizzly, and Killer Whale spirits, I shall use all my strength and will to do what is best for the clan."

After the ceremony honoring him, the head chief called his nephews to him. The first to receive an honor name was Galge.

"On you, Galge, a most deserving nephew, I confer the name of Caxna, held by many ancestral Grizzly Bear chiefs." He then related some of the past leaders' achievements.

"Most honored Chief, I accept this revered name and the responsibility that goes with it," the subdued Galge replied. "I shall try to prove worthy of this honor."

One by one, Kowishte called other nephews to come forward to receive honor names. On two of Galge's companions he conferred the names of former chiefs Skillat and Shustaks. Then it was time to present the gifts.

Beck, Mary Giraudo. "The Potlatch." In *Potlatch: Native Ceremony and Myth on the Northwest Coast*, 62–75. Anchorage: Alaska Northwest Books, 1993.

POST-READING PARS

1. What aspects of this story require more research on your part? How might you conduct this research in ways that serve Indigenous justice?
2. Research the history and meaning of the word "potlatch." Why is this term so problematic in anthropology, and why is it more culturally responsible to preserve the Tlingit term *ku.éex'*?
3. Are there insights in this story about Indigenous sovereignty, related to matters of protocol and ceremony, that become meaningful to you in your own place as you encounter Indigenous stories and cultures rooted in place?
4. Identify two or three passages in this narrative in which balance and reciprocal exchange are enacted through protocol.

from *Behistûn Inscription*

> **SNAPSHOT BOX**
>
> LANGUAGE: Old Persian, Elamite, and Babylonian
>
> DATE: c. 522–486 BCE
>
> LOCATION: Behistûn Mountain, Iran
>
> GENRE: History
>
> ETHNIC IDENTITY: Persian
>
> TAGS: Authority and Leadership; Conflict and War; Empire and Colonialism; Monument and Artifact; Rhetoric and Propaganda

Introduction

Darius I, also known as Darius the Great (522–486 BCE), monumentalized his ascension to the throne on a massive limestone cliff called *Bagastâna*, "seat of the gods," which we now know by the Anglicized forms "Behistûn" or "Bisotun." The Achaemenid Empire of Persia expanded in the fifth century BCE under Darius's leadership. He extended Persian rule westward to Greece, eastward to the Indus Valley, and north to the Black Sea. Along a well-traveled road through the Zagros Mountains in the Kermanshah Province, which separates Persia from Mesopotamia, Darius had reliefs and inscriptions carved in the three languages most relevant to the cliff's location: Old Persian for his own people, Elamite, spoken in the area where the cliff is located, and Old Babylonian for the travelers from Mesopotamia. There was originally a ledge along the Zagros mountain cliff for the workers who did the carving, but this was removed after the inscription was finally completed so that no further changes could be made. What do you think rulers are attempting to achieve through inscriptions on stone monuments?

In 1827, Henry Rawlinson, an English army officer with the British East India Company was sent to help the Shah of Persia (known as Iran since 1935) modernize and train his troops. Rawlinson was seventeen at the time and had already learned the modern Persian language. He was stationed in Kermanshah Province in the 1830s, when he decided to scale the mountain and make a copy of

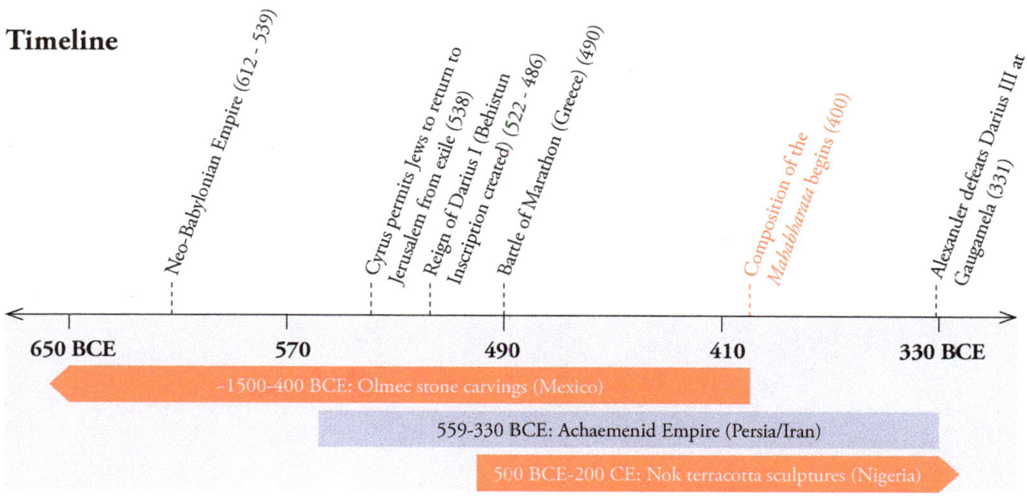

the great inscription carved there, starting with the Old Persian section (414 lines of text in five columns), which was the most accessible. Hanging precariously on ladders three hundred feet up a sheer cliff, he completed the Old Persian transcription in two years and returned later to complete the Elamite and Old Babylonian sections. Rawlinson's translation was the first in English.

The nineteenth century in Europe was a time of great interest in the languages of the East, such as Sanskrit, as well as Egyptian hieroglyphs, which were deciphered after the discovery of the trilingual Rosetta Stone in 1799. The trilingual Persian inscription served a similar role in the decipherment of Elamite and Old Babylonian, giving rise to the field of **Assyriology** (the study of ancient Southwest Asia that includes Syria and Mesopotamia) and enabling scholars to read the cuneiform texts of the *Epic of Gilgamesh*. The content of the inscription may be roughly divided into four sections: a short account of Darius's Achaemenid ancestry and a list of his conquests; a detailed account of the battles he fought and rebellions he put down to gain the Persian throne after the deaths of Cyrus the Great and his son Cambyses II; a recap of his conquests with an affirmation of its truth along with a litany of blessings and curses; and, finally, a short account of two new wars (an Elamite rebellion and war with the Scythians). The fourth column ends with a statement that the text of the inscription was also written on clay tablets and on parchment and was distributed throughout the Persian Empire. Although the many names of rulers and countries that Darius catalogues in the inscription are difficult for us to understand and appreciate today, they would have been as familiar to their ancient audience as a roll call of the fifty states would be for modern Americans. What kinds of responses to Darius' statements might different viewers from different parts of the empire have had?

The inscription surrounds a large central panel carved in relief. The top portion features a *faravahar*, a winged sun-disc with a central king figure that is believed to represent the **Zoroastrian** (ancient Persian religion revealed to the prophet Zoroaster) supreme deity Ahuramazda ("Wise Lord"). Below that is a montage of Darius and his court receiving the homage of conquered peoples, which borrows imagery from earlier Persian and Assyrian reliefs. The figure of Darius is larger than those who surround him. Behind him are his two most trusted men, his bow carrier Intaphrenes and his spear carrier Gobryas. Darius's right hand is raised in a gesture of authority. He holds his bow in his left hand and his left foot rests atop the body of his main rival Gaumata, while nine others, bound with a rope, stand in line before him. Short inscriptions above each man identifies him by name as a "lying king." What is Darius asserting through this visual imagery and why might he accuse his enemies of lying?

Lora Holland Goldthwaite
Department of Classics

PRE-READING PARS

1. What inscribed texts have we encountered in this course?
2. Brainstorm a few ideas about the historical differences between a king and a president. What leadership qualities work best for each?
3. Briefly describe two ways in which history is distinct from propaganda.

from Behistûn Inscription

Column 1

[1.1] I (am) Darius, the great king, the king of kings, the king in Persia, the king of countries, the son of Hystaspes, the grandson of Arsames, the Achaemenide.

[1.2] Says Darius the king: My father (is) Hystaspes, the father of Hystaspes (is) Arsames, the father of Arsames (is) Ariaramnes, the father of Ariaramnes (is Teispes), the father of Teispes (is) Achaemenes.

[1.3] Says Darius the king: Therefore we are called the Achaemenides; from long ago we have extended; from long ago our family have been kings.

[1.4] Says Darius the king: 8 of my family (there were) who were formerly kings; I am the ninth (9); long aforetime we were (lit. are) kings.

[1.5] Says Darius the king: By the grace of Ahuramazda I am king; Ahuramazda gave me the kingdom.

[1.6] Says Darius the king: These are the countries which came to me; by the grace of Ahuramazda I became king of them; Persia, Susiana, Babylonia, Assyria, Arabia, Egypt, the (lands) which are on the sea, Sparda, Ionia, [Media], Armenia, Cappadocia, Parthia, Drangiana, Aria, Chorasmia, Bactria, Sogdiana, Ga(n)dara, Scythia, Sattagydia, Arachosia, Maka; in all (there are) 23 countries.

[1.7] Says Darius the king: These (are) the countries which came to me; by the grace of Ahuramazda they became subject to me; they bore tribute to me; what was commanded to them by me this was done night and (lit. or) day.

[1.8] Says Darius the king: Within these countries what man was watchful, him who should be well esteemed I esteemed; who was an enemy, him who should be well punished I punished; by the grace of Ahuramazda these countries respected my laws; as it was commanded by me to them, so it was done.

[1.9] Says Darius the king: Ahuramazda gave me this kingdom; Ahuramazda bore me aid until I obtained this kingdom; by the grace of Ahuramazda I hold this kingdom.

[1.10] Says Darius the king: This (is) what (was) done by me after that I became king; Cambyses by name, the son of Cyrus (was) of our family; he was king here; of this Cambyses there was a brother Bardiya (i.e. Smerdis) by name possessing a common mother and the same father with Cambyses; afterwards Cambyses slew that

Bardiya; when Cambyses slew Bardiya, it was not known to the people that Bardiya was slain; afterwards Cambyses went to Egypt; when Cambyses went to Egypt, after that the people became hostile; after that there was Deceit to a great extent in the provinces, both in Persia and in Media and in the other provinces.

[1.11] Says Darius the king: Afterwards there was one man, a Magian, Gaumata by name; he rose up from Paishiyauvada; there (is) a mountain Arakadrish by name; from there - 14 days in the month Viyakhna were in course when he rose up; he thus deceived the people; I am Bardiya the son of Cyrus brother of Cambyses; afterwards all the people became estranged from Cambyses (and) went over to him, both Persia and Media and the other provinces; he seized the kingdom; 9 days in the month Garmapada were in course - he thus seized the kingdom; afterwards Cambyses died by a self-imposed death.

[1.12] Says Darius the king: This kingdom which Gaumata the Magian took from Cambyses, this kingdom from long ago was (the possession) of our family; afterwards Gaumata the Magian took from Cambyses both Persia and Media and the other provinces; he seized (the power) and made it his own possession; he became king.

[1.13] Says Darius the king: There was not a man neither a Persian nor a Median nor any one of our family who could make Gaumata the Magian deprived of the kingdom; the people feared his tyranny; (they feared) he would slay the many who knew Bardiya formerly; for this reason he would slay the people; "that they might not know me that I am not Bardiya the son of Cyrus"; any one did not dare to say anything against Gaumata the Magian until I came; afterwards I asked Ahuramazda for help; Ahuramazda bore me aid; 10 days in the month Bagayadish were in course I thus with few men slew that Gaumata the Magian and what men were his foremost allies; there (is) a stronghold Sikayauvatish by name; there is a province in Media, Nisaya by name; here I smote him; I took the kingdom from him; by the grace of Ahuramazda I became king; Ahuramazda gave me the kingdom.

[1.14] Says Darius the king: The kingdom which was taken away from our family, this I put in (its) place; I established it on (its) foundation; as (it was) formerly so I made it; the sanctuaries which Gaumata the Magian destroyed I restored; for the people the revenue(?) and the personal property and the estates and the royal residences which Gaumata the Magian took from them (I restored); I established the state on (its) foundation, both Persia and Media and the other provinces; as (it was) formerly, so I brought back what (had been) taken away; by the grace of Ahuramazda this I did; I labored that our royal house I might establish in (its) place; as (it was) formerly, so (I made it); I labored by the grace of Ahuramazda that Gaumata the Magian might not take away our royal house.

[1.15] Says Darius the king: This (is) what I did, after that I became king.

[1.16] Says Darius the king: When I slew Gaumata the Magian, afterwards there (was) one man Atrina by name, the son of Upadara(n)ma; he rose up in Susiana; thus he said to the people; I am king in Susiana; afterwards the people of Susiana became rebellious (and) went over to that Atrina; he became king in Susiana; and there (was) one man a Babylonian Nidintu-Bel by name, the son of Aniri,' he rose up in Babylon; thus he deceived the people; I am Nebuchadrezzar the son of Nabu-na'id; afterwards the whole of the Babylonian state went over to that Nidintu-Bel; Babylon became rebellious; the kingdom in Babylon he seized.

[1.17] Says Darius the king: Afterwards I sent forth (my army) to Susiana; this Atrina was led to me bound; I slew him.

[1.18] Says Darius the king: Afterwards I went to Babylon against that Nidintu-Bel who called himself Nebuchadrezzar; the army of Nidintu-Bel held the Tigris; there he halted and thereby was a flotilla; afterwards I placed my army on floats of skins; one part I set on camels, for the other I brought horses; Ahuramazda bore me aid; by the grace of Ahuramazdawe crossed the Tigris; there the army of Nidintu-Bel I smote utterly; 26 days in the month Atriyadiya were in course - we thus engaged in battle.

[1.19] Says Darius the king: Afterwards I went to Babylon; when I had not reached Babylon - there (is) a town Zazana by name along the Euphrates - there this Nidintu-Bel who called himself Nebuchadrezzar went with his army against me to engage in battle; afterwards we engaged in battle; Ahuramazda bore me aid; by the grace of Ahuramazda the army of Nidintu-Bel I smote utterly; the enemy were driven into the water; the water bore them away; 2 days in the month Anamaka were in course - we thus engaged in battle.

Column 2

[2.1] Says Darius the king: Afterwards Nidintu-Bel with (his) few horsemen went to Babylon; afterwards I went to Babylon; by the grace of Ahuramazda I both seized Babylon and seized that Nidintu-Bel; afterwards I slew that Nidintu-Bel at Babylon.

[2.2] Says Darius the king: While I was in Babylon, these (are) the provinces which became estranged from me, Persia, Susiana, Media, Assyria [Egypt], Parthia, Margiana, Sattagydia, Scythia.

[2.3] Says Darius the king: There (was) one man Martiya by name, the son of Cicikhrish - there (is) a town in Persia Kuganaka by name - here he dwelt; he rose up in Susiana; thus he said to the people; I am Imanish king in Susiana.

[2.4] Says Darius the king: Then I was on the march to Susiana; afterwards the Susians [feared] me; they seized that Martiya who was chief of them and slew him.

[2.5] Says Darius the king: One man Phraortes [by name, a Mede], he rose up in Media; thus he said to the people; [I am Khshathrita] of the family of Cyaxares; afterwards the Median people which [were in the palace] became estranged from me (and) went over to that Phraortes; he became [king] in Media.

[2.6] Says Darius the king: The Persian and the Median army, which was by me, it was small; afterwards I sent forth an army; Hydarnes by name, a Persian, my subject, him I made chief of them; thus I said to them; go, smite that Median army which does not call itself mine; afterwards this Hydarnes with the army went away; when he came to Media - there (is) a town in Media Marush by name - here he engaged in battle with the Medes; he who was the chief among the Medes did not there [withstand]; Ahuramazda bore me aid; by the grace of Ahuramazda my army smote that rebellious army utterly; 27 days in the month Anamaka were in course - the battle (was) thus fought by them; afterwards my army - there (is) a region Ka(m)pada by name - there awaited me until I went to Media.

[2.7] Says Darius the king: Dadarshish by name, an Armenian, my subject, him I sent forth to Armenia; thus I said to him; go, the rebellious army which does not call itself mine, smite it; afterwards Dadarshish went away; when he came to Armenia, afterwards the rebels came together (and) went against Dadarshish to engage in battle; there is a village [Zuzza] by name in Armenia - here they engaged in battle; Ahuramazda bore me aid; by the grace of Ahuramazda my army smote that rebellious army utterly; 8 days in the month Thuravahara were in course - thus the battle (was) fought by them.

[2.8] Says Darius the king: A second time the rebels came together (and) went against Dadarshish to engage in battle; there (is) a stronghold, Tigra by name, in Armenia - here they engaged in battle; Ahuramazda bore me aid; by the grace of Ahuramazda, my army smote that rebellious army utterly; 18 days in the month Thuravahara were in course - the battle (was) thus fought by them.

[2.9] Says Darius the king: A third time the rebels came together (and) went against Dadarshish to engage in battle; there (is) a stronghold, U[yam]a by name, in Armenia - here they engaged in battle; Ahuramazda bore me aid; by the grace of Ahuramazda my army smote that rebellious army utterly; 9 days in the month Thaigarcish were in course - thus the battle (was) fought by them; afterwards Dadarshish awaited me in Armenia until I came to Media.

[2.10] Says Darius the king: Afterwards Vaumisa by name, a Persian, my subject, him I sent forth to Armenia; thus I said to him; go, the rebellious army which does not call itself mine, smite it; afterwards Vaumisa went away; when he came to Armenia, afterwards the rebels came together (and) went against Vaumisa to engage in battle; there (is) a region I[zar]a by name, in Assyria - here they engaged in battle; Ahuramazda bore me aid; by the grace of Ahuramazda my army smote that rebellious army utterly; 15 days in the month Anamaka were in course - thus the battle (was) fought by them.

[2.11] Says Darius the king: A second time the rebels came together (and) went against Vaumisa to engage in battle; there (is) a region Autiyara by name in Armenia - here they engaged in battle; Ahuramazda bore me aid; by the grace of Ahuramazda my army smote that rebellious army utterly; at the end of the month Thuravahara - thus the battle (was) fought by them; afterwards Vaumisa awaited me in Armenia until I came to Media.

[2.12] Says Darius the king: Afterwards I went from Babylon; I went away to Media; when I went to Media - there (is) a town Ku(n)durush by name in Media - here this Phraortes who called himself king in Media went with (his) army against me to engage in battle; afterwards we engaged in battle; Ahuramazda bore me aid; by the grace of Ahuramazda I smote the army of Phraortes utterly; 25 days in the month Adukanisha were in course - we thus engaged in battle.

[2.13] Says Darius the king: Afterwards this Phraortes with a few horsemen fled; there is a region Raga by name in Media - along there he went; afterwards I sent forth my army in pursuit; Phraortes was seized (and) led to me; I cut off (his) nose and ears and tongue, and I put out his eyes; he was held bound at my court; all the people saw him; afterwards I put him on a cross at Ecbatana, and what men were his foremost allies, these I threw within a prison at Ecbatana.

[2.14] Says Darius the king: One man, Citra(n)takhma by name, a Sagartian, he became rebellious to me; thus he said to the people; I am king in Sagartia, of the family of Cyaxares; afterwards I sent forth the Persian and the Median army; Takhmaspada by name, a Mede, my subject, him I made chief of them, thus I said to them; go, the rebellious army, which does not call itself mine, smite it; afterwards Takhmaspada went away with the army (and) engaged in battle with Citra(n)takhma; Ahuramaz-dabore me aid; by the grace of Ahuramazda my army smote that rebellious army utterly and seized Citra(n)takhma (and) brought (him) to me; afterwards I cut off his nose and ears, and put out his eyes; he was held bound at my court; all the people saw him; afterwards I put him on a cross in Arbela.

[2.15] Says Darius the king: This (is) what (was) done by me in Media.

[2.16] Says Darius the king: Parthia and Hyrcania became rebellious to me and declared allegiance to Phraortes; my father Hystaspes, he was [in Parthia]; the people abandoned him (and) became rebellious; afterwards Hystaspes [went with his army] which was loyal; there is a town Vish[pa]uz[a]tish by name [in Parthia] - here he engaged in battle with the Parthians; Ahuramazda [bore] me [aid]; by the grace of Ahuramazda Hystaspes smote that rebellious army utterly; [22 days] in the month Viyakhna were in course - thus the battle was fought by them.

Column 3

[3.1] Says Darius the king: Afterwards I sent forth the Persian army to Hystaspes from Raga; when this army came to Hystaspes afterwards Hystaspes took that army (and) went away; there (is) a town Patigrabana by name in Parthia - here he engaged in battle with the rebels; Ahuramazda bore me aid; by the grace of Ahuramazda Hystaspes smote that rebellious army utterly; 1 day in the month Garmapada was in course - thus the battle (was) fought by them.

[3.2] Says Darius the king: Afterwards it became my province; this (is) what (was) done by me in Parthia.

[3.3] Says Darius the king: There (is) a region Margiana by name; it became rebel-lious to me; one man Frada, a Margian, him they made chief; afterwards I sent forth Dadarshish by name, a Persian, my subject, satrap in Bactria against him; thus I said to him; go, smite that army which does not call itself mine; afterwards Dadarshish with the army went away (and) engaged in battle with the Margians; Ahuramazda bore me aid; by the grace of Ahuramazda my army smote that rebellious army utterly; 23 days in the month Atriyadiya were in course - thus the battle {was) fought by them.

[3.4] Says Darius the king: Afterwards it became my province; this (is) what (was) done by me in Bactria.

[3.5] Says Darius the king: One man Vahyazdata by name; there (is) a town Tarava by name; there (is) a region Yutiya by name in Persia - here he dwelt; he was the second to rise against me in Persia; thus he said to the people; I am Bardiya the son of Cyrus; afterwards the Persian army which (was) in the palace cast aside their loyalty; they became estranged from me (and) went over to that Vahyazdata; he became king in Persia.

[3.6] Says Darius the king: Afterwards I sent forth the Persian and the Median army which was by me; Artavardiya by name, a Persian, my subject, him I made chief of them; the rest of the Persian army went with me to Media; afterwards Artavardiya with the army went to Persia; when he came to Persia - there (is) a town Rakha by name in Persia - here this Vahyazdata who called himself Bardiya went with (his) army against Artavardiya; afterwards they engaged in battle; Ahuramazda bore me aid; by the grace of Ahuramazda my army smote that army of Vahyazdata utterly; 12 days in the month Thuravahara were in course - thus the battle (was) fought by them.

[3.7] Says Darius the king: Afterwards this Vahyazdata with few horsemen fled (and) went to Paishiyauvada; from thence he took an army (and) again went against Artavardiya to engage in battle; there (is) a mountain Parga by name - here they engaged in battle; Ahuramazda gave me aid; by the grace of Ahuramazda my army smote that army of Vahyazdata utterly; 5 days in the month Garmapada were in course - thus the battle (was) fought by them and they seized that Vahyazdata and what men were his foremost allies they seized.

[3.8] Says Darius the king: Afterwards - there (is) a town in Persia Uvadaicaya by name - here, that Vahyazdata and what men were his foremost allies, them I put on a cross.

[3.9] Says Darius the king: This (is) what (was) done by me in Persia.

[3.10] Says Darius the king: This Vahyazdata, who called himself Bardiya, he sent forth an army to Arachosia - there (was) Vivana by name, a Persian, my subject, satrap in Arachosia - against him (he sent an army) and one man he made chief of them; thus he said to them; go, smite Vivana and that army which calls itself of Darius the king; afterwards this army, which Vahyazdata sent forth, went against Vivana to engage in battle; there (is) a stronghold Kapishakanish by name - here they engaged in battle; Ahuramazda bore me aid; by the grace of Ahuramazda my army smote that rebellious army utterly; 13 days in the month Anamaka were in course - thus the battle (was) fought by them.

[3.11] Says Darius the king: Again the rebels came together (and) went against Vivana to engage in battle; there (is) a region Ga(n)dutava by name - here they engaged in battle; Ahuramazda bore me aid; by the grace of Ahuramazda my army smote that rebellious army utterly; 7 days in the month Viyakhna were in course - thus the battle (was) fought by them.

[3.12] Says Darius the king: Afterwards this man, who was chief of that army which Vahyazdata sent against Vivana, he fled with a few horsemen (and) went away - there (is) a stronghold Arshada by name in Arachosia - he went thereby; afterwards Vivana, with an army went in pursuit of them; here he seized him and what men were his foremost allies he slew.

[3.13] Says Darius the king: Afterwards the province became mine; this (is) what (was) done by me in Arachosia.

[3.14] Says Darius the king: When I was in Persia and in Media, a second time the Babylonians became estranged from me; one man, Arakha by name, an Armenian son of Haldita, he rose up in Babylon; there (is) a region, Dubala by name - from here he thus lied to the people; I am Nebuchadrezzar, the son of Nabu-na'id; afterwards the Babylonian people became estranged from me (and) went over to that Arakha; he seized Babylon; he became king in Babylon.

[3.15] Says Darius the king: Afterwards I sent forth my army to Babylon; Intaphernes by name, a Persian, my subject, him I made chief of them; thus I said to them; go, smite that Babylonian army which does not call itself mine; afterwards Intaphernes with an army went to Babylon; Ahuramazda bore me aid; by the grace of Ahuramazda, Intaphernes smote the Babylonians; and [he led them bound to me]; 22 days in the month + + + +[137] were in course - that Arakha, who called himself Nebuchadrezzar, and the men who [were his foremost allies they seized and bound]; [this Arakha] and what men were his foremost allies were put on crosses at Babylon.

Column 4

[4.1] Says Darius the king: This (is) what was done by me in Babylon.

[4.2] Says Darius the king: This (is) what I did; by the grace of Ahuramazda it was (done) in every way; after that I became king, I engaged in 19 battles; by the grace of Ahuramazda I waged them and I seized 9 kings; there was one, Gaumata by name, a Magian; he lied; thus he said; I am Bardiya the son of Cyrus; he made Persia rebellious; there (was) one, Atrina by name, a Susian; he lied; thus he said; I am king in Susiana; he made Susiana rebellious to me; there (was) one, Nidintu-Bel by name, a Babylonian; he lied; thus he said; I am Nebuchadrezzar the son of Nabu-na'id; he made Babylon rebellious; there (was) one, Martiya by name, a Persian; he lied; thus he said; I am Imanish, king in Susiana; he made Susiana rebellious; there (was) one Phraortes by name, a Mede; he lied; thus he said; I am Khshathrita, of the family of Cyaxares; he made Media rebellious; there (was) one Citra(n)takhma by name, in Sagartia; he lied; thus he said; I am king in Sagartia, of the family of Cyaxares; he

137. Indicates missing text here and elsewhere in the reading.

made Sagartia rebellious; there (was) one Frada by name, a Margian; he lied; thus he said; I am king in Margiana; he made Margiana rebellious; there (was) one, Vahyazdata by name, a Persian; he lied; thus he said; I am Bardiya the son of Cyrus; he made Persia rebellious; there (was) one, Arakha by name, an Armenian; he lied; thus he said; I am Nebuchadrezzar the son of Nabu-na'id; he made Babylon rebellious.

[4.3] Says Darius the king: These 9 kings I seized within these battles.

[4.4] Says Darius the king: These (are) the provinces which became rebellious; the Lie made them rebellious so that these deceived the people; afterwards Ahuramazda gave them into my hand; as was my will so [I did] unto them.

[4.5] Says Darius the king: O thou who shalt be king in the future, protect thyself strongly from Deceit; whatever man shall be a deceiver, him who deserves to be punished, punish, if thus thou shalt think "may my country be secure."

[4.6] Says Darius the king: This (is) what I did; by the grace of Ahuramazda I did (it) in every way; O thou who shalt examine this inscription in the future, let it convince thee (as to) what (was) done by me; regard it not as lies.

[4.7] Says Darius the king: I appeal to Ahuramazda that this (is) true (and) not false (which) I did in every way.

[4.8] Says Darius the king: By the grace of Ahuramazda much else (was) done by me that (is) not written on this inscription; for this reason it (is) not written lest whoever shall examine this inscription in the future, to him what has been done by me should seem too much; and it should not convince him but he should think (it) false.

[4.9] Says Darius the king: Who were the former kings, while they lived, by these nothing (was) thus done as (was) done by me through the grace of Ahuramazda in every way.

[4.10] Says Darius the king: Now let it convince thee (as to) what (was) done by me; thus + + + + do not conceal this record; if thou shalt not conceal this record (but) tell (it) to the people, may Ahuramazda be a friend to thee and may there be unto thee a family abundantly and mayest thou live long.

[4.11] Says Darius the king: If thou shalt conceal this record (and) not tell (it) to the people, may Ahuramazda be a smiter unto thee and may there not be unto thee a family.

[4.12] Says Darius the king: This (is) what I did in every way; by the grace of Ahuramazda I did (it); Ahuramazda bore me aid and the other gods which are.

[4.13] Says Darius the king: For this reason Ahuramazda bore me aid and the other gods which are, because I was not an enemy, I was not a deceiver, I was not a wrong-doer, neither I nor my family; according to rectitude [I ruled] nor made I my power(?) an oppression to [those who praise me]; the man (who) helped my house, him who should be well esteemed, I esteemed; (the man) who would destroy it, him who should deserve punishment, I punished.

[4.14] Says Darius the king: O thou who shalt be king in the future, whatever man shall be a deceiver or a wrong-doer (be) not a friend to these; punish (them) with severe punishment.

[4.15] Says Darius the king: O thou who shalt see this inscription in the future which I have written or these sculptures, thou shalt not destroy (them) as long as thou shalt live; thus thou shalt guard them.

[4.16] Says Darius the king: If thou shalt see this inscription or these sculptures (and) shalt not destroy them and shalt guard them as long as thy family shall be, may Ahuramazda be a friend to thee and may there be unto thee a family abundantly and mayest thou live long and whatever thou shalt do, this for thee (let) Ahuramazda make [successful].

[4.17] Says Darius the king: If thou shalt see this inscription or these sculptures (and) shalt destroy; them and shalt not guard them as long as thy family shall be, may Ahuramazda be a smiter unto thee and may there not be unto thee a family and whatever thou shalt do, this let Ahuramazda destroy for thee.

[4.18] Says Darius the king: These (are) the men who were there then when I slew Gaumata the Magian, who called himself Bardiya; then these men cooperated as my allies; Intaphernes by name, the son of Vayaspara, a Persian; Otanes by name, the son of Thukhra, a Persian; Gobryas by name, the son of Mardonius, a Persian; Hydarnes by name, the son of Bagabigna, a Persian; Megabyzus by name, the son of Daduhya, a Persian; Ardumanish by name, the son of Vahauka, a Persian.

[4.19] Says Darius the king: O thou who shalt be king in the future, preserve + + + + +

[4.20] Says Darius the king: By the grace of Ahuramazda this inscription + + + + which I made + + + + + + + + + I have written; this inscription; + + + me afterwards the inscription + + + + + within the provinces + + + + + + + + +

The Behistan Inscription of King Darius. Translated by Herbert Cushing Tolman, 7–37. Nashville, TN: Vanderbilt University, 1908.

POST-READING PARS

1. How does Darius combine religion and war in his inscription? Find two examples.
2. What leadership qualities of kings and presidents that you identified earlier do you see displayed in the inscription?
3. Whom does Darius claim as his earliest ancestor?

Inquiry Corner

Content Question(s):	**Critical Question(s):**
Whom does Darius credit (besides himself) for his military successes, and what does this tell us about ancient Persian culture?	Can self-written history be an objective record of a person or event? Why or why not? In what ways do humans memorialize their ancestors and how does Darius's approach compare? How many generations of your ancestors can you name?
Comparative Question(s):	**Connection Question(s):**
The Roman emperor Augustus's self-eulogistic inscription *Res Gestae* offers some broad avenues of comparison to Darius's inscription: what are some of their similarities and differences? Which aspects of both seem propagandistic rather than strictly factual?	What monuments in America are carved into a mountain? Who created them and what do these monuments seek to commemorate? How accessible are they to public view, and how has technology changed that access?

Book of 1 Maccabees 1–4

SNAPSHOT BOX

LANGUAGE: Hebrew

DATE: c. 200 BCE

LOCATION: Judea

GENRE: Religious history

ETHNIC IDENTITY: Jewish

TAGS: Authority and Leadership; Community/Communal Identity; Conflict and War; Family; Identity; Religion

Introduction

When is societal change considered progress and when is it considered the destruction of tradition? This is the fundamental question in the *Book of Maccabees*. The excerpt below is from the first *Book of Maccabees*. It belongs to a set of texts known in English as **apocrypha** (from the Greek "hidden"), and in Hebrew, these are called **Sefarim Hachizonim** ("the outer books"). Most of these apocryphal texts were written by Jews during the Second Temple period and were excluded from the official **canon** of the Hebrew Bible when it was definitively set near the end of the first century CE. While Jews and Protestant Christians regard these books as apocrypha, they are accepted as part of the canons of other Christian denominations, including the Catholic and Eastern Orthodox churches.

Our reading recounts in detail the Maccabean revolt between the years 167 and 164 BCE. It begins some centuries before, when the Greeks, led by Alexander the Great, conquered the Jewish kingdom of Judea in 332 BCE. After Alexander's death, his empire was divided among his generals, and the Jews of Palestine became part of the eastern Seleucid dynasty. Judea functioned as a semiautonomous state until the reign of Antiochus IV Epiphanes (175–163 BCE), who affronted the Jews first by plundering the Jerusalem Temple and then by forcefully imposing Hellenistic culture—consisting of the Greek language, fashion, religious practices, and educational curriculum—on his subjects. What elements of culture might be more easily imposed or enforced by those in power? The Judeans were strongly divided in their attitude toward Hellenization. Many Judean

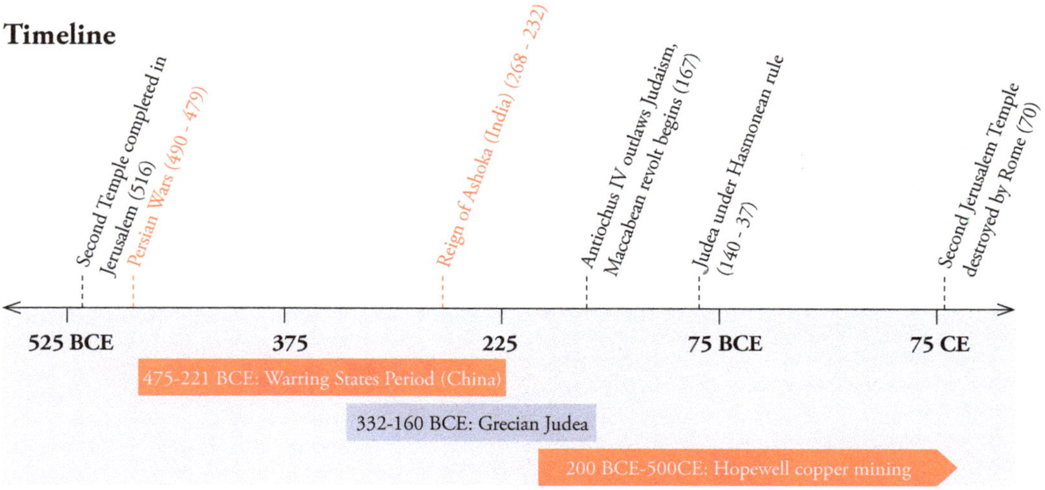

aristocrats, including members of the priesthood, were eager to assimilate to the ruling culture, viewing the adoption of Greek customs as a step toward modernizing Judea. Others strongly opposed this cultural and political imposition. When Antiochus IV issued an edict in 167 BCE that repealed the law of the Torah; outlawed common Jewish religious practices such as circumcision and observing the Sabbath rest; and converted the Jerusalem Temple into a Greek shrine where sacrifices of pork were offered on the altar, this opposition erupted into a revolt.

The rebellion was led by a conservative priestly family, made up of Mattathias and his five sons from the small village of Modein. When Mattathias died in 166 BCE, he was succeeded by his third son Judah, known as the **Maccabee** ("hammer"). Historical evidence attributes the Jewish victory to a deftly conducted guerrilla war and the happy coincidence that the Seleucid Empire was attending to a host of other conflicts. What might be some of the reasons given for Jewish success? Judah and his army successfully retook Jerusalem in 164 BCE, restored the desecrated temple, and eventually established a sovereign Jewish state led by his family, the Hasmoneans, also called the Maccabees. The military success of the Maccabees and the rededication of the temple in Jerusalem have been preserved in the collective memory of the Jews as the eight-day festival of **Hanukkah** ("dedication"), celebrated to this day by Jews the world over.

The story of the Maccabees foregrounds two themes that become central to Jewish civilization over the next two millennia. First, the conflict between those who supported and those who resisted Hellenization is emblematic of a larger tension between cultural assimilation and cultural separatism that has been a part of Jewish civilization from its inception. This tension is evident when one compares the books of First and Second Maccabees, which relate the same historical events from different perspectives. *First Maccabees* is written in Hebrew. It portrays non-Jewish rulers as wicked, assumes that all other peoples are hostile toward the Jews, and focuses on intra-Jewish conflicts. *Second Maccabees*, in contrast, is written in Greek and emphasizes magnanimous rulers, amicable relations with the non-Jewish world, and the harmonious unity of the Jewish community. Second, the Maccabees story marks the first time Judaism was persecuted as a religion, another theme that has dominated much of Jewish history. Before this point, any adversity the Jews had faced had been political, the result of living as a small nation among great powers. What might have been Antiochus's main motivations for outlawing Judaism? Given that he already had control of the Judean state, what other intended outcomes might result from attempts to quash Judean religion and culture?

Doria B. Killian
The Center for Jewish Studies and Department of Languages and Literatures

PRE-READING PARS

1. Brainstorm two ways in which religious practice/traditions are related to identity.
2. Consider a circumstance where cultural assimilation may be seen as positive and constructive, and another circumstance in which it might be seen as negative and detrimental.

Book of 1 Maccabees 1–4

1 Maccabees 1

1 After Alexander son of Philip, the Macedonian, who came from the land of Kittim,
had defeated King Darius of the Persians and the Medes, he succeeded him as king.
(He had previously become king of Greece.) 2 He fought many battles, conquered
strongholds, and put to death the kings of the earth. 3 He advanced to the ends of the
earth, and plundered many nations. When the earth became quiet before him, he was
exalted, and his heart was lifted up. 4 He gathered a very strong army and ruled over
countries, nations, and princes, and they became tributary to him.

5 After this he fell sick and perceived that he was dying. 6 So he summoned his
most honored officers, who had been brought up with him from youth, and divided
his kingdom among them while he was still alive. 7 And after Alexander had reigned
twelve years, he died. 8 Then his officers began to rule, each in his own place. 9 They
all put on crowns after his death, and so did their descendants after them for many
years; and they caused many evils on the earth.

Antiochus Epiphanes and Renegade Jews

10 From them came forth a sinful root, Antiochus Epiphanes, son of King Antiochus; he had been a hostage in Rome. He began to reign in the one hundred thirty-
seventh year of the kingdom of the Greeks.

11 In those days certain renegades came out from Israel and misled many, saying,
"Let us go and make a covenant with the Gentiles around us, for since we separated
from them many disasters have come upon us." 12 This proposal pleased them, 13
and some of the people eagerly went to the king, who authorized them to observe the
ordinances of the Gentiles. 14 So they built a gymnasium in Jerusalem, according to
Gentile custom, 15 and removed the marks of circumcision, and abandoned the holy
covenant. They joined with the Gentiles and sold themselves to do evil.

Antiochus in Egypt

16 When Antiochus saw that his kingdom was established, he determined to become
king of the land of Egypt, in order that he might reign over both kingdoms. 17 So he
invaded Egypt with a strong force, with chariots and elephants and cavalry and with
a large fleet. 18 He engaged King Ptolemy of Egypt in battle, and Ptolemy turned and
fled before him, and many were wounded and fell. 19 They captured the fortified cities in the land of Egypt, and he plundered the land of Egypt.

Persecution of the Jews

20 After subduing Egypt, Antiochus returned in the one hundred forty-third year.
He went up against Israel and came to Jerusalem with a strong force. 21 He arrogantly
entered the sanctuary and took the golden altar, the lampstand for the light, and
all its utensils. 22 He took also the table for the bread of the Presence, the cups for
drink offerings, the bowls, the golden censers, the curtain, the crowns, and the gold
decoration on the front of the temple; he stripped it all off. 23 He took the silver and
the gold, and the costly vessels; he took also the hidden treasures that he found. 24
Taking them all, he went into his own land.

He shed much blood,
    and spoke with great arrogance.
25 Israel mourned deeply in every community,
26 rulers and elders groaned,
young women and young men became faint,
    the beauty of the women faded.
27 Every bridegroom took up the lament;
    she who sat in the bridal chamber was mourning.
28 Even the land trembled for its inhabitants,
    and all the house of Jacob was clothed with shame.

29 Two years later the king sent to the cities of Judah a chief collector of tribute,
and he came to Jerusalem with a large force. 30 Deceitfully he spoke peaceable words
to them, and they believed him; but he suddenly fell upon the city, dealt it a severe
blow, and destroyed many people of Israel. 31 He plundered the city, burned it with
fire, and tore down its houses and its surrounding walls. 32 They took captive the
women and children, and seized the livestock. 33 Then they fortified the city of David with a great strong wall and strong towers, and it became their citadel. 34 They
stationed there a sinful people, men who were renegades. These strengthened their
position; 35 they stored up arms and food, and collecting the spoils of Jerusalem they
stored them there, and became a great menace,

36 for the citadel became an ambush against the sanctuary,
    an evil adversary of Israel at all times.

37 On every side of the sanctuary they shed innocent blood;
they even defiled the sanctuary.
38 Because of them the residents of Jerusalem fled;
she became a dwelling of strangers;
she became strange to her offspring,
and her children forsook her.
39 Her sanctuary became desolate like a desert;
her feasts were turned into mourning,
her sabbaths into a reproach,
her honor into contempt.
40 Her dishonor now grew as great as her glory;
her exaltation was turned into mourning.

41 Then the king wrote to his whole kingdom that all should be one people, 42
and that all should give up their particular customs. 43 All the Gentiles accepted the
command of the king. Many even from Israel gladly adopted his religion; they sacrificed to idols and profaned the sabbath. 44 And the king sent letters by messengers
to Jerusalem and the towns of Judah; he directed them to follow customs strange to
the land, 45 to forbid burnt offerings and sacrifices and drink offerings in the sanctuary, to profane sabbaths and festivals, 46 to defile the sanctuary and the priests,
47 to build altars and sacred precincts and shrines for idols, to sacrifice swine and
other unclean animals, 48 and to leave their sons uncircumcised. They were to make
themselves abominable by everything unclean and profane, 49 so that they would
forget the law and change all the ordinances. 50 He added, "And whoever does not
obey the command of the king shall die."

51 In such words he wrote to his whole kingdom. He appointed inspectors over all
the people and commanded the towns of Judah to offer sacrifice, town by town. 52
Many of the people, everyone who forsook the law, joined them, and they did evil in
the land; 53 they drove Israel into hiding in every place of refuge they had.

54 Now on the fifteenth day of Chislev, in the one hundred forty-fifth year, they
erected a desolating sacrilege on the altar of burnt offering. They also built altars in
the surrounding towns of Judah, 55 and offered incense at the doors of the houses
and in the streets. 56 The books of the law that they found they tore to pieces and
burned with fire. 57 Anyone found possessing the book of the covenant, or anyone
who adhered to the law, was condemned to death by decree of the king. 58 They kept
using violence against Israel, against those who were found month after month in
the towns. 59 On the twenty-fifth day of the month they offered sacrifice on the altar
that was on top of the altar of burnt offering. 60 According to the decree, they put
to death the women who had their children circumcised, 61 and their families and
those who circumcised them; and they hung the infants from their mothers' necks.

62 But many in Israel stood firm and were resolved in their hearts not to eat unclean food. 63 They chose to die rather than to be defiled by food or to profane the
holy covenant; and they did die. 64 Very great wrath came upon Israel.

1 Maccabees 2

2 In those days Mattathias son of John son of Simeon, a priest of the family of Joarib,
moved from Jerusalem and settled in Modein. 2 He had five sons, John surnamed
Gaddi, 3 Simon called Thassi, 4 Judas called Maccabeus, 5 Eleazar called Avaran,
and Jonathan called Apphus. 6 He saw the blasphemies being committed in Judah
and Jerusalem, 7 and said,

"Alas! Why was I born to see this,
    the ruin of my people, the ruin of the holy city,
and to live there when it was given over to the enemy,
    the sanctuary given over to aliens?
8 Her temple has become like a person without honor;
9 her glorious vessels have been carried into exile.
Her infants have been killed in her streets,
    her youths by the sword of the foe.
10 What nation has not inherited her palaces
    and has not seized her spoils?
11 All her adornment has been taken away;
    no longer free, she has become a slave.
12 And see, our holy place, our beauty,
    and our glory have been laid waste;
the Gentiles have profaned them.
13 Why should we live any longer?"

14 Then Mattathias and his sons tore their clothes, put on sackcloth, and mourned
greatly.

Pagan Worship Refused

15 The king's officers who were enforcing the apostasy came to the town of Modein to
make them offer sacrifice. 16 Many from Israel came to them; and Mattathias and his
sons were assembled. 17 Then the king's officers spoke to Mattathias as follows: "You
are a leader, honored and great in this town, and supported by sons and brothers. 18
Now be the first to come and do what the king commands, as all the Gentiles and the
people of Judah and those that are left in Jerusalem have done. Then you and your
sons will be numbered among the Friends of the king, and you and your sons will be
honored with silver and gold and many gifts."
19 But Mattathias answered and said in a loud voice: "Even if all the nations that live
under the rule of the king obey him, and have chosen to obey his commandments,
every one of them abandoning the religion of their ancestors, 20 I and my sons and
my brothers will continue to live by the covenant of our ancestors. 21 Far be it from us
to desert the law and the ordinances. 22 We will not obey the king's words by turning
aside from our religion to the right hand or to the left."

23 When he had finished speaking these words, a Jew came forward in the sight
of all to offer sacrifice on the altar in Modein, according to the king's command. 24
When Mattathias saw it, he burned with zeal and his heart was stirred. He gave vent
to righteous anger; he ran and killed him on the altar. 25 At the same time he killed
the king's officer who was forcing them to sacrifice, and he tore down the altar. 26
Thus he burned with zeal for the law, just as Phinehas did against Zimri son of Salu.

27 Then Mattathias cried out in the town with a loud voice, saying: "Let every one
who is zealous for the law and supports the covenant come out with me!" 28 Then he
and his sons fled to the hills and left all that they had in the town.

29 At that time many who were seeking righteousness and justice went down
to the wilderness to live there, 30 they, their sons, their wives, and their livestock,
because troubles pressed heavily upon them. 31 And it was reported to the king's officers, and to the troops in Jerusalem the city of David, that those who had rejected
the king's command had gone down to the hiding places in the wilderness. 32 Many
pursued them, and overtook them; they encamped opposite them and prepared for
battle against them on the sabbath day. 33 They said to them, "Enough of this! Come
out and do what the king commands, and you will live." 34 But they said, "We will
not come out, nor will we do what the king commands and so profane the sabbath
day." 35 Then the enemy quickly attacked them. 36 But they did not answer them or
hurl a stone at them or block up their hiding places, 37 for they said, "Let us all die in
our innocence; heaven and earth testify for us that you are killing us unjustly." 38 So
they attacked them on the sabbath, and they died, with their wives and children and
livestock, to the number of a thousand persons. 39 When Mattathias and his friends
learned of it, they mourned for them deeply. 40 And all said to their neighbors: "If we
all do as our kindred have done and refuse to fight with the Gentiles for our lives and
for our ordinances, they will quickly destroy us from the earth." 41 So they made this
decision that day: "Let us fight against anyone who comes to attack us on the sabbath
day; let us not all die as our kindred died in their hiding places."

Counter-Attack

42 Then there united with them a company of Hasideans, mighty warriors of Israel,
all who offered themselves willingly for the law. 43 And all who became fugitives to
escape their troubles joined them and reinforced them. 44 They organized an army,
and struck down sinners in their anger and renegades in their wrath; the survivors
fled to the Gentiles for safety. 45 And Mattathias and his friends went around and
tore down the altars; 46 they forcibly circumcised all the uncircumcised boys that
they found within the borders of Israel. 47 They hunted down the arrogant, and
the work prospered in their hands. 48 They rescued the law out of the hands of the
Gentiles and kings, and they never let the sinner gain the upper hand.

49 Now the days drew near for Mattathias to die, and he said to his sons: "Arrogance and scorn have now become strong; it is a time of ruin and furious anger. 50

Now, my children, show zeal for the law, and give your lives for the covenant of our
ancestors.

51 "Remember the deeds of the ancestors, which they did in their generations; and
you will receive great honor and an everlasting name. 52 Was not Abraham found
faithful when tested, and it was reckoned to him as righteousness? 53 Joseph in the
time of his distress kept the commandment, and became lord of Egypt. 54 Phinehas our ancestor, because he was deeply zealous, received the covenant of everlasting
priesthood. 55 Joshua, because he fulfilled the command, became a judge in Israel.
56 Caleb, because he testified in the assembly, received an inheritance in the land.
57 David, because he was merciful, inherited the throne of the kingdom forever. 58
Elijah, because of great zeal for the law, was taken up into heaven. 59 Hananiah,
Azariah, and Mishael believed and were saved from the flame. 60 Daniel, because of
his innocence, was delivered from the mouth of the lions.

61 "And so observe, from generation to generation, that none of those who put
their trust in him will lack strength. 62 Do not fear the words of sinners, for their
splendor will turn into dung and worms. 63 Today they will be exalted, but tomorrow
they will not be found, because they will have returned to the dust, and their plans
will have perished. 64 My children, be courageous and grow strong in the law, for by
it you will gain honor.

65 "Here is your brother Simeon who, I know, is wise in counsel; always listen to
him; he shall be your father. 66 Judas Maccabeus has been a mighty warrior from his
youth; he shall command the army for you and fight the battle against the peoples.
67 You shall rally around you all who observe the law, and avenge the wrong done
to your people. 68 Pay back the Gentiles in full, and obey the commands of the law."

69 Then he blessed them, and was gathered to his ancestors. 70 He died in the
one hundred forty-sixth year and was buried in the tomb of his ancestors at Modein.
And all Israel mourned for him with great lamentation.

1 Maccabees 3

3 Then his son Judas, who was called Maccabeus, took command in his place. 2 All
his brothers and all who had joined his father helped him; they gladly fought for
Israel.

3 He extended the glory of his people.
Like a giant he put on his breastplate;
he bound on his armor of war and waged battles,
protecting the camp by his sword.
4 He was like a lion in his deeds,
like a lion's cub roaring for prey.
5 He searched out and pursued those who broke the law;
he burned those who troubled his people.

6 Lawbreakers shrank back for fear of him;
all the evildoers were confounded;
and deliverance prospered by his hand.
7 He embittered many kings,
but he made Jacob glad by his deeds,
and his memory is blessed forever.
8 He went through the cities of Judah;
he destroyed the ungodly out of the land;
thus he turned away wrath from Israel.
9 He was renowned to the ends of the earth;
he gathered in those who were perishing.

10 Apollonius now gathered together Gentiles and a large force from Samaria
to fight against Israel. 11 When Judas learned of it, he went out to meet him, and he
defeated and killed him. Many were wounded and fell, and the rest fled. 12 Then they
seized their spoils; and Judas took the sword of Apollonius, and used it in battle the
rest of his life.

13 When Seron, the commander of the Syrian army, heard that Judas had gathered
a large company, including a body of faithful soldiers who stayed with him and went
out to battle, 14 he said, "I will make a name for myself and win honor in the kingdom. I will make war on Judas and his companions, who scorn the king's command."
15 Once again a strong army of godless men went up with him to help him, to take
vengeance on the Israelites.

16 When he approached the ascent of Beth-horon, Judas went out to meet him
with a small company. 17 But when they saw the army coming to meet them, they
said to Judas, "How can we, few as we are, fight against so great and so strong a multitude? And we are faint, for we have eaten nothing today." 18 Judas replied, "It is easy
for many to be hemmed in by few, for in the sight of Heaven there is no difference
between saving by many or by few. 19 It is not on the size of the army that victory in
battle depends, but strength comes from Heaven. 20 They come against us in great
insolence and lawlessness to destroy us and our wives and our children, and to despoil
us; 21 but we fight for our lives and our laws. 22 He himself will crush them before us;
as for you, do not be afraid of them."

23 When he finished speaking, he rushed suddenly against Seron and his army,
and they were crushed before him. 24 They pursued them down the descent of Beth-
horon to the plain; eight hundred of them fell, and the rest fled into the land of the
Philistines. 25 Then Judas and his brothers began to be feared, and terror fell on the
Gentiles all around them. 26 His fame reached the king, and the Gentiles talked of
the battles of Judas.

The Policy of Antiochus

27 When King Antiochus heard these reports, he was greatly angered; and he sent
and gathered all the forces of his kingdom, a very strong army. 28 He opened his
coffers and gave a year's pay to his forces, and ordered them to be ready for any need.
29 Then he saw that the money in the treasury was exhausted, and that the revenues
from the country were small because of the dissension and disaster that he had caused
in the land by abolishing the laws that had existed from the earliest days. 30 He feared
that he might not have such funds as he had before for his expenses and for the gifts
that he used to give more lavishly than preceding kings. 31 He was greatly perplexed
in mind; then he determined to go to Persia and collect the revenues from those
regions and raise a large fund.

32 He left Lysias, a distinguished man of royal lineage, in charge of the king's affairs from the river Euphrates to the borders of Egypt. 33 Lysias was also to take care
of his son Antiochus until he returned. 34 And he turned over to Lysias half of his
forces and the elephants, and gave him orders about all that he wanted done. As for
the residents of Judea and Jerusalem, 35 Lysias was to send a force against them to
wipe out and destroy the strength of Israel and the remnant of Jerusalem; he was to
banish the memory of them from the place, 36 settle aliens in all their territory, and
distribute their land by lot. 37 Then the king took the remaining half of his forces
and left Antioch his capital in the one hundred and forty-seventh year. He crossed
the Euphrates river and went through the upper provinces.

38 Lysias chose Ptolemy son of Dorymenes, and Nicanor and Gorgias, able men
among the Friends of the king, 39 and sent with them forty thousand infantry and
seven thousand cavalry to go into the land of Judah and destroy it, as the king had
commanded. 40 So they set out with their entire force, and when they arrived they
encamped near Emmaus in the plain. 41 When the traders of the region heard what
was said to them, they took silver and gold in immense amounts, and fetters, and
went to the camp to get the Israelites for slaves. And forces from Syria and the land
of the Philistines joined with them.

42 Now Judas and his brothers saw that misfortunes had increased and that the
forces were encamped in their territory. They also learned what the king had commanded to do to the people to cause their final destruction. 43 But they said to one
another, "Let us restore the ruins of our people, and fight for our people and the
sanctuary." 44 So the congregation assembled to be ready for battle, and to pray and
ask for mercy and compassion.

45 Jerusalem was uninhabited like a wilderness;
not one of her children went in or out.
The sanctuary was trampled down,
and aliens held the citadel;
it was a lodging place for the Gentiles.

Joy was taken from Jacob;
the flute and the harp ceased to play.

46 Then they gathered together and went to Mizpah, opposite Jerusalem, because
Israel formerly had a place of prayer in Mizpah. 47 They fasted that day, put on sackcloth and sprinkled ashes on their heads, and tore their clothes. 48 And they opened
the book of the law to inquire into those matters about which the Gentiles consulted
the likenesses of their gods. 49 They also brought the vestments of the priesthood
and the first fruits and the tithes, and they stirred up the nazirites who had completed
their days; 50 and they cried aloud to Heaven, saying,

"What shall we do with these?
Where shall we take them?
51 Your sanctuary is trampled down and profaned,
and your priests mourn in humiliation.
2 Here the Gentiles are assembled against us to destroy us;
you know what they plot against us.
53 How will we be able to withstand them,
if you do not help us?"

54 Then they sounded the trumpets and gave a loud shout. 55 After this Judas
appointed leaders of the people, in charge of thousands and hundreds and fifties and
tens. 56 Those who were building houses, or were about to be married, or were planting a vineyard, or were fainthearted, he told to go home again, according to the law.
57 Then the army marched out and encamped to the south of Emmaus.

58 And Judas said, "Arm yourselves and be courageous. Be ready early in the
morning to fight with these Gentiles who have assembled against us to destroy us
and our sanctuary. 59 It is better for us to die in battle than to see the misfortunes of
our nation and of the sanctuary. 60 But as his will in heaven may be, so shall he do."

1 Maccabees 4

4 Now Gorgias took five thousand infantry and one thousand picked cavalry, and
this division moved out by night 2 to fall upon the camp of the Jews and attack them
suddenly. Men from the citadel were his guides. 3 But Judas heard of it, and he and
his warriors moved out to attack the king's force in Emmaus 4 while the division was
still absent from the camp. 5 When Gorgias entered the camp of Judas by night, he
found no one there, so he looked for them in the hills, because he said, "These men
are running away from us."

6 At daybreak Judas appeared in the plain with three thousand men, but they
did not have armor and swords such as they desired. 7 And they saw the camp of the
Gentiles, strong and fortified, with cavalry all around it; and these men were trained
in war. 8 But Judas said to those who were with him, "Do not fear their numbers or

be afraid when they charge. 9 Remember how our ancestors were saved at the Red Sea, when Pharaoh with his forces pursued them. 10 And now, let us cry to Heaven, to see whether he will favor us and remember his covenant with our ancestors and crush this army before us today. 11 Then all the Gentiles will know that there is one who redeems and saves Israel."

12 When the foreigners looked up and saw them coming against them, 13 they went out from their camp to battle. Then the men with Judas blew their trumpets 14 and engaged in battle. The Gentiles were crushed, and fled into the plain, 15 and all those in the rear fell by the sword. They pursued them to Gazara, and to the plains of Idumea, and to Azotus and Jamnia; and three thousand of them fell. 16 Then Judas and his force turned back from pursuing them, 17 and he said to the people, "Do not be greedy for plunder, for there is a battle before us; 18 Gorgias and his force are near us in the hills. But stand now against our enemies and fight them, and afterward seize the plunder boldly."

19 Just as Judas was finishing this speech, a detachment appeared, coming out of the hills. 20 They saw that their army had been put to flight, and that the Jews were burning the camp, for the smoke that was seen showed what had happened. 21 When they perceived this, they were greatly frightened, and when they also saw the army of Judas drawn up in the plain for battle, 22 they all fled into the land of the Philistines. 23 Then Judas returned to plunder the camp, and they seized a great amount of gold and silver, and cloth dyed blue and sea purple, and great riches. 24 On their return they sang hymns and praises to Heaven—"For he is good, for his mercy endures forever." 25 Thus Israel had a great deliverance that day.

26 Those of the foreigners who escaped went and reported to Lysias all that had happened. 27 When he heard it, he was perplexed and discouraged, for things had not happened to Israel as he had intended, nor had they turned out as the king had ordered. 28 But the next year he mustered sixty thousand picked infantry and five thousand cavalry to subdue them. 29 They came into Idumea and encamped at Beth-zur, and Judas met them with ten thousand men. 30 When he saw that their army was strong, he prayed, saying, "Blessed are you, O Savior of Israel, who crushed the attack of the mighty warrior by the hand of your servant David, and gave the camp of the Philistines into the hands of Jonathan son of Saul, and of the man who carried his armor. 31 Hem in this army by the hand of your people Israel, and let them be ashamed of their troops and their cavalry. 32 Fill them with cowardice; melt the boldness of their strength; let them tremble in their destruction. 33 Strike them down with the sword of those who love you, and let all who know your name praise you with hymns."

34 Then both sides attacked, and there fell of the army of Lysias five thousand men; they fell in action. 35 When Lysias saw the rout of his troops and observed the boldness that inspired those of Judas, and how ready they were either to live or to die nobly, he withdrew to Antioch and enlisted mercenaries in order to invade Judea again with an even larger army.

36 Then Judas and his brothers said, "See, our enemies are crushed; let us go up

to cleanse the sanctuary and dedicate it." 37 So all the army assembled and went up to Mount Zion. 38 There they saw the sanctuary desolate, the altar profaned, and the gates burned. In the courts they saw bushes sprung up as in a thicket, or as on one of the mountains. They saw also the chambers of the priests in ruins. 39 Then they tore their clothes and mourned with great lamentation; they sprinkled themselves with ashes 40 and fell face down on the ground. And when the signal was given with the trumpets, they cried out to Heaven.

41 Then Judas detailed men to fight against those in the citadel until he had cleansed the sanctuary. 42 He chose blameless priests devoted to the law, 43 and they cleansed the sanctuary and removed the defiled stones to an unclean place. 44 They deliberated what to do about the altar of burnt offering, which had been profaned. 45 And they thought it best to tear it down, so that it would not be a lasting shame to them that the Gentiles had defiled it. So they tore down the altar, 46 and stored the stones in a convenient place on the temple hill until a prophet should come to tell what to do with them. 47 Then they took unhewn stones, as the law directs, and built a new altar like the former one. 48 They also rebuilt the sanctuary and the interior of the temple, and consecrated the courts. 49 They made new holy vessels, and brought the lampstand, the altar of incense, and the table into the temple. 50 Then they offered incense on the altar and lit the lamps on the lampstand, and these gave light in the temple. 51 They placed the bread on the table and hung up the curtains. Thus they finished all the work they had undertaken.

52 Early in the morning on the twenty-fifth day of the ninth month, which is the month of Chislev, in the one hundred forty-eighth year, 53 they rose and offered sacrifice, as the law directs, on the new altar of burnt offering that they had built. 54 At the very season and on the very day that the Gentiles had profaned it, it was dedicated with songs and harps and lutes and cymbals. 55 All the people fell on their faces and worshiped and blessed Heaven, who had prospered them. 56 So they celebrated the dedication of the altar for eight days, and joyfully offered burnt offerings; they offered a sacrifice of well-being and a thanksgiving offering. 57 They decorated the front of the temple with golden crowns and small shields; they restored the gates and the chambers for the priests, and fitted them with doors. 58 There was very great joy among the people, and the disgrace brought by the Gentiles was removed.

59 Then Judas and his brothers and all the assembly of Israel determined that every year at that season the days of dedication of the altar should be observed with joy and gladness for eight days, beginning with the twenty-fifth day of the month of Chislev.

60 At that time they fortified Mount Zion with high walls and strong towers all around, to keep the Gentiles from coming and trampling them down as they had done before. 61 Judas stationed a garrison there to guard it; he also fortified Beth-zur to guard it, so that the people might have a stronghold that faced Idumea.

"1 Maccabees 1–4." *New Revised Standard Version*. National Council of the Churches of Christ in the United States of America, 1989.

POST-READING PARS

1. How is religious practice linked with identity in the text? Compare it with your own understanding of the relationship between these two.
2. Identify two ways cultural assimilation is portrayed in the text. Do you think they are positive or negative?

Inquiry Corner

Content Question(s):	**Critical Question(s):**
What motivates Mattathias and his sons to rebel against the Seleucids? How do Mattathias and his sons justify turning their principled stand into a violent struggle?	How do we assess criteria for the justification of force or violence? Does one's position, identity, experiences validate these actions? How does your own understanding and assessment compare to the narrative presented in the text?
Comparative Question(s):	**Connection Question(s):**
How is the idea of religious freedom in this text and era similar to our understanding of religious freedom today? How is it different?	The Maccabean uprising was viewed on one side as an act of political terrorism and on the other as a struggle to free an oppressed people. What is the difference between these two? Is it ever clear-cut or is it always dependent on perspective?

BEYOND THE CLASSROOM

- Imagine you worked for a leader like Antiochus. How would it feel to stand up against this type of leader like Mattathias did? Would you do it, even if you knew it would come at a high cost?
- How would it feel to work in a team/organization/environment where the values of others differed greatly from your own? How could you be sure to stick to your own values? Would this be possible, or would you seek out another work environment?

from *Code of Hammurabi*

Introduction

The Law Code of Hammurabi consists of 282 edicts carved into a four-ton black stone stele, which is presently housed in the Louvre. At the top of the column is a relief of Hammurabi, the sixth king of the Babylon dynasty who reigned from 1792 to 1750 BCE, receiving the law from Shamash, the Babylonian god of justice. Below that is the code itself. Its content spans virtually all aspects of life, including family relations, criminal transgressions, the settlement of civil disputes, the giving of false testimony, and even relations between employers and employees in no particular order. An epilogue follows in which Hammurabi explains the overriding goal of his code.

A French expedition discovered Hammurabi's stele in excavations undertaken in the early part of the twentieth century. The stele was most likely erected either in the Esagila, the temple of the god Marduk in the city of Babylon, or in Ebabbar, the temple of the god Shamash in the city of Sippar, southwest of present-day Baghdad.

Hammurabi's reign was marked by the political consolidation of various territories neighboring the city-state of Babylon. There are strong indications that Hammurabi was active in the adjudication of various legal disputes. He maintained a steady correspondence with officials and judges throughout his kingdom, at times even questioning particular rulings.

SNAPSHOT

LANGUAGE: Akkadian

DATE: 1754 BCE

LOCATION: Sumer/Babylon

GENRE: Legal document

Artifact Material and Monument Type: Basalt stele

TAGS: Authority and Leadership; Class and Wealth; Community/Communal Identity; Deities and Spirits; Law and Punishment; Monument and Artifact

Timeline

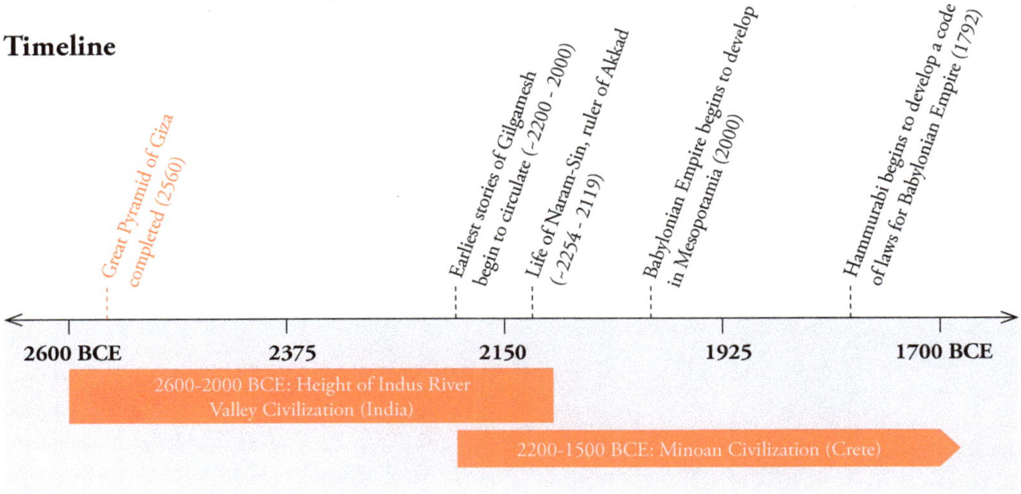

Each of the edicts has a conditional if-then form. For example, the very first law deals with false or unsubstantiated accusations or testimony: "If a man has accused another man and charges him with homicide but cannot bring proof against him, then the accuser shall be killed." What might be the impact on expected social behaviors when the edicts are phrased as conditional?

The "code" of Hammurabi should not be seen as the equivalent of the codified law that exists today, since historical records indicate that only a few actual trials made specific reference to the code itself. What purposes—cultural, religious, social, or other—could a code of law, set forth as directives by a sovereign authority, serve that are not purely legal?

By today's standards, the ***Code of Hammurabi*** demands a form of "rough justice," embodied in the edict of "an eye for an eye." However, the epilogue of Hammurabi stated below seems to offer us a different framework:

> That the strong might not injure the weak, in order to protect the widows and orphans, I have in Babylon the city where Anu and Bel raise high their head, in E-Sagil, the Temple, whose foundations stand firm as heaven and earth, in order to bespeak justice in the land, to settle all disputes, and heal all injuries, set up these my precious words, written upon my memorial stone, before the image of me, as king of righteousness . . . by the order of Marduk, my lord, let no destruction befall my monument. In E-Sagil, which I love, let my name be ever repeated.[138]

What does this epilogue consider to be the driving force behind the edicts? In its stated intentions to protect individuals and to maintain societal order, there may be a direct linkage between the ***Code of Hammurabi*** and present-day international human rights law, most notably, the Universal Declaration of Human Rights (1948).[139]

Mark Gibney
Department of Political Science

138. L. W. King, *The Code of Hammurabi*, the Avalon Project, Yale Law School, Avalon.law .yale.edu/ancient/hamframe.asp. E-Sagil is an alternative spelling for Esagila.

139. G. R. Driver and John Miles, *The Babylonian Laws*, vol. 2 (Oxford: Oxford University Press, 1960); Micheline Ishay, *The History of Human Rights: From Ancient Times to the Globalization Era* (Berkeley: University of California Press, 2004); Paul Gordon Lauren, *The Evolution of International Human Rights: Visions Seen* (Philadelphia: University of Pennsylvania Press, 1998).

PRE READING PARS

1. Do you think it is possible to develop a universal system of justice, and if so, what principles should it be based on?
2. What qualities or traits should a political leader possess?

The Code of Hammurabi, King of Babylon

Prologue

When the lofty Anu, king of the Anunnaki, and Bel, lord of heaven and earth, he who determines the destiny of the land, committed the rule of all mankind to Marduk, the chief son of Ea; when they made him great among the Igigi;[140] when they pronounced the lofty name of Babylon; when they made it famous among the quarters of the world and in its midst established an everlasting kingdom whose foundations were firm as heaven and earth—at that time, Anu and Bel called me, Hammurabi, the exalted prince, the worshiper of the gods, to cause justice to prevail in the land, to destroy the wicked and the evil, to prevent the strong from oppressing the weak, to go forth like the Sun over the Black Head Race,[141] to enlighten the land and to further the welfare of the people. Hammurabi, the governor named by Bel, am I, who brought about plenty and abundance; who stormed the four quarters of the world; who made the fame of Babylon great; who rejoiced the heart of Marduk, his lord; who daily served in Esagila; of the seed royal, which Sin begat; who filled the city of Ur with plenty; the pious and suppliant one, who brought abundance to E-gis-sir-gal; the diplomatic king, obedient to the mighty Shamash; the lord, who gave life to the city of Uruk; who supplied water in abundance to its inhabitants; who raised the turrets of Eanna; who brought riches to Anu and Nana; the divine protector of the land; who collected the scattered people of Nisin; who supplied E-gal-mah with luxurious abundance; who constructed the great shrines of Nana; the patron of the temple of Har-sag-kalama, the grave of the enemy; whose help brings victory; who extended the limits of Cutha; who enlarged Shid-lam in every way; the mighty bull, who gores the enemy; who stored up grain for the mighty Urash; the lord adorned with scepter and crown, whom the wise god Ma-ma has clothed with complete power; who defined the confines of Kish; who made sumptuous the splendid banquets in honor of Nin-tu; the wise and perfect one, who determined the pasture and watering places for Shir-pur-la (Lagash) and Girsu; who provided large sacrifices for the Temple of Fifty; who seizes the enemy; who made justice prevail and who ruled the race with right; who

140. Igigi is a collective term for the Babylonian gods, typically those that were chief in the pantheon.

141. This is a literal translation of the term used by the Sumerians to refer to themselves, for reasons that are not clear.

returned to Ashur its gracious protecting deity; who made the rising sun (?) to shine brilliantly; the ancient seed of royalty, the powerful king, the Sun of Babylon, who caused light to go forth over the lands of Sumer and Akkad; the king, who caused the four quarters of the world to render obedience; the favorite of Nana, am I. When Marduk sent me to rule the people and to bring help to the country, I established law and justice in the land and promoted the welfare of the people.

Selected Laws

Domestic Life

159. If a man, who has brought a present to the house of his father-in-law and has given the marriage settlement,[142] look with longing upon another woman and say to his father-in-law, "I will not take thy daughter"; the father of the daughter shall take to himself whatever was brought to him.

160. If a man brings a present to the house of his father-in-law and gives a marriage settlement and the father of the daughter says, "I will not give thee my daughter"; he (i.e., the father-in-law) shall double the amount which was brought to him and return it.

180. If a father does not give a dowry to his daughter, a bride or devotee, after her father dies she shall receive as her share in the goods of her father's house the portion of a son, and she shall enjoy it as long as she lives. After her (death) it belongs to her brothers.

Marriage

128. If a man takes a wife and does not arrange with her the (proper) contracts, that woman is not a (legal) wife.

145. If a man takes a wife and she does not present him with children and he sets his face to take a concubine, that man may take a concubine and bring her into his house. That concubine shall not rank with his wife.

148. If a man takes a wife and she becomes afflicted with disease, and if he sets his face to take another, he may. His wife, who is afflicted with disease, he shall not put away. She shall remain in the house which he has built and he shall maintain her as long as she lives.

142. The "marriage settlement" is what the groom gives to the family of the bride, sometimes called a "bride price" or "purchase price" in other translations and contexts. The dowry is what the bride brings from her father's house into the marriage.

Children

138. If a man would put away his wife who has not borne him children, he shall give her money to the amount of her marriage settlement and he shall make good to her the dowry which she brought from her father's house and then he may put her away.

194. If a man gives his son to a nurse and that son die in the hands of the nurse, and the nurse substitutes another son without the consent of his father or mother, they shall call her to account, and because she has substituted another son without the consent of his father or mother, they shall cut off her breast.

195. If a son strikes his father, they shall cut off his fingers.

185. If a man takes in his name a young child as a son and rear him, one may not bring claim for that adopted son.

186. If a man takes a young child as a son and, when he takes him, he is rebellious toward his father and mother (who have adopted him), that adopted son shall return to the house of his father.

188. If an artisan takes a son for adoption and teaches him his handicraft, one may not bring claim for him.

189. If he does not teach him his handicraft, that adopted son may return to his father's house.

Adultery

129. If the wife of a man be taken in lying with another man, they shall bind them and throw them into the water. If the husband of the woman would save his wife, or if the king would save his male servant (he may).

130. If a man forces the (betrothed) wife of another who has not known a male and is living in her father's house, and he lies in her bosom and they take him, that man shall be put to death and that woman shall go free.

131. If a man accuses his wife and she has not been taken in lying with another man, she shall take an oath in the name of god and she shall return to her house.

132. If the finger has been pointed at the wife of a man because of another man, and she has not been taken in lying with another man, for her husband's sake she shall throw herself into the river.

153. If a woman brings about the death of her husband for the sake of another man, they shall impale her.

Divorce

137. If a man sets his face to put away a concubine who has borne him children or a wife who has presented him with children, he shall return to that woman her dowry and shall give to her the income of field, garden and goods and she shall bring up her children; from the time that her children are grown up, from whatever is given to her

children they shall give to her a portion corresponding to that of a son and the man of her choice may marry her.

138. If a man would put away his wife who has not borne him children, he shall give her money to the amount of her marriage settlement and he shall make good to her the dowry which she brought from her father's house and then he may put her away.

139. If there were no marriage settlement, he shall give to her one mina of silver[143] for a divorce.

141. If the wife of a man who is living in his house, sets her face to go out and play the part of a fool, neglects her house, belittles her husband, they shall call her to account; if her husband says "I have put her away," he shall let her go. On her departure nothing shall be given to her for her divorce. If her husband says: "I have not put her away," her husband may take another woman. The first woman shall dwell in the house of her husband as a maid servant.

142. If a woman hates her husband, and says: "Thou shalt not have me," they shall inquire into her antecedents for her defects; and if she has been a careful mistress[144] and is without reproach and her husband has been going about and greatly belittling her, that woman has no blame. She shall receive her dowry and shall go to her father's house.

143. If she has not been a careful mistress, has gadded about, has neglected her house and has belittled her husband, they shall throw that woman into the water.

Widowhood

172. If her husband has not given her a gift, they shall make good her dowry and she shall receive from the goods of her husband's house a portion corresponding to that of a son. If her children scheme to drive her out of the house, the judges shall inquire into her antecedents and if the children be in the wrong, she shall not go out from her husband's house. If the woman sets her face to go out, she shall leave to her children the gift which her husband gave her; she shall receive the dowry of her father's house, and the husband of her choice may take her.

173. If that woman bears children to her later husband into whose house she has entered and later on that woman dies, the former and the later children shall divide her dowry.

177. If a widow, whose children are minors, sets her face to enter another house, she cannot do so without the consent of the judges. When she enters another house, the judges shall inquire into the estate of her former husband and they shall intrust the estate of her former husband to the later husband and that woman, and they

143. In Mesopotamia, silver was the most common metal used in currency. One mina equaled approximately 500 grams of silver.

144. That is, if she has been attentive to her household.

shall deliver to them a tablet (to sign). They shall administer the estate and rear the minors. They may not sell the household goods. He who purchases household goods belonging to the sons of a widow shall forfeit his money. The goods shall revert to their owner.

Inheritance

162. If a man takes a wife and she bears him children and that woman dies, her father may not lay claim to her dowry. Her dowry belongs to her children.

166. If a man take wives for his sons and does not take a wife for his youngest son, after the father dies, when the brothers divide, they shall give from the goods of the father's house to their youngest brother, who has not taken a wife, money for a marriage settlement in addition to his portion and they shall enable him to take a wife.

167. If a man takes a wife and she bears him children and that woman dies, and after her (death) he takes another wife and she bears him children and later the father dies, the children of the mothers shall not divide (the estate). They shall receive the dowries of their respective mothers and they shall divide equally the goods of the house of the father.

168. If a man sets his face to disinherit his son and say to the judges: "I will disinherit my son," the judges shall inquire into his antecedents, and if the son has not committed a crime sufficiently grave to cut him off from sonship, the father may not cut off his son from sonship.

169. If he has committed a crime against his father sufficiently grave to cut him off from sonship, they shall condone his first (offense). If he commits a grave crime a second time, the father may cut off his son from sonship.

Professional Life

215. If a physician operates on a man for a severe wound (or makes a severe wound upon a man) with a bronze lancet and saves the man's life; or if he open an abscess (in the eye) of a man with a bronze lancet and saves that man's eye, he shall receive ten shekels of silver (as his fee).

218. If a physician operates on a man for a severe wound with a bronze lancet and causes the man's death; or opens an abscess (in the eye) of a man with a bronze lancet and destroys the man's eye, they shall cut off his fingers.

221. If a physician sets a broken bone for a man or cures his diseased bowels, the patient shall give five shekels of silver to the physician.

224. If a veterinary physician operates on an ox or an ass for a severe wound and saves its life, the owner of the ox or ass shall give to the physician, as his fee, one-sixth of a shekel of silver.

228. If a builder builds a house for a man and completes it, (that man) shall give him two shekels of silver per SAR of house as his wage.

234. If a boatman builds a boat of 60 GUR for a man, he shall give to him two shekels of silver as his wage.

257. If a man hires a field-laborer, he shall pay him 8 GUR of grain per year.

258. If a man hires a herdsman, he shall pay him 6 GUR of grain per year.

271. If a man hires oxen, a wagon and a driver, he shall pay 180 KA of grain per day.

273. If a man hires a laborer, from the beginning of the year until the fifth month, he shall pay 6 SE of silver per day; from the sixth month till the end of the year he shall pay 5 SE of silver per day.

Religious Life

6. If a man steals the property of a god (temple) or palace, that man shall be put to death; and he who receives from his hand the stolen (property) shall also be put to death.

45. If a man rents his field to a tenant for crop-rent and receives the crop-rent of his field and later Adad (i.e., the Storm God) inundates the field and carries away the produce, the loss (falls on) the tenant.

110. If a priestess who is not living in a MAL.GE.A,[145] opens a wine-shop or enters a wine-shop for a drink, they shall burn that woman.

127. If a man points the finger at a priestess or the wife of another and cannot justify it, they shall drag that man before the judges and they shall brand his forehead.

249. If a man hires an ox and a god strikes it and it dies, the man who hired the ox shall take an oath before god and go free.

266. If a visitation of god happens to a fold, or a lion kills, the shepherd shall declare himself innocent before god, and the owner of the fold shall suffer the damage.

Property

199. If one destroys the eye of a man's slave or breaks a bone of a man's slave he shall pay one-half his price.

213. If he strikes the female slave of a man and brings about a miscarriage, he shall pay two shekels of silver.

219. If a physician operates on a slave of a freeman for a severe wound with a bronze lancet and causes his death, he shall restore a slave of equal value.

229. If a builder builds a house for a man and does not make its construction firm, and the house which he has built collapses and causes the death of the owner of the house, that builder shall be put to death.

233. If a builder builds a house for a man and does not make its construction meet the requirements and a wall falls in, that builder shall strengthen that wall at his own expense.

145. MAL.GE.A may refer to housing reserved for priestesses.

235. If a boatman builds a boat for a man and he do not make its construction seaworthy and that boat meets with a disaster in the same year in which it was put into commission, the boatman shall reconstruct that boat and he shall strengthen it at his own expense and he shall give the boat when strengthened to the owner of the boat.

237. If a man hires a boatman and a boat and freight it with grain, wool, oil, dates or any other kind of freight, and that boatman be careless and he sink the boat or wreck its cargo, the boatman shall replace the boat which he sank and whatever portion of the cargo he wrecked.

244. If a man hires an ox or an ass and a lion kill it in the field, it is the owner's affair.

245. If a man hires an ox and causes its death through neglect or abuse, he shall restore an ox of equal value to the owner of the ox.

Life at Court

1. If a man brings an accusation against a man, and charges him with a (capital) crime, but cannot prove it, he, the accuser, shall be put to death.

2. If a man charges a man with sorcery, and cannot prove it, he who is charged with sorcery shall go to the river, into the river he shall throw himself and if the river overcomes him, his accuser shall take to himself his house (estate). If the river shows that man to be innocent and he comes forth unharmed, he who charged him with sorcery shall be put to death. He who threw himself into the river shall take to himself the house of his accuser.[146]

3. If a man, in a case (pending judgment), bears false (threatening) witness, or does not establish the testimony that he has given, if that case be a case involving life, that man shall be put to death.

4. If a man (in a case) bears witness for grain or money (as a bribe), he shall himself bear the penalty imposed in that case.

5. If a judge pronounces a judgment, renders a decision, delivers a verdict duly signed and sealed and afterward alters his judgment, they shall call that judge to account for the alteration of the judgment which he had pronounced, and he shall pay twelve-fold the penalty which was in said judgment; and, in the assembly, they shall expel him from his seat of judgment, and he shall not return, and with the judges in a case he shall not take his seat.

146. This is an example of trial by ordeal. Here the River god judged the accused. Unlike the ordeal associated with medieval Europe, in which the accused was proven innocent if they drowned, in Mesopotamia, the accused was proven innocent if they survived.

Epilogue

The righteous laws, which Hammurabi, the wise king, established and (by which) he gave the land stable support and pure government. Hammurabi, the perfect king, am I. I was not careless, nor was I neglectful of the Black-Head people, whose rule Bel presented and Marduk delivered to me. I provided them with a peaceful country. I opened up difficult barriers and lent them support. With the powerful weapon which Za-má-má and Nana entrusted to me, with the breadth of vision which Ea allotted me, with the might which Marduk gave me, I expelled the enemy to the North and South; I made an end of their raids; I brought health to the land; I made the populace to rest in security; I permitted no one to molest them.

The great gods proclaimed me and I am the guardian governor, whose scepter is righteous and whose beneficent protection is spread over my city. In my bosom I carried the people of the land of Sumer and Akkad; under my protection I brought their brethren into security; in my wisdom I restrained (hid) them; that the strong might not oppose the weak, and that they should give justice to the orphan and the widow, in Babylon, the city whose turrets Anu and Bel raised; in Esagila, the temple whose foundations are firm as heaven and earth, for the pronouncing of judgments in the land, for the rendering of decisions for the land, and for the righting of wrong, my weighty words I have written upon my monument, and in the presence of my image as king of righteousness have I established.

The king, who is preeminent among city kings, am I. My words are precious, my wisdom is unrivaled. By the command of Shamash, the great judge of heaven and earth, may I make righteousness to shine forth on the land. By the order of Marduk, my lord, may no one efface my statutes, may my name be remembered with favor in Esagila forever. Let any oppressed man, who has a cause, come before my image as king of righteousness! Let him read the inscription on my monument! Let him give heed to my weighty words! And may my monument enlighten him as to his cause and may he understand his case! May he set his heart at ease! (and he will exclaim): "Hammurabi indeed is a ruler who is like a real father to his people; he has given reverence to the words of Marduk, his lord; he has obtained victory for Marduk in North and South; he has made glad the heart of Marduk, his lord; he has established prosperity for the people for all time and given a pure government to the land."

In the days that are yet to come, for all future time, may the king who is in the land observe the words of righteousness which I have written upon my monument! May he not alter the judgments of the land which I have pronounced, or the decisions of the country which I have rendered! May he not efface my statutes! If that man have wisdom, if he wish to give his land good government, let him give attention to the words which I have written upon my monument! And may this monument enlighten him as to procedure and administration, the judgments which I have pronounced, and the decisions which I have rendered for the land! And let him rightly rule his Black-Head people; let him pronounce judgments for them and render for them decisions! Let him root out the wicked and evildoer from his land! Let him promote the welfare of his people!

Hammurabi, the king of righteousness, whom Shamash has endowed with justice, am I. My words are weighty; my deeds are unrivaled If that man do not pay attention to my words which I have written upon my monument; if he forget my curse and do not fear the curse of god; if he abolish the judgments which I have formulated, overrule my words, alter my statutes, efface my name written thereon and write his own name; on account of these curses, commission another to do so—as for that man, be he king or lord, or priest-king or commoner, whoever he may be, may the great god, the father of the gods, who has ordained my reign, take from him the glory of his sovereignty, may he break his scepter, and curse his fate!

May Bel, the lord, who determines destinies, whose command cannot be altered, who has enlarged my dominion, drive him out from his dwelling through a revolt which his hand cannot control and a curse destructive to him. May he determine as his fate a reign of sighs, days few in number, years of famine, darkness without light, death staring him in the face! The destruction of his city, the dispersion of his people, the wresting away of his dominion, the blotting out of his name and memory from the land, may Bel order with his potent command!

May Ea, the great prince, whose decrees take precedence, the leader of the gods, who knows everything, who prolongs the days of my life, deprive him of knowledge and wisdom! May he bring him to oblivion, and dam up his rivers at their sources! May he not permit corn, which is the life of the people, to grow in his land!

May Shamash, the great judge of heaven and earth, who rules all living creatures, the lord (inspiring) confidence, overthrow his dominion; may he not grant him his rights! May he make him to err in his path, may he destroy the mass (foundation) of his troops! May he bring to his view an evil omen of the uprooting of the foundation of his sovereignty, and the ruin of his land.

May the blighting curse of Shamash come upon him quickly! May he cut off his life above (upon the earth)! Below, within the earth, may he deprive his spirit of water!

May Adad, the lord of abundance, the regent of heaven and earth, my helper, deprive him of the rain from heaven and the water-floods from the springs! May he bring his land to destruction through want and hunger! May he break loose furiously over his city and turn his land into a heap left by a whirlwind!

May Ishtar, goddess of battle and conflict, who makes ready my weapons, the gracious protecting deity, who loves my reign, curse his dominion with great fury in her wrathful heart, and turn good into evil for him! May she shatter his weapons on the field of battle and conflict! May she create confusion and revolt for him! May she strike down his warriors, may their blood water the earth! May she cast the bodies of his warriors upon the field in heaps! May she not grant his warriors (burial(?))! May she deliver him into the hands of his enemies, and may they carry him away bound into a hostile land!

May Nin-tu, the exalted mistress of the lands, the mother who bore me, deny him a son! May she not let him hold a name among his people, nor beget an heir!

Hammurabi. *The Code of Hammurabi King of Babylon about 2250 B.C.* by Robert Francis Harper. Chicago: University of Chicago Press, 1904. [Online] available from https://oll.libertyfund.org/titles/1276, accessed June 2, 2020.

POST READING PARS

1. How does the Code of Hammurabi fall short of contemporary ideals of justice?

Inquiry Corner

Content Question(s):	**Critical Question(s):**
What is a judicial code?	Do you think the Code of Hammurabi was more successful in protecting individual rights—or in maintaining (and perpetuating) social order?
Comparative Question(s):	**Connection Question(s):**
In what ways does the public monument of this stele compare to other public monuments in terms of what is communicated, by whom and for whom, and why?	Think about what would happen if you broke a law: Who would be involved? Who would take action? Where would you go? What would happen to you? How many of those roles and processes are present in the Code of Hammurabi?

BEYOND THE CLASSROOM

» Styles of leadership can be seen on a spectrum of authoritarian/dictatorial to communal/collectivist. What style of leadership do you think is the best? In what situations can you see the value in another style of leadership? How might leadership skills be combined across models?

» What is the value of context-specific laws versus universal laws? Can you think of policies in work environments that are context-specific and policies that are universal?

Cyrus Cylinder

Introduction

SNAPSHOT BOX

LANGUAGE: Babylonian Akkadian

DATE: c. 540 BCE

LOCATION: Babylon

GENRE: Official proclamation

ETHNIC IDENTITY: Persian and Babylonian

TAGS: Authority and Leadership; Deities and Spirits; Empire and Colonialism; Journey; Monument and Artifact; Religion; Rhetoric and Propaganda

Kurush II, the Shah of Persia (Iran), is known to the West as King Cyrus the Great. Greek sources credit him with founding the Achaemenid Empire (c. 550–330 BCE), a southern Persian dynasty that ruled the territory of the Ancient Near East from the Mediterranean Sea in the west to the Indus River in the east. Cyrus is a major figure in Persian, Greek, and Jewish traditions, but his rise to power was poorly understood and is often distorted by these sources. Jewish tradition portrays him as a savior figure while the Greek sources place him as the product of a traditional Greek education. In contemporary Persian chronicles, however, Cyrus is the shah of the city of Anshan, who expanded his rule by conquest. What might be some strategies for navigating sources with multiple perspectives?

The "Cyrus Cylinder" is a fragmentary baked clay barrel cylinder discovered in 1879 in the foundation of the temple in the ruins of Babylon. The proclamation inscribed into the clay begins with the reign of the Babylonian king Nebuchadnezzar (604–562 BCE), whose monumental building program in Babylon included the Esagila, a rich sanctuary of the city-god Marduk, the temple in which the cylinder was embedded. As was customary, Nebuchadnezzar relocated captives from cities that he conquered, including Jerusalem, to Babylon. After his death, a new ruler, Nabonidus (555–539 BCE) continued the building of monuments in the territories under his control, including temples to the moon-god Sin and the sun-god Shamash. Nabonidus also established the char-

Timeline

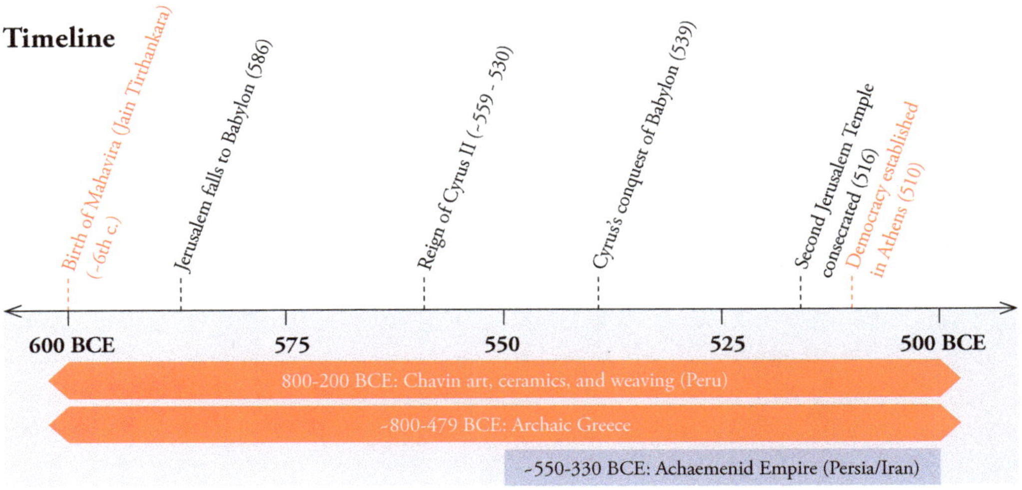

acteristic barrel-shaped cuneiform cylinder for disseminating information. During Nabonidus's reign in Babylon, Cyrus invaded the Median territory in northwestern Iran, and his continuing expansion west brought him finally to the conquest of Babylon. After Cyrus and his army prevailed in battle at the Mesopotamian cities of Opis on the Tigris and Sippar on the Euphrates, Babylon preemptively surrendered. Cyrus presented himself on the cylinder as entering the city as its liberator, justifying his conquest in the local form of an official proclamation: a barrel cylinder inscribed in Neo-Babylonian Akkadian cuneiform. Cyrus reassures the people that their ancestral cults and customs are secure under his reign, and that he is the restorer of the city much like the ancient Neo-Assyrian king Assurbanipal had been when he conquered Babylon. In other words, he issued propaganda, just as Darius the Great did in the Behistûn inscription and the Roman emperor Augustus in his ***Res Gestae***, in an attempt to portray his conquest as beneficence. However, Cyrus did allow foreign captives to return to their homes, for which he is celebrated in Jewish sources.

Lora Holland Goldthwaite
Department of Classics

PRE-READING PARS

1. If America were conquered by another national power, what two or three reassurances from the conquerors would you want to hear?
2. Identify two or three forms of authority leaders typically rely on to strengthen their position and power.

Cyrus Cylinder

[When ...] ... [... wor]ld quarters [...] ... a low person was put in charge of his country, but he set [a (...) counter]feit over them. He ma[de] a counterfeit of Esagil [and ...] ... for Ur and the rest of the cult-cities. Rites inappropriate to them, [impure] fo[od-offerings ...] [dis]respectful [...] were daily gabbled, and, intolerably, he brought the daily offerings to a halt; he inter[fered with the rites and] instituted [...] within the sanctuaries. In his mind, reverential fear of Marduk, king of the gods, ca[me to an e]nd. He did yet more evil to his city every day; [...] his [people...], he brought ruin on them all by a yoke without relief. Enlil-of-the-gods became extremely angry at their complaints, and [...] their territory. The gods who lived within them left their shrines, angry that he had made them enter into Babylon (Shuanna). Ex[alted Marduk, Enlil-of-the-Go]ds, relented. He changed his mind about all the settlements whose sanctuaries were in ruins and the population of the land of Sumer and Akkad who had become like corpses, and took pity on them. He inspected and checked all the countries, seeking for the upright king of his choice. He took under his hand Cyrus, king of the city of Anshan, and called him by his name, proclaiming him aloud for the kingship over all of everything. He made the land of the Qutu and all the Medean troops prostrate themselves at his feet, while he looked out in justice and righteousness for the black-headed people whom he had put under his care. Marduk, the great lord, who nurtures his people, saw with pleasure his fine deeds and true heart and ordered that he should go to his city, Babylon. He had him take the road to Tintir, and, like a friend and companion, he walked at his side. His vast troops whose number, like the water in a river, could not be counted, marched fully-armed at his side. He had him enter without fighting or battle right into Shuanna; he saved his city Babylon from hardship. He handed over to him Nabonidus, the king who did not fear him. All the people of Tintir, of all Sumer and Akkad, nobles and governors, bowed down before him and kissed his feet, rejoicing over his kingship and their faces shone. The lord through whose trust all were rescued from death and who saved them all from distress and hardship, they blessed him sweetly and praised his name.

I am Cyrus, king of the universe, the great king, the powerful king, king of Babylon, king of Sumer and Akkad, king of the four quarters of the world, son of Cambyses, the great king, king of the city of Anshan, grandson of Cyrus, the great king, ki[ng of the ci]ty of Anshan, descendant of Teispes, the great king, king of Anshan, the perpetual seed of kingship, whose reign Bel and Nabu love, and with whose kingship, to their joy, they concern themselves.

When I went as harbinger of peace i[nt]o Babylon I founded my sovereign residence within the royal palace amid celebration and rejoicing. Marduk, the great lord, bestowed on me as my destiny the great magnanimity of one who loves Babylon, and I every day sought him out in awe. My vast troops marched peaceably in Babylon, and the whole of [Sumer] and Akkad had nothing to fear. I sought the welfare of the city of Babylon and all its sanctuaries. As for the population of Babylon [..., w]ho as if without div[ine intention] had endured a yoke not decreed for them, I soothed their weariness, I freed them from their bonds(?). Marduk, the great lord, rejoiced at [my good] deeds, and he pronounced a sweet blessing over me, Cyrus, the king who fears him, and over Cambyses, the son [my] issue, [and over] my all my troops, that we might proceed further at his exalted [command]. All kings who sit on thrones, from every quarter, from the Upper Sea to the Lower Sea, those who inhabit [remote distric]ts (and) the kings of the land of Amurru who live in tents, all of them, brought their weighty tribute into Shuanna, and kissed my feet. From [Shuanna] I sent back to their places to the city of Ashur and Susa, Akkad, the land of Eshnunna, the city of Zamban, the city of Meturnu, Der, as far as the border of the land of Qutu—the sanctuaries across the river Tigris—whose shrines had earlier become dilapidated, the gods who lived therein, and made permanent sanctuaries for them. I collected together all of their people and returned them to their settlements, and the gods of the land of Sumer and Akkad which Nabonidus—to the fury of the lord of the gods—had brought into Shuanna, at the command of Marduk, the great lord, I returned them unharmed to their cells, in the sanctuaries that make them happy. May all the gods that I returned to their sanctuaries, every day before Marduk and Nabu, ask for a long life for me, and mention my good deeds, and say to Marduk, my lord, this: "Cyrus, the king who fears you, and Cambyses his son, may their ... [...] [.......]." The population of Babylon call blessings on my kingship, and I have enabled all the lands to live in peace. Every day I copiously supplied [... ge]ese, two ducks and ten pigeons more than the geese, ducks and pigeons [...]. I sought out to strengthen the guard on the wall Imgur-Enlil, the great wall of Babylon, and [...] the quay of baked brick on the bank of the moat which an earlier king had bu[ilt but not com]pleted, [I ...] its work. [... which did not surround the city] outside, which no earlier king had built, his troops, the levee from [his land, in/to] Shuanna. [... with bitume]n and baked brick I built anew, and [completed its wor]k. [...] great [doors of cedarwood] with copper cladding. [I installed all] their doors, threshold sla[bs and door fittings with copper par]ts. [...] I s[aw within it] an inscription of Ashurbanipal, a king who preceded me, [...] ... [...] ... [... for] ever.

Finkel, Irving, ed. and trans. *The Cyrus Cylinder: The Great Persian Edict from Babylon*, 4–7. London: I. B. Tauris, 2013.

POST-READING PARS

1. What reassurances does Cyrus provide to the Babylonian people?
2. What forms of authority did Cyrus rely on to strengthen his position of power?
3. What evidence does Cyrus provide that his victory is proof of the gods' favor?

Inquiry Corner

Content Question(s):	**Critical Question(s):**
What were some of the building activities that Cyrus ordered carried out in Babylon after his conquest?	The chief deity of Persia was Ahuramazda, yet in the Cyrus Cylinder, Cyrus prays to the Babylonian god Marduk for his blessing. What political and religious reasons might motivate this?
Comparative Question(s):	**Connection Question(s):**
Compare and contrast proclamations made by leaders about their achievements and actions (e.g., Hatshepsut, *Res Gestae*, Behistûn, etc.)	Shahs ruled in Persia (present-day Iran) for most of its history, from antiquity until 1979, when a Muslim Ayatollah overthrew the pro-Western government and imposed an Islamic theocracy. What evidence in the cylinder reflects what Cyrus might have thought of this internal power struggle?

BEYOND THE CLASSROOM

» What is the value of stating accomplishments? What are the best ways to acknowledge people's contributions to a team? What role do awards or other forms of recognition play in one's productivity?

Epic of Gilgamesh (Introduction only)

SNAPSHOT BOX

LANGUAGE: Akkadian

DATE: 13th century BCE (Standard Version)

LOCATION: Mesopotamia

GENRE: Epic

ETHNIC IDENTITY: Babylonian and Assyrian Empires

TAGS: Authority and Leadership; Conflict and War; Death; Deities and Spirits; Divination; Friendship; Identity; Journey; Love; Monument and Artifact; Nature; Oral Histories and Storytelling; Suffering and Compassion

Introduction

The *Epic of Gilgamesh* is the world's oldest extant literary masterpiece. It was written in Ancient Mesopotamia and read for centuries, until the traditional language and culture of Mesopotamia died out in the first few centuries CE. The epic's hero, the semi-divine Gilgamesh, is based on a historical king who ruled the city of Uruk, thought to be the world's oldest city, sometime between 2700 and 2500 BCE. "Epic," an ancient Greek term for a long narrative about the deeds of heroes told on a grand scale, is appropriate for *Gilgamesh*. Because of its antiquity, we might consider *Gilgamesh* to be **folklore,** a body of culturally meaningful stories circulated orally. There is, in fact, evidence of loosely connected legends called a **cycle** that grew up around the historical Gilgamesh, some of which were eventually collected and written down in Sumerian, the world's oldest written language, around 2000 BCE. Sumerian is related to no other known language. An earlier epic about Gilgamesh was composed during the age of Hammurabi (the Old Babylonian version) that survives only in fragments. The epic that you are reading, called the Standard Version by scholars today, was composed in the thirteenth century in Akkadian, a Semitic language that is an ancestor of Hebrew and Arabic. Its author was Sin-leqi-unninni, a scholar whose profession combined that of doctor, religious healer, priest, and reader of omens. Sin-leqi-unninni's text is indebted to the Old Babylonian version. Thus, *The Epic of Gilgamesh* is a work of literature that has roots reaching back into folklore.

Sin-leqi-unninni's epic had a name: "He Who Has Seen Everything,"

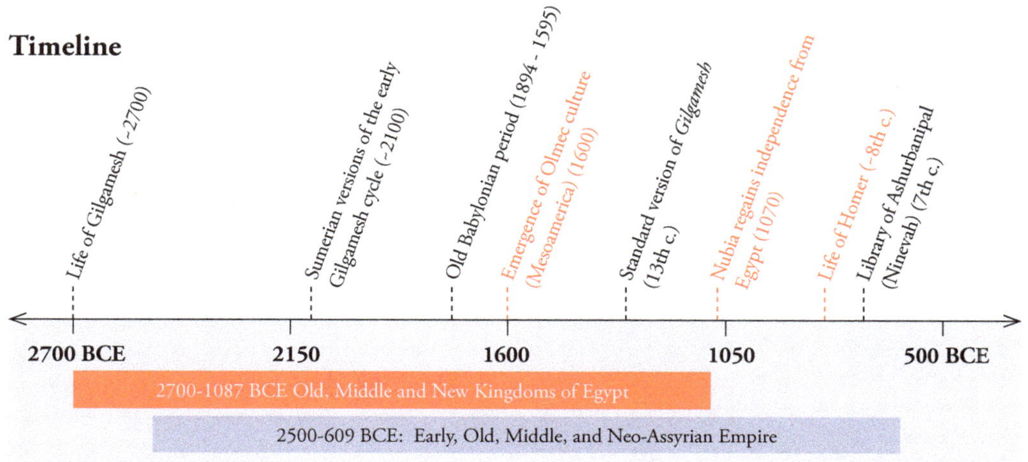

or, more literally, "He Who Has Seen the Deep."[147] This is, in fact, the first line of the epic. As you read, reflect on the evolving relevance of this title with the themes and events of the epic, and how the different supporting characters, including many powerful women, contribute to the internal and physical journeys Gilgamesh undertakes. *Gilgamesh* is a unified work, overtly thematic, symbolic, and psychological, adapting numerous oral and written genres of literature and speaking. A Mesopotamian reader would have recognized two major models of written literature in the epic: royal propaganda inscribed on monuments and walls, and fictional autobiographies of legendary figures, a popular genre known as ***naru***.[148] When you read the epic, you will encounter numerous genres used by the author to craft the story: prayers, visions, origin stories, myths, combat scenes, and more. What scenes or types of action do you expect from an epic?

We have dozens of surviving copies of the Standard Version of *Gilgamesh*, several of which were found in the ruins of the famous library of the king Ashurbanipal (d. 631 BCE) in the city of Nineveh (near modern-day Mosul, Iraq). Mesopotamian books took the form of pillow-shaped **clay tablets**, and writing was made by impressing shapes into the clay with a pen or **stylus** whose triangular tip left marks that are "wedge-shaped," the literal meaning of cuneiform, which is the oldest known form of writing. The Standard Version of *Gilgamesh* took up twelve tablets (the conceptual equivalent of a "book" in an epic like the *Odyssey*) containing about 250 lines of poetry each.[149] As you can tell when reading *Gilgamesh*, none of the tablets of the Standard Version has survived in complete form, although some are better preserved than others. Unlike Homer or the *Mahabharata*, the *Epic of Gilgamesh* did not exist as an enduring oral tradition, but was forgotten for nearly 2,000 years until copies were discovered in Iraq in the 1850s and the cuneiform script deciphered. As archaeological excavation continues in the Middle East, more fragmentary copies of the epic turn up—often, unfortunately, through looting—filling out our knowledge of the story.

Sin-leqi-unninni recast folktales about the hero and earlier epic fragments into a particular vision that reflects on what it means to be human and to straddle society and nature. *Gilgamesh* also presented wisdom from Ancient Mesopotamian culture, such as the nature of kingship, the importance of legacy, and more practical advice about living a meaningful life. One of the epic's enduring themes, friendship, was skillfully woven in by a clever transformation: a legendary servant of Gilgamesh

147. In Akkadian, this word refers to the source of rivers and springs. Here, it seems to be a metaphor for the outer reaches of the world and could be translated "abyss."

148. The word *naru* means "stele," a popular style of monument erected by rulers that contained both texts and images. A famous example is the Naram Sin stele. The *Code of Hammurabi* was also written on a stele.

149. Note that in Maureen Gallery Kovacs's translation, tablet 12, a later addition to the epic that sees Gilgamesh and Enkidu travel to the underworld, is omitted. The original epic, without a doubt, ended with tablet 11. It is not known whether Sin-leqi-unninni was responsible for the addition of the twelfth tablet or not.

known from Sumerian legends named Enkidu becomes his closest friend, and their relationship (which has unmistakable erotic overtones) blossoms into the dominant theme of the second half of the epic: mortality, leading the German poet Rainer Maria Rilke (1875–1926) to famously call *Gilgamesh* "an epic about the fear of death." This theme saturates the whole epic with a profound feeling of pity and sorrow, or **pathos**. Theoretically, Gilgamesh the character may not seem relatable to us, being far removed from our own experience, yet all of the epic's readers, past and present, share his human vulnerability: the inevitability of aging, loss, and death.

We should not get weighed down in the epic's depiction of human pathos at the expense of enjoying it as a work of storytelling. The epic narrative of *Gilgamesh* is made up of individual units that tell of mighty deeds, battles, long journeys, ominous dreams, and long-anticipated meetings that nevertheless build on each other toward a revelation that Gilgamesh experiences about death. It also raises muddier questions about human motivations in their relationships to the natural environment side by side with dazzling set pieces, such as when Gilgamesh traces the sun's path through the underworld, emerging into a dawn garden of jewels, and charming details, for example, offering an explanation for why snakes shed their skin. Equally memorable are several interludes, such as the entertaining telling of the myth of the Great Flood in tablet 11.[150] The epic was written by a sophisticated storyteller who knew how to introduce and flesh out characters, create suspense, and foster investment in the epic's themes and ideas on the part of the reader. In what different ways is Gilgamesh presented with the possibility of immortality, and how has his perspective on the meaning of life and his legacy evolved by the close of the epic? Do you think the ending is climactic or anticlimactic?

Joseph Cross
Humanities Program

[Content Notice: Non-consensual sex, may have outdated language related to sex work, violence]

Recommended Translation: *The Epic of Gilgamesh*. Translated with an introduction and notes by Maureen Kovacs. Stanford, CA: Stanford University Press, 1989.

150. The Great Flood was a popular myth in Mesopotamia and was known, either in its *Gilgamesh* version or in other text, by the author of the Noah story of the Book of Genesis (chapters 6–9).

"The Exaltation of Inana" by Enheduanna

Introduction

SNAPSHOT

LANGUAGE: Sumerian

DATE: c. 2300 BCE

LOCATION: Ur (southern Mesopotamia)

GENRE: Temple hymn

TAGS: Cosmology; Deities and Spirits; Love; Religion; Rhetoric and Propaganda; Women and Gender

Enheduanna (c. 2300 BCE) is the earliest named author that we know from antiquity. Her most well-known text, "The Exaltation of Inana," remains the best known of her prodigious literary output. Her numerous compositions appear to have formed the core reading list for ancient Sumerian students training to be **scribes**, a small but important professional class of people whose expertise in writing and reading made them crucial to the administration of Sumerian city-states. For several hundred years after Enheduanna's death, and more than 1,500 years before the ancient Athenians began teaching **rhetoric** (Greek *rhetorikē*, persuasive oratory), Mesopotamian students, mostly men, memorized, recited, and copied Enheduanna's texts as models of great literature.

Enheduanna was the high priest at a sanctuary devoted to the Sumerian moon god, Nanna (also called Ašimbabbar and, in Akkadian, Suen or Sin), in the southern city of Ur. She was appointed to this post by her father, the ruler Sargon of Akkad (c. 2371–2316 BCE), a northerner who conquered and consolidated the Sumerian city-states into the earliest recorded empire that spanned from present-day Turkey to the Persian Gulf. Sargon and his people spoke a language we now call Akkadian, rather than the language of the Sumerian people he conquered; intriguingly, however, the name "Enheduanna" is Sumerian and means "ornamented lord [or priest] of the heavens." In her role as high priest, Enheduanna led rituals that re-created Sumerian **myths**—stories that encode, express, and reinforce a culture's imagination about its values and truths.

Timeline

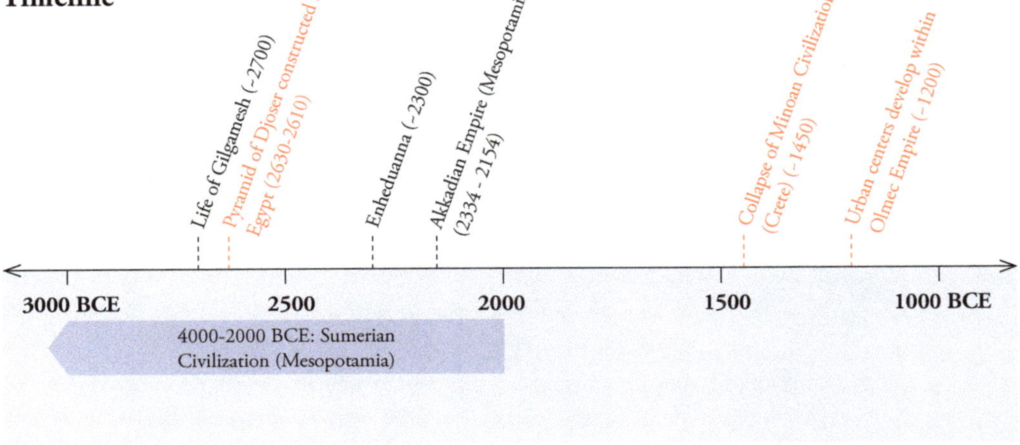

Enheduanna's hymns were composed and recorded in Sumerian, using the wedge-shaped writing system known as **cuneiform**. What political purposes are served by the appointment of Enheduanna, as well as the adoption of a conquered people's language and rituals?

The religious frameworks in the "Exaltation of Inana" highlight a goddess, yet also detail the political and personal experiences of Enheduanna. The poem refers to the goddess as Ninmešarra, "the Queen of all divine powers." She is Inana, the Sumerian goddess of war and fertility/sexuality, who was also worshipped as the Morning and Evening Star.[151] Interestingly, her name in Akkadian is Ishtar, a goddess we meet in the *Epic of Gilgamesh*. The poem also narrates and laments a political uprising against Enheduanna by a rival Sumerian ruler, Lugalanne, who deposed and exiled her. This political crisis leads Enheduanna to call on a number of male gods to restore her to power, including the moon god whose temple she oversees. The poem concludes with Enheduanna celebrating only Inana. In what ways do religion and politics intersect in this poem in relation to power and negotiating hierarchies?

Consider, too, the structure and style of the poem itself, particularly its **repetitions** and its **parallelisms,** lines that restate but elaborate on the same idea, both of which are distinctive features not only of Sumerian verse, but of ancient Near Eastern poetry more generally. What effect(s) might these elements have on audiences hearing or reading these texts? What might these features suggest about the literary or rhetorical qualities valued by ancient audiences, readers, teachers, and students?

Reading this multilayered poem from humanity's earliest named author offers us an excellent opportunity to ask a few broad questions. For example, what does Inana's prominence—as well as her association with both war and fertility—suggest about Ancient Mesopotamian attitudes toward women or the role of gender itself? How does Enheduanna's prominence and prodigious literary output square with our own assumptions about the status of women in antiquity?

Brian C. Graves
Department of English

151. Inana's name appears in Akkadian texts with various alternative spellings. Transliterations of the name into English (and related language using the Latin alphabet) include both Inana and Inanna.

The Exaltation of Inana (Inana B)

1–12. Lady of all the divine powers, resplendent light, righteous woman clothed in radiance, beloved of An and Uraš![152] Mistress of heaven, with the great diadem, who loves the good headdress befitting the office of high priestess, who has seized all seven of its divine powers! My lady, you are the guardian of the great divine powers! You have taken up the divine powers, you have hung the divine powers from your hand. You have gathered up the divine powers, you have clasped the divine powers to your breast. Like a dragon you have deposited venom on the foreign lands. When like Iškur[153] you roar at the earth, no vegetation can stand up to you. As a flood descending upon (?) those foreign lands, powerful one of heaven and earth, you are their Inana.

13–19. Raining blazing fire down upon the Land, endowed with divine powers by An, lady who rides upon a beast, whose words are spoken at the holy command of An! The great rites are yours: who can fathom them? Destroyer of the foreign lands, you confer strength on the storm. Beloved of Enlil,[154] you have made awesome terror weigh upon the Land. You stand at the service of An's commands.

20–33. At your battle-cry, my lady, the foreign lands bow low. When humanity comes before you in awed silence at the terrifying radiance and tempest, you grasp the most terrible of all the divine powers. Because of you, the threshold of tears is opened, and people walk along the path of the house of great lamentations. In the van of battle, all is struck down before you. With your strength, my lady, teeth can crush flint. You charge forward like a charging storm. You roar with the roaring storm, you continually thunder with Iškur. You spread exhaustion with the stormwinds, while your own feet remain tireless. With the lamenting balaĝ[155] drum a lament is struck up.

34–41. My lady, the great Anuna[156] gods fly from you to the ruin mounds like scudding bats. They dare not stand before your terrible gaze. They dare not confront your terrible countenance. Who can cool your raging heart? Your malevolent anger is too great to cool. Lady, can your mood be soothed? Lady, can your heart be gladdened? Eldest daughter of Suen,[157] your rage cannot be cooled!

42–59. Lady supreme over the foreign lands, who can take anything from your

152. Heaven and Earth, here understood as deities. In the Sumerian pantheon, they also figure as great-grandparents of Inana.

153. Sumerian storm god (Akkadian Adad), suggestive here of thunder.

154. Supreme Mesopotamian deity, associated with lordship and power; also Inana's grandfather.

155. An Akkadian gloss, here understood as a drum, but in other translations rendered as "harp."

156. A grouping of deities, here understood as the most important gods of the Sumerian pantheon.

157. Akkadian name for the moon god, Nanna.

province? {Once you have extended your province over the hills[158]}, vegetation there is ruined. Their {great gateways/palaces} are set afire. Blood is poured into their rivers because of you, and their people {could not drink[159]}. They must lead their troops captive before you, all together. They must scatter their élite regiments for you, all together. They must stand their able-bodied young men at your service, all together. Tempests have filled the dancing-places of their cities. They drive their young men before you as prisoners. Your holy command has been spoken over the city which has not declared "The foreign lands are yours!," wherever they have not declared "It is your own father's!"; and it is brought back under your feet. Responsible care is removed from its sheepfolds. Its woman no longer speaks affectionately with her husband; at dead of night she no longer takes counsel with him, and she no longer reveals to him the pure thoughts of her heart. Impetuous wild cow,[160] great daughter of Suen, lady greater than An, who can take anything from your province?

60–65. Great queen of queens, issue of a holy womb for righteous divine powers, greater than your own mother, wise and sage, lady of all the foreign lands, life-force of the teeming people: I will recite your holy song! True goddess fit for divine powers, your splendid utterances are magnificent. Deep-hearted, good woman with a radiant heart, I will enumerate {your divine powers[161]} for you!

66–73. I, En-ḫedu-ana the high priestess, entered my holy ĝipar[162] in your service. I carried the ritual basket, and intoned the song of joy. But {funeral offerings were[163]} brought, as if I had never lived there. I approached the light, but the light was scorching hot to me. I approached that shade, but I was covered with a storm. My honeyed mouth became scum. My ability to soothe moods vanished.

74–80. Suen, tell An about Lugal-Ane[164] and my fate! May An undo it for me! As soon as you tell An about it, An will release me. The woman will take the destiny away from Lugal-Ane; foreign lands and flood lie at her feet. The woman too is exalted, and can make cities tremble. Step forward, so that she will cool her heart for me.

81–90. I, En-ḫedu-ana, will recite a prayer to you. To you, holy Inana, I shall give free vent to my tears like sweet beer! I shall say to her {"Greetings!"[165]} Do not be anxious about Ašimbabbar.[166] In connection with the purification rites of holy An,

158. Phrases enclosed in curly brackets signal that variant readings exist in some manuscripts. Here, two manuscripts read instead, "If you frown at the mountains."

159. Most manuscripts read "must drink it."

160. The cow, whose horns resemble the crescent moon, was a principal symbol of Nanna, the moon god, though here it is associated with Inana.

161. Some manuscripts read "good divine powers" or "holy divine powers."

162. Akkadian gloss, apparently referring to some sacred space particular to Enheduanna.

163. One manuscript reads "my ritual meal was."

164. As noted in the intro, Lugalanne was the rival Sumerian ruler who deposed and exiled Enheduanna.

165. Other manuscripts read "Your decision!"

166. Another name for Nanna, the moon god, at whose temple Enheduanna served.

Lugal-Ane has altered everything of his, and has stripped An of the E-ana. He has not stood in awe of the greatest deity. He has turned that temple, whose attractions were inexhaustible, whose beauty was endless, into a destroyed temple. While he entered before me as if he was a partner, really he approached out of envy.

91–108. My good divine wild cow, drive out the man, capture the man! In the place of divine encouragement, what is my standing now? May An extradite the land which is a malevolent rebel against your Nanna! May An smash that city! May Enlil curse it! May its plaintive child not be placated by his mother! Lady, with the laments begun, may your ship of lamentation be abandoned in hostile territory. Must I die because of my holy songs? My Nanna has {paid no heed to me[167]}. He has destroyed me utterly in renegade territory. Ašimbabbar has certainly not pronounced a verdict on me. What is it to me if he has pronounced it? What is it to me if he has not pronounced it? He stood there in triumph and drove me out of the temple. He made me fly like a swallow from the window; I have exhausted my life-strength. He made me walk through the thorn bushes of the mountains. He stripped me of the rightful {crown[168]} of the high priestess. He gave me a knife and dagger, saying to me "These are appropriate ornaments for you."

109–121. Most precious lady, beloved by An, your holy heart is great; may it be assuaged on my behalf! Beloved spouse of Ušumgal-ana[169], you are the great lady of the horizon and zenith of the heavens. The Anuna have submitted to you. From birth you were the junior queen: how supreme you are now over the Anuna, the great gods! The Anuna kiss the ground with their lips before you. But my own trial is not yet concluded, although a hostile verdict encloses me as if it were my own verdict. I did not reach out my hands to {my[170]} flowered bed. I did not reveal the pronouncements of Ningal to anybody.[171] My lady beloved of An, may your heart be calmed towards me, the brilliant high priestess of Nanna!

122–138. It must be known! It must be known! Nanna has not yet spoken out! He has said, "He is yours!" Be it known that you are lofty as the heavens! Be it known that you are broad as the earth! Be it known that you destroy the rebel lands! Be it known that you roar at the foreign lands! Be it known that you crush heads! Be it known that you devour corpses like a dog! Be it known that your gaze is terrible! Be it known that you lift your terrible gaze! Be it known that you have flashing eyes! Be it known that you are unshakeable and unyielding! Be it known that you always stand triumphant! That Nanna has not yet spoken out, and that he has said "He is yours!"

167. One manuscript reads "has not decided my case."

168. One manuscript reads "garment."

169. Also known as Dumuzi or Tammuz, this god was the principal consort for Inana. In the sacred marriage ritual of ancient Mespotamia, a king and queen (or some other high-ranking woman) played the roles of Dumuzi and Inana to celebrate fertility.

170. Most manuscripts read "the."

171. Ningal was the wife of Nanna, the moon god, and thus Inana's mother; some translators see here a reference to dream interpretation.

has made you greater, my lady; you have become the greatest! My lady beloved by An, I shall tell of all your {rages[172]}! I have heaped up the coals in the censer, and prepared the purification rites. The E-ešdam-kug shrine awaits you.[173] Might your heart not be appeased towards me?

139–143. Since it was full, too full for me, great exalted lady, I have recited this song for you.[174] May a singer repeat to you at noon that which was recited to you at dead of night: "Because of your captive spouse, because of your captive child, your rage is increased, your heart unassuaged."

144–154. The powerful lady, respected in the gathering of rulers, has accepted her offerings from her. Inana's holy heart has been assuaged. The light was sweet for her, delight extended over her, she was full of fairest beauty. Like the light of the rising moon, she exuded delight. Nanna came out to gaze at her properly, and her mother Ningal blessed her. The door posts greeted her. Everyone's speech to the mistress is exalted. Praise be to the destroyer of foreign lands, endowed with divine powers by An, to my lady enveloped in beauty, to Inana!

The Exaltation of Inana (Inana B). Translated by the Faculty of Oriental Studies. Oxford: University of Oxford, 2006, accessed at https://etcsl.orinst.ox.ac.uk/cgi-bin/etcsl.cgi?text=t.4.07.2.

172. One manuscript reads "daises" i.e., seats of honor, thrones.

173. This may perhaps refer the sacred nuptial chamber where the sacred marriage ritual would have been enacted. (Whether it involved actual or merely symbolic sexual intercourse remains uncertain.)

174. Likely in a public recitation, perhaps celebrating Enheduanna's restoration as high priest.

from Hebrew Bible, Book of Daniel 1–6

Introduction

SNAPSHOT BOX

LANGUAGE: Hebrew and Aramaic

DATE: c. 4th–3rd century BCE

LOCATION: Judea

GENRE: Scripture

ETHNIC IDENTITY: Jewish

TAGS: Authority and Leadership; Divination; Identity; Journey; Religion

Do you have an "essential identity"? If so, how can your life change without changing that essential identity? The Book of Daniel in the Hebrew Bible offers explorations in response to these questions. It tells the story—or rather, several different stories—about Daniel and three other exiles who were taken to Babylon after the destruction of Judah in 586 BCE. The focus of their stories is about the forms of their faithfulness, but the broader context of the first six chapters excerpted below is about navigating choices around assimilating to Babylonian culture. The first chapter provides immediate examples of resistance and acceptance of changes forced on Jewish peoples as part of trying to thrive in exile.

The Book of Daniel presents many interpretive challenges. The Hebrew word for the text of the Hebrew Bible is *Tanakh*, an anagram of its contents: *Torah*, or Law; *Nevi'im*, or Prophets; and *Ketuvim*, or "Writings," to which belong books of poetry and history. Half of the Book of Daniel is devoted to dream prophecies, but it is considered one of the "Writings," not as one of the "Prophets." This brief book is really two books written in two languages: Hebrew and Aramaic, the language of Jesus. Of the twelve chapters, chapters 7–12 contain Daniel's **apocalyptic** dreams and prophecies and interpretations about political and cosmic upheavals and changes; and chapters 1 and 8–12 are written in Hebrew. Chapters 1–6 are stories *about* Daniel and other exiles from Jerusalem who are held in Babylon. Chapters 2–7 are written in Aramaic, a Semitic language like Hebrew that emerged from the Assyrian Empire.

Timeline

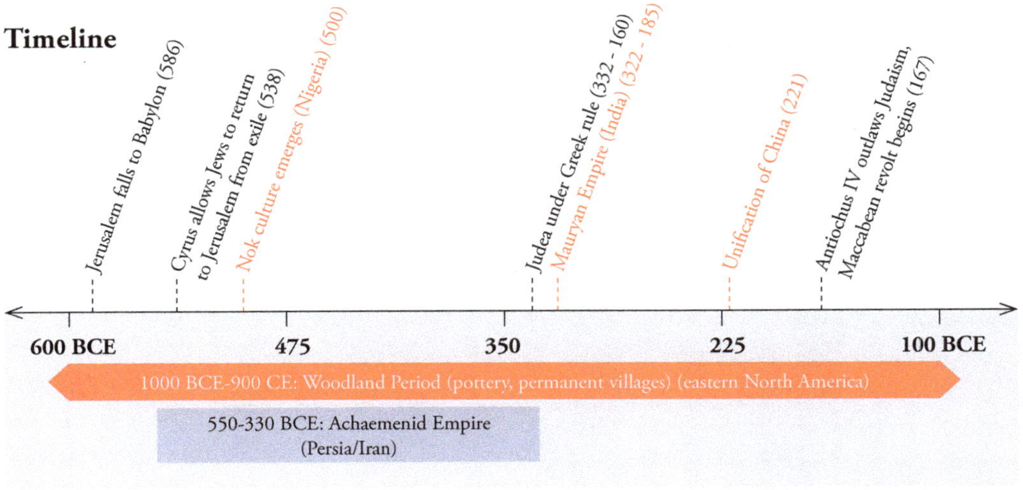

Very little is known about the original creation and composition of the text of the Book of Daniel. Scholars do not know whether there was an original version entirely in Hebrew or Aramaic; nor do we know exactly when the books were finally written down. The Book of Daniel reports events from about 605–537 BCE, and the later chapters present themselves as the first-person words of Daniel. However, historical inaccuracies in the first six chapters and certain historical details in Daniel's prophecies suggest a later composition or collation. The first six chapters may have existed as oral tales before they were written down, perhaps in the Hellenistic period between the fourth and third centuries BCE. Scholars often assign the later books to the early Maccabean period of persecution under Antiochus Epiphanes (167–164 BCE), when the Jews rebelled against and won independence from the Seleucid Empire, under the leadership of the family of Judas Maccabeus.

The Hebrew Bible has many accounts of the events that lead up to and follow the Babylonian exile of the Jewish peoples, but very few tales of the experience of exile itself. Other texts that address the experience of exile, like Psalm 139, express understandable sorrow and loss. The Jewish historian Josephus, writing in the first century CE, assumed that the noble young men like Daniel, who were taken into exile to serve the Babylonian king, were castrated (***Antiquities of the Jews*** 10.10.1), but if so, the Book of Daniel does not say so. Instead, we read success stories of the Jewish young men who thrive in the Babylonian courts. There is no attempt to describe the larger Jewish community in exile. For example, women are never mentioned in the text. For this reason, the first six chapters of Daniel have usually been read not as historical accounts but as moral narratives that provide examples of living one's Jewish identity in exile for its readers.

What moral lessons can you derive from these chapters, and how do they differ from the moral instruction of other cultures? What do Daniel and his companions do to acquire the favor and status that they have? Wisdom is an important component of Daniel's character. How does he gain it and how is it demonstrated? Whenever the Book of Daniel was composed, it appears to have been known to the author of I Maccabees. How do resistance and assimilation compare in these two books?

Brian S. Hook
Department of Classics

Book of Daniel 1–6

Daniel 1

Daniel's Training in Babylon

1 In the third year of the reign of Jehoiakim king of Judah, Nebuchadnezzar king of Babylon came to Jerusalem and besieged it. 2 And the Lord delivered Jehoiakim king of Judah into his hand, along with some of the articles from the temple of God. These he carried off to the temple of his god in Babylonia and put in the treasure house of his god.

3 Then the king ordered Ashpenaz, chief of his court officials, to bring into the king's service some of the Israelites from the royal family and the nobility— 4 young men without any physical defect, handsome, showing aptitude for every kind of learning, well informed, quick to understand, and qualified to serve in the king's palace. He was to teach them the language and literature of the Babylonians. 5 The king assigned them a daily amount of food and wine from the king's table. They were to be trained for three years, and after that they were to enter the king's service.

6 Among those who were chosen were some from Judah: Daniel, Hananiah, Mishael and Azariah. 7 The chief official gave them new names: to Daniel, the name Belteshazzar; to Hananiah, Shadrach; to Mishael, Meshach; and to Azariah, Abednego.

8 But Daniel resolved not to defile himself with the royal food and wine, and he asked the chief official for permission not to defile himself this way. 9 Now God had caused the official to show favor and compassion to Daniel, 10 but the official told Daniel, "I am afraid of my lord the king, who has assigned your food and drink. Why should he see you looking worse than the other young men your age? The king would then have my head because of you."

11 Daniel then said to the guard whom the chief official had appointed over Daniel, Hananiah, Mishael and Azariah, 12 "Please test your servants for ten days: Give us nothing but vegetables to eat and water to drink. 13 Then compare our appearance with that of the young men who eat the royal food, and treat your servants in accordance with what you see." 14 So he agreed to this and tested them for ten days.

15 At the end of the ten days they looked healthier and better nourished than any of the young men who ate the royal food. 16 So the guard took away their choice food and the wine they were to drink and gave them vegetables instead.

17 To these four young men God gave knowledge and understanding of all kinds of literature and learning. And Daniel could understand visions and dreams of all kinds.

18 At the end of the time set by the king to bring them into his service, the chief official presented them to Nebuchadnezzar. 19 The king talked with them, and he found none equal to Daniel, Hananiah, Mishael and Azariah; so they entered the king's service. 20 In every matter of wisdom and understanding about which the

king questioned them, he found them ten times better than all the magicians and enchanters in his whole kingdom.

21 And Daniel remained there until the first year of King Cyrus.

Daniel 2

Nebuchadnezzar's Dream

1 In the second year of his reign, Nebuchadnezzar had dreams; his mind was troubled
and he could not sleep. 2 So the king summoned the magicians, enchanters, sorcer-
ers and astrologers to tell him what he had dreamed. When they came in and stood
before the king, 3 he said to them, "I have had a dream that troubles me and I want
to know what it means."

4 Then the astrologers answered the king, "May the king live forever! Tell your
servants the dream, and we will interpret it."

5 The king replied to the astrologers, "This is what I have firmly decided: If you
do not tell me what my dream was and interpret it, I will have you cut into pieces and
your houses turned into piles of rubble. 6 But if you tell me the dream and explain
it, you will receive from me gifts and rewards and great honor.So tell me the dream
and interpret it for me."

7 Once more they replied, "Let the king tell his servants the dream, and we will
interpret it."

8 Then the king answered, "I am certain that you are trying to gain time, because you realize that this is what I have firmly decided: 9 If you do not tell me the
dream, there is only one penalty for you. You have conspired to tell me misleading
and wicked things, hoping the situation will change. So then, tell me the dream, and
I will know that you can interpret it for me."

10 The astrologers answered the king, "There is no one on earth who can do what
the king asks! No king, however great and mighty, has ever asked such a thing of any
magician or enchanter or astrologer.11 What the king asks is too difficult. No one can
reveal it to the king except the gods, and they do not live among humans."

12 This made the king so angry and furious that he ordered the execution of all
the wise men of Babylon.13 So the decree was issued to put the wise men to death, and
men were sent to look for Daniel and his friends to put them to death.

14 When Arioch, the commander of the king's guard, had gone out to put to
death the wise men of Babylon, Daniel spoke to him with wisdom and tact. 15 He
asked the king's officer, "Why did the king issue such a harsh decree?" Arioch then
explained the matter to Daniel. 16 At this, Daniel went in to the king and asked for
time, so that he might interpret the dream for him.

17 Then Daniel returned to his house and explained the matter to his friends Hananiah, Mishael and Azariah. 18 He urged them to plead for mercy from the God of
heaven concerning this mystery, so that he and his friends might not be executed with

the rest of the wise men of Babylon. 19 During the night the mystery was revealed to
Daniel in a vision. Then Daniel praised the God of heaven 20 and said:

"Praise be to the name of God for ever and ever;
wisdom and power are his.
21
He changes times and seasons;
he deposes kings and raises up others.
He gives wisdom to the wise
and knowledge to the discerning.
22
He reveals deep and hidden things;
he knows what lies in darkness,
and light dwells with him.
23
I thank and praise you, God of my ancestors:
You have given me wisdom and power,
you have made known to me what we asked of you,
you have made known to us the dream of the king."

Daniel Interprets the Dream

24 Then Daniel went to Arioch, whom the king had appointed to execute the wise
men of Babylon, and said to him, "Do not execute the wise men of Babylon. Take me
to the king, and I will interpret his dream for him."

25 Arioch took Daniel to the king at once and said, "I have found a man among
the exiles from Judah who can tell the king what his dream means."

26 The king asked Daniel (also called Belteshazzar), "Are you able to tell me what
I saw in my dream and interpret it?"

27 Daniel replied, "No wise man, enchanter, magician or diviner can explain to
the king the mystery he has asked about, 28 but there is a God in heaven who reveals
mysteries. He has shown King Nebuchadnezzar what will happen in days to come.
Your dream and the visions that passed through your mind as you were lying in bed
are these:

29 "As Your Majesty was lying there, your mind turned to things to come, and the
revealer of mysteries showed you what is going to happen. 30 As for me, this mystery
has been revealed to me, not because I have greater wisdom than anyone else alive,
but so that Your Majesty may know the interpretation and that you may understand
what went through your mind.

31 "Your Majesty looked, and there before you stood a large statue—an enormous,
dazzling statue, awesome in appearance. 32 The head of the statue was made of pure
gold, its chest and arms of silver, its belly and thighs of bronze, 33 its legs of iron, its

feet partly of iron and partly of baked clay. 34 While you were watching, a rock was cut out, but not by human hands. It struck the statue on its feet of iron and clay and smashed them. 35 Then the iron, the clay, the bronze, the silver and the gold were all broken to pieces and became like chaff on a threshing floor in the summer. The wind swept them away without leaving a trace. But the rock that struck the statue became a huge mountain and filled the whole earth.

36 "This was the dream, and now we will interpret it to the king. 37 Your Majesty, you are the king of kings. The God of heaven has given you dominion and power and might and glory; 38 in your hands he has placed all mankind and the beasts of the field and the birds in the sky. Wherever they live, he has made you ruler over them all. You are that head of gold.

39 "After you, another kingdom will arise, inferior to yours. Next, a third kingdom, one of bronze, will rule over the whole earth. 40 Finally, there will be a fourth kingdom, strong as iron—for iron breaks and smashes everything—and as iron breaks things to pieces, so it will crush and break all the others. 41 Just as you saw that the feet and toes were partly of baked clay and partly of iron, so this will be a divided kingdom; yet it will have some of the strength of iron in it, even as you saw iron mixed with clay. 42 As the toes were partly iron and partly clay, so this kingdom will be partly strong and partly brittle. 43 And just as you saw the iron mixed with baked clay, so the people will be a mixture and will not remain united, any more than iron mixes with clay.

44 "In the time of those kings, the God of heaven will set up a kingdom that will never be destroyed, nor will it be left to another people. It will crush all those kingdoms and bring them to an end, but it will itself endure forever. 45 This is the meaning of the vision of the rock cut out of a mountain, but not by human hands—a rock that broke the iron, the bronze, the clay, the silver and the gold to pieces.

"The great God has shown the king what will take place in the future. The dream is true and its interpretation is trustworthy."

46 Then King Nebuchadnezzar fell prostrate before Daniel and paid him honor and ordered that an offering and incense be presented to him. 47 The king said to Daniel, "Surely your God is the God of gods and the Lord of kings and a revealer of mysteries, for you were able to reveal this mystery."

48 Then the king placed Daniel in a high position and lavished many gifts on him. He made him ruler over the entire province of Babylon and placed him in charge of all its wise men. 49 Moreover, at Daniel's request the king appointed Shadrach, Meshach and Abednego administrators over the province of Babylon, while Daniel himself remained at the royal court.

Daniel 3

The Image of Gold and the Blazing Furnace

1 King Nebuchadnezzar made an image of gold, sixty cubits high and six cubits wide,
and set it up on the plain of Dura in the province of Babylon. 2 He then summoned
the satraps, prefects, governors, advisers, treasurers, judges, magistrates and all the
other provincial officials to come to the dedication of the image he had set up. 3 So
the satraps, prefects, governors, advisers, treasurers, judges, magistrates and all the
other provincial officials assembled for the dedication of the image that King Nebuchadnezzar had set up, and they stood before it.

4 Then the herald loudly proclaimed, "Nations and peoples of every language,
this is what you are commanded to do: 5 As soon as you hear the sound of the horn,
flute, zither, lyre, harp, pipe and all kinds of music, you must fall down and worship
the image of gold that King Nebuchadnezzar has set up. 6 Whoever does not fall
down and worship will immediately be thrown into a blazing furnace."

7 Therefore, as soon as they heard the sound of the horn, flute, zither, lyre, harp
and all kinds of music, all the nations and peoples of every language fell down and
worshiped the image of gold that King Nebuchadnezzar had set up.

8 At this time some astrologers came forward and denounced the Jews. 9 They
said to King Nebuchadnezzar, "May the king live forever! 10 Your Majesty has issued a decree that everyone who hears the sound of the horn, flute, zither, lyre, harp,
pipe and all kinds of music must fall down and worship the image of gold, 11 and
that whoever does not fall down and worship will be thrown into a blazing furnace.
12 But there are some Jews whom you have set over the affairs of the province of
Babylon—Shadrach, Meshach and Abednego—who pay no attention to you, Your
Majesty. They neither serve your gods nor worship the image of gold you have set up."

13 Furious with rage, Nebuchadnezzar summoned Shadrach, Meshach and Abednego. So these men were brought before the king, 14 and Nebuchadnezzar said to
them, "Is it true, Shadrach, Meshach and Abednego, that you do not serve my gods
or worship the image of gold I have set up? 15 Now when you hear the sound of the
horn, flute, zither, lyre, harp, pipe and all kinds of music, if you are ready to fall down
and worship the image I made, very good. But if you do not worship it, you will be
thrown immediately into a blazing furnace. Then what god will be able to rescue you
from my hand?"

16 Shadrach, Meshach and Abednego replied to him, "King Nebuchadnezzar, we
do not need to defend ourselves before you in this matter. 17 If we are thrown into
the blazing furnace, the God we serve is able to deliver us from it, and he will deliver
us from Your Majesty's hand. 18 But even if he does not, we want you to know, Your
Majesty, that we will not serve your gods or worship the image of gold you have
set up."

19 Then Nebuchadnezzar was furious with Shadrach, Meshach and Abednego,
and his attitude toward them changed. He ordered the furnace heated seven times

hotter than usual 20 and commanded some of the strongest soldiers in his army to
tie up Shadrach, Meshach and Abednego and throw them into the blazing furnace.
21 So these men, wearing their robes, trousers, turbans and other clothes, were bound
and thrown into the blazing furnace. 22 The king's command was so urgent and the
furnace so hot that the flames of the fire killed the soldiers who took up Shadrach, Meshach and Abednego, 23 and these three men, firmly tied, fell into the blazing furnace.

24 Then King Nebuchadnezzar leaped to his feet in amazement and asked his advisers,

"Weren't there three men that we tied up and threw into the fire?"

They replied, "Certainly, Your Majesty."

25 He said, "Look! I see four men walking around in the fire, unbound and unharmed, and the fourth looks like a son of the gods."

26 Nebuchadnezzar then approached the opening of the blazing furnace and shouted, "Shadrach, Meshach and Abednego, servants of the Most High God, come out! Come here!"

So Shadrach, Meshach and Abednego came out of the fire, 27 and the satraps,
prefects, governors and royal advisers crowded around them. They saw that the fire had not harmed their bodies, nor was a hair of their heads singed; their robes were not scorched, and there was no smell of fire on them.

28 Then Nebuchadnezzar said, "Praise be to the God of Shadrach, Meshach and
Abednego, who has sent his angel and rescued his servants! They trusted in him and
defied the king's command and were willing to give up their lives rather than serve
or worship any god except their own God. 29 Therefore I decree that the people of
any nation or language who say anything against the God of Shadrach, Meshach and Abednego be cut into pieces and their houses be turned into piles of rubble, for no other god can save in this way."

30 Then the king promoted Shadrach, Meshach and Abednego in the province of Babylon.

Daniel 4

Nebuchadnezzar's Dream of a Tree

1 King Nebuchadnezzar,

To the nations and peoples of every language, who live in all the earth:

May you prosper greatly!

2 It is my pleasure to tell you about the miraculous signs and wonders that the Most High God has performed for me.

3

How great are his signs,
how mighty his wonders!

His kingdom is an eternal kingdom;
his dominion endures from generation to generation.

4 I, Nebuchadnezzar, was at home in my palace, contented and prosperous. 5 I had a dream that made me afraid. As I was lying in bed, the images and visions that passed through my mind terrified me. 6 So I commanded that all the wise men of Babylon be brought before me to interpret the dream for me.7 When the magicians, enchanters, astrologers and diviners came, I told them the dream, but they could not interpret it for me. 8 Finally, Daniel came into my presence and I told him the dream. (He is called Belteshazzar, after the name of my god, and the spirit of the holy gods is in him.)

9 I said, "Belteshazzar, chief of the magicians, I know that the spirit of the holy gods is in you, and no mystery is too difficult for you. Here is my dream; interpret it for me. 10 These are the visions I saw while lying in bed: I looked, and there before me stood a tree in the middle of the land. Its height was enormous. 11 The tree grew large and strong and its top touched the sky; it was visible to the ends of the earth. 12 Its leaves were beautiful, its fruit abundant, and on it was food for all. Under it the wild animals found shelter, and the birds lived in its branches; from it every creature was fed.

13 "In the visions I saw while lying in bed, I looked, and there before me was a holy one, a messenger, coming down from heaven. 14 He called in a loud voice: 'Cut down the tree and trim off its branches; strip off its leaves and scatter its fruit. Let the animals flee from under it and the birds from its branches. 15 But let the stump and its roots, bound with iron and bronze, remain in the ground, in the grass of the field.

"'Let him be drenched with the dew of heaven, and let him live with the animals among the plants of the earth. 16 Let his mind be changed from that of a man and let him be given the mind of an animal, till seven times pass by for him.

17 "'The decision is announced by messengers, the holy ones declare the verdict, so that the living may know that the Most High is sovereign over all kingdoms on earth and gives them to anyone he wishes and sets over them the lowliest of people.'

18 "This is the dream that I, King Nebuchadnezzar, had. Now, Belteshazzar, tell me what it means, for none of the wise men in my kingdom can interpret it for me. But you can, because the spirit of the holy gods is in you."

Daniel Interprets the Dream

19 Then Daniel (also called Belteshazzar) was greatly perplexed for a time, and his thoughts terrified him. So the king said, "Belteshazzar, do not let the dream or its meaning alarm you."

Belteshazzar answered, "My lord, if only the dream applied to your enemies and its meaning to your adversaries! 20 The tree you saw, which grew large and strong, with its top touching the sky, visible to the whole earth, 21 with beautiful leaves and

abundant fruit, providing food for all, giving shelter to the wild animals, and having
nesting places in its branches for the birds— 22 Your Majesty, you are that tree! You
have become great and strong; your greatness has grown until it reaches the sky, and
your dominion extends to distant parts of the earth.

23 "Your Majesty saw a holy one, a messenger, coming down from heaven and
saying, 'Cut down the tree and destroy it, but leave the stump, bound with iron and
bronze, in the grass of the field, while its roots remain in the ground. Let him be
drenched with the dew of heaven; let him live with the wild animals, until seven
times pass by for him.'

24 "This is the interpretation, Your Majesty, and this is the decree the Most High
has issued against my lord the king: 25 You will be driven away from people and will
live with the wild animals; you will eat grass like the ox and be drenched with the
dew of heaven. Seven times will pass by for you until you acknowledge that the Most
High is sovereign over all kingdoms on earth and gives them to anyone he wishes.
26 The command to leave the stump of the tree with its roots means that your kingdom will be restored to you when you acknowledge that Heaven rules. 27 Therefore,
Your Majesty, be pleased to accept my advice: Renounce your sins by doing what is
right, and your wickedness by being kind to the oppressed. It may be that then your
prosperity will continue."

The Dream Is Fulfilled

28 All this happened to King Nebuchadnezzar. 29 Twelve months later, as the king
was walking on the roof of the royal palace of Babylon, 30 he said, "Is not this the
great Babylon I have built as the royal residence, by my mighty power and for the
glory of my majesty?"

31 Even as the words were on his lips, a voice came from heaven, "This is what is
decreed for you, King Nebuchadnezzar: Your royal authority has been taken from
you. 32 You will be driven away from people and will live with the wild animals; you
will eat grass like the ox. Seven times will pass by for you until you acknowledge that
the Most High is sovereign over all kingdoms on earth and gives them to anyone he
wishes."

33 Immediately what had been said about Nebuchadnezzar was fulfilled. He was
driven away from people and ate grass like the ox. His body was drenched with the
dew of heaven until his hair grew like the feathers of an eagle and his nails like the
claws of a bird.

34 At the end of that time, I, Nebuchadnezzar, raised my eyes toward heaven, and
my sanity was restored. Then I praised the Most High; I honored and glorified him
who lives forever.

His dominion is an eternal dominion;
  his kingdom endures from generation to generation.

35
All the peoples of the earth
are regarded as nothing.
He does as he pleases
with the powers of heaven
and the peoples of the earth.
No one can hold back his hand
or say to him: "What have you done?"

36 At the same time that my sanity was restored, my honor and splendor were
returned to me for the glory of my kingdom. My advisers and nobles sought me out,
and I was restored to my throne and became even greater than before. 37 Now I,
Nebuchadnezzar, praise and exalt and glorify the King of heaven, because everything
he does is right and all his ways are just. And those who walk in pride he is able to
humble.

Daniel 5

The Writing on the Wall

1 King Belshazzar gave a great banquet for a thousand of his nobles and drank wine
with them. 2 While Belshazzar was drinking his wine, he gave orders to bring in the
gold and silver goblets that Nebuchadnezzar his father had taken from the temple in
Jerusalem, so that the king and his nobles, his wives and his concubines might drink
from them. 3 So they brought in the gold goblets that had been taken from the temple
of God in Jerusalem, and the king and his nobles, his wives and his concubines drank
from them. 4 As they drank the wine, they praised the gods of gold and silver, of
bronze, iron, wood and stone.

5 Suddenly the fingers of a human hand appeared and wrote on the plaster of the
wall, near the lampstand in the royal palace. The king watched the hand as it wrote.
6 His face turned pale and he was so frightened that his legs became weak and his
knees were knocking.

7 The king summoned the enchanters, astrologers and diviners. Then he said to
these wise men of Babylon, "Whoever reads this writing and tells me what it means
will be clothed in purple and have a gold chain placed around his neck, and he will
be made the third highest ruler in the kingdom."

8 Then all the king's wise men came in, but they could not read the writing or tell
the king what it meant. 9 So King Belshazzar became even more terrified and his face
grew more pale. His nobles were baffled.

10 The queen, hearing the voices of the king and his nobles, came into the banquet hall. "May the king live forever!" she said. "Don't be alarmed! Don't look so
pale! 11 There is a man in your kingdom who has the spirit of the holy gods in him.
In the time of your father he was found to have insight and intelligence and wisdom

like that of the gods. Your father, King Nebuchadnezzar, appointed him chief of the magicians, enchanters, astrologers and diviners. 12 He did this because Daniel, whom the king called Belteshazzar, was found to have a keen mind and knowledge and understanding, and also the ability to interpret dreams, explain riddles and solve difficult problems. Call for Daniel, and he will tell you what the writing means."

13 So Daniel was brought before the king, and the king said to him, "Are you Daniel, one of the exiles my father the king brought from Judah? 14 I have heard that the spirit of the gods is in you and that you have insight, intelligence and outstanding wisdom. 15 The wise men and enchanters were brought before me to read this writing and tell me what it means, but they could not explain it. 16 Now I have heard that you are able to give interpretations and to solve difficult problems. If you can read this writing and tell me what it means, you will be clothed in purple and have a gold chain placed around your neck, and you will be made the third highest ruler in the kingdom."

17 Then Daniel answered the king, "You may keep your gifts for yourself and give your rewards to someone else. Nevertheless, I will read the writing for the king and tell him what it means.

18 "Your Majesty, the Most High God gave your father Nebuchadnezzar sovereignty and greatness and glory and splendor. 19 Because of the high position he gave him, all the nations and peoples of every language dreaded and feared him. Those the king wanted to put to death, he put to death; those he wanted to spare, he spared; those he wanted to promote, he promoted; and those he wanted to humble, he humbled. 20 But when his heart became arrogant and hardened with pride, he was deposed from his royal throne and stripped of his glory. 21 He was driven away from people and given the mind of an animal; he lived with the wild donkeys and ate grass like the ox; and his body was drenched with the dew of heaven, until he acknowledged that the Most High God is sovereign over all kingdoms on earth and sets over them anyone he wishes.

22 "But you, Belshazzar, his son, have not humbled yourself, though you knew all this. 23 Instead, you have set yourself up against the Lord of heaven. You had the goblets from his temple brought to you, and you and your nobles, your wives and your concubines drank wine from them. You praised the gods of silver and gold, of bronze, iron, wood and stone, which cannot see or hear or understand. But you did not honor the God who holds in his hand your life and all your ways. 24 Therefore he sent the hand that wrote the inscription.

25 "This is the inscription that was written:

mene, mene, tekel, parsin

26 "Here is what these words mean:

Mene: God has numbered the days of your reign and brought it to an end.

27 *Tekel*: You have been weighed on the scales and found wanting.

28 *Peres*: Your kingdom is divided and given to the Medes and Persians."

29 Then at Belshazzar's command, Daniel was clothed in purple, a gold chain
was placed around his neck, and he was proclaimed the third highest ruler in the
kingdom.

30 That very night Belshazzar, king of the Babylonians, was slain, 31 and Darius
the Mede took over the kingdom, at the age of sixty-two.

Daniel 6

Daniel in the Den of Lions

1 It pleased Darius to appoint 120 satraps to rule throughout the kingdom, 2 with
three administrators over them, one of whom was Daniel. The satraps were made
accountable to them so that the king might not suffer loss. 3 Now Daniel so distinguished himself among the administrators and the satraps by his exceptional qualities
that the king planned to set him over the whole kingdom. 4 At this, the administrators and the satraps tried to find grounds for charges against Daniel in his conduct
of government affairs, but they were unable to do so. They could find no corruption
in him, because he was trustworthy and neither corrupt nor negligent. 5 Finally these
men said, "We will never find any basis for charges against this man Daniel unless it
has something to do with the law of his God."

6 So these administrators and satraps went as a group to the king and said: "May
King Darius live forever!7 The royal administrators, prefects, satraps, advisers and
governors have all agreed that the king should issue an edict and enforce the decree
that anyone who prays to any god or human being during the next thirty days, except
to you, Your Majesty, shall be thrown into the lions' den. 8 Now, Your Majesty, issue
the decree and put it in writing so that it cannot be altered—in accordance with the
law of the Medes and Persians, which cannot be repealed." 9

So King Darius put the decree in writing

10 Now when Daniel learned that the decree had been published, he went home to
his upstairs room where the windows opened toward Jerusalem. Three times a day
he got down on his knees and prayed, giving thanks to his God, just as he had done
before. 11 Then these men went as a group and found Daniel praying and asking God
for help. 12 So they went to the king and spoke to him about his royal decree: "Did
you not publish a decree that during the next thirty days anyone who prays to any god
or human being except to you, Your Majesty, would be thrown into the lions' den?"

The king answered, "The decree stands—in accordance with the law of the
Medes and Persians, which cannot be repealed."

13 Then they said to the king, "Daniel, who is one of the exiles from Judah, pays
no attention to you, Your Majesty, or to the decree you put in writing. He still prays

three times a day." 14 When the king heard this, he was greatly distressed; he was determined to rescue Daniel and made every effort until sundown to save him.

15 Then the men went as a group to King Darius and said to him, "Remember, Your Majesty, that according to the law of the Medes and Persians no decree or edict that the king issues can be changed."

16 So the king gave the order, and they brought Daniel and threw him into the lions' den. The king said to Daniel, "May your God, whom you serve continually, rescue you!"

17 A stone was brought and placed over the mouth of the den, and the king sealed it with his own signet ring and with the rings of his nobles, so that Daniel's situation might not be changed. 18 Then the king returned to his palace and spent the night without eating and without any entertainment being brought to him. And he could not sleep.

19 At the first light of dawn, the king got up and hurried to the lions' den. 20
When he came near the den, he called to Daniel in an anguished voice, "Daniel, servant of the living God, has your God, whom you serve continually, been able to rescue you from the lions?"

21 Daniel answered, "May the king live forever! 22 My God sent his angel, and he shut the mouths of the lions. They have not hurt me, because I was found innocent in his sight. Nor have I ever done any wrong before you, Your Majesty."

23 The king was overjoyed and gave orders to lift Daniel out of the den. And when Daniel was lifted from the den, no wound was found on him, because he had trusted in his God.

24 At the king's command, the men who had falsely accused Daniel were brought in and thrown into the lions' den, along with their wives and children. And before they reached the floor of the den, the lions overpowered them and crushed all their bones.

25 Then King Darius wrote to all the nations and peoples of every language in all the earth:

"May you prosper greatly!

26 "I issue a decree that in every part of my kingdom people must fear and reverence the God of Daniel.

"For he is the living God
    and he endures forever;
his kingdom will not be destroyed,
    his dominion will never end.

27
He rescues and he saves;
    he performs signs and wonders
    in the heavens and on the earth.
He has rescued Daniel
    from the power of the lions."

28 So Daniel prospered during the reign of Darius and the reign of Cyrus the Persian.

from Hebrew Bible, Genesis 22 (The Akedah)

SNAPSHOT

LANGUAGE: Hebrew

DATE: Compiled and edited c. 480 and 250 BCE

LOCATION: Post-exilic Judah

TAGS: Family; Journey; Oral Histories and Storytelling; Sacrifice

Introduction

The Book of Genesis in the Hebrew Bible, the earliest collected sacred texts of Judaism, recounts the story of Abraham as the founder of what would become ancient Israel, and eventually ancient Judaism. Whether Abraham was a historical figure cannot be known, but most recent academic scholarship suggests that the character may have been a composite figure who embodied particular values important to the development of Judaism during and after the Babylonian Exile (597–539 BCE) as well as during the Persian and Hellenistic periods up until 250 BCE. It is during this time that the Jewish Temple was rebuilt under the Persians after having been destroyed by the Babylonians in 586 BCE.

Like the rest of the **Torah** (the first five books of the Hebrew Bible; *torah* is the Hebrew word for law), Abraham's story is composed from a variety of sources edited together during and after the time of exile in Babylon. Such a process of collection and re-editing texts is called **redaction**. The story of Abraham probably reflects the priorities of the redactors more than those of the people in the time the story is set, namely, over a thousand years before the Babylonian Exile.

The following excerpt from the life of Abraham involves a disturbing directive given by the Hebrew God YHWH to Abraham, asking him to sacrifice the son for whom he has waited most of his adult life, and who has finally been born to his wife, Sarah, in their old age. As horrible as this request is, the sacrifice of children was a ritual practiced in Ancient Mesopotamia, particularly for the Canaanite deity

Timeline

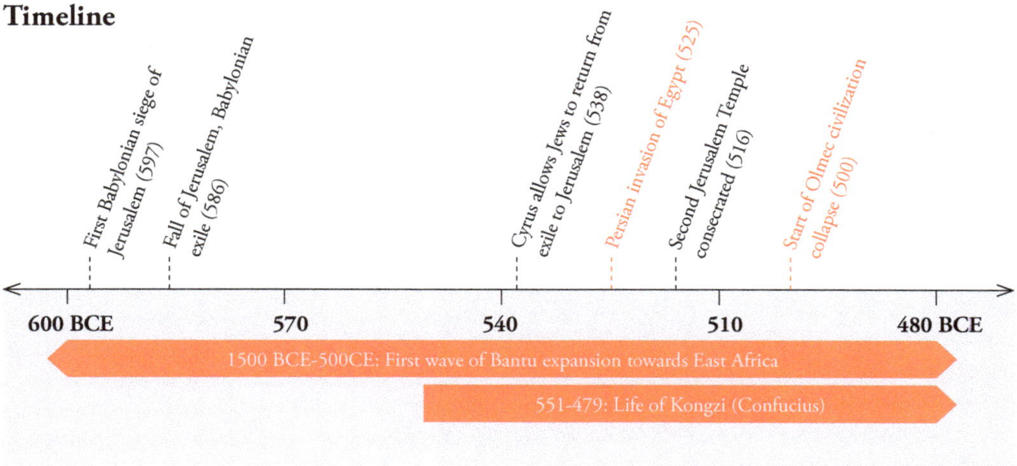

Molech. Abraham does not voice any objection to the request, though ultimately, he isn't required to carry it to its conclusion. Because the story abruptly changes direction at this crucial moment, there have long been questions about its meaning, its origins, and its implications for the moral and ethical development of Judaism. What moral conflicts arise in the tension between divine command and human love for one's family?

Despite the disturbing nature of God's request to Abraham, and despite Abraham's unwavering commitment to obey God without question no matter the cost, Jewish culture and other cultures have found moral clarity in the story. Obedience to God is portrayed as a moral imperative. In the absence of a temple, Judaism changed the focus of religious observance from animal sacrifice to the study of sacred text, and the Torah in particular. Study of the Torah as a way to worship God puts obedience to the Torah, and therefore to God, at the center of religious practice.

This story raises important questions about the way Jewish notions of God's character evolved over time, and about the editorial choices made by post-exilic redactors when preserving stories from Judaism before the exile. In the three Abrahamic religions (Judaism, Christianity, and Islam), Abraham has usually been seen as an example of great faith in the one God. Generations of Jewish scholars-commentators have noticed and speculated upon Abraham's blind obedience to God's problematic request, such as the following examples. First, Shlomo Yitzchaki (Rashi, 1040–1105) embraced the idea that Isaac is fully aware of what his father plans to do, but willingly goes along with it, making him a willing martyr. Then, Moses Ben Maimon (Maimonides/Rambam, 1135–1204) hinted that God's test of Abraham is possibly conducted in a dream state, and not actually in waking reality. Finally, Joseph H. Hertz (1872–1946), Chief Rabbi of Great Britain, suggested that this story represents an absolute rejection of human sacrifice. Do these interpretations resolve the ethical dissonance of the story? Do they reveal anything about the importance of this story in Jewish thought or culture?

Dennis Lundblad
Humanities Program

PRE-READING PARS

1. Are there any circumstances, for you or for anyone, in which absolute and unquestioning obedience is appropriate? Why or why not?
2. Have you ever had to make a choice between two difficult options? What principles guided your choice?

Genesis 22 (*The Akedah*)

1 Some time afterward, God put Abraham to the test. He said to him, "Abraham," and he answered, "Here I am." 2 And He said, "Take your son, your favored one, Isaac, whom you love, and go to the land of Moriah, and offer him there as a burnt offering on one of the heights that I will point out to you." 3 So early next morning, Abraham saddled his ass and took with him two of his servants and his son Isaac. He split the wood for the burnt offering, and he set out for the place of which God had told him. 4 On the third day Abraham looked up and saw the place from afar. 5 Then Abraham said to his servants, "You stay here with the ass. The boy and I will go up there; we will worship and we will return to you."

6 Abraham took the wood for the burnt offering and put it on his son Isaac. He himself took the firestone and the knife; and the two walked off together. 7 Then Isaac said to his father Abraham, "Father!" And he answered, "Yes, my son." And he said, "Here are the firestone and the wood; but where is the sheep for the burnt offering?" 8 And Abraham said, "God will see to the sheep for His burnt offering, my son." And the two of them walked on together. 9 They arrived at the place of which God had told him. Abraham built an altar there; he laid out the wood; he bound his son Isaac; he laid him on the altar, on top of the wood. 10 And Abraham picked up the knife to slay his son.

11 Then an angel of the LORD called to him from heaven: "Abraham! Abraham!" And he answered, "Here I am." 12 And he said, "Do not raise your hand against the boy, or do anything to him. For now I know that you fear God, since you have not withheld your son, your favored one, from Me." 13 When Abraham looked up, his eye fell upon a ram, caught in the thicket by its horns. So Abraham went and took the ram and offered it up as a burnt offering in place of his son. 14 And Abraham named that site Adonai-yireh, whence the present saying, "On the mount of the LORD there is vision." 15 The angel of the LORD called to Abraham a second time from heaven, 16 and said, "By Myself I swear, the LORD declares: Because you have done this and have not withheld your son, your favored one, 17 I will bestow My blessing upon you and make your descendants as numerous as the stars of heaven and the sands on the seashore; and your descendants shall seize the gates of their foes. 18 All the nations of the earth shall bless themselves by your descendants, because you have

obeyed My command."19 Abraham then returned to his servants, and they departed together for Beer-sheba; and Abraham stayed in Beer-sheba.

20 Some time later, Abraham was told, "Milcah too has borne children to your brother Nahor: 21 Uz the first-born, and Buz his brother, and Kemuel the father of Aram; 22 and Chesed, Hazo, Pildash, Jidlaph, and Bethuel"— 23 Bethuel being the father of Rebekah. These eight Milcah bore to Nahor, Abraham's brother. 24 And his concubine, whose name was Reumah, also bore children: Tebah, Gaham, Tahash, and Maacah.

"Genesis." In *Tanakh: A New Translation of the Holy Scriptures According to the Traditional Hebrew Text*, 11–25. Philadelphia, PA: The Jewish Publication Society, 1985.

POST-READING PARS

1. Identify all the options Abraham has in the face of YHWH's request. How might a story such as this function to clarify questions about identity and

Inquiry Corner

Content Question(s):	**Critical Question(s):**
What are the components of sacrifice in this passage?	How does the covenant provide a framework for interpreting the significance of this story?
Comparative Question(s):	**Connection Question(s):**
Compare the relationship between Abraham and Isaac with other parent-child interactions in our sources (e.g., *Epic of Gilgamesh, Life of the Buddha, Amenemope*).	Think about a time when you or others had to carry through on an action or an order that you or others did not agree with. What feelings did you experience around that action or witnessing those actions of others? What feelings might have been experienced by the people who were impacted by these actions?

relationships with the divine?

SNAPSHOT

LANGUAGE: Hebrew

DATE: c. 8th–6th centuries BCE

GENRE: Scripture

ETHNIC IDENTITY: Israelite (pre-6th century BCE), Judean/Jewish (post-6th century BCE)

TAGS: Cosmology; Deities and Spirits; Ethics and Morality; Family; Law and Punishment; Origin; Stories; Religion; Sacrifice

from Hebrew Bible, Selected Passages on Covenant

Introduction

The Hebrew Bible texts considered here illuminate a defining feature of ancient Israel's cosmology, their understanding of the structure or ordered reality of the world and universe. The central idea is that YHWH,[175] an elusive desert deity unknown to Israel's various oppressors, established an enduring **covenant**—a contract or treaty—with the Israelites after having delivered them from their enslavement to Egypt. Precisely why or how ancient Israel arrived at this understanding of YHWH remains unclear. Equally intriguing is the question of what role this unique relationship with YHWH may have played in the transformation of ancient Israelite religion into what would become Judaism and Christianity.

"Ancient Israel" refers to the peoples identified by the Hebrew Bible as having lived in the territories that came to be known as Judah (to the south, with its capital at Jerusalem) and Israel (or "Ephraim," to the north, with its capital at Samaria), in the period between the tenth and

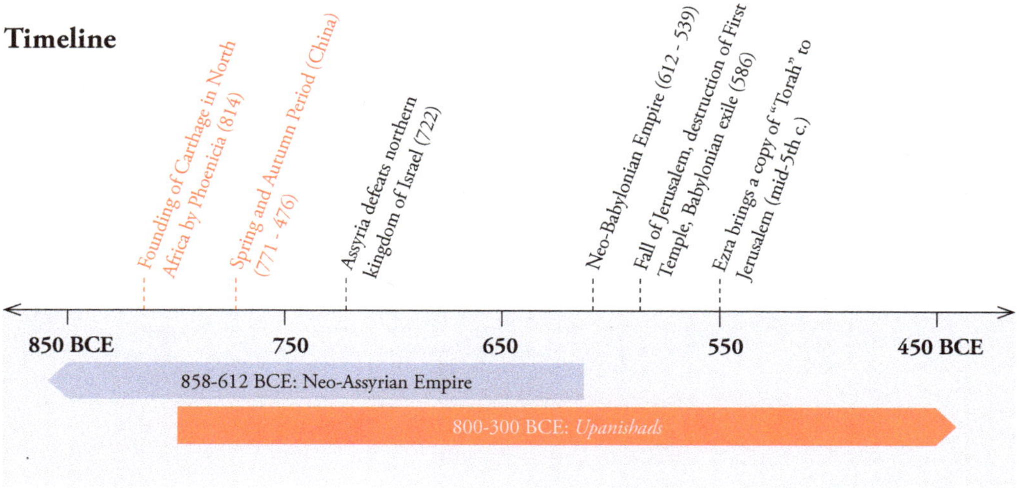

175. The Hebrew Bible uses several different names for the god of Israel, many of them variations on the Hebrew word for "god," *el*—El Shaddai, El Elyon, Elohim—but the *name* that most distinguishes this god from similar Canaanite deities is the four-consonant YHWH. Many scholars think the name may have been pronounced "Yahweh," but most English translations render it instead as "the Lord," as a deferential nod to the ancient Jewish tradition that, because of the name's holiness, it was best left unpronounced.

sixth centuries BCE. Many texts in the Hebrew Bible probably have their written origins during this period, following an eighth-century economic boom in the northern kingdom. As Samaria's wealth and geopolitical influence grew, so did the activity of two groups, prophets and scribes, though for different reasons. Prophets served as divine intermediaries, both in and outside of administrative power structures, delivering oracles that commented on present actions or problems, often in light of older traditions. Indeed, as the elites grew richer and more comfortable, the prophets grew more critical of them and their dealings with foreign empires. We only know this, however, because of the scribes who recorded the prophets' oracles—scribes whose work had itself become more important, ironically, precisely because of Israel's growing international fortunes. Scribes managed both administrative and diplomatic communication, particularly with the imperial authorities like Assyria, Egypt, or Babylonia. Like their Mesopotamian counterparts, the scribes of Israel and Judah trained by copying and revising classic texts, both legal (for example, Code of Hammurabi) and literary (for example, *Epic of Gilgamesh*). Many of the earliest biblical texts, from the Covenant Code (Exodus 21–23) to the songs of Deborah (Judges 5) and Moses (Deuteronomy 32), may even have originated as scribal training exercises.

Despite all this activity, we can date few, if any, extant texts exclusively to the Ancient Israelite period. Several factors account for this, including the impact of the outcomes of entanglement with three dominant empires: Assyria, Egypt, and Babylon. First, the northern kingdom's regional ascendancy came to a devastating halt in 722 BCE, when Samaria rebelled against Assyria, who promptly besieged and overthrew the kingdom. Many northern scribes took refuge in the southern kingdom of Judah, where their texts and traditions were revised and reinterpreted in light of southern perspectives and the events of 722. How often have you interpreted past events in terms of your current location and experiences? Second, the southern kingdom's efforts to navigate a growing power struggle between Egypt and Babylon led, perhaps inevitably, to the destruction of Judah in 597–586 BCE. When Judah's king shifted his allegiance to Egypt, Babylon retaliated. Nebuchadnezzar destroyed Jerusalem, razed the Temple of Solomon, and deported the ruling elites (including many scribes) to Babylon. All at once, the people lost their sovereignty, their temple, and their land. This insurmountable loss did not, however, put an end to the scribes' creative activity. Maybe these scribes carried written copies of their work with them, or maybe they re-created them from memory. Whatever the case, most Hebrew Bible texts as we now have them, even those with likely origins in the centuries before the exile, read as though they were compiled and edited during or after the sixth-century exile, reflecting interpretation of their traditions in light of these experiences of displacement. These compilations and reinterpretations also suggest the growing importance of written texts. We're still several hundred years away from the notion of a "Bible" as an authoritative library of sacred texts, but this exilic moment is crucial in understanding that development.

The **Torah,** a term used to reference the first five books of the Hebrew Bible, offers us a good example of the impact of these experiences of exile through **redaction**, a process that starts with compiling materials from various sources, followed by arranging and revising the texts. Thus, while the Torah is ascribed to Moses, the prophet who helped mediate YHWH's releasing of Israel from Egyptian slavery, it appears to have been redacted during the time of Ezra, a fifth-century Jewish priest and functionary of the Persian Empire, in order to offer an explanation for the exile itself. Even the **Psalms**, many of which read as hymns for worship in or near the temple, can be read as a response to the exile: Psalm 89, for example, asks the most pressing existential questions an exiled Jew might ask of YHWH—given all your promises to David, how could you let this happen to us? How long will you leave us bereft?—and Psalm 90 (the only one ascribed to Moses!) provides an answer: we have always, ultimately, found our home in YHWH. We can discern a central and recurring question: how are the ancient Israelites to understand their simultaneous experiences of YHWH's promise of "the Land" as a guarantee of the covenant alongside their devastating exile from that land?

Here are some questions to consider as you read these passages: What promises are made on both sides of the covenant? How do the details of those promises shift over each passage? What are the implications of the stories of YHWH's promises to Noah and Abraham? What is a person or community expected to do to keep their side of the covenant? Finally, and perhaps most important, what might have made this god—one that modern readers often find harsh and demanding—so appealing to ancient Israelites, particularly in the face of their recurring political defeat and displacement?

Brian C. Graves
Department of English

from Hebrew Bible, Selected Passages on Covenant

Genesis,[176] Chapter 9

[1] God blessed Noah and his sons, and said to them, "Be fertile and increase, and fill the earth.[177] [2] The fear and the dread of you shall be upon all the beasts of the earth and upon all the birds of the sky—everything with which the earth is astir—and upon all the fish of the sea; they are given into your hand. [3] Every creature that lives shall be yours to eat; as with the green grasses, I give you all these. [4] You must not, however, eat flesh with its life-blood in it.[178] [5] But for your own life-blood I will require a reckoning: I will require it of every beast; of man, too, will I require a reckoning for human life, of every man for that of his fellow man!

[6] Whoever sheds the blood of man,
By man shall his blood be shed;
For in His image
Did God make man.

[7] Be fertile, then, and increase; abound on the earth and increase on it."

[8] And God said to Noah and to his sons with him, [9] "I now establish My covenant with you and your offspring to come; [10] amd with every living thing that is with you—birds, cattle, and every wild beast as well—all that have come out of the ark, every living thing on earth. [11] I will maintain My covenant with you: never again shall all flesh be cut off by the waters of a flood, and never again shall there be a flood to destroy the earth."

[12] God further said, "This is the sign that I set for the covenant between Me and you, and every living creature with you, for all ages to come. [13] I have set My bow in the clouds, and it shall serve as a sign of the covenant between Me and the earth.[179] [14] When I bring clouds over the earth and the bow appears in the clouds, [15] I will remember My covenant between Me and you and every living creature among all flesh, so that the waters shall never again become a flood to destroy all flesh. [16] When the bow is in the clouds, I will see it and remember the everlasting covenant between God and all living creatures, all flesh that is on earth. [17] That," God said

176. Genesis is the first of the "Five Books of Moses," also known as the Torah (Hebrew, "instruction") or Pentateuch (Greek, "five books"). Most of the book consists of an extended narrative in two sections, the first focused on the creation of the world and the fraught beginnings of human civilization, the second on four generations of Israel's ancestors, culminating in their migration from Canaan to Egypt.

177. Noah, the central figure of the first part of Genesis, is portrayed both as a new Adam and an Israelite variation on Utnapishtim, the flood survivor in the Epic of Gilgamesh. God (here, elohim) offers this blessing after Noah and family have emerged from the ark. The directive to "be fertile and increase" echoes the very beginning of the creation story (Genesis 1:22, 28).

178. In contrast to Genesis 1:29–30, which limited the human diet to plants, God now permits them to eat animals, but only after its life—its blood—has been drained out.

179. This is the rainbow, of course, but can also be understood here as an emblem of the storm god's destructive arsenal, now set aside.

to Noah, "shall be the sign of the covenant that I have established between Me and all flesh that is on earth."

Genesis, Chapter 15

[1] Some time later, the word of the Lord[180] came to Abram[181] in a vision. He said,

"Fear not, Abram,
I am a shield to you;
Your reward shall be very great."

[2] But Abram said, "O Lord God, what can You give me, seeing that I shall die childless, and the one in charge of my household is Dammesek Eliezer!" [3] Abram said further, "Since You have granted me no offspring, my steward will be my heir." [4] The word of the Lord came to him in reply, "That one shall not be your heir; none but your very own issue shall be your heir." [5] He took him outside and said, "Look toward heaven and count the stars, if you are able to count them." And He added, "So shall your offspring be." [6] And because he put his trust in the Lord, He reckoned it to his merit.

[7] Then He said to him, "I am the Lord who brought you out from Ur of the Chaldeans to assign this land to you as a possession." [8] And he said, "O Lord God, how shall I know that I am to possess it?" [9] He answered, "Bring Me a three-year-old heifer, a three-year-old she-goat, a three-year-old ram, a turtledove, and a young bird." [10] He brought Him all these and cut them in two, placing each half opposite the other; but he did not cut up the bird. [11] Birds of prey came down upon the carcasses, and Abram drove them away. [12] As the sun was about to set, a deep sleep fell upon Abram, and a great dark dream descended upon him. [13] And He said to Abram, "Know well that your offspring shall be strangers in a land not theirs, and they shall be enslaved and oppressed four hundred years; [14] but I will execute judgment on the nation they shall serve, and in the end they shall go free with great wealth.[182] [15] As for you,

You shall go unto your fathers in peace,
You shall be buried at a ripe old age.

[16] And they shall return here in the fourth generation, for the iniquity of the Amorites is not yet complete."[183]

180. In most English translations, "the Lord" (in small or all caps) stands in for the name "YHWH" (or "YHVH").

181. A Mesopotamian descendent of Noah, Abram (or Abraham, "great father"), is chosen seemingly at random by YHWH and promised (Genesis 12:1–3) land, bountiful descendants, and a name (reputation) by which others would be blessed. Yet as we see here in chapter 15, the great tension of the narrative turns on Abram's and Sarai's persistent childlessness, even into their old age.

182. This "dark dream" foreshadows the Israelites' enslavement in Egypt and eventual release.

183. This is essentially a justification for dispossessing the Canaanites of their land because of their evil ways (compare Leviticus 18:24–25; Deuteronomy 9:4).

[17] When the sun set and it was very dark, there appeared a smoking oven, and a flaming torch which passed between those pieces. [18] On that day the Lord made a covenant with Abram, saying, "To your offspring I assign this land, from the river of Egypt to the great river, the river Euphrates: [19] the Kenites, the Kenizzites, the Kadmonites, [20] the Hittites, the Perizzites, the Rephaim, [21] the Amorites, the Canaanites, the Girgashites, and the Jebusites."[184]

Genesis, Chapter 17

[1] When Abram was ninety-nine years old, the Lord appeared to Abram and said to him, "I am El Shaddai.[185] Walk in My ways and be blameless. [2] I will establish My covenant between Me and you, and I will make you exceedingly numerous."

[3] Abram threw himself on his face; and God spoke to him further, [4] "As for Me, this is My covenant with you: You shall be the father of a multitude of nations. [5] And you shall no longer be called Abram, but your name shall be Abraham,[186] for I make you the father of a multitude of nations. [6] I will make you exceedingly fertile, and make nations of you; and kings shall come forth from you.[187] [7] I will maintain My covenant between Me and you, and your offspring to come, as an everlasting covenant throughout the ages, to be God to you and to your offspring to come. [8] I assign the land you sojourn in to you and your offspring to come, all the land of Canaan, as an everlasting holding. I will be their God."

[9] God further said to Abraham, "As for you, you and your offspring to come throughout the ages shall keep My covenant. [10] Such shall be the covenant between Me and you and your offspring to follow which you shall keep: every male among you shall be circumcised. [11] You shall circumcise the flesh of your foreskin, and that shall be the sign of the covenant between Me and you. [12] And throughout the generations, every male among you shall be circumcised at the age of eight days. As for the homeborn slave and the one bought from an outsider who is not of your offspring, [13] they must be circumcised, homeborn, and purchased alike. Thus shall My covenant be marked in your flesh as an everlasting pact. [14] And if any male who is uncircumcised fails to circumcise the flesh of his foreskin, that person shall be cut off from his kin; he has broken My covenant."

[15] And God said to Abraham, "As for your wife Sarai, you shall not call her Sarai, but her name shall be Sarah.[188] [16] I will bless her; indeed, I will give you a

184. To further signal the extent of the promised land, YHWH names several peoples who inhabited the land at the time Israel would appear, following their departure from Egypt and forty years in the wilderness. The two kingdoms of Judah and Israel, however, were never as extensive as this imagines.

185. Traditionally rendered "God Almighty." The name may mean "god of the mountains."

186. Understood as "father of a multitude."

187. Most famous of the kings descended from Abraham are David and Solomon, who held the two kingdoms together for some eighty years, 1000–922 BCE.

188. I.e., "princess."

son by her. I will bless her so that she shall give rise to nations; rulers of peoples shall issue from her." [17] Abraham threw himself on his face and laughed, and he said to himself, "Can a child be born to a man a hundred years old, or can Sarah bear a child at ninety?" [18] And Abraham said to God, "O that Ishmael[189] might live by Your favor!" [19] God said, "Nevertheless, Sarah your wife shall bear you a son, and you shall name him Isaac;[190] and I will maintain My covenant with him as an everlasting covenant for his offspring to come. [20] As for Ishmael, I have heeded you. I hereby bless him. I will make him fertile and exceedingly numerous. He shall be the father of twelve chieftains, and I will make of him a great nation. [21] But My covenant I will maintain with Isaac, whom Sarah shall bear to you at this season next year." [22] And when He was done speaking with him, God was gone from Abraham.

[23] Then Abraham took his son Ishmael, and all his homeborn slaves and all those he had bought, every male in Abraham's household, and he circumcised the flesh of their foreskins on that very day, as God had spoken to him. [24] Abraham was ninety-nine years old when he circumcised the flesh of his foreskin, [25] and his son Ishmael was thirteen years old when he was circumcised in the flesh of his foreskin. [26] Thus Abraham and his son Ishmael were circumcised on that very day; [27] and all his household, his homeborn slaves and those that had been bought from outsiders, were circumcised with him.

Exodus,[191] Chapter 15

[1] Then Moses[192] and the Israelites sang this song[193] to the Lord. They said:

I will sing to the Lord, for He has triumphed gloriously;
Horse and driver He has hurled into the sea.

189. Between chapters 15 and 17, in spite of having trusted YHWH's promises, Abram and Sarai take matters into their own hands and have Abram conceive a child, Ishmael ("God heeds"), with Hagar, an enslaved Egyptian.

190. Heb. Yishaq, from sahaq, "laugh."

191. The second of the Five Books of Moses, which introduces the character of Moses, narrates the Israelites' deliverance from Egyptian slavery and acceptance of YHWH's covenant, and details the building of the wilderness tabernacle (a mobile sacred dwelling place for YHWH in their midst).

192. Moses is the central human figure in four of the Five Books attributed to him, and a character of great significance in the biblical tradition, not least because he serves as the principal mediator between YHWH and Israel through their deliverance from Egypt, embrace of the covenant, and "stiff-necked" complaints and failures through forty years in the wilderness (as is previewed in verses 22–26 below). Moses is also the model prophet: one who speaks both for God to the people and on the people's behalf to God.

193. This ancient hymn celebrates Israel's deliverance from Egyptian slavery and YHWH's victory over Pharaoh and his army, with several echoes of an ancient Near Eastern myth in which the storm god defeats the powers of chaos—represented either by a sea monster or the sea itself. It is probably one of the oldest poems in the Hebrew Bible. Like the *Epic of Gilgamesh*, this poem is constructed largely by parallel lines, the second in each pair echoing or advancing the meaning of the first.

[2] The Lord is my strength and might;
He is become my deliverance.
This is my God and I will enshrine Him;
The God of my father, and I will exalt Him.
[3] The Lord, the Warrior—
Lord is His name!
[4] Pharaoh's chariots and his army
He has cast into the sea;
And the pick of his officers
Are drowned in the Sea of Reeds.
[5] The deeps covered them;
They went down into the depths like a stone.
[6] Your right hand, O Lord, glorious in power,
Your right hand, O Lord, shatters the foe!
[7] In Your great triumph You break Your opponents;
You send forth Your fury, it consumes them like straw.
[8] At the blast of Your nostrils the waters piled up,
The floods stood straight like a wall;
The deeps froze in the heart of the sea.
[9] The foe said, "I will pursue, I will overtake,
I will divide the spoil;
My desire shall have its fill of them.
I will bare my sword—
My hand shall subdue them."
[10] You made Your wind blow, the sea covered them;
They sank like lead in the majestic waters.
[11] Who is like You, O Lord, among the celestials;
Who is like You, majestic in holiness,
Awesome in splendor, working wonders!
[12] You put out Your right hand,
The earth swallowed them.
[13] In Your love You lead the people You redeemed;
In Your strength You guide them to Your holy abode.
[14] The peoples hear, they tremble;
Agony grips the dwellers in Philistia.
[15] Now are the clans of Edom dismayed;
The tribes of Moab—trembling grips them;
All the dwellers in Canaan are aghast.[194]

194. Philistia, Edom, and Moab all refer to neighboring peoples during Israel's time in the land. Goliath (of the famous story) was a Philistine. The stories of Genesis relate Edom and Moab to Israel's extended family, though as brothers or cousins in conflict with them.

[16] Terror and dread descend upon them;
Through the might of Your arm they are still as stone—
Till Your people cross over, O Lord,
Till Your people cross whom You have ransomed.
[17] You will bring them and plant them in Your own mountain,
The place You made to dwell in, O Lord,
The sanctuary, O Lord, which Your hands established.[195]
[18] The Lord will reign for ever and ever!

[19] For the horses of Pharaoh, with his chariots and horsemen, went into the sea; and the Lord turned back on them the waters of the sea; but the Israelites marched on dry ground in the midst of the sea.

[20] Then Miriam the prophetess, Aaron's sister, took a timbrel in her hand, and all the women went out after her in dance with timbrels.[196] [21] And Miriam chanted for them:

Sing to the Lord, for He has triumphed gloriously;
Horse and driver He has hurled into the sea.

[22] Then Moses caused Israel to set out from the Sea of Reeds. They went on into the wilderness of Shur; they traveled three days in the wilderness and found no water. [23] They came to Marah, but they could not drink the water of Marah because it was bitter; that is why it was named Marah. [24] And the people grumbled against Moses, saying, "What shall we drink?" [25] So he cried out to the Lord, and the Lord showed him a piece of wood; he threw it into the water and the water became sweet.

There He made for them a fixed rule, and there He put them to the test. [26] He said, "If you will heed the Lord your God diligently, doing what is upright in His sight, giving ear to His commandments and keeping all His laws, then I will not bring upon you any of the diseases that I brought upon the Egyptians, for I the Lord am your healer."

[27] And they came to Elim, where there were twelve springs of water and seventy palm trees; and they encamped there beside the water.

195. This mountain/place/sanctuary refers both to the land as a whole and to the cosmic, symbolic mountain at its center: Mt. Zion, the Temple mount, the navel of the universe and center of the Israelite cosmology, where YHWH sits enthroned.

196. Miriam is sister to both Aaron (ancestor of the priestly class) and Moses, and one of a handful of women named as prophets in the Hebrew Bible, along with Deborah (Judges 4–5) and Huldah (2 Kings 22). Note that Miriam's song echoes the first two lines of the longer poem attributed to Moses, even though the women were the traditional leaders of victory celebrations through song and dance.

Exodus, Chapter 19

[1] On the third new moon after the Israelites had gone forth from the land of Egypt, on that very day, they entered the wilderness of Sinai.[197] [2] Having journeyed from Rephidim, they entered the wilderness of Sinai and encamped in the wilderness. Israel encamped there in front of the mountain, [3] and Moses went up to God. The Lord called to him from the mountain, saying, "Thus shall you say to the house of Jacob and declare to the children of Israel: [4] 'You have seen what I did to the Egyptians, how I bore you on eagles' wings and brought you to Me.[198] [5] Now then, if you will obey Me faithfully and keep My covenant, you shall be My treasured possession among all the peoples. Indeed, all the earth is Mine, [6] but you shall be to Me a kingdom of priests and a holy nation.'[199] These are the words that you shall speak to the children of Israel."

[7] Moses came and summoned the elders of the people and put before them all that the Lord had commanded him. [8] All the people answered as one, saying, "All that the Lord has spoken we will do!" And Moses brought back the people's words to the Lord. [9] And the Lord said to Moses, "I will come to you in a thick cloud, in order that the people may hear when I speak with you and so trust you ever after." Then Moses reported the people's words to the Lord, [10] and the Lord said to Moses, "Go to the people and warn them to stay pure today and tomorrow. Let them wash their clothes. [11] Let them be ready for the third day; for on the third day the Lord will come down, in the sight of all the people, on Mount Sinai. [12] You shall set bounds for the people round about, saying, 'Beware of going up the mountain or touching the border of it. Whoever touches the mountain shall be put to death: [13] no hand shall touch him, but he shall be either stoned or shot; beast or man, he shall not live.' When the ram's horn sounds a long blast, they may go up on the mountain."

[14] Moses came down from the mountain to the people and warned the people to stay pure, and they washed their clothes. [15] And he said to the people, "Be ready for the third day: do not go near a woman."[200]

197. Mount Sinai appeared earlier in the Exodus narrative as the place where Moses first encountered YHWH in a burning bush and was commissioned (very reluctantly) to be this god's spokesperson and mediator both with Pharaoh and with the Israelites.

198. The instructions that are about to follow come in response to YHWH's saving act, delivering Israel from Egyptian servitude. This naming of the suzerain's mighty and beneficent acts is a typical opening statement in ancient Near Eastern vassal treaties. Note a similar move in 20:2.

199. Priests, of course, serve in many cultures as mediators between divine and human realms; because they live closer to the sacred center, priests are held to different standards for conduct, diet, language, and other ways of life. The idea here seems to be that Israel, even though they will have a priestly class, nonetheless will all be known as a "priestly" community, all set aside and held to distinctive expectations, because they all live closer than the rest of the world to YHWH at the sacred center of the universe.

200. Note that Moses (not YHWH) adds this last bit about avoiding women, seemingly addressing an exclusively male audience.

[16] On the third day, as morning dawned, there was thunder, and lightning, and a dense cloud upon the mountain, and a very loud blast of the horn; and all the people who were in the camp trembled. [17] Moses led the people out of the camp toward God, and they took their places at the foot of the mountain.

[18] Now Mount Sinai was all in smoke, for the Lord had come down upon it in fire; the smoke rose like the smoke of a kiln, and the whole mountain trembled violently. [19] The blare of the horn grew louder and louder. As Moses spoke, God answered him in thunder. [20] The Lord came down upon Mount Sinai, on the top of the mountain, and the Lord called Moses to the top of the mountain and Moses went up. [21] The Lord said to Moses, "Go down, warn the people not to break through to the Lord to gaze, lest many of them perish. [22] The priests also, who come near the Lord, must stay pure, lest the Lord break out against them." [23] But Moses said to the Lord, "The people cannot come up to Mount Sinai, for You warned us saying, 'Set bounds about the mountain and sanctify it.'" [24] So the Lord said to him, "Go down, and come back together with Aaron; but let not the priests or the people break through to come up to the Lord, lest He break out against them." [25] And Moses went down to the people and spoke to them.

Exodus, Chapter 20

[1] God spoke all these words, saying:

[2] I the Lord am your God who brought you out of the land of Egypt, the house of bondage: [3] You shall have no other gods besides Me.

[4] You shall not make for yourself a sculptured image, or any likeness of what is in the heavens above, or on the earth below, or in the waters under the earth. [5] You shall not bow down to them or serve them. For I the Lord your God am an impassioned God, visiting the guilt of the parents upon the children, upon the third and upon the fourth generations of those who reject Me, [6] but showing kindness to the thousandth generation of those who love Me and keep My commandments.

[7] You shall not swear falsely by the name of the Lord your God; for the Lord will not clear one who swears falsely by His name.

[8] Remember the sabbath day and keep it holy. [9] Six days you shall labor and do all your work, [10] but the seventh day is a sabbath of the Lord your God: you shall not do any work—you, your son or daughter, your male or female slave, or your cattle, or the stranger who is within your settlements. [11] For in six days the Lord made heaven and earth and sea, and all that is in them, and He rested on the seventh day; therefore the Lord blessed the sabbath day and hallowed it.

[12] Honor your father and your mother, that you may long endure on the land that the Lord your God is assigning to you.

[13] You shall not murder.

You shall not commit adultery.

You shall not steal.

You shall not bear false witness against your neighbor.

[14] You shall not covet your neighbor's house: you shall not covet your neighbor's wife, or his male or female slave, or his ox or his ass, or anything that is your neighbor's.

[15] All the people witnessed the thunder and lightning, the blare of the horn and the mountain smoking; and when the people saw it, they fell back and stood at a distance. [16] "You speak to us," they said to Moses, "and we will obey; but let not God speak to us, lest we die." [17] Moses answered the people, "Be not afraid; for God has come only in order to test you, and in order that the fear of Him may be ever with you, so that you do not go astray." [18] So the people remained at a distance, while Moses approached the thick cloud where God was.

[19] The Lord said to Moses:

Thus shall you say to the Israelites: You yourselves saw that I spoke to you from the very heavens: [20] With Me, therefore, you shall not make any gods of silver, nor shall you make for yourselves any gods of gold. [21] Make for Me an altar of earth and sacrifice on it your burnt offerings and your sacrifices of well-being, your sheep and your oxen; in every place where I cause My name to be mentioned I will come to you and bless you. [22] And if you make for Me an altar of stones, do not build it of hewn stones; for by wielding your tool upon them you have profaned them.[201] [23] Do not ascend My altar by steps, that your nakedness may not be exposed upon it.

Micah,[202] Chapter 6

[1] Hear what the Lord is saying:
Come, present [My] case before the mountains,
And let the hills hear you pleading.

[2] Hear, you mountains, the case of the Lord—
You firm foundations of the earth!
For the Lord has a case against His people,
He has a suit against Israel.[203]

201. Perhaps to preclude engraving images on the stones, which would run counter to the stipulation against creating images of YHWH (20:4).

202. Like his contemporary Isaiah, Micah was a prophet of the late eighth and early seventh centuries, a time when the southern kingdom was threatened by Assyrian aggression, following Samaria's destruction in 722 BCE. Micah's oracles suggest a driving ethical critique of the injustices and corruption of the elites—as well as of the politically popular theology that asserted YHWH would never abandon them or allow the Temple to be destroyed.

203. This oracle takes the form of a lawsuit, though the jury consists not of other celestial beings but of mountains, hills, and rocks.

[3] "My people!
What wrong have I done you?[204]
What hardship have I caused you?
Testify against Me.
[4] In fact,
I brought you up from the land of Egypt,
I redeemed you from the house of bondage,
And I sent before you
Moses, Aaron, and Miriam.[205]

[5] "My people,
Remember what Balak king of Moab
Plotted against you,
And how Balaam son of Beor
Responded to him.[206]
[Recall your passage] From Shittim to Gilgal[207]—
And you will recognize
The gracious acts of the Lord."

[6] With what shall I approach the Lord,
Do homage to God on high?
Shall I approach Him with burnt offerings,
With calves a year old?
[7] Would the Lord be pleased with thousands of rams,
With myriads of streams of oil?
Shall I give my first-born for my transgression,
The fruit of my body for my sins?

[8] "He has told you, O man, what is good,
And what the Lord requires of you:

204. Note the translators' choice to use quotation marks for vv. 3–5 and 8–9, understanding these lines to be the prophet's rendering of YHWH's words. Verses 6–7, then, represent a question from the audience.

205. "Moses, Aaron, and Miriam": See notes above on Exodus 15:1 and 15:20. Notice the prominence here of Miriam, seemingly equivalent to her brothers, in contrast to her comparably diminished role in the Torah narratives. (This text may well be older than the Torah.)

206. According to Numbers (chapters 22–24), Balak, the king of Moab, contacted Balaam, a famous Canaanite prophet (also known from other ancient Near Eastern texts), and asked him to curse the Israelites. Although the most memorable part of the story may be the talking donkey, the point there (and here) seems to be that what YHWH has decided to bless, no prophet can counter with a curse (Numbers 23:8).

207. I.e., the crossing of the Jordan; see Joshua 3:1, 14–4:19.

Only to do justice
And to love goodness,
And to walk modestly with your God;
[9] Then will your name achieve wisdom."[208]

Hark! The Lord
Summons the city:
Hear, O scepter;
For who can direct her [10] but you?[209]
Will I overlook, in the wicked man's house,
The granaries of wickedness
And the accursed short *ephah*?[210]
[11] Shall he be acquitted despite wicked balances
And a bag of fraudulent weights?—
[12] Whose rich men are full of lawlessness,
And whose inhabitants speak treachery,
With tongues of deceit in their mouths.

[13] I, in turn, have beaten you sore,
Have stunned [you] for your sins:
[14] You have been eating without getting your fill,
And there is a gnawing at your vitals;
You have been conceiving without bearing young,
And what you bore I would deliver to the sword.
[15] You have been sowing, but have nothing to reap;
You have trod olives, but have no oil for rubbing,
And grapes but have no wine to drink.
[16] Yet you have kept the laws of Omri,
And all the practices of the House of Ahab,
And have followed what they devised.

208. The hyperbole in verses 6–8 seems to emphasize the greater importance of ethics over sacrifices, though probably not to reject sacrifices altogether. Both Jewish and Christian readers have long found verse 8 to encapsulate the heart not only of the biblical prophetic literature, but of the Torah itself, distilling the 613 commandments to a mere three.

209. Verses 9–16, which may not be a part of the lawsuit oracle, do nonetheless articulate a fierce critique of, plus curses against, those wealthy merchants whose corruption reflects the wicked ways of "the laws of Omri / And all the practices of the House of Ahab," a ninth century dynasty of northern rulers judged by many biblical texts as emblematic of the northern kingdom's religious infidelities. Southern scribes and prophets assumed these religious failings were the cause of Samaria's destruction.

210. An ephah is a dry measure. The idea here is that the merchants' measures are off, to their own benefit. Cf. Amos 8:4–5.

Therefore I will make you an object of horror
And her inhabitants[211] an object of hissing;
And you shall bear the mockery of peoples.

Psalm 74[212]

[1] A maskil of Asaph.[213]
Why, O God, do You forever reject us,
do You fume in anger at the flock that You tend?
[2] Remember the community You made Yours long ago,
Your very own tribe that You redeemed,
Mount Zion, where You dwell.[214]
[3] Bestir Yourself because of the perpetual tumult,
all the outrages of the enemy in the sanctuary.
[4] Your foes roar inside Your meeting-place;
they take their signs for true signs.
[5] It is like men wielding axes against a gnarled tree;
[6] with hatchet and pike
they hacked away at its carved work.
[7] They made Your sanctuary go up in flames;
they brought low in dishonor the dwelling-place of Your presence.
[8] They resolved, "Let us destroy them altogether!"
They burned all God's tabernacles in the land.
[9] No signs appear for us;
there is no longer any prophet;
no one among us knows for how long.
[10] Till when, O God, will the foe blaspheme,
will the enemy forever revile Your name?
[11] Why do You hold back Your hand, Your right hand?
Draw it out of Your bosom![215]

[12] O God, my King from of old,
who brings deliverance throughout the land;

211. I.e., those of the city of v. 9, apparently Samaria.

212. This poem, in the form of a lament, calls on God (elohim) to respond to the destruction of Jerusalem.

213. The meaning of "maskil" is uncertain, though perhaps associated with wisdom, enlightenment, or teaching. Asaph, to whom several psalms are attributed, is named in 1 Chronicles 25 as a Levite (priestly clan) and is associated with a guild of Temple singers.

214. Mount Zion refers to the Temple in Jerusalem. See note above on Exodus 15:17.

215. "Draw it out of your bosom!": Meaning of Hebrew uncertain.

[13] it was You who drove back the sea[216] with Your might,
who smashed the heads of the monsters in the waters;[217]
[14] it was You who crushed the heads of Leviathan,[218]
who left him as food for the denizens of the desert;
[15] it was You who released springs and torrents,
who made mighty rivers run dry;
[16] the day is Yours, the night also;
it was You who set in place the orb of the sun;
[17] You fixed all the boundaries of the earth;
summer and winter—You made them.

[18] Be mindful of how the enemy blasphemes the Lord,
how base people revile Your name.
[19] Do not deliver Your dove[219] to the wild beast;
do not ignore forever the band of Your lowly ones.
[20] Look to the covenant!
For the dark places of the land are full of the haunts of lawlessness.
[21] Let not the downtrodden turn away disappointed;
let the poor and needy praise Your name.
[22] Rise, O God, champion Your cause;
be mindful that You are blasphemed by base men all day long.[220]
[23] Do not ignore the shouts of Your foes,
the din of Your adversaries that ascends all the time.

Selections from *Tanakh: A New Translation of the Holy Scriptures According to the Traditional Hebrew Text*, 11–25, 82–84, 87–89, 743–44, 828–29. Philadelphia, PA: The Jewish Publication Society, 1985.

216. "The sea": Hebrew Yamm, the name of the Canaanite sea-god.

217. Here, as in Exodus 15, the poet understands YHWH in light of the ancient Near Eastern myth of the storm god who defeats a watery chaos, establishes an ordered creation, and establishes a house (Temple) of rest.

218. Leviathan here seems to name the many-headed sea monster of Canaanite myth.

219. When poor families could not afford the preferred animals for Temple sacrifices, they could offer a dove instead (Leviticus 5:7).

220. In essence, the poet seems to suggest that YHWH's reputation is on the line.

from *Analects* (*Lunyu*)

SNAPSHOT

LANGUAGE: Classical Chinese

DATE: 5th century BCE

LOCATION: China

GENRE: Collection of quotations

Other CONTEXTUAL INFORMATION: Traditionally attributed to Confucius's students

TAGS: Authority and Leadership; Confucianism; Education; Ethics and Morality; Family; Philosophy; Sacrifice

Introduction

Confucius (551–479 BCE) considered himself a failure in life. Tradition has it that his pleas for employment were rejected by some seventy different rulers. When he failed to gain office he became a teacher, and the ideas that he developed were later widely adopted in China. Basically, he thought that the problems of his time—increasing violence and the breakup of society—could be countered with a return to the conventional morality of the past, by which he meant the aristocratic ways of the early Zhou dynasty (1046–256 BCE). He urged his students to study ancient history and literature, and he felt that if a ruler, typically presumed to be male, lived according to high ethical standards the people would naturally follow his example.

Confucius taught the importance of ritual and music in shaping moral sensibilities, and he advocated a benevolent sort of hierarchical social order. When the Duke of Qi asked him about government, he replied, "Let rulers be rulers, ministers be ministers, fathers fathers, and sons sons" (*Analects* 12.11). The idea is that if everyone knew their place in society and acted in accordance with their position, then things would run smoothly. If, for example, every father acted as a true father—caring for the welfare of his children, protecting, educating, and supporting them—and every son showed proper respect and obedience, families would be more stable and successful. Similarly, rulers and ministers should work together in a relationship that was unequal but nevertheless was character-

Timeline

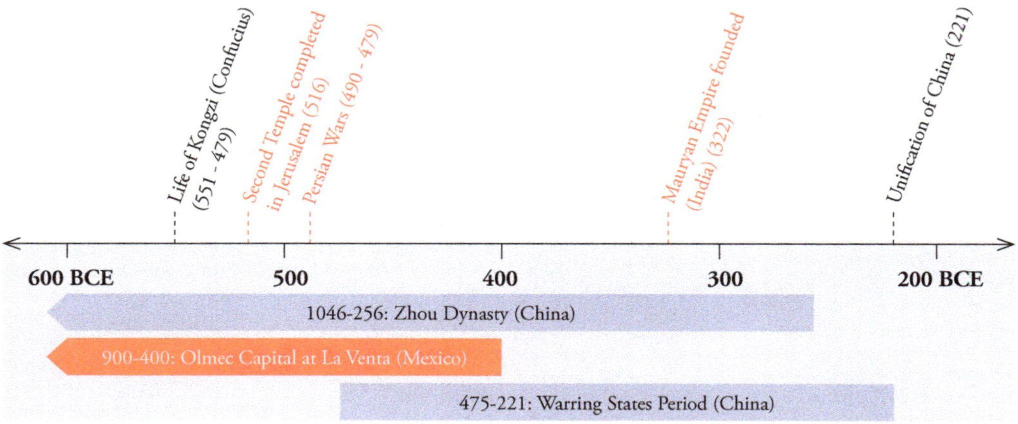

ized by generosity and mutual concern. What might reciprocity look like within the above-mentioned hierarchical relationship?

Key terms in Confucian thought include ***ren***, sometimes translated as "perfect virtue," "human-heartedness," or "humanity"; ***li*** or "ritual," which included not only ceremonial correctness but also proper etiquette and demeanor; and ***xiao***, usually rendered as "filial piety," referring to a respect for parents so strong that there is no already-existing equivalent term in English. In fact, Confucius believed that filial piety was the foundation of a well-ordered society.

In Chinese, Confucius is referred to as *Kongzi*, or "Master Kong" ("Confucius" is a Latinized form introduced by Jesuit missionaries) and his school of thought was called Ruism. The word *ru* meant something like "soft or weak" and referred to scholars and officials who had no military responsibilities. Confucius became the foremost teacher in this school, and he and his students gathered together the heritage of Chinese literary culture and became experts in their transmission and interpretation. The five **Confucian Classics** were the *Classic of Changes* (otherwise known as the *Yijing*—a divination text), the *Book of Songs* (or *Classic of Poetry*), the *Classic of History*, the *Record of Ritual*, and the *Spring and Autumn Annals*—a laconic history of Confucius's native state of Lu from 722 to 480 BCE. These texts were thought to have been edited by Confucius, and while modern scholars dispute this, there is broad consensus that our best source for Confucius's ideas is the *Analects*, a collection of short sayings of Confucius that was put together after his death by his students. In this way, our knowledge of Confucius is like our understanding of Buddha, Socrates, and Jesus, none of whom wrote anything themselves.

The Chinese text is known in China as the *Lunyu*, or "collected sayings." The term *Analects* is derived from a Greek word meaning "a gathering up" and was used as the title by the first English translator, James Legge, in 1861. Legge wanted to convey the idea that the sayings of Confucius had a status in Chinese culture similar to Classics of Greece and Rome in the West. However, it was only with the philosopher Zhu Xi (1130–1200 CE) that the **Four Books** (the *Analects*, along with the *Mencius*, the *Great Learning*, and the *Doctrine of the Mean*) became the core texts of the Chinese educational system—a position they held until the end of the imperial civil service exams in 1905.

As presented in the *Analects*, Confucius makes no attempt at systematic philosophy. He responds to specific inquiries from students or rulers (sometimes we get just the answers without questions), and his primary concern seems to be inspiring and motivating his disciples. Different students sometimes get different answers to the same question, and Confucius is not overly concerned with contradictions. Perhaps he is still trying to figure things out himself as he engages in ongoing conversation about the issues that really matter in life. What might that tell us about Confucius's process of arriving at truths? The 511 sayings in the *Analects* are organized into twenty chapters that treat a variety of topics in a somewhat haphazard, even random order. I have organized the following selections by theme, but the original is much more wide ranging. Through it all comes a portrait of a teacher — patient usually, frustrated sometimes, curious, dedicated, generous, judgmental, and, above all, committed to identifying true virtue and putting it into practice.

Grant Hardy
Department of History

PRE-READING PARS

1. Which is more important in an inspiring teacher, engaging ideas or personality?
2. Is it better to bring order to society by laws, or by customs and traditions? Which is more likely to be long-lasting?
3. How much does music shape your mood? Do you ever use music deliberately to alter your mood? Can listening to good music make you a better person?

From Analects (Lunyu)

Education

1.1 The Master said, "Is it not pleasant to learn with a constant perseverance and application? Is it not delightful to have friends coming from distant quarters? Is he not a man of complete virtue, who feels no discomposure though men may take no note of him?"

2.15 The Master said, "Learning without thought is labor lost; thought without learning is perilous."

2.17 The Master said, "Zilu [one of Confucius's students], shall I teach you what knowledge is? When you know a thing, to hold that you know it; and when you do not know a thing, to allow that you do not know it;—this is knowledge."

5.13 When Zilu heard anything, if he had not yet succeeded in carrying it into practice, he was only afraid lest he should hear something else.

6.18 The Master said, "They who know the truth are not equal to those who love it, and they who love it are not equal to those who delight in it."

7.8 The Master said, "I do not open up the truth to one who is not eager to get knowledge, nor help out anyone who is not anxious to explain himself. When I have presented one corner of a subject to anyone, and he cannot from it learn the other three, I do not repeat my lesson."

15.38 The Master said, "In teaching there should be no distinction of classes."

17.2 The Master said, "By nature, men are nearly alike; by practice, they get to be wide apart."

Government

2.3 The Master said, "If the people be led by laws, and uniformity sought to be given them by punishments, they will try to avoid the punishment, but have no sense of shame. If they be led by virtue, and uniformity sought to be given them by the rules of propriety [*li*], they will have the sense of shame, and moreover will become good."

2.20 Lord Ji Kang asked how to cause the people to reverence their ruler, to be faithful to him, and to go on to nerve themselves to virtue. The Master said, "Let him preside over them with gravity;—then they will reverence him. Let him be filial and kind to all;—then they will be faithful to him. Let him advance the good and teach the incompetent;—then they will eagerly seek to be virtuous."

12.7 Zigong [a student] asked about government. The Master said, "The requisites of government are that there be sufficiency of food, sufficiency of military equipment, and the confidence of the people in their ruler." Zigong said, "If it cannot be helped, and one of these must be dispensed with, which of the three should be foregone first?" "The military equipment," said the Master. Zigong again asked, "If it cannot be helped, and one of the remaining two must be dispensed with, which of them should be foregone?" The Master answered, "Part with the food. From of old, death has been the lot of an men; but if the people have no faith in their rulers, there is no standing for the state."

12.11 Duke Jing, of Qi, asked Confucius about government. Confucius replied, "There is government, when the prince is prince, and the minister is minister; when the father is father, and the son is son." "Good!" said the duke; "if, indeed, the prince be not prince, the minister not minister, the father not father, and the son not son, although I have my revenue, can I enjoy it?"

12.18 Lord Ji Kang, distressed about the number of thieves in the state, inquired of Confucius how to do away with them. Confucius said, "If you, sir, were not covetous, although you should reward them to do it, they would not steal."

12.19 Lord Ji Kang asked Confucius about government, saying, "What do you say to killing the unprincipled for the good of the principled?" Confucius replied, "Sir, in carrying on your government, why should you use killing at all? Let your evinced desires be for what is good, and the people will be good. The relation between superiors and inferiors is like that between the wind and the grass. The grass must bend, when the wind blows across it."

13.9 When the Master went to Wei, Ran Qiu acted as driver of his carriage. The Master observed, "How numerous are the people!" Ran Qiu said, "Since they are thus numerous, what more shall be done for them?" "Enrich them," was the reply. "And when they have been enriched, what more shall be done?" The Master said, "Teach them."

The Superior Man (or Gentleman)

2.13 Zigong asked what constituted the superior man. The Master said, "He acts before he speaks, and afterwards speaks according to his actions."

4.5 The Master said, "Riches and honors are what men desire. If it cannot be obtained in the proper way, they should not be held. Poverty and meanness are what men dislike. If it cannot be avoided in the proper way, they should not be avoided. If a superior man abandon virtue [*ren*], how can he fulfill the requirements of that name? The superior man does not, even for the space of a single meal, act contrary to virtue. In moments of haste, he cleaves to it. In seasons of danger, he cleaves to it."

4.16 The Master said, "The mind of the superior man is conversant with righteousness; the mind of the mean man is conversant with gain."

7.36 The Master said, "The superior man is satisfied and composed; the mean man is always full of distress."

9.13 The Master was wishing to go and live among the nine wild tribes of the east. Someone said, "They are rude. How can you do such a thing?" The Master said, "If a superior man dwelt among them, what rudeness would there be?"

15.20 The Master said, "What the superior man seeks, is in himself. What the mean man seeks, is in others."

16.7 Confucius said, "There are three things which the superior man guards against. In youth, when the physical powers are not yet settled, he guards against lust. When he is strong and the physical powers are full of vigor, he guards against quarrelsomeness. When he is old, and the animal powers are decayed, he guards against covetousness."

Morality

4.17 The Master said, "When we see men of worth, we should think of equaling them; when we see men of a contrary character, we should turn inwards and examine ourselves."

4.23 The Master said, "The cautious seldom err."

5.19 Lord Ji Wen thought thrice, and then acted. When the Master was informed of it, he said, "Twice may do."

13.18 The Duke of She informed Confucius, saying, "Among us here there are those who may be styled upright in their conduct. If their father have stolen a sheep, they will bear witness to the fact." Confucius said, "Among us, in our part of the country, those who are upright are different from this. The father conceals the misconduct of the son, and the son conceals the misconduct of the father. Uprightness is to be found in this."

13.24 Zigong asked, saying, "What do you say of a man who is loved by all the people of his neighborhood?" The Master replied, "We may not for that accord our approval of him." "And what do you say of him who is hated by all the people of his neighborhood?" The Master said, "We may not for that conclude that he is bad. It is better than either of these cases that the good in the neighborhood love him, and the bad hate him."

14.36 Someone said, "What do you say concerning the principle that injury should be recompensed with kindness?" The Master said, "With what then will you recompense kindness? Recompense injury with justice, and recompense kindness with kindness."

15.23 Zigong asked, saying, "Is there one word which may serve as a rule of practice for all one's life?" The Master said, "Is not 'reciprocity' such a word? What you do not want done to yourself, do not do to others."

16.10 Confucius said, "The superior man has nine things which are subjects with him of thoughtful consideration. In regard to the use of his eyes, he is anxious to see clearly. In regard to the use of his ears, he is anxious to hear distinctly. In regard to his countenance, he is anxious that it should be benign. In regard to his demeanor, he is anxious that it should be respectful. In regard to his speech, he is anxious that it should be sincere. In regard to his doing of business, he is anxious that it should be reverently careful. In regard to what he doubts about, he is anxious to question others. When he is angry, he thinks of the difficulties (his anger may involve him in). When he sees gain to be got, he thinks of righteousness."

Humanity [*ren*]

3.3 The Master said, "If a man be without the virtues proper to humanity [*ren*], what has he to do with the rites of propriety [*li*]? If a man be without the virtues proper to humanity, what has he to do with music?"

4.2 The Master said, "Those who are without virtue [*ren*] cannot abide long either in a condition of poverty and hardship, or in a condition of enjoyment. The virtuous rest in virtue; the wise desire virtue."

4.3 The Master said, "It is only the (truly) virtuous man [*ren*], who can love, or who can hate, others."

6.21 The Master said, "The wise find pleasure in water; the virtuous [*ren*] find pleasure in hills. The wise are active; the virtuous are tranquil. The wise are joyful; the virtuous are long-lived."

Filial Piety

1.11 The Master said, "While a man's father is alive, look at the bent of his will; when his father is dead, look at his conduct. If for three years he does not alter from the way of his father, he may be called filial."

2.6 Ziyou [a student] asked what filial piety was. The Master said, "The filial piety nowadays means the support of one's parents. But dogs and horses likewise are able to do something in the way of support;—without reverence, what is there to distinguish the one support given from the other?"

4.18 The Master said, "In serving his parents, a son may remonstrate with them, but gently; when he sees that they do not incline to follow his advice, he shows an increased degree of reverence, but does not abandon his purpose; and should they punish him, he does not allow himself to murmur."

4.19 The Master said, "While his parents are alive, the son may not go abroad to a distance. If he does go abroad, he must have a fixed place to which he goes."

4.21 The Master said, "The years of parents [i.e. how old they are] may by no means not be kept in the memory, as an occasion at once for joy and for fear."

Ritual/Music

8.2 The Master said, "Respectfulness, without the rules of propriety [*li*], becomes laborious bustle; carefulness, without the rules of propriety, becomes timidity; boldness, without the rules of propriety, becomes insubordination; straightforwardness, without the rules of propriety, becomes rudeness. When those who are in high stations perform well all their duties to their relations, the people are aroused to virtue. When old friends are not neglected by them, the people are preserved from meanness."

8.8 The Master said, "It is by the Classic of Poetry that the mind is aroused. It is by the rules of propriety that the character is established. It is from music that the finish is received."

11.12 Zilu asked about serving the spirits of the dead. The Master said, "While you are not able to serve men, how can you serve their spirits?" Zilu added, "I venture to ask about death?" He was answered, "While you do not know life, how can you know about death?"

12.1 1. Yan Hui [Confucius' favorite student] asked about perfect virtue [*ren*]. The Master said, "To subdue one's self and return to propriety, is perfect virtue. If a man can for one day subdue himself and return to propriety, all under heaven will ascribe perfect virtue to him. Is the practice of perfect virtue from a man himself, or is it from others?" Yen Hui said, "I beg to ask the steps of that process." The Master replied, "Look not at what is contrary to propriety; listen not to what is contrary to propriety; speak not what is contrary to propriety; make no movement which is contrary to propriety." Yen Hui then said, "Though I am deficient in intelligence and vigor, I will make it my business to practice this lesson."

17.25 The Master said, "Of all people, girls and servants are the most difficult to behave to. If you are familiar with them, they lose their humility. If you maintain a reserve towards them, they are discontented."

Confucius the Man

2.4 The Master said, "At fifteen, I had my mind bent on learning. At thirty, I stood firm. At forty, I had no doubts. At fifty, I knew the decrees of Heaven. At sixty, my ear was an obedient organ for the reception of truth. At seventy, I could follow what my heart desired, without transgressing what was right."

2.21 Someone addressed Confucius, saying, "Sir, why are you not engaged in the government?" The Master said, "What does the *Classic of Poetry* say of filial piety?—'You are filial, you discharge your brotherly duties. These qualities are displayed in government.' This then also constitutes the exercise of government. Why must there be *that*—making one be in the government?"

5.27 The Master said, "In a hamlet of ten families, there may be found one honorable and sincere as I am, but not so fond of learning."

7.18 The Duke of She asked Zilu about Confucius, and Zilu did not answer him. The Master said, "Why did you not say to him,—He is simply a man, who in his eager pursuit of knowledge forgets his food, who in the joy of its attainment forgets his sorrows, and who does not perceive that old age is coming on?"

7.19 The Master said, "I am not one who was born in the possession of knowledge; I am one who is fond of antiquity, and earnest in seeking it there."

7.31 When the Master was in company with a person who was singing, if he sang well, he would make him repeat the song, while he accompanied it with his own voice.

7.33 The Master said, "The sage and the man of perfect virtue [*ren*];—how dare I rank myself with them? It may simply be said of me, that I strive to become such without satiety, and teach others without weariness." Gongxi Chi said, "This is just what we, the disciples, cannot imitate you in."

10.8 Although his food might be coarse rice and vegetable soup, he would offer a little of it in sacrifice with a grave, respectful air.

11.8 When Yan Hui [Confucius' favorite student] died, the Master said, "Alas! Heaven is destroying me! Heaven is destroying me!"

13.10 The Master said, "If there were (any of the princes) who would employ me, in the course of twelve months, I should have done something considerable. In three years, the government would be perfected."

17.20 Ru Bei wished to see Confucius, but Confucius declined, on the ground of being sick, to see him. When the bearer of this message went out at the door, (the master) took his lute and sang to it, in order that [the messenger] might hear him.

Confucius. Selections from *The Chinese Classics: Confucian Analects (in Chinese and English).* Translated by James Legge. London: Trübner & Co., 1861.

POST-READING PARS

1. How would you describe Confucius as a teacher based on your reading of the *Analects*? What inspires more, his ideas or his personality?
2. According to Confucius, where do ideas of right and wrong come from? How can people be persuaded to adopt particular points of morality?
3. Are there ethical concerns that Confucius does not consider?

Inquiry Corner

Content Question(s):	Critical Question(s):
What are the responsibilities of a ruler, according to Confucius? What sorts of specific behaviors are required for filial piety?	In what ways could Confucius be considered a traditionalist (upholding the status quo)? Are there ways in which he might also be thought of as a reformer?
Comparative Question(s):	**Connection Question(s):**
Compare Confucius's teachings about how to be in harmonious relationship with others with a source from another culture (e.g., Eastern Band of Cherokee Origin Stories—"Origin of Strawberries" (Cherokee), Sermon on the Mount, *Bhagavad Gita*, etc.). Some readers have seen Confucius's statement, "What you do not want done to yourself, do not do to others" (15.23) as equivalent to the Golden Rule. Do you agree?	Where is the locus of morality—in the individual, the community, or some other source? Would the world be a better place if most people were more Confucian?

BEYOND THE CLASSROOM

- Do you experience parental or societal pressure to pursue a specific major/career? Or to support your family?
- What aspects (e.g., family, money, fame, etc.) take priority when choosing a career path? When working for someone else?
- How many positions have you applied for and been rejected from? Why did you carry on applying? What (if anything) did you learn from the rejections?
- Confucius and others have said if you choose a job you love, you will never have to work a day in your life. Do you agree?

from *Book of Songs*

SNAPSHOT BOX

LANGUAGE: Chinese

DATE: 12th–7th century BCE

LOCATION: China

GENRE: Poetry

TAGS: Aesthetics; Confucianism; Love; Nature; Women and Gender

Introduction

The *Book of Songs*, or *Classic of Poetry* (*Shijing*), is one of the five **Confucian Classics** (see the introduction to the *Analects*). The traditional account is that the king sent messengers into the countryside to collect folksongs from the common people as a way of gauging their attitudes and concerns, that is, as a sort of early public opinion survey. Out of the 3,000 songs that were brought back to the capital, Confucius (551–479 BCE) chose the 305 best for inclusion in the *Book of Songs*. The story of Confucius's editing is probably not accurate, but he and his followers became experts in this anthology of ancient Chinese poetry, which included songs from the twelfth–seventh century BCE. In the generations preceding Confucius, it had become an expectation for educated courtiers to memorize the *Book of Songs*, and interstate relations were sometimes conducted through allusions to the text. Diplomats would have to recognize quoted lines, remember the entire poem, and then apply it to the situation at hand. After the time of Confucius, familiarity with the *Book of Songs* became even more essential for literary and political endeavors. Are there any cultural artifacts—text, song, image, meme—that you would expect everyone to understand?

Confucius highlighted the role of the *Book of Songs* in his educational program, as can be seen in this quote from the *Analects*:

> The Master said, "My students, why do you not study the *Songs*? The *Songs* can stir your emotions, enhance your observations, smooth social interactions, and

Timeline

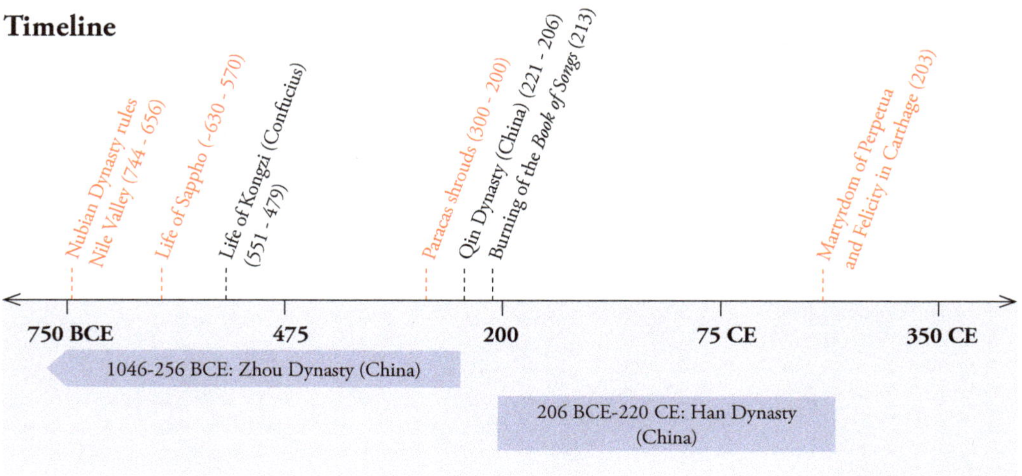

give expression to complaints. Close at hand, they enable service to parents; at a distance, service to a ruler. Through them you can become acquainted with the names of birds and animals, plants and trees."[221]

Can songs teach us about nature? If not, why does Confucius think that his students can learn about nature from them?

The close association of the *Book of Songs* with Confucianism in later centuries resulted in scholars interpreting individual poems as allegories or illustrations of orthodox Confucian values. For instance, a reference to "a mere glimpse of a plain coat" that could "stab my heart with grief" was explained as anguish caused by the sight of someone dressed in inappropriate clothes during the time they should be mourning for their parents (an important aspect of **filial piety**). In actuality, it was probably just a love song, as can be seen in the next line: "Enough! Take me with you to your home."

The poems themselves are mostly short—nothing quite like the **epic poetry** of Homer emerged in ancient China—and were originally set to music, although the melodies have long since been lost. They are generally organized into stanzas of four-character lines, with even-numbered lines ending with rhyming syllables. This may be the oldest example of rhyming poetry in world literature. It is common for a poem to highlight a metaphor or parallel from nature, and the lines are often rather repetitive. As you read, pay attention to the repetitions and variations from stanza to stanza.

The topics, especially in the first half of the collection, tend to come from everyday life—as one might expect from folksongs. There are descriptions of love, marriage, agricultural labors, hunting, feasting, war, and complaints about the government. In the latter half of the work there are somewhat longer poems that seem to have accompanied court ceremonies and sacrifices, sometimes making reference to dynastic legends or to specific historical events among the nobility. For modern readers, the folksongs probably spark the most interest, particularly since so many of them were written by women (always a rarity in the ancient world), or at least were spoken by a female persona (perhaps composed by men who were trying to imagine a woman's perspective; although even this was a rarity at the time). These are **lyric poems** that express a personal emotion, though often without a lot of details about context. It is up to readers to imagine the sorts of situations that might have called forth such feelings.

The *Book of Songs*, along with other works of literature and philosophy, was banned by the First Emperor in 213 BCE and only survived into the next generation because of a few scholars who had memorized the entire text. For what reasons

221. 17.9; my translation.

might rulers ban or burn books? As you read, consider what could have made *this* book so dangerous.

Grant Hardy
Department of History

from the Book of Songs

Mao #20 [Waley #17]

Plop fall the plums; but there are still seven.
Let those gentlemen that would court me
Come while it is lucky!

Plop fall the plums; there are still three.
Let any gentleman that would court me
Come before it is too late!

Plop fall the plums; in shallow baskets we lay them.
Any gentleman who would court me
Had better speak while there is time.

Mao #23 [Waley #63]

In the wilds there is a dead doe;
With white rushes we cover her.
There was a lady longing for the spring;
A fair knight seduced her.

In the wood there is a clump of oaks,
And in the wilds a dead deer
With white rushes well bound;
There was a lady fair as jade.

"Heigh, not so hasty, not so rough;
Heigh, do not touch my handkerchief.[222]
Take care, or the dog will bark."

222. Which was worn at the girdle [translator note].

Mao #61 [Waley #44]

Who says that the River is broad?
On a single reed you could cross it.[223]
Who says that Sung[224] is far away?
By standing on tip-toe I can see it.

Who says that the River is broad?
There is not room in it even for a skiff.
Who says that Sung is far away?
It could not take you so much as a morning.

Mao #66 [Waley #100]

My lord is on service;[225]
He did not know for how long.
Oh, when will he come?
The fowls are roosting in their holes,
Another day is ending,
The sheep and cows are coming down.
My lord is on service;
How can I not be sad?

My lord is on service;
Not a matter of days, nor months.
Oh, when will he be here again?
The fowls are roosting on their perches,
Another day is ending,
The sheep and cows have all come down,
My lord is on service;
Were I but sure that he gets drink and food!

Mao #76 [Waley #24]

I beg of you, Chung Tzu,
Do not climb into our homestead,
Do not break the willows we have planted.
Not that I mind about the willows,

223. The speaker seems to be reproving an absent lover for making excuses.

224. The state of Sung lay south of the Yellow River, and Wei (where this song comes from) to the North [translator note].

225. That is, my husband is away at war.

But I am afraid of my father and mother.
Chung Tzu I dearly love;
But of what my father and mother say
Indeed I am afraid.

I beg of you, Chung Tzu,
Do not climb over our wall,
Do not break the mulberry-trees we have planted.
Not that I mind about the mulberry-trees,
But I am afraid of my brothers.
Chung Tzu I dearly love;
But of what my brothers say
Indeed I am afraid.

I beg of you, Chung Tzu,
Do not climb into our garden,
Do not break the hard-wood we have planted.
Not that I mind about the hard-wood,
But I am afraid of what people will say.
Chung Tzu I dearly love;
But of all that people will say
Indeed I am afraid.

Mao #113 [Waley #276]

Big rat, big rat,
Do not gobble our millet!
Three years we have slaved for you,
Yet you take no notice of us.
At last we are going to leave you
And go to that happy land;
Happy land, happy land,
Where we shall have our place.

Big rat, big rat,
Do not gobble our corn![226]
Three years we have slaved for you,
Yet you give us no credit.
At last we are going to leave you
And go to that happy kingdom;

226. Wheat

Happy kingdom, happy kingdom,
Where we shall get our due.

Big rat, big rat,
Do not eat our rice-shoots!
Three years we have slaved for you,
Yet you did nothing to reward us.
At last we are going to leave you
And go to those happy borders;
Happy borders, happy borders,
Where no sad songs are sung.

Mao #147 [Waley #10]

That the mere glimpse of a plain cap
Could harry me with such longing,
Cause pain so dire!

That the mere glimpse of a plain coat
Could stab my heart with grief!
Enough! Take me with you to your home.

That a mere glimpse of plain leggings
Could tie my heart in tangles!
Enough! Let us two be one.

Mao #245 [Waley #238]

She who in the beginning gave birth to the people,
This was Chiang Yüan.
How did she give birth to the people?
Well she sacrificed and prayed
That she might no longer be childless.
She trod on the big toe of God's footprint,
Was accepted and got what she desired.
Then in reverence, then in awe
She gave birth, she nurtured;
And this was Hou Chi.[227]

227. Or Hou Ji ("Lord Millet"), who was the god of agriculture and the legendary ancestor of the clan that became the Zhou royal family.

Indeed, she had fulfilled her months,
And her first-born came like a lamb
With no bursting or rending,
With no hurt or harm.
To make manifest His magic power
God on high gave her ease.
So blessed were her sacrifice and prayer
That easily she bore her child.

Indeed, they put it in a narrow lane;
But oxen and sheep tenderly cherished it.
Indeed, they[228] put it in a far-off wood;
But it chanced that woodcutters came to this wood.
Indeed, they put it on the cold ice;
But the birds covered it with their wings.
The birds at last went away,
And Hou Chi began to wail.

Truly far and wide
His voice was very loud.
Then sure enough he began to crawl;
Well he straddled, well he reared,
To reach food for his mouth.
He planted large bean;
His beans grew fat and tall.
His paddy-lines were close set,
His hemp and wheat grew thick,
His young gourds teemed.

Truly Hou Chi's husbandry
Followed the way that had been shown.[229]
He cleared away the thick grass,
He planted the yellow crop.
It failed nowhere, it grew thick,
It was heavy, it was tall,
It sprouted, it eared,
It was firm and good,
It nodded, it hung—

228. The ballad does not tell us who exposed the child. According to one version it was the mother herself; according to another, her husband [translator note].

229. By God [translator note]

He made house and home in T'ai.

Indeed, the lucky grains were sent down to us,
The back millet, the double-kernelled,
Millet pink-sprouted and white.
Far and wide the black and the double-kernelled
He reaped and acred;[230]
Far and wide the millet pink and white
He carried in his arms, he bore on his back,
Brought them home, and created the sacrifice.

Indeed, what are they, our sacrifices?
We pound the grain, we bale it out,
We sift, we tread,
We wash it—soak, soak;
We boil it all steamy.
Then with due care, due thought
We gather southernwood, make offering of fat,
Take lambs for the rite of expiation,
We roast, we broil,
To give a start to the coming year.

High we load the stands,
The stands of wood and of earthenware.
As soon as the smell rises
God on high is very pleased:
"What smell is this, so strong and good?"
Hou Chi founded the sacrifices,
And without blemish or flaw
They have gone on till now.

Waley, Arthur, trans. *The Book of Songs: The Ancient Chinese Classic of Poetry*, 30, 35, 48, 60, 92, 244–43, 309. New York: Grove, 1938 [1960]. [Mao numbers, referring to the ancient Mao version of the text, are the standard scholarly way to cite specific poems; Waley used his own numbering system.]

230. The yield was reckoned by acre [translator note]

from *Daodejing* and *Zhuangzi*

Introduction

The Daodejing of Laozi

How do people live together in harmony? This is the fundamental question that Chinese philosophy attempted to answer. Two prominent answers are provided by Confucius and Laozi. If Confucius comes across as a real person, Laozi (Master Lao) is a mystery. His name may not even be a name, for it might simply mean "The Old Master." We have no idea when he lived, or even if he lived. What we do have is a book, sometimes called the *Laozi*, and sometimes referred to as the *Daodejing* ("The Classic of the Way and Virtue/Power"),[231] and its author(s) is conventionally identified as Laozi. Laozi advocates a return to the **Dao**—often translated as "the Way." The Dao is a bit hard to describe since Laozi taught that it was beyond words, but it acts according to natural principles and it encompasses all opposites. This is the concept behind the famous **yin/yang** symbol, representing the two opposite but interdependent forces that make up the natural world. So although we tend to judge things as being weak or strong, hard or soft, desirable or repugnant, from the perspective of nature these artificial, human distinctions do not mean much. For instance, which is more valuable, gold or dirt? Both are natural products

SNAPSHOT BOX

LANGUAGE: Classical Chinese

DATE: Late 4th century BCE

LOCATION: China

GENRE: Aphorisms (*Daodejing*)

Philosophical discourse: (*Zhuangzi*)

TAGS: Aesthetics; Cosmology; Death; Ethics and Morality; Freedom and Harmony; Nature; Philosophy

Timeline

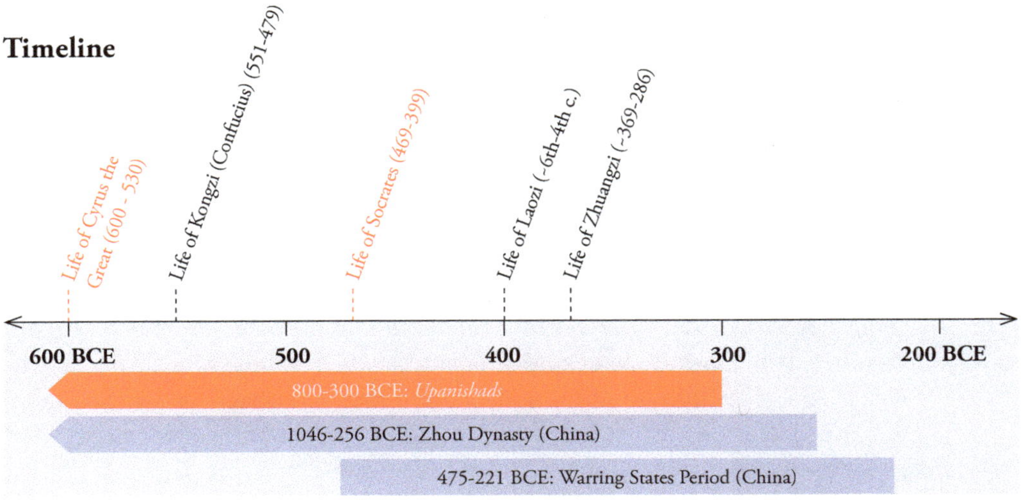

231. *De*, or "virtue/power," is a difficult term to translate and refers to a sort of spiritual force or moral charisma.

and both have their uses, but people are willing to lie and steal and even murder to get gold. But can you grow crops in a field of gold? If people could ignore such conventional value judgments, would everyone be happier?

According to Laozi, a harmonious society would be one made up of small villages whose inhabitants were basically content with what they had (see ch. 80). It is desire and ambition that get us into trouble, and they are hardly ever worth it. Even more striking, Laozi suggests that many opposites are illusory. Thus water appears soft and weak, but for wearing away mountains and digging canyons, there is nothing like it. And opposites always come in pairs, so that when we praise someone as being beautiful, we are also implying that everyone who looks different is ugly. So also, Laozi complains that whenever the Confucians emphasize a virtue, they also highlight a vice. For example, would anyone elevate filial piety as a virtue if the lack of respect for parents were not already a major problem?

Laozi offers advice for ordinary people, but he also has suggestions for rulers. In political terms, the best government is one that does not do much, because trying to change things too quickly will always bring a backlash of resentment. Laozi promotes a vision of simplicity, contentment, and quietism, and he specifically advocates **wu-wei**, or "non-action." This probably does not literally mean doing nothing. Rather, we should avoid doing anything that takes too much effort. Relax. Go with the flow. Don't worry, be happy.

Most Chinese traditionally have been both Confucian and Daoist to some degree. When times are good and hard work seems to pay off, Confucianism provides direction and encouragement to make things even better. But when times are bad and the government is corrupt, Daoism functions as a sort of safety valve, an ideology that allows one to withdraw from public life and concentrate on simple pleasures. But Confucius and Laozi were not exactly opposites, since they shared many assumptions. They both rejected competition and strife, they communicated their ideas through aphorisms rather than detailed arguments, and they believed that an intuitive, spontaneous sort of harmony would naturally arise from their principles.

The Zhuangzi

Zhuang Zhou, or Zhuangzi (Master Zhuang), can be reliably dated to the late fourth century BCE. His book, also called the *Zhuangzi*, was probably augmented by later writers, but the first seven chapters seem to be by the same person. Because his ideas are similar to those of Laozi (he may, in fact, have been earlier than Laozi), Chinese scholars in the first century BCE categorized both of them as Daoists. Their styles, however, are very different. Zhuangzi wrote long, fantastic narratives and dialogues, full of language games, that humorously poke holes in our everyday notions of value and truth. Perspective is everything, he seems to say. How can language be used to destabilize meaning and alter perspectives?

The *Daodejing* is somewhat contradictory. Laozi argues that there is no real difference between opposites like weak and strong, but in the end he has a clear preference as he gives advice to rulers. Take the weaker position (like water), he suggests, because then you will survive longer. Zhuangzi really seems to have no preferences. Dream and reality; power and powerlessness; even life and death are all the same to him. The following few excerpts, particularly on this last theme, will illustrate this.

Grant Hardy
Department of History

PRE-READING PARS

1. What would a life without ambition look like? Does striving ever get in the way of living well?
2. To what degree is thinking in dualities or binaries a helpful way of understanding human experience? How is it a limiting way of understanding human experience?
3. Can you think of any other influential texts that do not exactly have an author? Does it make a difference in how we read such works?

from *Daodejing* and *Zhuangzi*

from the Daodejing of Laozi, Book One (The Way)

Chapter 1

A Way that can be followed is not a constant Way.
A name that can be named is not a constant name.
Nameless, it is the beginning of Heaven and Earth;
Named, it is the mother of the myriad creatures.
And so,
    Always eliminate desire in order to observe its mysteries
    Always have desires in order to observe its manifestations.
These two come forth in unity but diverge in name.
Their unity is known as an enigma.
Within this enigma is yet a deeper enigma.
The gate of all mysteries!

Chapter 2

Everyone in the world knows that when the beautiful strives to be beautiful, it is repulsive.
Everyone knows that when the good strives to be good, it is no good.[232]
And so,
    To have and to lack generate each other.
    Difficult and easy give form to each other.
    Long and short off-set each other.
    High and low incline into each other.

232. An alternative translation is: "When the people of the world all know beauty as beauty, / There arises the recognition of ugliness. / When they all know the good as good, / There arises the recognition of evil. [Wing-Tsit Chan, trans.]

Note and rhythm harmonize with each other.
Before and after follow each other.
This is why sages abide in the business of nonaction,
and practice the teaching that is without words.
They work with the myriad creatures and turn none away.
They produce without possessing.
They act with no expectation of reward.
When their work is done, they do not linger.
And by not lingering, merit never deserts them.

Chapter 3

Not paying honor to the worthy leads the people to avoid contention.
Not showing reverence to precious goods leads them to not steal.
Not making a display of what is desirable leads their hearts away from chaos.
This is why sages bring things to order by opening people's hearts
and filling their bellies.
They weaken the people's commitments and strengthen their bones;
They make sure that the people are without knowledge or desires;
And that those with knowledge do not dare to act.
Sages enact nonaction and everything becomes well ordered.

Chapter 9

To hold a vessel upright in order to fill it is not as good as to stop in time.
If you make your blade too keen it will not hold its edge.
When gold and jade fill the hall none can hold on to them.
To be haughty when wealth and honor come your way is to bring disaster upon yourself.
To withdraw when the work is done is the Way of Heaven.

Chapter 11

Thirty spokes are joined in the hub of a wheel.
But only by relying on what is not there, do we have the use of the carriage.
By adding and removing clay we form a vessel.
By carving out doors and windows we make a room.
But only by relying on what is not there, do we have use of the room.
And so, what is there is the basis for profit;
What is not there is the basis for use.

Chapter 19

Cut off sageliness, abandon wisdom, and the people will benefit one hundred fold.
Cut off benevolence, abandon righteousness, and the people will return to being filial and kind.
Cut off cleverness, abandon profit, and robbers and thieves will be no more.
This might leave the people lacking in culture;
So give them something with which to identify:
Manifest plainness.
Embrace simplicity.
Do not think just of yourself.
Make few your desires.

Chapter 36

What you intend to shrink, you first must stretch.
What you intend to weaken, you first must strengthen.
What you intend to abandon, you first must make flourish.
What you intend to steal from, you first must provide for.
This is called subtle enlightenment.
The supple and weak overcome the hard and the strong.
Fish should not be taken out of the deep pools.
The sharp implements of the state should not be shown to the people.

From the Daodejing of Laozi, Book Two (Virtue/Power)

Chapter 42

The Way produces the One.
The One produces two.
Two produces three.
Three produces the myriad creatures.
The myriad creatures shoulder yin and embrace yang,
and by blending these *qi* ("vital energies") they attain harmony.
People most despise being orphaned, desolate, or forlorn,
and yet barons and kings take these as their personal appellations.
And so sometimes diminishing a thing adds to it;
What others teach, I too teach: "The violent and overbearing will not die a natural death."
I shall take this as the father of all my teachings.

Chapter 47

Without going out the door, one can know the whole world.
Without looking out the window, one can see the Way of Heaven.
The farther one goes, the less one knows.
This is why sages
    Know without going abroad,
    Name without having to see,
    Perfect through nonaction.

Chapter 48

In the pursuit of learning, one does more each day;
In the pursuit of the Way, one does less each day;
One does less and less until one does nothing;
One does nothing yet nothing is left undone.
Gaining the world always is accomplished by following no activity.
As soon as one actively tries, one will fall short of gaining the world.

Chapter 71

To know that one does not know is best;
Not to know but to believe that one knows is a disease.
Only by seeing this disease as a disease can one be free of it.
Sages are free of this disease;
Because they see this disease as a disease, they are free of it.

Chapter 76

When alive human beings are supple and weak;
When dead they are stiff and strong.
When alive the myriad creatures, plants, and trees are supple and weak;
When dead they are withered and dry.
And so the stiff and the strong are the disciples of death;
The supple and weak are the disciples of life.
This is why,
    A weapon that is too strong will not prove victorious;
    A tree that is too strong will break.
The strong and the mighty reside down below;
The soft and the supple reside on top.

Chapter 78

In all the world, nothing is more supple or weak than water;
Yet nothing can surpass it for attacking what is stiff and strong.
And so nothing can take its place.
That the weak overcome the strong and the supple overcomes the hard,
These are things everyone in the world knows but none can practice.
This is why sages say,
    Those who can take on the disgrace of the state
    Are called lords of the altar to the soil and grain.
    Those who can take on the misfortune of the state,
    Are called kings of all the world.
Straightforward words seem paradoxical.

Chapter 80

Reduce the size of the state;
Lessen the population.
Make sure that even though there are labor saving tools, they are never used.
Make sure that the people look upon death as a weighty matter and never move to distant places.
Even though they have ships and carts, they will have no use for them.
Even though they have armor and weapons, they will have no reason to deploy them.
Make sure that the people return to the use of the knotted cord.
Make their food savory,
Their clothes fine,
Their houses comfortable,
Their lives happy.
Then even though neighboring states are within sight of each other,
Even though they can hear the sounds of each other's dogs and chickens,
Their people will grow old and die without ever having visited one another.

Chapter 81

Words worthy of trust are not beautiful;
Words that are beautiful are not worthy of trust.
The good do not engage in disputation;
Those who engage in disputation are not good.
Those who know are not full of knowledge;
Those full of knowledge do not know.
Sages do not accumulate.

The more they do for others, the more they have;
The more they give to others, the more they possess.
The Way of Heaven is to benefit and not harm.
The Way of the sage is to act but not contend.

from the Zhuangzi

from Chapter 2: "The Adjustment of Controversies"

Zhuangzi replied ...

"How do I know that the love of life is not a delusion? and that the dislike of death is not like a young person's losing his way, and not knowing that he is really going home? Lady Li was a daughter of the border guard of Ai. When the ruler of the state of Jin first got possession of her,[233] she wept till the tears wetted all the front of her dress. But when she came to the place of the king, shared with him his luxurious couch, and ate his grain-and-grass-fed meat, then she regretted that she had wept. How do I know that the dead do not repent of their former craving for life?

"Those who dream of the pleasures of drinking may in the morning wail and weep; those who dream of wailing and weeping may in the morning be going out to hunt. When they were dreaming they did not know it was a dream; in their dream they may even have tried to interpret it; but when they awoke they knew that it was a dream. And there is the great awaking, after which we shall know that this life was a great dream. All the while, the stupid think they are awake, and with nice discrimination insist on their knowledge; now playing the part of rulers, and now of shepherds. Bigoted was that Confucius! He and you are both dreaming. I who say that you are dreaming am dreaming myself. These words seem very strange; but if after ten thousand ages we once meet with a great sage who knows how to explain them, it will be as if we met him unexpectedly some morning or evening.

"Since you made me enter into this discussion with you, if you have got the better of me and not I of you, are you indeed right, and I indeed wrong? If I have got the better of you and not you of me, am I indeed right and you indeed wrong? Is the one of us right and the other wrong? Are we both right or both wrong? Since we cannot come to a mutual and common understanding, men will certainly continue in darkness on the subject.

"Whom shall I employ to adjudicate in the matter? If I employ one who agrees with you, how can he, agreeing with you, do so correctly? And the same may be said, if I employ one who agrees with me. It will be the same if I employ one who differs from us both or one who agrees with us both. In this way I and you and those others would all not be able to come to a mutual understanding; and shall we then wait for that great sage? We need not do so. To wait on others to learn how conflicting opinions are changed is simply like not so waiting at all. The harmonizing of them

233. She was taken captive in 671 BCE.

is to be found in the invisible operation of Heaven, and by following this on into the unlimited past. It is by this method that we can complete our years without our minds being disturbed.

* * * * *

"Formerly, I, Zhuang Zhou (Zhuangzi), dreamt that I was a butterfly, a butterfly flying about, feeling that it was enjoying itself. I did not know that it was Zhuang Zhou. Suddenly I awoke, and was myself again, the veritable Zhuang Zhou. I did not know whether it had formerly been Zhuang Zhou dreaming that he was a butterfly, or it was now a butterfly dreaming that it was Zhuang Zhou. But between Zhuang Zhou and a butterfly there must be a difference. This is a case of what is called the Transformation of Things."

from Chapter 6: "The Great and Most Honored Master"

Ziji, Ziyu, Zili, and Zilai, these four men were talking together when one of them said, "Who can suppose the head to be made from nothing, the spine from life, and the rump-bone from death? Who knows how death and birth, living on and disappearing, compose the one body? I will be friends with him!" The four men looked at one another and laughed, but no one seized with his mind the drift of the questions. All, however, were friends together.

No long after, Ziyu fell ill and Ziji went to inquire for him. "How great," said the sufferer, "is the Creator! That he should have made me the deformed object that I am!" He was a crooked hunchback; his five viscera were squeezed into the upper part of his body; his chin bent over his navel; his shoulder was higher than his head; on his head was a ponytail pointing to the sky; his breath came and went in gasps—yet he was easy in his mind, and made no trouble of his condition. He limped to a well, looked at himself in it, and said, "Alas that the Creator should have made me the deformed object that I am!"

Ziji said, "Do you dislike your condition?"

He replied, "No, why should I dislike it? If He were to transform my left arm into a rooster, I should be watching with it the time of the night; if He were to transform my right arm into a cross-bow, I should then be looking for an owl to bring down and roast; if He were to transform my rump-bone into a wheel, and my spirit into a horse, I should then be mounting it, and would never need a carriage again. Moreover, when we have got what we are to do, there is the time of life in which to do it; when we lose that at death, submission is what is required. When we rest in what the time requires, and manifest that submission, neither joy nor sorrow can find entrance to the mind. This would be what the ancients called 'loosing the cord by which the life is suspended.' But one hung up cannot loose himself; he is held fast by his bonds. And that creatures cannot overcome Heaven (the inevitable) is a long-acknowledged fact. Why should I hate my condition?"

Before long Zilai fell ill, and lay gasping at the point of death, while his wife and children stood around him wailing. Zili went to ask for him, and said to them, "Hush! Get out of the way! Do not disturb him as he is passing through his change." Then, leaning against the door, he said to the dying man, "Great indeed is the Creator! What will He now make you to become? Where will He take you to? Will He make you the liver of a rat, or the arm of an insect?" Zilai replied, "Wherever a parent tells a son to go, east, west, south, or north, he simply follows the command. The yin and yang are more to a man than his parents are. If they are hastening my death, and I do not quietly submit to them, I shall be obstinate and rebellious. There is the great mass of Nature—I find the support of my body in it; my life is spent in toil on it; my old age seeks ease on it; at death I find rest on it. What has made my life a good, will make my death also a good.

"Here now is a great founder, casting his metal. If the metal were to leap up in the pot and say, "I must be made into a sword like Moye,"[234] the great founder would be sure to regard it as uncanny. So again, when a form is being fashioned in the mold of the womb, if it were to say, "I must become a man; I must become a man," the Creator would be sure to regard it as uncanny. When we once understand that heaven and earth are a great melting-pot, and the Creator a great founder, where can we have to go that shall not be right for us? We are born as from a quiet sleep, and we die to a calm awaking."

from Chapter 17: "The Floods of Autumn"

Zhuangzi was once fishing in the river Pu, when the king of Chu sent two great officers to him, with the message, "I wish to trouble you with the charge of all within my territories." Zhuangzi kept on holding his rod without looking round, and said, "I have heard that in Chu there is a spirit-like tortoise-shell, the wearer of which died 3000 years ago, and which the king keeps, in his ancestral temple, in a hamper covered with a cloth. Was it better for the tortoise to die, and leave its shell to be thus honored? Or would it have been better for it to live, and keep on dragging its tail through the mud?" The two officers said, "It would have been better for it to live, and draw its tail after it over the mud." "Go your ways. I will keep on drawing my tail after me through the mud."

* * * * *

Zhuangzi and Huizi were walking on the dam over the Hao River, when the former said, "These minnows come out, and play about at their ease—that is the enjoyment of fishes." The other said, "You are not a fish; how do you know what constitutes the enjoyment of fishes?" Zhuangzi rejoined, "You are not I. How do you know that I do not know what constitutes the enjoyment of fishes?" Huizi said, "I am not you; and though indeed I do not fully know you, you certainly are not a fish, and the argument is complete against your knowing what constitutes the happiness

234. A famous named sword, like Excalibur.

of fishes." Zhuangzi replied, "Let us keep to your original question. You said to me, 'How do you know what constitutes the enjoyment of fishes?' You knew that I knew it, and yet you put your question to me—well, I know it from our enjoying ourselves together over the River Hao."

from Chapter 18: "Perfect Enjoyment"

When Zhuangzi's wife died, Huizi went to condole with him, and, finding him squatted on the ground, drumming on the basin, and singing, said to him, "When a wife has lived with her husband, and brought up children, and then dies in her old age, not to wail for her is enough. When you go on to drum on this basin and sing, is it not an excessive and strange demonstration?" Zhuangzi replied, "It is not so. When she first died, was it possible for me to be singular and not affected by the event? But I reflected on the commencement of her being. She had not yet been born to life; not only had she no life, but she had no bodily form; not only had she no bodily form, but she had no breath. During the intermingling of the waste and dark chaos, there ensued a change, and there was breath; another change, and there was the bodily form; another change, and there came birth and life. There is now a change again, and she is dead. The relation between these things is like the procession of the four seasons from spring to autumn, from winter to summer. There now she lies with her face up, sleeping in the Great Chamber; and if I were to fall sobbing and going on to wall for her, I should think that I did not understand what was appointed for all. I therefore restrained myself!"

Selections from *The Daodejing of Laozi*. Edited and translated by Philip J. Ivanhoe, 159–60, 163–64, 167–68, 176–77, 181, 183–84, 196, 198–200. Indianapolis, IN: Hackett, 2002.

James Legge, trans., *The Texts of Taoism*, Sacred Books of the East, vols. 39–40. Oxford: Clarendon Press, 1891, 1:194–97; 247–50; 390–92; 2:4–5 [with spelling and other slight modifications by the present editor].

POST-READING PARS

1. Try to explain the idea of wu-wei (non-action) in your own words.
2. Can you give examples of the benefits and the drawbacks of thinking in the duality of labeling actions as good and bad?

Inquiry Corner

Content Question(s):	**Critical Question(s):**
Identify some blatant contradictions in the *Daodejing*. Is there any way to reconcile them? How does Zhuangzi's understanding of dreaming shape his views about life in general?	What common assumptions do Laozi and Zhuangzi attempt to subvert? Explain how Zhuangzi's rejection of a narrow human perspective might affect human values. What is the role of knowledge in Daoist thought? How do you know when you have it?
Comparative Question(s):	**Connection Question(s):**
How are Laozi's warnings about desire similar to or different from those of the Buddha? What about the concept of "waking up" in Zhuangzi and the Buddha? Besides the Dao, what other concepts or phenomena might be beyond words?	Can you think of examples when actions lead to the opposite outcome of what was intended? How might the idea of progress be undermined by teachings about contentment and detachment? Is that a good or a bad thing?

from *Han Feizi* and *Qin Law*

SNAPSHOT BOX

LANGUAGE: Classical Chinese

DATE: 3rd century BCE

LOCATION: China

GENRE: Philosophical Discourse (Han Feizi) and Legal Code (Qin Law)

TAGS: Authority and Leadership; Law and Punishment; Philosophy

Introduction

At times of public unrest and chaos, what seems most needed to re-establish harmony? In Chinese history Han Feizi (c. 280–233 BCE) and Qin Law articulate one particularly harsh approach known as Legalism among many offering a response to this question during a turbulent period. The late Zhou dynasty in China, comprising the Spring and Autumn period (722–481 BCE) and the Warring States period (403–221 BCE), was a time of social chaos, when multiple feudal states violently competed for power and domination. During that turbulent era, a number of political theorists traveled from state to state offering to advise anxious rulers. Confucius (551–479 BCE) was one of the earliest of these thinkers, followed by Mozi (c. 480–390 BCE), who taught that universal love or "impartial caring" was the key to social harmony, and Daoists such as Laozi and Zhuangzi (both in the fourth century BCE). Eventually there were also Cosmologists, Logicians, Militarists, Agriculturalists, and many others, in a cultural flowering that came to be known as the "Hundred Schools of Thought." The end came when the state of Qin, adopting Legalist techniques to control the assumed prevalence of universally bad behavior of humans, conquered all its rivals and unified China under the First Emperor in 221 BCE.

The Legalists regarded both Confucians and Daoists as hopelessly idealistic. They argued that rulers cannot truly motivate their people with vague concepts of mo-

Timeline

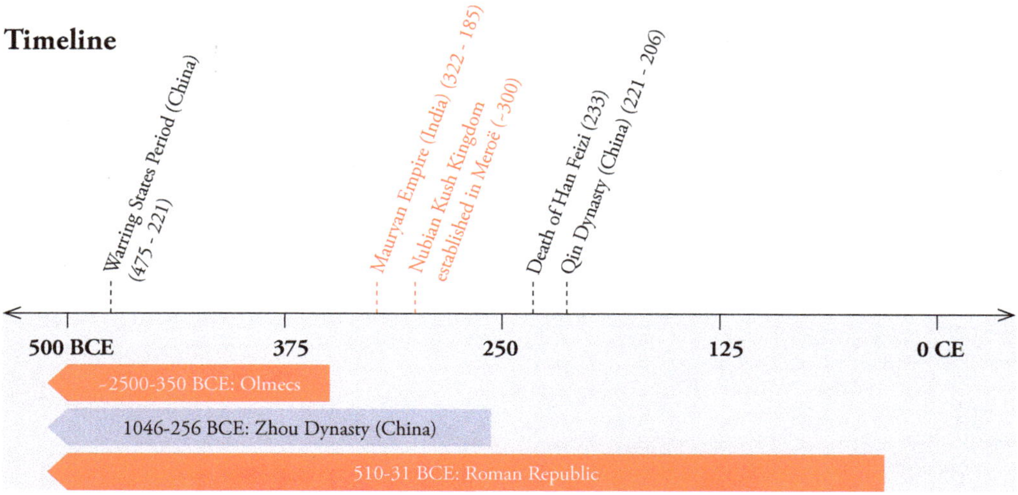

rality or visions of a simpler world; the real motivators will always be punishments and rewards. Legalist scholars would approach a worried ruler and rather than saying "think of the state as a family and set a good example" (as did Confucians) or "relax and don't worry so much" (the Daoist approach), they would suggest that if they were allowed to set up the legal code, the ruler could enjoy himself while the country pretty much ran on its own. Laws, they argued, should be objective or quantifiable, widely publicized, and strict, although a portion of the actual law code that was discovered in 1975 in a tomb sealed in 217 BCE reveals a surprisingly sophisticated view of the law, with gradations and categories, as you will read in the excerpt on penal servitude. In addition, the laws should be applied impartially and impersonally. If a ruler wanted his people to fight hard in battle, he should offer a reward—say, a piece of gold for each enemy head the soldier brought in. It might be a gruesome method of accounting, but it had the advantage of being clear-cut and easily administered. And family background was irrelevant; whether someone's father was a general or a peasant, four heads were worth four pieces of gold. On the other hand, running away in battle was punishable by death. Later Chinese assumed that the laws of the Qin dynasty must have been harsh and unfair, with the death penalty meted out for most infractions.

What ends should laws serve? Legalists are often regarded as the villains of Chinese philosophy because they taught techniques of government that relied on raw power and came with no moral justifications. By applying rewards and punishments they could make people do whatever the ruler wanted—good or bad—and most rulers were interested in success in war. Legalists therefore increased the power of the state, and they disdained history and philosophy as a waste of time, though that did not prevent Han Feizi, one of the most famous of Legalist philosophers, from appealing to historical precedent to argue that rulers need not appeal to historical precedent. Because Han was a stutterer, he had to rely on carefully crafted essays to communicate his ideas. He argued that rulers need to be wary of delegating power to their ministers, and he directly criticized the ideas of his Confucian, Mohist, and Daoist competitors. Han eventually was invited to advise the king of Qin, but the prime minister there, one of his former schoolmates, became jealous and slandered him, which led to his arrest and execution.

Although the king later regretted his decision, he nevertheless adopted the sort of harsh realistic approach to social order that Han Feizi had advocated. In fact, had Han lived another dozen years, he would have seen the king go on to become the First Emperor of China. The dynasty he founded came to be known as the Qin dynasty. Within the law code, there were four grades of penal servitude in Qin China (from least to most severe): debt worker, convict servant, convict worker, and convict laborer. In the last category, men could either be "intact" or "mutilated" (by tattooing or losing one or both feet). Male convict laborers usually worked on government construction projects such as building roads, defensive walls, or canals. Female convicts were assigned to other tasks such as sifting or pounding grain.

The Qin dynasty only lasted fifteen years before it was overthrown by popular rebellions. Arguably, the Qin regime was too harsh and tried to change too much, too fast. Consequently, Legalism might seem a failure, but the combination of Legalist administrative practices and Confucian moral principles provided the political foundation for Imperial China from the succeeding Han dynasty until the twentieth century.

Grant Hardy
Department of History

PRE-READING PARS

1. What are two main reasons governments use laws?
2. How important are punishments and rewards in your life? What alternative sorts of motivations might there be?

From Han Feizi and Qin Law

from Han Feizi

from Chapter 7: "The Two Handles"

The way an enlightened ruler controls his ministers is through the use of two handles, and nothing more.[235] These two handles are punishment and favor. What is meant by punishment and favor? To kill or execute—this is what is meant by "punishment." To venerate or reward—this is what is meant by "favor." Those who serve as ministers are fearful of execution and penalties and regard being venerated or rewarded as something beneficial. So if the ruler of men personally exercises his power to punish and grant favors, then the assembled ministers will all fear his might and turn to the benefits he offers them.

With the corrupt ministers of the age, however, this is not the case. When they hate someone, they are able to obtain the power to punish from their ruler and accuse him, and when they love someone, they are able to obtain the power to grant favors from their ruler and reward him. Now if the ruler of men does not make it so that the might and benefits that derive from rewards and penalties come only from him, and instead listens to his ministers when carrying out rewards and penalties, then the people of the state will all fear their ministers while dismissing their ruler, and turn to their ministers while departing from their ruler. This is the misfortune that comes when the ruler of men loses the power to punish and grant favors. The reason why the tiger can subdue the dog is because he has claws and fangs. But if the tiger loses his claws and fangs and allows the dog to use them, then the tiger will instead be subdued by the dog. A ruler of men is someone who uses punishments and favor to control his ministers. Now if the ruler of men loses his power to punish and grant favors and allows his ministers to use them, then the ruler will instead be controlled by his ministers.

235. The imagery here is of a two-handled plow.

from Chapter 49: "The Five Vermin"[236]

Among the people of Song[237] there was a farmer who had a stump in the middle of his field. One day, a rabbit running across the field crashed into the stump, broke its neck, and died. Seeing this, the man put aside his plow and took up watch next to the stump, hoping that he would get another rabbit in the same way. But of course he could not get another rabbit like this, and he soon became the laughing-stock of the entire state of Song. Now if one wants to use the government of the former kings to bring order to the people of the current age, this is all just so much stump-watching.

* * * * *

The past and the present have different customs; the new and the old require different preparations. If one wants to use a lax and lenient government to bring order to the people of a tense age, this is like trying to drive a spirited horse without reins or a whip. This is the kind of calamity that comes from not understanding.

Now the Confucians and Mohists all claim that the former kings loved everyone in the whole world equally, and looked upon the people like parents look upon their own children. How do they show that this was the case? They say, "When the Minister of Crime was carrying out a punishment, the ruler would not hold any musical entertainment. When he heard report of a death sentence, the ruler would always shed tears." This is how they praise the former kings. But if one holds that when ruler and subject are like father and son there will always be order, this implies that there is never any disorder between fathers and sons. In the nature and disposition of human beings nothing is more primary than the love of parents for their children. All children are loved by their parents, and yet children are not always well behaved. Even if one loves a child deeply, how does that prevent the child from being unruly? Now the love of the former kings of the people was not greater than the love of parents for their children, so if children are not always well behaved even when they are loved, how could the people have been made well-ordered simply by loving them?

Furthermore, when punishments are carried out according to the law and the ruler sheds tears because of it, this is in order to demonstrate the ruler's benevolence,[238] and not for the sake of creating order. To shed tears and not want to punish is benevolence, but to not allow offenses not to be punished is the law. The former kings allowed their laws to prevail and did not listen to their tears, so clearly benevolence cannot be relied on to produce order.

People naturally submit to the power of position, but few are able to yield to righteousness. Confucius was a great sage of the world. He travelled throughout the land

236. The title refers to five categories of people that Han Feizi considered politically dangerous or socially useless: classical scholars (i.e., Confucians), wandering debaters, private swordsmen, draft dodgers, and merchants. He recommended getting rid of all of them (though he himself, of course, was a wandering debater).

237. One of the feudal states.

238. Benevolence (*ren*) was a key Confucian virtue.

within the four seas refining people's conduct and elucidating the Way.[239] Everyone in the land within the four seas was pleased by his benevolence and praised him for his righteousness, but those who followed him number only seventy men. It seems those who value benevolence are rare while those with the ability to be righteous are difficult to find. Thus, even with the vastness of the whole world, there were only seventy men who followed Kongzi,[240] and only one man who was truly benevolent and righteous.[241]

Duke Ai of Lu was an inferior ruler, but when he faced south and became ruler of the state, none of the people within the borders of Lu dared to not be his subjects. People naturally submit to the power of position, and using the power of position it is truly easy to make people submit. Thus, Kongzi served as Duke Ai's subject despite his moral superiority, and Duke Ai acted as Kongzi's ruler despite his inferiority as a ruler. Kongzi did not yield to the Duke's righteousness, he submitted to the power of the duke's superior position. Thus, if Duke Ai had depended on his righteousness, Kongzi would not have submitted to him, but by taking advantage of the power of his position, he was able to make Kongzi his subject.

These days when scholars counsel the rulers of men, they do not tell them to take advantage of the invincible power of their position as rulers. Instead, they tell them that by striving to practice benevolence and righteousness they can become kings. This is to demand that the rulers of men must be equal to Kongzi and to regard the ordinary people of the world as if they were all comparable to his disciples. This is a scheme that is bound to fail.

Now suppose there is some no-good child. His parents scold him, but he will not reform his behavior because of their anger; his fellow villagers reprimand him, but he is not moved by what they say; his teachers and elders try to educate him, but he does not change his ways despite their instruction. So even with love of his parents, the actions of his fellow villagers, and the wisdom of his teachers and elders—these three "beautiful things"—acting on him, in the end he remains unmoved and will not change so much as a hair on his neck. But when the civil officers of the local magistrate take up the weapons of their office, enforce the public law, and go out looking for evil-doers, he then becomes fearful, changing his demeanor and altering his conduct. Thus, the love of parents is not enough to teach a child to be good. It must be backed up by the harsh punishments of the local magistrate. People naturally grow proud when loved, and become obedient only through coercion.

Even the agile Lou Ji could not climb over a wall ten spans in height because the face is too steep, but a lame sheep can easily graze on a thousand-span mountain if the slope is gradual. Therefore, an enlightened ruler makes sure that his laws are steep

239. Confucians, like Daoists, talked about "the Way (*dao*)," but in their case it was "the Way of the Former Kings."

240. Confucius

241. That is, Confucius himself.

and his punishments are severe. Any ordinary person will not throw away so much as a yard or two of silk cloth, but even the notorious Robber Zhi would not take a hundred taels[242] of molten bronze.[243] Where there is no certainty of harm, even a few yards of cloth will not be thrown away, but when one is sure to injure one's hand, even a hundred taels of bronze will not be taken. Thus, an enlightened ruler makes sure that his punishments are always carried out.

For this reason, when handing out rewards, it is best to make them substantial and dependable, so that the people will prize them; when assigning penalties, it is best to make them heavy and inescapable, so that the people will fear them; when framing laws, it is best to make them unequivocal and fixed, so that the people will understand them. Thus, if a ruler dispenses rewards and does not revoke them, carries out punishments and does not pardon them, supports his rewards with praise, and accompanies his penalties with condemnation, then both the worthy and the unworthy will do their utmost to serve him.

The Laws of Qin [Excerpts]

If they hide healthy youths[244] or are negligent about declaring the disabled, the [village] chieftain and elders pay [the punishment] of having their beards shaved off.[245] For those who dare to deceive or defraud [the state] by [declaring themselves] old when it is not warranted, or, upon reaching old age [by removing themselves from the tax rolls], without bothering to request [a release], the fine is two suits of armor. If the chieftain and elders do not indict them, they are each fined one suit; the members of their "group of five" are to be fined one shield per household; and all are to be exiled. Enrollment Statute.[246]

A husband steals 1,000 [units of] cash and hides 300 in his wife's quarters. How is the wife to be sentenced? If the wife hid [the booty] knowing that the husband had stolen it, the warranted [punishment] is for having stolen 300 [cash]. If she did not know, she [is sentenced] for receiving [stolen goods].[247]

[Someone] accuses another of stealing 110 [units of cash]. The inquiry [reveals] that he stole 100 [cash]; how is the accuser to be sentenced? [The error] warrants a fine of two suits of armor. Suppose the [the criminal] stole 100 [cash] and [the ac-

242. A unit of weight.

243. Or gold.

244. Such as would be eligible for military service. [All notes are from the translator.]

245. As opposed to having their entire heads shaved, which would have been considered a more severe humiliation.

246. The so-called group of five, which reappears below, was an institution of collective responsibility: if one member of the group committed a crime, the other members might all be subject to reprisals. "Enrollment" refers to registration on the tax rolls.

247. The punishment for stealing was significantly more severe than that for receiving stolen goods.

cuser] intentionally added 10 cash to the stolen amount, then the question is: How is the accuser to be sentenced? [This crime] warrants a fine of one shield; the fine of one shield satisfies the statute. However, the practice of the court is to sentence those who bring false charges; the fine is two suits of armor.[248]

"For killing a child on one's own authority,[249] [the punishment] is to be tattooed and made a penal laborer or grain-pounder.[250] If the child is newborn and has strange marks on its body or is deformed, it is not a crime to kill it." Suppose someone gives birth to a child, and the child's body is not deformed and does not have strange marks, but [the family] does not want the child merely because it has many children. They do not raise it, but kill it—what is the sentence? It is for killing a child.

Commoner A was in a fight. Drawing his sword, he hacked and lopped off another's hair-knot.[251] What is the sentence? [The crime] warrants penal labor, but he is left intact.

If one draws a sheathed lance, halberd, or spear in a fight, but without causing injury, the sentence is as though [the weapon] were a sword.

If [someone] uses a poker, a *shu*-poker, or an awl in a fight, and injures another with that poker, *shu*-poker, or awl, how is he to be sentenced in each case?[252] If [the crime] is [the consequence] of a fight, it warrants a fine of two suits of armor; if it is premeditated, it warrants tattooing and penal labor.

"If members of a 'group of five' indict each other to avoid guilt by bringing a false charge, they are to be found guilty of the crime which they were [trying to] avoid." [The statutes] also say, "If one cannot determine the guilty party, and indicts someone else, this is bringing a false charge." Suppose A says that B, a member of his "group of five," has committed premeditated murder.

248. The principle of this item is clear: a defendant may not be charged for a crime greater than what he or she committed, and an accuser or prosecutor who exaggerates the severity of a crime is liable to be punished. The details, however, are confusing. On the one hand, the text seems to draw a distinction between cases in which the accuser overestimates the value of the stolen goods through sheer carelessness and those in which the accuser does so deliberately. However, the statutory fine for negligence (two suits of armor) sounds far heavier than that for intentionally misrepresenting the magnitude of a crime (one shield), though one would naturally expect the latter error to be considered more serious. Finally, the text asserts here, exceptionally, that the court may enforce a fine different from that mandated by the statutes; perhaps it was recognized that a penalty of one shield was too lenient in this case.

249. As we shall see, an irate father could petition the court for authority to slay his unfilial son, but this right had to be granted beforehand, or else the father would be convicted "for killing a child on his own authority."

250. Women were sentenced to be convict "grain-pounders" whereas men were sent to penal labor camps.

251. In other words, without causing any serious wounds—in which case the criminal would be mutilated as well as sentenced to penal labor.

252. The sentence for using these kinds of weapons is lighter because they do not have a sheath. Removing a weapon from its sheath is understood as a sign of some degree of premeditation. (A *shu* is defined as "a long poker.")

After B has been arrested, [it is determined] as a result of questioning that he did not commit the murder. A brought a false charge—is the warranted sentence that for bringing a false charge, or that for [the crime] which he [was trying to] avoid?[253] The warranted sentence is for what he [was trying to] avoid.

Bandits entered A's house and wounded him. A cried "Burglars!" but his four neighbors, [village] chieftain, and elders had all gone out and were not present, so they did not hear him cry "Burglars!" Question: Does this warrant sentencing or not? If the investigation [shows that his four neighbors] were not present, a sentence is not warranted; but for the chieftain and elders, even though they were not present, a sentence is warranted. What is meant by "four neighbors"? The "four neighbors" are the other members of his "group of five."

When one appeals for an inquest,[254] either for oneself or for another person, is the [appeal] heard after the case has been adjudicated, or is it heard even before the case has been adjudicated? It is heard after the case has been adjudicated.

How many rat burrows in a granary warrant a sentence or reprimand?[255] The practice of the court is to fine one shield for three or more rat burrows and to reprimand for two or fewer. Three mouse burrows count as one rat burrow.

Trying cases. In trying cases, if it is possible to track down the words [of a witness] by means of documents, it is better to obtain facts from a person without flogging him. Flogging is inferior because where there is fear, [the case] fails.

Interrogating in a case. While interrogating in a case, one must always first hear [witnesses'] words completely and write them down as each one lays out his statement. Even when you know that [a witness] is lying, there is no need to cross-examine hastily. If he cannot explain himself once his statement has been written down completely, cross-examine those points that are [vulnerable to] cross-examination. In cross-examination, once again, listen to his explanatory statements and have them written down. Again review the unexplained points and perform another cross-examination. If the cross-examination comes to an end and [the witness] has repeatedly lied or changed his words without acknowledging [the inconsistencies], then, in cases where the statutes warrant flogging,[256] flog him. The flogging must be recorded as follows: "Deposition: Since So-and-so repeatedly changed his words without an explanatory statement, he has been interrogated with the bastinado."

Accusing a son. Deposition: Commoner A of such-and-such a village indicted [his son], saying, "My natural son (Commoner C of the same village) is unfilial. Call-

253. In other words, assuming that there was a murder and that A shared some blame in the affair, should he be tried for bringing false charges against B or for having committed premeditated murder himself?

254. The accused or a relative of the accused was regularly allowed to demand a second inquest into the case if there was reason to doubt the justice or fairness of the first.

255. I.e., of the functionaries in charge of the granary.

256. In other words, even a perjurer cannot be flogged except in accordance with the predetermined statutes.

ing on [the court] for his death, I dare to indict him." Prefectural Clerk E was ordered to go and arrest him. Prefectural Clerk E's deposition: "With Prison Bondservant So-and-so I arrested C, apprehending him in the house of So-and-so." When Deputy So-and-so interrogated C, his statement was, "I am A's natural son. I have truly been unfilial to A. I have not been convicted of any other crime."[257]

Ivanhoe, Philip J., and Bryan W. Van Norden, eds. *Readings in Classical Chinese Philosophy*, 2nd ed., 323, 340–43. Indianapolis, IN: Hackett, 2001.

"The Laws of Qin before the Empire." In *Hawaii Reader in Traditional Chinese Culture*, edited by Victor H. Mair, Nancy S. Steinhardt, and Paul R. Goldin, 148–50. Honolulu: University of Hawai'i Press, 2005.

POST-READING PARS

1. Give two examples of internal and/or external motivations that cause good behavior.
2. What areas of social life do you think require laws?

Inquiry Corner

Content Question(s):	**Critical Question(s):**
How does Han Feizi use analogies to make his points? Which analogies do you think are the most effective? List the various types of punishments mentioned in the Qin Law excerpt.	What allowances are made in Qin law for family relations or slavery? What do those accommodations tell us about social values of the time? Are the legal principles taken into account in the Qin law effective in judging crimes?
Comparative Question(s):	**Connection Question(s):**
How do the Qin laws compare with the laws of Hammurabi?	How was the life of convict laborers in Qin China different from prisoners in our current justice system?

257. The text does not relate the resolution of this conflict. The "Prison Bondservant" was apparently required to assist the Prefectural Clerk as part of his sentence.

Lessons for Women by Ban Zhao

SNAPSHOT BOX

LANGUAGE: Classical Chinese

DATE: c. 100 CE

LOCATION: China

GENRE: Wisdom literature

CONTEXTUAL INFORMATION: Parental advice

TAGS: Confucianism; Ethics and Morality; Family; Women and Gender

Introduction

We can ask of any text if it affirms the dominant values of the society in which it is embedded, or if it questions and challenges those values. For many texts, the answer is clear. For others, it is difficult to tell, and *Lessons for Women* falls into this category. Its author, Ban Zhao (c. 45–120 CE), whose name is spelled *Pan Chao* in the reading, had a life that was both traditional and exceptional for her time. She was married to Cao Shishu at the age of fourteen. After she had given birth to several children, her husband died young and she never remarried. But she was born into a well-connected scholarly family. She received an education at home, with instruction in history, literature, geography, astronomy, and mathematics. Her father and her oldest brother were noted historians. Her second oldest brother was a famous general. Unusually, after she became a widow she did not stay with her husband's family but was invited to come to the royal palace to work in the imperial library. When her oldest brother died in prison, where he had been held on politically motivated charges, she completed his groundbreaking *History of the Han Dynasty*. She later became an adviser to the empress and royal consorts.

Sometime around 100 CE, she wrote *Lessons for Women*, a book of advice for the young women in her family concerning their domestic duties. It is the earliest surviving text written by a Chinese woman and was influential in China, Japan, and Korea for nearly two thousand years. The book is short, with seven brief chapters, included in its entirety here. Ban Zhao takes a mainly Confucian point of view, with an emphasis on hierarchy and harmony, though she draws upon Daoist yin-yang

Timeline

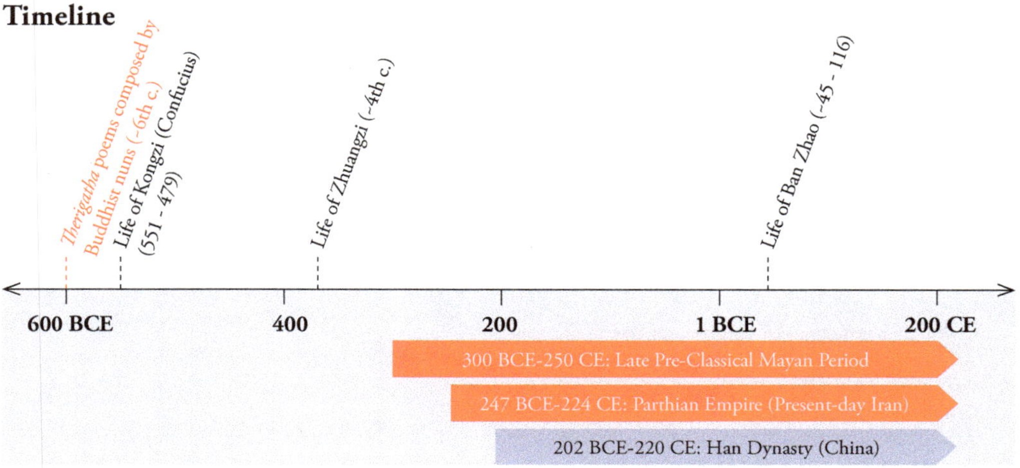

ideas as well as quotations from the Five Confucian Classics, including the *Book of Songs*, the *Record of Rites*, and the *Classic of Changes*.

Female humility, deference, and obedience were central to the ancient Chinese family life that Ban Zhao was navigating. Marriages were arranged by parents as a way to unify two families and took place when the bride and groom were teenagers. Marriages were also **patrilocal**, meaning that the wife moved into her young husband's home, where he lived with his parents, his brothers and their wives, and any unmarried sisters. What strategies might women engage to negotiate successfully with this type of complex family living situation?

The fundamental religion of ancient China was ancestor worship, and the various rites had to be performed by married couples, which meant that a woman worshipped her husband's ancestors rather than her own parents and grandparents. Widows were discouraged from remarrying because that would have sent them into another family line and disrupted that generational chain necessary for worshipping the ancestors of their first husbands. In addition, baby boys were more valued than girls because daughters would eventually make offerings to other people's ancestors, leaving parents who only had daughters to the tragic fate of becoming "hungry ghosts."

The ancient Chinese conception of family life centered on wives successfully enacting their responsibilities. Divorce was considered more disruptive to ancestor worship than death and was strongly stigmatized and restricted, at least theoretically. In the Han dynasty, the responsibilities of a wife were outlined in the seven possible grounds to divorce one's wife (while men could divorce their wives, women could not divorce their husbands). Prominent among the seven possible grounds is disobedience to in-laws since they could force their son to divorce even if he himself wanted to stay married. The other possible justifications included infertility, adultery, jealousy (men were allowed multiple wives), disease, talking too much, and theft. However, a wife could not be divorced if she met any one of three conditions: her parents had died and she had no home to return to, she had observed the three-year mourning period for her deceased in-laws, or her husband was poor when they married and was now rich. In her *Lessons for Women*, Ban Zhao focuses on the responsibilities of women as wives, daughters-in-law, and mothers. How might Ban Zhao's advice for wives include indirect guidance for other family members?

Ban Zhao's views on proper roles for women appear conservative and traditional, yet at the same time she advocates for female education, she denounces domestic violence, and she argues that women should be judged by their actions rather than their sexual attractiveness. Most important, she treats women as moral agents, fully capable of choosing right or wrong. Confucius, by contrast, hardly mentions women in the *Analects*. As you read, where do you see her accept the status quo or creatively assert independent thinking?

Grant Hardy
Department of History

PRE-READING PARS

1. Identify two or three ways that gender is shaped by culture.
2. In your family, are there gender-specific family responsibilities?

Lessons for Women: Instructions in Seven Chapters for a Woman's Ordinary Way of Life in the First Century C.E.

Introduction

I, the unworthy writer, am unsophisticated, unenlightened, and by nature unintelligent, but I am fortunate both to have received not a little favor from my scholarly father, and to have had a cultured mother and instructresses upon whom to rely for a literary education as well as for training in good manners. More than forty years have passed since at the age of fourteen I took up the dustpan and the broom[258] in the Ts'ao family. During this time with trembling heart I feared constantly that I might disgrace my parents, and that I might multiply difficulties for both the women and the men of my husband's family. Day and night I was distressed in heart, but I labored without confessing weariness. Now and hereafter, however, I know how to escape from such faults.

Being careless, and by nature stupid, I taught and trained my children without system. Consequently I fear that my son Ku may bring disgrace upon the Imperial Dynasty by whose Holy Grace he has unprecedentedly received the extraordinary privilege of wearing the Gold and the Purple,[259] a privilege for the attainment of which by my son, I a humble subject never even hoped. Nevertheless, now that he is a man and able to plan his own life, I need not again have concern for him. But I do grieve that you, my daughters,[260] just now at the age for marriage, have not at this time had gradual training and advice; that you still have not learned the proper customs for married women. I fear that by failure in good manners in other families you will humiliate both your ancestors and your clan. I am now seriously ill, life is uncertain. As I have thought of you all in so untrained a state, I have been uneasy many a time for you. At hours of leisure I have composed in seven chapters these instructions under the title *Lessons for Women*. In order that you may have something wherewith to benefit your persons, I wish every one of you, my daughters, each to write out a copy for yourself.

From this time on, every one of you strive to practice these lessons.

258. A conventional expression for the inferior position of the daughter-in-law in relation to her parents-in-law. [All notes are from the translator.]

259. Gold seal and purple robe (symbols of high nobility).

260. Not necessarily her own daughters only, but girls of her family as a whole.

Chapter 1: Humility

On the third day after the birth of a girl the ancients observed three customs: first to place the baby below[261] the bed; second to give her a potsherd with which to play;[262] and third to announce her birth to her ancestors by an offering. Now to lay the baby below the bed plainly indicated that she is lowly and weak, and should regard it as her primary duty to humble herself before others. To give her potsherds with which to play indubitably signified that she should practice labor and consider it her primary duty to be industrious. To announce her birth before her ancestors clearly meant that she ought to esteem as her primary duty the continuation of the observance of worship in the home.

These three ancient customs epitomize a woman's ordinary way of life and the teachings of the traditional ceremonial rites and regulations. Let a woman modestly yield to others; let her respect others; let her put others first, herself last. Should she do something good, let her not mention it; should she do something bad, let her not deny it. Let her bear disgrace; let her even endure[263] when others speak or do evil to her. Always let her seem to tremble and to fear. When a woman follows such maxims as these, then she may be said to humble herself before others.

Let a woman retire late to bed, but rise early to duties; let her not dread tasks by day or by night. Let her not refuse to perform domestic duties whether easy or difficult. That which must be done, let her finish completely, tidily, and systematically. When a woman follows such rules as these, then she may be said to be industrious.

Let a woman be correct in manner and upright in character in order to serve her husband. Let her live in purity and quietness of spirit, and attend to her own affairs. Let her love not gossip and silly laughter. Let her cleanse and purify and arrange in order the wine and the food for the offerings to the ancestors. When a woman observes such principles as these, then she may be said to continue ancestral worship.

No woman who observes these three fundamentals of life has ever had a bad reputation or has fallen into disgrace. If a woman fails to observe them, how can her name be honored; how can she but bring disgrace upon herself?

Chapter 2: Husband and Wife

The Way of husband and wife is intimately connected with yin and yang, and relates the individual to gods and ancestors. Truly it is the great principle of Heaven and Earth, and the great basis of human relationships. Therefore the *Rites* honor union of man and woman; and in the *Classic Book of Poetry*, the "First Ode" manifests the

261. On the floor or the ground.

262. In the *Classic of Odes*, it is written that "daughters . . . shall have tiles to play with." Since potsherds were used as spindle weights, they served both as toys for little girls and as an early introduction to domesticity.

263. Literally, "let her hold filth in her mouth," i.e., let her swallow insult.

principle of marriage. For these reasons the relationship cannot but be an important one.

If a husband be unworthy, then he possesses nothing by which to control his wife. If a wife be unworthy, then she possesses nothing with which to serve her husband. If a husband does not control his wife, then the rules of conduct manifesting his authority are abandoned and broken. If a wife does not serve her husband, then the proper relationship between men and women and the natural order of things are neglected and destroyed. As a matter of fact, the purpose of these two, the controlling of women by men and the serving of men by women, is the same.

Now examine the gentlemen of the present age. They only know that wives must be controlled and that the husband's rules of conduct manifesting his authority must be established. They therefore teach their boys to read books and study histories. But they do not in the least understand that husbands and masters must also be served, and that the proper relationship and the rites should be maintained. Yet only to teach men and not to teach women—is that not ignoring the essential relation between them? According to the *Rites*, it is the rule to begin to teach children to read at the age of eight years, and by the age of fifteen years they ought then to be ready for cultural training.[264] Only why should it not be that girls' education as well as boys' be according to this principle?

Chapter 3: Respect and Caution

As yin and yang are not of the same nature, so man and woman have different characteristics. The distinctive quality of the yang is rigidity; the function of the yin is yielding. Man is honored for strength; a woman is beautiful on account of her gentleness. Hence there arose the common saying: "A man though born like a wolf may, it is feared, become a weak monstrosity; a woman though born like a mouse may, it is feared, become a tiger."

Now for self-culture nothing equals respect for others. To counteract firmness nothing equals compliance. Consequently it can be said that the Way of respect and acquiescence is woman's most important principle of conduct. So respect may be defined as nothing other than holding on to that which is permanent; and acquiescence nothing other than being liberal and generous. Those who are steadfast in devotion know that they should stay in their proper places; those who are liberal and generous esteem others, and honor and serve them.

If husband and wife have the habit of staying together, never leaving one another, and following each other around within the limited space of their own rooms, then they will lust after and take liberties with one another. From such action improper language will arise between the two. This kind of discussion may lead to licentious-

264. Not merely literary studies, but all the accomplishments of a gentleman: ceremonies, music, archery, horsemanship, writing, and numbers.

ness. Out of licentiousness will be born a heart of disrespect to the husband. Such a result comes from not knowing that one should stay in one's proper place.

Furthermore, affairs may be either crooked or straight; words may be either right or wrong. Straightforwardness cannot but lead to quarreling; crookedness cannot but lead to accusation. If there are really accusations and quarrels, then undoubtedly there will be angry affairs. Such a result comes from not esteeming others, and not honoring and serving them.

If wives suppress not contempt for husbands, then it follows that such wives rebuke and scold their husbands. If husbands stop not short of anger, then they are certain to beat their wives. The correct relationship between husband and wife is based upon harmony and intimacy, and conjugal love is grounded in proper union. Should actual blows be dealt, how could matrimonial relationship be preserved? Should sharp words be spoken, how could conjugal love exist? If love and proper relationship both be destroyed, then husband and wife are divided.

Chapter 4: Womanly Qualifications

A woman ought to have four qualifications: 1. womanly virtue, 2. womanly words, 3. womanly bearing, and 4. womanly work. Now what is called womanly virtue need not be brilliant ability, exceptionally different from others. Womanly words need be neither clever in debate nor keen in conversation. Womanly appearance requires neither a pretty nor a perfect face and form. Womanly work need not be work done more skillfully than that of others.

To guard carefully her chastity, to control circumspectly her behavior, in every motion to exhibit modesty, and to model each act on the best usage—this is womanly virtue.

To choose her words with care, to avoid vulgar language, to speak at appropriate times, and not to weary others with much conversation may be called the characteristics of womanly words.

To wash and scrub filth away, to keep clothes and ornaments fresh and clean, to wash the head and bathe the body regularly, and to keep the person free from disgraceful filth may be called the characteristics of womanly bearing.

With wholehearted devotion to sew and to weave, to love not gossip and silly laughter, in cleanliness and order to prepare the wine and food for serving guests may be called the characteristics of womanly work. These four qualifications characterize the greatest virtue of a woman. No woman can afford to be without them. In fact they are very easy to possess if a woman only treasure them in her heart. The ancients had a saying: "Is Love far off? If I desire love, then love is at hand!"[265] So can it be said of these qualifications.

265. This is a direct quote from the *Analects* (7.29) of Confucius. The word translated here as "love" [*ren*] is usually rendered as "benevolence" but is more accurately represented by "humaneness."

Chapter 5: Wholehearted Devotion

Now in the *Rites* is written the principle that a husband may marry again, but there is no canon that authorizes a woman to be married the second time. Therefore it is said of husbands as of Heaven, that as certainly as people cannot run away from Heaven, so surely a wife cannot leave a husband's home.[266]

If people in action or character disobey the spirits of Heaven and of Earth, then Heaven punishes them. Likewise if a woman errs in the rites and in the proper mode of conduct, then her husband esteems her lightly. The ancient book, *A Pattern for Women*, says: "To obtain the love of one man is the crown of a woman's life; to lose the love of one man is to miss the aim in woman's life."[267] For these reasons a woman cannot but seek to win her husband's heart. Nevertheless, the beseeching wife need not use flattery, coaxing words, and cheap methods to gain intimacy.

Decidedly nothing is better to gain the heart of a husband than wholehearted devotion and correct manners. In accordance with the rites and the proper mode of conduct, let a woman live a pure life. Let her have ears that hear not licentiousness and eyes that see not depravity. When she goes outside her own home, let her not be conspicuous in dress and manners. When at home let her not neglect her dress. Women should not assemble in groups, not gather together, for gossip and silly laughter. They should not stand watching in the gateways. If a woman follows these rules, she may be said to have wholehearted devotion and correct manners.

If, in all her actions, she is frivolous, she sees and hears only that which pleases herself. At home her hair is disheveled and her dress is slovenly. Outside the home she emphasizes her femininity to attract attention; she says what ought not to be said; and she looks at what ought not to be seen: If a woman does such as these, she may be said to be without wholehearted devotion and correct manners.

Chapter 6: Implicit Obedience

Now "to win the love of one man is the crown of a woman's life; to lose the love of one man is her eternal disgrace." This saying advises a fixed will and a wholehearted devotion for a woman. Ought she then to lose the hearts of her father- and mother-in-law?

There are times when love may lead to differences of opinion between individuals; there are times when duty may lead to disagreement. Even should the husband say that he loves something, when the parents-in-law say "no," this is called a case of duty leading to disagreement. This being so, then what about the hearts of the parents-in-law? Nothing is better than an obedience that sacrifices personal opinion.

266. Even after the death of her husband, the worthy wife does not leave the home of his extended family.

267. More literally, this may be rendered as: "To become of like mind with one man may be said to be the final end; to fail to become of like mind with one man may be said to be the eternal end."

Whenever the mother-in-law says, "Do not do that," and if what she says is right, unquestionably the daughter-in-law obeys. Whenever the mother-in-law says, "Do that," even if what she says is wrong, still the daughter-in-law submits unfailingly to the command.

Let a woman not act contrary to the wishes and opinions of parents-in-law about right and wrong; let her not dispute with them what is straight and what is crooked. Such docility may be called obedience that sacrifices personal opinion. Therefore the ancient book, *A Pattern for Women*, says: "If a daughter-in-law who follows the wishes of her parents-in-law is like an echo and a shadow, how could she not be praised?"

Chapter 7: Harmony with Younger Brothers- and Sisters-in-Law

In order for a wife to gain the love of her husband, she must win for herself the love of her parents-in-law. To win for herself the love of her parents-in-law, she must secure for herself the good will of younger brothers- and sisters-in-law. For these reasons the right and the wrong, the praise and the blame of a woman alike depend upon younger brothers- and sisters-in-law. Consequently it will not do for a woman to lose their affection.

They are stupid both who know not that they must not lose the hearts of younger brothers- and sisters-in-law, and who cannot be in harmony with them in order to be intimate with them. Excepting only the Holy Men, few are able to be faultless. Now Yen Tzu's[268] greatest virtue was that he was able to reform. Confucius praised him for not committing a misdeed the second time. In comparison with him a woman is the more likely to make mistakes.

Although a woman possesses a worthy woman's qualifications and is wise and discerning by nature, is she able to be perfect? Yet if a woman lives in harmony with her immediate family, unfavorable criticism will be silenced within the home. But if a man and woman disagree, then this evil will be noised abroad. Such consequences are inevitable. The *Classic of Changes* says:

Should two hearts harmonize,
The united strength can cut gold.
Words from hearts which agree,
Give forth fragrance like the orchid.

This saying may be applied to harmony in the home.

Though a daughter-in-law and her younger sisters-in-law are equal in rank, nevertheless they should respect each other; though love between them may be sparse, their proper relationship should be intimate. Only the virtuous, the beautiful, the modest, and the respectful young women can accordingly rely upon the sense of duty to make their affection sincere, and magnify love to bind their relationships firmly.

268. Yen Hui, the favorite disciple of Confucius.

Then the excellence and the beauty of such a daughter-in-law becomes generally known. Moreover, any flaws and mistakes are hidden and unrevealed. Parents-in-law boast of her good deeds; her husband is satisfied with her. Praise of her radiates, making her illustrious in district and in neighborhood; and her brightness reaches to her own father and mother.

But a stupid and foolish person as an elder sister-in-law uses her rank[269] to exalt herself; as a younger sister-in-law, because of parents' favor, she becomes filled with arrogance. If arrogant, how can a woman live in harmony with others? If love and proper relationships be perverted, how can praise be secured? In such instances the wife's good is hidden and her faults are declared. The mother-in-law will be angry, and the husband will be indignant. Blame will reverberate and spread in and outside the home. Disgrace will gather upon the daughter-in-law's person, on the one hand to add humiliation to her own father and mother, and on the other to increase the difficulties of her husband.

Such then is the basis for both honor and disgrace, the foundation for reputation or for ill-repute. Can a woman be too cautious? Consequently, to seek the hearts of young brothers- and sisters-in-law decidedly nothing can be esteemed better than modesty and acquiescence.

Modesty is virtue's handle; acquiescence is the wife's most refined characteristic. All who possess these two have sufficiency for harmony with others. In the *Classic of Poetry* it is written that "Here is no evil; there is no dart." So it may be said of these two, modesty and acquiescence.

Pan Chao. "Lessons for Women." Translated by Nancy Lee Swann. In *The Columbia Anthology of Traditional Chinese Literature*, edited by Victor H. Mair, 534–41. New York: Columbia University Press, 1994.

POST-READING PARS

1. Identify two areas in which Han Chinese culture may be shaping gender expectations in Ban Zhao's *Lessons*.
2. List two or three ways that marriages could go wrong in *Lessons for Women*.
3. The extreme humility expressed in the first two paragraphs is striking; what difference would it make to know that Chinese men of the time period wrote in the same way?

269. In the *Record of Rites (Li chi)*, the power of control over the other sons' wives is accorded to the eldest daughter-in-law.

Inquiry Corner

Content Question(s):	Critical Question(s):
What were the primary responsibilities of women in Chinese families, according to Ban Zhao? Do any of these still apply in modern America?	When a young bride moved in with her husband's family, she was vulnerable to mistreatment, especially before she gave birth to a son herself. Could *Lessons for Women* be read as a survival manual?
Comparative Question(s):	**Connection Question(s):**
How does Ban Zhao's advice to her daughters compare with Amenemope's advice to his son?	Do Ban Zhao's justifications for education align with your own reasons for pursuing a college degree? What other reasons might you add?

BEYOND THE CLASSROOM

- What roles/jobs in work environments are often undervalued and who usually occupies those roles?
- Think of a time when you were expected to know something that you didn't know. How were you supposed to know it? Did you fail to learn or were you uninformed?
- How have you seen gender inequalities play out in the workplace?

from *The Achievements of the Divine Augustus* (*Res Gestae Divi Augusti*) by Augustus

SNAPSHOT BOX

LANGUAGE: Latin

DATE: Before 13 CE

LOCATION: Rome

GENRE: Funeral oration/eulogy

CONTEXTUAL INFORMATION: Inscription, public account of reign

TAGS: Authority and Leadership; Class and Wealth; Conflict and War; Empire and Colonialism; Hagiography; Monument and Artifact; Rhetoric and Propaganda

Introduction

What would you include if you wrote your own eulogy: your relationships, your character, your accomplishments? Of course, eulogies are usually composed by others, but the emperor Augustus (63 BCE–14 CE)—the first Roman emperor—left his own, and we know a little about the circumstances of its creation. In the last paragraph of his *Life of Augustus*, the Roman biographer Suetonius reports that when Augustus died, the priestesses of Vesta, goddess of Rome's hearth, produced four documents that Augustus had deposited with them. The documents included his will and three other scrolls. All were unsealed and read in the Roman Senate. Suetonius says that one scroll contained "an account of the things achieved by him," which he wanted carved into bronze tablets and placed before his tomb in Rome. From this source and the opening line we assign the title *Res Gestae Divi Augusti*, "The Achievements of the Divine Augustus," to this work.

This text did not survive in a manuscript, and the original bronze tablets are long gone. In 1555, a Dutch scholar saw the ruins of a temple dedicated to Rome and Augustus in Ankara, Turkey. The walls of the temple were covered with a bilingual inscription in Latin and Greek, and he recognized it as a copy of the lost *Res Gestae*. Because of the ruined state of the temple walls, some gaps in the text remain; but since then other copies of the inscription, in Latin and a Greek paraphrase, have been found in other cities in the province

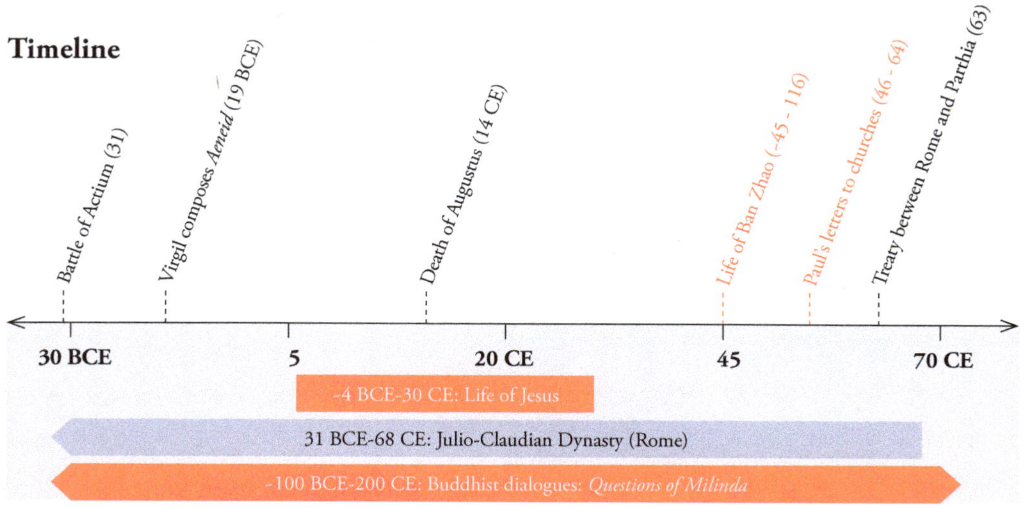

of Galatia, which is located in what is now north central Turkey, and they allow a fairly complete restoration. Augustus's accomplishments may have been published all over the Roman Empire at his death; but the worship of "Rome and Augustus" was limited to the Roman East, so our inscribed sources come from there.

Augustus wrote this in Latin for a Roman audience. It was translated into multiple languages based on the location of its inscription in order to communicate to the many different populations throughout the Roman Empire. For example, Augustus claims at the beginning that he "subjected the world to Roman rule," and that included the lands where this inscription appeared. What might the Galatians, part of the Roman Empire but not Roman themselves, have thought about having such a temple and such an inscription? What does this suggest about the political and social culture of the cities where the inscription was found?

Augustus writes with no particular chronological structure: he is largely cataloging his achievements. The question is whether he is doing so for documentation or persuasion. Is he simply giving a public rendering of the final "balance sheet" of his long reign? Is he making a bid for the deification that he later received? His intentions do emerge here and there; for example, he speaks of reviving "many exemplary practices of our ancestors that were disappearing in our time" and of handing down "exemplary practices to posterity for their imitation" (*RG* 8.5). What forms of "revival" do you find in the text? And more important, what does it mean for a participant in civil wars to declare that he has restored a country to its former glory?

Notice that Augustus is cautious when mentioning Rome's civil wars. He fought in them (*RG* 3.1) and ended them (*RG* 34.1). He was "avenging the crime" of the murder of Julius Caesar, his adoptive father (*RG* 2), for example, not fighting against the Republican armies of Brutus and Cassius. He mentions the Battle of Actium, in which he defeated Mark Antony and Cleopatra, without naming them (*RG* 25.2); Egypt's conquest lacks mention of Cleopatra (*RG* 27.1); he alludes to Mark Antony only once as "the man against whom I had waged war" (*RG* 24.1). When reading the text, where is Augustus making the boldest statements about his own actions and where is he silent about them? Given its focus on Augustus himself and his silence about certain details, should we consider this work a historical account? There are many texts and material objects that illuminate the Augustan period, including architecture, sculpture, and coins, along with the works of Vergil, Horace, and others, but little historical writing survives from those years. If we consider this as a historical account, what kinds of cautions are necessary? Should we regard it as political propaganda? Even if we question some of the events and the way they are presented in the *Res Gestae*, can you detect particular themes that Augustus chose to emphasize about war and peace, tradition, power, religion, empire? Do you see any similarities with the Behistûn inscription of Darius, which is also a kind of "self-eulogy"?

Brian S. Hook and Lora Holland Goldthwaite
Department of Classics

from *The Achievements of the Divine Augustus* (*Res Gestae Divi Augusti*)

A copy below of the deeds of the divine Augustus, by which he subjected the whole wide earth to the rule of the Roman people, and of the money which he spent for the state and Roman people, inscribed on two bronze pillars, which are set up in Rome.

1. In my nineteenth year, on my own initiative and at my own expense, I raised an army with which I set free the state, which was oppressed by the domination of a faction. For that reason, the senate enrolled me in its order by laudatory resolutions, when Gaius Pansa and Aulus Hirtius were consuls[270] (43 B.C.E.), assigning me the place of a consul in the giving of opinions, and gave me the *imperium*. With me as propraetor, it ordered me, together with the consuls, to take care lest any detriment befall the state. But the people made me consul in the same year, when the consuls each perished in battle, and they made me a triumvir for the settling of the state.

2. I drove the men who slaughtered my father [Julius Caesar] into exile with a legal order, punishing their crime, and afterwards, when they waged war on the state, I conquered them in two battles.

3. I often waged war, civil and foreign, on the earth and sea, in the whole wide world, and as victor I spared all the citizens who sought pardon. As for foreign nations, those which I was able to safely forgive, I preferred to preserve than to destroy. About five hundred thousand Roman citizens swore an oath of allegiance to me. I led more than three hundred thousand of them into colonies and I returned them to their cities, after their stipend had been earned, and I assigned all of them fields or gave them money for their military service. I captured six hundred ships in addition to those smaller than triremes.

4. Twice I triumphed with an ovation, and three times I enjoyed a full triumph, and twenty one times I was named "Victorious General." When the senate decreed more triumphs for me, I abstained from all of them. I placed the laurel from the fasces[271] in the Capitol, when the vows which I pronounced in each war had been fulfilled. On account of the things successfully done by me and through my officers, under my auspices, on earth and sea, the senate decreed fifty-five times that there be sacrifices to the immortal gods. Moreover there were 890 days on which the senate decreed there would be sacrifices. In my triumphs kings and nine children of kings were led before my chariot. I had been consul thirteen times, when I wrote this, and I was in the thirty-seventh year of tribunician power[272] (14 C.E.).

5. When the dictatorship was offered to me, both in my presence and my absence,

270. The consuls were the highest officers in Rome's "ladder" of annual magistrates. There were two elected each year, and years are designated by the consuls who served during them.

271. A bundle of sticks with an axe that was carried in front of Roman magistrates to symbolize their authority to punish and execute. This symbol was appropriated in Italy by Mussolini's authoritarian party in the 1920s and from that source gives us the term "fascism."

272. Augustus was granted the power of the office of a tribune of the people without holding the office, and without having it renewed annually. This allowed him to summon the senate or people, submit motions, propose or veto legislation or the actions of magistrates, etc. This tribuni-

by the people and senate, when Marcus Marcellus and Lucius Arruntius were consuls (22 B.C.E.), I did not accept it. I did not evade the curatorship of grain in the height of the food shortage, which I so arranged that within a few days I freed the entire city from the present fear and danger by my own expense and administration. When the annual and perpetual consulship was then again offered to me, I did not accept it.

6. When Marcus Vinicius and Quintus Lucretius were consuls (19 B.C.E.), then again when Publius Lentulus and Gnaeus Lentulus were (18 B.C.E.), and third when Paullus Fabius Maximus and Quintus Tubero were (11 B.C.E.), although the senate and Roman people consented that I alone be made curator of the laws and customs with the highest power, I accepted no magistracy offered that was contrary to the customs of the ancestors. What the senate then wanted to accomplish through me, I did through tribunician power, and five times on my own accord I both requested and received from the senate a colleague in such power.

7. I was triumvir for the settling of the state for ten continuous years. I was first of the senate up to that day on which I wrote this, for forty years. I was high priest, augur, one of the Fifteen for the performance of rites, one of the Seven of the sacred feasts, brother of Arvis, fellow of Titus, and Fetial.

8. When I was consul the fifth time (29 B.C.E.), I increased the number of patricians by order of the people and senate. I revised the roll of the senate three times, and in my sixth consulate (28 B.C.E.) I made a census of the people with Marcus Agrippa as my colleague.[273] I conducted a *lustrum*,[274] after a forty-one year gap, in which were counted 4,063,000 Roman citizens. Then again, with consular imperium I conducted a *lustrum* alone when Gaius Censorinus and Gaius Asinius were consuls (8 B.C.E.), in which were counted 4,233,000 Roman citizens. And the third time, with consular *imperium*,[275] I conducted a lustrum with my son Tiberius Caesar as colleague, when Sextus Pompeius and Sextus Appuleius were consuls (14 A.C.E.), in which were counted 4,937,000 Roman citizens. By new laws passed with my sponsorship, I revived many traditions of the ancestors, which were falling into disuse in our age, and myself I handed on precedents of many things to be imitated in later generations.

9. The senate decreed that vows be undertaken for my health by the consuls and priests every fifth year. In fulfillment of these vows they often celebrated games for my life; several times the four highest colleges of priests, several times the consuls. Also both privately and as a city all the citizens unanimously and continuously prayed at all the shrines for my health.

cian power was the most elastic and explicit one that Augustus held, and it became a traditional statement of imperial authority for all emperors.

273. By revising the roll of the senate and conducting a census Augustus was undertaking the duties of a censor, another Roman office. As with his tribunician power, Augustus exercised the authority of a censor without holding the office.

274. A lustrum is a purification ritual conducted at the end of a census.

275. The technical term for "the authority of an office."

10. By a senate decree my name was included in the Salian Hymn[276], and it was sanctified by a law, both that I would be sacrosanct for ever, and that, as long as I would live, the tribunician power would be mine. I was unwilling to be high priest in the place of my living colleague; when the people offered me that priesthood which my father had, I refused it. And I received that priesthood, after several years, with the death of him who had occupied it since the opportunity of the civil disturbance, with a multitude flocking together out of all Italy to my election, so many as had never before been in Rome, when Publius Sulpicius and Gaius Valgius were consuls (12 B.C.E.).

11. The senate consecrated the altar of Fortune the Bringer-back[277] before the temples of Honor and Virtue at the Campanian gate for my return, on which it ordered the priests and Vestal virgins to offer yearly sacrifices on the day when I had returned to the city from Syria (when Quintus Lucretius and Marcus Vinicius were consuls (19 B.C.E.), and it named that day Augustalia after my cognomen.

12. By the authority of the senate, a part of the praetors and tribunes of the plebs, with consul Quintus Lucretius and the leading men, was sent to meet me in Campania, which honor had been decreed for no one but me until that time. When I returned to Rome from Spain and Gaul, having successfully accomplished matters in those provinces, when Tiberius Nero and Publius Quintilius were consuls (13 B.C.E.), the senate voted to consecrate the altar of August Peace[278] in the field of Mars for my return, on which it ordered the magistrates and priests and Vestal virgins to offer annual sacrifices.

13. Our ancestors wanted [the temple of] Janus Quirinus to be closed when throughout all the empire of the Roman people, by land and sea, peace had been secured through victory. Although before my birth it had been closed twice in all recorded memory from the founding of the city, the senate voted three times in my principate that it be closed.

14. When my sons Gaius and Lucius Caesar, whom fortune stole from me as youths, were fourteen, the senate and Roman people made them consuls-designate on behalf of my honor, so that they would enter that magistracy after five years, and the senate decreed that on that day when they were led into the forum they would be included in public councils. Moreover the Roman knights[279] together named each of them first of the youth and gave them shields and spears.

276. As if Augustus were a god.

277. Fortuna Redux, not simply because Augustus returned after three years but because he brought back the Roman standards which had been lost to the Parthians in defeat in 53 BCE. See *RG* 29.

278. The first fragments of this Ara Pacis were found in 1568 but the complete excavation and restoration was not completed until 1938. It is recognized as a significant work of Augustan art and propaganda.

279. The "equestrian order" or "knights" were the social class just below the senate in Roman society. Augustus recognized them by reviving some of their privileges and traditions.

15. I paid to the Roman plebs, HS 300 per man[280] from my father's will, and in my own name gave HS 400 from the spoils of war when I was consul for the fifth time (29 B.C.E.); furthermore I again paid out a public gift of HS 400 per man, in my tenth consulate (24 B.C.E.), from my own patrimony; and, when consul for the eleventh time (23 B.C.E.), twelve doles of grain personally bought were measured out;[281] and in my twelfth year of tribunician power (12–11 B.C.E.) I gave HS 400 per man for the third time. And these public gifts of mine never reached fewer than 250,000 men. In my eighteenth year of tribunician power, as consul for the twelfth time (5 B.C.E.), I gave to 320,000 plebs of the city HS 240 per man. And, when consul the fifth time (29 B.C.E.), I gave from my war-spoils to colonies of my soldiers each HS 1000 per man; about 120,000 men in the colonies received this triumphal public gift. Consul for the thirteenth time (2 B.C.E.), I gave HS 240 to the plebs who then received the public grain; they were a few more than 200,000.

16. I paid the towns money for the fields which I had assigned to soldiers in my fourth consulate (30 B.C.E.) and then when Marcus Crassus and Gnaeus Lentulus Augur were consuls (14 B.C.E.); the sum was about HS 600,000,000 which I paid out for Italian estates, and about HS 260,000,000 which I paid for provincial fields. I was the first and only one who did this among all who founded military colonies in Italy or the provinces according to the memory of my age.[282] And afterwards, when Tiberius Nero and Gnaeus Piso were consuls (7 B.C.E.), and likewise when Gaius Antistius and Decius Laelius were consuls (6 B.C.E.), and when Gaius Calvisius and Lucius Passienus were consuls (4 B.C.E.), and when Lucius Lentulus and Marcus Messalla were consuls (3 B.C.E.), and when Lucius Caninius and Quintus Fabricius were consuls (2 B.C.E.), I paid out rewards in cash to the soldiers whom I had led into their towns when their service was completed, and in this venture I spent about HS 400,000,000.

17. Four times I helped the senatorial treasury with my money, so that I offered HS 150,000,000 to those who were in charge of the treasury. And when Marcus Lepidus and Lucius Arruntius were consuls (6 C.E.), I offered HS 170,000,000 from my personal assets to the military treasury, which was founded by my advice and from which rewards were given to soldiers who had served twenty or more years.

18. From that year when Gnaeus and Publius Lentulus were consuls (18 B.C.E.), when the taxes fell short, I gave out contributions of grain and money from my granary and personal assets, sometimes to 100,000 men, sometimes to many more.

19. I built the senate-house and the Chalcidicum which adjoins it and the temple

280. HS is the abbreviation for "sesterces." The annual pay for a Roman legionary soldier at this time was 900 sesterces, so Augustus' gift was a considerable sum for many recipients.

281. In other words, Augustus supplemented the monthly grain rations available to a limited number of adult male Roman residents. The need in 23 BCE arose in part from a flood of the Tiber that destroyed some of Rome's stored grain reserves.

282. Previous victorious generals had simply appropriated land for their soldiers without paying for it.

of Apollo on the Palatine with porticos, the temple of divine Julius, the Lupercal, the portico at the Flaminian circus, which I allowed to be called by the name Octavian, after he who had earlier built in the same place, the state box at the great circus, the temple on the Capitoline of Jupiter Subduer and Jupiter Thunderer, the temple of Quirinus, the temples of Minerva and Queen Juno and Jupiter Liberator on the Aventine, the temple of the Lares at the top of the holy street, the temple of the gods of the Penates on the Velian, the temple of Youth, and the temple of the Great Mother on the Palatine.

20. I rebuilt the Capitol and the theater of Pompey, each work at enormous cost, without any inscription of my name. I rebuilt aqueducts in many places that had decayed with age, and I doubled the capacity of the Marcian aqueduct by sending a new spring into its channel. I completed the Forum of Julius and the basilica which he built between the temple of Castor and the temple of Saturn, works begun and almost finished by my father. When the same basilica was burned with fire I expanded its grounds and I began it under an inscription of the name of my sons, and, if I should not complete it alive, I ordered it to be completed by my heirs. Consul for the sixth time (28 B.C.E.), I rebuilt eighty-two temples of the gods in the city by the authority of the senate, omitting nothing which ought to have been rebuilt at that time. Consul for the seventh time (27 B.C.E.), I rebuilt the Flaminian road from the city to Ariminum and all the bridges except the Mulvian and Minucian.

21. I built the temple of Mars Ultor on private ground and the forum of Augustus from war-spoils. I built the theater at the temple of Apollo on ground largely bought from private owners, under the name of Marcus Marcellus, my son-in-law. I consecrated gifts from war-spoils in the Capitol and in the temple of divine Julius, in the temple of Apollo, in the temple of Vesta, and in the temple of Mars Ultor, which cost me about HS 100,000,000. I sent back gold crowns weighing 35,000 pounds to the towns and colonies of Italy, which had been contributed for my triumphs, and later, however many times I was named emperor, I refused gold crowns from the towns and colonies which they equally kindly decreed, and before they had decreed them.

22. Three times I gave shows of gladiators under my name and five times under the name of my sons and grandsons; in these shows about 10,000 men fought. Twice I furnished under my name spectacles of athletes gathered from everywhere, and three times under my grandson's name. I celebrated games under my name four times, and furthermore in the place of other magistrates twenty-three times. As master of the college I celebrated the secular games for the college of the Fifteen,[283] with my colleague Marcus Agrippa, when Gaius Furnius and Gaius Silanus were consuls (17 B.C.E.). Consul for the thirteenth time (2 B.C.E.), I celebrated the first games of Mars, which after that time thereafter in following years, by a senate decree and a law,

283. The "college of Fifteen" oversaw foreign cults at Rome, including the consultation of the Sibylline books, which allegedly proclaimed these "secular" or "once a century" games (saeculum = century).

the consuls were to celebrate. Twenty-six times, under my name or that of my sons and grandsons, I gave the people hunts of African beasts in the circus, in the forum, or in the amphitheater; in them about 3,500 beasts were killed.

23. I gave the people the spectacle of a naval battle, in the place across the Tiber where the grove of the Caesars is now, with the ground excavated in length 1,800 feet, in width 1,200, in which thirty beaked ships, biremes or triremes, but many smaller, fought among themselves; in these ships about 3,000 men fought in addition to the rowers.

24. In the temples of all the cities of the province of Asia, as victor, I replaced the ornaments which he with whom I fought the war[284] had possessed privately after he despoiled the temples. Silver statues of me—on foot, on horseback, and standing in a chariot--were erected in about eighty cities, which I myself removed, and from the money I placed golden offerings in the temple of Apollo under my name and of those who paid the honor of the statues to me.

25. I restored peace to the sea from pirates. In that slave war[285] I handed over to their masters for the infliction of punishments about 30,000 captured, who had fled their masters and taken up arms against the state. All Italy swore allegiance to me voluntarily, and demanded me as leader of the war which I won at Actium;[286] the provinces of Gaul, Spain, Africa, Sicily, and Sardinia swore the same allegiance. And those who then fought under my standard were more than 700 senators, among whom 83 were made consuls either before or after, up to the day this was written, and about 170 were made priests.

26. I extended the borders of all the provinces of the Roman people which neighbored nations not subject to our rule. I restored peace to the provinces of Gaul and Spain, likewise Germany, which includes the ocean from Cadiz to the mouth of the river Elbe. I brought peace to the Alps from the region which is near the Adriatic Sea to the Tuscan, with no unjust war waged against any nation. I sailed my ships on the ocean from the mouth of the Rhine to the east region up to the borders of the Cimbri,[287] where no Roman had gone before that time by land or sea, and the Cimbri and the Charydes and the Semnones and the other Germans of the same territory sought by envoys the friendship of me and of the Roman people. By my order and auspices two armies were led at about the same time into Ethiopia and into that part

284. Mark Antony.

285. In 43 BCE, the senate authorized Sextus Pompey, the son of Pompey the Great, to wage war on Mark Antony; when Antony joined forces with Octavian/Augustus, they proscribed Sextus Pompey, who then took control of Sicily and used his fleet to blockade and disrupt trade and supplies. Pompey's forces were not defeated until 36 BCE. Augustus celebrates this victory by raising the fear of a "slave revolt" and denigrating his opponents as pirates and slaves.

286. The victory over the forces of Mark Antony and Cleopatra in 31 BCE, which left him as sole ruler.

287. I.e. present-day Denmark.

of Arabia which is called Fortunate,[288] and the troops of each nation of enemies were slaughtered in battle and many towns captured. They penetrated into Ethiopia all the way to the town Nabata, which is near to Meroe; and into Arabia all the way to the border of the Sabaei, advancing to the town Mariba.

27. I added Egypt to the rule of the Roman people. When Artaxes, king of Greater Armenia, was killed, though I could have made it a province, I preferred, by the example of our elders, to hand over that kingdom to Tigranes, son of king Artavasdes, and grandson of King Tigranes, through Tiberius Nero, who was then my step-son. And the same nation, after revolting and rebelling, and subdued through my son Gaius, I handed over to be ruled by King Ariobarzanes son of Artabazus, King of the Medes, and after his death, to his son Artavasdes; and when he was killed, I sent Tigranes, who came from the royal clan of the Armenians, into that rule. I recovered all the provinces which lie across the Adriatic to the east and Cyrene, with kings now possessing them in large part, and Sicily and Sardina, which had been occupied earlier in the slave war.

28. I founded colonies of soldiers in Africa, Sicily, Macedonia, each Spain,[289] Greece, Asia, Syria, Narbonian Gaul, and Pisidia, and furthermore had twenty-eight colonies founded in Italy under my authority, which were very populous and crowded while I lived.

29. I recovered from Spain, Gaul, and Dalmatia the many military standards lost through other leaders, after defeating those enemies. I compelled the Parthians to return to me the spoils and standards of three Roman armies, and as suppliants to seek the friendship of the Roman people. Furthermore I placed those standards in the sanctuary of the temple of Mars Ultor.[290]

30. As for the tribes of the Pannonians,[291] before my principate no army of the Roman people had entered their land. When they were conquered through Tiberius Nero, who was then my step-son and emissary, I subjected them to the rule of the Roman people and extended the borders of Illyricum to the shores of the river Danube. On the near side of it the army of the Dacians was conquered and overcome under my auspices, and then my army, led across the Danube, forced the tribes of the Dacians to bear the rule of the Roman people.

31. Emissaries from the Indian kings were often sent to me, which had not been seen before that time by any Roman leader. The Bastarnae, the Scythians, and the Sarmatians, who are on this side of the river Don and the kings further away, and the kings of the Albanians, of the Iberians, and of the Medes, sought our friendship through emissaries.

288. Arabia Felix was the southern part of the Arabian peninsula, including parts of present-day Saudi Arabia and Yemen.

289. That is, Nearer and Further Spain, the two provinces into which Rome had divided the Spanish peninsula.

290. "Mars the Avenger," a temple that Augustus built; see *RG* 21.

291. They occupied parts of present-day Hungary, Austria, Slovakia, Slovenia, and Croatia.

32. To me were sent supplications by kings: of the Parthians, Tiridates and later Phraates son of king Phraates, of the Medes, Artavasdes, of the Adiabeni, Artaxares, of the Britons, Dumnobellaunus and Tincommius, of the Sugambri, Maelo, of the Marcomanian Suebi (...). King Phraates of the Parthians, son of Orodes, sent all his sons and grandsons into Italy to me, though defeated in no war, but seeking our friendship through the pledges of his children. And in my principate many other peoples experienced the faith of the Roman people, of whom nothing had previously existed of embassies or interchange of friendship with the Roman people.

33. The nations of the Parthians and Medes received from me the first kings of those nations which they sought by emissaries: the Parthians, Vonones son of king Phraates, grandson of king Orodes, the Medes, Ariobarzanes, son of king Artavasdes, grandson of king Ariobarzanes.

34. In my sixth and seventh consulates (28–27 B.C.E.), after putting out the civil war, having obtained all things by universal consent, I handed over the state from my power to the control of the senate and Roman people. And for this merit of mine, by a senate decree, I was called Augustus and the doors of my temple were publicly clothed with laurel and a civic crown was fixed over my door and a gold shield[292] placed in the Julian senate-house, and the inscription of that shield testified to the virtue, mercy, justice, and piety, for which the senate and Roman people gave it to me. After that time, I exceeded all in influence, but I had no greater power than the others who were colleagues with me in each magistracy.

35. When I administered my thirteenth consulate (2 B.C.E.), the senate and equestrian order[293] and Roman people all called me father of the country, and voted that the same be inscribed in the vestibule of my temple, in the Julian senate-house, and in the forum of Augustus under the chariot which had been placed there for me by a decision of the senate. When I wrote this I was seventy-six years old.

Appendix: Written after Augustus' death.

1. All the expenditures which he gave either into the treasury or to the Roman plebs or to discharged soldiers: HS 2,400,000,000.

2. The works he built: the temples of Mars, of Jupiter Subduer and Thunderer, of Apollo, of divine Julius, of Minerva, of Queen Juno, of Jupiter Liberator, of the Lares, of the gods of the Penates, of Youth, and of the Great Mother, the Lupercal, the state box at the circus, the senate-house with the Chalcidicum, the forum of Augustus, the Julian basilica, the theater of Marcellus, the Octavian portico, and the grove of the Caesars across the Tiber.

292. This shield (clipeus virtutis) appears on many of Augustus' coins and a marble copy was found in Arles.

293. I.e. the "Roman knights" of *RG* 14.

3. He rebuilt the Capitol and holy temples numbering eighty-two, the theater of Pompey, waterways, and the Flaminian road.

4. The sum expended on theatrical spectacles and gladiatorial games and athletes and hunts and mock naval battles and money given to colonies, cities, and towns destroyed by earthquake and fire or per man to friends and senators, whom he raised to the senate rating: innumerable.

Thurinus, Gaius Octavius. "Res Gestae Divi Augusti (The Deeds of the Divine Augustus)." Translated by Thomas Bushnell, BSG. Copyright 1998. Available at: http://classics.mit.edu/Augustus/deeds.html, accessed June 10, 2021.

Apology of Socrates by Plato (Introduction only)

Introduction

SNAPSHOT

LANGUAGE: Ancient Greek

DATE: c. 390 BCE

LOCATION: Athens

GENRE: Philosophy

TAGS: Death; Divination; Ethics and Morality; Identity; Law and Punishment; Philosophy; Ways of Knowing; Wisdom

In Greek, an "apologia" is not an expression of regret or repentance. It is a defense speech. Socrates is on trial, charged with corrupting the young and "innovating about the gods" rather than worshipping the traditional gods of the city. The content of these charges is fluid: try to establish what they are as you read. Socrates was seventy years old when he was brought to trial in 399 BCE, but he had been known in Athens for more than twenty-five years as a philosopher, soldier, conversationalist, and social irritant. We do not have the speeches of the prosecutors, but we have two versions of what Socrates is alleged to have said in his defense. The earlier and more famous version is Plato's.

Socrates was judged by a jury of five hundred (or 501) and many others were in attendance, including Plato. This is the only time Plato places himself in any of his twenty-six or so dialogues. Many of the others are clearly fictions, since they are set early in Plato's life or before his birth, and many consist of conversations between Socrates and one other individual with no others present. By contrast, the *Apology of Socrates* invites us to consider it as something like a transcript of the event, since Plato places himself in the audience and includes apparent addresses to the audience. But Plato was not a reporter, and this is probably Plato's defense of Socrates more than Socrates's defense of himself.

Although the *Apology* is included among Plato's dialogues, it is fundamentally a monologue. The exception to this monologue is Socrates's brief cross-examination of one of his accusers, Meletus. That passage reveals a condensed version of the "Socratic method" of ***elenchus***, or **cross-examination**, in which Socrates asks questions about the knowledge and opinions of others, usually without claiming particu-

Timeline

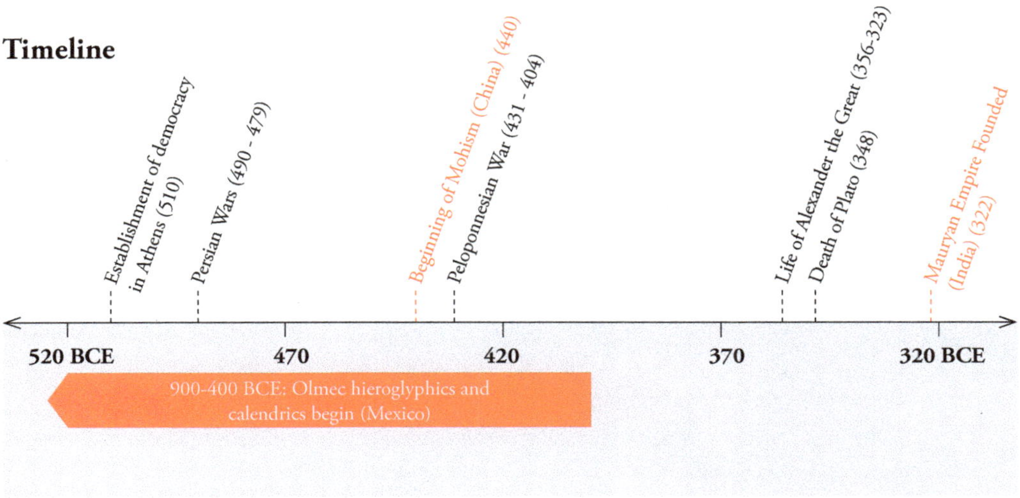

lar knowledge himself. Through the questioning, Socrates shakes the certainty of those he talks to until they reach a state of ***aporia***, a kind of **intellectual impasse**, at which point they confess that they do not know what they thought they knew. For Socrates, this seems to be the starting place for knowledge; for the others, as with Meletus in the *Apology*, it is often an embarrassing source of anger.

Socrates uses familiar terms like knowledge and wisdom, but he often regards them as if they were unfamiliar and difficult concepts and worth investigating. Most Athenians must have assumed that they knew what wisdom, knowledge, and moral goodness were, even intuitively. Socrates does not dismiss intuition or other kinds of knowledge. For example, early on in this dialogue, what sources and kinds of knowledge does Socrates grant to the poets and the craftsmen (22a–e) or to himself (23a–b)? Throughout the trial, he continues to test the knowledge and wisdom of others and finds that it is partial and fallible. As you read, look for indications of Socrates's own knowledge and his claims of wisdom. What does he know and not know? If Socrates thinks "that he does not know" (e.g., *Apol.* 21d), how can he be so certain about moral matters and that he is doing the right thing? How can he encourage the Athenians to take certain moral actions, like "caring for their souls" (*Apol.* 30a–b)? How are his disclaimers of knowledge compatible with his moral certainty?

It can be difficult to know how sincere Socrates is at times: what does he mean that he knows only that he doesn't know, or that he was never anyone's teacher? This is the source of Socrates's famous **irony**, which often straddles or combines a serious and sincere meaning and something more playful and allusive. Socratic irony is rarely simple irony that means the opposite of what it says. To take another small example, Socrates says that the rich young men imitate him (23c–d). We understand that they are mimicking his irritating interrogations. At a deeper level, can they truly imitate Socrates? If they are and aren't imitating Socrates, how might this be an example of irony?

These kinds of questions seem to be fundamental to the process of reading a Platonic dialogue, most of which recreate the experience of having a philosophical dialogue rather than providing conclusions or answers. Like many good teachers, Socrates and Plato seem interested in getting us to ask questions. Plato was not the first or only writer of Socratic dialogues, but only his and those of Xenophon, a later writer who borrowed from Plato, survive. We have fragments of other Socratic writers, some of them substantial, and they suggest that cross-examination and the use of irony were practices of Socrates and not inventions of Plato. As for their philosophies, however, it is impossible to distinguish a Socratic doctrine from a Platonic one: Socrates wrote nothing, and Plato is absent and silent in his dialogues.

Brian S. Hook
Department of Classics

Recommended Translation:

Plato. *The Trial and Death of Socrates: Four Dialogues*. Translated by Benjamin Jowett. New York: Dover, 1992.

The Bacchae by Euripides (Introduction only)

Introduction

SNAPSHOT BOX

LANGUAGE: Ancient Greek

DATE: 405 BCE

LOCATION: Greece

GENRE: Tragic drama

TAGS: Authority and Leadership; Community/Communal Identity; Conflict and War; Death; Deities and Spirits; Emotion; Nature; Religion; Women and Gender

In order to understand the plot of the *Bacchae*, one must know something about Dionysus's human family, which is associated with the Greek city of Thebes. In myth, Cadmus is the brother of Europa, the maiden from Sidon who was abducted by Zeus disguised as a bull and carried to Europe. When Cadmus fails to find his sister, he consults the oracle of Apollo at Delphi. The oracle tells him to follow a cow that leads him to a spot in northern Greece that will become the city of Thebes. In this place he comes upon a dragon guarding a spring of fresh water. Cadmus slays it and on the advice of the goddess Athena, sows its teeth in the ground. The teeth produce a crop of "earth-born" men who attempt to kill him, but Zeus saves him. Cadmus atones for killing the sacred dragon and is given a wife, Harmonia, daughter of Ares and Aphrodite. They produce four daughters, Autonoe, Semele, Agave, and Ino, and a son, Polydorus. Many of their descendants are featured in Greek tragedies.

Dionysus and his antagonist in the *Bacchae*, Pentheus, are cousins. Semele, the mother of Dionysus, is the only mortal woman in Greek myth to become the mother of a major deity. She has a relatively long-term relationship with Zeus whose affairs with mortal women are usually brief, until Hera in disguise convinces Semele to ask Zeus to reveal himself to her in all his immortal glory. By this time, Semele is pregnant. She is unable to endure the fiery thunderbolt of Zeus and is incinerated; but Zeus "delivers" the unborn baby and sews him into his thigh as a surrogate womb until he is ready to be born again. This is why Dionysus is some-

Timeline

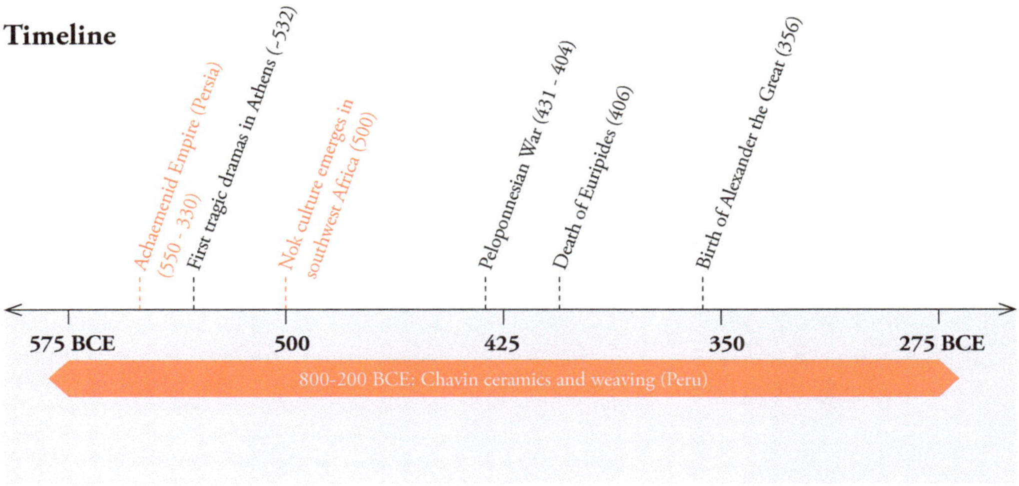

times called "twice-born" and is associated with rebirth and salvation in mystery cults. Ecstasy (from Greek, "to stand outside oneself"), a heightened consciousness experienced as joyful rapture, was a primary component of his worship, along with dancing, music, and singing hymns.

In the *Bacchae*, Dionysus is represented as a "new" god from the east, not one of the traditional gods in the Greek pantheon although the name Dionysus appears in Linear B Greek as early as 1300 BCE, and he was a very important god in Athens. The main festivals in Athens and environs in his honor were the Lenaia, a winter festival that featured dramatic competition and wine drinking; the Anthesteria, a celebration of the opening of the new wine jars; and the great City Dionysia in March, whose central event was the presentation of the great Athenian dramas. Smaller festivals happened at other times, and secret cults, including mysteries, emerged over time. The mythic dismemberment of Dionysus by the Titans and his re-embodiment gave rise to the idea that he could offer eternal life to those "reborn" into his cult.

Some key terms from the *Bacchae* introduce us to the worship of Dionysus:

- Bacchae, Bacchantes—Greek term for the female followers of Dionysus, so-called from their ritual cry "io, Bacche!" In the play, they are represented as eastern women who accompany the god, and who are then joined by the women of Thebes.
- Maenads—another term for Bacchae, derived from mania, "madness," in reference to the ecstatic frenzy the god provokes.
- *thyrsus*—Greek term for the Bacchic staff (sometimes these staffs have strands of wool clinging to them, suggestive of the normal role of Greek women weaving at the loom in their homes).
- Satyrs—half-goat, half-human men who join in the rites.

Both men and women worshipped Dionysus, participating in the nocturnal cultic practices that included making music, dancing, carrying the thyrsus and pine torches in the *thiasos* (procession), and so forth, as we see in the *Bacchae*. When the Bacchantes gather on Mt. Cithaeron in the play, however, the rituals are for female eyes only. Gender-specific ritual was not uncommon in Greek religion. For example, in Athens women regularly gathered to celebrate the Thesmophoria, a festival in honor of Demeter, which men were not permitted to attend or watch.

Dancing, music, and singing praises to the god help to bring the participants into an ecstatic state of mind. Ecstatic states have a wide range of practices, from internal meditative stillness to partaking in external communal behaviors. Euripides describes two Dionysiac practices as especially exotic and threatening that fall within the more extreme range of ecstatic behaviors:

- *sparagmos*—Greek term for rending a live animal from limb to limb. The Bacchantes generally do this to small animals, such as fawns, during their frenzy.

- *omophagia*—Greek term for eating raw flesh, an act generally associated with the *sparagmos*. <BL>

In Greek myth, wine was the gift of Dionysus to humankind. As a god of wine, then, we can understand the role of intoxication as a way to ecstasy as well. Why do you think that the use of mind-altering substances also features in many religions, ancient and modern? Dionysus is often depicted holding a wine cup and on Greek vases intoxicated satyrs carouse, have sex, chase maenads, make music, and participate in various cultic activities, often in the presence of the god Dionysus. There is a duality to wine in this cult: in the *Bacchae* the god of wine is praised for bringing sleep and for quieting the cares of mortals; but wine is also described as the blood of the grapevine. This connection between wine and blood helps us to understand the frequent presence of death in his cult. Dionysus himself, however, is not depicted as drinking or drunk in the play. Instead, he is completely in control of himself and of others. Indeed, as you will notice, some of the characters' symptoms of drunkenness in the play might in fact be a reflection of Dionysus having taken complete control over their minds and bodies. As you read, which characters in the play display the most consistent symptoms of drunkenness: difficulty walking and talking, double vision, and so on, in your opinion?

Dionysus is represented in various forms in Greek literature and art. First, simply as a mask, usually hung on a column and draped with cloth. There were two basic masks of Dionysus: the god who causes frenzy and the mild god who brings joy to mortals. During the Archaic period, Dionysus was often depicted on Greek vases as bearded and mature. But by the mid-fifth century BCE, he features prominently in art and literature in the form of a sensuous, androgynous youth. Satyrs' faces were often depicted as masks as well. Masks were worn by the actors in Greek drama. In this way, mask and actor merge (*persona* is the Latin word for "mask"), just as the god and his female votary fluidly merge into one, called by the same name (Bacchus/ Bacche). How do the masks of tragedy and comedy, still used today to represent modern theater, ultimately represent the dual nature of the god Dionysus himself?

Lora Holland Goldthwaite
Department of Classics

[Content Notice: violence]

Recommended Translation: Euripides's *Bacchae*. Translated with introduction and notes by Stephen Esposito. New York: Hackett, 1998.

from *The Handbook of Epictetus* (*Enchiridion*) by Epictetus

SNAPSHOT

LANGUAGE: Ancient Greek

DATE: c. 100 CE

GENRE: Philosophy

Cultural identity: Greco-Roman

TAGS: Deities and Spirits; Desire and Happiness; Emotion; Ethics and Morality; Freedom and Harmony; Wisdom

Introduction

What does it mean to be "free"? This question was a personal one for Epictetus. According to his biographical tradition, Epictetus was born in Phrygia in what is modern-day Turkey, probably as a slave. At some point he became a servant to Epaphroditus, one of Nero's own former slaves and administrators, in Rome. Epaphroditus also served later emperors, including Vespasian and Domitian. Epictetus says in one of his *Discourses* (1.9.29) that while still a slave he was allowed to attend the lectures of the Stoic Musonius Rufus. Some time after this, Epaphroditus gave Epictetus his freedom, but we have no information about the reasons or circumstances. Presumably with Musonius Rufus's support, Epictetus began to teach in Rome. In 95 CE, the emperor Domitian expelled all philosophers from Italy, and Epictetus probably left at that time. He set up a school in northwestern Greece, which attracted wealthy Roman citizens, and he taught there until his death. From his *Discourses*, we can see how his experiences of slavery and freedom, of politics and the imperial court, shaped his thinking and teaching for the rest of his life.

For all Stoics, virtue (***aretê*** in Greek) is the only good, and it consists in "living according to Nature." Epictetus repeatedly distinguishes the things that are "up to us" or in our control—our judgments, impulses, desires, and aversions—from those things that are not "up to us"—our health, wealth, reputation, and status (Chapter 1). By locating so few things in our control, Epictetus radically limits the extent of our freedom, but also defines and empowers it. For example, how much are you

Timeline

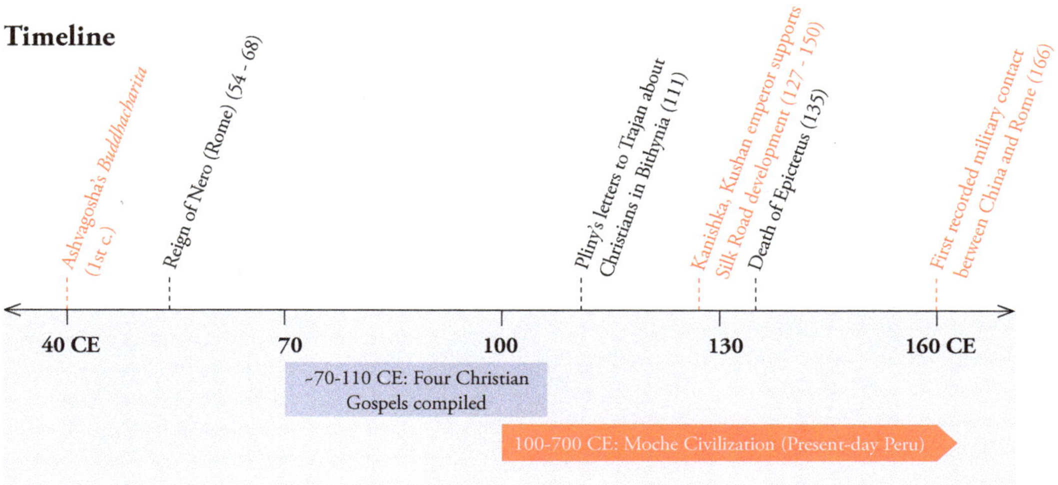

in control of what others say about you? And how much do you control the effect on you of what others say? Epictetus applies the same questions to our financial status, our health, our relationships, and everything else that is external to us. The goal of Stoicism is not simply self-discipline, but rather inner tranquility and happiness. Epictetus's essential insight, that our happiness is bound up with our valuation of things, resembles contemporary cognitive behavioral therapy. This approach, popular in psychotherapy, encourages patients to identify negative or inaccurate perceptions and patterns of thinking, and to replace them with more helpful and accurate ones.

Epictetus himself, like Socrates, apparently wrote nothing. The source below comes from his student Arrian who recorded Epictetus's oral teachings. While the four books of *Discourses* express more of Epictetus's biography, personality, and his relationship with students, the excerpt below comes from a smaller epitome distilled from the *Discourses*, called the *Enchiridion* or the *Handbook* that succinctly conveys his philosophical reflections on Stoicism.

Stoicism was developed in Athens by Zeno of Citium (in Cyprus) in the fourth century BCE. The first Stoics elaborated their doctrines in stark terms. If virtue was identical to rationality, and no misfortune affected one's virtue, then the Stoic wise man could not call torture a bad thing—and could even be content while suffering it. Other philosophers, like the Skeptics and Academics, pointed out that some circumstances, like health and good government, were more amenable to the practice of virtue than others; so how could health and government be immaterial to virtue? Later Stoics adapted to these criticisms, and to new social circumstances such as the dominance of Rome. Modern scholars identify early, middle, and late periods of Stoic philosophy. Epictetus, with the Romans Seneca (c. 4 BCE–65 CE) and the emperor Marcus Aurelius (121–180 CE), represents the late Stoa. They emphasize practical ethics, rather than physics and logic as the earlier Stoics did, and theirs are the only complete Stoic works to survive from antiquity. Nevertheless, much of Epictetus's Stoicism is consistent with what we know of the teachings of the early Stoics, who lived nearly four centuries before him and whom he cites regularly.

Brian S. Hook
Department of Classics

PRE-READING PARS

1. Identify two or three scenarios or contexts that come to mind when you hear or read the word "virtue."
2. Consider the common phrase, "It is what it is." Name three to five emotions or attitudes, negative and positive, that you associate with such a phrase.

from *Handbook of Epictetus*

1. Some things are up to us and some are not up to us. Our opinions are up to us, and our impulses, desires, aversions—in short, whatever is our own doing. Our bodies are not up to us, nor are our possessions, our reputations, or our public offices, or, that is, whatever is not our own doing. The things that are up to us are by nature free, unhindered, and unimpeded; the things that are not up to us are weak, enslaved, hindered, not our own. So remember, if you think that things naturally enslaved are free or that things not your own are your own, you will be thwarted, miserable, and upset, and will blame both gods and men. But if you think that only what is yours is yours, and that what is not your own is, just as it is, not your own, then no one will ever coerce you, no one will hinder you, you will blame no one, you will not accuse anyone, you will not do a single thing unwillingly, you will have no enemies, and no one will harm you, because you will not be harmed at all.

As you aim for such great goals, remember that you must not undertake them by acting moderately, but must let some things go completely and postpone others for the time being. But if you want both those great goals and also to hold public office and to be rich, then you may perhaps not get even the latter just because you aim at the former too; and you certainly will fail to get the former, which are the only things that yield freedom and happiness.

From the start, then, work on saying to each harsh appearance,[294] "You are an appearance, and not at all the thing that has the appearance." Then examine it and assess it by these yardsticks that you have, and first and foremost by whether it concerns the things that are up to us or the things that are not up to us. And if it is about one of the things that is not up to us, be ready to say, "You are nothing in relation to me."

2. Remember, what a desire proposes is that you gain what you desire, and what an aversion proposes is that you not fall into what you are averse to. Someone who fails to get what he desires is *un*fortunate, while someone who falls into what he is averse to has met *mis*fortune. So if you are averse only to what is against nature among the things that are up to you, then you will never fall into anything that you are averse to; but if you are averse to illness or death or poverty, you will meet misfortune. So

294. In Greek, *phantasia*, which may also be translated impression or presentation; that is, something perceptible to the senses.

detach your aversion from everything not up to us, and transfer it to what is against nature among the things that are up to us. And for the time being eliminate desire completely, since if you desire something that is not up to us, you are bound to be unfortunate, and at the same time none of the things that are up to us, which it would be good to desire, will be available to you. Make use only of impulse and its contrary, rejection, though with reservation, lightly, and without straining.

3. In the case of everything attractive or useful or that you are fond of, remember to say just what sort of thing it is, beginning with the least little things. If you are fond of a jug, say "I am fond of a jug!" For then when it is broken you will not be upset. If you kiss your child or your wife, say that you are kissing a human being; for when it dies you will not be upset. [...]

5. What upsets people is not things themselves but their judgments about the things. For example, death is nothing dreadful (or else it would have appeared dreadful to Socrates), but instead the judgment about death that it is dreadful—*that* is what is dreadful. So when we are thwarted or upset or distressed, let us never blame someone else but rather ourselves, that is, our own judgments. An uneducated person accuses others when he is doing badly; a partly educated person accuses himself, an educated person accuses neither someone else nor himself. [...]

7. On a voyage when your boat has anchored, if you want to get fresh water you may pick up a small shellfish and a vegetable by the way, but you must keep your mind fixed on the boat and look around frequently in case the captain calls. If he calls you must let all those other things go so that you will not be tied up and thrown on the ship like livestock. That is how it is in life too: if you are given a wife and a child instead of a vegetable and a small shellfish, that will not hinder you; but if the captain calls, let all those things go and run to the boat without turning back; and if you are old, do not even go very far from the boat, so that when the call comes you are not left behind.

8. Do not seek to have events happen as you want them to, but instead want them to happen as they do happen, and your life will go well. [...]

15. Remember, you must behave as you do at a banquet. Something is passed around and comes to you: reach out your hand politely and take some. It goes by: do not hold it back. It has not arrived yet: do not stretch your desire out toward it, but wait until it comes to you. In the same way toward your children, in the same way toward your wife, in the same way toward public office, in the same way toward wealth, and you will be fit to share a banquet with the gods. But if when things are set in front of you, you do not take them but despise them, then you will not only share a banquet with the gods but also be a ruler along with them. For by acting in this way Diogenes and Heraclitus[295] and people like them were deservedly gods and were deservedly called gods. [...]

295. Both Greek philosophers—a Cynic and a pre-Socratic, respectively—admired by the Stoics.

17. Remember that you are an actor in a play, which is as the playwright wants it to be: short if he wants it short, long if he wants it long. If he wants you to play a beggar, play even this part skillfully, or a cripple, or a public official, or a private citizen. What is yours is to play the assigned part well. But to choose it belongs to someone else. [...]

21. Let death and exile and everything that is terrible appear before your eyes every day, especially death; and you will never have anything contemptible in your thoughts or crave anything excessively. [...]

23. If it ever happens that you turn outward to want to please another person, certainly you have lost your plan of life. Be content therefore in everything to be a philosopher, and if you want to seem to be one, make yourself appear so to yourself, and you will be capable of it. [...]

29. For each action, consider what leads up to it and what follows it, and approach it in the light of that. Otherwise you will come to it enthusiastically at first, since you have not borne in mind any of what will happen next, but later when difficulties turn up you will give up disgracefully. You want to win an Olympic victory? I do too, by the gods, since that is a fine thing. But consider what leads up to it and what follows it, and undertake the action in the light of that. You must be disciplined, keep a strict diet, stay away from cakes, train according to strict routine at a fixed time in heat and in cold, not drink cold water, not drink wine when you feel like it, and in general you must have turned yourself over to your trainer as to a doctor, and then in the contest "dig in," sometimes dislocate your hand, twist your ankle, swallow a lot of sand, sometimes be whipped, and, after all that, lose. Think about that and then undertake training, if you want to. Otherwise you will be behaving the way children do, who play wrestlers one time, gladiators another time, blow trumpets another time, then act a play. In this way you too are now an athlete, now a gladiator, then an orator, then a philosopher, yet you are nothing wholeheartedly, but like a monkey you mimic each sight that you see, and one thing after another is to your taste, since you do not undertake a thing after considering it from every side, but only randomly and half-heartedly.

In the same way when some people watch a philosopher and hear one speaking like Euphrates (though after all who can speak like him?), they want to be philosophers themselves. Just you consider, as a human being, what sort of thing it is; then inspect your own nature and whether you can bear it. You want to do the pentathlon, or to wrestle? Look at your arms, your thighs, inspect your loins. Different people are naturally suited for different things. Do you think that if you do those things you can eat as you now do, drink as you now do, have the same likes and dislikes? You must go without sleep, put up with hardship, be away from your own people, be looked down on by a little slave boy, be laughed at by people who meet you, get the worse of it in everything, honor, public office, law course, every little thing. Think about whether you want to exchange these things for tranquillity, freedom, calm. If not, do not embrace philosophy, and do not like children be a philosopher at one time, later a tax-collector, then an orator, then a procurator of the emperor. These things do not go together. You must be one person, either good or bad. You must either work on your ruling principle, or work on externals, practice the art either of what is inside or of what is outside, that is, play the role either of a philosopher or of a non-philosopher.

30. Appropriate actions[296] are in general measured by relationships. He is a father: that entails taking care of him, yielding to him in everything, putting up with him when he abuses you or strikes you. "But he is a bad father." Does nature then determine that you have a good father? No, only that you have a father. "My brother has done me wrong." Then keep your place in relation to him; do not consider his action, but instead consider what you can do to bring your own faculty of choice into accord with nature. Another person will not do you harm unless you wish it; you will be harmed at just that time at which you take yourself to be harmed. In this way, then, you will discover the appropriate actions to expect from a neighbor, from a citizen, from a general, if you are in the habit of looking at relationships.

31. The most important aspect of piety toward the gods is certainly both to have correct beliefs about them, as beings that arrange the universe well and justly, and to set yourself to obey them and acquiesce in everything that happens and to follow it willingly, as something brought to completion by the best judgment. For in this way you will never blame the gods or accuse them of neglecting you. And this piety is impossible unless you detach the good and the bad from what is not up to us and attach it exclusively to what is up to us, because if you think that any of what is not up to us is good or bad, then when you fail to get what you want and fall into what you do not want, you will be bound to blame and hate those who cause this. For every animal by nature flees and turns away from things that are harmful and from what causes them, and pursues and admires things that are beneficial and what causes them. There is therefore no way for a person who thinks he is being harmed to enjoy what he thinks is harming him, just as it is impossible to enjoy the harm itself. Hence a son even abuses his father when the father does not give him a share of things that he thinks are good; and thinking that being a tyrant was a good thing is what made enemies of Polyneices and Eteocles.[297] This is why the farmer too abuses the gods, and the sailor, and the merchant, and those who have lost their wives and children. For wherever someone's advantage lies, there he also shows piety. So whoever takes care to desire as he might and to have aversions, in the same way also cares about being pious. And it is always appropriate to make libations and sacrifices and give firstfruits according to the custom of one's forefathers, in a manner that is pure and neither slovenly nor careless, nor indeed cheaply nor beyond one's means. [...]

33. Set up right now a certain character and pattern for yourself which you will preserve when you are by yourself and when you are with people. Be silent for the most part, or say what you have to in a few words. Speak rarely, when the occasion requires speaking, but not about just any topic that comes up, not about gladiators,

296. Actions in accordance with nature.

297. Sons of Oedipus who killed each other in a battle over who would rule in Thebes.

horse-races, athletes, eating or drinking—the things that always come up; and especially if it is about people, talk without blaming or praising or comparing. Divert by your own talk, if you can, the talk of those with you to something appropriate. If you happen to be stranded among strangers, do not talk. Do not laugh a great deal or at a great many things or unrestrainedly. Refuse to swear oaths, altogether if possible, or otherwise as circumstances allow. Avoid banquets given by those outside philosophy. But if the appropriate occasion arises, take great care not to slide into their ways, since certainly if a person's companion is dirty the person who spends time with him, even if he happens to be clean, is bound to become dirty too. Take what has to do with the body to the point of bare need, such as food, drink, clothing, house, household slaves, and cut out everything that is for reputation or luxury. As for sex stay pure as far as possible before marriage, and if you have it do only what is allowable. But do not be angry or censorious toward those who do engage in it, and do not always be making an exhibition of the fact that you do not.

If someone reports back to you that so-and-so is saying bad things about you, do not reply to them but answer, "Obviously he didn't know my other bad characteristics, since otherwise he wouldn't just have mentioned these."

For the most part there is no need to go to public shows, but if ever the right occasion comes do not show your concern to be for anything but yourself; that is to say, wish to have happen only what does happen, and for the person to win who actually does win, since that way you will not be thwarted. But refrain completely from shouting or laughing at anyone or being very much caught up in it. After you leave, do not talk very much about what has happened, except what contributes to your own improvement, since that would show that the spectacle had impressed you.

Do not go indiscriminately or readily to people's public lectures, but when you do be on guard to be dignified and steady and at the same time try not to be disagreeable.

When you are about to meet someone, especially someone who seems to be distinguished, put to yourself the question, "What would Socrates or Zeno have done in these circumstances?" and you will not be at a loss as to how to deal with the occasion. When you go to see someone who is important, put to yourself the thought that you will not find him at home, that you will be shut out, that the door will be slammed, that he will pay no attention to you. If it is appropriate to go even under these conditions, go and put up with what happens, and never say to yourself, "It wasn't worth all that!" For that is the way of a non-philosopher, someone who is misled by externals.

In your conversations stay away from making frequent and longwinded mention of what you have done and the dangers that you have been in, since it is not as pleasant for others to hear about what has happened to you as it is for you to remember your own dangers.

Stay away from raising a laugh, since this manner slips easily into vulgarity and at the same time is liable to lessen your neighbors' respect for you. It is also risky to fall into foul language. So when anything like that occurs, if a good opportunity arises, go so far as to criticize the person who has done it, and otherwise by staying silent and blushing and frowning you will show that you are displeased by what has been said. 34. Whenever you encounter some kind of apparent pleasure, be on guard, as in the case of other appearances, not to be carried away by it, but let the thing wait for you and allow yourself to delay. Then bring before your mind two times, both the time when you enjoy the pleasure and the time when after enjoying it you later regret it and berate yourself; and set against these the way you will be pleased and will praise yourself if you refrain from it. But if the right occasion appears for you to undertake the action, pay attention so that you will not be overcome by its attractiveness and pleasantness and seductiveness, and set against it how much better it is to be conscious of having won this victory against it. [...]

46. Never call yourself a philosopher and do not talk a great deal among non-philosophers about philosophical propositions, but do what follows from them. For example, at a banquet do not say how a person ought to eat, but eat as a person ought to. Remember that Socrates had so completely put aside ostentation that people actually went to him when they wanted to be introduced to philosophers, and he took them. He was that tolerant of being overlooked. And if talk about philosophical propositions arises among non-philosophers, for the most part be silent, since there is a great danger of your spewing out what you have not digested. And when someone says to you that you know nothing and you are not hurt by it, then you know that you are making a start at your task. Sheep do not show how much they have eaten by bringing the feed to the shepherds, but they digest the food inside themselves, and outside themselves they bear wool and milk. So in your case likewise do not display propositions to non-philosophers but instead the actions that come from the propositions when they are digested. [...]

48. The position and character of a non-philosopher: he never looks for benefit or harm to come from himself but from things outside. The position and character of a philosopher: he looks for all benefit and harm to come from himself.

Signs of someone's making progress:[298] he censures no one; he praises no one; he blames no one; he never talks about himself as a person who amounts to something or knows something. When he is thwarted or prevented in something, he accuses himself. And if someone praises him he laughs to himself at the person who has praised him; and if someone censures him he does not respond. He goes around like an invalid, careful not to move any of his parts that are healing before they have become firm. He has kept off all desire from himself, and he has transferred all aversion onto what is against nature among the things that are up to us. His impulses toward everything are diminished. If he seems foolish or ignorant, he does not care. In a single phrase, he is on guard against himself as an enemy lying in wait. [...]

298. Epictetus uses this phrase to mean someone behaving in accordance with nature; being a philosopher.

50. Abide by whatever task is set before you as if it were a law, and as if you would be committing sacrilege if you went against it. But pay no attention to whatever anyone says about you, since that falls outside what is yours. [...]

53. On every occasion you must have these thoughts ready:

Lead me, Zeus, and you too, Destiny,
Wherever I am assigned by you;
I'll follow and not hesitate,
But even if I do not wish to,
Because I'm bad, I'll follow anyway.
Whoever has complied well with necessity
Is counted wise by us, and understands divine affairs.
Well, Crito, if it is pleasing to the gods this way, then let it happen
this way.
Anytus and Meletus can kill me, but they can't harm me.[299]

From *Handbook of Epictetus*. Edited and translated by Nicholas White, 11–13, 15–17, 19–24, 26–29. Indianapolis, IN: Hackett, 1983

POST-READING PARS

1. What is Epictetus's understanding of virtue? How does it compare to your own understanding?
2. Name a few consequences of "wanting things to be as they are." What are the personal and social consequences? Are they positive or negative?

299. Cleanthes, a Greek Stoic; tragic playwright Euripides; Plato's *Crito*; Plato's *Apology*.

Inquiry Corner

Content Question(s):	Critical Question(s):
What characteristics of tranquility does Epictetus suggest? What approaches does he recommend in cultivating them?	What are the sources of authority in Epictetus's world and worldview? How does he use analogies to support his arguments?
Comparative Question(s):	**Connection Question(s):**
Examine the similarities and differences between Epictetus's instruction and Buddha's teaching. For example, what do they say about desire and attachment? What are their respective goals of life?	How does Epictetus's instruction resemble a kind of behavioral training or therapy? What other religious or philosophical practices from the ancient world also cultivate changes of attitude or behavior?

BEYOND THE CLASSROOM

» Epictetus advises acceptance and adaptation, assuming that circumstances are as they must be. When would you accept and adapt to a difficult working environment, and when would you feel that you should oppose or leave it?

» One might argue that in advising us to only focus on things that are in our control, Stoicism wants us not to try things that we might not succeed at. How might a Stoic approach a new work environment with a lot of unknowns?

from *History of the Peloponnesian War*, "Funeral Oration of Pericles" by Thucydides

SNAPSHOT BOX

LANGUAGE: Ancient Greek

DATE: c. 430–400 BCE

LOCATION: Athens, Greece

GENRE: Historiography

TAGS: Community/Communal Identity; Conflict and War; Death; Empire and Colonialism; Rhetoric and Propaganda

Introduction

The funeral speech that Thucydides puts in Pericles's mouth has become one of the most famous and most frequently quoted ancient Greek texts, and many modern ideas about life in ancient Athens are based on it. However, the custom of commemorating the war dead of Athens with funeral rites and a speech was an annual Athenian tradition that started around 470 BCE, a few years after the end of the Greco-Persian wars. So this funeral speech by Pericles was not unique, but just one version of a fairly standardized narrative that listeners would have heard every year from Athenian politicians. Although these addresses are always called funeral speeches, their central subject is the city of Athens itself, as much as remembrance of the men who died in the service of the city. Thucydides does not give us anything like a transcript of what Pericles actually said in this speech, but its broader themes of national identity have always been considered to offer a unique insight into some of the values and beliefs that most Athenians would have held about their city.

Thucydides's *History of the Peloponnesian War* is the source for Pericles's funeral oration. One of the major themes of Thucydides's work is the process by which Athens's relationship to the rest of Greece gradually changed throughout the fifth century BCE. During the Persian Wars, Athens was one of the leaders of the Greek resistance against invaders from the Persian Empire. Over the next fifty years, Athens itself became the target of resistance from some of the other Greek cities

Timeline

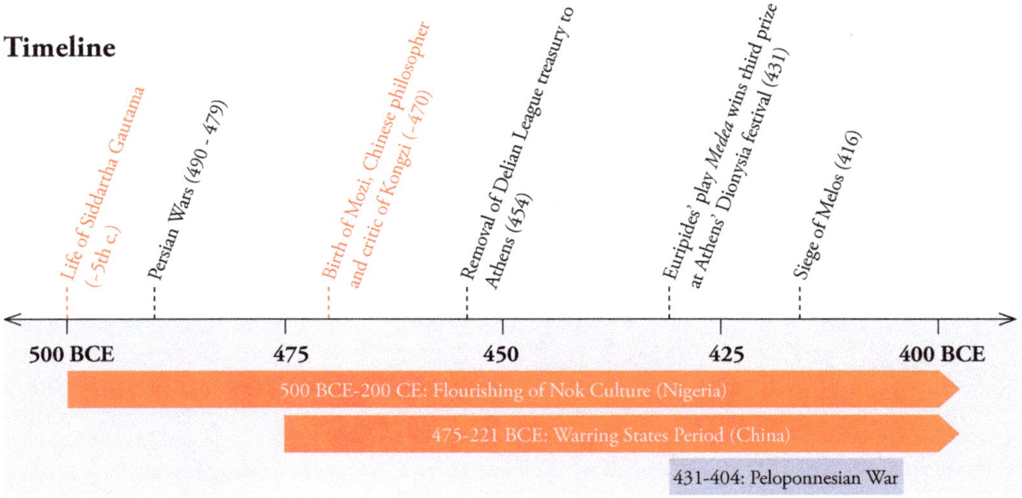

who perceived it as becoming an increasingly oppressive force within Greece. These former allies of equal status resented Athens's demands for financial contributions which consolidated Athens's power even further. Some themes in Pericles's funeral speech—of Athenian exceptionalism and preeminence in wartime and peace—represent the closest Athens has to a "national" history. What sort of connections can you see between Pericles's claims about Athenian democracy in this speech and other Greeks' perception of Athens as a tyrant?

Much of Pericles's speech articulates Athenian exceptionalism through an implied contrast to its arch-enemy Sparta, its chief rival for dominance in Greece. For example, Pericles claims that Athens is an open, tolerant city that welcomes strangers. Can you think of ways that we define America positively or negatively in contrast to other countries? Athens was significantly different from Sparta in many aspects, notably in its political system of democracy, as opposed to Sparta's oligarchy. In Athens any free, male Athenian citizen had the right of speaking in the political assembly and the responsibility to help govern his city.

However, other values that Pericles claims as uniquely Athenian would be recognized by most Greeks as generally Greek values. For example, he claims that Athens is the only city that wins friends by doing favors rather than receiving them, but most Greek men would have much preferred to be benefactors to others than receivers of others' benefactions. To be an active benefactor and savior is to be like Heracles and other heroes, while to receive benefits from others is to be dangerously passive, the sort of behavior that the Greeks attributed to women and one that Greek males would shun. In what ways are gendered Greek values being prioritized as reflecting the values of the Athenian state here?

Sophie Mills
Department of Classics

PRE-READING PARS

1. Create a list of three to five values/principles that guide the national identity of the United States.
2. Identify two types of sources that we value as authentic historical evidence.

"Funeral Oration of Pericles"

XXXIV. In the course of the same winter the Athenians, following the custom of their fathers, celebrated at the public expense the funeral rites of the first who had fallen in this war. The ceremony is as follows. The bones of the departed lie in state for the space of three days in a tent erected for that purpose, and each one brings to his own dead any offering he desires. On the day of the funeral coffins of cypress wood are borne on wagons, one for each tribe, and the bones of each are in the coffin of his tribe. One empty bier, covered with a pall, is carried in the procession for the missing whose bodies could not be found for burial. Anyone who wishes, whether citizen or stranger, may take part in the funeral procession, and the women who are related to the deceased are present at the burial and make lamentation. The coffins are laid in the public sepulcher, which is situated in the most beautiful suburb of the city; there they always bury those fallen in war, except indeed those who fell at Marathon; for their valor the Athenians judged to be preeminent and they buried them on the spot where they fell. But when the remains have been laid away in the earth, a man chosen by the state, who is regarded as best endowed with wisdom and is foremost in public esteem, delivers over them an appropriate eulogy. After this the people depart. In this manner they bury; and throughout the war, whenever occasion arose, they observed this custom. Now over these, the first victims of the war, Pericles son of Xanthippus was chosen to speak. And when the proper time came, he advanced from the sepulcher and took his stand upon a platform which had been built high in order that his voice might reach as far as possible in the throng, and spoke as follows:

XXXV. "Most of those who have spoken here in the past have commended the law-giver who added this oration to our ceremony, feeling that it is right that it should be spoken at their burial over those who have fallen in war. To me, however, it would have seemed sufficient, when men have proved themselves brave by valiant acts, by act only to make manifest the honors we render them—such honors as today you have witnessed in connection with these funeral ceremonies solemnized by the state—and not that the valor of many men should be hazarded on one man to be believed or not according as he spoke well or ill. For it is a hard matter to speak in just measure on an occasion where it is with difficulty that belief in the speaker's accuracy is established. For the hearer who is cognizant of the facts and partial to the dead will perhaps think that scant justice has been done in comparison with his own wishes and his own knowledge, while he who is not so informed, whenever he hears of an exploit which goes beyond his own capacity, will be led by envy to think there is some exaggeration. And indeed eulogies of other men are tolerable only in so far as each hearer thinks that he too has the ability to perform any of the exploits of which he hears; but whatever goes beyond that at once excites envy and unbelief. However, since our forefathers approved of this practice as right and proper, I also, rendering obedience to the law, must endeavor to the best of my ability to satisfy the wishes and beliefs of each of you.

XXXVI. "I shall speak first of our ancestors, for it is right and at the same time fitting, on an occasion like this, to give them this place of honor, in recalling what they did. For this land of ours, in which the same people have never ceased to dwell in an unbroken line of successive generations, they by their valor transmitted to our times a free state. And not only are they worthy of our praise, but our fathers still more; for they, adding to the inheritance which they received, acquired the empire we now possess and bequeathed it, not without toil, to us who are alive today. And we ourselves here assembled, who are now for the most part still in the prime of life, have further strengthened the empire in most respects, and have provided our city with all resources, so that it is sufficient for itself both in peace and in war. The military exploits whereby our several possessions were acquired, whether in any case it were we ourselves or our fathers that valiantly repelled the onset of war, Barbarian or Hellenic, I will not recall, for I have no desire to speak at length among those who know. But I shall first set forth by what sort of training we have come to our present position, and with what political institutions and as the result of what manner of life our empire became great, and afterwards proceed to the praise of these men; for I think that on the present occasion such a recital will be not inappropriate and that the whole throng, both of citizens and of strangers, may with advantage listen to it.

XXXVII. "We live under a form of government which does not emulate the institutions of our neighbors; on the contrary, we are ourselves a model which some follow, rather than the imitators of other peoples. It is true that our government is called a democracy, because its administration is in the hands, not of the few, but of the many; yet while as regards the law all men are on an equality for the settlement of their private disputes, as regards the value set on them it is as each man is in any way distinguished that he is preferred to public honors, not because he belongs to a particular class, but because of personal merits; nor, again, on the ground of poverty is a man barred from a public career by obscurity of rank if he but has it in him to do the state a service. And not only in our public life are we liberal, but also as regards our freedom from suspicion of one another in the pursuits of everyday life; for we do not feel resentment at our neighbor if he does as he likes, nor yet do we put on sour looks which, though harmless, are painful to behold. But while we thus avoid giving offence in our private intercourse, in our public life we are restrained from lawlessness chiefly through reverent fear, for we render obedience to those in authority and to the laws, and especially to those laws which are ordained for the succor of the oppressed and those which, though unwritten, bring upon the transgressor a disgrace which all men recognize.

XXXVIII. "Moreover, we have provided for the spirit many relaxations from toil: we have games and sacrifices regularly throughout the year and homes fitted out with good taste and elegance; and the delight we each day find in these things drives away sadness. And our city is so great that all the products of all the earth flow in upon us, and ours is the happy lot to gather in the good fruits of our own soil with no more home-felt security of enjoyment than we do those of other lands.

XXXIX. "We are also superior to our opponents in our system of training for warfare, and this in the following respects. In the first place, we throw our city open to all the world and we never by exclusionary acts debar any one from learning or seeing anything which an enemy might profit by observing if it were not kept from his sight; for we place our dependence, not so much upon prearranged devices to deceive, as upon the courage which springs from our own souls when we are called to action. And again, in the matter of education, whereas they from early childhood by a laborious discipline make pursuit of manly courage, we with our unrestricted mode of life are none the less ready to meet any equality of hazard. And here is the proof: When the Lacedaemonians invade our territory they do not come alone but bring all their confederates with them, whereas we, going by ourselves against our neighbors' territory, generally have no difficulty, though fighting on foreign soil against men who are defending their own homes, in overcoming them in battle. And in fact our united forces no enemy has ever yet met, not only because we are constantly attending to the needs of our navy, but also because on land we send our troops on many enterprises; but if they by chance engage with a division of our forces and defeat a few of us, they boast that they have repulsed us all, and if the victory is ours, they claim that they have been beaten by us all. If, then, by taking our ease rather than by laborious training and depending on a courage which springs more from manner of life than compulsion of laws, we are ready to meet dangers, the gain is all ours, in that we do not borrow trouble by anticipating miseries which are not yet at hand, and when we come to the test we show ourselves fully as brave as those who are always toiling; and so our city is worthy of admiration in these respects, as well as in others.

XL. "For we are lovers of beauty yet with no extravagance and lovers of wisdom yet without weakness. Wealth we employ rather as an opportunity for action than as a subject for boasting; and with us it is not a shame for a man to acknowledge poverty, but the greater shame is for him not to do his best to avoid it. And you will find united in the same persons an interest at once in private and in public affairs, and in others of us who give attention chiefly to business, you will find no lack of insight into political matters. For we alone regard the man who takes no part in public affairs, not as one who minds his own business, but as good for nothing; and we Athenians decide public questions for ourselves or at least endeavor to arrive at a sound understanding of them, in the belief that it is not debate that is a hindrance to action, but rather not to be instructed by debate before the time comes for action. For in truth we have this point also of superiority over other men, to be most daring in action and yet at the same time most given to reflection upon the ventures we mean to undertake; with other men; on the contrary, boldness means ignorance and reflection brings hesitation. And they would rightly be adjudged most courageous who, realizing most clearly the pains no less than the pleasures involved, do not on that account turn away from danger. Again, in nobility of spirit, we stand in sharp contrast to most men; for it is not by receiving kindness, but by conferring it, that we acquire our friends. Now he who confers the favor is a firmer friend, in that he is disposed, by continued goodwill toward the recipient, to keep the feeling of obligation alive in him; but he who owes it is more listless in his friendship, knowing that when he repays the kindness it will count, not as a favor bestowed, but as a debt repaid. And, finally, we alone confer our benefits without fear of consequences, not upon a calculation of the advantage we shall gain, but with confidence in the spirit of liberality which actuates us.

XLI. "In a word, then, I say that our city as a whole is the school of Hellas, and that, as it seems to me, each individual amongst us could in his own person, with the utmost grace and versatility, prove himself self-sufficient in the most varied forms of activity. And that this is no mere boast inspired by the occasion, but actual truth, is attested by the very power of our city, a power which we have acquired in consequence of these qualities. For Athens alone among her contemporaries, when put to the test, is superior to the report of her, and she alone neither affords to the enemy who comes against her cause for irritation at the character of the foe by whom he is defeated, nor to her subject cause for complaint that his masters are unworthy. Many are the proofs which we have given of our power and assuredly it does not lack witnesses, and therefore we shall be the wonder not only of the men of today but of after times; we shall need no Homer to sing our praise nor any other poet whose verses may perhaps delight for the moment but whose presentation of the facts will be discredited by the truth. Nay, we have compelled every sea and every land to grant access to our daring, and have everywhere planted everlasting memorials both of evil to foes and of good to friends. Such, then, is the city for which these men nobly fought and died, deeming it their duty not to let her be taken from them; and it is fitting that every man who is left behind should suffer willingly for her sake.

XLII. "It is for this reason that I have dwelt upon the greatness of our city; for I have desired to show you that we are contending for a higher prize than those who do not enjoy such privileges in like degree, and at the same time to let the praise of these men in whose honor I am now speaking be made manifest by proofs. Indeed, the greatest part of their praise has already been spoken; for when I lauded the city, that was but the praise wherewith the brave deeds of these men and men like them have already adorned her; and there are not many Hellenes whose fame would be found, like theirs, evenly balanced with their deeds. And it seems to me that such a death as these men died gives proof enough of manly courage, whether as first revealing it or as affording its final confirmation. Aye, even in the case of those who in other ways fell short of goodness, it is but right that the valor with which they fought for their country should be set before all else; for they have blotted out evil with good and have bestowed a greater benefit by their service to the state than they have done harm by their private lives. And no one of these men either so set his heart upon the continued enjoyment of wealth as to become a coward, or put off the dreadful day, yielding to the hope which poverty inspires, that if he could but escape it he might yet become rich; but, deeming the punishment of the foe to be more desirable than these things, and at the same time regarding such a hazard as the most glorious of all, they chose, accepting the hazard, to be avenged upon the enemy and to relinquish these other things, trusting to hope the still obscure possibilities of success, but in action, as to the issue that was before their eyes, confidently relying upon themselves. And then when the moment of combat came, thinking it better to defend themselves and suffer death rather than to yield and save their lives, they fled, indeed, from the shameful word of dishonor, but with life and limb stood stoutly to their task, and in the brief instant ordained by fate, at the crowning moment not of fear but of glory, they passed away.

XLIII. "And so these men then bore themselves after a manner that befits our city; but you who survive, though you may pray that it be with less hazard, should resolve that you will have a spirit to meet the foe which is no whit less courageous; and you must estimate the advantage of such a spirit not alone by a speaker's words, for he could make a long story in telling you—what you yourselves know as well as he—all the advantages that are to be gained by warding off the foe. Nay rather you must daily fix your gaze upon the power of Athens and become lovers of her, and when the vision of her greatness has inspired you, reflect that all this has been acquired by men of courage who knew their duty and in the hour of conflict were moved by a high sense of honor, who, if ever they failed in any enterprise, were resolved that at least their country should not find herself deserted by their valor, but freely sacrificed to her the fairest offering it was in their power to give. For they gave their lives for the common weal, and in so doing won for themselves the praise which grows not old and the most distinguished of all sepulchers—not that in which they lie buried, but that in which their glory survives in everlasting remembrance, celebrated on every occasion which gives rise to word of eulogy or deed of emulation. For the whole world is the sepulcher of famous men, and it is not the epitaph upon monuments set up in their own land that alone commemorates them, but also in lands not their own there abides in each breast an unwritten memorial of them, planted in the heart rather than graven on stone. Do you, therefore, now make these men your examples, and judging freedom to be happiness and courage to be freedom, be not too anxious about the dangers of war. For it is not those that are in evil plight who have the best excuse for being unsparing of their lives, for they have no hope of better days, but rather those who run the risk, if they continue to live, of the opposite reversal of fortune, and those to whom it makes the greatest difference if they suffer a disaster. For to a manly spirit more bitter is humiliation associated with cowardice than death when it comes unperceived in close company with stalwart deeds and public hopes.

XLIV. "Wherefore, I do not commiserate the parents of these men, as many of you as are present here, but will rather try to comfort them. For they know that their lives have been passed amid manifold vicissitudes; and it is to be accounted good fortune when men win, even as these now, a most glorious death—causing you grief—and when life has been meted out to them to be happy in no less than to die in. It will be difficult, I know, to persuade you of the truth of this, when you will constantly be reminded of your loss by seeing others in the enjoyment of blessings in which you too once took delight; and grief, I know, is felt, not for the want of the good things which a man has never known, but for what is taken away from him after he has once become accustomed to it. But those of you who are still of an age to have offspring should bear up in the hope of other children; for not only to many of you individually will the children that are born hereafter be a cause of forgetfulness of those who are gone, but the state also will reap a double advantage—it will not be left desolate and it will be secure. For they cannot possibly offer fair and impartial counsel who, having no children to hazard, do not have an equal part in the risk. But as for you who have passed your prime, count as gain the greater portion of your life during which you were fortunate and remember that the remainder will be short; and be comforted by the fair fame of these your sons. For the love of honor alone is untouched by age, and when one comes to the ineffectual period of life it is not 'gain' as some say, that gives the greater satisfaction, but honor.

XLV. "But for such of you here present as are sons and brothers of these men, I see the greatness of the conflict that awaits you—for the dead are always praised—and even were you to attain to surpassing virtue, hardly would you be judged, I will not say their equals, but even a little inferior. For there is envy of the living on account of rivalry, but that which has been removed from our path is honored with a good-will that knows no antagonism.

"If I am to speak also of womanly virtues, referring to those of you who will henceforth be in widowhood, I will sum up all in a brief admonition: Great is your glory if you fall not below the standard which nature has set for your sex, and great also is hers of whom there is least talk among men whether in praise or in blame.

XLVI. "I have now spoken, in obedience to the law, such words as I had that were fitting, and those whom we are burying have already in part also received their tribute in our deeds; besides, the state will henceforth maintain their children at the public expense until they grow to manhood, thus offering both to the dead and to their survivors a crown of substantial worth as their prize in such contests. For where the prizes offered for virtue are greatest, there are found the best citizens. And now, when you have made due lament, each for his own dead, depart."

Thucydides. "History of the Peloponnesian War: Books I and II." *Thucydides*. Translated by Charles Forster Smith, vol. 1. Cambridge, MA: William Heinemann LTD and Harvard University Press, [1921] 1956.

POST-READING PARS

1. How do the values underlying the identity of the United States you listed earlier compare with the values you think underlie Pericles's speech?
2. What types of historical evidence does Pericles claim to draw upon for his account?
3. Given that this oration was spoken to honor all the dead killed in wars fought by Athens over the year, what passages directly mention the dead and the impact on their relatives?

Inquiry Corner

Content Question(s):	**Critical Question(s):**
What justifications for Athenian predominance in the Greek world does Thucydides offer? Why does Pericles lay such emphasis on Athens's generosity to the world?	This speech has had a huge influence on later perceptions of fifth-century Athens and for the way that people from later cultures have imagined themselves as latter-day "Athenians." Critically identify two elements from Pericles's speech that might explain its enduring values.
Comparative Question(s):	**Connection Question(s):**
Compare/contrast the use of persuasive rhetoric in Thucydides's speech with the rhetoric of Cyrus, Augustus, or other state documents by national leaders.	How would a modern speechwriter use this oration as a model for making a similar case (regardless if you agree or disagree), about the United States?

from *History of the Peloponnesian War*, "Melian Dialogue" by Thucydides

Introduction

SNAPSHOT BOX

LANGUAGE: Ancient Greek

DATE: c. 430 BCE–400 BCE

LOCATION: Greece

GENRE: History

TAGS: Authority and Leadership; Conflict and War; Empire and Colonialism; Law and Punishment; Rhetoric and Propaganda

Melos is a small island in the Aegean Sea. It is a part of a group of islands in the eastern Mediterranean Sea that forms a rough circle around the island of Delos where there was an important temple of Apollo. Most islands in the Aegean had ties to Athens through supposed ancestral racial connections (as **Ionians**). Furthermore, since Athens ruled over most of these islands in the fifth century BCE, Athens required them to acknowledge Athenian dominance by paying a yearly financial tribute. Residents of Melos resisted this Athenian demand, since its citizens were proud of their shared ancestral **Dorian** connections with Sparta, the other dominant Greek city-state at this time. Ionic and Doric were two dialects of ancient Greek, used by their speakers—Ionians and Dorians, respectively—to create their own political and cultural identities.

In the conflict of the Peloponnesian War (431–404 BCE) between Athens and Sparta, most Greek cities lined up as allies to one or the other side. But Melos was the rare city-state that chose neutrality, at least according to Thucydides. What reasons do you imagine might have convinced Melos to attempt to stay neutral? Melos's neutrality displeased the Athenians and several times in the 420s BCE, Athens unsuccessfully attempted to bring them into submission. In 421 BCE, after ten years of an exhausting war of attrition, Athens and Sparta agreed on temporary peace terms that allowed Melos to experience a short-lived moment of safety.

Timeline

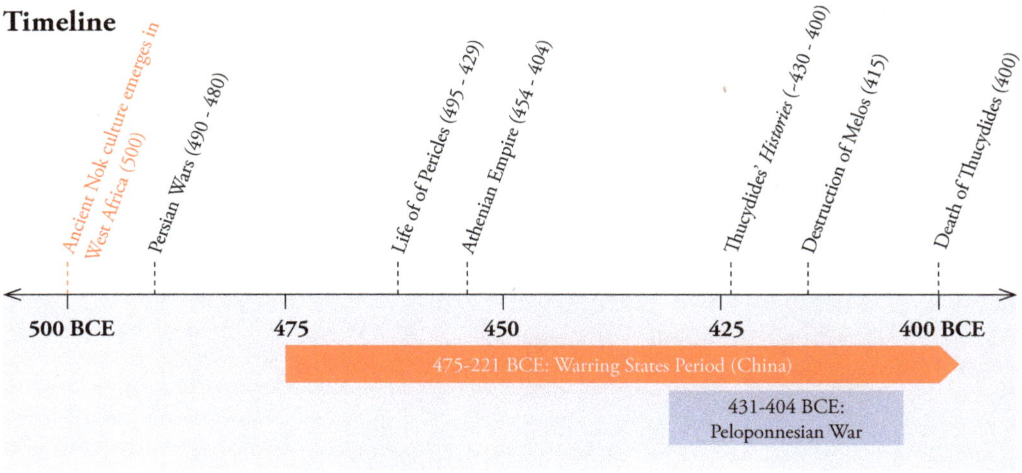

But the peace could not hold as Athens and Sparta were determined to annihilate each other, and in the summer of 416 BCE, Athens sent a large army composed of 3,400 soldiers, including 1,500 of their allies, to try once more to force Melos into submission. Thucydides positions the Melian dialogue in the context of this expedition. The military action that this dialogue explores took place in 416 BCE, though the actual words of the dialogue are probably mostly Thucydides's invention. As you read the dialogue, what types of justifications do Melians give for not surrendering once Athens has their warships pointed at them? The Athenians besieged the city for five months until treachery from within Melos enabled them to take control. The Athenians executed all the adult males and enslaved the women and children and took possession of the island.

In the Melian dialogue the Athenians offer reasons to the Melians why they should surrender. It has retained lasting relevance for later historians and political scientists. Famously, the Athenians claim that justice is meaningless where there is a large imbalance of power, thus reducing concepts of disgrace or honor to mere abstractions. Is this actually true, or is it simply part of the rhetorical strategy Athens uses to persuade the Melians that their resistance is futile? The Melians respond to the Athenians' strategy with their own arguments, which are focused on expediency and not on justice. Which city makes the more convincing arguments?

The Athenians were the greatest power in Greece and ruled over many Greek city-states, and yet somehow the fact that Melos wished to be neutral was perceived as an affront. Melos is weak, but how strong is Athens? Athens acquired dominance in Greece to a large extent because of the respect and gratitude of other Greeks for Athens' courage and self-sacrifice in the earlier Persian wars (490–479 BCE) against Darius and Xerxes. Athenian power was justified by reminding other Greeks that Athens chose to fight for the ideal of freedom in the face of terrible threats from a mighty Persian army. How might one explain why the Athenians who value their own freedom will not extend the same value to other Greek city-states, especially Melos?

Sophie Mills
Department of Classics

PRE-READING PARS

1. Think of a time when you were in an inferior position to someone. How did they justify their orders to you? Or, think of a time when you were in a position of power over someone else and required them to follow particular actions. How did you persuade them that they had to do as they were told?
2. Take five minutes to brainstorm what you know about ancient Athens and its culture.

Melian Dialogue

LXXXIV. The next summer Alcibiades sailed to Argos with twenty ships and seized such Argives as seemed to be still open to suspicion and to favor the side of the Lacedaemonians [Spartans], to the number of three hundred men; and these the Athenians deposited in the adjacent islands over which they had sway. The Athenians also made an expedition against the island of Melos with thirty ships of their own, six Chian and two Lesbian, and twelve hundred Athenian hoplites, three hundred bowmen, and twenty mounted archers, and from their allies and the islanders about fifteen hundred hoplites. Now the Melians are colonists of the Lacedaemonians, and were unwilling to obey the Athenians like the rest of the islanders. At first they remained quiet as neutrals; then when the Athenians tried to force them by ravaging their land, they went to war openly. Accordingly, having then camped in their territory with the forces just mentioned, the Athenian commanders, Cleomedes son of Lycomedes and Teisias son of Teisimachus, before doing any harm to the land, sent envoys to make proposals to the Melians. These envoys the Melians did not bring before the popular assembly, but bade them tell in the presence of the magistrates and the few[300] what they had come for. The Athenian envoys accordingly spoke as follows:

LXXXV. "Since our proposals are not to be made before the assembly, your purpose being, as it seems, that the people may not hear from us once for all, in an uninterrupted speech, arguments that are seductive and untested, and so be deceived—for we see the few—do you who sit here adopt a still safer course? Take up each point, and do not you either make a single speech, but conduct the inquiry by replying at once to any statement of ours that seems to be unsatisfactory. And first state whether our proposal suits you."

LXXXVI. The commissioners of the Melians answered: "The fairness of the proposal, that we shall at our leisure instruct one another, is not open to objection, but these acts of war, which are not in the future, but already here at hand, are manifestly at variance with your suggestion. For we see that you are come to be yourselves judges

300. Probably the chief governing body, a chamber of oligarchs, to which the magistrates belonged.

of what is to be said here, and that the outcome of the discussion will in all likelihood be, if we win the debate by the righteousness of our cause and for that very reason refuse to yield, war for us, whereas if we are persuaded, servitude."

LXXXVII. ATH. "Well, if you have met to argue from suspicions about what may happen in the future, or for any other purpose than to consult for the safety of your city in the light of what is present and before your eyes, we may as well stop; but if you have this end in view, we may speak on."

LXXXVIII. MEL. "It is natural and pardonable for me in such a position as ours to resort to many arguments and many suppositions. This conference, however, is here to consider the question of our safety; so let the discussion, if it please you, proceed in the way that you propose."

LXXXIX. ATH. "Well, then, we on our part will make use of no fair phrases, saying either that we hold sway justly because we overthrew the Persians, or that we now come against you because we are injured, offering in a lengthy speech arguments that would not be believed; nor, on the other hand do we presume that you will assert, either that the reason why you did not join us in the war was because you were colonists of the Lacedaemonians, or that you have done us no wrong. Rather we presume that you aim at accomplishing what is possibly in accordance with the real thoughts of both of us, since you know as well as we know that what is just is arrived at in human arguments only when the necessity on both sides is equal, and that the powerful exact what they can, while the weak yield what they must."

XC. MEL. "As we think, at any rate, it is expedient (for we are constrained to speak of expediency, since you have in this fashion, ignoring the principle of justice, suggested that we speak of what is advantageous) that you should not rule out the principle of the common good, but that for him who is at the time in peril what is equitable should also be just, and though one has not entirely proved this point he should still derive some benefit therefrom. And this is not less for your interest than for our own, inasmuch as you, if you shall ever meet with a reverse, would not only incur the greatest punishment, but would also become a warning example to others."

XCI. ATH. "But we on our part, so far as our empire is concerned, even if it should cease to be, do not look forward to the end with dismay. For it is not those who rule over others, as the Lacedaemonians also do—though our quarrel is not now with the Lacedaemonians—that are a terror to the vanquished, but subject peoples who may perchance themselves attack and get the better of their rulers. And as far as that is concerned, you must permit us to take the risk. But that it is for the benefit of our empire that we are here, and also the safety of your city that we now propose to speak, we shall make plain to you, since what we desire is to have dominion over you without trouble to ourselves, and that you should be saved to the advantage of both."

XCII. MEL. "And how could it prove as advantageous for us to become slaves, as it is for you to have dominion?"

XCIII. ATH. "Because it would be to your advantage to submit before suffering the most horrible fate, and we should gain by not destroying you."

XCIV. MEL. "And so, you mean, you would not consent to our remaining at peace and being friends instead of enemies, but allies of neither combatant?"

XCV. ATH. "No; for your hostility does not injure us so much as your friendship; for in the eyes of our subjects that would be a proof of our weakness, whereas your hatred is a proof of our power."

XCVI. MEL. "Do your subjects regard equity in such a way as to put in the same category those that do not belong to you at all and those—your own colonists in most cases and in others revolted subjects—who have been subdued by you?"

XCVII. ATH. "As to pleas of justice, they think that neither the one nor the other lacks them, but that those who preserve their freedom owe it to their power, and that we do not attack them because we are afraid. So that, to say nothing of our enlarging our empire, you would afford us security by being subdued, especially if you, an insular power, and weaker than other islanders, should fail to show yourselves superior to a power which is master of the sea."

XCVIII. MEL. "But do you not think there is security in the other course? For here also it is necessary, just as you force us to abandon all pleas of justice and seek to persuade us to give ear to what is to your own interest, that we, too, tell you what is to our advantage and try to persuade you to adopt it, if that happens to be to your advantage also. How, we say, shall you not make enemies of all who are now neutral, as soon as they look at our case and conclude that some day you will come against them also? And in this what else are you doing but strengthening the enemies you already have, and bringing upon you, against their inclination, others who would never have thought of becoming your enemies?"

XCIX. ATH. "Not so, for we do not reckon those as the more dangerous to us who, dwelling somewhere on the mainland and being free men, will defer for a long time taking any precautions against us, but rather those who dwell in some of the islands, both these who, like you, are subject to no control, and those who are already exasperated by the necessity of submission to our rule. For it is these who are most likely to give way to recklessness and bring both themselves and us into danger which they cannot but foresee."

C. MEL. "Surely, then, if you and your subjects brave so great a risk, you in order that you may not lose your empire, and they, who are already your slaves, in order that they may be rid of it, for us surely who still have our freedom it would be the height of baseness and cowardice not to resort to every expedient before submitting to servitude."

CI. ATH. "No, not if you take a sensible view of the matter; for with you it is not a contest of equal terms to determine a point of manly honor, so as to avoid incurring disgrace; rather the question before you is one of self-preservation—to avoid offering resistance to those who are far stronger than you."

CII. MEL. "But we know that the fortune of war is sometimes impartial and not in accord with the difference in numbers. And for us, to yield is at once to give up hope; but if we make an effort, there is still hope that we may stand erect."

CIII. ATH. "Hope is indeed a solace in danger, and for those who have other resources in abundance, though she may injure, she does not ruin them; but for those who stake their all on a single throw—hope being by nature prodigal—it is only when disaster has befallen that her true nature is recognized, and when at last she is known, she leaves the victim no resource wherewith to take precautions against her in future. This fate, we beg of you, weak as you are and dependent on a single turn of the scale, do not willingly incur; nor make yourselves like the common crowd who, when it is possibly still to be saved by human means, as soon as distress comes and all visible grounds of hope fail them, betake themselves to those that are invisible—to divination, oracles, and the like, which, with the hopes they inspire, bring men to ruin."

CIV. MEL. "We, too, be well assured, think it difficult to contend both against your power and against fortune, unless we shall be impartial; but nevertheless we trust that, in point of fortune, we shall through the divine favor be at no disadvantage because we are god-fearing men standing our ground against men who are unjust; and as to the matter of power, that the alliance of the Lacedaemonians will supply what we lack, since that alliance must aid us, if for no other reason, because of our kinship with them and for very shame. So our confidence is not altogether so irrational as you may suppose."

CV. ATH. "Well, as to the kindness of the divine favor, neither do we expect to fall short of you therein. For in no respect are we departing from men's observances regarding that which pertains to the divine or from their desires regarding that which pertains to themselves, in aught that we demand or do. For the gods we hold the belief, and of men we know, that by a necessity of their nature wherever they have power they always rule. And so in our case since we neither enacted this law nor when it was enacted were the first to use it, but found it in existence and we expect to leave it in existence for all time, so we make use of it, well aware that both you and others, if clothed with the same power as we are, would do the same thing. And so with regard to the divine favor, we have good reason not to be afraid that we shall be at a disadvantage. But as to your expectation regarding the Lacedaemonians, your confident trust that out of shame forsooth they will aid you—while we admire your simplicity, we do not envy you your folly. We must indeed acknowledge that with respect to themselves and the institutions of their own country, the Lacedaemonians practice virtue in a very high degree; but with respect to their conduct towards the rest of mankind, while one might speak at great length, in briefest summary one may declare that of all men with whom we are acquainted they, the most conspicuously, consider what is agreeable to be honorable, and what is expedient just. And yet such an attitude is not favorable to your present unreasonable hope of deliverance."

CVI. MEL. "But we find in this very thing our strongest ground of confidence —that in their own interest the Lacedaemonians will not be willing to betray the Melians who are their colonists, and so incur, on the one hand, the distrust of all the Hellenes who are well-disposed towards them, and, on the other, give aid to their enemies."

CVII. ATH. "Do you not think, then, that self-interest goes hand in hand with security, while justice and honor are practiced with danger—a danger the Lacedaemonians are in general the least disposed to risk?"

CVIII. MEL. "Nay, but even the dangers we believe they would be more ready to incur for our sakes, and that they would consider them less hazardous than if incurred for others, inasmuch as we lie close to the Peloponnesus when anything is to be undertaken there and on account of affinity of sentiment are more to be trusted than any others."

CIX. ATH. "But for men who are about to take part in a struggle, that which inspires their confidence is clearly not the good will of those who call them to their aid, but such marked superiority in actual power of achievement as they may possess; and to this superiority the Lacedaemonians give heed rather more than do the rest of mankind. At any rate, they so mistrust their own resources that they always associate themselves with many allies when they attack their neighbors; so that it is not likely they will ever cross over to an island while we are masters of the sea."

CX. MEL. "But there are others whom they might send; besides, the Cretan sea is wide, so that upon it the capture of a hostile squadron by the masters of the sea will be more difficult than it would be to cross over in security for those who wish to elude them. And if they should fail in this attempt they could turn against your territory and against any of the rest of your allies whom Brasidas did not reach; and then you would have to exert yourselves, not for the acquisition of territory that never belonged to you, but for preservation of your own confederacy, aye, and your own country."

CXI. ATH. "Of these contingencies one or another might indeed happen; but they would not be new to our experience, and you yourselves are not unaware that the Athenians have never in a single instance withdrawn from a siege through fear of any foe. However, we cannot but reflect that, although you said that you would take counsel concerning your deliverance, you have not in this long discussion advanced a single argument that ordinary men would put their confidence in if they expected to be delivered. On the contrary, your strongest grounds for confidence are merely cherished hopes whose fulfilment is in the future, whereas your present resources are too slight, compared with those already arrayed against you, for any chance of success. And you exhibit a quite unreasonable attitude of mind if you do not even now, after permitting us to withdraw, come to some decision that is wiser than your present purpose. For surely you will not take refuge in that feeling which most often brings men to ruin when they are confronted by dangers that are clearly foreseen and therefore disgraceful—the fear of such disgrace. For many men, though they can still clearly foresee the dangers into which they are drifting, are lured on by the power of a seductive word—the thing called disgrace—until, the victims of a phrase, they are indeed plunged, of their own act, into irretrievable calamities, and thus incur in addition a disgrace that is more disgraceful, because associated with folly rather than with misfortune. Such a course you will avoid, if you take wise counsel, and you will not consider it degrading to acknowledge yourselves inferior to the most powerful state when it offers you moderate terms—to become allies, keeping your own territory but paying tribute—and, when a choice is given to you of war or safety, not to hold out stubbornly for the worse alternative. Since those who, while refusing to submit to their equals, yet comport themselves wisely towards their superiors and are moderate towards their inferiors—these, we say, are most likely to prosper. Consider, then, once more after our withdrawal, and reflect many times in your deliberations that your fatherland is at stake, your one and only fatherland, and that upon one decision only will depend her fate for weal or woe."

CXII. So the Athenians retired from the conference; and the Melians, after consulting together in private, finding themselves of much the same opinion as they had expressed before, answered as follows: "Men of Athens, our opinion is no other than it was at first, nor will we in a short moment rob of its liberty a city which has been inhabited already seven hundred years; but trusting to the future which by divine favor has preserved her hitherto, and to such help as men, even the Lacedaemonians, can give, we shall try to win our deliverance. But we propose to you that we be your friends, but enemies to neither combatant, and that you withdraw from our territory, after making such a truce as may seem suitable for both of us."

CXIII. Such was the answer of the Melians; and the Athenians, as they were quitting the conference, said: "Then, as it seems to us, judging by the result of these deliberations of yours, you are the only men who regard future events as more certain that what lies before your eyes, and who look upon that which is out of sight, merely because you wish it, as already realized. You have staked your all, putting your trust in the Lacedaemonians, in fortune and in hopes; and with your all you will come to ruin."

CXIV. So the Athenian envoys returned to the army; and their generals, as the Melians would not yield, immediately commenced hostilities, and drew a wall round about the city of Melos, distributing the work among the several states. Afterwards, leaving some of their own troops and of their allies to keep guard both by land and by sea, they withdrew with the greater part of the army, while the rest remained behind and besieged the place.

CXV. About the same time the Argives invaded Phliasia; but being ambushed by the Phliasians and the Argive exiles they lost about eighty men. Also the Athenians at Pylos took much booty from the Lacedaemonians; but even this did not move the Lacedaemonians to renounce the treaty and make war upon them. They made proclamation, however, that any one of their own people who wished might make reprisals upon the Athenians. The Corinthians also went to war with the Athenians on account of some private differences; but the rest of the Peloponnesians kept quiet. The Melians, too, took the part of the Athenian wall over against the market-place by a night assault; then having slain some of the men and brought in grain and as many other necessaries as they could, they withdrew and kept quiet. After that the Athenians maintained a better watch. So the summer ended.

CXVI. The following winter the Lacedaemonians were on the point of invading Argive territory, but as the sacrifices for crossing the boundaries were not favorable they returned home. On account of this intention on the part of the Lacedaemonians, the Argives, suspecting certain men in their city, seized some of them, but the rest escaped. About the same time the Melians again at another point took a part of the Athenian encompassing wall, the garrison not being numerous. But later, in consequence of these occurrences, another force came from Athens, of which Philocrates son of Demeas was commander, and the Melians, being now closely besieged—some treachery, too, having made its appearance among them—capitulated to the Athenians on the condition that these should determine their fate. The Athenians thereupon slew all the adult males whom they had taken and made slaves of the children and women. But the place they then peopled with new settlers from Athens, sending thither at a later time five hundred colonists.

Thucydides. "History of the Peloponnesian War: Books V and VI." *Thucydides.* Translated by Charles Forster Smith, vol. 3, 155–79. Cambridge MA: William Heinemann LTD and Harvard University Press, [1921] 1959.

POST-READING PARS

1. Thucydides specifically says that this dialogue was held between the Athenians and the leaders of the Melians in closed session, not in front of the whole community. What aspects of his account might be realistic or not?
2. To what extent did this extract from Thucydides confirm or change your impressions of the ancient Athenians?
3. What attitudes toward hope are evident in this dialogue? Is it presented as good or harmful?

Inquiry Corner

Content Question(s):	**Critical Question(s):**
Explain in your own words three arguments that the Athenians use to persuade the Melians to surrender to them.	The Melians could have saved themselves by simply agreeing to be part of the Athenian Empire. Should they have done so or not, and why? Do you think Thucydides is endorsing or critiquing the Athenians' point of view?
Comparative Question(s):	**Connection Question(s):**
Read or reread "Funeral Oration of Pericles," also written by Thucydides, found in this Reader. Which themes are shared and how do the approaches to those themes overlap or differ?	Looking at either other ancient civilizations or specific modern political situations, are Thucydides's Athenians unusual or the norm in their political self-assertion over others?

BEYOND THE CLASSROOM

» Much of the text could be seen as the negotiations prior to a hostile takeover, where the Athenians were trying to convince the Melians to acquiesce to the power of the Athenians without going to war. What skills do you think would be most valuable in situations where a hostile takeover seems imminent?

Letters between Pliny and Trajan on Christians

Introduction

SNAPSHOT BOX

LANGUAGE: Latin

DATE: 111 CE

LOCATION: Bithynia (present-day Turkey)

GENRE: Letter

TAGS: Authority and Leadership; Death; Empire and Colonialism; Identity; Law and Punishment; Religion

When do the differences in a society lead to division rather than diversity of perspectives and experiences? At its height in the early second century CE, the Roman Empire encompassed over two million square miles from Britain to North Africa, from Spain to Afghanistan. Its perhaps seventy million inhabitants spoke dozens of languages and worshipped dozens of gods. Such pluralism suggests tolerance. But it was not infinite. Rome's official encounter with Christianity tested the limits.

Pliny, called "the Younger" by modern scholars to distinguish him from his uncle Pliny "the Elder," was sent by the Roman emperor Trajan in 110 CE to serve as a special imperial representative to Bithynia, a province in the north central region of what we know as Turkey. Pliny's responsibilities included a review of the finances of the province and a general consideration of the political situation. Although Pliny represented Trajan, he wrote him frequent letters asking for approval and guidance—surprising given that a letter needed about two months to reach Rome from Bithynia, and its response required the same to return. Some of Pliny's questions seem trivial, almost as if he is worried about doing anything that Trajan might disapprove of. The correspondence between Pliny and Trajan is found in the tenth book of Pliny's *Letters*.

In Letter 10.96, Pliny refers a matter to Trajan that he regards as serious and confusing. Several people in Bithynia were accused of being Christians, and once accusations began, they multiplied. Soon an anonymous list was published. Pliny

Timeline

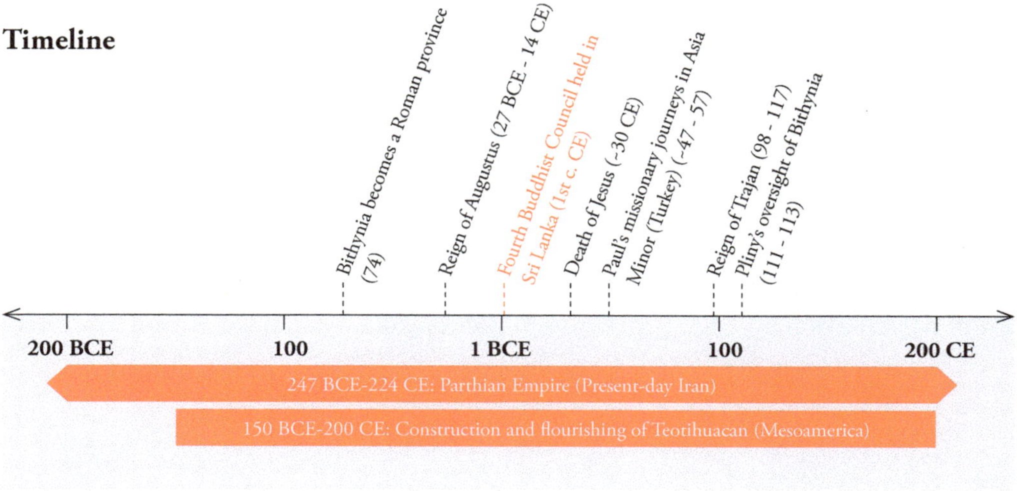

investigates and reports what he learns to Trajan, but he is not sure what the real crime is, if any, and how he should respond to it. His letter is invaluable because it is the earliest source describing Christian worship and Christian community outside of the New Testament. As you read the letter, can you determine who were members of the Christian community and suggest who were not? What did the Christian community do (and not do)?

It is worth noting that Pliny's "discovery" of subjects practicing Christianity in Bithynia is belated. Some of those accused of being Christians tell him that they had ceased to practice Christianity twenty-five years earlier. Indeed, the following passage in the New Testament, written before Pliny, attests to the presence of Christians in Bithynia: "To the exiles of the Dispersion in Pontus, Galatia, Cappadocia, Asia, and Bithynia, who have been chosen and destined by God the Father and sanctified by the Spirit to be obedient to Jesus Christ and to be sprinkled with his blood" (I Peter 1:1–2). And Paul addressed a letter to the Christians in Rome some time before 60 CE—written in Greek. What does the lack of awareness by Roman magistrates and rulers, such as Pliny and Trajan, tell us about the spread of Christianity and its adherents?

Another exchange in an earlier letter with Trajan helps explain Pliny's concern about the "secret" meetings of Christians. In Letter 10.33, Pliny tells Trajan that he visited a town near Nicomedia, the capital city of Bithynia, where fire had damaged homes, the "Gerousia" (Elders' Council building), and the temple of Isis. The problem, Pliny reports, was lack of fire-fighting equipment, but even more, the inaction of the populace, who stood around and watched. Pliny tells Trajan that he has ordered the purchase of hoses and buckets, but he wants Trajan's approval for a brigade of firemen, no more than 150, whose organization he will personally attend to. In his response (Letter 10.34), Trajan commends Pliny for the equipment, but he denies the brigade: "Let's remember that that province, and those cities especially, have been disturbed by factions of that sort. When men have been organized for one purpose, whatever name we give them and for whatever cause, they soon become political groups." Why do you think Trajan wants to suppress "political groups"? What assumptions does this imply, and what does Trajan's concern communicate about the Roman attitude toward pluralism and diversity? Why would a temple to Isis, the Egyptian goddess, be acceptable but Christianity forbidden?

Brian S. Hook
Department of Classics

Letters between Pliny and Trajan on Christians

Letters of the Younger Pliny

XCVIII — To Trajan.

It is my custom, Sire, to refer to you in all cases where I do not feel sure, for who can better direct my doubts or inform my ignorance? I have never been present at any legal examination of the Christians, and I do not know, therefore, what are the usual penalties passed upon them, or the limits of those penalties, or how searching an inquiry should be made. I have hesitated a great deal in considering whether any distinctions should be drawn according to the ages of the accused; whether the weak should be punished as severely as the more robust; whether if they renounce their faith they should be pardoned, or whether the man who has once been a Christian should gain nothing by recanting; whether the name itself, even though otherwise innocent of crime, should be punished, or only the crimes that gather round it.

In the meantime, this is the plan which I have adopted in the case of those Christians who have been brought before me. I ask them whether they are Christians; if they say yes, then I repeat the question a second and a third time, warning them of the penalties it entails, and if they still persist, I order them to be taken away to prison. For I do not doubt that, whatever the character of the crime may be which they confess, their pertinacity and inflexible obstinacy certainly ought to be punished. There were others who showed similar mad folly whom I reserved to be sent to Rome, as they were Roman citizens.

Subsequently, as is usually the way, the very fact of my taking up this question led to a great increase of accusations, and a variety of cases were brought before me. A pamphlet was issued anonymously, containing the names of a number of people. Those who denied that they were or had been Christians and called upon the gods in the usual formula, reciting the words after me, those who offered incense and wine before your image, which I had given orders to be brought forward for this purpose, together with the statues of the deities—all such I considered should be discharged, especially as they cursed the name of Christ, which, it is said, those who are really Christians cannot be induced to do. Others, whose names were given me by an informer, first said that they were Christians and afterwards denied it, declaring that they had been but were so no longer, some of them having recanted many years before, and more than one so long as twenty years back. They all worshipped your image and the statues of the deities, and cursed the name of Christ. But they declared that the sum of their guilt or their error only amounted to this, that on a stated day they had been accustomed to meet before daybreak and to recite a hymn among themselves to Christ, as though he were a god, and that so far from binding themselves by oath to commit any crime, their oath was to abstain from theft, robbery, adultery, and from breach of faith, and not to deny trust money placed in their keeping when called upon to deliver it.

When this ceremony was concluded, it had been their custom to depart and meet again to take food, but it was of no special character and quite harmless, and they had ceased this practice after the edict in which, in accordance with your orders, I had forbidden all secret societies. I thought it the more necessary, therefore, to find out what truth there was in these statements by submitting two women, who were called deaconesses, to the torture, but I found nothing but a debased superstition carried to great lengths.

So I postponed my examination, and immediately consulted you. The matter seems to me worthy of your consideration, especially as there are so many people involved in the danger. Many persons of all ages, and of both sexes alike, are being brought into peril of their lives by their accusers, and the process will go on. For the contagion of this superstition has spread not only through the free cities, but into the villages and the rural districts, and yet it seems to me that it can be checked and set right. It is beyond doubt that the temples, which have been almost deserted, are beginning again to be thronged with worshippers, that the sacred rites which have for a long time been allowed to lapse are now being renewed, and that the food for the sacrificial victims is once more finding a sale, whereas, up to recently, a buyer was hardly to be found. From this it is easy to infer what vast numbers of people might be reclaimed, if only they were given an opportunity of repentance.

XCIX — Trajan to Pliny.

You have adopted the proper course, my dear Pliny, in examining into the cases of those who have been denounced to you as Christians, for no hard and fast rule can be laid down to meet a question of such wide extent. The Christians are not to be hunted out; if they are brought before you and the offence is proved, they are to be punished, but with this reservation—that if any one denies that he is a Christian and makes it clear that he is not, by offering prayers to our deities, then he is to be pardoned because of his recantation, however suspicious his past conduct may have been. But pamphlets published anonymously must not carry any weight whatever, no matter what the charge may be, for they are not only a precedent of the very worst type, but they are not in consonance with the spirit of our age.

Pliny, The Younger. *The Letters of the Younger Pliny.* Edited by John B. Firth and Heinrich Keil. London: W. Scott, 1900. Available at https://hdl.handle.net/2027/umn.31951002237967y?urlappend=%3Bseq=30 (Hathi Trust, Version 2018-12-05 17:40 UTC, accessed March 21, 2020).

BEYOND THE CLASSROOM

» Consider the response from Trajan, "But anonymously posted accusations ought to have no place in any prosecution," and imagine yourself in a position of leadership. How do you tell the difference between information relevant to a co-worker's performance and irrelevant gossip about that person?

Martyrdom of the Saints Perpetua and Felicity

SNAPSHOT BOX

LANGUAGE: Latin and Greek

DATE: 206–209 CE

LOCATION: Carthage (Tunisia)

GENRE: Religious testimonial

ETHNIC IDENTITY: Roman

TAGS: Death; Divination; Empire and Colonialism; Family; Hagiography; Sacrifice; Women and Gender

Introduction

What might make you prioritize some elements of your identity over others? How many elements of your identity are you allowed to choose and change? This source provides one exploration of these questions. Vibia Perpetua was a Roman woman living in Carthage at the beginning of the third century CE. As part of an aristocratic household, she may have had access to literacy education, something that would have been unusual for women at the time. A Christian **catechumen** (a person studying for baptism and admission to the church), Perpetua was awaiting baptism when she and a number of other young people were arrested, imprisoned, and eventually executed because their newly adopted religious beliefs precluded acts that were required of Roman citizens, such as declaring allegiance to the emperor. Perpetua was newly married, implying that she was quite young, and had an infant who had not yet been weaned.

Part of the text is represented as Perpetua's own words, though we cannot know how much of the document is her own composition. It is clear that the words passed through the hands of an unnamed **redactor**, someone who edits or compiles a text for publication, on their way to the most recent form. As is true with similar writings from the ancient world, there are several versions of the text: both Latin and Greek manuscripts as well as long and short versions. The larger document represents the work of at least three authors: Perpetua herself, Saturus, her fellow martyr, and the unnamed editor who

Timeline

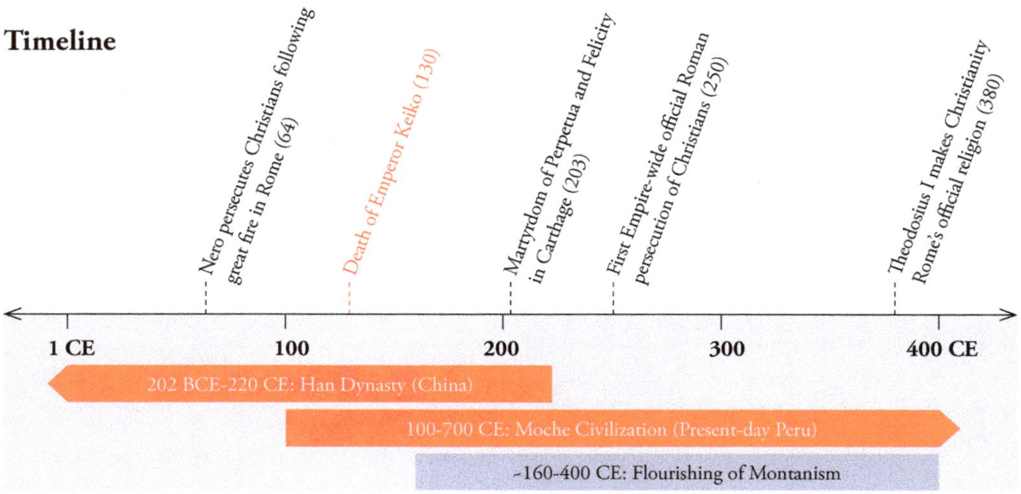

put it all together. If the presumed date of Perpetua's martyrdom (March 7, 203 CE) during the reign of Emperor Septimius Severus is correct, the document made its way into Christian readership fairly quickly, since it is mentioned in Tertullian's *De Anima (On the Soul)* around 210 CE and a number of other documents after that. It would have been of interest to Tertullian because Perpetua's experience could be interpreted to support the basic principle of **Montanism**, a Christian heresy that claimed new prophecies could be equal with or even surpass in authority those that came before. Augustine of Hippo also makes mention of Perpetua in *A Treatise on the Soul and Its Origin* more than two centuries after her martyrdom.

The text itself unfolds in four broad units: A brief introduction written by the unnamed redactor (Ch. 1), a section from Perpetua's own account of her story (Chs. 2–9), a section about the other martyrs who were with Perpetua (Chs. 10–16), and an account of events on the day of the games at which they are killed (Chs. 17–21).

Perpetua's gender is important in two ways. First, it may be the earliest and most extensive extant writing by a female author within Christianity, and thus of particular value to scholars inside and outside Christianity. Second, its language invites consideration of gender roles and norms shaping Roman society in the third century. The prescribed role of motherhood for women in her society allows us to appreciate the gravity of her choices. What does the celebration of Perpetua's martyrdom suggest about the role of gender in the Christian faith? Finally, Perpetua's visions also offer an opportunity to see the possible complexity in expressions of gender. Most noticeably, she "becomes a man" when she does battle in the arena with a gladiator. As you read, what other expressions of gender fluidity can you detect in Perpetua's visions and choices?

Dennis Lundblad
Humanities Program

PRE-READING PARS

1. What are two images or ideas that come to mind when you think about martyrdom?
2. What might be a context in which you choose not to identify with your own family?

The Martyrdom of Saints Perpetua and Felicity

I. If the old examples of the faith, which testify to the grace of God and lead to the edification of men, were written down so that by reading them God should be honored and man comforted—as if through a reexamination of those deeds—should we not set down new acts that serve each purpose equally? For these too will some day also be venerable and compelling for future generations, even if at the present time they are judged to be of lesser importance, due to the respect naturally afforded the past. But let those who would restrict the singular power of the one spirit to certain times understand this: that newer events are necessarily greater because they are more recent, because of the overflow of grace promised for the end of time. In the last days, says the Lord, "I will pour out my Spirit on all flesh; and their sons and daughters shall prophesy; and I will pour out my Spirit on my servants and handmaidens; and your young men shall see visions and your old men shall dream dreams." And we, who also acknowledge and honor the new prophecies and new visions as well, according to the promise, and regard the other virtues of the Holy Spirit as intended for the instruction of the church (to which church the same spirit was sent distributing all gifts to all, just as the Lord grants to each one); therefore, out of necessity we both proclaim and celebrate them in reading for the glory of God, lest any person who is weak or despairing in their faith should think that only the ancients received divine grace (either in the favor of martyrdom or of revelations), since God always grants what he has promised, as a proof to the unbelievers and as a kindness to believers. And so we also announce to you, our brothers and little sons, that which we have heard and touched, so that you who were present may be reminded of the glory of the Lord, and that you who know it now through hearing may have a sharing with the holy martyrs, and through them with our Lord Jesus Christ, to whom be glory and honor for ever and ever. Amen.

II. Some young catechumens were arrested: Revocatus and Felicity, his fellow slave; Saturninus; and Secundulus. And among these was also Vibia Perpetua—a woman well born, liberally educated, and honorably married, who had a father, mother, and two brothers, one of whom was also a catechumen. She had an infant son still at the breast and was about twenty-two years of age. From this point there follows a complete account of her martyrdom, as she left it, written in her own hand and in accordance with her own understanding.

III. "While," she said, "we were still with the prosecutors, my father, because of his love for me, wanted to change my mind and shake my resolve. 'Father,' I said, 'do you see this vase lying here, for example, this small water pitcher or whatever?' 'I see it,' he said. And I said to him: 'Can it be called by another name other than what it is?' And he said: 'No.' 'In the same way, I am unable to call myself other than what I am, a Christian.' Then my father, angered by this name, threw himself at me, in order to gouge out my eyes. But he only alarmed me and he left defeated, along with the arguments of the devil. Then for a few days, freed from my father, I gave thanks to the Lord and was refreshed by my father's absence. In the space of a few days we were baptized. The Spirit told me that nothing else should be sought from the water other than the endurance of the body. After a few days we were taken into the prison. I was terrified because I had never before known such darkness. Oh cruel day! The crowding of the mob made the heat stifling; and there was the extortion of the soldiers. Last of all, I was consumed with worry for my infant in that dungeon. Then Tertius and Pomponius, the blessed deacons who ministered to us, arranged by a bribe that we should be released for a few hours to revive ourselves in a better part of the prison. Then all left the prison and sought some time for themselves. I nursed my baby, who was now weak from hunger. In my worry for him, I spoke to my mother concerning the baby and comforted my brother. I entrusted my son to them. I suffered grievously when I saw how they suffered for me. I endured such worry for many days, and I arranged for my baby to stay in prison with me. Immediately I grew stronger, and I was relieved of the anxiety and worry I had for my baby. Suddenly the prison became my palace, so that I wanted to be there rather than anywhere else.

IV. "Then my brother said to me: 'Lady my sister, you are now greatly esteemed, so much so that you might ask for a vision, and it may be shown to you whether there will be suffering or freedom.' And I, who knew that I was able to speak with the Lord, whose great benefits I had known, confidently promised him, saying: 'Tomorrow, I will tell you.' And I asked, and this was shown to me. I see a bronze ladder of great length, reaching up to heaven, but so narrow that people could only climb up one at a time. And on the sides of the ladder, iron implements of every kind were attached. There were swords, lances, hooks, knives, and daggers, so that if anyone climbed up carelessly, or not looking upwards, he was torn to pieces and his flesh clung to the iron weapons. And there was a serpent of great size lying at the foot of the ladder, which would lie in wait for those who climbed and deterred them from climbing. And the first to go up was Saturus. (Because he had been our teacher and because he had not been present when we were seized, he later voluntarily handed himself over for our sake.) And he reached the top of the ladder and he turned back to me and said: 'Perpetua, I am waiting for you, but be careful that the serpent does not bite you.' And I said: 'In the name of Jesus Christ, he will not hurt me.' And from beneath the ladder itself, the serpent slowly stuck out its head, as if it feared me, and I stepped on its head and climbed up, as if it were the first step. And I saw an enormous garden and a white-haired man sitting in the middle of it dressed in shepherd's clothes, a big man, milking sheep. And standing around were many thousands dressed in white. And he raised his head, looked at me, and said: 'You are welcome here, child.' And he called me, and from the cheese that he had milked he gave me as it were a mouthful. And I received it in my cupped hands and ate it. And all those standing around said: 'Amen.' And I woke up at the sound of their voice, still eating some unknown sweet. And at once I told this to my brother. And we knew we would suffer, and we ceased to have any hope in this world.

V. "A few days later, a rumor circulated that we were to be given a hearing. My father arrived from the city, worn with worry; he climbed up to me, in order to change my mind, saying: 'My daughter, have pity on my gray hair, have pity on your father, if I am worthy to be called father by you, if with these hands I have raised you to this flower of youth, if I have preferred you to all your brothers, do not shame me among men. Think about your brothers, think about your mother and your mother's sister, think about your son who will not be able to live without you. Give up your pride; do not destroy us all. For, if you are punished, none of us will be able to speak freely again.' My father said these things to me, as a father would, out of his love for me, kissing my hands and throwing himself at my feet. Weeping, he no longer called me daughter, but lady. And I grieved for my father's anguish, because he alone of all my family would not rejoice in my suffering. And I tried to comfort him saying: 'What God has willed shall be done in the prisoner's platform. Know that we are no longer in our own power but in God's.' And in great sadness he left me.

VI. "On another day, while we were eating lunch, we were suddenly rushed off for a hearing. We arrived at the forum and immediately a rumor circulated throughout the neighborhood surrounding the forum, and a huge crowd had gathered. We climbed the platform. The others, having been questioned, confessed. Then they came to me. And my father appeared in that very place with my son and dragged me from the step saying: 'Offer the sacrifice. Have pity on your baby.' And Hilarianus, the procurator, who at that time had received the right of the sword on the death of proconsul Minucius Timinianus, said: 'Spare the gray hair of your father, spare your infant son. Offer the sacrifice for the health of the emperors.' 'I will not,' I answered. Hilarianus then said: 'Are you a Christian?' 'I am a Christian,' I replied. And when my father persisted in his efforts to change my mind, Hilarianus ordered him to be thrown to the ground and beaten with a rod. My father's suffering made me sad, almost as if I had been beaten. I grieved for his pitiable old age. Then Hilarianus pronounced sentence on us all and condemned us to the beasts. And we descended the platform and returned cheerfully to prison. But because my baby had become accustomed to nurse at my breasts and to stay with me in prison, I immediately sent Pomponius, the deacon, to ask my father for the child. But my father would not give him back. And as God willed, the baby no longer desired my breasts, nor did they ache and become inflamed, so that I might not be tormented by worry for my child or by the pain in my breasts.

VII. "A few days later while we were all praying, suddenly, in the midst of our prayer a voice came to me, and I cried out the name of Dinocrates. I was shocked because never before then had his name entered my mind, and I grieved as I remembered his fate. And I knew at once that I was worthy and that I ought to pray for him. And I began to pray intensely for him and groan before the Lord. Immediately, on that very night this vision was shown to me. I saw Dinocrates coming out of a dark place where there were many others; he was very hot, thirsting, and his face was covered with dirt and his skin was pale. And he had that wound on his face which was there when he died. This Dinocrates was my brother in the flesh, who died horribly at the age of seven from a cancer of the face. All men who saw it loathed the manner of his death. Therefore I prayed for him. But between him and me there was a great gulf so that we were not able to get close to each other. Moreover, in that place where Dinocrates was, there was a pool full of water with a rim that was higher than the height of the boy. And Dinocrates stretched himself up as if to drink. I was saddened because, although the pool had water in it, he was not able to drink because of the height of the rim. And I awakened, and I knew that my brother was suffering. But I trusted that I could help him in his suffering. And I prayed for him every day until we were transferred to the military prison, for we were to fight in the military games; it was on the birthday of Geta Caesar. And I prayed day and night for my brother with groans and tears so that this gift might be given to me.

VIII. "On the day on which we were kept in the stocks, this vision was shown to me. I saw that place which I had seen before, but now there was Dinocrates, his body clean, well dressed and refreshed, and where the wound was, I saw a scar. And that pool which I had seen earlier, I now saw with its rim lowered to the boy's navel, and he drew water from it without ceasing. And above the rim there was a golden cup full of water. And Dinocrates began to drink from it, but the cup never emptied. And when his thirst was quenched, he began to play in the water, rejoicing in the manner of children. And I woke up. I knew then that he was freed from his suffering.

IX. "Then after a few days, Pudens, the military adjutant, who was in charge of the prison, began to show us considerable respect, recognizing that there was some great power in us. He allowed many to visit us so that we were able to comfort one another. Now when the day of the games drew near, my father, devastated with worry, came to visit me, and he began to tear out his beard and to throw it on the ground. He then threw himself on his face and, cursing his years, spoke such words to me as might move creation itself. I grieved for his unhappy old age.

X. "On the day before we were to fight, I saw this in a vision: Pomponius, the deacon, had come to the door of the prison, and was knocking loudly. And I went out and opened the door for him. He was wearing a white unbelted robe, and multilaced sandals. And he said to me: 'Perpetua, we are awaiting you: come.' And he took me by the hand and we began to walk through places that were rugged and winding. And finally, after great difficulty, we arrived at the amphitheatre, all out of breath, and he led me into the middle of the arena, and he said to me 'Don't be afraid: I am here with you, and I will struggle with you.' And he went away. And I saw many people who were astonished; and, because I knew that I had been condemned to the beasts, I was puzzled that the beasts were not being turned loose on me. And a certain Egyptian, foul in appearance and intending to fight with me, came out against me, surrounded by his helpers. Handsome young men came to me as my helpers and supporters. And I was stripped naked, and I became a man. And my supporters began to rub me with oil, as they are accustomed to do for a match. And I saw that Egyptian on the other side rolling in the dust. Next there came out a man of such great size that he exceeded the height of the amphitheatre. He was wearing an unbelted robe, a purple garment with two stripes running down the middle of his chest, and decorated shoes made of gold and silver, and carrying a rod or wand as if a gladiator trainer, and a green branch on which there were golden apples. And he asked for silence and said: 'This Egyptian, if he defeats this woman, will kill her with the sword, but if she defeats him, she shall receive this branch.' And he departed. And we drew near to each other and began to throw punches at each other. He kept trying to grab hold of my feet while I kept kicking him in his face with my heels. And I was raised up into the air, and I began to strike him stepping on his face, as though I were unable to step on the ground. But when I saw that there was a hesitation, I joined my hands so that my fingers were knit together and I grabbed hold of his head. And he fell on his face and I stepped on his head. And the crowd began to shout and my supporters began to sing hymns. And I went to the gladiator trainer, and I took the branch. And he kissed me and he said to me: 'Daughter, peace be with you.' And I began to walk in triumph to the Gate of Life. And then I woke up. And I knew that I was going to fight with the devil and not with the beasts; but I knew that victory was to be mine. This is the story of what I did the day before the final conflict. But concerning the outcome of that contest, let whoever wishes to write about it, do so."

XI. But blessed Saturus made known his own vision, which he himself wrote. "We had suffered," he said, "and we departed from the flesh and we began to be carried towards the east by four angels, whose hands were not touching us. But we were moving, not on our backs facing upwards, but as if we were climbing a gentle hill. And when we were freed from this world, we saw a great light, and I said to Perpetua (for she was at my side): 'This is what the Lord promised us: we have received the promise.' And while we were being carried by the four angels, a great space appeared before us, which was like a formal garden, having rose trees and flowers of all sorts. The height of the trees was like that of cypress trees, and their leaves were falling without ceasing. There in the garden were four other angels more radiant than the others. When they saw us, they gave us honor, and they said with admiration to the other angels: 'Look, they are here, they are here.' And those four angels who were carrying us became fearful and put us down. And on foot we crossed the park by a broad path. There we found Jocundus and Saturninus and Artaxius, who were burned alive in the same persecution, and Quintus, who had died as a martyr in prison. And we asked of them where the rest were. And the angels said to us: 'First come, enter and greet the Lord.'

XII. "And we came near a place whose walls seemed to be made of light; and in front of the door of that place stood four angels, who clothed those who entered in white robes. And we entered in, and we heard a choir of voices chanting continually: 'Holy, Holy, Holy.' And we saw sitting in the same place what appeared to be an aged man. He had white hair and a youthful face, but we could not see his feet. And on his right and on his left were four elders, and behind them were standing many other elders. And entering in a spirit of wonder we stood before the throne, and four angels lifted us up, and we kissed him. And he stroked our faces with his hand. And the other elders said to us: 'Let us stand'; and we stood and offered each other the sign of peace. And the elders said to us: 'Go and play.' And I said to Perpetua: 'You have what you want.' And she said to me: 'Thanks be to God, because just as I was happy in the flesh, I am even happier here now.'

XIII. "And we went out and we saw in front of the gates Optatus the bishop on the right-hand side and Aspasius the priest and teacher on the left, separated and sorrowful. And they threw themselves at our feet and said: 'Make peace between us, for you have gone away and left us in this state.' And we said to them: 'Are you not our father and our priest? How can you throw yourselves at our feet?' And we were greatly moved and embraced them. And Perpetua began to speak to them in Greek, and we led them into a park under a rose tree. And while we were speaking with them, the angels said to them: 'Let them rest; and if you have any disagreements among yourselves, forgive one another.' And the angels admonished them and said to Optatus: 'Rebuke your people, because they are gathering around you, just as if they were returning from the chariot races, arguing about the different teams.' And it seemed to us as if they wanted to shut the gates. And we began to recognize there many of our brothers, and martyrs also. We were all nourished by an indescribable fragrance that satisfied us. Then, rejoicing, I awoke."

XIV. These were the extraordinary visions of the most blessed martyrs Saturus and Perpetua, which they themselves wrote. As for Secundulus, God called him from this world while still in prison, and by his earlier death, one not without favor, so that he might escape the fight with the beasts. Yet his flesh, if not his soul, knew the sword.

XV. As for Felicity, the Lord's favor touched her in this way. She was now in her eighth month (for she was pregnant when she was arrested). As the day of the games drew near, she was in agony, fearing that her pregnancy would spare her (since it was not permitted to punish pregnant women in public), and that she would pour forth her holy and innocent blood afterwards, along with common criminals. But also her fellow martyrs were deeply saddened that they might leave behind so good a friend, their companion, to travel alone on the road to their shared hope. And so, two days before the games, they joined together in one united supplication, groaning, and poured forth their prayer to the Lord. Immediately after their prayer her labor pains came upon her. And when—because of the natural difficulty associated with an eighth-month delivery—she suffered in her labor, one of the assistant jailers said to her: "If you are suffering so much now, what will you do when you are thrown to the beasts which you scorned when you refused to sacrifice?" And she replied: "Now I alone suffer what I am suffering, but then there will be another inside me, who will suffer for me, because I am going to suffer for him." And she gave birth to a baby girl, whom a certain sister brought up as her own daughter.

XVI. Therefore, since the Holy Spirit has given permission that the narrative of this contest be written down, and by such permission has willed it, although we are unworthy to add to the description of such great glory, nevertheless we shall carry out the command of the most holy Perpetua, or rather her sacred trust, adding one further example of her resolve and sublimity of spirit. The tribune treated them with great cruelty because of the warnings of the most devious of men. He feared that they would be carried off from prison through magical incantations. Perpetua said directly to his face: "Why do you not permit us to refresh ourselves—we, the most noble of the condemned belonging to Caesar, who are to fight on his birthday? Would it not be to your credit, if we were brought forth well fed?" The Tribune was horrified and flushed; and he ordered them to be treated more humanely, so that her brothers, and the others, might be granted the chance to visit and be refreshed with the prisoners, for now even the adjutant in charge of the prison was a believer.

XVII. And then on the day before the games, when at that last meal which they call "free," they partook, as far as it was possible, not of a "free meal" but a "love-feast." They boldly flung their words at the mob, threatening them with the judgment of God, bearing witness to the happiness they found in their suffering and mocking the curiosity of those who jostled to see them. Saturus said: "Will not tomorrow be enough for you? Why do you long to see that which you hate? Today our friends, tomorrow our enemies. But take a good look at our faces, so that you will be able to recognize us on that day." And so the crowd left the prison stunned, and many of them became believers.

XVIII. The day of their victory dawned, and they marched from the prison to the amphitheatre, joyously, as if going to heaven, their faces radiant; and if by chance they trembled, it was from joy and not from fear. Perpetua followed, with a shining face and a calm step, as a wife of Christ and darling of God, and the intensity of her stare caused the spectators to look away. Likewise Felicity rejoiced that she had given birth safely, so that she might fight with the beasts—advancing from blood to blood, from the midwife to a net-bearing gladiator—now to be washed after child-birth in a second baptism. And when they were led to the gate, they were forced to put on costumes; the men, those of the priests of Saturn, and the women, those of the priestesses of Ceres. But that nobleminded woman fiercely resisted this to the end. She said: "We came here freely, so that our freedom might not be violated, and we handed over our lives so that we would not be forced to do anything like this. We had this agreement with you." Injustice recognized justice. The tribune agreed that they should be brought in dressed simply as they were. Perpetua was singing a hymn, already trampling on the head of the Egyptian. Revocatus, Saturninus, and Saturus were threatening the spectators. Then, when they passed under the gaze of Hilarianus, they began to say to him through gestures and nods: "You [judge] us but God will [judge] you." The crowd, angered by this, demanded that they be whipped along a line of beast-hunting gladiators. And they gave thanks that they had obtained some share in the Lord's sufferings.

XIX. But he who said: "Ask and you shall receive" gave to those who asked the death that each desired. For whenever they spoke among themselves concerning their desire for martyrdom, Saturninus declared that he wished to be thrown to all the different kinds of beasts so that he might wear a more glorious crown. And so at the beginning of the spectacle, he and Revocatus were attacked by a leopard, and then while on the platform, they were charged by a bear. Saturus hated nothing more than a bear, and now he was confident that he would die from one bite of a leopard. However, he was offered to a wild boar. Yet it was the hunter who had tied him to the wild boar who was gored by the same beast, and died a few days after the games. Saturus himself was only dragged. And when he was tied on the bridge awaiting the bear, the bear refused to leave its cage. And so Saturus, unhurt, was called back for the second time.

XX. For the young women, however, the devil prepared a wild cow—not a traditional practice—matching their sex with that of the beast. And so stripped naked and covered only with nets, they were brought out again. The crowd shuddered, seeing that one was a delicate young girl and that the other had recently given birth, as her breasts still dripping with milk. So they were called back and dressed in unbelted robes. Perpetua was thrown down first and fell on her loins. Then sitting up, she noticed that her tunic was ripped on the side, and so she drew it up to cover her thigh, more mindful of her modesty than her suffering. Then she requested a pin and she tied up her tousled hair; for it was not right for a martyr to suffer with disheveled hair, since it might appear that she was grieving in her moment of glory. Then she got up; and when she saw Felicity crushed to the ground, she went over to her, gave her her hand and helped her up. And the two stood side by side. The cruelty of the crowd now being sated, they were called back to the Gate of Life. There Perpetua was received by a certain Rusticus, also a catechumen, who clung to her side. She awakened, as if from a sleep—she was so deep in the spirit and in ecstasy—and looked about her, and said, to the amazement of all: "When are we to be thrown to the mad cow, or whatever it is?" And when she heard that it had already happened, she refused at first to believe it until she noticed certain marks of physical violence on her body and her clothing. Then after calling her brother and the catechumen, she spoke to them, saying: "Stand fast in faith and love one another, and do not lose heart because of our sufferings."

XXI. At another gate, Saturus was exhorting the soldier Pudens, saying: "It is exactly," he said, "as I imagined and predicted. Until now no beast has touched me. And now you must believe this with all your heart: See, I will go in there and be killed by one bite from a leopard." And immediately at the end of the game, a leopard rushed out and bit Saturus. He was so covered with blood from one bite that as he was returning, the crowd roared in witness to his second baptism: "A saving bath, a saving bath." For truly one was saved who had bathed in such manner. Then he said to the soldier Pudens: "Farewell, remember the faith and me; and do not let these things trouble you but strengthen you." At the same time he asked Pudens for the small ring from his finger, and dipping it into his wound, he returned it to him as a legacy, leaving it to him as a pledge and a memorial of his blood. Then, being now unconscious, he was thrown with the others in the accustomed place to have his throat cut. But the crowd demanded that they be brought back to the middle of the arena, so that as the sword penetrated the bodies of the martyrs their eyes might be accomplices to the murder. The martyrs got up unaided and moved to where the crowd wished them to be. First they kissed each other so that the ritual of peace would seal their martyrdom. The others, in silence and without moving, received the sword's thrust, and particularly Saturus, who had first climbed up the ladder, was the first to give up his spirit. For once again he was waiting for Perpetua. Perpetua, however—so that she might taste something of the pain—screamed out in agony as she was pierced between the bones. And when the right hand of the novice gladiator wavered, she herself guided it to her throat. Perhaps such a woman, feared as she was by the unclean spirit, could not have been killed unless she herself had willed it. O bravest and most blessed martyrs! O truly called and chosen for the glory of our Lord Jesus Christ! Anyone who praises, honors, and adores his glory surely should read these deeds, which are no less worthy than the old ones for building up the church. For these new deeds of courage too may witness that one and the same Holy Spirit is always working among us even now, along with God, the Father almighty, and his Son, our Lord, Jesus Christ, to whom is glory and endless power for ever and ever. Amen.

The Passion of Perpetua and Felicity. Translated by Thomas J. Heffernan, 125–35. New York: Oxford University Press, 2012.

POST-READING PARS

1. What aspects of martyrdom in this reading were similar to or contrasted with your own images or ideas?
2. Why do you think Perpetua's father is so upset about her choice? Why do you think her mother and husband have such limited roles in the story?

Inquiry Corner

Content Question(s):	**Critical Question(s):**
In what ways is Perpetua's gender significant or irrelevant in her story? What social standing and relationships exist among various people mentioned in the story, including the original group of catechumens, family members, fellow martyrs, and even the Roman officials who were in charge of the prison and the games? How does Christianity affect these relationships?	Why and how might an act of martyrdom and the story about it be important for a community? What is the role of agency in choosing death?
Comparative Question(s):	**Connection Question(s):**
Compare and contrast with other course readings in which religion clashes with politics, gender, class, or other social structures of identity.	In what ways is the act of compromising positive or negative? What are some of the factors you consider when you decide whether to compromise or not?

from the New Testament, Matthew 5–7 (Sermon on the Mount)

SNAPSHOT

LANGUAGE: Koine Greek

DATE: 70–90 CE

LOCATION: Palestine

GENRE: Wisdom literature

TAGS: Class and Wealth; Ethics and Morality; Rhetoric and Propaganda

Introduction

What is a **gospel**? The word "gospel" is derived from an Old English word meaning "good news," which is a direct translation of the Greek word *euangelion*. This "good news" was a new genre created by early Christian authors that combined elements of **hagiography** (biography of religious figures from an insider perspective), didactic teaching, and thaumaturgy (miracle stories) and other genres. The four Gospels that became canonized—those of Matthew, Mark, Luke, and John—were not the only ones written, but these were considered the oldest and most authoritative, since they were perceived to be written by those with direct knowledge of Jesus's life.

The Sermon on the Mount appears in the Gospel of Matthew, chapters 5–7; it received that name from St. Augustine, who wrote the first commentary devoted exclusively to those chapters in 393 CE. There is similar material in the Gospel of Luke 6:17–49, but it is far less extensive. In Matthew, the Sermon on the Mount is presented as one event, but it seems more likely that it is a compilation, or **epitome**, of Jesus's basic teachings that his followers should know. It probably represents the sorts of things that Jesus said frequently in many settings. It is the source of many familiar, even proverbial, lines, such as "turning the other cheek" (Matt. 5:39), "the salt of the earth" (Matt. 5:13), and "wolves in sheep's clothing" (Matt. 7:15). Also in these chapters we find the Beatitudes (Matt. 5:3–10), the so-called Lord's Prayer (Matt. 6:9–13), and the "Golden Rule," with which Jesus

Timeline

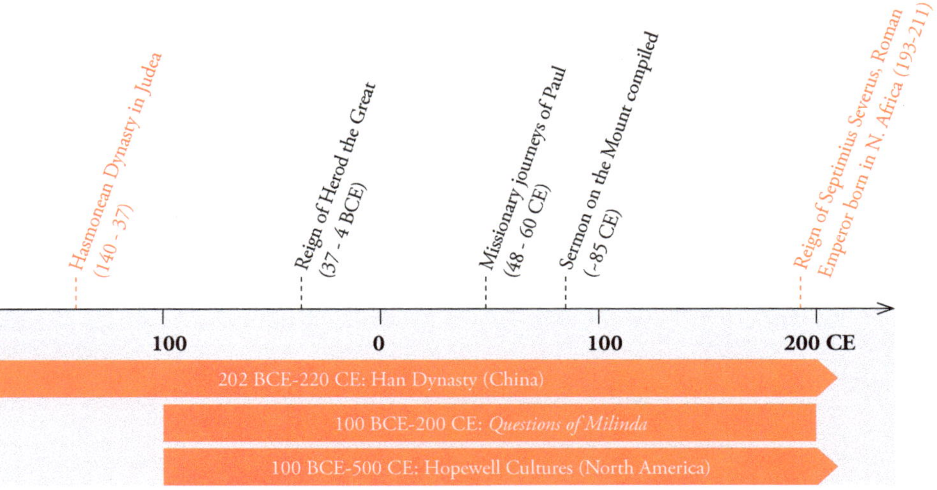

sums up "the Law and the Prophets" by saying that we should treat others as we want to be treated (Matt. 7:12). Have you encountered versions of the golden rule in other contexts?

A general theme that animates much of the Sermon on the Mount prioritizes one's internal and private processes and attitudes over the external and public behaviors. This may seem counterintuitive: isn't the right action more important than the right attitude? Jesus is not diminishing the importance of actions but rather emphasizing the role of our motivations and dispositions in relation to those actions. In several cases, Jesus broadens specific instructions of the **Torah**, or Law, in ways that move from behavior to attitude. For example, the Law prohibits murder and adultery, but Jesus condemns anger and lust as well. At other times, Jesus extends the reach of the moral instruction, as when he takes the commandment to love one's neighbor and says that his followers should love their enemies as well (Matt. 5:43–44). He claims that he has "not come to abolish" the Law and the Prophets "but to fulfill them" (Matt. 5:17). What he meant by "fulfilling" is not completely clear, but it may imply some "reframing" of the moral instructions. How does he reframe attitudes toward the poor, the grieving, the oppressed, and all other marginalized groups?

Jesus's emphasis on our internal motivations and attitudes is not unique. Buddha, Confucius, and Aristotle, among others, taught that a virtuous character was a process of ethical cultivation and habitual practice. But Jesus is working in a different context. He often contrasts his approach with that of the **Pharisees**, a Jewish sect that prescribed strict adherence to the written texts and the traditions surrounding them. Pharisaic righteousness apparently consisted of this strict legal adherence. Jesus cites examples of Pharisees being generous, or praying, for the sake of being seen and praised. In response, Jesus tells his followers that they should act "in secret" and that their righteousness must exceed the "righteousness of the Pharisees" if they want to enter the "kingdom of heaven" (Matt. 5:20). How does this compare to other ethical systems? Does Confucius or Aristotle teach that one can do the "right" thing for the "wrong" reason?

While some of the Sermon on the Mount stresses simplification, it presents a very high ethical standard. What resources do humans draw on to cultivate mental and embodied ethical dispositions in order to love enemies, avoid anger and lust, and not to worry about tomorrow? Jesus pushed even further: "Be perfect, therefore, as your heavenly Father is perfect" (Matt. 5:48). Jesus seems to regard these instructions as possible. What might "perfection" mean as a process, and how do other ethical systems approach that idea? The Sermon on the Mount concludes with another now familiar image. Jesus says that those who hear his words and do them are like those who build a house on rock, while those who hear but do not do them have built a house on sand.

Brian S. Hook
Department of Classics

PRE-READING PARS

1. Note three to five qualities that come to mind when thinking of a "good" person.
2. In what areas of your life are you required to follow a set of rules? How do you personally respond to those rules?

Sermon on the Mount

Matthew 5

Introduction to the Sermon on the Mount

Now when Jesus saw the crowds, he went up on a mountainside and sat down. His
disciples came to him, 2 and he began to teach them.

The Beatitudes

He said:

3 "Blessed are the poor in spirit, for theirs is the kingdom of heaven.
4 Blessed are those who mourn, for they will be comforted.
5 Blessed are the meek, for they will inherit the earth.
6 Blessed are those who hunger and thirst for righteousness, for they will be filled.
7 Blessed are the merciful, for they will be shown mercy.
8 Blessed are the pure in heart, for they will see God.
9 Blessed are the peacemakers, for they will be called children of God.
10 Blessed are those who are persecuted because of righteousness, for theirs is the
kingdom of heaven.
11 "Blessed are you when people insult you, persecute you and falsely say all kinds
of evil against you because of me. 12 Rejoice and be glad, because great is your reward
in heaven, for in the same way they persecuted the prophets who were before you.

Salt and Light

13 "You are the salt of the earth. But if the salt loses its saltiness, how can it be made
salty again? It is no longer good for anything, except to be thrown out and trampled
underfoot.
14 "You are the light of the world. A town built on a hill cannot be hidden. 15 Neither do people light a lamp and put it under a bowl. Instead they put it on its stand,
and it gives light to everyone in the house. 16 In the same way, let your light shine
before others, that they may see your good deeds and glorify your Father in heaven.

The Fulfillment of the Law

17 "Do not think that I have come to abolish the Law or the Prophets; I have not come to abolish them but to fulfill them. 18 For truly I tell you, until heaven and earth disappear, not the smallest letter, not the least stroke of a pen, will by any means disappear from the Law until everything is accomplished. 19 Therefore anyone who sets aside one of the least of these commands and teaches others accordingly will be called least in the kingdom of heaven, but whoever practices and teaches these commands will be called great in the kingdom of heaven. 20 For I tell you that unless your righteousness surpasses that of the Pharisees and the teachers of the law, you will certainly not enter the kingdom of heaven.

Murder

21 "You have heard that it was said to the people long ago, 'You shall not murder, and anyone who murders will be subject to judgment.' 22 But I tell you that anyone who is angry with a brother or sister[301] will be subject to judgment. Again, anyone who says to a brother or sister, 'Raca,'[302] is answerable to the court. And anyone who says, 'You fool!' will be in danger of the fire of hell.

23 "Therefore, if you are offering your gift at the altar and there remember that your brother or sister has something against you, 24 leave your gift there in front of the altar. First go and be reconciled to them; then come and offer your gift.

25 "Settle matters quickly with your adversary who is taking you to court. Do it while you are still together on the way, or your adversary may hand you over to the judge, and the judge may hand you over to the officer, and you may be thrown into prison. 26 Truly I tell you, you will not get out until you have paid the last penny.

Adultery

27 "You have heard that it was said, 'You shall not commit adultery.' 28 But I tell you that anyone who looks at a woman lustfully has already committed adultery with her in his heart. 29 If your right eye causes you to stumble, gouge it out and throw it away. It is better for you to lose one part of your body than for your whole body to be thrown into hell. 30 And if your right hand causes you to stumble, cut it off and throw it away. It is better for you to lose one part of your body than for your whole body to go into hell.

301. The Greek word for brother or sister (*adelphos*) refers here to a fellow disciple, whether man or woman; also in verse 23.

302. An Aramaic term of contempt.

Divorce

31 "It has been said, 'Anyone who divorces his wife must give her a certificate of divorce.' 32 But I tell you that anyone who divorces his wife, except for sexual immo-
rality, makes her the victim of adultery, and anyone who marries a divorced woman
commits adultery.

Oaths

33 "Again, you have heard that it was said to the people long ago, 'Do not break your
oath, but fulfill to the Lord the vows you have made.' 34 But I tell you, do not swear
an oath at all: either by heaven, for it is God's throne; 35 or by the earth, for it is his
footstool; or by Jerusalem, for it is the city of the Great King. 36 And do not swear by
your head, for you cannot make even one hair white or black. 37 All you need to say
is simply 'Yes' or 'No'; anything beyond this comes from evil.

Eye for Eye

38 "You have heard that it was said, 'Eye for eye, and tooth for tooth.' 39 But I tell you,
do not resist an evil person. If anyone slaps you on the right cheek, turn to them the
other cheek also. 40 And if anyone wants to sue you and take your shirt, hand over
your coat as well. 41 If anyone forces you to go one mile, go with them two miles.
42 Give to the one who asks you, and do not turn away from the one who wants to
borrow from you.

Love for Enemies

43 "You have heard that it was said, 'Love your neighbor and hate your enemy.' 44
But I tell you, love your enemies and pray for those who persecute you, 45 that you
may be children of your Father in heaven. He causes his sun to rise on the evil and
the good, and sends rain on the righteous and the unrighteous. 46 If you love those
who love you, what reward will you get? Are not even the tax collectors doing that?
47 And if you greet only your own people, what are you doing more than others? Do
not even pagans do that? 48 Be perfect, therefore, as your heavenly Father is perfect.

Matthew 6

Giving to the Needy

"Be careful not to practice your righteousness in front of others to be seen by them.
If you do, you will have no reward from your Father in heaven.

2 "So when you give to the needy, do not announce it with trumpets, as the hypocrites do in the synagogues and on the streets, to be honored by others. Truly I tell

you, they have received their reward in full. 3 But when you give to the needy, do not let your left hand know what your right hand is doing, 4 so that your giving may be in secret. Then your Father, who sees what is done in secret, will reward you.

Prayer

5 "And when you pray, do not be like the hypocrites, for they love to pray standing in the synagogues and on the street corners to be seen by others. Truly I tell you, they have received their reward in full. 6 But when you pray, go into your room, close the door and pray to your Father, who is unseen. Then your Father, who sees what is done in secret, will reward you. 7 And when you pray, do not keep on babbling like pagans, for they think they will be heard because of their many words. 8 Do not be like them, for your Father knows what you need before you ask him.

9 "This, then, is how you should pray: "'Our Father in heaven, hallowed be your name, 10 your kingdom come, your will be done, on earth as it is in heaven. 11 Give us today our daily bread. 12 And forgive us our debts, as we also have forgiven our debtors. 13 And lead us not into temptation,[303] but deliver us from evil.'

14 For if you forgive other people when they sin against you, your heavenly Father will also forgive you. 15 But if you do not forgive others their sins, your Father will not forgive your sins.

Fasting

16 "When you fast, do not look somber as the hypocrites do, for they disfigure their faces to show others they are fasting. Truly I tell you, they have received their reward in full. 17 But when you fast, put oil on your head and wash your face, 18 so that it will not be obvious to others that you are fasting, but only to your Father, who is unseen; and your Father, who sees what is done in secret, will reward you.

Treasures in Heaven

19 "Do not store up for yourselves treasures on earth, where moths and vermin destroy, and where thieves break in and steal. 20 But store up for yourselves treasures in heaven, where moths and vermin do not destroy, and where thieves do not break in and steal. 21 For where your treasure is, there your heart will be also.

22 "The eye is the lamp of the body. If your eyes are healthy,[304] your whole body will be full of light. 23 But if your eyes are unhealthy, your whole body will be full of darkness. If then the light within you is darkness, how great is that darkness!

24 "No one can serve two masters. Either you will hate the one and love the other,

303. The Greek word for *temptation* can also mean *testing*.

304. The Greek word for *healthy* here implies *generous*, and *unhealthy* implies *stingy*.

or you will be devoted to the one and despise the other. You cannot serve both God and money.

Do Not Worry

25 "Therefore I tell you, do not worry about your life, what you will eat or drink; or about your body, what you will wear. Is not life more than food, and the body more than clothes? 26 Look at the birds of the air; they do not sow or reap or store away in barns, and yet your heavenly Father feeds them. Are you not much more valuable than they? 27 Can any one of you by worrying add a single hour to your life?

28 "And why do you worry about clothes? See how the flowers of the field grow. They do not labor or spin. 29 Yet I tell you that not even Solomon in all his splendor was dressed like one of these. 30 If that is how God clothes the grass of the field, which is here today and tomorrow is thrown into the fire, will he not much more clothe you—you of little faith? 31 So do not worry, saying, 'What shall we eat?' or 'What shall we drink?' or 'What shall we wear?' 32 For the pagans run after all these things, and your heavenly Father knows that you need them. 33 But seek first his kingdom and his righteousness, and all these things will be given to you as well. 34 Therefore do not worry about tomorrow, for tomorrow will worry about itself. Each day has enough trouble of its own.

Matthew 7

Judging Others

1 "Do not judge, or you too will be judged. 2 For in the same way you judge others, you will be judged, and with the measure you use, it will be measured to you.

3 "Why do you look at the speck of sawdust in your brother's eye and pay no attention to the plank in your own eye? 4 How can you say to your brother, 'Let me take the speck out of your eye,' when all the time there is a plank in your own eye? 5 You hypocrite, first take the plank out of your own eye, and then you will see clearly to remove the speck from your brother's eye.

6 "Do not give dogs what is sacred; do not throw your pearls to pigs. If you do, they may trample them under their feet, and turn and tear you to pieces.

Ask, Seek, Knock

7 "Ask and it will be given to you; seek and you will find; knock and the door will be opened to you. 8 For everyone who asks receives; the one who seeks finds; and to the one who knocks, the door will be opened.

9 "Which of you, if your son asks for bread, will give him a stone? 10 Or if he asks for a fish, will give him a snake? 11 If you, then, though you are evil, know how to give

good gifts to your children, how much more will your Father in heaven give good gifts
to those who ask him! 12 So in everything, do to others what you would have them
do to you, for this sums up the Law and the Prophets.

The Narrow and Wide Gates

13 "Enter through the narrow gate. For wide is the gate and broad is the road that
leads to destruction, and many enter through it. 14 But small is the gate and narrow
the road that leads to life, and only a few find it.

True and False Prophets

15 "Watch out for false prophets. They come to you in sheep's clothing, but inwardly
they are ferocious wolves. 16 By their fruit you will recognize them. Do people pick
grapes from thornbushes, or figs from thistles? 17 Likewise, every good tree bears
good fruit, but a bad tree bears bad fruit. 18 A good tree cannot bear bad fruit, and
a bad tree cannot bear good fruit. 19 Every tree that does not bear good fruit is cut
down and thrown into the fire. 20 Thus, by their fruit you will recognize them.

True and False Disciples

21 "Not everyone who says to me, 'Lord, Lord,' will enter the kingdom of heaven,
but only the one who does the will of my Father who is in heaven. 22 Many will say
to me on that day, 'Lord, Lord, did we not prophesy in your name and in your name
drive out demons and in your name perform many miracles?' 23 Then I will tell them
plainly, 'I never knew you. Away from me, you evildoers!'

The Wise and Foolish Builders

24 "Therefore everyone who hears these words of mine and puts them into practice is
like a wise man who built his house on the rock. 25 The rain came down, the streams
rose, and the winds blew and beat against that house; yet it did not fall, because it had
its foundation on the rock. 26 But everyone who hears these words of mine and does
not put them into practice is like a foolish man who built his house on sand. 27 The
rain came down, the streams rose, and the winds blew and beat against that house,
and it fell with a great crash."

28 When Jesus had finished saying these things, the crowds were amazed at his
teaching, 29 because he taught as one who had authority, and not as their teachers
of the law.

POST-READING PARS

1. How does the "righteousness of the Pharisees" contrast with the "righteousness" that Jesus urges his followers to have?
2. Identify two or three teaching techniques or rhetorical methods Jesus uses to connect with his audience.

Inquiry Corner

Content Question(s):	**Critical Question(s):**
In what sense are the "poor in spirit" and "those who mourn" supposed to be blessed?	Does the ethical content of the Sermon on the Mount seem focused on the community or on the individual? If it is communally oriented, what sort of community is envisioned?
Comparative Question(s):	**Connection Question(s):**
How does Jesus's ethical instruction in the Sermon on the Mount compare with Buddha's instructions in the Four Noble Truths, especially in the Eightfold Path, or with Confucius's *Analects*?	Contemporary activists including Mahatma Gandhi and Dr. Martin Luther King Jr. were inspired by the Sermon on the Mount in articulating their versions of the nonviolence resistance movement. What do you see in these passages that would support working toward social transformation?

from New Testament, Selected Passages on Wealth and Poverty

Introduction

What does it mean to be wealthy? Is wealth a sign of divine blessing or a manifestation of human vice? It is not surprising that both perspectives are present in different religious texts, because such texts present complex views of the relationship between the human and divine worlds. These include views of the ways of attaining salvation, of our relationships to each other, and to the material world. The Christian New Testament presents complex views on many of these subjects, including the topics of wealth and poverty.

It is important to note that in the ancient Mediterranean world, the setting of the following passages, wealth primarily takes the form of land—no one rose into a "middle class" by starting a successful carpentry business. Land was usually inherited, and wealth was concentrated in the hands of a very few elite. They also held most of the political power. The vast majority of people lived lives of basic subsistence and had minimal political power. Theirs was a poverty of access to power and opportunity as well as a poverty of material goods. What contemporary connections do you see between wealth and political power?

The New Testament Gospels attribute complex views of wealth and poverty to Jesus. He clearly advocates for the poor—but he never calls for revolution. It is not always easy to draw a general paradigm from anything that Jesus says about possessions. At first glance, the stories of the rich young man in Mark 10:17–27 and

SNAPSHOT BOX

LANGUAGE: Koine Greek

DATE: 60–90 CE

LOCATION: Eastern Mediterranean

GENRE: Scripture

ETHNIC/RELIGIOUS IDENTITY: Jewish

TAGS: Asceticism; Class and Wealth

Timeline

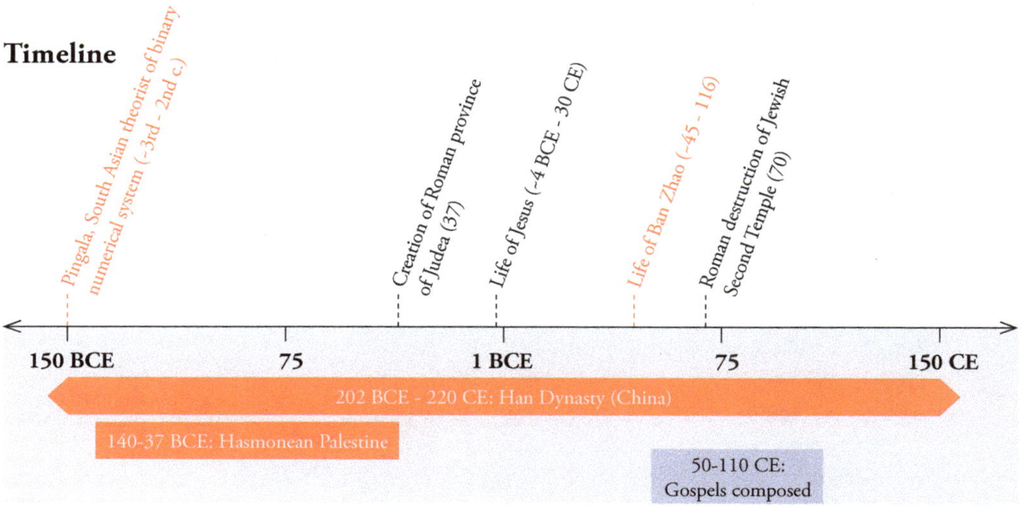

of the rich man and Lazarus in Luke 16:19–31 seem to advocate for **asceticism** in maintaining that if one denies or is denied material comforts, one will be better for it and will even receive treasures in heaven (Matthew 6:19–21). However, other New Testament scriptures, including those attributing miracles to Jesus of turning water into wine and feeding at least 5,000 people with five loaves of bread and two fish, recognize value in material goods and basic human needs.

The story of the rich man and Lazarus raises some questions. For instance, to what extent should cost-benefit analysis of laying up treasures in heaven be part of one's moral calculus? Should believers be as shrewd in calculating faith and material goods as others are in calculating expenses and financial matters, as Jesus seems to suggest in the parable of the dishonest manager told in Luke 16:1–13? Is the different treatment of the rich man and Lazarus due to differences in their earthly wealth, or might the issue be how the rich acquire their wealth, as other passages suggest (James 5:1–6)?

In Mark 10:17–27 the rich young man, at least in his own eyes, has fully adhered to God's commandments. Yet, Jesus says he is still found lacking if he does not sell all of his possessions and give to the poor. What lessons might we learn from this story? Might there be gradations of living the good life, and relinquishment of goods might be a step toward perfection as the same story in Matthew 19:16–22 suggests? Might the issue not be with material goods themselves, but with our relationship to them? In considering this, note that Jesus did not ask the wealthy Zacchaeus to sell all of his possessions in Luke 19:1–10 as he did with the rich young man, but Zacchaeus willingly offered to give the poor half of his possessions and to restore anyone he had defrauded fourfold. More directly, might the issue be the love of money rather than the possession of it?[305]

The earliest interpreters of Christian scripture, the Patristic writers who lived between the first and fifth centuries CE, saw a range of different lessons reflected in passages such as the story of the rich young man.[306] These interpretations ranged from taking the story figuratively to literally. Clement of Alexandria advocated that one should be indifferent or unattached to one's own wealth.[307] Alternately, Basil the Great contended that the rich young man was even lying when he claimed he follows the law since he did not share his wealth. Basil understood the story in social rather than individual terms: how could one love one's neighbor as the law required (Matt. 22:36–40) if one does not share wealth?[308] In the early Church, described in

305. See, for example, 1 Timothy 6:10 and Hebrews 13:5.

306. Translation of relevant Patristic writings can be found in Helen Rhee, ed., *Wealth and Poverty in Early Christianity. Ad Fontes: Early Christian Sources*. Minneapolis, MN: Fortress Press, 2017.

307. Clement of Alexandria, "The Rich Man's Salvation," in *Wealth and Poverty in Early Christianity*, 15.

308. Basil the Great, "Homily 7: To the Rich," in *Wealth and Poverty in Early Christianity*, 61, 63.

the New Testament's Acts of the Apostles, early Christians in and around Jerusalem sold their possessions and held everything in common (Acts 4:32–5:11). But Ananias and Sapphira held back some of their possessions, lied that they did not, and were seemingly struck dead by God as a result. Certainly, questions we should ask include: Were the selling of possessions and holding everything in common dictates of the faith or responses to it? Did Ananias and Sapphira die because they held back possessions or because they lied about it? Whatever the answers, the story still matters. For instance, some of the great modern debates about socialism and capitalism find roots in different interpretations of this scripture. In particular, the slogan popularized by Karl Marx, "from each according to his ability, to each according to his need," draws directly from Acts 2:44–45 and 4:34–35.[309] Yet, the act of giving in these passages is generally understood to be voluntary rather than required.

Robert Tatum
Department of Economics

309. Craig L. Blomberg, "Neither Capitalism nor Socialism: A Biblical Theology of Economics," *Journal of Markets and Morality* 15, 1 (Spring 2012): 210–11.

New Testament Passages on Wealth and Poverty

Matthew 6:19–34

Treasures in Heaven

19 "Do not store up for yourselves treasures on earth, where moths and vermin destroy, and where thieves break in and steal. 20 But store up for yourselves treasures in heaven, where moths and vermin do not destroy, and where thieves do not break in and steal. 21 For where your treasure is, there your heart will be also. 22 "The eye is the lamp of the body. If your eyes are healthy,[310] your whole body will be full of light. 23 But if your eyes are unhealthy,[311] your whole body will be full of darkness. If then the light within you is darkness, how great is that darkness! 24 "No one can serve two masters. Either you will hate the one and love the other, or you will be devoted to the one and despise the other. You cannot serve both God and money.

Do Not Worry

25 "Therefore I tell you, do not worry about your life, what you will eat or drink; or about your body, what you will wear. Is not life more than food, and the body more than clothes? 26 Look at the birds of the air; they do not sow or reap or store away in barns, and yet your heavenly Father feeds them. Are you not much more valuable than they? 27 Can any one of you by worrying add a single hour to your life?[312] 28 "And why do you worry about clothes? See how the flowers of the field grow. They do not labor or spin. 29 Yet I tell you that not even Solomon in all his splendor was dressed like one of these. 30 If that is how God clothes the grass of the field, which is here today and tomorrow is thrown into the fire, will he not much more clothe you—you of little faith? 31 So do not worry, saying, 'What shall we eat?' or 'What shall we drink?' or 'What shall we wear?' 32 For the pagans run after all these things, and your heavenly Father knows that you need them. 33 But seek first his kingdom and his righteousness, and all these things will be given to you as well. 34 Therefore do not worry about tomorrow, for tomorrow will worry about itself. Each day has enough trouble of its own.

Mark 10:17–27

The Rich and the Kingdom of God

17 As Jesus started on his way, a man ran up to him and fell on his knees before him. "Good teacher," he asked, "what must I do to inherit eternal life?" 18 "Why do you

310. Matthew 6:22. The Greek word for *healthy* here implies *generous*.
311. Matthew 6:23. The Greek word for *unhealthy* here implies *stingy*.
312. Matthew 6:27. Or *single cubit to your height*.

call me good?" Jesus answered. "No one is good—except God alone. 19 You know the commandments: 'You shall not murder, you shall not commit adultery, you shall not steal, you shall not give false testimony, you shall not defraud, honor your father and mother.'"[313] 20 "Teacher," he declared, "all these I have kept since I was a boy." 21 Jesus looked at him and loved him. "One thing you lack," he said. "Go, sell everything you have and give to the poor, and you will have treasure in heaven. Then come, follow me." 22 At this the man's face fell. He went away sad, because he had great wealth. 23 Jesus looked around and said to his disciples, "How hard it is for the rich to enter the kingdom of God!" 24 The disciples were amazed at his words. But Jesus said again, "Children, how hard it is[314] to enter the kingdom of God! 25 It is easier for a camel to go through the eye of a needle than for someone who is rich to enter the kingdom of God." 26 The disciples were even more amazed, and said to each other, "Who then can be saved?" 27 Jesus looked at them and said, "With man this is impossible, but not with God; all things are possible with God."

Luke 16:19–31

The Rich Man and Lazarus

19 "There was a rich man who was dressed in purple and fine linen and lived in luxury every day. 20 At his gate was laid a beggar named Lazarus, covered with sores 21 and longing to eat what fell from the rich man's table. Even the dogs came and licked his sores. 22 "The time came when the beggar died and the angels carried him to Abraham's side. The rich man also died and was buried. 23 In Hades, where he was in torment, he looked up and saw Abraham far away, with Lazarus by his side. 24 So he called to him, 'Father Abraham, have pity on me and send Lazarus to dip the tip of his finger in water and cool my tongue, because I am in agony in this fire.' 25 "But Abraham replied, 'Son, remember that in your lifetime you received your good things, while Lazarus received bad things, but now he is comforted here and you are in agony. 26 And besides all this, between us and you a great chasm has been set in place, so that those who want to go from here to you cannot, nor can anyone cross over from there to us.' 27 "He answered, 'Then I beg you, father, send Lazarus to my family, 28 for I have five brothers. Let him warn them, so that they will not also come to this place of torment.' 29 "Abraham replied, 'They have Moses and the Prophets; let them listen to them.' 30 "'No, father Abraham,' he said, 'but if someone from the dead goes to them, they will repent.' 31 "He said to him, 'If they do not listen to Moses and the Prophets, they will not be convinced even if someone rises from the dead.'"

313. Mark 10:19; Exodus 20:12–16; Deuteronomy 5:16–20.

314. Mark 10:24. Some manuscripts *is for those who trust in riches.*

Acts 4:32–5:11

The Believers Share Their Possessions

32 All the believers were one in heart and mind. No one claimed that any of their possessions was their own, but they shared everything they had. 33 With great power the apostles continued to testify to the resurrection of the Lord Jesus. And God's grace was so powerfully at work in them all 34 that there were no needy persons among them. For from time to time those who owned land or houses sold them, brought the money from the sales 35 and put it at the apostles' feet, and it was distributed to anyone who had need. 36 Joseph, a Levite from Cyprus, whom the apostles called Barnabas (which means "son of encouragement"), 37 sold a field he owned and brought the money and put it at the apostles' feet.

Ananias and Sapphira

Now a man named Ananias, together with his wife Sapphira, also sold a piece of property. 2 With his wife's full knowledge he kept back part of the money for himself, but brought the rest and put it at the apostles' feet. 3 Then Peter said, "Ananias, how is it that Satan has so filled your heart that you have lied to the Holy Spirit and have kept for yourself some of the money you received for the land? 4 Didn't it belong to you before it was sold? And after it was sold, wasn't the money at your disposal? What made you think of doing such a thing? You have not lied just to human beings but to God." 5 When Ananias heard this, he fell down and died. And great fear seized all who heard what had happened. 6 Then some young men came forward, wrapped up his body, and carried him out and buried him. 7 About three hours later his wife came in, not knowing what had happened. 8 Peter asked her, "Tell me, is this the price you and Ananias got for the land?" "Yes," she said, "that is the price." 9 Peter said to her, "How could you conspire to test the Spirit of the Lord? Listen! The feet of the men who buried your husband are at the door, and they will carry you out also." 10 At that moment she fell down at his feet and died. Then the young men came in and, finding her dead, carried her out and buried her beside her husband. 11 Great fear seized the whole church and all who heard about these events.

from *Nicomachean Ethics* by Aristotle

Introduction

Aristotle was born in Macedonia, around 384 BCE. He was a student of Plato in Plato's Academy and later went on to found his own school, the Lyceum. One of Aristotle's most famous students was the Macedonian king, Alexander the Great. The *Nicomachean Ethics* is named after Aristotle's son and father who were both called Nicomachus.

Aristotle wrote and lectured on just about every area of inquiry available to him. An ancient biographer reported that Aristotle wrote 150 different texts, on a range of subjects, including logic, rhetoric, ethics, politics, constitutional history, psychology, physiology, biology, chemistry, astronomy, mathematics, metaphysics, and epistemology. About thirty-one of those works survive, all of them in a form that suggests they are meant for his students; what we have seem to be Aristotle's lecture notes or first drafts rather than polished works. Many of his works were translated into different languages (e.g., Arabic, Armenian, Ge'ez, Hebrew, Latin, Persian, Syriac) in the late antique and medieval periods, and again in many more languages in the modern periods, including Chinese and Japanese. His works, especially on logic and language, became standard texts in educational curricula. Aristotle made significant contributions in many of the disciplines. In particular, in the field of ethics, his concept of virtue ethics is still a prominent perspective on what it means to be moral, and his discussion of friendship within an ethical framework was the most extensive and in-depth for many centuries. Although we have significantly expanded on and often revised many of Aristotle's claims, we continue to benefit from his insights and arguments.

SNAPSHOT BOX

LANGUAGE: Ancient Greek

DATE: c. 340 BCE

LOCATION: Athens, Greece

GENRE: Philosophy

ETHNIC IDENTITY: Macedonian

TAGS: Desire and Happiness; Ethics and Morality; Friendship; Philosophy

Timeline

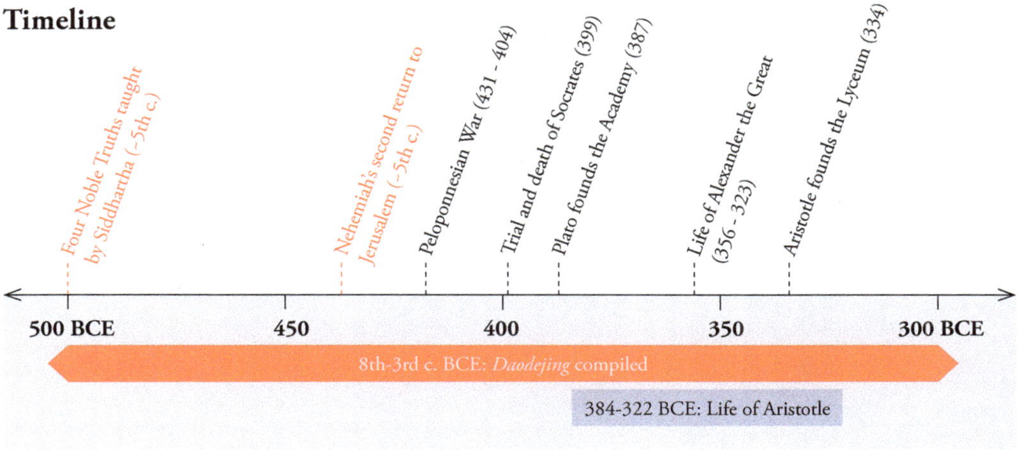

Aristotle distinguished three kinds of knowledge: knowledge for its own sake (theoretical knowledge), knowledge for the sake of doing something (practical knowledge), and knowledge for the sake of producing something (productive knowledge). The kind of knowledge that the *Nicomachean Ethics* offers is practical knowledge. The *Nicomachean Ethics* is intended to help you to know how you should act and what you should feel in order to live an overall excellent, that is, virtuous, human life. How might we understand the role of excellence or virtue in living a good human life? Aristotle understands excellence or virtue in terms of knowing and feeling what is intermediate between the extremes of excess and deficiency in a given context of human life. To identify and define a virtue requires that we refer to a context of human life, and the vice of excess and the vice of deficiency in that context. For example, one context is when human beings are threatened and they respond by feeling fear or confidence. In this context, the vice of excess is being rash, the vice of deficiency is being cowardly, and the virtue—which is intermediate between these vices—is being brave. As Aristotle says in book 2, chapter 6, "We can be afraid, for instance, or be confident, or have appetites, or get angry, or feel pity, and in general have pleasure or pain, both too much and too little, and in both ways not well. But having these feelings at the right times, about the right things, toward the right people, for the right end, and in the right way, is the intermediate and best condition, and this is proper to virtue." To understand what is virtuous requires us to know about all of these circumstances of our actions and feelings.

In the first selection of the *Nicomachean Ethics* given below, Aristotle claims that all of our daily activity is aimed at some ultimate goal or end. How is your life shaped by goals? Aristotle calls this ultimate goal **eudaimonia**, which is often translated as "happiness." This eudaimonia is the product of excellence in every context of one's life, including how we relate to ourselves, family, friends, guests, strangers, and political arenas. This excellence is a communal pursuit since we depend on others to achieve eudaimonia.

Aristotle argues that in each context of one's life there is a virtuous way to *be,* defined as voluntarily cultivated dispositions or habits, to *act*, and to *feel.* In book 2, we find Aristotle explaining what virtue-in-general is. After defining virtue-in-general, he subdivides the genus of virtue into two species, virtue of character and of thought. After this, Aristotle gives us a chart of different contexts of human life, and briefly the virtue and vices—the latter understood in terms of the two extremes of deficiency and excess—for each context. Aristotle explains that virtue is cultivated through habits, actions, and feelings; becoming virtuous is something we choose to cultivate. The last part of the selected readings is a case study on a human being's relation to bodily pleasure. The virtue in this context is "temperance" (sometimes translated as "moderation"), which is intermediate between overindulgence and insensibility. How does Aristotle's general definition of "virtue" help him to understand human relations to bodily pleasures?

Aristotle believes that ethics is an inexact practical science because it deals with particular people living within particular human histories. Nonetheless, Aristotle maintains that ethical knowledge helps us to know how to live excellent human lives in our own particular circumstances.

Scott M. Williams
Department of Philosophy

PRE-READING PARS

1. Is the acquisition of virtue a process? If so, can you identify some defining features of that process?
2. What resources do you use to help you figure out what an excellent human life would be like?

from *Nicomachean Ethics*

1. Bk. 1, ch. 7, 1097a24–1097b22. Distinction between subordinate ends and an ultimate end; identifies happiness with the ultimate end

Our argument, then, has followed a different route to reach the same conclusion. But we must try to make this still more perspicuous. Since there are apparently many ends, and we choose some of them (for instance, wealth, flutes, and, in general, instruments) because of something else, it is clear that not all ends are complete. But the best good is apparently something complete. And so, if only one end is complete, the good we are looking for will be this end; if more ends than one are complete, it will be the most complete end of these.

We say that an end pursued in its own right is more complete than an end pursued because of something else, and that an end that is never choiceworthy because of something else is more complete than ends that are choiceworthy both in their own right and because of this end. Hence an end that is always choiceworthy in its own right, never because of something else, is complete without qualification.

Now happiness, more than anything else, seems complete without qualification. For we always choose it because of itself, never because of something else. Honor, pleasure, understanding, and every virtue we certainly choose because of themselves, since we would choose each of them even if it had no further result; but we also choose them for the sake of happiness, supposing that through them we shall be happy. Happiness, by contrast, no one ever chooses for their sake, or for the sake of anything else at all.

The same conclusion (that happiness is complete) also appears to follow from self-sufficiency. For the complete good seems to be self-sufficient. What we count as self-sufficient is not what suffices for a solitary person by himself, living an isolated life, but what suffices also for parents, children, wife, and, in general, for friends and fellow citizens, since a human being is a naturally political [animal]. Here, however, we must impose some limit; for if we extend the good to parents' parents and children's children and to friends of friends, we shall go on without limit; but we must examine this another time.

Anyhow, we regard something as self-sufficient when all by itself it makes a life choiceworthy and lacking nothing; and that is what we think happiness does. Moreover, we think happiness is most choiceworthy of all goods, [since] it is not counted as one good among many. [If it were] counted as one among many, then, clearly, we think it would be more choiceworthy if the smallest of goods were added; for the good that is added becomes an extra quantity of goods, and the larger of two goods is always more choiceworthy.

Happiness, then, is apparently something complete and self-sufficient, since it is the end of the things achievable in action.

2. Bk. 1, ch. 8, 1098b13–1098b23 - distinction between three kinds of goods: external goods, goods of the soul, goods of the body

Goods are divided, then, into three types, some called external, some goods of the soul, others goods of the body. We say that the goods of the soul are goods most fully, and more than the others, and we take actions and activities of the soul to be [goods] of the soul. And so our account [of the good] is right, to judge by this belief anyhow—and it is an ancient belief, and accepted by philosophers.

Our account is also correct in saying that some sort of actions and activities are the end; for in that way the end turns out to be a good of the soul, not an external good.

The belief that the happy person lives well and does well also agrees with our account, since we have virtually said that the end is a sort of living well and doing well.

3. Bk. 1, ch. 8, 1099a25–1099b9 - associates happiness with the best, the fine, and the pleasant; introduces the need for friends and external resources

Happiness, then, is best, finest, and most pleasant, and the Delian inscription is wrong to distinguish these things: 'What is most just is finest; being healthy is most beneficial; but it is most pleasant to win our heart's desire.' For all three features are found in the best activities, and we say happiness is these activities, or (rather) one of them, the best one.

Nonetheless, happiness evidently also needs external goods to be added, as we said, since we cannot, or cannot easily, do fine actions if we lack the resources. For, first of all, in many actions we use friends, wealth, and political power just as we use instruments. Further deprivation of certain [externals]—for instance, good birth, good children, beauty—mars our blessedness. For we do not altogether have the character of happiness if we look utterly repulsive or are ill-born, solitary, or childless; and we have it even less, presumably, if our children or friends are totally bad, or were good but have died.

And so, as we have said, happiness would seem to need this sort of prosperity added also. That is why some people identify happiness with good fortune, and others identify it with virtue.

4. Bk. 1, ch. 13, 1102a5–1102a7 - states the connection between happiness and virtues

Since happiness is a certain sort of activity of the soul in accord with complete virtue, we must examine virtue; for that will perhaps also be a way to study happiness better.

5. Bk. 2, ch. 1, 1103a15–1103b2 - distinguishes moral virtue and intellectual virtue; describes in general how one can become virtuous

Virtue, then, is of two sorts, virtue of thought and virtue of character. Virtue of thought arises and grows mostly from teaching; that is why it needs experience and time. Virtue of character [i.e., of ēthos] results from habit [ethos]; hence its name 'ethical,' slightly varied from 'ethos.'

Hence it is also clear that none of the virtues of character arises in us naturally. For if something is by nature in one condition, habituation cannot bring it into another condition. A stone, for instance, by nature moves downwards, and habituation could not make it move upwards, not even if you threw it up ten thousand times to habituate it; nor could habituation make fire move downwards, or bring anything that is by nature in one condition into another condition. And so the virtues arise in us neither by nature nor against nature. Rather, we are by nature able to acquire them, and we are completed through habit.

Further, if something arises in us by nature, we first have the capacity for it, and later perform the activity. This is clear in the case of the senses; for we did not acquire them by frequent seeing or hearing, but we already had them when we exercised them, and did not get them by exercising them. Virtues, by contrast, we acquire, just as we acquire crafts, by having first activated them. For we learn a craft by producing the same product that we must produce when we have learned it; we become builders, for instance, by building, and we become harpists by playing the harp. Similarly, then, we become just by doing just actions, temperate by doing temperate actions, brave by doing brave actions.

6. Bk. 2, ch. 6, 1106b9–1107a9 - introduction of the threefold distinction between what is excessive, intermediate, and deficient, in order to give a general definition of virtue

This, then, is how each science produces its product well, by focusing on what is intermediate and making the product conform to that. This, indeed, is why people regularly comment on well-made products that nothing could be added or subtracted; they assume that excess or deficiency ruins a good [result], whereas the mean preserves it. Good craftsmen also, we say, focus on what is intermediate when they produce their product. And since virtue, like nature, is better and more exact than any craft, it will also aim at what is intermediate.

By virtue I mean virtue of character; for this is about feelings and actions, and these admit of excess, deficiency, and an intermediate condition. We can be afraid, for instance, or be confident, or have appetites, or get angry, or feel pity, and in general have pleasure or pain, both too much and too little, and in both ways not well. But having these feelings at the right times, about the right things, toward the right people, for the right end, and in the right way, is the intermediate and best condition, and this is proper to virtue. Similarly, actions also admit of excess, deficiency, and an intermediate condition.

Now virtue is about feelings and actions, in which excess and deficiency are in error and incur blame, whereas the intermediate condition is correct and wins praise, which are both proper to virtue. Virtue, then, is a mean, insofar as it aims at what is intermediate.

Moreover, there are many ways to be in error—for badness is proper to the indeterminate, as the Pythagoreans pictured it, and good to the determinate. But there is only one way to be correct. That is why error is easy and correctness is difficult, since it is easy to miss the target and difficult to hit it. And so for this reason also excess and deficiency are proper to vice, the mean to virtue; 'for we are noble in only one way, but bad in all sorts of ways.'

Virtue, then, is a state that decides, consisting in a mean, the mean relative to us, which is defined by reference to reason, that is to say, to the reason by reference to which the prudent person would define it. It is a mean between two vices, one of excess and one of deficiency.

It is a mean for this reason also: Some vices miss what is right because they are deficient, others because they are excessive, in feelings or in actions, whereas virtue finds and chooses what is intermediate.

That is why virtue, as far as its essence and the account stating what it is are concerned, is a mean, but, as far as the best [condition] and the good [result] are concerned, it is an extremity.

7. Bk. 2, ch. 7, 1107b29–1108b7 - rough outline of different moral virtues, including Temperance; uses the threefold distinction to describe these

However, we must not only state this general account but also apply it to the particular cases. For among accounts concerning actions, though the general ones are common to more cases, the specific ones are truer, since actions are about particular cases, and our account must accord with these. Let us, then, find these from the chart.

First, then, in feelings of fear and confidence the mean is bravery. The excessively fearless person is nameless (indeed many cases are nameless), and the one who is excessively confident is rash. The one who is excessive in fear and deficient in confidence is cowardly.

In pleasures and pains—though not in all types, and in pains less than in pleasures—the mean is temperance and the excess intemperance. People deficient in pleasure are not often found, which is why they also lack even a name; let us call them insensible.

In giving and taking money the mean is generosity, the excess wastefulness and the deficiency ungenerosity. Here the vicious people have contrary excesses and defects; for the wasteful person is excessive in spending and deficient in taking, whereas the ungenerous person is excessive in taking and deficient in spending. At the moment we are speaking in outline and summary, and that is enough; later we shall define these things more exactly.

In questions of money there are also other conditions. Another mean is magnificence; for the magnificent person differs from the generous by being concerned with large matters, while the generous person is concerned with small. The excess is ostentation and vulgarity, and the deficiency is stinginess. These differ from the vices related to generosity in ways we shall describe later.

In honor and dishonor the mean is magnanimity, the excess something called a sort of vanity, and the deficiency pusillanimity. And just as we said that generosity differs from magnificence in its concern with small matters, similarly there is a virtue concerned with small honors, differing in the same way from magnanimity, which is concerned with great honors. For honor can be desired either in the right way or more or less than is right. If someone desires it to excess, he is called an honor-lover, and if his desire is deficient he is called indifferent to honor, but if he is intermediate he has no name. The corresponding conditions have no name either, except the condition of the honor-lover, which is called honor-loving.

This is why people at the extremes lay claim to the intermediate area. Moreover, we also sometimes call the intermediate person an honor-lover, and sometimes call him indifferent to honor; and sometimes we praise the honor-lover, sometimes the person indifferent to honor. We will mention later the reason we do this; for the moment, let us speak of the other cases in the way we have laid down.

Anger also admits of an excess, deficiency, and mean. These are all practically nameless; but since we call the intermediate person mild, let us call the mean mildness. Among the extreme people, let the excessive person be irascible, and his vice irascibility, and let the deficient person be a sort of irascible person, and his deficiency inirascibility.

There are also three other means, somewhat similar to another, but different. For they are all concerned with common dealings in conversations and actions, but differ insofar as one is concerned with truth telling in these areas, the other two with sources of pleasure, some of which are found in amusement, and the others in daily life in general. Hence we should also discuss these states, so that we can better observe that in every case the mean is praiseworthy, whereas the extremes are neither praiseworthy nor correct, but blameworthy. Most of these cases are also nameless, and we must try, as in the other cases also, to supply names ourselves, to make things clear and easy to follow.

In truth-telling, then, let us call the intermediate person truthful, and the mean truthfulness; pretense that overstates will be boastfulness, and the person who has it boastful; pretense that understates will be self-deprecation, and the person who has it self-deprecating.

In sources of pleasure in amusements let us call the intermediate person witty, and the condition wit; the excess buffoonery and the person who has it a buffoon; and the deficient person a sort of boor and the state boorishness.

In the other sources of pleasure, those in daily life, let us call the person who is pleasant in the right way friendly, and the mean state friendliness. If someone goes to excess with no [ulterior] aim, he will be ingratiating; if he does it for his own advantage, a flatterer. The deficient person, unpleasant in everything, will be a sort of quarrelsome and ill-tempered person.

There are also means in feelings and about feelings. Shame, for instance, is not a virtue, but the person prone to shame as well as [the virtuous people we have described] receives praise. For here also one person is called intermediate, and another—the person excessively prone to shame, who is ashamed about everything—is called excessive; the person who is deficient in shame or never feels shame at all is said to have no sense of disgrace; and the intermediate one is called prone to shame.

Proper indignation is the mean between envy and spite; these conditions are concerned with pleasure and pain at what happens to our neighbors. For the properly indignant person feels pain when someone does well undeservedly; the envious person exceeds him by feeling pain when anyone does well, while the spiteful person is so deficient in feeling pain that he actually enjoys [other people's misfortunes].

There will also be an opportunity elsewhere to speak of these. We must consider justice after these. Since it is spoken of in more than one way, we shall distinguish its two types and say how each of them is a mean. Similarly, we must also consider the virtues that belong to reason.

8. Bk. 3, ch. 5, 1113b4–1113b14 - summarizes why becoming virtuous is up to us

We have found, then, that we wish for the end, and deliberate and decide about things that promote it; hence the actions concerned with things that promote the end are in accord with decision and are voluntary. The activities of the virtues are concerned with these things [that promote the end].

Hence virtue is also up to us, and so also, in the same way, is vice. For when acting is up to us, so is not acting, and when no is up to us, so is yes. And so if acting, when it is fine, is up to us, not acting, when it is shameful, is also up to us; and if not acting, when it is fine, is up to us, then acting, when it is shameful, is also up to us. But if doing, and likewise not doing, fine or shameful actions is up to us, and if, as we saw, [doing or not doing them] is [what it is] to be a good or bad person, being decent or base is up to us.

9. Bk. 3, ch. 5, 1114b22–1114b30 - summarizes virtue and vice as voluntary

Now the virtues, as we say, are voluntary. For in fact we are ourselves in a way jointly responsible for our states of character, and the sort of character we have determines the sort of end we lay down. Hence the vices will also be voluntary, since the same is true of them.

We have now discussed the virtues in common. We have described their genus in outline; they are means, and they are states. Certain actions produce them, and they cause us to do these same actions in accord with the virtues themselves, in the way that correct reason prescribes. They are up to us and voluntary.

10. Bk. 3, ch. 10–12, 1117b24–1119b21 - on the moral virtue of Temperance

Let us discuss temperance next; for bravery and temperance seem to be the virtues of the nonrational parts. Temperance, then, is a mean concerned with pleasures, as we have already said; for it is concerned less, and in a different way, with pains. Intemperance appears in this same area too. Let us, then, now distinguish the specific pleasures that concern them.

First, let us distinguish pleasures of the soul from those of the body. Love of honor and of learning, for instance, are among the pleasures of the soul; for though a lover of one of these enjoys it, only his thought, not his body, is at all affected. Those concerned with such pleasures are called neither temperate nor intemperate. The same applies to those concerned with any of the other non-bodily pleasures; for lovers of tales, storytellers, those who waste their days on trivialities, are called babblers, but not intemperate. Nor do we call people intemperate if they feel pain over money or friends.

Temperance, then, will be about bodily pleasures, but not even about all of these. For those who find enjoyment in objects of sight, such as colors, shapes, a painting, are called neither temperate nor intemperate, even though it would also seem possible to enjoy these either rightly or excessively and deficiently. The same is true for hearing; no one is ever called intemperate for excessive enjoyment of songs or playacting, or temperate for the right enjoyment of them.

Nor is this said about someone enjoying smells, except coincidentally. For someone is called intemperate not for enjoying the smell of apples or roses or incense, but rather for enjoying the smell of perfumes or cooked delicacies. For these are the smells an intemperate person enjoys because they remind him of the objects of his appetite. And we can see that others also enjoy the smells of food if they are hungry. It is the enjoyment of the things [that he is reminded of by these smells] that is proper to an intemperate person, since these are the objects of his appetite.

Nor do other animals find pleasures from these senses, except coincidentally. What a hound enjoys, for instance, is not the smell of a hare, but eating it; but the hare's smell made the hound perceive it. And what a lion enjoys is not the sound of the ox, but eating it; but since the ox's sound made the lion perceive that it was near, the lion appears to enjoy the sound. Similarly, what pleases him is not the sight of 'a deer or a wild goat,' but the prospect of food.

The pleasures that concern temperance and intemperance are those that are shared with the other animals, and so appear slavish and bestial. These pleasures are touch and taste.

However, they seem to deal even with taste very little or not at all. For taste discriminates flavors—the sort of thing that wine tasters and cooks savoring food do; but people, or intemperate people at any rate, do not much enjoy this. Rather, they enjoy the gratification that comes entirely through touch, in eating and drinking and in what are called the pleasures of sex. That is why a glutton actually prayed for his throat to become longer than a crane's, showing that he took pleasure in the touching. And so the sense that concerns intemperance is the most widely shared, and seems justifiably open to reproach, since we have it insofar as we are animals, not insofar as we are human beings.

To enjoy these things, then, and to like them most of all, is bestial. For indeed the most civilized of the pleasures coming through touch, such as those produced by rubbing and warming in gymnasia, are excluded from intemperance, since the touching that is proper to the intemperate person concerns only some parts of the body, not all of it.

Some appetites seem to be shared [by everyone], while others seem to be additions that are distinctive [of different people]. The appetite for nourishment, for instance, is natural, since everyone who lacks nourishment, dry or liquid, has an appetite for it, sometimes for both; and, as Homer says, the young in their prime [all] have an appetite for sex. Not everyone, however, has an appetite for a specific sort of food or drink or sex, or for the same things. That is why an appetite of this type seems to be distinctive of [each of] us. Still, this also includes a natural element, since different sorts of people find different sorts of things more pleasant, and there are some things that are more pleasant for everyone than things chosen at random would be.

In natural appetites few people are in error, and only in one direction, toward excess. Eating indiscriminately or drinking until we are too full is exceeding the quantity that accords with nature; for [the object of] natural appetite is the filling of a lack. That is why these people are called 'gluttons,' showing that they glut their bellies past what is right; that is how especially slavish people turn out.

With the pleasures that are distinctive of different people, many make errors and in many ways; for people are called lovers of something if they enjoy the wrong things, or if they enjoy something in the wrong way. And in all these ways intemperate people go to excess. For some of the things they enjoy are hateful, and hence wrong; distinctive pleasures that it is right to enjoy they enjoy more than is right, and more than most people enjoy them.

Clearly, then, with pleasures excess is intemperance, and is blameworthy. With pains, however, we are not called temperate, as we are called brave, for standing firm against them, or intemperate for not standing firm. Rather, someone is intemperate because he feels more pain than is right at failing to get pleasant things; and even this pain is produced by the pleasure [he takes in them]. And someone is temperate because he does not feel pain at the absence of what is pleasant, or at refraining from it.

The intemperate person, then, has an appetite for all pleasant things, or rather for the most pleasant of them, and his appetite leads him to choose these at the cost of the other things. That is why he also feels pain both when he fails to get something and when he has an appetite for it, since appetite involves pain. It would seem absurd, however, to suffer pain because of pleasure.

People who are deficient in pleasures and enjoy them less than is right are not found very much. For that sort of insensibility is not human; indeed, even the other animals discriminate among foods, enjoying some but not others. If someone finds nothing pleasant, or preferable to anything else, he is far from being human. The reason he has no name is he is not found much.

The temperate person has an intermediate state in relation to these [bodily pleasures]. For he finds no pleasure in what most pleases the intemperate person, but finds it disagreeable; he finds no pleasure at all in the wrong things. He finds no intense pleasure in any [bodily pleasure], suffers no pain at their absence, and has no appetite for them, or only a moderate appetite, not to the wrong degree or at the wrong time or anything else at all of that sort. If something is pleasant and conducive to health or fitness, he will desire this moderately and in the right way; and he will desire in the same way anything else that is pleasant, if it is no obstacle to health and fitness, does not deviate from the fine, and does not exceed his means. For the opposite sort of person likes these pleasures more than they are worth; that is not the temperate person's character, but he likes them as correct reason prescribes.

Intemperance is more like a voluntary condition than cowardice; for it is caused by pleasure, which is choiceworthy, whereas cowardice is caused by pain, which is to be avoided. Moreover, pain disturbs and ruins the nature of the sufferer, while pleasure does nothing of the sort; intemperance, then, is more voluntary. That is why it is also more open to reproach. For it is also easier to acquire the habit of facing pleasant things, since our life includes many of them and we can acquire the habit with no danger; but with frightening things the reverse is true.

However, cowardice seems to be more voluntary than particular cowardly actions. For cowardice itself involves no pain, but the particular actions disturb us because of the pain [that causes them], so that people actually throw away their weapons and do all the other disgraceful actions. That is why these actions even seem to be forced [and hence involuntary].

For the intemperate person the reverse is true. The particular actions are the result of his appetite and desire, and so they are voluntary; but the whole condition is less voluntary [than the actions], since no one has an appetite to be intemperate.

We also apply the name of intemperance to the errors of children, since they have some similarity. Which gets its name from which does not matter for our present purposes, but clearly the posterior is called after the prior.

The name would seem to be quite appropriately transferred. For the things that need to be tempered are those that desire shameful things and tend to grow large. Appetites and children are most like this; for children also live by appetite, and desire for the pleasant is found more in them than in anyone else.

If, then, [the child or the appetitive part] is not obedient and subordinate to its rulers, it will go far astray. For when someone lacks understanding, his desire for the pleasant is insatiable and seeks indiscriminate satisfaction. The [repeated] active exercise of appetite increases the appetite he already had from birth, and if the appetites are large and intense, they actually expel rational calculation. That is why appetites must be moderate and few, and never contrary to reason. This is the condition we call obedient and temperate. And just as the child's life must follow the instructions of his guide, so too the appetitive part must follow reason.

Hence the temperate person's appetitive part must agree with reason; for both [his appetitive part and his reason] aim at the fine, and the temperate person's appetites are for the right things, in the right ways, at the right times, which is just what reason also prescribes.

So much, then, for temperance.

Aristotle. Selections from *Nicomachean Ethics*. Translated by Terence Irwin, 7–8, 10–11, 16, 18–19, 24–27, 37, 39, 45–49. Indianapolis, IN: Hackett, 2019.

POST-READING PARS

1. Identify two transformational processes that Aristotle notes for cultivating virtue.
2. What are the signs or circumstances of temperance and intemperance, according to Aristotle?

Inquiry Corner

Content Question(s):	Critical Question(s):
What does Aristotle mean when he claims that virtue is "intermediate" between an excess and a deficiency? What are the ways that one can be excessive, or deficient, when one performs an action, according to Aristotle? Give examples.	What are some salient features of Aristotle's virtue ethics? Can these features be applied to contemporary contexts? Why or why not?
Comparative Question(s):	**Connection Question(s):**
Compare Aristotle's understanding of virtue with insights about how to live a good life in *Amenemope*, *Analects*, *Daodejing*, or other wisdom literature?	Imagine that all citizens had an opportunity to cultivate the virtues of character and the virtues of thought. How might this impact citizens' civic and communal engagement?

BEYOND THE CLASSROOM

- Does the virtue of the golden mean have a role in the workplace? Which virtues would be most important to creating a fulfilling career? How would one cultivate those virtues?
- What role do friendships play in work environments?

Pythagorean Women: Theano I, Perictione I, Theano II, Aesara of Lucania, Phintys of Sparta

Introduction

Although many ancient Greek philosophical schools considered women inferior to men, the followers of Pythagoreanism, a school founded by **Pythagoras**, welcomed women as equals to men in their intellectual abilities and their capacity for **arete**, or virtue. Consequently, there are more women known to history as Pythagorean philosophers than in any other philosophical school of the ancient Greek world; one important source names 218 male Pythagoreans, and lists by name seventeen of the "most famous" women Pythagoreans.[315] Pythagoras himself treated his wife and daughters as intellectual equals and trusted disciples (he is said to have entrusted his daughter with keeping his notes for him), and thus set the model for his followers.

The principles that the Pythagoreans were expected to follow (and keep secret) included some that required full cooperation of the wives and children of male members. For example, there were very strict dietary rules that the whole household would have followed, which women, as overseers of the household, had to be aware of in order

SNAPSHOT BOX

LANGUAGE: Ancient Greek

DATE: c. 6th–1st century BCE

LOCATION: Greece and colonies, especially southern Italy

GENRE: Philosophical treatise and letters

TAGS: Ethics and Morality; Freedom and Harmony; Philosophy; Wisdom; Women and Gender

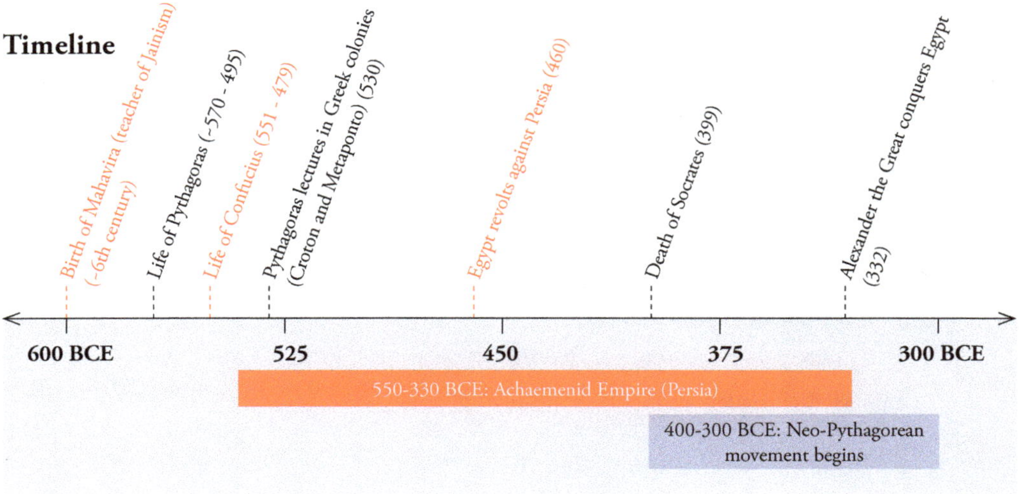

315. Iamblichus, *Life of Pythagoras*, translated by Thomas Taylor (Rochester, VT: Inner Traditions International, 1986). Iamblichus lived circa 250–330 CE, so considerably later than the Pythagoreans, but is an important source of information on them. However, there is significant debate in the traditional literature about which of the Pythagoreans and Neo-Pythagoreans are genuine, and some scholars believe that most if not all of the women's writings may be forgeries. I am following the work of scholars such as Mary Ellen Waithe and Sarah Pomeroy (as well as the authority of Iamblichus and other ancient sources) in believing the work of these Pythagorean women to be genuine.

that the entire household would be able to live up to the Pythagorean standards of proper living. There were also strict regulations about proper clothing; for example, clothes were to be made of plant fibers, not wool, and should be white, with little ornamentation. What might have been the intended functions of these practices? Pythagoras, at the urging of the women of his community, even declared that the usual sexual double standard of the ancient Greek world was wrong, and that the men must give up their concubines and practice monogamy, as was traditionally expected of women in the ancient Mediterranean world. What areas of equality between men and women does this leave out?

Pythagorean women were generally literate and well educated and participated in philosophical debate and activity with their male relatives and partners. As is the case with most early philosophy, we have very little of what they actually wrote, but what we do have takes several forms. They wrote in **apothegms**, or short, pithy "sayings"; **treatises**, or longer, formal expositions; and letters, which they appear to have frequently exchanged with other members of the Pythagorean extended community. The apothegms and treatises probably concerned the same topics as those treated by male philosophers, but the letters were often **exhortation**, written to provide advice and urge good conduct to the specific women they were addressed to and to women generally.

Pythagorean women wrote about typical topics of Greek philosophy, including the "scientific" study of the nature of the cosmos, mathematics, and music. However, the Pythagorean school is the first Greek school for which we have evidence of significant attention to **ethics**, or the study of proper living. They investigated the right actions to take, the right person to become, and the best characteristics to cultivate in order to become that person. The goal of ethics in the ancient Greek world was to know how to live well, and this knowledge constituted **wisdom**, or the understanding of what goals in life should be sought and how to attain them. Wisdom thus encompasses both theoretical knowing (what is true or good) and practical knowing (how to act well, how to achieve ends). Does this combination of theoretical and practical knowing seem to you like a good basis for living well? What do you think living well means?

Pythagorean women also examined women's ethics, that is, what women in particular need to know and to do in order to live well. They recognized that since women are responsible for the earliest teaching of the next generation, it was crucial that women be well educated on practical subjects like household management and on "big questions" like the nature of the soul and justice in the cosmos and in human communities. They believed that since the human world should be a reflection of the cosmic order, they must understand these matters in order to understand how to properly order their relationships with others, including their parents, husbands, neighbors, and children. Their writing often includes discussion of how to achieve the highest virtue for women: **sophrosyne**. This term means moderation and the ability to exercise self-control, which was of course necessary for men as well as women, but also has connotations of chastity and modesty, which were considered especially important for women. As you read, consider how the recommendations for women's proper behavior compare to your experience today: are there still "special" virtues for women? For men?

Melissa Burchard
Department of Philosophy

PRE-READING PARS

1. Think of two to three virtues or characteristics that are important for your ability to live well.
2. What do you see as the difference between knowledge and wisdom?
3. Brainstorm three ideas about how relationships, and which relationships, make it possible for you to live well.

Pythagorean Women

Theano I

On Piety

"I have learned that many Greeks think Pythagoras said everything is created from number. This statement itself raises a question. How can what does not exist think and reproduce? But he did not say everything is derived from number, but everything is generated according to number, that the primary order is in number. By being part of it [the primary order], a first and second and the rest that follow are the order for things that are counted." (67)

Apophthegm[316]

"There are things which it is fine to discuss; about these things it is shameful to remain silent. There are also things which it is shameful to discuss; about these things it is preferable to remain silent." (68)

Perictione I

On the Harmonious Woman

"We should neither speak ill of our parents nor do them harm, but obey those who generated us in both trivial and important matters, and in every state of the soul and body, in inner and external matters, both in peace and in war, in health and in sickness, and in wealth and poverty, in fame and obscurity, whether they are private individuals or public officials. It is necessary to keep in step and never desert them, but to obey them even to the point of madness. Such conduct is considered wise and honorable by pious people.

"If someone should have contempt for her parents, plotting any sort of evil in private, her wrongdoing is recorded by the gods whether she is living or dead. People

316. This is an alternate spelling for the term "apothegm," and means the same thing.

will hate her, and with the impious in their place under the earth forever she will be harmed by evils in behalf of justices and of the gods below who are appointed to supervise these matters.

"Divine and beautiful is the sight of one's parents, so too is the reverence and the care of them, as great as the sight of the sun and all the stars which heaven wears and twirls, and whatever else anyone may consider something greater to view. It seems to me not even the gods are angry when they see this occur. It is necessary to revere them when they are living and when they have departed and never to mutter against them even when they behave senselessly because of illness or deception, but rather exhort and teach and in no way hate them. There is no greater error and injustice among human beings than not to revere one's parents." (77)

Theano II

Letter to Euboule

"I hear that you are raising your children in luxury. The mark of a good mother is not attention to the pleasure of her children, but education with a view to temperance. Look out lest you accomplish not the work of a loving mother, but that of a doting one. When pleasure and children are brought up together, it makes the children undisciplined. What is sweeter to the young than familiar pleasure? One must take care, my friend, lest the upbringing of one's children become their downfall. Luxury perverts nature when children become lovers of pleasure in spirit and sensualists in body, mentally afraid of toil and physically soft. A mother must also exercise her charges in the things they dread—even if this causes them some pain and distress—so that they shall not become the slaves of their feelings, greedy for pleasure and shrinking from pain; but rather, shall honor virtue above everything and be able both to abstain from pleasure and to withstand pain.

"Don't let them be sated with nourishment, nor gratified in their every pleasure. Such lack of restraint in childhood makes them unbridled; it lets them say anything and try everything; especially if you take alarm every time they cry out, and always take pride in their laughter—smiling indulgently even if they strike their nurse or taunt you—and if you insist on keeping them unnaturally cool in summer and warm in winter, giving them every luxury. Poor children have no experience of such things; yet they grow up readily enough. They grow no less, and become stronger by far. But you nurse your children like the scions of Sardanapalus,[317] enfeebling their manly natures with pleasures. What would one make of a child who, if he does not eat sooner, clamors; who, whenever he eats, craves the delights of delicacies; who wilts in the heat and is felled by the cold; who, if someone finds fault with him, fights back; who, if someone does not cater to his every pleasure, is aggrieved; who, if he does not

317. Sardanapalus was traditionally understood to be a king of Assyria in the seventh century BCE, who was believed to have lived and died in extreme decadence and overindulgence.

chew on something, is discontent; who gets into mischief just for the fun of it, and stutters about without living in an articulate way?

"Take care, my friend—conscious of the fact that children who live licentiously become slaves when they grow to manhood—to deprive them of such pleasures. Make their nourishment austere rather than sumptuous; let them endure both hunger and thirst, both cold and heat, and even shame before their peers or their overseers. This is how they turn out to be brave in spirit no matter whether they are exalted or tormented. Hardships, my dear, serve as a hardening-up process for children, a process by which virtue is perfected. Those who have been dipped sufficiently in them bear the tempering bath of virtue as a natural thing. So look out, dear, lest, just as vines which have been improperly tended are deficient in fruit, your children produce the evil fruit of licentiousness and utter worthlessness, all because of luxury. Farewell." (78–79)

Letter to Callisto: the text on managing household slaves

"To you younger women, just as soon as you are married, authority is granted by law to govern the household. But, to do well, instruction about household management is needed from older women, a continual source of advice. It is well to learn what you do not know ahead of time and to deem most proper the advice of older women; in these matters a young soul must be brought up from girlhood. The primary authority of women in the household is authority over the slaves. And the greatest thing, my dear, is good will on the slaves' part. For this possession is not bought along with their bodies; rather, intelligent mistresses bring it about in time. Just usage is the cause of this—seeing to it that they are neither worn out by toil nor incapacitated by deprivation.

"For they are human in nature. There are some women who suppose the profitable to be what is most unprofitable: maltreatment of their slaves, overburdening them with tasks to be done, and depriving them of the things they need. And then, having made much of an obol's[318] profit, they pay the price in enormous damages: ill-will and the worst treacheries. As for you, let there be ready at hand a measure of food that is proportionate to the amount of woolwork[319] produced by a day's work. With respect to the diet of your slaves, this will suffice. As for undisciplined behavior, one must assist to the utmost what is fitting for you, not what is advantageous to them. For it is necessary to estimate one's slaves at their proper worth. On the one hand, cruelty will not bring gratitude to a soul; on the other hand, reasoning, no less than righteous indignation, is an effective means of control. But if there is too much unconquerable vice on the part of the slaves, one must send them away to be sold. Let what is alien to the needs [of the house] be estranged from its mistress as

318. An obol was a Greek coin worth approximately eight dollars.

319. "Woolwork" refers to the amount of spinning and/or weaving produced in the household.

well [lit. "Let what is alien to the need be estranged from the (female) proper judge as well"].

"Let proper judgment of this take precedence so that you will determine the true facts of wrongdoing in keeping with the justice of the condemnation, and the magnitude of wrongdoing in proportion to the proper punishment. But sometimes the mistress' forgiveness and kindness towards those who have erred will release them from penalties. In this way, too, you will preserve a fitting and appropriate mode of life. There are some women, my dear, who because they are cruel—brutalized by jealousy or anger—even whip the bodies of their slaves as if they were inscribing the excess of their bitterness as a memorandum. In time, some of these [female slaves] are used up, utterly worked out; others procure safety by escaping; but some stop living, withdrawing into death with their own hands. In the end, the isolation of the mistress, bewailing her lack of domestic consideration, finds desolate repentance. But, my dear, likening yourself to musical instruments, know what sound they make when they are loosened too much, but that they are snapped asunder when stretched too tight. It is the same way for your slaves. Too much license creates dissonance in the matter of obedience, but the stretching of forceful necessity causes the dissolution of nature itself. One must meditate on this: 'Right measure is best in everything.' Farewell." (85–86)

Aesara of Lucania

On Human Nature

"Human nature seems to me to provide a standard of law and justice both for the home and for the city. By following the tracks within himself whoever seeks will make a discovery: law is in him and justice, which is the orderly arrangement of the soul. Being threefold, it is organized in accordance with triple functions: that which effects judgment and thoughtfulness is [the mind], that which effects strength and ability is [high spirit], and all that effects love and kindliness is desire. These are all so disposed relatively to one other, that the best part is in command, the most inferior is governed, and the one in between holds a middle place; it both governs and is governed.

The god thus contrived these things according to principle in both the outline and completion of the human dwelling place, because he intended man alone to become a recipient of law and justice, and none other of mortal animals. A composite unity of association could not come about from a single thing, nor indeed from several which are all alike. (For it is necessary, since the things to be done are different, that the parts of the soul also be different, just as in the case of the body [the organs of touch and] sight and hearing and taste and smell differ, for these do not all have the same affinity with everything.)

Nor could such a unity come from several dissimilar things at random, but rather, from parts formed in accordance with the completion and organization and fitting together of the entire composite whole. Not only is the soul composed from several dissimilar parts, these being fashioned in conformity with the whole and complete, but in addition these are not arranged haphazardly and at random, but in accordance with rational attention.

For if they had an equal share of power and honor, though being themselves unequal—some inferior, some better, some in between—the association of parts throughout the soul could not have been fitted together. Or, even if they did have an unequal share, but the worse rather than the better had the greater share, there would be great folly and disorder in the soul. And even if the better had the greater, and the worse the lesser, but each of these had not the proper proportion, there could not be unanimity and friendship and justice throughout the soul, since when one is arranged in accordance with the suitable proportion, this sort of arrangement I assert to be justice.

And indeed a certain unanimity and agreement in sentiment accompanies such an arrangement. This sort would justly be called good order of the soul, whichever, due to the better part's ruling and the inferior's being ruled, should add the strength of virtue to itself. Friendship and love and kindliness, cognate and kindred, will sprout from these parts. For a closely-inspecting mind persuades, love desires, and high spirit is filled with strength; once seething with hatred, it becomes friendly to desire.

Mind having fitted the pleasant together with the painful, mingling also the tense and robust with the slight and relaxed portion of the soul, each part is distributed in accordance with its kindred and suitable concern for each thing: mind closely inspecting and tracking out things, high spirit adding impetuosity and strength to what is closely inspected, and desire, being akin to affection, adapts to the mind, preserving the pleasant as its own, and giving up the thoughtful to the thoughtful part of the soul. By virtue of these things the best life for man seems to me to be whenever the pleasant should be mixed with the earnest and pleasure with virtue. Mind is able to fix these things to itself, becoming lovely through systematic education and virtue." (100–101)

Phintys of Sparta

On the Moderation of Women, fragment 1

"A woman must be altogether good and orderly; without excellence [arete] she would never become so. The excellence appropriate to each thing makes superior that which is receptive of it: the excellence appropriate to the eyes makes the eyes so; that appropriate to hearing, the faculty of hearing; that appropriate to a horse, a horse; that appropriate to a man, a man. So too the excellence appropriate to a woman makes a woman excellent. The excellence most appropriate to a woman is moderation [sophrosyne]. For, on account of this virtue, she will be able to honor and love her husband.

Now, perhaps many think that it is not fitting for a woman to philosophize, just as it is not fitting for her to ride horses or speak in public. But I think that some things are peculiar to a man, some to a woman, some are common to both, some belong more to a man than a woman, some more to a woman than a man. Peculiar to a man are serving in battle, political activity, and public speaking; peculiar to a woman are staying at home and indoors, and welcoming and serving her husband. But I say that courage [andreia] and justice and wisdom are common to both. Excellences of the body are appropriate for both a man and a woman, likewise those of the soul. And just as it is beneficial for the body of each to be healthy, so too, it is beneficial for the soul to be healthy. The excellences of the body are health, strength, keenness of perception, and beauty. Some of these are more fitting for a man to cultivate and possess, some more for a woman. For courage and wisdom are more appropriate for a man, both because of the constitution of his body and because of his strength of soul, while moderation is more appropriate for a woman.

Therefore one must discover the nature of the woman who is trained in moderation, and make known the number and kinds of things which confer this good upon a woman. I say this comes from five things: first, from piety and reverence concerning her marriage bed; second, from decency with respect to her body; third, from the processions of those from her own household; fourth, from not indulging in mystery rites and celebrations of Cybele; and fifth, from being devout and correct in her sacrifices to the divine.

Of these, that which most of all causes and preserves moderation is being incorruptible in respect to her marriage, and not getting mixed up with a strange man. For, first, a woman who thus transgresses does an injustice to the gods of her race, providing not genuine, but spurious, allies to her house and family. She does an injustice to the natural gods by whom she swore, along with her ancestors and kin, to share in a common life and the lawful procreation of children. She also does an injustice to her fatherland, by not abiding among those who were duly appointed for her. Then she is wont to err over and above those for whom death, the greatest of penalties, is determined. On account of the magnitude of injustice to do wrong and commit outrages for the sake of pleasure is unlawful and least deserving of mercy. The issue of all outrage is destruction" (104–5).

Pomeroy, Sarah B. *Pythagorean Women: Their History and Writings*, 67–68, 77–79, 85–86, 100–101, 104–5. Baltimore, MD: Johns Hopkins University Press, 2013.

POST-READING PARS

1. Which virtues or characteristics do the Pythagorean women note as important for living well?
2. Did your ideas about knowledge and/or wisdom seem to match the discussion in the readings?
3. Are the relationships that you noted before reading the same as any of those the Pythagorean women saw as important? Is it significant that the importance of some relationships has remained constant through time?

Inquiry Corner

Content Question(s):

What are the three parts of human nature/the soul that Aesara describes, and how do they work together to form justice in the soul?

Critical Question(s):

What does the advice regarding enslaved peoples tell us about the culture the Pythagoreans lived in generally? What picture does it give us of the socioeconomic status of the Pythagoreans, and how might that status be affecting their ideas about things like virtue and justice?

Comparative Question(s):

How is the advice to women in these texts different from and similar to the advice we see in the reading from Ban Zhao in ancient China?

How do the relationships that are emphasized in these readings compare to the ones emphasized in the Confucian tradition?

Connection Question(s):

How does gender difference affect a culture's ideas about education, social roles, sexuality, and ethics?

Sappho's Poetry

Introduction

SNAPSHOT BOX

LANGUAGE: Ancient Greek

DATE: c. 630–570 BCE

LOCATION: Lesbos, Greece

GENRE: Lyric poetry

TAGS: Aesthetics; Community/Communal Identity; Emotion; Love; Suffering and Compassion

Sappho is unique in the ancient Greek world for being a female **lyric** poet whose works have survived, if only in fragments. Unlike the grand narrative of Homeric epic, lyric poetry tends to be smaller scale and subjective. It is often written in the first person and treats subjects such as love, beauty, wine, and so forth. Sappho's poetry appears to describe a society that celebrated relationships between women. But because she is so unlike any other ancient Greek writer, it is hard to place her very clearly in the context of women's lives and experiences in archaic Greece, and appreciation of her poetry has sometimes been obscured by an obsession with her sexuality. Older scholars often tried to ignore or explain away her apparent references to romantic relationships between women, while in some modern readings, questions about her sexual orientation become the most important aspect of her identity.

Sappho's poetry, with its emphasis on beauty, song, leisure, and love, strongly suggests that she was from an aristocratic background but otherwise we know little about women's lives on ancient Lesbos that would have enabled the recognition and promotion of her talent. We know that in **archaic** Greece (eighth century BCE–480 BCE), aristocratic young women were trained to sing and dance in choruses, probably with a ritual focus. While some of Sappho's poems, such as poem 1, have an intensely first-person, individual focus, it is likely that she also wrote for women's choruses like these. Thus traditional accounts of Sappho imagine her as some kind of educator, teaching young women music and dance and perhaps the arts of beauty or sexuality as well. In poem 96, Sappho apparently refers to a

Timeline

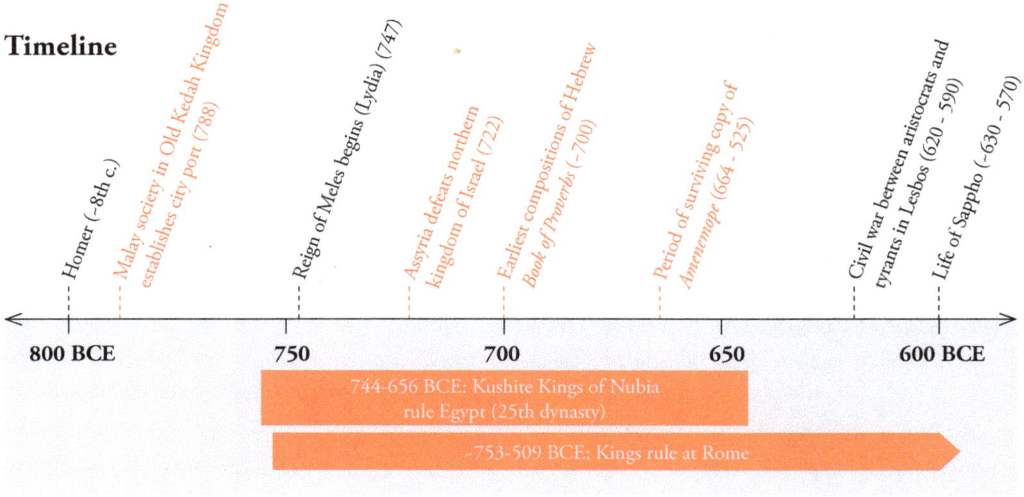

community of women with religious and artistic interests, which one woman has now left, perhaps to get married. But her departure was apparently unwilling, since Sappho says that she now misses a woman called Atthis.

Additionally, the content of the poems seems emotionally intense and some of the language of the Greek certainly implies erotic feelings between women. However, many modern songwriters use a first-person persona that does not necessarily reflect directly their own experiences and feelings. How do we distinguish between an artist's personal voice and a role that they are playing? In ancient Greece the symposium (see introduction to Plato's *Symposium*) was another venue where singer-poets performed, and some intimate, first-person poetry by men has come down to us, but as far as we know, aristocratic, free-born women did not participate in these events. If Sappho had regularly participated in symposia as a performer, she would have been highly unusual.

There is a strong biographical tradition that Sappho was married and had a child, although that tradition calls her husband Kerkylas of Andros. This is apparently a joke name, which translates roughly to "Dick Allcock of the Isle of Man," and it may have derived from (now lost) plays of later comic writers that portray Sappho as enthusiastically and indiscriminately heterosexual. What exactly was the source and possibly purpose of humor in this portrayal of the great female poet whose work, as best we can tell, prized the community and emotions of women? In short, Sappho is a mystery, but it is safe to say that she has been an inspiration through the ages for women who are attracted to other women—even to the extent that her birthplace of Eressos in Lesbos has become a major women's tourist destination in the past forty years. Many feminist scholars have suggested that Sappho's poetry is qualitatively different from the poetry of contemporary male writers, contrasting more masculine patterns of hierarchical control with the mutuality of desire between participants in Sappho. From the poems selected here, if we did not know that Sappho was in fact a unique female poet, would we suspect that there was something different about this poetry?

Sophie Mills
Department of Classics

PRE-READING PARS

1. Give two to three examples of poetry that you love.
2. Identify two to three features of a poem that in your opinion make it personally meaningful or relatable to you.

Sappho's Poetry

Poem 1[320]

Aphrodite, queen of the painted throne
Child of Zeus, wile-weaving, I beseech you,
don't subdue my heart with pain and troubles—
Mistress, I beg you.
But come here now, if all those years ago
I cried my prayer to you and you listened.
Leaving your father's golden palace
you came to help me
Harnessing your chariot; lovely birds drew it.
Sparrows swiftly speeding over the coal-black earth
whirling feathery wings, descending
down through the heavens.
They came swiftly. And you, O holy one
face immortal, smiling, looking down,
asked me, "Not again! Who hurts you?
What must I do now?
And what do you want most to happen
In your crazy heart? Who now must I persuade
And bring her back to your love?
Sappho, who wrongs you?
If she runs away now, soon she'll pursue you.
If she rejects your gifts, soon she'll give them.
If she hates you now, soon she'll love you,
Whether she wants to
Or not." So come again now and free me
from cruel love, and make happen
Whatever my heart desires: do it. Goddess,
Now, be my ally.

320. Note: These poems are mostly written in a very loose approximation of the meters used by Sappho.

Poem 16

Some say knights in armor, some say footsoldiers
and others claim a navy on the dark earth
are the most glorious sights. But I think it's
whoever you love most.
It's easy enough to understand this
for anyone. Just think of stunning Helen,
loveliest of all women, who abandoned
great Menelaus
And left her home to sail to Troy with Paris,
Forgetting she had a child and parents
Altogether. But somehow love enticed her ...
... but my mind's on Anactoria.
She's gone away now.
I'd rather see her drawing near me,
Her sparkling eyes and shining face,
Than all the Lydians' chariots, all those heroes
fighting in armor.

Poem 31

Godlike that man seems to me—
the one across the table
sitting and hearing your voice
talking so sweetly
and laughing adorably. It's made
my heart in my breast tremble.
As soon as I see you, my speech
falters within me
My tongue freezes in silence,
a light fire runs under my skin,
I'm blind; I'm deaf; a roaring
blares in my ears,
cold sweat pours down me; trembling
grabs my whole body. Greener than grass
my skin. I think I'm going to die
Any moment now
But all must be endured; even a poor man ...

Poem 94

Truly, I just want to die.
She cried when she left me.
She told me many things.
What awful luck we've had—
Sappho, I can't bear to leave you.
And I told her in response,
"Go, be happy, don't forget me,
for you know what you meant to me.
If you've forgotten, I'll remind you ...
... we had so much fun
So many garlands of violets
Roses and crowns of crocus ...
... you sat by my side
And winding wreaths fashioned from flowers
Around your soft neck
And ... pouring rich, royal perfumes
you anointed and ...
on soft beds you satisfied desire
And never was there any temple or grove ... dancing ...

Poem 96

... Sard[is] ...
often turning her mind this way ...
... like a true goddess, she rejoiced in your song and dance
Now she shines among the Lydian women
Just as when the sun goes down
Up comes the moon, rosy-fingered,
outshining all the stars. A light
spreads over the salty sea
and over the flowering fields.
And the dew comes down, so lovely,
the roses bloom and the soft chervil
and the leafy, honey-rich clover.
Pacing back and forth, remembering
gentle Atthis with desire,
and her tender spirit is consumed by your fate...

Translated by Sophie Mills, Department of Classics

[Greek text from *Greek Lyric Poetry: A Selection of Early Greek Lyric, Elegiac and Iambic Poetry*, edited by David A. Campbell, 40–51. London: Bristol Classical Press, 1982.]

POST-READING PARS

1. After reading these poems, how would you characterize Sappho's poetry?
2. How does Sappho's poetry compare to the features you identified as relatable in the pre-PAR?

Inquiry Corner

Content Question(s):	Critical Question(s):
What sort of poetic imagery is typical for Sappho?	What can we deduce about life for women in seventh-century BCE Lesbos from Sappho's poetry? To what degree is her experience likely to have been typical for women and what other sources might give us a fuller or different picture?
Comparative Question(s):	**Connection Question(s):**
What other ancient women's voices have you heard (whether directly or indirectly through the writings of men), and what do we learn from them about their lives?	Consider one of your favorite songs about love and compare and contrast its lyrics with Sappho's expressions about love.

from *Symposium* by Plato

Introduction

When we say that we "love" chocolate, our parents, our partner, or our cat, are these all the same kinds of love? And if not, how would we define "love" in a way that can apply to all of these? How do we know who, what, and how we love? The Athenian philosopher Plato was intensely interested in exploring concepts central to human life and well-being, such as love, justice, beauty, and so on, and conveyed his ideas through dramatic dialogues centered on a fictionalized portrayal of his mentor Socrates (470–399 BCE). By portraying the relationships between Socrates's opinions and those of other Athenian intellectuals, Plato explores some central philosophical and humanistic concepts and opens up his readers' understanding of their complexity. His dialogue *Symposium* explores the nature of love from many different angles, and this extract discusses the origin of love and its role in human existence as imagined by Aristophanes, an Athenian comic playwright, perhaps best known today for his sex comedy *Lysistrata*. Does his account of love seem entirely serious, comic, or somewhere in between?

SNAPSHOT BOX

LANGUAGE: Ancient Greek

DATE: c. 385–370 BCE

LOCATION: Athens, Greece

GENRE: Philosophical dialogue

TAGS: Body; Deities and Spirits; Love; Oral Histories and Storytelling; Origin Stories; Women and Gender

The *Symposium* is a work of philosophy rather than a literal account of one evening in Athens, but Plato's characters are real Athenians and his narrative includes many realistic details of Athenian male upper-class life. The date is 416 BCE and the tragic playwright Agathon has just won his first victory at the dramatic competitions at Athens' Festival of Dionysus. Agathon and his longtime lover Pausanias are cel-

Timeline

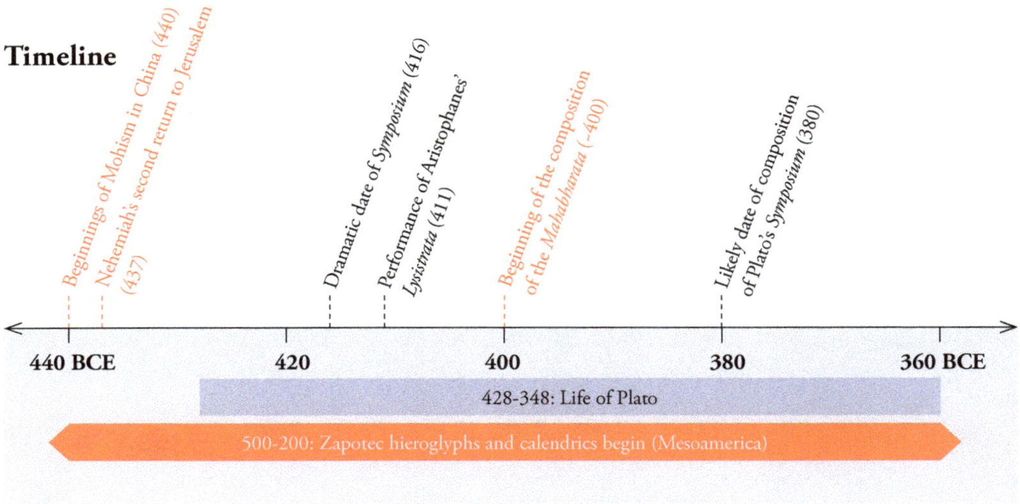

ebrating with a group of their distinguished Athenian friends, including Socrates and Aristophanes, at a **symposium**. This Greek word literally means "drinking together," and symposia had many functions in ancient Greece. They were social events for men and could be wild, drunken affairs: the "respectable" free women of the host's household were barred from attending, but other women of lower social status or slaves were available for male musical and/or sexual entertainment. But symposia could also offer the opportunity for citizens with a shared political outlook to bond with each other, or be venues for performance of music and lyric poetry, some of which survives in fragmentary form to this day.[321]

Early on in this dialogue, Plato's characters decide that, as they had all drunk too much the night before, they should stay sober and instead entertain themselves with speeches praising Love. Each man takes his turn speaking, and Socrates's speech is clearly intended to be the most important, although it remains unclear whether or not the reader is intended to reject the other speakers' ideas about love, and consider Socrates's ideas (which look nothing like conventional ideas of love, ancient or modern) as true and ideal.

Aristophanes's claim that humans are always looking for their "other half" may seem natural to modern readers, but it may be worth setting this claim alongside other evidence for the way that relationships were conducted in Greece and wondering whether it would have been so to Aristophanes's contemporaries or Plato's readers. Aristophanes imagines three types of original creatures—those composed of a male-male pairing, those of a female-female pairing, and those of a male-female pairing—but does not explore each of them in equal detail. Which does he focus on and is it possible to explain his choice? We know that it was the custom among upper-class Athenian males that an older man would take an adolescent boy (perhaps between thirteen and seventeen) as a lover, but once the boy attained adulthood, he was expected to marry a woman to produce children and then in his turn become the older lover of a younger male. How far does Aristophanes's description of male-male pairings conform to this convention?

Sophie Mills
Department of Classics

321. Compare the introduction to Sappho.

PRE-READING PARS

1. Think about your understanding of love between two people. Do you believe that there is one ideal person, "the One" for you?
2. Think back to some of the creation myths you have already read. What roles do gods play in them?

The Speech of Aristophanes

First you must learn what Human Nature was in the beginning and what has happened to it since, because long ago our nature was not what it is now; but very different. There were three kinds of human beings, that's my first point—not two as there are now, male and female. In addition to these, there was a third, a combination of those two; its name survives, though the kind itself has vanished. At that time, you see, the word "androgynous" really meant something: a form made up of male and female elements, though now there's nothing but the word, and that's used as an insult. My second point is that the shape of each human being was completely round, with back and sides in a circle; they had four hands each, as many legs as hands, and two faces, exactly alike, on a rounded neck. Between the two faces, which were on opposite sides, was one head with four ears. There were two sets of sexual organs, and everything else was the way you'd imagine it from what I've told you. They walked upright, as we do now, whatever direction they wanted. And whenever they set out to run fast, they thrust out all their eight limbs, the ones they had then, and spun rapidly, the way gymnasts do cartwheels, by bringing their legs around straight.

Now here is why there were three kinds, and why they were as I described them: The male kind was originally an offspring of the sun, the female of the earth, and the one that combined both genders was an offspring of the moon, because the moon shares in both. They were spherical, and so was their motion, because they were like their parents in the sky.

In strength and power, therefore, they were terrible, and they had great ambitions. They made an attempt on the gods, and Homer's story about Ephialtes and Otos was originally about them: how they tried to make an ascent to heaven so as to attack the gods. Then Zeus and the other gods met in council to discuss what to do, and they were sore perplexed. They couldn't wipe out the human race with thunderbolts and kill them all off, as they had the giants, because that would wipe out the worship they receive, along with the sacrifices we humans give them. On the other hand, they couldn't let them run riot. At last, after great effort, Zeus had an idea.

"I think I have a plan" he said, "that would allow human beings to exist and stop their misbehaving: they will give up being wicked when they lose their strength. So I shall now cut each of them in two. At one stroke they will lose their strength and also become more profitable to us, owing to the increase in their number. They shall walk upright on two legs. But if I find they still run riot and do not keep the peace," he said, "I will cut them in two again, and they'll have to make their way on one leg, hopping."

So saying, he cut those human beings in two, the way people cut sorb-apples before they dry them or the way they cut eggs with hairs. As he cut each one, he commanded Apollo to turn its face and half its neck towards the wound, so that each person would see that he'd been cut and keep better order. Then Zeus commanded Apollo to heal the rest of the wound, and Apollo did turn the face around, and he drew skin from all sides over what is now called the stomach, and there he made one mouth, as in a pouch with a drawstring, and fastened it at the center of the stomach. This is now called the navel. Then he smoothed out the other wrinkles, of which there were many, and he shaped the breasts, using some such tool as shoemakers have for smoothing wrinkles out of leather on the form. But he left a few wrinkles around the stomach and the navel, to be a reminder of what happened long ago.

Now, since their natural form had been cut in two, each one longed for its own other half, and so they would throw their arms about each other, weaving themselves together, wanting to grow together. In that condition they would die from hunger and general idleness, because they would not do anything apart from each other. Whenever one of the halves died and one was left, the one that was left still sought another and wove itself together with that. Sometimes the half he met came from a woman, as we'd call her now, sometimes it came from a man; either way, they kept on dying.

Then, however, Zeus took pity on them, and came up with another plan: he moved their genitals around to the front! Before then, you see, they used to have their genitals outside, like their faces, and they cast seed and made children, not in one another, but in the ground, like cicadas. So Zeus brought about this relocation of genitals, and in doing so he invented interior reproduction, by the man in the woman. The purpose of this was so that, when a man embraced a woman, he would cast his seed and they would have children; but when male embraced male, they would have at least have the satisfaction of intercourse, after which they could stop embracing, return to their jobs, and look after their other needs in life. This, then, is the source of our desire to love each other; Love is born into every human being; it calls back the halves of our original nature together; it tries to make one out of two and heal the wound of human nature.

Each of us, then, is a "matching half" of a human whole, because each was sliced like a flatfish, two out of one, and each of us is always seeking the half that matches him. That's why a man who is split from the double sort (which used to be called "androgynous") runs after women. Many lecherous men have come from this class, and so do the lecherous women who run after men. Women who are split from a woman, however, pay no attention at all to men; they are oriented more towards women, and lesbians come from this class. People who are split from a male are male-oriented. While they are boys, because they are chips off the male block, they love men and enjoy lying with men and being embraced by men; those are the best of boys and lads, because they are the most manly in their nature. Of course, some say such boys are shameless, but they're lying. It's not because they have no shame that such boys do this, you see, but because they are bold and brave and masculine, and they tend to cherish what is like themselves. Do you want me to prove it? Look, these are the only kind of boys who grow up to be politicians. When they're grown men, they are lovers of young men, and they naturally pay no attention to marriage or to making babies, except insofar as they are required by local custom. They, however, are quite satisfied to live their lives with one another unmarried. In every way, then, this sort of man grows up as a lover of young men and a lover of Love, always rejoicing in his own kind.

And so, when a person meets the half that is his very own, whatever his orientation, whether it's to young men or not, then something wonderful happens: the two are struck from their senses by love, by a sense of belonging to one another, and by desire, and they don't want to be separated from one another, not even for a moment.

These are the people who finish out their lives together and still cannot say what it is they want from one another. No one would think it is the intimacy of sex--that mere sex is the reason each lover takes so great and deep a joy in being with the other. It's obvious that the soul of every lover longs for something else; his soul cannot say what it is, but like an oracle it has a sense of what it wants, and like an oracle it hides behind a riddle. Suppose two lovers are lying together and Hephaestus stands over them with his mending tools, asking, "What is it you human beings really want from each other?" And suppose they're perplexed, and he asks them again: 'Is this your heart's desire, then—for the two of you to become parts of the same whole, as near as can be, and never to separate, day or night? Because if that's your desire, I'd like to weld you together and join you into something that is naturally whole, so that the two of you are made into one. Then the two of you would share one life, as long as you lived, because you would be one being, and by the same token, when you died, you would be one and not two in Hades, having died a single death. Look at your love, and see if this is what you desire: wouldn't this be all the good fortune you could want?"

Surely you can see that no one who received such an offer would turn it down; no one would find anything else that he wanted. Instead, everyone would think he'd found out at last what he had always wanted to come together and melt together with the one he loves, so that one person emerged from two. Why should this be so? It's because, as I said, we used to be complete wholes in our original nature, and now "Love" is the name for our pursuit of wholeness, for our desire to be complete.

Long ago we were united, as I said; but now the god has divided us as punishment for the wrong we did him, just as the Spartans divided the Arcadians. So there's a danger that if we don't keep order before the gods, we'll be split in two again, and then we'll be walking around in the condition of people carved on gravestones in bas-relief, sawn apart between the nostrils, like half dice. We should encourage all men, therefore, to treat the gods with all due reverence, so that we may escape this fate and find wholeness instead. And we will, if Love is our guide and our commander. Let no one work against him. Whoever opposes Love is hateful to the gods, but if we become friends of the god and cease to quarrel with him, then we shall find the young men that are meant for us and win their love, as very few men do nowadays.

Now don't get ideas, Eryximachus, and turn this speech into a comedy. Don't think I'm pointing this at Pausanias and Agathon. Probably, they both do belong to the group that are entirely masculine in nature. But I am speaking about everyone, men and women alike, and I say there's just one way for the human race to flourish: we must bring love to its perfect conclusion, and each of us must win the favors of his very own young man, so that he can recover his original nature. If that is the ideal, then, of course, the nearest approach to it is best in present circumstances, and that is to win the favor of young men who are naturally sympathetic to us.

If we are to give due praise to the god who can give us this blessing, then, we must praise Love. Love does the best that can be done for the time being: he draws us towards what belongs to us. But for the future, Love promises the greatest hope of all: if we treat the gods with due reverence, he will restore to us our original nature, and by healing us, he will make us blessed and happy.

Plato. "The Speech of Aristophanes." In *Symposium*. Translated by Alexander Nehamas and Paul Woodruff, 25–30. Indianapolis, IN: Hackett, 1989.

POST READING PARS

1. To what extent does Aristophanes's account of love ring true to you from your understanding? To what extent does it seem different?
2. What elements of creation myths can you see in Aristophanes's narrative?

Inquiry Corner

Content Question(s):

Look at the detailed language in which Aristophanes describes the gods' interventions in shaping the original human beings. What effects could this have on his readers?

Critical Question(s):

This speech has historically been cited in the fight for LGBTQ equality as a glorification of same-sex relationships and its celebration of male same-sex relationships in Athens as a model for modern society to aspire to. Are you convinced by such a reading?

Comparative Question(s):

What other reading from the ancient world places gender and sexuality at the heart of their understanding of love? How do these sources compare with Aristophanes's account?

Connection Question(s):

To what extent do Aristophanes's notions of gender and sexuality map onto your understanding/beliefs?

Bhagavad Gita (Introduction only)

Introduction

The *Bhagavad-Gita* (Song of the Lord) is a part of the sixth chapter of the Hindu epic *Mahabharata*. Popularly referred to as the *Gita*, it is traditionally considered to have been authored by the sage Vyasa. Scholars think that the *Gita* was composed somewhere between 400 BCE and 400 CE, although they recognize that many parts of the *Mahabharata*, along with the outline of the conversation captured in the *Gita*, were probably circulating orally in different parts of the Indian subcontinent much earlier. The core story of the *Mahabharata* narrates the battle for control of an ancient northern Indian kingdom of Hastinapur. This battle was between two sets of cousins—the Pandavas and the Kauravas—of the same Aryan clan named Bharata. The main characters of the *Gita* are Arjuna, the third Pandava brother, an unparalleled archer who is arguably the most important warrior on their side, and Krishna, Arjuna's dear friend and his charioteer during the battle. It becomes evident in the course of the *Gita* that Krishna is an incarnation of the Hindu god Vishnu. Have you encountered another character like Krishna in your various readings for this course?

Written in poetic Sanskrit, the *Gita*'s welcoming style, vivid imagery, and clear message reflect Krishna's deep caring not only for Arjuna but for all his devotees and for humanity. Among Hindu religious texts, the *Gita* enjoys an exceptional popularity. It has been translated into most of the regional languages of India, and almost all major philosophers and thinkers of classical and modern India have written interpretations of the *Gita*. It is also integral to

SNAPSHOT BOX

LANGUAGE: Sanskrit

DATE: c. 400 BCE–400 CE

LOCATION: South Asia

GENRE: Epic poetry, philosophy

RELIGIOUS IDENTITY: Hindu

TAGS: Class and Wealth; Conflict and War; Death; Deities and Spirits; Ethics and Morality; Freedom and Harmony; Love; Philosophy; Religion; Sacrifice; Ways of Knowing

Timeline

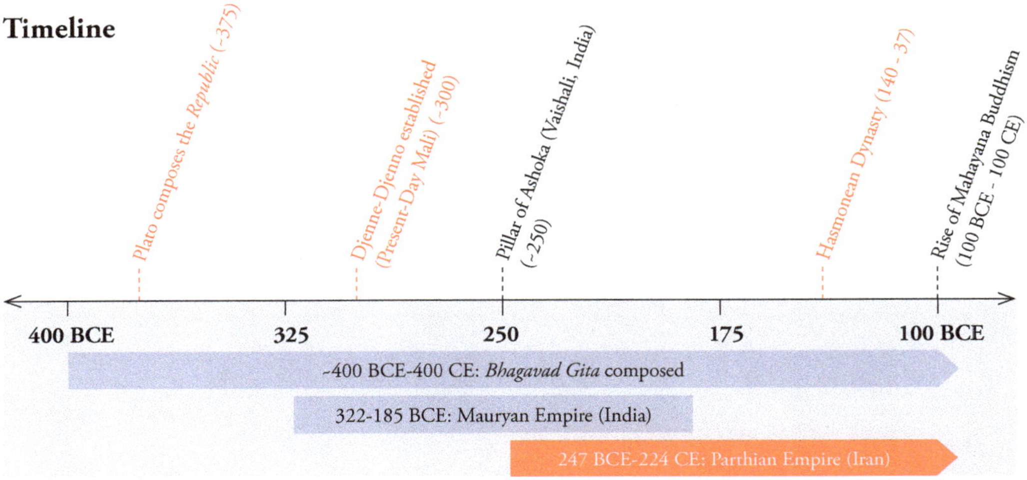

everyday rituals and religiosity, offering meaning and solace to countless Hindus. Mahatma Gandhi underscores the *Gita*'s relevance and potential by crediting it as the sole source and inspiration behind his revolutionary concept of nonviolent resistance. How might it be possible for Krishna's positive counsel about war to co-exist with messages of nonviolence?

The opening chapter of the *Gita* presents Arjuna's passionate arguments for not joining the impending battle. Arjuna is dejected because joining the battle would require him to take up arms against and ultimately kill his teachers, relatives, and friends, who had joined the battle on the Kaurava side. The rest of the *Gita* contains Krishna's counsel that not only convinces Arjuna to join the battle by the end but also offers peace, certainty, and comfort. If you imagine yourself in Arjuna's position compelled to make a decision that would cause harm to those you love, what could your companion say that would offer you peace and comfort?

There are a few concepts that will facilitate a deeper engagement with the *Gita*. First is the interrelated concept of rebirth and the theory of karma. Rebirth, simply speaking, stands for the Hindu belief that when one dies, the enduring, eternal part of one—***atman*** (which in the West is often called the soul, but in its Hindu context is better translated as the self) generally recycles back to the universe in another physical form. Hindus consider this cycle of birth and rebirths to be beginningless. If one has to be reborn, then how is it determined whether one should be reborn as a human or a lion or a skunk or even as an ant? The answer lies in the law of karma. It is a universal moral law that maintains that every intentional action produces a trace or residue that has to be faced by its agent. According to the theory of karma, the accumulated karmic residue operates as an inescapable rut that guarantees our future births.

There are at least two sets of reasons behind the enduring value of Krishna's counsel. The first set follows from the *Gita*'s skillful molding together of the metaphysical (having to do with the fundamental nature of reality), the ethical (offering ways one must live one's life), and the spiritual (having to do with the ultimate goal of human life). In metaphysics, Krishna draws on the central Hindu concept of ***Brahman*** or the ultimate reality as the foundation for everything. Krishna identifies himself as the highest *Brahman* as well as the *atman* living in every embodied being. In ethics, Krishna utilizes the multidimensional concept of ***yoga***, a popular Sanskrit term that literally means union. The *Gita* is celebrated for its inclusive and expansive use of this concept, which it uses not only as a way or means to arrive at the final goal of a Hindu life, but also as the goal itself. Finally, the *Gita* draws from the Hindu concept of ***moksha*** (freedom from *samsara* or the cycle of rebirth) in outlining the ultimate goal of a human life. Krishna declares that one attains *moksha* by becoming one with Krishna, by realizing the true identity of one's *atman* with *Brahman* and Krishna. As you read the *Gita*, ascertain the occasions that articulate this core message of unity.

The second set of reasons for the *Gita*'s enduring resonance within Hinduism follows from its unique ability to synthesize many different and often divergent strands of various Hindu philosophical and religious themes. Some Hindu philosophies emphasize renunciation, the idea of abandoning our societal and familial responsibilities for a life of retreat, asceticism, and quiet contemplation. They further emphasize that only renunciation will grant a person knowledge about their true nature—their identity with Krishna and that knowledge alone allows them to attain *moksha*. Others emphasize the importance of action—rituals involving the worship of the numerous gods and goddesses of Hinduism, and assigned caste duties among others—as a way to arrive at this same freedom. The *Gita* almost effortlessly weaves these two themes together by narrowing the gap between the two and arguing that both knowledge and action, when performed with the appropriate mental attitude, will prepare one for liberation from *samsara*. The *Gita* identifies these two as the ***yoga* of knowledge** and ***yoga* of action**, respectively, and assures that both deliver the same end of becoming one with Krishna. Finally, the *Gita* introduces the ***yoga* of *bhakti*** or devotion as an important third way of attaining *moksha* or oneness with Krishna. This *yoga* underscores Krishna's role as the personal divinity for his devotees to worship him with complete surrender, tender love, and deepest trust. Among the three *yoga*s the *Gita* champions, is there one that, in your opinion, might best suit the life of a college student?

No introduction to the *Gita* can be complete without addressing its central concept of ***samatvam*** or equanimity. It refers to our ability to see everything with an equal eye and requires us to love everyone and care for friend and foe equally. Many scholars of the *Gita* identify equanimity as the most fundamental virtue that the *Gita* proposes. Krishna clarifies that it is the necessary virtue that enables the successful performance of every *yoga*: the performance of action without attachment, without worrying about results; the pursuit of self-knowledge through meditation and deep contemplation; and devotion with complete submission. What are some situations where a response with equanimity might offer you the best strategy? How might a cultivation of equanimity allow us to learn skills useful in our public liberal arts educational contexts?

Keya Maitra
Department of Philosophy

Recommended Translations:

Philosophy of the Bhagavad Gita: A Contemporary Introduction. Transated by Keya Maitra. New York: Bloomsbury Academic, 2018.

Bhagavad Gita: Krishna's Counsel in Time of War. Translated by Barbara Stoler Miller. New York: Bantam Classics, 1986.

Kisagotami

SNAPSHOT BOX

LANGUAGE: Sinhalese

DATE: c. 5th century CE

LOCATION: Sri Lanka

GENRE: Oral narrative

TAGS: Class and Wealth; Death; Desire and Happiness; Ethics and Morality; Oral Histories and Storytelling; Suffering and Compassion; Wisdom; Women and Gender

Introduction

Kisagotami was one of the first women to join the *sangha*, or Buddhist monastic community. Her poems appeared in the earliest Buddhist teachings, the Pali Canon, and she is best known for her encounter with death and journey of discovery about the nature of suffering (Pali: *dukkhah*; Sanskrit: *duḥkha*) that leads to her eventual enlightenment narrated here. This narrative is from a collection of stories about exemplary women in early Buddhism that has a complex translation history. After starting as an oral tradition in Sinhalese, the everyday language of Sri Lanka, it was translated into Pali, back into Sinhalese, and then into English.

The story of Kisagotami follows a familiar pattern within the genre of enlightenment narratives with karma and nirvana as the main framing concepts. **Karma**, or "action," refers typically to the consequences of people's behaviors from previous lives or this lifetime, that serve to set up the conditions for lifetimes that follow. ***Nirvana*** literally means to extinguish or blow out the conditions of karma. A person becomes an ***arahant***, or ***arhat***, after reaching nirvana thus becoming enlightened. In Buddhism, enlightenment narratives highlight the context and special qualities or character of the person that are the result of their karma. These types of narratives often interweave aspects of how the karma of different people lead up to a particular intersecting event or moment. For example, this story about Kisagotami begins with an embedded mini-narrative about a merchant and

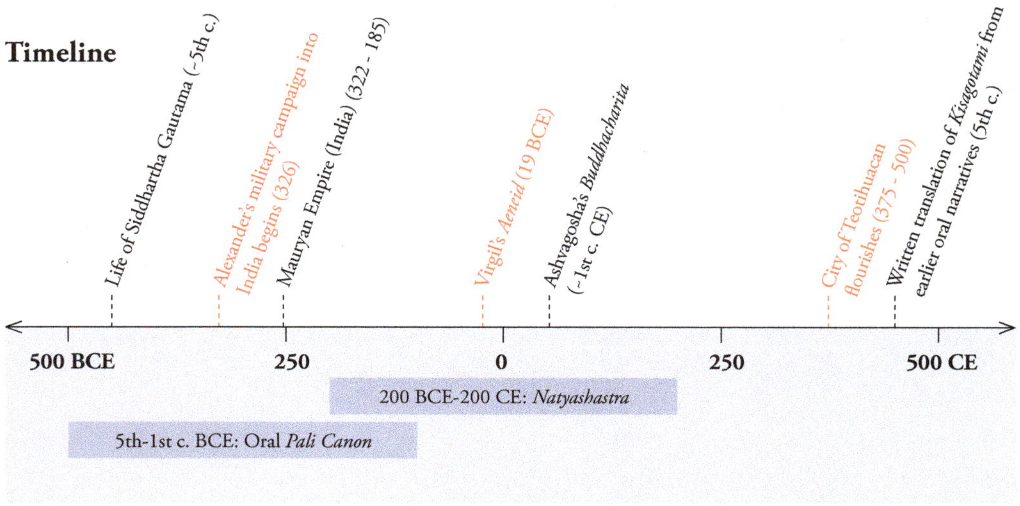

his karmic conditions. How does this mini-narrative involving the merchant establish information about Kisagotami's karma?

In the main narrative, a particularly tragic event sends Kisagotami looking for answers. Because this experience of loss is so personal, Kisagotami is not able to see the bigger picture at first. When she approaches the Buddha for answers, what strategies might the Buddha suggest to help her understand this loss on a more universal scale for herself?

It is through engaging the Buddha's strategy that Kisagotami can let go of her different levels of attachments, another key theme of Buddhism, and turn toward a monastic life. Becoming a ***sovan***, meaning "stream-enterer," indicates that she has stepped onto the path, or river, leading to nirvana or enlightenment. Women were at first not allowed to become monastics, but with the intervention of Siddhartha's aunt/stepmother, Mahaprajapati, and Siddhartha's closest assistant monk, Ananda, a women's monastic structure was established with extra rules meant to navigate public perception about mixed-gender interactions current in ancient India. While the rules point to institutional gender disparities and an unbalanced burden of propriety placed on the nuns, in that time period it created the first designated space for women to practice monasticism communally, as well as acknowledged that *nirvana* was possible for all genders, castes, and classes.

As you read this narrative, keep in mind that narratives are received and interpreted differently in cultures that encounter Buddhist ideas. The tension between the personal experience of death and its universal nature may be one common way to read the narrative. In China, however, it is read more through a lens that highlights the community's role in our experiences of loss. What American metaphors and values might change the interpretation of this story to make it relevant in our contemporary context today?

Katherine C. Zubko
Department of Religious Studies

PRE-READING PARS

1. What do you think the role of a teacher is? Brainstorm three to five ideas.
2. Make a list of three to five people you know who have authority in different contexts. What criteria, factors, or qualifications lead them to have authority in that situation?

The Story of Kisagotami

Moreover, to illustrate that wisdom becomes a refuge in every situation we shall relate the tale of Kisagotami. How does it go?

The home of a certain noble merchant in the city of Savat together with his entire wealth of about four hundred million all turned to charcoal as a result of what was left of some past bad karma. Greatly depressed by what had happened, the noble merchant refused all food and took to his bed. A friend came to visit him and inquired, "My good friend why are you depressed?" He learned the cause and added, "Friend, do not be upset. What has now become charcoal was once your wealth. By some expedient is it not possible for the charcoal to turn again into wealth? I know a way to turn that charcoal into wealth. Even what is not gold or silver can be turned into gold and silver by certain devices. Do as I tell you."

"What shall I do?" he asked.

"Order some mats for your store, spread them out, heap that charcoal on the mats, and sit there as if you were selling it. If people come up and say, 'Others sell oil, honey, jaggery,[322] clothes, and such things. You sell charcoal,' reply, 'If I don't sell what I have what should I sell?' Now if someone else comes along and says, 'Others sell clothes and such like goods. You sell gold and silver,' reply, 'What gold and silver?' When they say, 'Why, like this you have here, say,' 'Then give it to me,' and get them to bring it to you. Thus whatever they bring when it reaches your hand will (as if secretly) turn to gold. Now if the person who gives you the gold is a young woman, then bring her to your household (since the association will be beneficial) and give your son in marriage to her and also your four hundred million in wealth.' Live on what she gives you. If the person who gives you the gold and silver happens to be a man, then marry your young daughter to him and give the four hundred million to your son-in-law, just as with a daughter-in-law. Take what he gives and live on it. Don't try to keep ownership of your wealth or enjoy it except in this way."

He took the advice, heaped the charcoal outside his shop, and sat as if selling it. At that time a very poor young woman who was named Kisagotami because she was

322. Jaggery is a type of brown sugar.

physically lean (though she was very strong in Merit[323]) came to the fair to buy something. She saw the noble merchant and said, "Others keep cloth and such things for sale but why do you sell gold? These are things one should buy even if one sells all else?"

"My child, where is the gold?"

"You are like one who while traveling along the road asks where the road is. Those piles you have there are gold."

"If that is so my child, give me some in my hand."

As the young woman picked up a handful of charcoal it turned to gold by the power of her Merit just as the Venerable Pilindivacca's[324] garland turned into a golden necklace by the power of his psychic powers and by the merit of those in the monastery. Even what was put in the merchant's hands remained gold, and did not turn back into charcoal.[325]

"My child, where do you live?" asked the noble merchant. When she told him he inquired if there were suitors for her hand and when he learned there weren't any he then paid all the expenses and gave her in marriage to his son. He gave the four hundred million as a dowry as the piles of charcoal had all turned into silver and gold.

Some time after her marriage, she conceived a child not destined to live long. After ten months she gave birth to a son, who was like a visitor who came for a limited time. Just at the age when he began to take his first steps he died. Kisagotami had not seen a dead person before so she stopped those who were to take her son for burial or burning, saying, "I'll go ask for some medicine for my child."

Carrying her dead child on her shoulder she set out. She went from house to house asking, "Do you know of a medicine to cure my child?"

Those she spoke to would answer, "Child, are you crazy to seek medicine for a dead child?" In spite of whatever anyone said, she kept asking for the medicine she was seeking.

One wise man saw her and thought, 'This is perhaps her firstborn so she has not seen a dead child before. I must try to be of help to her.' He said to her, "My child, I do not know of such a medicine but I do know of a place where you can find such a medicine."

"O Father,[326] who is it who knows such a medicine?" she asked.

"Child, the Lord Buddha, teacher of the Three Worlds,[327] knows everything.

323. Merit refers to what is accrued through good actions, or beneficial actions done without attachment.

324. It is common in South Asian storytelling to make brief, unexplained references to other characters and events the audience would be aware of, and that invite a wider nexus of interconnections.

325. The assumption is that he regains his lost wealth through the magical powers of the woman.

326. The use of "father" here is a term of respect used for male elders who are not biologically related.

327. Refers to the formless realm (*arupa*) or heaven, the human world of form (*rupa*), and hell or the spirit world of (*kama*) lust.

Therefore, would he not know of such medicines and cures? He knows cures for everything. Go there and ask him," he said.

"Good," she said and went to the Buddha. She worshiped[328] him in greeting and standing on one side she said, "Your Reverence, do you know a cure for my child?"

"I who knows the deathless state[329] and the cure for birth, decay, and the sufferings of life, why would I not know that? I do know," he said.

"What then is needed [for the cure?]," she asked.

"A pinch of fresh mustard seed,"[330] he replied.

"Isn't it easy to find that? From what sort of place should I get it?" she asked.

The power of her intelligence could be gauged from the fact that she did not set off to look for mustard seed merely on being told to get it but asked some basic questions.

"Listen Gotami, I do not want it collected from any household at random. If there is a household that has not lost a daughter or a son, get it from such a house," he said.

"Good," she replied, and worshiping the Buddha and carrying her dead child on her shoulder she left for the inner city. At the first house she asked, "Do you have any mustard seeds? It is to make a medicine for my son." When the people replied that they did, she asked them for some. As they brought it to her she asked, "Have you lost a son or daughter in this household?"

"My child what can I say? There are as many more who have died here as there are living."

"In that case your mustard seed will not be a cure for my child," she said and gave it back.

In this manner she walked to every house in the village inquiring but could not find what she wanted from a single house. Toward evening she thought, 'Alas, it seems impossible to do. I think only of my son dying. But in this village there seem to be more sons and daughters who have died than there are living.' As she thought thus she realized that there was no other cure for the disease of death and her ailment of overpowering affection for her child eased somewhat. As the grief arising from her strong affection eased little by little her heart became strong. Just as ashram-dwelling yogis discard a corpse once it passes the swollen stage[331] so she buried the corpse of her son and went to the Buddha, worshiped him, and stood on one side.

The Buddha, knowing that she had not obtained it, asked, "Did you find the handful of mustard seed?"

328. By worship what is meant is to give honor to him through appropriate greetings and respect.

329. In Theravada Buddhism, the deathless state is the state of being enlightened, as one no longer is accruing the karma that would create the circumstances for another lifetime, and thus if there is not a birth into a next life, there is also no death.

330. A common household cooking spice.

331. This practice of observing a corpse as a form of meditation was sometimes done in order to understand the impermanence of the body. Ascetics, or those who had renounced their householder lives, had already conducted their own "funeral" when they became a yogi, and so at their physical death, their bodies were not cremated but placed in the river.

"Your Reverence I did not. There were as many dead sons and daughters in this village as there were living."

"If you cannot find the medicinal ingredients we need, then what can we do? Just as you could not obtain such mustard seed so there is no cure for the dead. What one can do is find a medicine to stop one from dying," and he recited a stanza from the twentieth Magga (Path).

At the end of the stanza Kisagotami became a *sovan*, partook of the medicine of nirvana and rid herself of the three ailments, such as the belief in the body as a personal possession. Many others, too, attained to the state of *sovan* and other states.

Having become a *sovan* she asked to be ordained so she could find the cure for the ills of birth and suffering through the monastic order. The Buddha sent her to the nuns and she was ordained and conferred Higher Ordination. Having obtained the status of seniority she became known as the Elder Nun Kisagotami.

One day when it was her turn to do the observances at the temple she made the offering of lights and as she saw the flames die down and rekindle again she thought, 'We beings, if we cannot stop the continuous rebirth process, will be born again and again. Since death is inevitable, all creatures born must die. Only those who attain nirvana become extinct leaving no residual matter. She made the lighted lamp, like a weapon come to hand, an object of meditation.

The Buddha, seated in his perfumed chamber, sent out a ray of light to her and as if he were talking to her in her presence, said, "Gotami, it is so. Other than Designatory Form and Characteristic Form all other types of Form have a lifespan of not more than seventeen mental moments. Formless entities are also subject to the three characteristics, namely, birth, existence, and destruction. Hence these beings die an instant death or by death as a [sequential] process. Those who die are born again. That does not happen even after a long time when one attains nirvana.[332] Therefore if one were to live a hundred years (which is the longest one can live in this era) without understanding nirvana it is of no use. But to live for one day having seen nirvana is blessed, because such a one has no fear of hell and fear of samsara is lessened."

At the end of the teaching Kisagotami, even as she sat there, reached the final stage of *arahat* with the Fourfold Analytic Powers. Though she was physically lean she filled out in goodness.

Thus good men though they are lacking in physical fitness should acquire mental fitness, free themselves from Acts of Demerit, perform Acts of Merit, and cultivate goodness.

Obeyesekere, Ranjani, trans. *Portraits of Buddhism Women: Stories from the Saddharmaratnavaliya (Jewel of the Doctrine)*, 134–37. New York: SUNY Press, 2001.

332. This is a fairly condensed reference to a technical Theravada approach explaining the nature of impermanence in relation to what appears to be solid and consistent forms, whether physical matter or mental ideas.

POST-READING PARS

1. In what ways does the approach of the Buddha compare with your expectations of the role of a teacher?
2. Who has authority in the narrative? How do they compare to what you discovered in the list about authority and criteria you made before reading?

Inquiry Corner

Content Question(s):	**Critical Question(s):**
What is a *sovan*? Who has authority in the narrative, and why and how do you know?	What forms of knowledge create authority in this story? What is the relationship between death and self-knowledge in this story?
Comparative Question(s):	**Connection Question(s):**
What is the function of death in the story of Kisagotami in comparison to its role in *Gilgamesh*? How do Hindu and Buddhist understandings of dharma align or come into conflict in the story of Kisagotami?	When have you gained knowledge or wisdom from interacting with a community instead of from a teacher or on your own?

from *Life of the Buddha* (*Buddhacarita*) by Ashvaghosha

Introduction

SNAPSHOT

LANGUAGE: Sanskrit

DATE: 1st century CE

LOCATION: South Asia

GENRE: Poetry

TAGS: Asceticism; Deities and Spirits; Desire and Happiness; Ethics and Morality; Family; Freedom and Harmony; Hagiography; Identity; Journey; Rhetoric and Propaganda; Suffering and Compassion; Women and Gender

Ashvaghosa provides us with one of the earliest written documents detailing the life of Siddhartha Gautama Sakya, who would become the Buddha, or "one who is awake." The only other earlier sources about the life of the Buddha are connected to the oral scriptural traditions of the Pali Canon, passed down in the vernacular language of Pali for centuries. The earliest dating of Ashvaghosha's text is first century CE, over five hundred years after the historical life of the Buddha. How might this distance from the lifetime of the Buddha impact what is told in the narrative?

Ashvaghosa was born a Hindu **brahmin**—a member of the priestly caste—and had achieved some fame as a learned scholar of the Vedas and well-respected poet. Later in life he took vows of celibacy and joined a Buddhist monastery while living in the northern kingdom of the Kushanas, rulers who were great patrons of Buddhist institutions.

This text is what could be called an ***apologia***, a genre that seeks to defend a particular position against its detractors. In this case, Ashvaghosa is making an argument for presenting Buddhism as the next step in the evolution of Hindu Brahmanism (an early Vedic ritual system focused on fire sacrifice performed by brahmins). Because of this focus, Ashvaghosa utilizes several forms of authority in his rhetoric that would have resonated with Hindu brahmins, the main audience he was trying to convince. For example, he composes the text in Sanskrit, the language of the Vedas, rather

Timeline

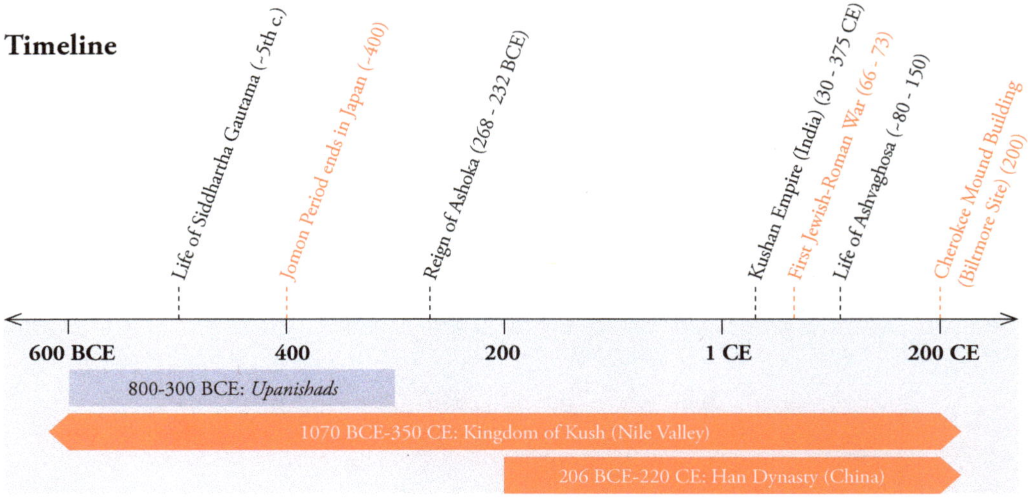

than a vernacular language. Hindu deities, usually in disguise, are constantly intervening in the story to move Siddhartha to the next step of his journey. Both Siddhartha's father, Suddhodana, and Siddhartha are referred to as the equivalent of Indra or other deities.

These examples would have placed the story of Siddhartha's life squarely within a recognizable Hindu framework and help Ashvaghosa make the argument that even Hindu deities are helping Buddhism to emerge as a valid path. The use of Hindu frameworks as an apologia is closely linked to another genre evident in this text, namely ***hagiography.*** It is defined as a biography of a religious figure from the perspective of a believer within the tradition that often emphasizes miraculous aspects. What types of physical features and actions of Siddhartha that Ashvaghosa highlights make the Buddha-to-be stand out as extraordinary?

This chapter, "The Departure," comes at a point in the narrative just after Siddhartha has encountered three of the **four passing sights**: an old person, a sick person, and a corpse. These have stirred in Siddhartha a deep existential crisis about the human condition. It is now that he first encounters the fourth sight, an **ascetic**, or one that has renounced their worldly ***dharma***, or duties, to pursue religious insight. This exchange with the ascetic gives Siddhartha a pathway of how to begin the search for answers to his own troubling questions.

Before Siddhartha leaves his home, as a good dutiful son, he goes and asks his father, the king, for permission. This passage is an important example of an apologia. Note how Siddhartha's father argues in several ways why Siddhartha should not leave and become an ascetic. He utilizes mostly Hindu understandings of dharma, or duty, in contrast to Siddhartha's focus on changing the definition of dharma toward a Buddhist understanding of "teachings" and the pursuit of experiential truths.

On a final note, at the end of the chapter, there is a key passage that is often troublesome regarding the depiction of women. In these verses, what patterns do you see in how women are being described? Do they have any personal voice or names? Ashvaghosa, as a male celibate monk, may be utilizing the idea of "women" to serve particular rhetorical purposes in relation to Buddhist teachings. What do you think those might be? Even Buddhists today wrestle with these passages, but knowing about Ashvaghosa's own context may point to some possible interpretations.

Katherine C. Zubko
Department of Religious Studies

PRE-READING PARS

1. Identify two or three examples of when leaving home and family is socially acceptable.
2. Think of a role model or person you admire who is no longer living. What two or three features do you choose to highlight about that person and why?

The Departure (Canto 5)

1: Although, in this way, the Shakya king's son
was enticed with priceless objects of sense,
yet he got no content, found no relief,
like a lion shot in the heart
with a poison-tipped arrow.
2: Then one day, with the consent of the king,
he went outside to see the wooded groves,
along with able sons of ministers
and friends good at narrating vivid tales,
yearning to find peace.
3: He set out mounted on the good horse Kánthaka—
the bells hanging from its bit were made of new gold,
its gold trappings made charming with
    flowing chowries—
like the glint of *drumábja* mounted on a flag.[333]
4: Love of the woods and the exquisite land
drew him deep into the distant forest;
there he saw the earth being plowed, with furrows
resembling the rippling waves on water.
5: Clumps of grass dug up by the plow littered the earth,
covered with tiny dead creatures, insects and worms;
as he beheld the earth with all these strewn about,
he grieved greatly, as if a kinsman had been killed.
6: Seeing the men plowing the fields,
    their bodies discolored
by the wind, the dust, the scorching
    rays of the sun,

333. The *drumábja* is also known as *karnikára*, whose fragrant yellow flowers are used for dressing the hair. They were put at the top of a flag pole carried into battle. Sleeping women at 5.51 are compared to karnikára branches torn down by an elephant. This may be an allusion to their wearing karnikára flowers in their hair.

oxen wearied by the toil of pulling the plows,
great compassion overwhelmed that great noble man.
7: Getting down from the horse, then, he began to pace
slowly across that land, deeply engulfed by grief,
reflecting on the birth and death of all creatures;
and deeply anguished, he cried out:
"How wretched, indeed, is this world!"
8: Getting rid of those friends who accompanied him,
wishing to reach some clarity in his own mind,
he reached the foot of a rose apple tree in a
lonely spot with charming leaves rustling all around.
9: On that pure ground with grass the color of beryl,
he sat down, and as he began to contemplate
the origin and destruction of all creatures,
he embarked upon the path of mental stillness.
10: Achieving at once the state of mental stillness,
and freedom from worries, such as sensual desire,
he attained the first trance—
with thought and reflection,
tranquil, uninfluenced by the evil inflows.[334]
11: Thereupon, he attained absorption of the mind,
born of discernment, with the joy of supreme bliss;
knowing rightly in his mind the course of the world,
thereafter he pondered over this very thing:
12: "How wretched that ignorant man,
blinded by pride,
who, though himself powerless
and subject to the law
Of disease, old age, and death,
should treat with contempt
another who's sick, dead, or oppressed by old age!
13: If I, being myself like that,
should treat with contempt
another man here with a nature just like that,
It would not befit me, and it would not be right,
I who have come to fathom
this supreme dharma."
14: As he thus saw rightly the evils of the world,
the evils of disease, old age, and death,

334. The "evil inflows" are caused by desire and action, which are tendencies that produce rebirth.

pride of self in an instant departed from him,
pride resulting from his strength, youth, and life.
15: He did not give in to dejection or delight;
he did not give in to doubt, or to sloth or sleep;
he felt no attachment to sensual delights;
he did not hate others or treat them with contempt.
16: As this awareness, stainless and free of passion,
began to wax strong in that noble man,
a man approached him wearing a mendicant's garb,
unseen by any of the other men.
17: The son of the king then questioned that man:
"Tell me. Who are you?"
And the man gave him this reply:
"Frightened by birth and death, bull among men,
I have gone forth as a recluse,
for the sake of release.
18: I seek release within this perishable world,
I seek that holy and imperishable state,
I regard my own people and others alike,
love and hate of sensual things
have been extinguished in me.
19: Dwelling anywhere at all—under trees,
a deserted temple, forest or hill—
I wander without possessions or wants,
living on almsfood I happen to get,
in search of the supreme goal."
20: Having said this, he flew into the sky,
even as the son of the king looked on;
for he was a deity who in that form
had seen other Buddhas[335] and had come down
to arouse the attention of the prince.
21: When he had flown to the sky like a bird,
that foremost of men was thrilled and amazed;
then, perceiving that emblem of dharma,[336]
he set his mind on how he might leave home.

335. By the time Ashvaghosa composes his text, Siddhartha is not the only Buddha, or "awakened one," especially within the cosmology of Mahayana Buddhism.

336. The mendicant garb is the emblem of dharma, that is, a sign that the man wearing it is devoted to renunciation. This emblem showed the way to release, as a result of which the Buddha decided to leave home.

22: Then, that Indra's equal,[337]
who had controlled the horses of senses,
mounted his horse to enter the city;
out of concern for his men he did not
go directly to the forest he loved.
23: Intending to destroy old age and death,
his mind set on living the forest life,
he entered the city again
unwillingly, like an elephant king
from the forest entering a corral.
24: On seeing him entering along the road,
a royal maiden, her palms joined, exclaimed:
"Happy, indeed, and fulfilled is the wife,
O Long-eyed One,[338]
Who has for her husband here such a man!"
25. Then, as he heard this voice,
he obtained supreme calm,
he whose voice was like that of a great thunder cloud;
for, as he heard the word "fulfilled," he set his mind
on the means to final Nirvanic fulfillment.
26: Then, in stature like the peak of the golden mount,
arms of an elephant, voice of a thunder cloud,
eyes of a bull, gait of a lion, face like the moon,
he reached the dwelling place
with his yearning aroused
for the dharma that's imperishable.
27: Then he, with the gait of the king of beasts, approached
the king attended by the group of ministers,
as Sanat-kumára in the third heaven approached
Indra shining in the council of the Maruts.[339]
28: He prostrated himself with his palms joined and said:
"Kindly grant me permission, O god among men;
to gain release, I desire the wandering life,
For separation is appointed for this man."
29: Hearing his words, the king began to shake,

337. Indra is the chief Hindu Vedic god. As Ashvaghosa was writing for a Hindu brahmin audience, he makes many references that compare Siddhartha and his father to Hindu gods, such as Indra and Rama, to emphasize the power and stature of Siddhartha.

338. Long-eyed One (referring to Siddhartha) is an honorific referring to the beautiful shaped eyes that are elongated like a lotus petal.

339. Sanat-kumára is the fourth mind-born son of the Hindu god Brahma. The Maruts are gods of wind and storm that accompany Indra.

like a tree struck down by an elephant;
grasping his hands that looked like lotus buds,
the king uttered these words, choking with tears:

30: "Turn back, my son, from this resolution,
for it's not the time for you
to give yourself to dharma;
For, when you're young and your mind is fickle,
there are many dangers, they say,
in the practice of dharma.

31: As objects of sense tend to excite his senses,
as he can't be firm facing the hardships of vows,
A young man's mind turns away
from the wilderness,
above all as he is not used to solitude.

32: But for me it is the time for dharma,
after conferring on you sovereignty,
you who possess the marks of sovereignty
O lover of dharma;
But if you leave your father by violating
the right order, you whose courage is firm,
your dharma will turn into *adharma*.[340]

33: So, give up this resolution of yours,
give yourself for now to household dharma;
For, when one goes to the ascetic grove
after he has enjoyed the joys of youth,
it's truly a wonderful sight!"

34: Hearing these words of the king, he gave this reply,
in a voice like that of a *kalavínka* bird[341]:
"If you will become a surety for me
in four things, O King,
I will not go to the ascetic grove.

35: My life shall never be subject to death,
disease shall not steal this good health of mine,
Old age shall never overtake my youth,
no mishap shall rob this fortune of mine."

36: To his son making such a hard request,
the king of the Shakyas made this response:
"Withdraw this your request, it is inordinate;

340. By placing an "a" in front of the term *dharma*, it creates the opposite meaning, thus *adharma* means unrighteous or against one's duty.

341. A *kalavínka* bird is likely a sparrow or finch.

An extravagant wish is improper and extreme."
37: Then that one, mighty as Meru[342], told his father:
"If that's not possible, don't hold me back;
for it is not right to obstruct a man,
Who's trying to escape from a burning house.
38: When separation is the fixed rule for this world,
is it not far better for dharma's sake
to make that separation on my own?
Will death not separate me as I stand
helpless and unfulfilled,
without reaching my goal?"
39: When the king thus ascertained the resolve
of his son in search of final release,
he exclaimed, "He shall not leave!"
and made arrangements for security,
and provided him with choicest pleasures.
40: But when the ministers had duly counseled him,
according to scriptures, with deep respect and love;
and his father had stopped him,
shedding copious tears,
sorrowfully, then, he entered his residence—
41: while young women, their faces kissed by their
dangling earrings, their breasts throbbing with deep
and constant sighs, their eyes darting hither
and thither, gazed up at him like young does.
42: For he, as bright as the golden mountain
bewitching the hearts of those peerless girls,
enthralled their ears and limbs, their eyes and selves,
with his speech and touch, beauty and virtues.
43: Then, as the day came to an end,
his body shining like the sun,
he climbed up to the high palace,
like the rising sun Mount Meru,
so as to dispel the darkness
with the light of his self.
44: Going up to his inner chamber
filled with incense of the best black aloe,
lit by candelabra glistening with gold,
he sat on a splendid seat made of gold
and bespeckled with streaks of diamonds.

342. Meru is the mountain at the center of the world in Hindu and Buddhist cosmologies.

45: Then, during that night, splendid girls
playing their musical instruments
entertained that equal of Indra, that splendid man,
as on the Himalayan peak as white as the moon,
large throngs of *apsarases*[343] entertained
the son of the Lord of Wealth.[344]
46: But even that music of the finest instruments,
rivaling those of heaven,
did not bring him mirth or joy;
the sole desire of that good man was to leave his home
in search of ultimate joy;
therefore, he did not rejoice.
47: Then, Akaníshtha deities,[345] who
practiced the best austerities,
became aware of his resolve;
at once they made those young women succumb
to sleep,
and in unsightly postures positioned their limbs—
48: one was reclining there resting her cheek
on her unsteady hand, tossing her lute
adorned with gold leaf resting on her lap
as if in anger, though she loved it much;
49: another sparkled, a flute in her hand,
lying down, her white gown slipping
from her breasts,
looking like a river, its banks laughing with foam,
its lotuses relished by a straight row of bees;[346]
50: another slept embracing her tambour,
as if it were her lover, with her hands
tender as the hearts of new lotuses,
glistening gold armlets linked to each other;
51: others too, decked with jewelry of new gold,
dressed in peerless yellow clothes,
fell down helpless overcome by deep sleep,
like a *karnikára* branch
torn down by an elephant;

343. The *apsarases* are female divine beings associated with water and known for their beauty and expertise in dance.

344. The Lord of Wealth is Kubera.

345. Akaníshtha deities are one of the highest classes of deities in Buddhist cosmology.

346. The simile appears as follows: the river is the body/chest, the foam is the white dress, the breasts are the lotuses, and the row of bees is the flute.

52: another slept leaning on a window,
her slender body was bent like a bow;
she sparkled, her lovely necklace dangling,
looking like a *shala* plucker
carved upon a gateway;[347]
53: another had her lotus-face bent down,
her jeweled earrings scraping
the decorative lines on her face,
looking like a lotus with its stalk half bent down,
pushed by the perching of a *karandava* coot;[348]
54: others were resplendent—
lying down where they sat,
bodies bent down by the weight of their breasts,
embracing each other with entwined arms
adorned with golden bracelets;
55: one girl in deep sleep embraced her large lute
as if it were her girl-friend,
as she rolled, her gold chains shook,
her earrings in disarray on her face;
56: another girl was lying down
laying her drum between her thighs—
        the drum's beautiful cord
        slipping from her shoulder—
like a lover lying exhausted
after making passionate love;
57: but others, though their brows were pretty,
and their eyes were large,
displayed no beauty with their eyes closed,
like lotuses with their flower-buds closed
after the setting of the sun;
58: another girl likewise was lying there,
her hair disheveled and hanging loose,
her clothes and ornaments slipping down
from her waist, her necklaces scattered,
        like a statue of a girl
        trampled by an elephant;
59: although genteel and endowed with beauty,

347. The simile here is taken from sculpture, probably the gateways around a stupa, or memorial mound, such as those of Sanchi. There women bent to a side and touching a *shala* tree are depicted at the very edge of the gateway as if they were almost about to fall down.

348. The simile appears to be as follows: the lotus is the face, the stalk is the neck, the bird is the earring. *Karandava* is probably the common coot, a medium-size water bird.

others were snoring with their mouths agape,
without any shame and out of control,
with limbs distorted and arms extended,
sleeping in immodest pose;
60: others looked revolting, lying as if dead,
their jewelry and their garlands fallen down,
unconscious, with eyes unblinking,
the whites gazing in a fixed stare;
61: another was lying as if she was drunk,
mouth wide open and saliva oozing,
legs wide open and genitals exposed,
body distorted, looking repulsive.
62: Thus, in diverse postures those enticing girls slept,
each in keeping with her nature,
her family and pedigree;
in appearance they resembled a pond,
with its lilies knocked down, crushed by the wind.
63: When he saw those girls sleeping in such poses,
their bodies distorted, movements unrestrained,
the king's son gave vent to his utter contempt—
    though their bodies were exquisite,
    and the way they spoke was so sweet:
        64: "Dirty and distorted lies here exposed
            the true nature of women in this world;
        Deluded by their nice clothes and jewelry,
            men become infatuated with them.
        65: If men reflect on women's true nature
            and this mutation brought about by sleep,
        Surely their passion for them would not wax;
            yet, struck by the thought of their elegance,
            they become infatuated with them."
66: When he understood thus their difference,
the urge to depart surged in him that night;
when the gods discerned his intention, then,
they opened the door of his residence.
67: Then, he came down from the palace roof-top,
in utter contempt of those sleeping girls;
having come down, then, resolute,
he went out to the first courtyard.
68: He woke up Chándaka and told
that quick-footed groom of his horse:
    "Quickly bring the horse Kánthaka!

I want to leave this place today,
To arrive at the deathless state.[349]
69: Contentment has arisen in my heart,
and resolve has taken hold of my mind;
Even in a deserted place
I do have some sort of a guide;
The goal I yearn for has appeared
before my eyes, that is certain.
70: Abandoning modesty and deference,
the girls slept right in front of me;
And the doors were thrown open on their own—
so today is the time I must
depart from this place, that's certain."
71: Then, although he knew well the king's decree,
he acceded to his master's command;
and he made up his mind to bring the horse,
his mind as if goaded by someone else.
72: Then, he brought to his lord that sterling steed,
a horse endowed with strength, heart, speed, and breed—
its mouth was furnished with a golden bit,
its back was covered with a soft bedspread,
73: its chine, rump, and fetlocks were long,
hair, tail, and ears were short and still,
with sunken back, bulging belly and flanks,
and with wide nostrils, forehead, hips and chest.
74: The wide-chested prince then embraced that horse,
caressing it with his lotus-like hand;
he ordered it in a sweet voice, as if
wishing to charge into enemy lines:
75: "Many a time did the sovereign mount you,
and vanquish in battle his foes;
that is well known;
So act in such a way, O best of steeds,
that I too may obtain the deathless state.
76: Companions are easy to find to fight a war,
to win riches or to enjoy sensual delights;
But they are hard to find when one is in dire straits,
or when one takes to the path of dharma.

349. The deathless state refers to enlightenment, and a state in which no more karma is produced that would create the causation that would set up the conditions for rebirth. If one is not born, one does not die, thus a deathless state.

77: The companions of a man in this world
in foul acts or in the path of dharma,
They too will doubtless partake of the fruits,
this is what I'm told by my inner self.
78: Knowing, therefore, that my exit from here
is connected with dharma
and for the good of the world,
Strive, you best of horses, with speed and dare,
for your own welfare
and that of the world."
79: Wishing to enter the forest, that finest king
thus instructed in his duty that finest horse,
as if he were a friend;
and that handsome prince, who was blazing like a fire,
mounted the white horse, like the sun
an autumn cloud.
80: Then, the good horse went without making any sound
that would cause alarm in the night
or awaken the attendants;
his jaws made no noise and his neighing
was suppressed;
he walked with unwavering steps.
81: *Yakshas*,[350] then, bending their bodies low, supported
the horse's hooves with the tips of their
trembling hands,
hands that resembled lotus buds,
forearms adorned with golden bands,
so that it seemed they were scattering lotuses.
82: As the prince made his way, the city's gates
opened noiselessly on their own,
gates that were closed with heavy iron bars,
gates not easily burst open
even by elephants.
83: He then left the city of his father,
firm in his resolve and unwavering,
leaving his loving father and young son,
his devout subjects and highest fortune.
84: Then he, with long eyes like white lotuses,
caught sight of the city
and roared this lion-roar:

350. *Yakshas* are a class of divine beings related to nature.

"I will not enter this city called Kápila,
Before I've seen the farther shore of birth and death."
85: Hearing these words of his, the retinue
of the court of the Lord of Wealth rejoiced,
and hosts of deities, their minds filled with joy,
announced to him the success of his vow.
86: Other fiery-bodied denizens of heaven,
knowing his vow was exceedingly hard to keep,
shined a light on his frosty path,
like moonbeams coming down through
an opening in a cloud.
87: As that steed sped along like the steed of the sun,
its mind as if spurred on, he traveled many leagues,
before the stars became faint in the sky
at the coming of the dawn.
Thus ends the fifth canto named "The Departure"
of the great poem *Life of the Buddha*.

Asvaghosa (Ashvaghosha). *Life of the Buddha*. Translated by Patrick Olivelle, 124–57. New York: New York University Press, 2008 (every other page, Sanskrit removed).

POST-READING PARS

1. How would you characterize the interactions Siddhartha has with family in this reading?
2. What two or three aspects of Siddhartha's life are most prominently being highlighted? Which aspects highlight his humanity and which highlight his specialness as a unique role model?

Inquiry Corner

Content Question(s):	Critical Question(s):
What types of Hindu elements do you recognize in the text? Which forms of Hindu dharma (based on stage of life, caste, gender, family, or societal roles) are being challenged by Siddhartha's actions?	Desire is identified as the primary cause of suffering in the Four Noble Truths, the main teaching of Buddhism. In what ways is Siddhartha encountering and responding to desire and suffering in this reading?
Comparative Question(s):	**Connection Question(s):**
How does the interaction between Siddhartha and his father, Suddodhana, compare to other parent-child interactions you have explored in this class (Gilgamesh and his mother Rimat-Ninsun, Abraham and Isaac, Amenemope giving wisdom to his youngest son, etc.)?	What types of encounters with ideas, experiences, nature, or people have urged you to make a huge change in your life? If you haven't had such an encounter, what types of events do you think might be persuasive?

The Recognition of Shakuntala (*Abhijnanasakuntalam*) by Kalidasa (Introduction only)

SNAPSHOT BOX

LANGUAGE: Sanskrit
DATE: c. 4th–5th century CE
LOCATION: South Asia
GENRE: Play
TAGS: Aesthetics; Authority and Leadership; Emotion; Friendship; Identity; Love; Nature; Women and Gender

Introduction

Kalidasa is one of the most well-known, earliest Sanskrit playwrights of South Asia whose works are extant. His poetic and theatrical works were likely supported through the patronage of the local rulers of the Gupta dynasty in present-day northern India, in particular Chandragupta II (r. 380–415 CE). Biographical information about Kalidasa is speculative, including theories about where he lived based on his extensive knowledge of the regional plants described in his poems and plays. There are only three of his plays we have in their entirety, the most famous being *Abhijñanaśākuntalam* (*The Recognition of Shakuntala*), commonly referred to as Shakuntala.

The play features the character of Shakuntala, a young female heroine with human and celestial heritage mentioned in a brief narrative within the Hindu epic, the *Mahabharata* (400 BCE–400 CE), and provides a full expansion and exploration of her narrative—a story of love, loss, and reunited love again. The strategy of expansion on a known character is common among South Asian authors who give breathing space to intriguing characters nestled into the dense layers of story in the epics. The play also follows a typical Sanskrit storyline, namely that a heroine and hero in love will experience several obstacles but will almost always be united triumphantly in the end. If audiences already know and expect particular endings, what elements would be the source of enjoyment for people watching the play?

Timeline

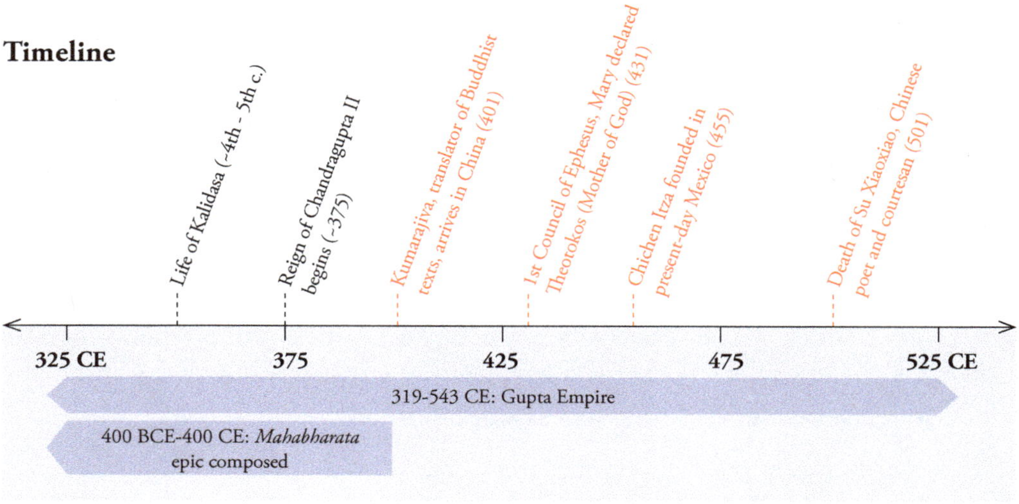

Since the emphasis for enjoyment is not on plot twists or even complexity of psychological character development, actor-dancers performing *Shakuntala* and other plays focus on developing the range of emotional nuance and expression of key characters and their range of play within various tropes (e.g., the responsibilities and behaviors of a king, the hospitality of a daughter to guests, etc.). For more information on the aesthetics of emotional nuance used in South Asian theater, see the entry in this Reader on the *Natyashastra, the Science of Dance-Drama* (page 473), a source that details the relationship between actor-dancers' use of gestures, expressions and postures, and emotions they express. Other defining features of Sanskrit theater involve wordplay, including regional dialects—much of this gets lost in translation, along with any staged physical humor in the written version—as well as opportunities for song and dance and contrasting symmetrical tensions between opposites that are reconfigured over the arc of the play.

The play begins with King Dushyanta hunting deer in the forest with his courtier, a clownish sidekick who constantly complains and often is the only character who directly and indirectly teases the king for his human fallibilities. This common sidekick character to the hero is often also a brahmin, a member of the highest caste responsible for religious knowledge and rituals, creating enjoyment by depicting what should be a more somber, learned figure as a bit gullible and bumbling in contrast to the stately king. While hunting, the king crosses over into an ***ashram***, a place of residence for a community of religious ascetics living in the forests, and upon seeing Shakuntala falls immediately in love with her. What follows involves gathering information as indirectly as possible about who Shakuntala is and whether she is an ascetic or not, and thus whether she is "available." He disguises himself to test Shakuntala's feelings and employs the help of Shakuntala's friends to create an opportunity for a rendezvous. Are these types of plot devices similar or different to those that enhance our own enjoyment of today's modern love stories?

Many of the antics in *Shakuntala* are colored by humor at the king's lovesickness, friends' and courtier's teasing and good-hearted machinations, and the play between what is hidden from one person or the other but is fully known to the audience. The shared moment of passion is brief and not shown or elaborated. What kind of nonverbal gestures and actions convey desire, love, and/or attraction in your culture? How is desire, love, and/or attraction conveyed nonverbally in *Shakuntala*? (Hint: Pay attention to the stage cues.) After their tryst, the king returns to his palace but promises to send for Shakuntala to join his court. In the meantime, Shakuntala learns she is pregnant.

What follows is a series of mishaps that result in the king forgetting who Shakuntala is. The remainder of the play works out his loss of memory through some carefully placed human and divine interventions, because love will always win even in the face of seemingly impossible circumstances. Think about a memorable love relationship in a book or movie: what role did suffering, missed connections, challenges, and/or misunderstandings play in leading to a stronger bond?

The symmetrical tensions of the play create prominent themes, such as the dual contexts of the religious ashram and the royal court. The dharma or duties of a king are often juxtaposed with the responsibilities and actions of ascetics, creating an important blending of the two. In what ways do the activities, character, and emotional life of King Dushyanta compare with rulers we have encountered in other sources? A second notable theme centers on the role of nature, which functions as its own character at times, and certainly as a substitute to indicate emotions of desire, love, and physical expressions of intimacy. Shakuntala's special relationship with the plants and animals of the forest speaks to underlying assumptions about gender and nature worth exploring further. In what ways is our understanding of nature gendered? How is nature gendered in ***Shakuntala***? Perhaps a final primary theme to consider throughout the play is the conceptual nexus of memory and remembrance, and their opposites of hiddenness and disguise. What is revealed, when, and how creates some of the most delightful moments of the play. How might remembering or having something revealed after a time of forgetting or not knowing heighten one's enjoyment?

Katherine C. Zubko
Department of Religious Studies

Recommended Translation: Miller, Barbara Stoler. *Theater of Memory: The Plays of Kalidasa*, 85–176. New York: Columbia University Press, 1984.

from *Science of Dance-Drama* (*Natyashastra*) attributed to Bharata

Introduction

The *Natyashastra*, or *Science of Dance-Drama*, is a 2,000-year-old compendium of South Asian theatrical elements attributed to the sage Bharata. In its broadest understanding, the Sanskrit term ***natya*** encompasses dance, music, verbal speech, and acting. As a ***shastra***, this Sanskrit philosophical-religious genre is charged with trying to capture every component and perspective on a topic. *Natyashastra* offers an encyclopedic knowledge of dance-drama that includes lists and technical descriptions of movements, aesthetic theory about how audiences experience art, and the role of Hindu gods and goddesses in the creation and purpose of the performing arts.

In the opening chapter of the *Natyashastra*, you hear the narrative of how the gods approached Brahma, a Hindu god of creation, with a request to create a pastime that is "both visible and audible," later also noted as a "poem that is seen." Brahma draws upon aspects found in the four Vedas, the primary authoritative religious compositions used by priests in the earliest development of Hindu traditions, to create a fifth Veda, the Natyaveda. The Natyaveda is considered an authoritative form of the Vedas that is still accessible to all. Indra, the head god of the Vedic pantheon, notes that gods are unfit to be able to learn and practice dance-drama and so Brahma calls upon the human sage Bharata, who in his wisdom is able to learn natya and teach his one hundred sons the artform. Why do you think humans instead of gods would be better suited to performing natya?

SNAPSHOT BOX

LANGUAGE: Sanskrit

DATE: 200 BCE–200 CE

LOCATION: South Asia

GENRE: Compendium on theatrical arts

TAGS: Aesthetics; Body; Deities and Spirits; Education; Emotion; Music; Origin Stories; Religion; Women and Gender

Timeline

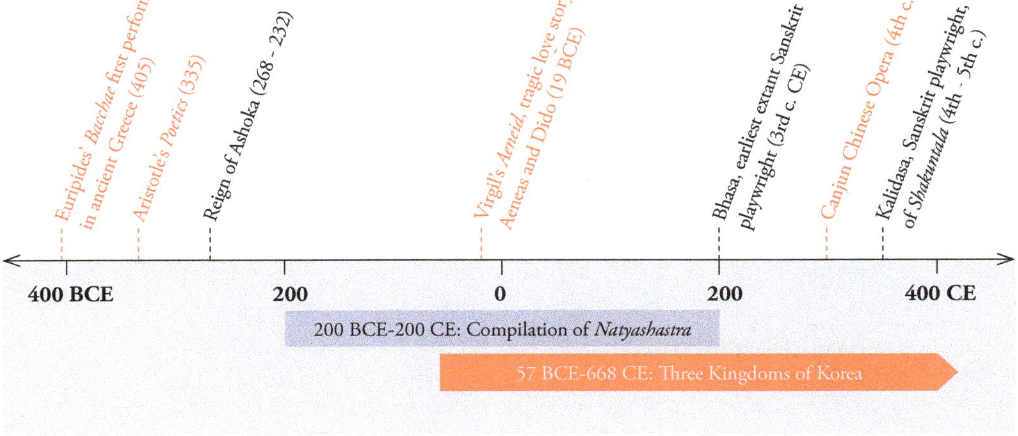

The very first dance-drama, according to the ***Natyashastra***, is performed at the festival of Indra, with gods and demigods in attendance. It is the narrative of the Churning of the Ocean in which the gods and the demigods, sometimes referred to as demons who are powerful beings with flaws, had to cooperate with each other so that the nectar of immortality would emerge from the ocean and become available for both groups of powerful beings to consume. When cooperation breaks down because the demigods steal the nectar, the dance-drama also falls apart because the demigods in the audience object to the way they are being portrayed and storm the stage, disrupting the performance.

Brahma weighs in on this dispute, telling the demigods to not be angry, as he made natya to not only be entertaining, but also educational by showing the character and behaviors of all beings: "the art of drama will promote virtue, bring fame and longevity, provide benefit, increase intelligence, and contain proper advice to the world" (1: 116). Brahma then names different gods to protect every part of the stage and stagecraft, from the lights to the colors used on costumes, so that the performance space itself becomes sacred space, and dance-drama also is underscored further as a religious activity. In what ways might the performing arts be connected to religious activities today?

Performing stories about the Hindu gods and goddesses and their devotees is the first topic of central prominence in Sanskrit theater traditions and classical dance forms whose practitioners connect their art to the heritage and authority of the ***Natyashastra***. A second primary focus is on two experiences of love: love in separation from and love in union with one's beloved. These two experiences are detailed through the gendered character perspective of a female heroine in relationship to a male hero. The heroine embodies a metaphorical substitution for humans experiencing both a yearning to be close to a god they feel separated from, and the blissful fulfillment of being in union with the divine. The aesthetic focus is almost entirely on the development of the heroine's experience. To support narrative expression (***abhinaya***) of these themes, there are chapters describing hand gestures that create an adaptable vocabulary, while other chapters focus on individual movements of the eyes, torso, foot positions, and the 108 steps (***karanas***) choreographed by the Hindu god Shiva.

The 1930s was a time of great change in South Asian dance-drama traditions. British colonialism had diminished traditional avenues of patronage of local dance traditions by rulers and wealthy merchants. The rising nationalism of the independence movement used these dance traditions in an effort to identify and glorify classical, national art forms. This led to a form of internal cultural appropriation as dancers from upper castes and classes began learning local, hereditary dance forms and performing them on concert stages. This led to a shift from the traditional cultural practice of specialized artists from lower castes typically performing these dances in temples, courts, and homes. ***Natyashastra*** plays a strategic role in this shift. Dancers employed the ***Natyashastra***, as an authoritative Sanskrit text, to further distance the art form from its traditional home and its lower-caste practitioners. One approach was to modify movements to align with their textual descriptions found in the ***Natyashastra*** as a strategy to create a sense of ancient authenticity. Making visible the processes and impact of disenfranchisement and disruption to hereditary artistic traditions and practitioners is an ongoing focus of scholars and artists today. They are faced with having to reconcile this history of systemic disenfranchisement with these classical art forms that now represent a form of high culture in India and its diaspora. What other art forms do you know that have a history of disenfranchisement?

The excerpt below comes from the chapter that details the aesthetic theory of ***rasa*** (flavor, sentiment) experienced by audience members through the dancers' physical portrayal of eight primary emotions. The eight rasas discussed in the ***Natyashastra*** are love, humor, anger, fear, disgust, courage, wonder, and compassion, with a ninth rasa of peacefulness added later. The chapter proposes an idealized formula for how rasa may be created and portrayed on stage. A combination of three components are used to depict the primary emotion: the context for developing the mood or sentiment, details of the physical responses of actor-dancers, and additional fleeting subsidiary emotional states that would enhance the primary emotion being portrayed. For each of the rasas you will see the development of these three components in light of differences such as character, class, and gender. If an actor-dancer is skilled in their portrayal, the audience member would savor the rich nuances and subtleties as a form of aesthetic enjoyment, even if the topic was fear or disgust, much like some of us enjoy horror movies. How precisely do you think emotion can be portrayed through gesture, posture, and facial expressions? What might the ***Natyashastra***'s dissection of these elements on stage reveal about a South Asian perspective on the relationship between body, mind, and heart?

Katherine C. Zubko
Department of Religious Studies

PRE-READING PARS

1. List six to eight emotions/sentiments that you consider to be experienced by most human beings, even if they have culturally distinct expressions.
2. Identify two or three types of movements (gestures, facial expressions, postures) that are considered gendered within your own cultural background or context.

from *The Science of Dance Drama (Natyashastra)*

The Eight Rasas (Aesthetic Sentiments/Moods)[351]

The eight sentiments recognized in drama are as follows: erotic, comic, compassionate, furious, heroic, terrible, odious, and marvelous.

These eight are the sentiments named by [the Hindu god] Brahma. I shall now speak of the three types of *bhavas*—the durable psychological-emotional states, the complementary or fleeting psychological-emotional states, and the *sattvika* [involuntary] ones, [as expressed physically through enacted gestures].

Three Types of Bhavas

The durable psychological-emotional states are known to be the following: love, mirth, sorrow, anger, energy, fear, disgust, and astonishment.

The thirty-three complementary psychological-emotional states are known to be the following: discouragement, weakness, apprehension, envy, intoxication, weariness, indolence, depression, anxiety, distraction, recollection, contentment, shame, inconstancy, joy, agitation, stupor, arrogance, despair, impatience, sleep, uncontrollable shaking, dreaming, awakening, indignation, dissimulation, cruelty, assurance, sickness, insanity, death, fright, and deliberation....

The eight *sattvika* states: paralysis, perspiration, horripilation,[352] change of voice, trembling, change of color, weeping, and fainting.

Rasas Explained

In that connection I shall first of all explain the aesthetic sentiments/moods *(rasas)*. No poetic meaning proceeds from speech without some kind of sentiment. Now the

351. Sentiment is related to, but is qualitatively different from, "feeling" in real life. It is the experience produced in the spectator's mind by the portrayal of a feeling in drama. *Rasa* is also defined as flavor, and relates to taste—both in terms of cooking and aesthetic enjoyment.

352. A bristling of the hair on the head and the body because of terror, cold, or illness, also called gooseflesh.

sentiment is produced from a combination of determinants [the contextual causes or factors bringing about certain feelings], consequents [the visible physical signs accompanying particular feelings], and complementary psychological-emotional states. Is there any instance parallel to it? Yes, it is said that, as taste *(rasa)* results from a combination of various spices, vegetables, and other ingredients, and as six tastes are produced by these ingredients, such as raw sugar or spices or vegetables, so the durable psychological states, when they come together with various other psychological-emotional states, attain the quality of a sentiment [i.e., produces an aesthetic mood]. Now one enquires, "What is the meaning of the word *rasa*?" It is said in reply [that *rasa* is so called] because it is capable of being tasted, "How is *rasa* tasted?" In reply it is said that just as well-disposed persons, while eating food cooked with many kinds of spice, enjoy its tastes and attain pleasure and satisfaction, so the cultured people taste the durable psychological-emotional states while they see them represented by an expression of the various emotions with words, gestures, and other contributors to the physical enactment of the emotional state, and derive pleasure and satisfaction....

Just as connoisseurs of cooked food, while eating food which has been prepared from various spices and other ingredients taste it, so the learned people taste in their heart the durable psychological-emotional states (such as love, sorrow, etc.) when they are represented by an expression of the psychological-emotional states with gestures. Hence these durable psychological-emotional states (*bhavas*) in a drama create aesthetic sentiments (*rasas*).

Relation between Sentiments and Psychological-Emotional States[353]

Now one enquires, "Do the psychological-emotional states come out of the sentiments or the sentiments come out of the psychological-emotional states?" On this point, some are of the opinion that they arise from their mutual contact. But this is not so. Why?

It is apparent that the sentiments arise from the psychological-emotional states and not the psychological-emotional states from the sentiments. For on this point there are traditional couplets, such as [the following].

The psychological-emotional states are so called by experts in drama, for they make one feel the sentiments in connection with various modes of dramatic representation. Just as by many ingredients of various kinds, cooked eatables [meat and fish] are brought forth, so the psychological states, along with different kinds of theatrical enacted representation will cause the sentiments to be felt.

There can be no sentiment prior to (without) the psychological-emotional states,

353. The following section explores what different theorists have considered in their inquiries into the relationships between *bhavas* and *rasas*, starting with what is the causal relationship between the two, if any.

and no psychological-emotional states without the sentiments following it, and during the theatrical representations they result from their interaction....

Just as a tree grows from a seed, and flowers and fruits from a tree, ... likewise the psychological-emotional states exist as the source of all the sentiments.

Eight Sentiments from Four Original Ones

Now we shall describe the origin, colors, presiding deities,[354] and examples of these sentiments. Sources of these eight sentiments are the four original sentiments (i.e., erotic, furious, heroic, and odious).

The comic sentiment arises from the erotic, the compassionate from the furious, the marvelous from the heroic, and the terrible from the odious.

A mimicry of the erotic sentiment is called the comic, and the result of the furious sentiment is the compassionate, the result of the heroic sentiment is called the marvelous, and that which is odious to see, results in the terrible.

The erotic sentiment is light green; the comic sentiment, white; the compassionate sentiment, grey; the furious sentiment, red; the heroic sentiment, yellowish; the terrible sentiment, black; the odious sentiment, blue; and the marvelous sentiment, yellow.

Presiding Deities of Sentiments

Vishnu is the god of the erotic, Pramathas of the comic, Rudra of the furious, Yama of the compassionate, Mahakala (Shiva) of the odious, Kala of the terrible, Indra of the heroic, and Brahma of the marvelous sentiments.[355]

Thus have been described the origin, colors, and deities of these sentiments. Now we shall explain the determinants, the consequents, the complementary psychological-emotional states, and their combination, definition, and examples.

We shall now enumerate the *bhavas* - the durable psychological-emotional states that create different sentiments.

354. These deities are all Hindu gods. Vishnu is the god who preserves creation; Rudra, the god of storms; Yama, the god of death and the underworld; Shiva, the destroyer and fertility god; Kala, the god of time; and Indra, the chief Vedic god.

355. Bharata lists the various feelings conventionally associated with the different gods and other mythical figures in the Hindu pantheon, including Vishnu, Shiva, or Mahakala, and Brahma. Pramathas are a class of demigods attendant on Shiva. Rudra is a very complex deity, often visualized as the god of storms, called the howler, roarer, or terrible. Yama is the god of death; Kala, the god of time; and Indra, the great Vedic chief god.

The Erotic Sentiment

Of these, the erotic sentiment proceeds from the durable psychological-emotional state of love, and it has as its basis a bright attire; for whatever in this world is pure, bright, and beautiful is appreciated in terms of the durable psychological-emotional state of love. For example, one who is elegantly dressed is called a lovely person. Just as persons are named after the profession of their father, mother, or family in accordance with the traditional authority, so the sentiments, the psychological-emotional states, and other objects connected with drama are given names in pursuance of the practice and the traditional authority. Hence the erotic sentiment has been so named on account of its usually being associated with a bright and elegant attire. It owes its origin to men and women and relates to the fullness of youth. It has two bases: union and separation. Of these two, the erotic sentiment in union arises from determinants like the pleasures of the season, the enjoyment of garlands, unguents, ornaments, the company of beloved persons, objects of senses, splendid mansions, going to a garden and enjoying oneself there, seeing the beloved one, hearing his or her words, playing and dallying with him or her. It should be represented on the stage by consequents such as clever movement of eyes, eyebrows, glances, soft and delicate movement of limbs, and sweet words, and similar other things. Complementary psychological-emotional states in it do not include fear, indolence, cruelty, and disgust. The erotic sentiment in separation should be represented on the stage by consequents, such as indifference, languor, fear, jealousy, fatigue, anxiety, yearning, drowsiness, sleep, dreaming, awakening, illness, insanity, epilepsy, inactivity, fainting, death, and other conditions.

Now it has been asked, "If the erotic sentiment has its origin in love, why does it sometimes manifest itself through compassionate conditions?" In reply to this it is said, "It has been mentioned before that the erotic sentiment has its basis in union as well as in separation. Authorities on the arts of love have mentioned ten conditions of the persons separated from their beloved ones, which are compassionate...." The compassionate sentiment relates to a condition of despair owing to the affliction under a curse, separation from dear ones, loss of wealth, death, or captivity; while the erotic sentiment, based on separation, relates to a condition of retaining optimism arising out of yearning and anxiety. Hence the compassionate sentiment and the erotic sentiment in separation differ from each other. And this is the reason why the erotic sentiment includes conditions available in all other sentiments.

And the sentiment called erotic is generally happy; connected with desired objects, enjoyment of seasons, garlands and similar other things, and it relates to the union of two lovers.[...] The erotic sentiment arises in connection with music and poetry, and going to the garden and roaming there. It should be represented on the stage by means of composure of the eyes and the face, sweet and smiling words, satisfaction and delight, and graceful movements of limbs.

The Comic Sentiment

Now the comic has as its basis the durable psychological-emotional state of laughter. This is created by determinants, such as showing unseemly dress or ornament, impudence, greediness, quarrel, use of irrelevant words, mentioning of different faults, and similar other things. This (the comic sentiment) is to be represented on the stage by consequents like the throbbing of the lips, the nose, and the cheek, opening the eyes wide or contracting them, perspiration, color of the face, and taking hold of the sides. Complementary psychological-emotional states in it are indolence, dissimulation, drowsiness, sleep, dreaming, insomnia, envy, and the like. This sentiment is of two kinds: self-centered and centered in others. When a person himself laughs, it relates to the self-centered (comic sentiment), but when he makes others laugh, it (the comic sentiments therein) is centered in others.

As one laughs with an exhibition of oddly placed ornaments, uncouth behavior, words and dress and strange movements of limbs, it is called the comic sentiment. As this makes other people laugh by means of his uncouth behavior, words, movement of the limbs, and strange dress, it is known as the comic sentiment.

This sentiment is mostly to be seen in women and men of the lower type, and it has six varieties of which I shall speak presently.

They are: slight smile, smile, gentle laughter, laughter of ridicule, vulgar laughter, and excessive laughter. Two by two they belong respectively to the superior, the middling, and the lower types of persons.

In Persons of the Superior Type

To persons of the superior type belong the slight smile and the smile; to those of the middling type, the gentle laughter and the laughter of ridicule; and to those of the lower type, the vulgar laughter and the excessive laughter.

There are verses on this subject:

The slight smile of the people of the superior type should be characterized by slightly blown cheeks and elegant glances, and in it teeth are not to be made visible.

Their smile should be distinguished by blooming eyes, face, and cheeks, and in it teeth should be slightly visible.

In Persons of the Middling Type

The gentle laughter should have slight sound and sweetness and should be suitable to the occasion, and in it eyes and cheeks should be contracted and the face joyful.

During the laughter of ridicule the nose should be expanded, eyes should be squinting, and the shoulder and the head should be bent.

In Persons of the Lower Type

The laughter on occasions not suitable to it, the laughter with tears in one's eyes, or with the shoulder and the head violently shaking, is called the vulgar laughter.

The excessive laughter is that in which the eyes are expanded and tearful sound is loud and excessive, and the sides are covered by hands.

Comic situations which may arise in the course of a play, for persons of the superior, middling, or lower type are thus to be given expression to....

The Compassionate Sentiment

Now the compassionate sentiment arises from the durable psychological-emotional state of sorrow. It grows from determinants such as affliction under a curse, separation from dear ones, loss of wealth, death, captivity, flight accidents, or any other misfortune. This is to be represented on the stage by means of consequents such as shedding tears, lamentation, dryness of the mouth, change of color, drooping limbs, being out of breath, loss of memory, and the like. Complementary psychological-emotional states connected with it are indifference, languor, anxiety, yearning, excitement, delusion, fainting, sadness, dejection, illness, inactivity, insanity, epilepsy, fear, indolence, death, paralysis, tremor, change of color, weeping, loss of voice, and the like.

The compassionate sentiment arises from seeing the death of a beloved person, or from hearing something very unpleasant, and these are its determinants.

This is to be represented on the stage by consequents like weeping loudly, fainting, lamenting and bewailing, exerting the body, or striking it.

The Furious Sentiment

Now the furious sentiment has as its basis the durable psychological-emotional state of anger. It owes its origin to *raksasas, danavas,*[356] and haughty men, and is caused by fights. This is created by determinants such as anger, rape, abuse, insult, untrue allegation, exorcizing, threatening, revengefulness, jealousy, and the like. Its actions are beating, breaking, crushing, fighting, drawing of blood, and similar other deeds. This is to be represented on the stage by means of consequents such as red eyes, knitting of eyebrows, defiance, biting of the lips, movement of the cheeks, pressing one hand with the other, and the like. Complementary psychological-emotional states in it are presence of mind, determination, energy, indignation, restlessness, fury, perspiration, trembling, horripilation, choking voice, and the like.

Now one enquires, "Is it to be assumed from the above statement about *raksasas* that they only give rise to the furious sentiment, and that this sentiment does not

356. *Raksasas* and *danavas* are beings that cause harm, sometimes powerful like titans and other times more mischievous and trickster-like.

relate to others?" [Reply] "No, in case of others too, this sentiment may arise. But in the case of *raksasas* it is to be understood as their special function. They are naturally furious, for they have many arms, many mouths, standing and unkempt hairs of brown color, and prodigious physical frame of dark complexion. Whatever they attempt, be it their speech, movement of limbs or any other effort, is by nature furious. Even in their lovemaking they are violent. It is to be easily inferred that persons who imitate them give rise to the furious sentiment from their fights and battles."

On these points there are two verses:

The furious sentiment is created by striking, cutting, mutilation, and piercing in fights, and tumult of the battle, and the like.

It should be represented on the stage by special acts, such as the release of many weapons, cutting off the head, the trunk and the arms.

Such is the furious sentiment viewed by experts; it is full of conflict of arms, and in it words, movement, and deeds are terrible and fearful.

The Heroic Sentiment

Now the heroic sentiment relates to the superior type of persons and has energy as its basis. This is created by determinants, such as presence of mind, perseverance, diplomacy, discipline, military strength, aggressiveness, reputation of might, influence, and the like. It is to be represented on the stage by consequents such as firmness, patience, heroism, charity, diplomacy, and the like. Complementary psychological-emotional states in it are contentment, judgment, pride, agitation, energy, determination of purpose, indignation, remembrance, horripilation, and the like. There are two verses [on these points]:

The heroic sentiment arises from energy, perseverance, optimism, absence of surprise, and presence of mind, and such other special conditions of the spirit.

This heroic sentiment is to be properly represented on the stage by firmness, patience, heroism, pride, energy, aggressiveness, influence, and censuring words.

The Terrible Sentiment

Now the terrible sentiment has as its basis the durable psychological state of fear. This is created by determinants like hideous noise, sight of ghosts, panic, and anxiety due to untimely cry of jackals and owls, staying in an empty house or forest, sight of death or captivity of dear ones, or news of it, or discussion about it. It is to be represented on the stage by consequents such as trembling of the hands and the feet, horripilation, change of color, and loss of voice. Its complementary psychological states are paralysis, perspiration, choking voice, horripilation, trembling, loss of voice, change of color, fear, stupefaction, dejection, agitation, restlessness, inactivity, fear, epilepsy and death, and the like.

On these points there are two traditional verses:

The terrible sentiment is created by hideous noise, sight of ghosts, battle, entering an empty house or forest, and offending one's superiors or the king.

Terror is characterized by looseness of the limbs, the mouth, and the eyes; paralysis of the thighs; looking around with uneasiness; dryness of the drooping mouth; palpitation of the heart; and horripilation.

This is the character of natural fear; the artificially shown fear also should be represented by these conditions. But in case of the feigned fear all efforts for its representation should be milder.

This terrible sentiment should be always represented by tremor of hands and feet; paralysis; shaking of the body; palpitation of the heart; dryness of the lips, the mouth, the palate, and the throat.

The Odious Sentiment

Now the odious sentiment has as its basis the durable psychological-emotional state of disgust. It is created by determinants like hearing of unpleasant, offensive, impure, and harmful things or seeing them or discussing them. It is to be represented on the stage by consequents such as stopping movement of all the limbs, narrowing down of the mouth, vomiting, spitting, shaking the limbs [in disgust], and the like. Complementary psychological-emotional states in it are uncontrollable shaking, delusion, agitation, fainting, sickness, death, and the like. On these points there are two traditional verses:

The odious sentiment arises in many ways from disgusting sight, tastes, smell, touch, and sound which cause uneasiness.

This is to be represented on the stage by narrowing down the mouth and the eyes, covering the nose, bending down the head, and walking imperceptibly.

The Marvelous Sentiment

The marvelous sentiment has as its basis the durable psychological-emotional state of astonishment. It is created by determinants such as sight of heavenly beings or events, attainment of desired objects, entry into a superior mansion, temple, audience hall, and seven-storied palace, and seeing illusory and magical acts. It is to be represented on the stage by consequents such as wide opening of eyes; looking with fixed gaze; horripilation; tears of joy; perspiration; joy; uttering words of approbation; making gifts; crying incessantly "ha, ha, ha"; waving the end of *dhoti* or *sari*;[357] and movement of fingers and the like. Complementary psychological-emotional states in it are weep-

357. A *dhoti* is a sheet of material worn below the waist, usually by men. A *sari*, too, is a long sheet of cloth, part of it wrapped around the waist and part covering the head and the rest of the upper body, usually worn by women.

ing, paralysis, perspiration, choking voice, horripilation, agitation, hurry, inactivity, death, and the like.

On this point there are two traditional verses:

The marvelous sentiment is that which arises from words, character, deed, and personal beauty.

This is to be represented on the stage by a gesture of feeling; sweet smell; joyful shaking of limbs; and uttering "ha, ha, ha" sounds; speaking words of approbation; tremor; choking voice; perspiration; and the like.

Bharata. *Natyasastra*. Translated and edited by Manmohan Ghosh, 102–3, 105–17. Calcutta: Manisha Granthalaya, 1951 [1967].

POST-READING PARS

1. How does your list of emotions compare/contrast to the eight universalized sentiments described in the *Natyashastra*?
2. Identify two passages that intentionally describe differences in gendered movement patterns. How do these movements or expressions compare to the ones you identified in your own cultural context?

Inquiry Corner

Content Question(s):

Choose one of the rasas (e.g., fear, wonder, etc.) and identify the features in the three-part formula that contribute to how dancer-actors would potentially create that rasa for audience members.

What roles do the gods play in the creation and performance of dance-drama?

Critical Question(s):

The *Natyashastra* intentionally translates oral/kinesthetic knowledge into textual knowledge. What are the challenges in this transfer? What gets lost? Who do you think the main audience of this text is?

How is art used as part of nationalism or national identity?

Comparative Question(s):

Shastra is a form used to convey authority in its attempts to cover all aspects of a topic like an encyclopedic compendium. What ways have other sources we've read this semester conveyed authority?

Connection Question(s):

Take a passage out of an epic, dialogue, or play you've read for this course or a two-minute clip of a TV episode or movie and identify which of the rasas are present. How does tracking the nuances of emotions instead of character development or plot line change what you notice?

from *Upanishads*

Introduction

The *Upanishads* are part of the Vedas, an orally composed body of religious knowledge in Sanskrit that evolved over multiple centuries. The Vedas may be translated as "knowledge," indicating the most sacred religious knowledge held by the highest caste, the priestly **brahmins**. The *Upanishads* reflect the last and latest of the additions to the Vedas. Most of the early portions of the Vedas convey hymns of praise to the Vedic gods, such as Agni, the god of fire. These hymns that predate the *Upanishads* were chanted as part of the main Vedic ritual, a fire sacrifice. Nomadic Aryans from the northwest Caucasus region brought these earliest parts of the Vedas into South Asia.

In the early Vedic period (1500–800 BCE), kings, wealthy merchants, and those with resources would hire brahmins to perform a fire sacrifice to achieve a particular goal, such as victory in battle, an increase in trade and profits, or the birth of a healthy child. The logic was that if the brahmin chanted every Sanskrit syllable from the Vedic hymn correctly and made the right offerings, the gods were obligated to comply with the request. This religious system, known to modern-day scholars as Brahminism, was the main aspect of ritual we know about from the Vedic period. We know very little about the religious practices of the average person at this time.

We see a huge shift in the late Vedic period (800–300 BCE) toward more philosophical speculation about how a person navigates and understands their role and purpose in relation to the sacred, as evidenced in the *Upanishads*. The term "upa-

SNAPSHOT BOX

LANGUAGE: Sanskrit

Dates: 900–300 BCE

LOCATION: South Asia

GENRE: Late Vedic philosophy

TAGS: Asceticism; Cosmology; Education; Nature; Ways of Knowing; Wisdom

Timeline

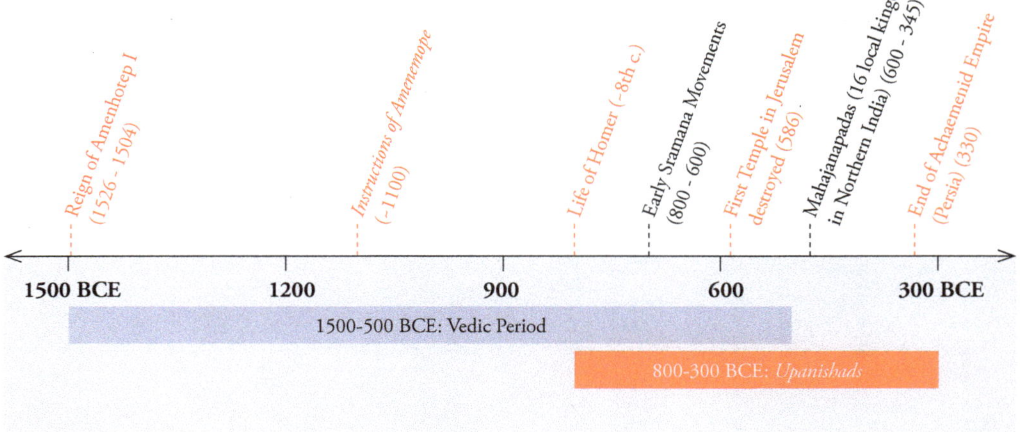

nishad" translates "to sit down near" and the presumption is that it is a student sitting near a teacher in a natural environment, under a tree or by a river, exploring particular types of existential questions including "who am I?" These teachers were mostly **ascetics**, those who utilized physical or mental practices of self-denial, such as fasting and celibacy, in order to turn their mental attention inward to explore various questions. How do you think engagement in ascetic practices supports an internal orientation to inquire into the "big questions" about life? What types of questions do you think students seeking out these ascetic teachers would ask?

What you see in the *Upanishads* are dialogues between teachers and students, wordplay, riddles, and experiential learning strategies in which a student is not given a verbal explanation, but instead sent off to engage in a task in response to a question they pose to the teacher. In what ways do you think experiential and personalized forms of learning support or hinder one's own growth?

Students are taught about two concepts without direct explanation: ***Brahman*** and ***atman***. Brahman is the Absolute, sacred Reality that pervasively exists in everything and sustains the world. It is not a god, but a more abstract divine essence. Atman is the spark of Brahman that exists in humans, indicating the most important core of a person or self in relation to Brahman. Within the worldview of the *Upanishads*, the atman is what is reborn back into the world (***samsara***) over and over again until it gains an experiential understanding of its oneness with Brahman. With the bliss of finally realizing one's own divine nature, a person is released from the cycles of rebirth and attains ***moksha***, or liberation, ultimately being reabsorbed into Brahman.

Several major Hindu philosophical schools develop in relation to different insights into the interrelation between Brahman and atman. As you read the following excerpts, look for which metaphors and characteristics are used to describe Brahman and how teachers attempt to help students understand how their own atman is related to Brahman. What do these excerpts help us appreciate about one of the possible models of relationship between humans and the sacred in ancient South Asia?

Katherine C. Zubko
Department of Religious Studies

PRE-READING PARS

1. Identify two or three sources that provide you with wisdom.
2. What are two or three important insights that you have learned from nature?
3. Identify two or three metaphors you would use to describe your understanding of being human in the world.

from *Chandogya* and *Taittiriya Upanishads*

The Individual Self (Atman) is One with the Supreme Brahman

Chandogya 3, Section 14

1. This whole world is *Brahman*, from which he comes forth, without which he will be dissolved and in which he breathes. Tranquil, one should meditate on it.[358] Now truly, a person consists of purpose. According to the purpose a person has in this world, so does he become on departing upon death. So let him frame for himself the following purpose:

2. He who consists of mind, whose body is life (*prana*),[359] whose form is light, whose conception is truth, whose self is space, containing all works, containing all desires, containing all odors, containing all tastes, encompassing this whole world, being without speech and without concern.

3. This is my Self (*atman*) within my heart, smaller than a grain of rice, than a barley corn, than a mustard seed, than a grain of millet or than the kernel of a grain of a millet. This is my Self within the heart, greater than the earth, greater than the atmosphere, greater than the sky, greater than these worlds.

4. Containing all worlds, containing all desires, containing all odors, containing all tastes, encompassing this whole world, without speech, without concern, this is the Self of mine within the heart; this is *Brahman*. Into *Brahman*, I shall enter, on departing upon death. He who believes this purpose, will have no more doubts. Thus used to say Sandilya.[360]

358. The whole world should be meditated on as *jalan*, which is defined as waters, usually referring to great cosmic, endless bodies of water.

359. *Prana* is the breath, life force.

360. Sandilya was a great *risi*, or wise seer.

The Primacy of Being

Chandogya 6, Section 2

1. In the beginning, my dear, this was being alone, one only without a second. Some people say 'in the beginning this was non-being alone, one only; without a second. From that non-being, being was produced.'

2. But how, indeed, my dear, could it be thus? said he, how could being be produced from non-being? On the contrary, my dear, in the beginning this was being alone, one only, without a second.

3. It thought, may I be many, may I grow forth. It sent forth heat. That heat thought, may I be many, may I grow forth. It sent forth water. Therefore, whenever a person grieves or perspires, water is produced from heat.

4. That water thought, may I be many, may I grow forth. It sent forth food. Therefore, whenever it rains anywhere then there is abundant food. So food for eating is produced from water alone.

The Indwelling Spirit

Chandogya 6, Section 9

1. Just as, my dear one, the bees prepare honey by collecting the essences (juices) of different trees and reducing them into one essence.

2. And as these (juices) possess no discrimination (so that they might say) 'I am the essence of this tree, I am the essence of that tree,' even so, indeed, my dear one, all these creatures though they reach Being do not know that they have reached the Being.

3. Whatever they are in this world, tiger or lion or wolf or boar or worm or fly or gnat or mosquito, that they become.

4. That which is the subtle essence, this whole world has as its self. That is the truth. That is the self (atman). That is what you are, Shvetaketu. 'Please, respected teacher, instruct me still further.' 'So be it, my dear one,' said he.

Chandogya 6, Section 10

1. These rivers, my dear, flow the eastern toward the east, the western toward the west. They go just from sea to sea. They become the sea itself. Just as these rivers while there do not know 'I am this one,' 'I am that one.'

2. In the same manner, my dear one, all these creatures even though they have come forth from Being do not know that 'we have come forth from Being.' Whatever they are in this world, tiger or lion or wolf or boar or worm or fly or gnat or mosquito that they become.

3. That which is the subtle essence, this whole world has as its self. That is the

truth. That is the self (atman). That is what you are, Shvetaketu. 'Please, respected teacher, instruct me still further.' 'So be it, my dear one,' said he.

Chandogya 6, Section 11

1. Of this mighty tree, my dear one, if someone should strike at the root it would bleed but still live: if someone should strike at the middle, it would bleed but still live. If someone should strike at the top, it would bleed but still live. Being pervaded by its living self, it stands firm, drinking in its moisture (which nourishes it) and rejoicing.

2. If the life leaves one branch of it, then it dries up; if it leaves a second, then that dries up; if it leaves a third, then that dries up. If it leaves the whole, the whole dries up. Even so, indeed, my dear one, understand,' said he.

3. Indeed, this body dies, when deprived of the living self, but the living self does not die. That which is the subtle essence, this whole world has as its self. That is the truth. That is the self (atman). That is what you are, Shvetaketu. 'Please, respected teacher, instruct me still further.' 'So be it, my dear one,' said he.

Illustrations of the Nyagrodha (Fig) Tree

Chandogya 6, Section 12

1. 'Bring hither a fruit of that *nyagrodha* tree.' 'Here it is, respected teacher.' 'Break it.' 'It is broken, respected teacher.' 'What do you see there?' 'These extremely fine seeds, respected teacher.' 'Of these, please break one.' 'It is broken, respected teacher.' 'What do you see there?' 'Nothing at all, respected teacher.'

2. Then he said to him, 'My dear one, that subtle essence which you do not perceive, truly, my dear one, from that very essence this great *nyagrodha* tree exists. Believe me, my dear one.

3. That which is the subtle essence, this whole world has as its self. That is the truth. That is the self (atman). That is what you are, Shvetaketu. 'Please, respected teacher, instruct me still further.' 'So be it, my dear one,' said he.

Illustration of Salt and Water

Chandogya 6, Section 13

1. Place this salt in the water and come to me in the morning. Then he did so. Then he said to him, 'That salt you placed in the water last evening, please bring it hither.' Having looked for it he found it not, as it was completely dissolved.

2. 'Please take a sip of it from this end.' He said, 'How is it?' 'Salt.' 'Take a sip from the middle. How is it?' 'Salt.' 'Take a sip from the other end. How is it?' 'Salt!' 'Throw it away and come to me.' He did so. It is always the same. Then he said to him, 'Truly, indeed, my dear one, you do not perceive Pure Being here. Truly, indeed, it is here.'

3. That which is the subtle essence, this whole world has as its self. That is the truth. That is the self (atman). That is what you are, Shvetaketu. 'Please, respected teacher, instruct me still further.' 'So be it, my dear one,' said he.

Bhrgu Undertakes Investigation of Brahman

Taittiriya 3, Sections 1–6

Bhrgu, the son of Varuna,[361] approached his father Varuna and said, 'Respected teacher, teach me *Brahman*.'

He explained to him thus: matter, life, sight, hearing, mind, speech.

To him, he said further: 'That from which these beings are born, that by which, when born they live, that into which, when departing upon death, they enter. That, seek to know. That is *Brahman*."

He performed austerities.[362] Having performed austerities, he knew that food (anna) is *Brahman*. For truly, beings here are born from food, when born, they live by food, and into food, when departing upon death they enter.

Having known that, he again approached his father Varuna and said, 'Respected teacher, teach me *Brahman*.'

To Bhrgu he said, 'Through austerity, seek to know *Brahman*. *Brahman* is austerity.'

Bhrgu performed austerities; having performed austerities, he knew that life-breath (prana) is *Brahman*. For truly, beings here are born from life, when born they live by life, and into life, when departing upon death they enter.

Having known that, he again approached his father Varuua, and said: 'Venerable Sir, teach me *Brahman*.'

To him he said, 'Through austerity, seek to know *Brahman*. *Brahman* is austerity.'

He performed austerities; having performed austerities, he knew that mind (manas) is *Brahman*. For truly, beings here are born from mind, when born, they live by mind and into mind, when departing upon death, they enter.

Having known that, he again approached his father Varuna and said: 'Respected teacher, teach me *Brahman*.'

To him, he said, 'Through austerity seek to know *Brahman*. *Brahman* is austerity.'

He performed austerities; having performed austerities, he knew that perception (vijnanam) is *Brahman*. For truly, beings here are born from perception, when born, they live by perception and into perception, when departing upon death, they enter.

361. The term "son" is a form of endearment, usually addressed toward a student, but there were also a few teachers who previously had families before becoming ascetics, such as in this exchange.

362. Austerities are defined as asceticism, practices of physical or mental forms of self-denial for religious purposes.

Having known that, he again approached his father Varuna, and said, 'Respected teacher, teach me *Brahman*.'

To him, he said, 'Through austerity, seek to know *Brahman*. *Brahman* is austerity.'

He performed austerities; having performed austerities, he knew that *Brahman* is bliss (ananda). For truly, beings here are born from bliss, when born, they live by bliss and into bliss, when departing upon death, they enter.

This wisdom of Bhrgu and Varuna, established in the highest realms, he who knows this, becomes established. He becomes possessor of food and eater of food. He becomes great in offspring and cattle and in the splendor of sacred wisdom; great in fame.

The Principal Upaniṣads. Translated and edited by Sarvepalli Radhakrishnan, 391–92, 447–49, 459–62, 553–57. Atlantic Highlands, NJ: Humanities Press, 1992.

POST-READING PARS

1. How does the format of the *Upanishads* contribute or detract from the wisdom being conveyed?
2. Choose two to three passages where nature is utilized in the Upanishadic understanding of who we are and our place in the cosmology.
3. Identify two to three metaphors that are used in these passages to describe the relationship between atman and Brahman?

Inquiry Corner

Content Question(s):	**Critical Question(s):**
What is the role of the teacher in these passages? How do they go about "teaching"? What is expected of the student?	In what ways does nature or natural elements become a form of knowledge?
Comparative Question(s):	**Connection Question(s):**
How does the relationship of humans to Brahman compare/contrast to humans' relationship to the sacred in other systems (e.g., orisha, YHWH, etc.)	Go find a tree to sit under or take a walk where you pay attention to your senses interacting with nature. How might exercises like these deepen your knowledge about an idea or topic that is on your mind?

BEYOND THE CLASSROOM

- What are the typical ways you go about learning new skills in a work environment? Are the strategies used by the Upanishadic teachers in use or could they be useful?
- What lessons from observing nature could transfer into healthy work habits and/or relationships with colleagues?

SOURCES AND PERMISSIONS

The editors and publisher gratefully acknowledge the permission granted to reproduce the copyrighted material in this book. Every effort has been made to trace copyright holders and to obtain their permission for the use of copyrighted material. The publisher apologizes for any errors or omissions in the list below and would be grateful if notified of any corrections that should be incorporated in future reprints or editions of this book.

The Achievements of the Divine Augustus: Thurinus, Gaius Octavius. "Res Gestae Divi Augusti." Translated by Thomas Bushnell, BSG, copyright 1998. http://classics.mit.edu/Augustus/deeds.html. The Internet Classics Archive, accessed June 8, 2021. Reprinted by permission of the translator.

AFRICAN SONGS ABOUT FAMILY:

Blessing Upon an Infant: Field, M. J. Selection from *Religion and Medicine of the Gã People*, 171–73. Oxford: Oxford University Press, 1961.

Mother's Song: "Mother's Song." In *Seven Days to Lomaland*, translated by Esther Warner, 180. Boston: Houghton Mifflin, 1954.

A Mother to Her First-Born: "A Mother to Her First-Born." In *Initiation: Translations from Poems of the Didinga and Lango Tribes*, translated by J. H. Driberg, 16–17. London: Golden Cockerel Press, 1932. Reprinted by permission of Associated University Presses. [Public Domain]

African Work Songs for Pounding Grain: "Lazybones" and "A Shared Husband I Do Not Want": "Pounding Songs." In *Oral Poetry from Africa: An Anthology*, compiled by Jack Mapanje and Landeg White, adviser, Isidore Okpewho, 55, 93. New York: Longman, 1983.

Analects: Confucius. Selections from *The Chinese Classics: Confucian Analects (in Chinese and English)*. Translated by James Legge. London: Trübner & Co., 1861. [Public Domain]

***Ananseseɛm*: Stories of Ananse:** Asihene, Emmanuel V. Selections from *Traditional Folk-Tales of Ghana*, 17–18, 33–36, 55–57. Lewiston, NY: Edwin Mellen Press, 1997. Reprinted by permission of the publisher.

Behistûn Inscription: *The Behistan Inscription of King Darius*. Translated by Herbert Cushing Tolman, 7–37. Nashville, TN: Vanderbilt University, 1908. [Public Domain]

Book 1 Maccabees 1–4: "1 Maccabees 1–4." *New Revised Standard Version*. 1989. [Scripture quotations are from] New Revised Standard Version Bible, copyright © 1989 National Council of the Churches of Christ in the United States of America. Used by permission. All rights reserved worldwide.

***Book of Songs*:** *The Book of Songs: The Ancient Chinese Classic of Poetry*. Translated by Arthur Waley, 30, 35, 48, 60, 92, 244–43, 309. New York: Grove, 1938 [1960]. [Public Domain]

Code of Hammurabi: Hammurabi. *The Code of Hammurabi King of Babylon about 2250 B.C.*, by Robert Francis Harper. Chicago: University of Chicago Press, 1904. [Online] available from https://oll.libertyfund.org/titles/1276, accessed June 2, 2020. [Public Domain]

Creation Myths:
Dayrell, Elphinstone. "Why the Sun and Moon Live in the Sky." In *Folk Stories from Southern Nigeria West Africa*, 64–65. London: Longmans Green and Co., 1910. [Public Domain]

Duncan, Barbara. "How the World Was Made" as told by Kathi Smith Littlejohn. In *Living Stories of the Cherokee*, 40–43. Chapel Hill: University of North Carolina Press, 1998. Used by permission of the publisher.

"Genesis 1–2." In *Tanakh: The New Translation of the Holy Scriptures According to the Traditional Hebrew Text*, 3–5. Philadelphia, PA: The Jewish Publication Society, 1985. Jewish Publication Society Copyright © 1985, Used by permission of University of Nebraska Press.

"Purusa-Sukta." In *The Rig Veda: An Anthology*. Selected, translated, and edited by Wendy Doniger O'Flaherty, 29–32. New York: Penguin Books, 1981, Penguin Classics, 2005. Copyright © Wendy Doniger O'Flaherty 1981. Reproduced by permission of Penguin Books Ltd. ©

Radhakrishnan, Sarvepalli. "Section 19: The Cosmic Egg." In *The Principal Upanisads*, 399–400. Atlantic Highlands, NJ: Humanities Press, 1992. Reprinted by permission of Brill Academic Publishers.

Cyrus Cylinder: Used with permission of I.B. Tauris & Co., *The Cyrus Cylinder: The Great Persian Edict from Babylon*. Edited and translated by Irving Finkel, 4–7.

London: I.B. Tauris & Co., 2013. Permission conveyed through Copyright Clearance Center, Inc.

***Daodejing* and *Zhuangzi*:**
Daodejing: Selections from *The Daodejing of Laozi*. Edited and translated by Philip J. Ivanhoe, 159–60, 163–64, 167–68, 176–77, 181, 183–84, 196, 198–200. Indianapolis, IN: Hackett, 2002. Reprinted by permission of Hackett Publishing Company, Inc. All rights reserved.

Zhuangzi: Legge, James, trans., *The Texts of Taoism*, Sacred Books of the East, vols. 39–40, 1:194–97; 247–250; 390–92; 2:4–5. Oxford: Clarendon Press, 1891 [Public Domain]

Eastern Band of Cherokee Origin Stories and Nature Stories: Duncan, Barbara. In *Living Stories of the Cherokee*, 32–34, 40–43, 55–58, 100–101, 201–12, 226–31. Chapel Hll: University of North Carolina Press, 1998. Used by permission of the publisher, www.uncpress.org.

Egyptian Love Poetry: "Egyptian Love Poems (From Papyrus Chester Beatty I, Poem 1)." In *Ancient Egyptian Literature. A Book of Readings: The New Kingdom*, edited by Miriam Lichtheim, 182–85. Berkeley: University of California Press, 2006. Reproduced with permission of the Licensor through PLSclear.

"The Exaltation of Inana": *The Exaltation of Inana (Inana B)*. Translated by the Faculty of Oriental Studies. Oxford: University of Oxford, 2006. Available at https:// https://etcsl.orinst.ox.ac.uk/cgi-bin/etcsl.cgi?text=t.4.07.2#.

Han Feizi and Qin Law:
Han Feizi: "Han Feizi." In *Readings in Classical Chinese Philosophy*, edited by Philip J. Ivanhoe and Bryan W. Van Norden, 2nd ed., 323, 340–43. Indianapolis, IN: Hackett, 2001. Reprinted by permission of Hackett Publishing Company., Inc. All rights reserved.

Qin Law: Used by permission of University of Hawai'i Press. "The Laws of Qin before the Empire." In *Hawaii Reader in Traditional Chinese Culture*, edited by Victor H. Mair, Nancy S. Steinhardt, and Paul R. Goldin, 148–50. Honolulu: University of Hawai'i Press, 2005., Permission conveyed through Copyright Clearance Center, Inc.

Handbook of Epictetus, selections: *Handbook of Epictetus*. Edited and translated by Nicholas White, 11–13, 15–17, 19–24, 26–29. Indianapolis, IN: Hackett Publishing Company, 1983. Reprinted by permission of Hackett Publishing Company, Inc. All rights reserved.

Hebrew Bible, Daniel 1–6: "Daniel 1–6." In the Holy Bible, New International Version®, **NIV® Copyright © 1973, 1978, 1984, 2011 by Biblica, Inc.® Used by permission. All rights reserved worldwide.**

Hebrew Bible, Genesis 22: "Genesis." In *Tanakh: The New Translation of the Holy Scriptures According to the Traditional Hebrew Text,* 11–25. Philadelphia, PA: The Jewish Publication Society, 1985. Jewish Publication Society Copyright © 1985, Used by permission of University of Nebraska Press.

Hebrew Bible, Selected Passages on Covenant: Selections from *Tanakh: The New Translation of the Holy Scriptures According to the Traditional Hebrew Text,* 11–25, 82–84, 87–89, 743–44, 828–29. Philadelphia, PA: The Jewish Publication Society, 1985. Jewish Publication Society Copyright © 1985, Used by permission of University of Nebraska Press.

History of the Peloponnesian War, "The Funeral Oration of Pericles": Thucydides. "History of the Peloponnesian War: Books I and II." *Thucydides.* Translated by Charles Forster Smith, Vol. 1, 317–41. Cambridge, MA: William Heinemann LTD and Harvard University Press, [1921] 1956. [Public Domain]

History of the Peloponnesian War, "Melian Dialogue": Thucydides. "History of the Peloponnesian War: Books V and VI." *Thucydides.* Translated by Charles Forster Smith, Vol. 3, 155–79. Cambridge, MA: William Heinemann LTD and Harvard University Press, [1921] 1959. [Public Domain]

Ifá Divination Poems: Abimbola, Wande. *Ifá Divination Poetry,* 61, 63, 65, 79, 99, 101, 103, 121, 123, 125, 151, 153. New York: NOK Publishers, 1977.

***Instructions of Amenemope*:** Simpson, W. K., and R. K. Ritner, *The Literature of Ancient Egypt: An Anthology of Stories, Instructions, Stelae, Autobiographies, and Poetry,* 223–43. New Haven, CT: Yale University Press, 2003. Reproduced with permission of the Licensor through PLSclear.

Kisagotami: Ranjani Obeyesekere, trans. *Portraits of Buddhism Women: Stories from the Saddharmaratnavaliya (Jewel of the Doctrine),* 134–37. New York: SUNY Press, 2001. Reprinted by permission of State University of New York Press.

Laughing Warrior Girl: Selection from *Tewa Tales,* edited by Elsie Clews Parsons, 191–92. New York: American Folk-Lore Society and G.E. Stechert and Co., 1926.

Lessons for Women: Used with permission of Columbia University Press. Pan Chao. "Lessons for Women." In *The Columbia Anthology of Traditional Chinese Literature,* translated by Nancy Lee Swann, edited by Victor H. Mair, 534–41. New York: Columbia University Press, 1994. Permission conveyed through Copyright Clearance Center, Inc.

Letters between Pliny and Trajan on Christians: Pliny, The Younger. *The Letters of the Younger Pliny.* Edited by John B. Firth and Heinrich Keil, 270–73. London: W. Scott, 1900. https://hdl.handle.net/2027/umn.31951002237967y?urlappend=%3Bseq=30. Hathi Trust, Version 2018-12-05 17:40 UTC, accessed March 21, 2020. [Public Domain]

Life of the Buddha (The Departure): Asvaghosa (Ashvaghosha), *Life of the Buddha.* Translated by Patrick Olivelle, 124–157 (every other page, no Sanskrit). New York: New York University Press, 2008. Reprinted by permission of NYU Press.

The Martyrdom of Saints Perpetua and Felicity**:** *The Passion of Perpetua and Felicity.* Translated by Thomas J. Heffernan, 125–35. New York: Oxford University Press, 2012. Reproduced with permission of the Licensor through PLSclear.

New Testament, Matthew 5–7 (Sermon on the Mount): All scripture quotations, unless otherwise indicated, are taken from the Holy Bible, New International Version®, NIV®. Copyright ©1973, 1978, 1984, 2011 by Biblica, Inc.™ Used by permission of Zondervan. All rights reserved worldwide. www.zondervan.com. The "NIV" and "New International Version" are trademarks registered in the United States Patent and Trademark Office by Biblica, Inc.™

New Testament on wealth and poverty: Mark 10:17–27; Luke 16:19–31; Acts 4:32–5:11: All scripture quotations, unless otherwise indicated, are taken from the Holy Bible, New International Version®, NIV®. Copyright ©1973, 1978, 1984, 2011 by Biblica, Inc.™ Used by permission of Zondervan. All rights reserved worldwide. www.zondervan.com. The "NIV" and "New International Version" are trademarks registered in the United States Patent and Trademark Office by Biblica, Inc.™

Nicomachean Ethics: Aristotle. Selections from *Nicomachean Ethics.* Translated by Terence Irwin, 7–8, 10–11, 16, 18–19, 24–27, 37, 39, 45–49. Indianapolis, IN: Hackett, 2019. Reprinted by permission of Hackett Publishing Company, Inc. All rights reserved.

Pop Wuj**, "Descent to Xibalba":** Used with permission of University of Oklahoma Press. *Popol Vuh: The Sacred Book of the Maya.* Translated by Allen J. Christenson, 141–77. Norman: University of Oklahoma Press, 2007. Permission conveyed through Copyright Clearance Center, Inc.

Potlatch: Beck, Mary Giraudo. "The Potlatch." In *Potlatch: Native Ceremony and Myth on the Northwest Coast*, 62–75. Anchorage: Alaska Northwest Books, 1993. Reprinted by permission of West Margin Press. All rights reserved.

Pythagorean Women: Used with permission of Johns Hopkins University Press. Pomeroy, Sarah B. In *Pythagorean Women: Their History and Writings*, 67–68, 77–79, 85–86, 100–101, 104–5. Baltimore, MD: Johns Hopkins University Press, 2013. Permission conveyed through Copyright Clearance Center, Inc.

Sappho: Sappho. *Selected Poems.* Translated by Sophie Mills, 2020 [unpublished].

Science of Dance-Drama (Natyashastra): Bharata. *Natyasastra.* Translated and edited by Manmohan Ghosh, 102–3, 105–17. Calcutta: Manisha Granthalaya, 1951 [1967].

Song for Dance of Young Girls: Driberg, J. H. "Song for Dance of Young Girls." In *People of the Small Arrow*, 320–24. New York: Payson and Clarke, 1930. [Public Domain]

Song of Gimmile: Courlander, Harold. "Song of Gimmile." In *The King's Drum and Other African Stories*, 9, 11–12. San Diego, CA: Harcourt Brace Jovanovich, 1962.

Speech of the Queen, Hatshepsut: Used with permission of the University of California Press, copyright 1973–80 by the regents, from Hatshepsut. "Speech of the Queen." In *Ancient Egyptian Literature*, edited by Miriam Lichtheim, 337–39. Oakland: University of California Press, 1973–80. Permission conveyed through Copyright Clearance Center, Inc.

***Symposium*, "Speech of Aristophanes":** Plato. "The Speech of Aristophanes." In *Symposium*. Translated by Alexander Nehamas and Paul Woodruff, 25–31. Indianapolis, IN: Hackett, 1989. Reprinted by permission of Hackett Publishing Company, Inc. All rights reserved.

***Upanishads*:** *The Principal Upaniṣads*. Translated and edited by Sarvepalli Radhakrishnan, 391–92, 447–49, 459–62, 553–57. Atlantic Highlands, NJ: Humanities Press, 1992. Reprinted by permission of Brill Academic Publishers.

TAG GLOSSARY

Aesthetics: perception of; beauty; principles governing appreciation of beauty; poetry; **see also Music**

Book of Songs
Daodejing/Zhuangzi
Ifá Divination Poetry
Sappho
Song for Dance of Young Girls
Cherokee Nature Stories
Egyptian Love Poetry
Recognition of Shakuntala
Science of Dance-Drama

Asceticism: physical and mental forms of self-denial for religious purposes; experience of; metaphors related to; criteria for; expected outcomes of; **see also Body; Desire and Happiness; Religion; Sacrifice; Suffering and Compassion**

Life of the Buddha
Upanishads
New Testament (Wealth/Poverty)

Authority and Leadership: governance; power; rule; origin of; legitimacy of; political institutions; government; structure of; resistance to; **see also Class and Wealth; Law and Punishment; Rhetoric and Propaganda**

Achievements/Augustus
Bacchae
Code of Hammurabi
Epic of Gilgamesh
Hebrew Bible (Daniel)
Laughing Warrior Girl
Maccabees
Recognition of Shakuntala
Speech of the Queen
Analects
Behistûn Inscription
Cyrus Cylinder
Han Feizi/Qin Law
History (Melian)
Letters/Pliny and Trajan
Potlatch
Song of Gimmile

Body: work; play; dance; experience; memory; performance; feelings; embodied experience; cosmic; personhood; **see also Music; Nature; Sacrifice; Ways of Knowing; Wisdom**

African Work Songs
Cosmogonic Myths
Song for Dance of Young Girls
Anansesɛm
Science of Dance-Drama
Symposium

Class and Wealth: social hierarchy; social inequality; caste system; possessions; rank; power; conflict, resource distribution, money, sharing, greed, economy, poverty; **see also Authority and Leadership; Community/Communal Identity**

Achievements/Augustus
Bhagavad Gita
Code of Hammurabi
Instruction of Amenemope
Kisagotami
New Testament (Matthew)
New Testament (Wealth/Poverty)
Potlatch

Community/Communal Identity: group identity, social cohesion, tradition, shared experience, nationalism; **see also Class and Wealth; Conflict and War; Freedom and Harmony; Law and Punishment**

African Work Songs
Bacchae
Cherokee Origin Stories
Code of Hammurabi
History (Pericles)
Maccabees
Potlatch
Sappho

Conflict and War: disagreement, agitation, violence, courage, justification for, consequences of, heroism, experience of; **see also Empire and Colonialism; Authority and Leadership; Monument and Artifact; Rhetoric and Propaganda**

Achievements/Augustus
Anansesɛm
Bacchae
Behistûn Inscription
Bhagavad Gita
Cherokee Origin Stories
Epic of Gilgamesh
History (Melian)
History (Pericles)
Ifá Divination Poetry
Laughing Warrior Girl
Maccabees
Pop Wuj

Confucianism: a Chinese worldview, mode of governance, social hierarchy; **see also Authority and Leadership; Education; Ethics and Morality; Philosophy; Women and Gender**

Analects
Book of Songs
Lessons for Women

Cosmology: worldview, creation, nature, reality, order; **see also Deities and Spirits; Origin Stories**

Cherokee Nature Stories
Cosmogonic Myths
Daodejing/Zhuangzi
Exaltation of Inana
Hebrew Bible (Covenant)
Pop Wuj
Upanishads

Death: loss, extinction, acceptance of, martyrdom, reincarnation, rebirth, underworld, immortality, afterlife, mortuary rites; **see also Sacrifice; Conflict and War; Suffering and Compassion; Family**

Anansesɛm
Apology of Socrates
Bacchae
Bhagavad Gita
Cherokee Nature Stories
Daodejing/Zhuangzi
Epic of Gilgamesh
History (Pericles)
Ifá Divination Poetry
Kisagotami
Letters/Pliny and Trajan
Martyrdom of Perpetua
Pop Wuj
Potlatch

Deities and Spirits: gods, lords; power of, obedience to, devotion; relationships with, actions of, sanctioned by; **see also Religion**

Anansesɛm
Bacchae
Bhagavad Gita
Cherokee Nature Stories
Cherokee Origin Stories
Code of Hammurabi
Cyrus Cylinder
Epic of Gilgamesh
Exaltation of Inana
Handbook of Epictetus
Hebrew Bible (Covenant)
Ifá Divination Poetry
Laughing Warrior Girl
Life of the Buddha
Pop Wuj
Science of Dance-Drama
Symposium

Desire and Happiness: impulse, urge, want, detachment from, fulfilment, satisfaction, flourishing; **see also Asceticism; Philosophy; Ethics and Morality; Wisdom**

African Family Songs
Handbook of Epictetus
Instruction of Amenemope
Kisagotami
Life of the Buddha
Nicomachean Ethics

Divination: consultation, divine will, dreams, revelation, future; **see also Ways of Knowing; Religion**

Apology of Socrates
Epic of Gilgamesh
Hebrew Bible (Daniel)
Ifá Divination Poetry
Martyrdom of Perpetua

Education: instructive texts; didactic; teacher-student, elders, transmission of knowledge; **see also Ways of Knowing; Philosophy; Ethics and Morality**

African Work Songs
Analects
Anansesɛm
Cherokee Nature Stories
Cherokee Origin Stories
Instruction of Amenemope
Science of Dance-Drama
Upanishads

Emotion: feelings, mind, perception, experience, performance of, control of; **see also Women and Gender; Love; Family; Desire and Happiness; Aesthetics**

Bacchae
Cherokee Nature Stories
Egyptian Love Poetry
Handbook of Epictetus
Recognition of Shakuntala
Sappho
Science of Dance-Drama
Song for Dance of Young Girls

Empire and Colonialism: founding of; expansion; colonization; enslavement; legacy building; administration of; settler colonialism; **see also Authority and Leadership; Rhetoric and Propaganda; Indigeneity; Law and Punishment**

Achievements/Augustus
Behistûn Inscription
Cyrus Cylinder
History (Melian)
History (Pericles)
Letters/Pliny and Trajan
Martyrdom of Perpetua
Pop Wuj
Potlatch

Ethics and Morality: how to live well; narrative ethics; situatedness of; reflecting on; virtue, good, moderation, duty, right conduct; **see also Philosophy; Desire and Happiness; Freedom and Harmony; Wisdom**

Analects
Anansesɛm
Apology of Socrates
Bhagavad Gita
Cherokee Nature Stories
Cherokee Origin Stories
Daodejing/Zhuangzi
Handbook of Epictetus
Hebrew Bible (Covenant)
Instruction of Amenemope
Kisagotami
Lessons for Women
Life of the Buddha
New Testament (Matthew)
Nicomachean Ethics
Pythagorean Women

Family: relationship, conflict with, instruction by, tradition, filial reverence, ancestors, elders; **see also Women and Gender; Identity; Education; Love**

African Family Songs
African Work Songs
Analects
Anansesɛm
Cherokee Nature Stories
Cherokee Origin Stories
Cosmogonic Myths
Egyptian Love Poetry
Hebrew Bible (Covenant)
Hebrew Bible (Genesis 22)
Ifá Divination Poetry
Instruction of Amenemope
Lessons for Women
Life of the Buddha
Maccabees
Martyrdom of Perpetua
Pop Wuj
Potlatch
Song for Dance of Young Girls

Freedom and Harmony: choice, one's own actions, renunciation, reason, balance, order; **see also Philosophy; Nature; Wisdom; Ethics and Morality**

Bhagavad Gita
Cherokee Nature Stories
Daodejing/Zhuangzi
Handbook of Epictetus
Life of the Buddha
Pythagorean Women

Friendship: companionship, ideal, support, affection, go-between, shared experiences, relationality; **see also Love; Ethics and Morality**

Epic of Gilgamesh
Nicomachean Ethics
Recognition of Shakuntala
Song for Dance of Young Girls

Hagiography: biographical narrative emphasizing the miraculous; journey; revelation; magnified self-narrative; **see also Identity; Origin Stories; Rhetoric and Propaganda**

Achievements/Augustus
Life of the Buddha
Martyrdom of Perpetua

Identity: self-fashioning; defining of; transformation; examination of self; assimilation; cross-cultural encounters; memory/remembering; **see also Community/ Communal Identity; Ways of Knowing; Women and Gender**

Anansesɛm
Apology of Socrates
Epic of Gilgamesh
Hebrew Bible (Daniel)
Ifá Divination Poetry
Letters/Pliny and Trajan
Life of the Buddha
Maccabees
Pop Wuj
Recognition of Shakuntala
Song for Dance of Young Girls

Indigeneity: place; language; Indigenous perspectives; oppression of; **see also Empire and Colonialism; Oral Histories and Storytelling; Origin Stories; Ways of Knowing**

Cherokee Nature Stories
Cherokee Origin Stories
Laughing Warrior Girl
Pop Wuj
Potlatch

Journey: pilgrimage; exile; travel; adventure; departure; home; captive; cross-cultural encounters; **see also Empire and Colonialism; Identity**

Anansesɛm
Cherokee Nature Stories
Cherokee Origin Stories
Cosmogonic Myths
Cyrus Cylinder
Epic of Gilgamesh
Hebrew Bible (Daniel)
Hebrew Bible (Genesis 22)
Ifá Divination Poetry
Life of the Buddha
Pop Wuj

Law and Punishment: trial; debate; social order; crime; investigation; justice; **see also Authority and Leadership**

Apology of Socrates
Code of Hammurabi
Han Feizi/Qin Law
Hebrew Bible (Covenant)
History (Melian)
Letters/Pliny and Trajan

Love: intimacy; expression of; loss of; devotion; union; sexuality; **see also Emotion; Family; Friendship; Religion; Ways of Knowing; Women and Gender**

Bhagavad Gita
Book of Songs
Cherokee Origin Stories
Egyptian Love Poetry
Epic of Gilgamesh
Exaltation of Inana
Recognition of Shakuntala
Sappho
Symposium

Monument and Artifact: physical objects representing cultures; memorial; public declaration; inscriptions; **see also Authority and Leadership; Rhetoric and Propaganda**

Achievements/Augustus
Behistûn Inscription
Code of Hammurabi
Cyrus Cylinder
Epic of Gilgamesh
Speech of the Queen

Music: dance; song; performance; musical instruments; **see also Aesthetics; Emotion**

African Family Songs
African Work Songs
Cherokee Nature Stories
Science of Dance-Drama
Song of Gimmile

Nature: animals; beauty; balance; creation; food; diversity; interdependence; source of instruction; **see also Cosmology; Freedom and Harmony; Indigeneity**

Anansesɛm
Bacchae
Book of Songs
Cherokee Nature Stories
Cherokee Origin Stories
Cosmogonic Myths
Daodejing/Zhuangzi
Epic of Gilgamesh
Potlatch
Recognition of Shakuntala
Upanishads

Oral Histories and Storytelling: oral traditions; folklore; myths; orature; performance of; explanation; knowledge; narrative; **see also Ethics and Morality; Origin Stories; Ways of Knowing; Wisdom**

African Family Songs
Anansesɛm
Cherokee Nature Stories
Cherokee Origin Stories
Cosmogonic Myths
Epic of Gilgamesh
Hebrew Bible (Genesis 22)
Ifá Divination Poetry
Kisagotami
Laughing Warrior Girl
Pop Wuj
Potlatch
Song for Dance of Young Girls
Song of Gimmile
Symposium

Origin Stories: explanations; etiology; social order; human nature; **see also Cosmology; Oral Histories and Storytelling; Religion**

Cherokee Origin Stories
Cosmogonic Myths
Hebrew Bible (Covenant)
Pop Wuj
Science of Dance-Drama
Symposium

Philosophy: nature of reality; meaning of life; fundamental questions; political theory; epistemology; writing about; **see also Education; Ethics and Morality; Ways of Knowing; Wisdom**

Analects
Apology of Socrates
Bhagavad Gita
Cherokee Nature Stories
Daodejing/Zhuangzi
Han Feizi/Qin Law
Nicomachean Ethics
Pythagorean Women

Religion: organized systems of belief and practice; orientations to the sacred; Christianity; Buddhism; Hinduism; (Ancient Israelite) Judaism; Zoroastrianism; teachings of; laws about; afterlife; **see also Cosmology; Deities and Spirits; Ethics and Morality; Love**

Bacchae
Bhagavad Gita
Cherokee Nature Stories
Cosmogonic Myths
Cyrus Cylinder
Exaltation of Inana
Hebrew Bible (Covenant)
Hebrew Bible (Daniel)
Ifá Divination Poetry
Laughing Warrior Girl
Letters/Pliny and Trajan
Maccabees
Science of Dance-Drama

Rhetoric and Propaganda: persuasion; communication; power; justification; instruction; proclamation; explanation; audience for; history; **see also Authority and Leadership; Law and Punishment; Monument and Artifact**

Achievements/Augustus
Behistûn Inscription
Cyrus Cylinder
Exaltation of Inana
History (Melian)
History (Pericles)
Life of the Buddha
New Testament (Matthew)
Speech of the Queen

Sacrifice: offerings to gods; renunciation; detachment; obedience; **see also Asceticism; Deities and Spirits; Religion**

Analects
Bhagavad Gita
Cosmogonic Myths
Hebrew Bible (Covenant)
Hebrew Bible (Genesis 22)
Ifá Divination Poetry
Martyrdom of Perpetua
Pop Wuj

Suffering and Compassion: pain; longing; loss; empathy; responses to; grief; **see also Asceticism; Death; Desire and Happiness**

Epic of Gilgamesh
Kisagotami
Life of the Buddha
Sappho

Ways of Knowing: epistemologies; perspectives; tradition; reality; embodied knowledge; **see also Cosmology; Indigeneity; Oral Histories and Storytelling; Origin Stories; Philosophy; Women and Gender**

African Work Songs
Anansesɛm
Apology of Socrates
Bhagavad Gita
Cherokee Nature Stories
Upanishads

Wisdom: knowledge; self-knowledge; nature of reality; revelation; experience; teacher-student; **see also Education; Ethics and Morality; Philosophy; Ways of Knowing**

Apology of Socrates
Cherokee Origin Stories
Handbook of Epictetus
Instruction of Amenemope
Kisagotami
Pythagorean Women
Upanishads

Women and Gender: gender roles; power and agency; gender identity; women's experiences; gender fluidity; marriage; children; sexuality; **see also Family; Love; Ways of Knowing**

African Family Songs
Bacchae
Book of Songs
Cherokee Nature Stories
Cosmogonic Myths
Exaltation of Inana
Kisagotami
Laughing Warrior Girl
Lessons for Women
Life of the Buddha
Martyrdom of Perpetua
Pythagorean Women
Recognition of Shakuntala
Science of Dance-Drama
Song for Dance of Young Girls
Speech of the Queen
Symposium

INDEX

CPSIA information can be obtained
at www.ICGtesting.com
Printed in the USA
LVHW070751290622
722365LV00006B/43